Wisconsin Riffs

Wisconsin Riffs

Jazz Profiles from the Heartland

Kurt Dietrich

Wisconsin Historical Society Press

Published by the Wisconsin Historical Society Press
Publishers since 1855

The Wisconsin Historical Society helps people connect to the past by collecting, preserving, and sharing stories. Founded in 1846, the Society is one of the nation's finest historical institutions.
Join the Wisconsin Historical Society: wisconsinhistory.org/membership

Front cover photos (top to bottom): Al Jarreau, courtesy of Ripon College; Brian Lynch and Art Blakey, photo by Teri Bloom; Lynne Arriale, photo by Jean Marc Lubrano; Woody Herman, courtesy of the William P. Gottlieb/Ira and Leonore S. Gershwin Fund Collection, Music Division, Library of Congress; and Sue Orfield, photo by Joel Christopherson. Back cover photos (left to right): Joe Sanders, © Hamza Djenat; Wisconsin Conservatory faculty (left to right): Eddie Baker, Manty Ellis, Jessie Hauck, Berkeley Fudge, Jeff Pietrangelo, Scott Preston (student), and Reggie Willis, courtesy of the Wisconsin Conservatory of Music; and Ben Sidran, photo by Jordan Makow. Front flap photo: Kelly and Doc De Haven, photo by Bill Fritsch.

Printed in Canada
Cover design by Percolator Graphic Design
Interior Typesetting by Integrated Composition Systems

22 21 20 19 18   1 2 3 4 5

Library of Congress Cataloging-in-Publication Data

Names: Dietrich, Kurt author.
Title: Wisconsin riffs : jazz portraits from the heartland / Kurt Dietrich.
Description: Madison : Wisconsin Historical Society Press, 2018. | Includes bibliographical references and index. |
Identifiers: LCCN 2017042188 (print) | LCCN 2017042750 (ebook) | ISBN 9780870208546 (E-book) | ISBN 9780870208539 (hardcover : alk. paper)
Subjects: LCSH: Jazz—Wisconsin—History and criticism. | Jazz musicians—Wisconsin.
Classification: LCC ML3508.7.W6 (ebook) | LCC ML3508.7.W6 D54 2018 (print) | DDC 781.6509775—dc23
LC record available at https://lccn.loc.gov/2017042188

♾ The paper used in this publication meets the minimum requirements of the American National Standard for Information Sciences—Permanence of Paper for Printed Library Materials, ANSI Z39.48-1992.

Contents

JAZZ AROUND THE STATE

Introduction

When I started work on this book, it was my intention to write a history of jazz in Wisconsin. Having previously written two books and a number of articles on jazz history, I was under no illusions that history, especially jazz history, is neat and clean. Despite what some revisionists would have us believe, a music, particularly one as rich and diverse as jazz, by no means evolves in a straight stylistic or chronological line. Also, there is considerable disagreement today about what music should (and should not) be considered as jazz.

Nonetheless, I was confident that I could combine approaches to weave a somewhat coherent narrative tracing how jazz and jazz players have developed in Wisconsin. I started by writing the sections on some of the icons of Wisconsin jazz—Bunny Berigan, Woody Herman, and Les Paul (the last of whom, incidentally, some don't consider a jazz player). These profiles became the first three chapters, and the information on those figures (as well as some others later on) came from a variety of secondary sources.

When I got into the interview process, however, things changed. I began interviewing important jazz musicians from Wisconsin who have made a splash on the national and international scene. Early on, I spoke with Carl Allen, Brian Lynch, and others. But I had always intended to make this book about the less famous as well—specifically, the jazz musicians who were born in Wisconsin and are still here, or are back here after time away, or who may have moved here from elsewhere, and who make today's Wisconsin jazz scene much more vibrant than outsiders might suspect. As I conducted more and more interviews with local musicians, they, of course, led me to many other area musicians. The stories I heard were even richer than I expected. And some of the most interesting stories were from musicians who—based strictly on musical ability, reputation, and/or influence—are not the most important Wisconsin musicians.

At that point, I began realizing that *Wisconsin Riffs* was becoming, and in fact has now become, a book of stories of jazz musicians rather than a history of the music and its development in our state.

Here's a short version of my own story. While less compelling than many others in the book, it gives you an idea of where I have come from, how I got here, and, perhaps, why I have written this book.

I was born and grew up in southwestern Virginia, where my father was a college professor; he led a church choir, and at home sang songs, often accompanied by my mother on piano. Although living in a small town in the boondocks, I took part in a strong school band program, beginning on my grandfather's trombone. My high school jazz band (called the "dance band" in those days, when *jazz* was an even dirtier word than *dance* in the Bible Belt) played at school festivals in North Carolina, Tennessee, and West Virginia. I enrolled at Lawrence University in Appleton, Wisconsin, in 1969 with the expectation of becoming a math or science major, but the inspiration of professors Marge Irvin, Derald DeYoung, and Fred "Prof" Schroeder and my fellow students convinced me that music was the way to go. When jazz pianist and composer John Harmon (see chapter 18) joined the Lawrence faculty in 1971, my fate was sealed.

After graduating from Lawrence, I earned a master's degree at Northwestern University, studying with legendary Chicago Symphony trombonist Frank Crisafulli. At school and in the Chicago Civic Orchestra, I rubbed elbows with future luminaries in the classical music world. In the spring of my one academic year at Northwestern, I got "the call" from John Harmon, saying that the guys were forming a band and that I was expected to be in it. The story of Matrix is told in chapter 12.

When Matrix quit traveling in 1979, I returned to the Fox Valley where my new wife, Maria, was a piano technician. I did temp work, played the few jobs available to a trombonist in the area, taught lessons, and worked at Henri's Music. I joined the Fox Valley Symphony and became a member of the Lawrence Brass Quintet. In 1980, I started teaching brass lessons at Ripon College, and I took over as director of the Symphonic Wind Ensemble the next year. I signed a full-time contract in 1982 and

Matrix in 1979. Left to right, top row: John Kirchberger, Michael Murphy, and Mike Hale; middle row: Jeff Pietrangelo, Kurt Dietrich, Randy Tico, and John Harmon; bottom row: Larry Darling and Brad McDougall. COURTESY OF JOHN KIRCHBERGER

have been at Ripon ever since. I earned a doctorate at the University of Wisconsin–Madison in 1989; my dissertation led to my first book, which, like my second, was about jazz trombone history.

I was active for many years in the Wisconsin chapter of the International Association for Jazz Education (and its predecessors), serving a long stint as newsletter editor and a term as president. (The group presented me with a Lifetime Achievement Award in 2007.) As director of Chamber

Music and Jazz at Ripon, I have brought many jazz acts to Ripon College, musicians from around the nation (Jazz at Lincoln Center, Fred Hersch, and Delfeayo Marsalis, to name a few) and from Wisconsin (Chuck Hedges, John Harmon, Mark Davis, Janet Planet, Mary Louise Knutson, and many others). I continue to perform in the classical and jazz areas, the latter usually along with my mentor and close friend John Harmon. I have had the great good fortune of performing alongside more than fifty other musicians in this book, in bands large and small, in jam sessions, or just "sitting in."

Now, with a mixture of trepidation and pride, I watch my son Paul, a talented trumpeter and composer/arranger, carve out a life in jazz in Madison. My other son Erik plays bass in a couple of amateur jazz bands while sensibly holding down an IT job.

Once it became clear to me that this book was about individual stories in Wisconsin, I decided to include as many names of people and places as I could, with the idea that by doing so I could engage readers who would recognize these Wisconsin names and places, even if they never thought of themselves as jazz fans. The featured musicians fall within a very wide range of backgrounds, ages, stylistic schools, experiences, and outlooks. The lengths of the profiles vary considerably, based on what I was told in conversations of various lengths, and what, in turn, I thought would be interesting to readers—who might range from jazz professionals to fans to those just interested in Wisconsin history and culture. Furthermore, the stories of some musicians are told largely in their own words, while I have narrated others in third person, spiced with only a few quotes from the subjects. I made these choices based on how I was presented with the information, and how I felt I could best tell the stories.

Some chapters of the book are arranged by musical styles and schools, others by geographical areas, and others by groups of musicians who have worked or developed together. They are told in more or less detail, based on my conversations, but also my prior or acquired knowledge about the schools in question (for example, the lengthy jazz rock chapter). There are so many different strands of the Wisconsin jazz story, including

Kurt Dietrich and Al Jarreau at Ripon College in 2012. PHOTO BY MARC HEALY

individuals who are decidedly outliers, that the book eventually became very messy. But history is messy, and jazz is messy, so the book accurately reflects that. I trust that there is enough coherence to keep readers invested. Some may prefer reading the book from cover to cover, while others may enjoy jumping from one section to another, reading the individual stories that speak to them on a personal level.

Needless to say, after conducting interviews with more than one hundred musicians and others involved in the music, I had to leave a great deal out of this book. And there are so many wonderful musicians with whom I did not speak—many of whom are quite prominent and may justly feel unfairly left out. I could start interviewing fifty additional worthy choices tomorrow. I will add that the western part of the state is underrepresented in this volume, as are the genres of traditional jazz and Latin jazz. I regret the omissions but invite readers to enjoy what I have uncovered, discovered (or rediscovered), and brought, I hope, to a brighter light.

DISCOGRAPHY

Much of the discussion of the music itself appears in an online discography at www.kurtdietrich.net. Here the musicians have chosen their recorded music that they want others to hear. *Wisconsin Riffs* celebrates the people who make the music, but also the music they make. Purchase and listen to the recordings, but even more importantly—go hear these musicians perform in person.

Wisconsin Icons

1

Bunny Berigan

The Miracle Man of Swing

The great trumpeter Bunny Berigan is one of Wisconsin's most legendary jazz musicians. Like Bix Beiderbecke, one of Berigan's heroes and another star of early jazz, Berigan grew up in the Midwest; exploded onto the jazz scene in New York seemingly out of nowhere, dazzling audiences and fans with what was often thought of as an outsized natural talent; became a legendary drinker; and died young.[1] (As Gunther Schuller said when writing of Berigan, "Jazz loves its legends, especially its alcoholic martyrs."[2]) Much of Berigan's story has basis in fact, of course, but legends are rarely as complicated as their real-life counterparts.

Roland Bernard Berigan was born in Hilbert, in east central Wisconsin, on November 2, 1908. At the time, his father, William "Cap" Berigan, was working for the US Express Company.[3] But before Bunny was a year old, his father gave up that job to become a salesman for the Badger Tobacco & Candy Company, and the Berigans moved southwest to Fox Lake.

Bunny's mother, Mayme, played piano and organ and taught piano lessons to local children. His grandfather, John Schlitzberg, ran a furniture store and was an undertaker in Fox Lake, but he also led a community band and ran a local dance hall. When Schlitzberg, with whom the Berigans periodically lived, brought home a violin one day, six-year-old Bunny picked it up and learned to play. His grandfather (who played violin and cornet) and mother served as Bunny's music instructors until he started lessons with a respected teacher in the area, "Professor" Clarence H. Wagner.

From left to right: Donald Berigan, Bernard "Bunny" Berigan, and Charles Casey Jr.
UNIVERSITY OF WISCONSIN DIGITAL COLLECTIONS, BUNNY BERIGAN, FOX LAKE'S OWN

Grandfather Schlitzberg also gave Bunny his first instrument (either a trumpet or a cornet) when the boy was about eleven. A photograph of the Fox Lake Juvenile Band from around this time shows Berigan holding an alto horn, but the trumpet was to be his instrument. According to Berigan biographer Robert Dupuis, the Juvenile Band "played for community concerts and enjoyed an excellent reputation in the area. . . . [Among other things,] they were called upon to welcome soldiers returning from overseas duty [at the end of World War I]."[4] By 1920, Berigan was playing dance jobs in a family band, which included his mother on piano, brother Don on drums, and occasionally an aunt and uncle on other horns.

Some Fox Lake residents recalled Berigan as a boy who was "a little sickly" (he had appendicitis at age eleven) and who did not take part in sports as many of the other boys did (something Bunny's brother disputes), but everyone remembered him practicing music tirelessly and assiduously. He listened to whatever new records he could find in Fox Lake, a small but busy resort town with many summer visitors from Chicago and Milwaukee.

Berigan played many of his first professional jobs with Merrill Owen and his Pennsylvanians, a quintet that was not from Pennsylvania, but rather from the Fox Lake–Beaver Dam area. And a popular band it was—the summer that Berigan joined, at the age of fourteen or fifteen, the band reportedly played seventy-one straight nights. As fall of 1924 and the start of the school year approached, the young trumpeter was torn between what he wanted to do—play with a band—and what he needed to do—attend school. He ended up leaving school for two quarters to play, and then attending school for the other two, during which he took part in school music activities. Over the next couple of years, he continued to play with Owen's band, as well as Si Mahlberg's Fond du Lac–based band.

In the fall of 1925, Bunny moved to Madison to live with his uncle, "Big Bob" Berigan. The move was designed to have two benefits: Bunny could play with bands that were more advanced musically, and the change of scenery and schools was intended to improve his attitude toward schoolwork. It is safe to say that the musical goal was met, but the academic goal was not. Uncle Bob was a drummer on the Madison scene, and he was able to get Bunny involved right away. Bunny worked for a while with the University of Wisconsin Skyrockets, led by Jesse Cohen, but soon he was playing with the Berigan-Smith Band, with his uncle Bob and local reed player Erle Smith.[5] Bunny also freelanced with a variety of other bands that played at venues in Madison, including the fraternity houses of the University of Wisconsin. After spending a couple of years improving his music reading, he was able to build a reputation, and probably obtain better-paying jobs, in the pit orchestras of the Orpheum Theater and the Capitol Theater, which opened in 1928. One of Bunny's favorite hangouts in Madison was the Ward-Brodt music store, where musicians awaited new records by their favorites—in Berigan's case, Louis Armstrong and Bix Beiderbecke.

In early 1928, Keith "Curly" Roberts, a trombonist from Lancaster, Wisconsin, and one of Berigan's bandmates, moved to New York City. When Frank Cornwell was forming a new band in the Big Apple, Roberts called Berigan to join. The band became the Janssen's Hofbrau Orchestra, named for the fancy new restaurant in Philadelphia where they played from the time of the restaurant's opening in April until the beginning of September. The band also played regularly on radio broadcasts. After they broke up later that year, Berigan returned to Wisconsin.

Berigan briefly resumed his busy musical life in Madison, working gigs with bands that sometimes included his name, as in Mr. B. and His Orchestra, and, for the University of Wisconsin Military Ball, Bunny Berrigan's [*sic*] 12 Piece Band. He worked in Illinois, Ohio, and Kentucky with territory bands. But soon, while leading a band at the Club

Chanticleer in September 1929, Berigan was called back to New York by Frank Cornwell. The big city became his primary home for the rest of his life.

He returned to Cornwell's band at the original New York location of Janssen's Hofbrau. Not only did the band play in a popular nightspot, they also appeared regularly on WOR radio. While Berigan sometimes played violin, he primarily used his time in the band to build his reputation as a solid trumpeter. After hours, Berigan started building another reputation—that of fun-loving drinking companion. One night at the club, he met a lovely young dancer named Donna McArthur and they began to date, occasionally double-dating with Cornwell and his wife.

In the spring of 1930, Berigan left Cornwell's band to join Hal Kemp's band, just in time to sail to England for several months of engagements. The trip also led to performances in Paris and Ostend, Belgium. Kemp's band returned to New York at the end of September and began another long-term engagement in Greenwich Village. When the band took part in a series of recording sessions, Berigan found his musical home for the next several years—the studios of New York. On one of the Kemp sides, "Them There Eyes," Berigan recorded one of his first widely praised solos, showing Louis Armstrong–like rhythmic ease and bravura.

Records had been the most common way that people consumed music in the 1920s, but with the onset of the Great Depression, the bottom fell out of the record business. However, the popularity of free music on the radio grew directly in proportion to the decline of record sales. When Berigan was hired by the Columbia Broadcasting System (CBS) in 1931, he was assured a great deal of good-paying work. The studio orchestras for the radio networks worked many hours a week playing for live broadcasts, yet not so many that the musicians couldn't also do plenty of freelancing on record sessions, as well as after-hours jamming in the city's clubs, in their free time. Among those on staff at CBS during Berigan's employment were future stars Jimmy and Tommy Dorsey, Artie Shaw, and Glenn Miller. Berigan worked in the studios and on live gigs with other excellent jazzmen such as Joe Venuti, Jack Teagarden, and Benny Goodman. It was an exciting and busy life.

To add to the excitement, in May 1931 Bunny and Donna got married in her hometown of Syracuse, New York. They had reconnected after he returned from Europe with the Kemp band. Their outlook was good, as Berigan's biographer explained: "If ever a couple seemed to have it made, they were that couple. Good looks, talent, big money, promising future, exciting and satisfying work—they had it all."[6]

But in a questionable career decision, Berigan left CBS in the fall of 1931 at the invitation of the Dorsey brothers, who were leading a band for the new show *Everybody's Welcome*. Berigan was still able to play some sessions, but the security of the CBS work was gone. Following the close of the show, Berigan recorded for some time in the American Record Company studios. Tommy Dorsey was the unofficial leader of this unofficial house band. For some months, the band of then-popular singer Smith Ballew provided Berigan with steady work.

A much more prestigious association for Berigan developed in November 1932, when he joined the band of Paul Whiteman, the so-called "King of Jazz." While Whiteman's band hardly played any real jazz at this time, it was one of the most famous, popular, and profitable bands in the country. So great was Whiteman's fame that even the residents of Fox Lake took notice, and Berigan's new position was noted in the local paper, the *Representative*. Berigan's signing with Whiteman was eerily reminiscent of the earlier relationship between Berigan's hero, Bix Beiderbecke, and the same band. Berigan, although a more well-rounded trumpet player than Beiderbecke, was known primarily for his inventive jazz solos, as Beirderbecke was. And Whiteman's band didn't provide Berigan with many opportunities for this type of improvisational playing. Fortunately, he seemed to suffer no lasting effects from this musical straitjacket. When Whiteman's orchestra was not on the road, Berigan remained active in the studios.

One Whiteman tour led to a concert at Madison's Capitol Theater in May 1933, where Berigan's friends and family turned out in droves to celebrate the return of their hometown hero. During this tour, Donna and their daughter, Pat (who had been born the previous July), stayed in Fox Lake with the Berigan family, establishing a pattern that would be repeated during future tours. After the tour ended in Chicago, Berigan joined Donna and Pat in Fox Lake for almost three weeks. Sadly, on November 2, the Berigans' second daughter, Barbara, died almost immediately after birth.

Shortly after this tragedy, Berigan left Whiteman and joined Abe Lyman's band—a popular group, but not in the same league as Whiteman's. Berigan's stay with Lyman was brief, however, and soon he was back with CBS.

Historian Richard Sudhalter writes about Berigan's solos from this period on records with Mildred Bailey as "alternately stately, eloquent, and hair-raising in their flair for the dramatic."[7] It wasn't much longer before his recorded solos had developed to the point that Sudhalter's praise goes even further:

> Berigan was now one of the most polished and versatile trumpet men in the music business. His range was big, glowing, and secure all the way up to his high G. His control of high-note lip-trills was nonpareil. His flexibility was remarkable even by today's [1999's] advanced standards of technique: he could vault from the lowest to the highest reaches of his horn with the same matter-of-factness displayed on [his earlier records], but with ever greater confidence and polish, and no loss of tonal size or quality.[8]

During much of 1934 and 1935, Berigan worked the early shift at CBS, the so-called "morning band" that played for radio shows broadcast in the morning and afternoon. Groups featuring Berigan sprang up in the studios—most famously, Bunny's Blue Boys. Regular listeners followed these groups; they could also hear Berigan with such radio stars as singer Kate Smith. Working this day job allowed Berigan to play gigs at night, and to participate in legendary jam sessions at clubs like the Onyx, where he was a regular with many of the usual suspects—the Dorsey brothers, Jack and Charlie Teagarden, Benny Goodman, and the Onyx's house pianist, jazz giant Art Tatum. Berigan also worked with an early version of the Dorseys' big band.

In late 1934, a series of events led to the flowering of the Swing Era. Benny Goodman, who had the itch to lead a big band, put together a band for the Saturday night nationwide radio broadcasts of *Let's Dance*. Berigan played some of the early broadcasts but was dropped from the band after a few weeks, very possibly because he was drinking to excess before or during the show. However, Berigan continued his freelancing, recording in the first half of 1935 with the Mound City Blue Blowers, Red Norvo's octet, Glenn Miller's new band, and Gene Gifford's orchestra. And when the Goodman band cut its first records, Goodman realized Berigan was just the soloist he needed. Berigan played two of his most famous solos on the July 1 recordings of "Sometimes I'm Happy" and "King Porter Stomp."

When the Goodman band began its legendary cross-country tour in July 1935, Goodman decided he had to take the trumpet powerhouse with him. However, the tour was largely unsuccessful, as audiences were not ready for this brand of hot jazz. Still, music journalist Helen Oakley raved about Berigan after hearing him at Milwaukee's Modernistic Ballroom, saying that only Louis Armstrong was comparable. And after a series of lukewarm receptions, the tour climaxed in much different fashion in late August at the Palomar Ballroom in Los Angeles. The West Coast audience that had been listening for months to the "hottest" hours of the *Let's Dance* broadcasts (the hours after most listeners on the East Coast had gone to bed) was ready to catapult Goodman's band to stardom. This memorable show is often acknowledged as the beginning of the Swing Era.

As had been their custom with earlier tours, Donna and Pat stayed in Fox Lake while Berigan was out on the road with Goodman. When the family returned to New York in mid-October, Berigan jumped right back into the scene, working at CBS and recording with saxophonist Bud Freeman and vocalist Mildred Bailey. On December 13, Berigan recorded his first date as a leader, with his Blue Boys for the Decca label. In 1936, he continued making records; one of the most meaningful was made on February 4 with jazz's greatest practitioner, and Berigan's early idol, Louis Armstrong.

A brief but celebrated association for Berigan began on February 10, 1936, when he joined Red McKenzie, Eddie Condon, and Joe Bushkin opening at the Famous Door, one of the hippest jazz clubs on the hippest jazz street in the world—New York's Fifty-Second Street. Berigan was still busy at CBS and in the recording studios, but he also made money playing gigs for special occasions, like composer Hoagy Carmichael's wedding reception. The Famous Door band was successful enough, and musically rewarding enough, that Berigan decided to resign from CBS, his real cash cow, in March of 1936. In April, he cut his first recording as leader of what was to become his signature tune, Vernon Duke and Ira Gershwin's "I Can't Get Started." Although this version was later eclipsed in popularity by his 1937 recording of the tune, it was named one of the best jazz records of 1936 by *Metronome*.[9]

Also in April, the Berigan family grew to four when Donna gave birth to another girl, Joyce. But what could have been a happy time for the family soon became tumultuous.

The Famous Door closed suddenly in May. Around the same time, Berigan started an affair with singer Lee Wiley that went on for several years and seriously weakened his marriage, though Berigan and Donna never divorced. After losing his regular gig at the club, he began rehearsing a big band, but it played only a few jobs before disbanding.

Luckily, Berigan managed to slip back in at CBS in June, just in time for the debut of a prime-time program, *Saturday Night Swing Club*. He remained busy for the rest of 1936 with *SNSC* and in the studios, recording more dates as leader and as a sideman, perhaps most notably on Billie Holiday's first date as a leader.

At the end of the year, Berigan signed on with a relatively new band that was about to make a splash in the business, just as he had previously done with Goodman. After years of working in the studios, Tommy and Jimmy Dorsey had put together a big band in 1933. It became a full-time venture in 1934 and seemed to be on the brink of stardom when the brothers had a very public falling out at the Glen Island Casino in the spring of 1935. Jimmy kept the band, but Tommy quickly put together his own unit, and Berigan's luminescent trumpet style was just the ingredient Tommy needed to spark the band. Never one to turn down that sort of challenge, Berigan signed up in December 1936. About this time, Berigan also won the "hot trumpet" chair in the annual poll conducted by *Metronome* magazine.

Although Berigan was still occasionally making records with his own big band in 1937, he garnered much more attention that year from records he made with Dorsey. Two Dorsey hits were recorded on January 29, and Berigan made crucial contributions to both. "Song of India" became one of Dorsey's jazzed-up classics. The arrangement is largely memorable for the introductory tom-tom figure and Dorsey's statement of the melody in clear-tone mute, with one startling exception—Berigan's hot solo in the middle.[10] "Marie" is notable for Dorsey's flawless melodic exposition and the call-and-response vocal between Jack Leonard and the rest of the band. But Berigan's solo, beginning with an electric octave jump to high F (E-flat in concert pitch), inserted jazz into what was an otherwise sweet arrangement and further built the reputations of both the Dorsey band and Berigan.

Sudhalter puts the landmark "Marie" solo in context, writing:

> [Berigan's] solo here, pursued at a remarkably consistent level of inventiveness and execution, is more than just a piece of jazz improvisation. With its daring reaches into the topmost range of the horn, its imaginative, bold figures, . . . its heraldic, Armstrong-inspired *bel canto* statements, . . . it is a composition, a paraphrase and a development of the original.[11]

It is difficult to pin down when Berigan officially left Dorsey's band, as he was in and out for some months. Dorsey was notorious as a dictatorial leader and disciplinarian, and Berigan's laissez-faire attitude, not to mention his drinking, put the two on a collision course. But while Berigan was recording and playing dance dates with Dorsey, he was also rehearsing his own band (with occasional recordings), holding down a job back at CBS, and working freelance gigs, including the remarkable pickup session from March 31 that included Fats Waller and his classic "Honeysuckle Rose." Eventually, Berigan's stint with the Dorsey band came to a close.

However, a great new chapter in his career was about to open. Although he had made recordings leading a band, the real Bunny Berigan Orchestra was born on April 1, 1937. On this date, the band recorded four tracks for RCA Victor that would establish its reputation and kick off several years of work. Berigan's sidemen on this landmark session included reedman Clyde Rounds, young saxophone star Georgie Auld, pianist/arranger Joe Lippman, drummer George Wettling, and guitarist Tom Morgan. Early reviews of its live performances were unflattering, to say the least. But within a few months, other notables had joined the band, including clarinetist and saxophonist Joe Dixon and trombonist Sonny Lee. The crowning achievement for the new band was a long-term opening gig at the Pennsylvania Hotel's Madhattan Room, a prestigious location in New York.

The Bunny Berigan Orchestra finally started to receive strong reviews in the trade and New York–area papers for their recordings, broadcasts, and live performances. The signature recording session was on August 7, 1937, when the band re-recorded Berigan's monumental hit, Duke and Gershwin's "I Can't Get Started." Because Lippman's arrangement is somewhat minimally scored, Berigan steals the show with his oddly affecting vocals (including a slight modification of Gershwin's sophisticated lyrics about a high-achieving man who can't make any inroads with the object of his desire) and his remarkable trumpet solo. While this is the record that virtually everyone associates with Berigan, "The Prisoner's Song" on the record's reverse side was also a commercial and artistic success.

By the end of the year, the band had completed a smash engagement at the Paramount Theater and had cut more successful records, including four excellent tracks from a session on December 23: "In a Little Spanish Town," "Black Bottom," "Trees," and "Russian Lullaby." As a big-name bandleader, Berigan began appearing in advertisements for the Selmer Company, one of the country's leading instrument manufacturers. He was arguably at the height of his career.

Unfortunately, 1938 was not quite as good a year. The band started the year with a long delay, due to Berigan's bout with the flu and the serious illness of one of his daughters. His manager, Arthur Michaud of the Music Corporation of America (MCA) agency, who also handled Tommy Dorsey, took on a new bandleader, Gene Krupa, leaving him less time to attend to Berigan. However, after a successful engagement at Philadelphia's Arcadia International Restaurant, the Bunny Berigan Orchestra became the first jazz band to be booked at another choice New York spot, the Paradise Restaurant, where Berigan was billed as "the Miracle Man of Swing." In addition to playing nightly at dances, the band was broadcast regularly on WOR and held popular jam sessions in the restaurant on Sundays.

As was common with bands of this era, the orchestra's personnel was somewhat fluid. Among those who contributed to the Berigan outfit were ace drummers Dave Tough, Johnny Blowers, and Buddy Rich, and the noted trombonist and soon-to-be-famous arranger Ray Conniff. Joe Lippman and Joe Bushkin moved in and out of the piano spot. Many consider the summer of 1938 to be the musical peak of the band's history.

When the job at the Paradise ended in May, the band played at the Paramount Theater and recorded another hit, "The Wearin' of the Green." Gigs, mostly one-nighters, filled much of the band's summer, in cities such as Cincinnati, Atlantic City, Detroit, Pittsburgh, and Syracuse, New York. But problems slowly began to creep in. The band lost a prime show job for entrepreneur Billy Rose in New York and traveled to the wrong city for a job in Connecticut. Dixon, the steady saxophonist, left the band. And a hurricane hit Boston in September, canceling almost two weeks of important work.[12] Berigan was forced to lay off the band for a short time. When the band finally reassembled, Berigan showed up with his leg in a cast, apparently having broken something (an ankle or a leg) while roughhousing with his daughters.

Despite these setbacks, the band cut some good records, including "Sobbin' Blues" and "Jelly Roll Blues" on November 22. At the end of November, a scaled-down version of the band recorded five compositions of Bix Beiderbecke, a project that was unprecedented in its scope—the material filled three full records, front and back—and historical nature, that of reprising and reinterpreting the work of an earlier jazz figure. The records were very well received, even if they were not best sellers. But changes in personnel continued, including the loss of the vital Auld.

Berigan participated in another historical recording session in January 1939. George Simon, longtime editor of *Metronome*, recorded the winners of the magazine's annual readers' poll of jazz favorites on each instrument. Berigan, voted jazz favorite on trumpet, played with the All-Star Band that included Tommy Dorsey, Benny Goodman, Jack Teagarden, Harry James, Charlie Spivak, and Sonny Dunham. "Blue Lou," recorded on that date, displays Berigan in prime form.

But this was a highlight following an otherwise tough year. In late 1938, rumors emerged about Berigan threatening to reduce the size of the band, more likely a fabrication of the press than an actual statement by Berigan. The big band remained intact, but with continuing changes in personnel. Among those who shuffled in and out of the band were

A poster used by MCA to promote Bunny Berigan, ca. 1938. UNIVERSITY OF WISCONSIN DIGITAL COLLECTIONS, BUNNY BERIGAN, FOX LAKE'S OWN

Wisconsinites Vic Hauprich, a saxophonist who had worked with Berigan in Madison, and another Madison saxophonist, Doc De Haven.

On the home front, Donna, like Bunny, was battling alcoholism. Some claimed that she was farming out the Berigan daughters to others for foster care. After an incident of possible child abuse involving the girls' caretaker, Bunny's parents decided to move to New York to live with the family.

The band continued to play a few successful gigs, and it produced some good recordings on March 15, 1939. By most accounts (and the evidence of broadcasts), it was playing at a high level. The band spent most of the first half of the year playing one-nighters all over the eastern half of the United States, at "ballrooms, hotels, theaters, armories, clubs, auditoriums, halls, pavilions, casinos and academic institutions."[13] Occasionally, the band would have the luxury of spending a week or two on location, but these did not always turn out well. Joe Bushkin recalled a particularly ugly job near Pittsburgh when the band had to get a police escort to and from the gig for several nights to avoid direct confrontation with an angry group of men armed with "lead pipes and broomsticks and baseball bats."[14] Bookings in Wisconsin included a date in little Clintonville, and at the Orpheum Theater in Madison in June, as the band continued its tour.

Two successful visits to Detroit led to a plum booking for six weeks at the Panther Room of the Sherman Hotel in Chicago in July. There were radio broadcasts from the hotel on both the NBC and ABC affiliates in the city. Fox Lake was near enough that Berigan could get back home on days off (often to play golf), and he regularly took some of the sidemen with him. But Berigan's notorious lack of business acumen caught up with him and the band during what should have been a period of professional success and reward.

Because Berigan owed money to MCA, and the agency was charging him excessive interest—as well as the fact that the agency was collecting the pay from the hotel—the men in the band were paid only partially for several weeks. When Berigan explained to the men what was going on, they appealed to powerful labor boss James Petrillo, the head of the Chicago musicians' union. Petrillo had the clout to get the band members paid what they were owed. But this did not include Berigan, the leader. Berigan was fined by the American Federation of Musicians and forced to file for bankruptcy.[15]

The filing did not take place until the end of August, after the ill-fated—but at least steady—six weeks at the Sherman, as well as an outstanding reception at the Modernistic Ballroom at the State Fair Park in Milwaukee. The band started another successful gig at New York's Loew's State Theater during the last week of August. The unending changes in personnel continued, and Berigan was forced to quell rampant rumors that the band was about to disband.

September and October consisted mostly of one-nighters, in the northeast and then the south, before a return to New York to play at a casino associated with the 1939 World's Fair. When the band returned to the studio for their last recording session for RCA on November 28, they had not recorded since March. With an almost completely new band, and mediocre material, the four sides they recorded did not appear on the market for almost a year, at which time they received tepid reviews.

In December, there were two weeks of work—one at the Apollo Theater and another starting on Christmas Eve at the Mosque Ballroom in Newark, New Jersey. After the unsettled fall, the location work during the holiday season must have been welcome to the band members. During the Mosque engagement, Berigan was taken to a hospital in New York where he stayed for ten days, experiencing painful swelling throughout his body. He attributed the affliction to arthritis. In his absence, the band was fronted by Wingy Manone and then Jack Teagarden.

After Berigan's release from the hospital, perhaps sobered up to a certain degree as well as relieved of some of the swelling pain, he led the band through theater and hotel jobs in New York and Boston. But eventually, in late February, after a few more one-nighters, Berigan faced the inevitable and disbanded the group. There simply was no work and no money.

Amazingly, Berigan's recovery—both physical and psychological—was quick and spectacular, perhaps partly because he was relieved of the burden of being a leader. He rejoined Tommy Dorsey's band on March 3, 1940, at the Meadowbrook in Cedar Grove, New Jersey—the very same location where Berigan's band had played its first job three years earlier. This reunion was big news in the music business, with all the trade magazines weighing in, uniformly praising the move. Though the popularity of Dorsey's outfit had waned since its earlier peak, it was still very popular. And with budding superstar Frank Sinatra as the "boy singer" backed by the popular vocal group the Pied Pipers, it was about to peak again. Though Berigan received special billing on the band's engagements, he still felt at home with the other sidemen, several of whom had come to Dorsey from Berigan's band.

By all reports, Berigan was playing very well when he came back to Dorsey's band, both in the lead trumpet chair and as a soloist. "East of the Sun," recorded April 23, showcases his typically relaxed swing feel and his innate mastery of solo construction. But there were problems, too. Berigan received only a small portion of his weekly salary; the rest was funneled through the musicians' union to pay off debts to his former band members and other creditors. And after a period of relative sobriety, he resumed his heavy drinking, with the predictable ill effects on his health and playing. To make matters worse, the notoriously egotistical Dorsey began to become envious of Berigan, a star stealing some of the attention from the leader, and became understandably unhappy about Berigan's inconsistency and unprofessionalism on the stand. The two could not coexist. In August, either Dorsey fired Berigan or Berigan quit.

After parting ways with Dorsey, Berigan put together a small group that worked for a few weeks. But he felt the need to work with a big band again, and that new band, with no recognizable names among the sidemen, debuted in late September. This new incarnation of the Bunny Berigan Orchestra played for several weeks in the New York area before heading south for a series of one-nighters. Eventually, the band settled into a four-week engagement in Jacksonville, Florida, late in the year.

Bunny Berigan (standing, top left) with Tommy Dorsey's band, 1940. UNIVERSITY OF WISCONSIN DIGITAL COLLECTIONS, BUNNY BERIGAN, FOX LAKE'S OWN

The band struggled through a patchy schedule for the first half of 1941. *Metronome* printed two reviews of the band during this period; one was a rave, the other a blistering pan. The band was wildly inconsistent, and Berigan's increasingly destructive alcoholism was probably the primary cause.

The summer offered the promise of more steady work, but even with location gigs, Berigan couldn't pay the band. He even ended up in jail in Atlantic City for his inability to pay a hotel bill. By the end of July, much of the band mutinied and left Berigan without a working unit.

But only days later, largely by raiding a New Jersey bandleader of his musicians, Berigan put together a new band of very young, inexperienced players, sometimes referred to as the "Kids' Band," which played a month at Buckeye Lake, Ohio. On September 4, a one-nighter in Pulaski, Virginia, turned into a reunion with Louis Armstrong. Armstrong had recently reported to *Down Beat* magazine that Berigan was first among his favorite trumpet players, saying, "Now there's a boy whom I've always admired for his tone, soul, technique, his sense of 'phrasing' and all. To me, Bunny can't do no wrong in music."[16] This must have been a highlight during a trying period in Berigan's career.

Heading back to Jacksonville for a location date, the youngsters in the band did their best to keep their leader off the juice. Even if they had some success, it was a losing battle. After an autumn of tough traveling from gig to far-flung gig, Berigan was called back to Fox Lake, where his father had died of cardiac failure on November 11. Berigan was clearly not well—his appearance had declined to such a degree that it shocked his family. Back with his band after his father's funeral, he was sometimes too ill to show up for the gigs.

At the beginning of 1942, Berigan was invited to California to play for the soundtrack of a movie called *Syncopation*. Away from the monitoring of his bandmates, his drinking worsened. His decline had reached the point that trumpeter George Thow, who sat next to Berigan in the studio, had to dub in parts that Berigan couldn't handle.

Somehow, the band carried on for a month without their leader. After Berigan returned, the band continued to struggle, barely keeping its collective head above water, until Berigan was admitted to a hospital near Pittsburgh on April 20, where he was diagnosed as having pneumonia.

While Berigan remained in the hospital, the band played a job in Pittsburgh, then went to Baltimore for a three-week engagement. During the Baltimore gig, Berigan's agent insisted that Berigan wasn't too terribly ill, and threatened that dates would be canceled if the leader didn't join his band. Despite all of his problems during the previous few years, Berigan retained a strong work ethic, and he left the hospital prematurely to go to work. Doctors had told him not to play his horn, but he ignored the warnings. He was noticeably ill and his playing was weaker than ever.

The band played a couple of one-nighters before going to Boston for a week. By this time, Berigan had to sit down during performances, even while soloing. While in Norfolk, Virginia, for three nights, another story was added to the legend. According to radio personality Jack Pyle, Bunny was called up for one more great performance of "I Can't Get Started," which he played with "flawless precision," evoking a five-minute ovation from the audience after the stunning climax.[17]

The band traveled from Norfolk to Milford, Connecticut (without a day in between), and then to Scranton, Pennsylvania. The next night was scheduled for Pottstown, Pennsylvania, but the band bus got lost on the way. Berigan arrived in a car with a couple of the sidemen, but the rest of the band arrived hours late, after the gig had already been canceled. Reportedly, by the time the rest of the band had arrived, Berigan had already downed a whole bottle of booze. The next night, the band was booked in New York City, but Berigan was too sick to make the gig.

The following day, June 1, Berigan was taken to Polyclinic Hospital. Ironically, that date's edition of *Down Beat* featured an article announcing the return of Berigan's band, and stating that the leader was "completely recovered from . . . pneumonia." By the next morning, he was dead.[18]

Whatever the stated cause, Berigan's death was almost certainly the result of cirrhosis of the liver, brought on by his alcoholism. Drinking was such a dominating aspect of his life that his biographer, Dupuis, devotes a whole chapter to Berigan's relationship to drink, with testimonies from his friends, family, and musical associates. These conflicting reports reflect denial, ignorance, and enabling. Clearly, though, drinking was the cause of Berigan's professional downfall, physical breakdown, and eventual death. It is a tragic part of the Berigan legend.

Berigan's wife, Donna, accompanied his body on the long train ride back from New York to Wisconsin. He was buried on June 6 in an unmarked grave in Fox Lake's St. Mary's Cemetery.

Berigan's untimely death set off a string of articles that appeared in newspapers and trade journals expressing regret, sadness, incriminations, and recriminations. Musicians and writers tried to celebrate what had been while speculating on what might have been. Due to his business troubles, Berigan left behind a considerable amount of debt, which would affect his family for years. There were arguments about who contributed to the family in their time of need. Tommy Dorsey was widely reported to have helped with the financial arrangements, which Donna denied. Eventually the Berigan band's library slipped away, and even Berigan's trumpet was lost under questionable circumstances, disappearing into obscurity.

Many people, however, voiced appropriate and heartfelt tributes to one of the great figures of the Swing Era. In the July issue of *Metronome*, George Simon compared Berigan to his celebrated predecessor:

> One of these years they're going to start talking about Bunny Berigan the way they now talk about Bix Beiderbecke. They're going to

> rave about his trumpeting feats; they're going to dig out his records, and they're going to play them for the next generation, pointing out this passage and that passage to prove that Bunny was one of the true Greats of All Jazz.[19]

Years later, Richard Sudhalter wrote about Berigan's early days in New York:

> Bunny Berigan seemed to have everything: strength, limitless endurance, a huge, singing tone. His hot solos fused Beiderbecke's lyricism with Armstrong's sense of drama. . . . He seemed to achieve expressive heights few trumpeters, black or white, had approached before.[20]

Forty years after Berigan's death, the poetic Whitney Balliett wrote about Berigan for the *New Yorker*:

> One side of Berigan's style was lyrical, romantic, melodramatic, and garrulous. It had a kind of Irish cast. The other side was blue, emotional, down, funky. He would root around in his lowest register, playing heavy, resonant notes—gravestone notes. He would play blue note after blue note. Both sides of his style would appear in a single solo. He might start two choruses of the blues in his down style. He would stay in his low register, . . . growling and circling like a bear. He would use four or five notes, shaping them into short, insistent reiterated phrases. These would summon up the baying of hounds, the call of train whistles. At the start of his second chorus, he would suddenly jump to a high C or D, go into a flashy descending arpeggio, and wing through a couple of large intervals. His vibrato would become noticeable, and his tone would become generous and sunny. He might dip into his low register at the end of the solo, but he'd finish with a ringing Irish high C. Berigan had superb technique. His sense of dynamics was unmatched, and his beautiful tone had the same texture and thickness and luxuriousness no matter what register he was in. His execution was almost flawless. He was a daring and advanced improviser, who fooled with

> offbeat and behind-the-beat rhythms and with all sorts of tonal effects. Yet his melodic lines were invariably long, logical, and graceful. There was an outsize quality to all Berigan's playing. He sounded like a three-man trumpet section pressed into one. He dominated every group he was in: on Benny Goodman's recordings of "Sometimes I'm Happy" and "King Porter Stomp" and on Tommy Dorsey's of "Marie" and "Song of India" his famous solos stand like oaks on a plain.[21]

Berigan's presence is still felt in Wisconsin. Almost every year since 1974, his hometown of Fox Lake has hosted what is now known as the Bunny Berigan Jazz Jubilee. The event takes place over the weekend of the third Sunday of May, which was declared Bunny Berigan Day in Wisconsin by Governor Patrick Lucey.

A huge collection of Berigan materials, under the title "Bunny Berigan, Fox Lake's Own," is available online through the University of Wisconsin Digital Collections. Former Fox Lake librarian Julie Flemming (who is also the driving force behind the Berigan Jazz Jubilee) oversaw the transfer of the original collection, which she lovingly curated, to digital. The original, and larger, collection is still housed in the Fox Lake library, in the Harriet O'Connell Historical Room. New material is continually added to the collection.

Over a hundred years after Berigan's birth, it remains astounding to consider that small-town Wisconsin produced this tall, handsome, charismatic musician. Seemingly simple but surely complex, unschooled but musically brilliant, gentle but troubled, Bunny Berigan was undeniably one of the great talents of the Swing Era.

2

Woody Herman

Road Father

Bunny Berigan notwithstanding, Woody Herman is probably the best-known jazz artist to have been born and raised in Wisconsin. He led a vital big jazz band for over fifty years, a record rivaled only (but not surpassed) by Duke Ellington in the annals of jazz history.

Woody was born May 16, 1913, and named Woodrow Charles Thomas Herrmann.[1] His father, Otto Herrmann, was a lifelong Milwaukee resident, and his mother, Myrtle Bartoszewich Herrmann, moved to the city from Poland with her family when she was about one year old. Otto worked for the United Shoe Machine Company, installing shoe manufacturing machines and instructing workers in their use.

According to Woody's boyhood friend Ray Sherman, the Herrmanns lived west of the Locust Street viaduct when Woody was born, renting a flat from Sherman's grandfather. They later moved to the Lower East Side, one of many moves by a family that always rented and never owned a home. Woody recalled living above a music store for a while, and later, a grocery store. He said, "Living with my family in Milwaukee as a child was like being on the road."[2] He also remembered a magical summer living in a home rented from the Uihlein family, of Schlitz beer fame. The family's extensive property bordered on the Milwaukee River in the northern part of the city. Woody and Ray Sherman swam in the river and in a public pool at Pleasant Valley. According to Herman's biographer, Gene Lees, "[Woody] and the Sherman boys played marbles, spun tops, flew kites, pretended to be streetcar motormen, and had fights with slingshots, firing hickory nuts."[3] Woody liked to swim, ice-skate, and ride bicycles. He would ride horses at the farm of relatives in Wales, Wisconsin. Bicycles and horses gave way to an interest in auto racing, and he was reportedly driving by age twelve.

Otto moved from United Shoe Machine to Milwaukee's famed Nunn Bush shoe company, eventually working his way into an executive position there. He was an amateur singer who performed with a number of groups, including the Melpomene Four, named after one of the Greek Muses, and later, the Cream City Four. He also owned a player piano, and Woody remembered learning a lot of music from his father's wide variety of piano rolls.

Woody attended live shows by the time he was six, and at age nine he won an audition that got him into a revue based on the Booth Tarkington story that was made into the movie *School Days*. Woody sang, danced, and acted. The group toured Wisconsin and Michigan, working in theater settings described by Erv Sherman, Ray's brother, as "small-time girlie revues, mainly four girls in the chorus line, and then usually one and sometimes two comedians, a juggler, and then some artist who would come out and play the saw."[4]

Young Woody took piano lessons, and probably bought his first saxophone from the money earned from the *School Days* show. He studied saxophone with Art Buech, who also steered him to clarinet. At age twelve or thirteen, Woody had a lesson with the famous saxophone virtuoso Rudy Wiedoeft, which made a lasting impression. He also studied dance at more than one Milwaukee dance school.

Woody experienced difficulties with school officials because of his involvement with show business, even though he worked only during summers at first. He transferred to St. John's Cathedral Grade School, where the youth believed that things would be easier for a budding entertainer. One of his schoolmates was Hildegarde Loretta Sell, who later became "The Incomparable Hildegarde," an internationally renowned singer and entertainer.

In Lees's biography, there is text of a court order allowing fourteen-year-old Woodrow Herman (note the new spelling), then a student at Cathedral High School, to take part in some musical and theatrical productions. Herman was by then a true vaudevillian; he sang, danced, and played his saxophone in theaters in Milwaukee, Chicago, and elsewhere in the Midwest, billed as "The Boy Wonder." But his interest was shifting from song and dance to jazz. He listened to records and music on the radio—Duke Ellington, Andy Kirk and His Twelve Clouds of Joy, and Don Redman. Herman began studying the saxophone with Arthur Krueger, who led a band that made remote broadcasts from the Badger Room at the Wisconsin Hotel. As Herman strived to be a "hot player," Red McKenzie (of the Mound City Blue Blowers) and C-melody saxophonist Frankie Trumbauer became new influences. Herman formed a small band in high school that later made broadcasts on WTMJ radio.

Herman was struggling in school, having trouble staying awake in class after late nights of performing. But one of his teachers, Sister Fabian Riley, remained his protector and champion. She recognized his gifts and encouraged him in his musical pursuits. He would never forget the woman, about whom he said, "Without her defending me all the time and encouraging me in my music, who knows what might have become of me?"[5]

Herman mentioned working in such Milwaukee venues as the Blue Heaven Roadhouse, Pick's Madrid Club, and the Modernistic, which was on the state fairgrounds. His weekends were spent in such exotic locales as Waupaca and Oshkosh. When Herman joined Joie Lichter's ten-piece band, which had been the house band at the Strand Theater, the band moved to a five-nighter at the Eagles Ballroom, later known as the Million Dollar. There, Herman was able to hear traveling bands, including name bands such as the Coon-Sanders band and Paul Whiteman's star-studded outfit. Lichter's group traveled to cities like Lexington, Kentucky; Toledo, Ohio; Tulsa, Oklahoma; and Kansas City.

In high school, Herman was perfecting his skills, including music reading, preparing himself, consciously or not, to move up in the music business. The Tom Gerun band came to Milwaukee to work at the Schroeder Hotel, and Herman ended up being offered a position with the band. He accepted, left high school, and joined Gerun in Chicago on January 3, 1931.

This was the rough-and-tumble world of Depression-era—and gangster-era—Chicago, and Herman managed to get shot in the leg one night in a post-gig confrontation after listening to Earl Hines's great band at the Grand Terrace ballroom. However, Herman and Gerun's band were on the move; they played Pittsburgh and then settled in for a long residence in San Francisco. In California, Herman became friends with other up-and-coming musicians such as Phil Harris, Bob Crosby, and Red Norvo. One of his closest friends at this time was saxophonist Al Morris, who later became known as singer Tony Martin. Herman also met a beautiful young dancer, Charlotte Neste, and immediately fell in love.

After about a year, the band left San Francisco and went to Chicago, playing at the World's Fair during the day and at clubs at night. Herman's parents could come visit from Milwaukee, and Charlotte also stopped in during one cross-country tour. While he primarily played tenor and baritone saxophone in Gerun's band, Herman also played alto, his first love, and some jazz clarinet. When the band traveled to New York after Chicago, he finally recorded his first vocals.

Herman left Gerun in July 1934, hoping, according to Lees, to become a bandleader. But the time was not yet right for the twenty-one-year-old. After some time at home in Milwaukee, he joined Harry Sosnick's band, before switching to Gus Arnheim's band, which had recently been the home of the young Stan Kenton. During this tenure, Herman began to be known as much for his singing and dancing as for his instrument playing.

Making a decision that would ultimately change the course of his career as a musician, Herman left Arnheim's band in 1934 to join Isham Jones's big band. Jones was a successful and well-known songwriter of this golden age of American song, composing such standards as "It Had to Be You" and "I'll See You in My Dreams." His band (if not particularly jazzy) was respected as one of the tightest and most professional of the 1930s dance outfits, but Jones seems to have been little impressed by his success and was somewhat ill-suited as a leader. In 1936, he decided to call it quits, leaving a band full of musicians out of work. A core of this group decided to save the band, and to continue as Woody Herman and His Orchestra, with each of the founding members owning a share of the group. Herman was finally a leader.

Before the premiere of the new band in November 1936, Herman decided that it was time for him and Charlotte to get married. After Charlotte arrived in New York on a night train and a justice of the peace refused to marry them at the late hour, the couple raced out to Armonk, New York, where another justice performed the ceremony at two a.m. on September 27. They reportedly spent their honeymoon going from club to club on Fifty-Second Street, New York's center of jazz during that era.[6]

Though he was the youngest of the new band cooperative, Herman had as much professional experience as any of the others. Besides his ability as a saxophonist and clarinetist, he could also sing, dance, and serve as a convincing front man. As the charter members dropped out over time (a usual occurrence for big bands during this era), Herman bought the shares of those who left, and within a period of just a few years, he owned the band.

Herman's band, which became known as "the Band That Plays the Blues," struggled to find an original voice and an audience in its early days, playing sweet and hot music as well as vocal novelties, at which Herman was skilled. The band liked and excelled at playing arrangements by Joe Bishop and possessed a strong rhythm section. Trombonist Neal Reid, saxophonist Saxie Mansfield, and Herman were all strong soloists.

After more than two years of living on the edge, the band, largely on the strength of a simple riff blues tune, "Woodchopper's Ball," experienced enough success to make a go of it in the exciting but very competitive era of the big bands. Recorded on April 12, 1939, "Woodchopper's Ball" eventually sold about two million copies in three years.[7] It was the biggest hit that Herman ever recorded, and his band continued to play it almost nightly until the very end.

Vocalist Mary Ann McCall, the first of a series of female singers, became another selling feature for the band. In May 1939, the band recorded "Blue Flame," which later became its theme song. During these years, the band grew and evolved musically, becoming tighter and jazzier. Cappy Lewis (see chapter 5), another Wisconsinite, joined the trumpet section and became a valued soloist. While Herman primarily played clarinet in these early years, his alto saxophone playing eventually became an important part of the band's unique mix of styles.

By 1940, the readers of the industry magazine *Billboard* rated the Herman band the sixth-best band in the "sweet music" category and third best in "swing,"[8] yet the band was still not experiencing nearly the commercial success of the bands led by Benny Goodman, Tommy Dorsey, or Glenn Miller, nor the musical success of the great black bands of the era led by Duke Ellington, Count Basie, or Jimmie Lunceford.

Arguably the peak year of the big band era, 1941, also marked the high point for the Band That Plays the Blues. By that time, Herman, like other prominent big band leaders, was a celebrity, appearing at high-profile events with famous people. The band even appeared in motion pictures. "Blues in the Night," featuring Herman's vocals, became another big hit. Following the trend of other leaders such as Goodman and Dorsey, Herman formed the Woodchoppers, a small band created from within the big band, and they recorded extensively. Around the same time, he made a few recordings with an even smaller group, Woody Herman and His Four Chips. Billie Rogers joined the big band as both a singer and, rare among the predominantly male big bands, a trumpeter. The future was looking rosy for Herman and his orchestra.

But the bombing of Pearl Harbor in December 1941 brought the United States into World War II and changed everything, including the big band business. The draft disrupted every band in the country, and Herman's was no exception. Almost half the members of the band were eventually drafted. While turnover was constant in big bands even before the war, things got much worse in 1942 and beyond. Men were yanked out of their bands (and some, of course, enlisted), only to have their replacements drafted in turn. The very best musicians who were not in the armed forces could name their price and pit one band against another for their services.

Excellent musicians came and went in the Herman band: vocalists Anita O'Day and Frances Wayne, pianist Jimmy Rowles, saxophonist Budd Johnson, and trombonist Eddie Bert. Herman was deeply infatuated with the music of Duke Ellington during this time, and hired Ellington sidemen Ben Webster, Johnny Hodges, Juan Tizol, and Ray Nance, who were all looking for more work, for some recordings.

Despite the continually shifting personnel, the war years were not all bad for Herman and his sidemen. Music continued to be in great demand throughout the United States, with the added venues of USO (United Service Organizations) shows at military bases all over the country. There were new radio opportunities as well, with the Armed Forces Radio

Woody Herman in a 1942 publicity photo. COURTESY OF KURT DIETRICH

Service. However, soldiers were not buying many records. And with the rationing of gasoline and tires, travel was challenging for touring bands.

The ill-fated 1942 American Federation of Musicians strike against the record labels, organized by union boss James Petrillo in the name of protecting musicians' royalty payments, also contributed to the demise of the Big Band Era. During the strike, bands did not record for the labels, but they did record radio transcriptions on so-called V-Discs for distribution to the troops. These records, however, were not commercial—

there were no fees for the musicians, and the products were given away, not sold. Like the free performances for the USO, this was part of the unified war effort. An ultimate result of the strike was the rise in popularity of singers and the demise of the popularity of instrumental music.

Even before the decline of the Band That Plays the Blues, it had been referred to as a Herman Herd. During the war years, one by one, the building blocks for the band that would become known as the First Herd came into Herman's orbit. First, bassist Chubby Jackson joined Herman in September 1943 and became a recruiter for a number of those who followed. In 1944, composer/arranger/pianist Ralph Burns and composer/arranger/trumpeter Neal Hefti both joined. Next came guitarist Billy Bauer, then veteran drummer Dave Tough, tenor saxophonist Flip Phillips, trombonist Bill Harris, and young trumpeter Pete Candoli. Soon Herman welcomed another excellent woman instrumentalist to the band, vibraphonist Marjorie Hyams. In late December, another brilliant young trumpeter, Sonny Berman, was brought into the fold.

The First Herd earned a reputation as one of the outstanding musical units of the 1940s and one of the great big bands in jazz history. It featured a crack ensemble and had the power of great soloists—Phillips, Harris, Berman, Candoli, and later Shorty Rogers. Its library of music, much of it written by Hefti and Burns, was new and fresh. With the drive of a rhythm section fueled by Tough and Jackson, the musical output of the First Herd was regarded at the time of its creation as among the most exciting in jazz, and in the more than seventy years since, it has taken on almost legendary status.

The classic recordings that the band made during 1945 and 1946 showcase all of these elements. While Burns and Hefti wrote and shaped much of the material, many of the best-known pieces were "head charts"—arrangements put together without written music. Among the pieces that still sound fresh after many decades are "Apple Honey" (named for the trademark spice in the tobacco blend of cigarette brand, and radio show sponsor, Old Gold), "Goosey Gander," "Northwest Passage," "Your Father's Moustache," "Wild Root" (for the hair-care cream oil sponsor of the Herd's next radio showcase), "Blowin' Up a Storm," and "Caldonia." "Caldonia" was played during almost every one of the band's shows up until Herman's death four decades later.

The band's commercial records, though less jazz oriented, were equally, if not more, important to the band's reputation and livelihood. Many featured Herman's vocals. David Raskin's beguiling "Laura," cut at the band's first recording session for Columbia Records in January 1945, became the most popular. A month later came another popular hit, "Happiness Is Just a Thing Called Joe," featuring Frances Wayne's vocal.

Some good players were lost along the way, but the replacements—pianists Tony Aless and Jimmy Rowles, Don Lamond on drums, and the great Red Norvo on vibes—were equally strong. The addition of Shorty Rogers and lead player Conrad Gozzo made a strong trumpet section even stronger. And after leaving the band in 1945, Burns continued to supply the First Herd with exceptional material, including the Bill Harris feature, "Bijou," and a three-part suite, *Summer Sequence*. Among Hefti's gems was "The Good Earth."

Things could hardly have been better for the band. According to historian Robert Kriebel, "By the end of 1945, the First Herd reigned as America's top swing band. It grossed twenty thousand dollars a week from radio, records, and stage shows and often set records for theater, hotel, and ballroom crowds. It won the best-band polls in *Down Beat* and *Metronome*."[9]

Eventually, the band took on legendary status. Eminent jazz historian Gunther Schuller, in his definitive *The Swing Era*, states that "in 1945 [Herman produced] one of the finest orchestras jazz has ever known and through it [caused] the creation of a body of works that stand to this day as classics of the post-Swing Era."[10]

In fact, the band was so well known in its heyday that through an unlikely series of events, Igor Stravinsky—arguably the greatest classical composer of the twentieth century—wrote a work for this Herman Herd. The work, called *Ebony Concerto*, is not a jazz piece, although the rhythm may indicate some jazz influence. The piece's demands on Herman's players necessitated frantic rehearsals in the weeks preceding the premiere, which the band squeezed in between the six to eight shows they were performing daily at New York's Paramount Theater.

The premiere took place on March 25, 1946, at Carnegie Hall—a measure of the Herd's prestige, as it was still the rare jazz group that appeared in this most famous of American concert halls. The program

Woody Herman, 1946, probably in Carnegie Hall. WILLIAM P. GOTTLIEB/IRA AND LEONORE S. GERSHWIN FUND COLLECTION, MUSIC DIVISION, LIBRARY OF CONGRESS

primarily consisted of typical Herman fare—the exciting instrumentals for which it was known, a few vocal features for Herman, several tunes by the Woodchoppers, and features for the primary soloists. The band also premiered Burns's extended *Summer Sequence*. The reception of *Ebony Concerto* was lukewarm, but as it turned out, Stravinsky and Herman were neighbors in southern California, and they became quite close after this event.

Despite rumors of unrest, some personnel changes, and the continued demise of the Big Band Era as it had existed before World War II, 1946 was another very good year for the band. They made more good records, including a series of lauded recordings by the Woodchoppers as small-group jazz was poised to replace big bands as the preferred vehicle of progressive music.

December 1946 marked a watershed in jazz and American popular music. The decline of the big bands—brought on by the musicians' union strike, the shortage of musicians during World War II, and the vagaries of the public's changing taste—came to a symbolic head. The bands of Benny Goodman, Tommy Dorsey, Harry James, Les Brown, Jack Teagarden, Benny Carter, and Ina Ray Hutton all dissolved, and the great First Herd joined these ranks. Furthermore, Herman's wife, Charlotte, living alone most of the time in the beautiful Hollywood Hills home that the Hermans bought from Humphrey Bogart and Lauren Bacall, was battling addictions to drugs and alcohol. Herman needed to be home with her.

Herman's activity in early 1947 was described by Kriebel like this: "Herman stayed home, played golf, dined with his wife, played with Ingie [his daughter, Ingrid], subbed for KLAC disc jockey Al Jarvis, and loafed around Los Angeles."[11] But Herman had been in show business and on the road for a long time, and an idle life was not for him. He formed a booking agency. He appeared on radio broadcasts with singer Peggy Lee. While there was no Herd, Herman still recorded for Columbia as a vocalist, occasionally playing clarinet and alto.

He continued to go out to enjoy live music, and hearing the young trumpeter Ernie Royal contributed to Herman's itch to start another band. He was inspired by the sound of a band in which Gene Roland and Jimmy Giuffre were writing for a saxophone section of four tenor players. The next step was inevitable. Herman's Second Herd debuted on October 16, 1947.

The new band included a few carryovers from the First Herd, but it was a much different band in many respects. Adherents of the music that emerged in the mid-1940s, "modern jazz" or bebop, hold an even higher regard for this unit than for its forerunner. The signature sound of the group came from the saxophone section (three tenors and a baritone), referenced in the title of one of the band's popular records, "Four Brothers," a composition by Jimmy Giuffre. The original Brothers included Herbie Steward and future jazz stars Stan Getz and Zoot Sims on tenor, and the short-lived but highly regarded Serge Chaloff on baritone. Al Cohn came in for Steward some months later. When the original Brothers left, Gene Ammons, with his burly, bluesy Chicago sound and style, became the featured tenor soloist. Besides Royal, the trumpet section included Shorty Rogers again, and bop star Red Rodney; Bill Harris returned to the trombone section, joining the young modernist Earl Swope. The rhythm section was also loaded with talent; Don Lamond and Chubby Jackson were early members, but more bop-oriented stars such as pianist Lou Levy, vibist Terry Gibbs, drummer Shelly Manne, and bassist Oscar Pettiford also put in time driving this new unit.

The recording history of the Second Herd was distorted by a second musicians' union strike, which lasted most of 1948. This band did not produce commercial hits like the First Herd, or even the Band That Plays the Blues, but it did create some classic recordings. Ralph Burns added a fourth movement to *Summer Sequence* that featured Getz on a solo that caught many ears. Soon this movement was reworked, and the result,

"Early Autumn," was a minor hit with an even better-known Getz solo. "Four Brothers" became a famous record. Underrated vocalist Mary Ann McCall returned to the band and produced a couple of lovely ballad performances in "Detour Ahead" and "More Than You Know."

Despite all of the solo firepower, many believe that the music of the Second Herd was dominated by the writers, not the players. Burns and Hefti, so important to the First Herd's sound, remained central to the library, but Shorty Rogers was increasingly integral to its works. Among his contributions were the originals "Keen and Peachy" (with Burns), "Keeper of the Flame," "Lollipop" (with Terry Gibbs), and "More Moon," but Rogers was also responsible for many arrangements. Al Cohn and Johnny Mandel made few contributions but were highly regarded by the beboppers in the band.

One of the unfortunate facts of life in the Second Herd was the prevalence of heroin abuse, the scourge of the wider culture of bebop. For much of this Herd's existence, approximately half of the band's members were known users. It created a division in the band, between the "junkies" and the "straights." Drug use also led to embarrassing personal experiences (nodding off during performances and damaging hotel rooms, not to mention destroying personal relationships) and brushes with the law, though amazingly, very few musical compromises. Even in the most trying times, the band seemed to perform at an extremely high level.

Still, by the middle of 1949, this great band playing exciting new music was hemorrhaging money at an alarming rate. In the late 1940s, big bands just were not making enough money to support up to twenty touring musicians. A fall tour on a double bill with Nat King Cole could not save the day. The band again won the *Down Beat* poll for top big band of 1949, but, despite his love for this Herd, Herman had to call it quits in early December.

It didn't take Herman long, however, to form another band. By early 1950, a new Herd existed. There was very little carryover in personnel from the Second Herd to the Third, but this was not a clean break from the past—Ralph Burns remained the chief writer for the band, and some of the music of the First and Second Herds remained in the book. The thrust of the band, however, was different. According to Kriebel, "Herman's goal remained to regain lost fans and money—to endure. . . . This band, although resembling the Four Brothers Band, . . . stayed mainstream, and even catered to broader, less discriminating tastes."[12]

The big band did not tour continuously, and Herman recorded with others in his spare time, including leading a Dixieland group billed as Chuck Thomas. Frustrated by existing record companies, Herman formed his own, Mars Records, which released most of the Third Herd's recordings between 1952 and 1954. Some of the records were solid, swinging jazz, but others were clearly intended for dancers, not listeners, and there continued to be a variety of commercial-sounding releases, with or without vocals. According to jazz critic Doug Ramsey, Herman was "always looking for a hit."[13]

When listening to the recordings of the Third Herd, one is struck by the precision and trademark excitement of Herman units, yet there is not the spark of originality or newness that made the first two Herds special. Herman carried on, perhaps because he knew no other way. Among the outstanding players who went through the various early editions of this band were trombonists Urbie Green and Carl Fontana, tenor saxophonist Bill Perkins, and trumpeter Don Fagerquist. Ernie Royal occasionally returned to contribute his stellar lead trumpet work. The rhythm section featured drummer Sonny Igoe and pianist Dave McKenna. In October 1951, Nat Pierce took over the piano chair, where he was to remain a fixture for many years; he also became an important arranger and occasional composer for the band.

One of the qualities always associated with Herman was his ability as a talent scout. Especially starting with the First Herd, excellent jazz talents—who were usually young, relative unknowns when they played with Herman—were a feature of every group that he led. In addition, many of these younger players considered Herman a father figure, and eventually referred to him as Road Father.

Herman was back with Capitol Records before the end of 1954, and while his bands that recorded over the next few years never forged a lasting identity, the fine players kept coming, including trumpeter Al Porcino, bass trumpeter Cy Touff, and saxophonists Richie Kamuca and Jack Nimitz.

While continuing to tour whenever possible, Herman signed with the minor label Everest Records in the late 1950s. Still searching for commercial success, he created new stereo versions of his earlier bands' hits, an album that joined forces with upcoming Latin jazz star Tito Puente, and another with guitarist Charlie Byrd. Two small group sessions for Verve Records featured Herman with star-laden sidemen singing great standards on *Songs for Hip Lovers*.

By the latter half of the 1950s, the number of touring big bands had been reduced to a precious few, many of them "ghost bands"—groups that continued to play the music of the 1930s and 1940s, and whose leaders were no longer living. Perhaps more ominously for the big bands, rock and roll was here to stay. Many in the business concluded that big bands were dead, never to live again.

Herman, however, had a surprise in store for the doubters and doomsayers. After a period with a small group, he could not resist putting together a big band for a date at the Metropole, a crowded midtown Manhattan bar. The biggest stars of the new unit, eventually known as the Swinging (or Swingin') Herd, were the powerhouse lead trumpet player Bill Chase, sensational trombonist Phil Wilson, and one of Herman's hardest-driving tenor players, Sal Nistico. The rhythm section, as in earlier Herds, was key, with Nat Pierce back on piano and the brilliant Jake Hanna on drums. The trumpet section included two other excellent soloists and writers, Don Rader and the Yugoslav Duško Gojković. Other notables who eventually joined were trombonist Henry Southall and tenor man Andy McGhee. Pierce wrote the bulk of the library, with important contributions from Bill Holman.

By the early 1960s, European label Philips Records was ready to take a chance on Herman. *Woody Herman 1963* became a surprisingly good-selling album. Following in quick succession were more albums for Philips, including *Encore*, which won Herman his first Grammy award, and *Woody Herman 1964*. After the Philips contract ran out, the Swingin' Herd cut two superb albums for Columbia: *My Kind of Broadway* and *Woody's Winners*. But even with this crack outfit, times were not easy. As Ralph Gleason wrote in 1965 in the liner notes to *My Kind of Broadway*,

> In contemporary America it is a difficult thing to keep a big band alive and flourishing. Jazz clubs become fewer each year. The days when two- and three-month tours could be made up out of theater

> bookings are only a dim memory. In order to survive, a big band today—more than any other time in history—must be prepared to play every possible kind of engagement. High-school proms, Elks [Club] dances, jazz concerts followed by two hours of dancing. Anything.[14]

A look at Herman's itinerary from these years shows that Gleason described precisely what the Swingin' Herd was doing. Occasionally the band would play a week of shows backing singers such as Mel Tormé or Tony Bennett. And it played short tours of Europe just about every year. But most of the year was spent on the road, playing one-nighters and traveling uncomfortable distances.

By the mid-1960s, the Swingin' Herd's burst of success was starting to diminish. The British Invasion (most notably the Beatles) was in full force. Among the revolving personnel during this difficult period was Wisconsin jazz trumpet star Dick Ruedebusch. But Ruedebusch, whom Herman had discovered in Milwaukee, didn't care for life on the road and left the Herd after about a year (see chapter 10).

In the fall of 1967, the Monterey Jazz Festival honored Herman by bringing him to their tenth annual festival to play a new major work commissioned just for the occasion. Bill Holman wrote the twenty-minute, three-movement *Concerto for Herd*, but the Herd that premiered this distinguished work featured only one regular band member, Sal Nistico. Evidently, at that time Herman did not have a traveling band that he could bring to the auspicious event.

Around this time, Herman began to suffer financial losses from which he would never recover. Band manager Abe Turchen, who had worked with Herman since the First Herd, had bailed the band out of financial difficulties more than once, getting the group through some financial emergencies on the strength of his impressive ability to win sports bets and make money playing cards. However, times were not always good for Turchen and his betting, and he'd been bailing himself out with the band's earnings for some time. Sometime in the mid-1960s, the Internal Revenue Service sent Herman a bill for more than a million dollars for unpaid payroll taxes, penalties, and interest. Herman was hounded by the IRS and his financial problems for the rest of his life.

If anything, though, Herman was a musical survivor, and in the late 1960s, he made a concession to the realities of the market that assured the viability of the band for the remainder of his career. No longer would Herman play and record "straight" jazz for audiences that were far removed from the Swing Era. His 1968 album on Cadet, *Light My Fire*, featured a couple of popular songs, a lovely ballad, and a burning Nistico feature that wasn't unusual for Herman's more traditional repertoire. But in a new vein for Herman was the title cut, a hit by the Doors, and other rock and soul hits including "MacArthur Park," Deep Purple's "Hush," and Smoky Robinson's "Here I Am Baby."

A similar formula was used for two more Cadet albums. *Heavy Exposure* and *Woody* included covers of hits by Stevie Wonder, the Isley Brothers, the Temptations, Blood, Sweat & Tears, as well as the hit "Aquarius" from the rock musical *Hair*. Electric guitar and bass were prominently featured on these records, and Herman frequently soloed on soprano saxophone, which he had taken up in the 1960s under the influence of John Coltrane. Despite the presence of Bill Chase and Nistico, this late-1960s Herd was a much different band from the Herd of the early 1960s. Key figures were trombonist Bobby Burgess, tenor saxophonist Frank Tiberi, trumpeter Tony Klatka, and drummer Ed Soph. Perhaps the most important band member for several years was a young pianist from New Zealand, Alan Broadbent, an excellent soloist who wrote a significant portion of this band's book. He arranged rock tunes, but he also crafted a gargantuan new arrangement of Herman's 1940s hit "Blues in the Night."

In his performances, Herman walked a fine line, trying to appeal to a young audience with the new material, but also trying to maintain tradition and keep his older fans. Concerts and dances would include "Light My Fire" and "MacArthur Park," juxtaposed with old standbys such as "Woodchopper's Ball" and "Four Brothers." The band also started moving into an important new venue for remaining big bands—the concert-clinic circuit at high schools and colleges, an area that had been developed most notably by Stan Kenton and his orchestra. The band would work with student musicians during the day, introducing them to the world of jazz and developing their fledgling skills, then present a concert in the evening for the wider community. Occasionally, the Herd had the luxury of spending several weeks at a time at Caesars Palace in Las Vegas.

Opening at both the Fillmore East and Fillmore West rock clubs for the Who in 1969 was an indication of how Herman's status as a musician had changed.

Around 1970, Herman moved to the West Coast label Fantasy, which combined the Herd with blues-rock guitarist Mike Bloomfield, who appears on *Brand New*. While the pairing brought a contemporary electric sound to the album, Bloomfield and Herman primarily played the blues (featuring Herman's vocals), which had been the backbone of Herman's bands since the 1930s. The succeeding albums from the early 1970s continued in a similar vein to those of the late 1960s, but the number of jazz compositions on the records came into a stronger balance with the rock and pop pieces. The band performed new arrangements of works by John Coltrane, Herbie Hancock, Keith Jarrett, and Chick Corea as well as originals by band members. New instrumental stars included trombonist Jim Pugh; tenor saxophonist, flutist, and piccolo player Greg Herbert; and trumpeter/composer/arranger Bill Stapleton. Other major talents who passed through the group included Tom Harrell, Alphonso Johnson, Harold Danko, Andy LaVerne, and Joe LaBarbera. Herman won two more Grammy awards for 1973's *Giant Steps* and 1974's *Thundering Herd*, respectively. A live album from the Montreux Jazz Festival in Switzerland followed.

For several months during this period, two-thirds of the Herd's rhythm section was Wisconsin born and bred: pianist Lyle Mays (see chapter 7) and drummer Steve Houghton (see chapter 8). Herman plucked them and bassist Marc Johnson from the high-powered jazz program at North Texas State University.

Work was steady, yet it continued to be a mixture of jobs: a series of one-nighters (many of them school gigs), a week or two in Vegas, a short tour with Sinatra in 1974, a jazz festival, and a trip to Europe where the band played more one-nighters and festivals. In 1975, Herman returned to Milwaukee to set up the Sister Fabian Riley scholarship fund for young musicians. This memorial to his childhood teacher would bring the band back to Milwaukee annually for a fund-raising concert and to work with young musicians in Herman's home city.

Herman celebrated his fortieth year as a bandleader in 1976. The public commemoration of this milestone was a concert in Carnegie Hall. It featured the current working Herd, as well as alumni of the First and Second Herds. The recording of the concert reflects the fun had by all in a fitting tribute to Herman and his exceptional accomplishment.

Unfortunately, two life-changing events followed this time of celebration in the late 1970s. For years, Herman had been driving his car cross-country, enjoying the freedom of his own automobile, rather than traveling in the bus with the band. Occasionally, he would have Charlotte along, or sometimes a member of the band, but most frequently he drove by himself. The countless hours behind the wheel caught up with him on March 27, 1977. He fell asleep driving across Kansas and ended up in a head-on collision that crushed his leg. He had steel pins implanted up to his hip, remained in the hospital for weeks, then recuperated (with therapy) at his home in California.[15] While Herman recovered from the accident, Frank Tiberi fronted the band. Herman flew to Boston to receive an honorary degree from the Berklee College of Music in May and joined the band later in the month. He did not play until later, in June.

Around the same time, in another terrible blow, it was discovered that Herman's dear Charlotte had cancer.[16] Though he continued his seemingly endless touring with the band after his recovery from the car accident, he called Charlotte every day.[17]

The band continued its one-nighters across America, a few big shows and concerts, and tours of Europe. But they did not record commercially in the United States for all of 1977. In January 1978, the Herd recorded three albums for Century Records. One featured the three-movement *Suite for a Hot Band* by star pianist Chick Corea and tunes by the progressive rock band Steely Dan. These ended up being the last studio sessions for the Herd for over two years. Many players came and went, including some very fine ones who left a mark on the Herman legacy. Saxophonist Gary Anderson became the principal writer in the band, and excellent players from the period included trombonists Birch Johnson and Larry Farrell; saxophonists Joe Lovano, Bruce Johnstone, Bob Belden, and Gary Smulyan; trumpeters Allen Vizzutti and Dennis Dotson; pianists/keyboardists Pat Coil and Dave Lalama; bassist Marc Johnson; and drummer Jeff Hamilton.

An appearance at the Monterey Jazz Festival in 1979 featured big-name guest artists Stan Getz, Dizzy Gillespie, Slide Hampton, and Woody

Shaw. The band played a straight-ahead jazz program (no rock or funk in sight). And an appearance by the band in New Orleans at Mardi Gras in 1980 resulted in the hope of a promising new regular gig. The Hyatt Regency hotel was building a performance room, and an entrepreneur believed that Herman and the band could make this a profitable home base. The band could be in residence at the club for much of the year and tour the rest of the year for higher fees than they had been earning, as their absence from the road would create a higher demand when they were available. Herman and the Herd were game.

While arrangements in New Orleans moved forward, Herman got a record deal with the fledgling Concord Jazz label, and in 1980 the label released a jam session with Herman and some of its other artists. In 1981, another jam album was recorded and released, featuring some notable alumni of the band, but with Herman present in name only.

When an album of the music from the 1979 Monterey Festival was finally released in 1981, it broke a drought of over two years for the big band without a record release. By the time the full band finally recorded for Concord live in August 1981, pianist John Oddo had taken over the bulk of the writing duties, and soloists included trombonists Gene Smith and John Fedchock, and trumpeter and vocalist George Rabbai. Former Four Brothers saxophonists Stan Getz and Al Cohn were guest soloists. Almost the same group recorded in Japan in September 1982 with guests Cohn, Med Flory, Sal Nistico, and Flip Phillips.

To considerable fanfare, Herman and the band opened at their new, not fully outfitted home in New Orleans in late December 1981 (three months later than scheduled). After an abbreviated "season" at the club, the band hit the road again in May. Following the usual tours and festival appearances, they returned to the Hyatt Regency club in October 1982. However, by early November, for lack of funding, the club folded.

Before the month was out, Charlotte, after a long battle with cancer, died in Hollywood. Though her death was an inevitability that had been foreseen for months, it was certainly a crushing blow to Herman. And he reacted in what may have been the only way he could: he went back to work.

The band hit the road again in January 1983, engaged in its typical fashion at schools, hotels, clubs, and the occasional festival. The band

Woody Herman and his band at Disneyland, 1984. COURTESY OF MARK LEWIS

served as backup for an album by vocalist Rosemary Clooney and played shows with Natalie Cole and Tony Bennett, before another European jaunt.

The next year, 1984, brought a similar mix. Herman's "elder statesman of jazz" role became more prominent as he was inducted into the Big Band Hall of Fame. "Four Brothers" was also tapped for the Hall of Fame of the National Academy of Recording Arts and Sciences (NARAS). The band played its first jazz cruise on the SS *Norway*. The standard end-of-the-year break was followed in January 1985 with a small group engagement in New York.

The next few years were a mixed bag. There were more periods when the band didn't tour, and Herman was not always in the best of health—physically or mentally. However, high-profile jobs still popped up and the band continued to play at a high level. The big band re-formed briefly in April 1985, before breaking up again. Another cruise followed in October. By the end of the month, the band was rehearsing with classical clarinetist Richard Stoltzman, and a series of concerts featured the big band by itself, Stoltzman by himself, and then a collaboration on the long dormant *Ebony Concerto*.

Herman passed his ownership of the band and its music to his daughter, Ingrid, trying to forestall its takeover by the IRS. But the agency took Herman's beloved Hollywood home and auctioned it off at a fraction of its worth. The new owner tried to move Herman out of the house, but a protracted legal battle kept him in it.

Herman's fiftieth year as a bandleader was celebrated in 1986 in appropriate style. Live recordings from March reveal yet another excellent band, playing vital, contemporary big band jazz. Articles celebrating the anniversary appeared in publications as diverse as *Down Beat*, the *Atlantic*, and the *New York Daily News*. Herman spent enough time with Stuart Troup to create a slender autobiography, which didn't appear in print until 1990. The grandest event was a concert in July at the Hollywood Bowl, with the current Young Thundering Herd; a host of band alumni; and other guests, including Stoltzman and Clooney.

Sadly, this celebration marked the beginning of the end for the seventy-three-year-old Herman. He was rushed to the hospital in New York in November with heart and breathing problems.[18] The band continued working without him before he appeared at a couple of jobs in December. The band resumed life on the road in January 1987, but Herman didn't rejoin until March. The last album on which Herman appeared was recorded on March 3. Although it is another very fine big band album, Herman's contribution is minimal and—uncharacteristically, but not surprisingly—weak. He soldiered on with the band for several more weeks but was finally in no condition to go on. He spent weeks in the hospital before returning to his home, where he was put on life support. While the band continued its travels, Herman was not to leave his home again. He hung on for months. When the end was near, the IRS made another attempt to evict him from the house. When this news was made public, Herman's fans were furious, and various fund-raisers were organized to collect money for his medical bills and the IRS. NARAS honored Herman with a lifetime achievement award.

Herman's body finally gave out on October 29, 1987, thus ending the life and career of one of the great bandleaders in the history of jazz, and Wisconsin's most noted and acclaimed jazz figure.

In 2013, Herman's centennial year, at least two events in Milwaukee commemorated the occasion. On March 9, the Woody Herman Centennial Celebration was held at Waukesha South High School. Former Herd star trumpeter Allen Vizzutti performed with the 132nd Army Patriot Jazz Band; earlier that day, he'd worked with four area high school jazz groups. Trombonist John Fedchock spent April 5 at UW–Milwaukee (UWM) conducting the sixth annual Woody Herman Jazz Educational Workshop. On April 6, Fedchock soloed with the UWM jazz ensembles and the Milwaukee Jazz Orchestra.

While some have recently acknowledged Herman's place in jazz history, Gunther Schuller's judgment from over twenty years ago unfortunately still holds true today:

> The fact that Herman [was] an excellent, at times superior clarinetist/saxophonist/singer—certainly never less than professional—and that his 1944–46 band was as exciting and influential an orchestra as jazz has seen is generally ignored or suppressed. . . . Woody Herman ought to be given credit where it is due (and in the measure it is due) as an outstanding figure in jazz, whose contributions to the music have often been important and never less than honest.[19]

Herman's career as one of the most important big band leaders and talent scouts in jazz history stands as one of Wisconsin's great contributions to American music.

3

Les Paul

The Wizard of Waukesha

Les Paul, one of the seminal figures in American popular music, is not regarded as a jazz musician by many "jazzers." And many, if not most, of the people who know of Paul do not even know that he was a jazz musician. But early in his career, and in the last three and a half decades of his life as a performer, he played jazz almost exclusively.

Paul certainly didn't start out as a jazz musician, though. Born in Waukesha on June 9, 1915, as Lester William Polfuss (although, legally, the family name was still the tongue-twisting Polsfuss), Lester grew up in a home with a hardworking, ambitious mother and an often-absent father.[1] When Lester was little, his father, George, ran a successful auto repair service—when automobiles were practically new—and what must have been one of the first cab services in Wisconsin. However, when George's drinking, gambling, and womanizing finally became too much, his wife, Evelyn, kicked him out of the family home on West St. Paul Avenue, where she continued to raise Lester and his older brother, Ralph. By all accounts, the diminutive Evelyn was a strong woman, steeped in Wisconsin's tradition of progressive politics but largely focused on raising her boys right and eventually promoting her younger son's career with all her might.

Reportedly, the first sign of young Lester's interest in music was his sitting rapt by a harmonica-playing construction worker who was laying sewage pipe on St. Paul Avenue. At the end of the encounter, the worker gave the eight-year-old boy his instrument, and a lifelong career began.

Once Lester had the harmonica, his schoolwork began to suffer, an early episode in what would become a checkered educational career.

In addition to his passion for music, Lester at an early age started cultivating his other passion: tinkering. After experimenting with his mother's player piano, modifying and adding to the piano rolls, he eventually took apart the whole instrument, trying to power it with the family vacuum cleaner rather than the standard but cumbersome foot pedals. Although the experiment failed, Lester put everything back in proper order with no help or instruction, at the age of only nine or ten. Wanting to learn how to play the instrument led to a few unhappy lessons with Mrs. Williams, the local piano teacher, which constituted the extent of his formal music training. He never learned to read music.

This was the age of radio, and young Lester listened for hours at a time. His favorite shows were the broadcasts from Nashville's Grand Ole Opry. Inspired by what he heard, he started playing his harmonica around Waukesha for tips. Apparently, even at this early age, Lester had a natural ability to relate to crowds—they loved him, and he loved them. His fascination with machines—especially radios and phonographs—also grew, as he was seemingly always tearing something apart to understand how it worked. He even cobbled together and set up a primitive radio station in his basement that could transmit to other houses in the neighborhood. His knowledge grew as he made friends with the engineer at the WTMJ transmission tower outside of Waukesha.[2] When Lester was eleven, he obtained a guitar. His inspiration was Pie Plant Pete, a radio personality on Chicago's powerful WLS. Pete (whose real name was Claud J. Moye) told stories and jokes, sang, and played his guitar and harmonica on several shows, as well as with the station's touring group, the WLS Showboat. The band featured old-time songs, but mostly Lester's favorite, then referred to as "hillbilly music." When Evelyn drove Lester to one of the live shows, he met his hero backstage. Pete showed Lester some of his favorite guitar tricks, and the boy became even more hooked on the instrument. According to Pete, in a matter of months, Lester, who was a frequent attendee of the shows, had already exceeded his hero's guitar skills.

Although Lester was quite athletic as a young teen (he was captain of his youth football team), everything else fell by the wayside once he became focused on the guitar. He designed a brace that hung on his shoulders so that he could play both sides of a double-sided harmonica while he played guitar. He was soon working the circuit of civic clubs by day and taverns by night, performing as Red Hot Red. According to biographer Mary Alice Shaughnessy, by about age thirteen, "He performed for schoolmates at Wednesday afternoon assemblies and worked the crowds at local dance halls, stock pavilion shows, movie theaters, festivals—anyplace that called for live entertainment."[3] When Lester was fourteen, Red Hot Red and His Five Aces played New Year's Eve at the Firefly Inn.

In 1931, Lester heard his next hero, Sunny Joe Wolverton, at a dance hall in nearby Genesee, Wisconsin. Wolverton showed the boy some more "fancy stuff" on guitar, awakening his imagination to the instrument's possibilities. A year later, Lester took Wolverton's place with Rube Tronson's Cowboys, playing his first job in Escanaba, Michigan, and his first radio broadcast in nearby Iron Mountain. That summer, he also designed and built a public address system for announcing the band's appearances. But after this first glorious taste of life on the road, he returned to Waukesha and high school that fall.

However, Lester's days as a student were all but over. In early October 1932, he and his mother boarded the bus for St. Louis. Wolverton had secured a job for Lester with him at powerful KMOX radio. Beginning with the morning farm report, the station played musical interludes all day long. According to Shaughnessy, "Sunny Joe Wolverton and His Scalawags were . . . the audience's undisputed favorites."[4] With Wolverton on fiddle, banjo, guitar, and mandolin; Ken Wright on organ and accordion; and Lester, the newly dubbed "Rhubarb Red," on guitar, jug, and harmonica, this "hillbilly" band was versatile enough to fill many musical roles at the station, while also playing dance halls and fairs in the area. Fully embracing his new nickname, Lester highlighted his naturally red hair with regular applications of henna.

When KMOX cut back on musicians, Wolverton and Lester resurfaced in Springfield, Missouri, as a duo—the Ozark Apple Knockers. Paul got his first Gibson guitar and started learning such challenging standard tunes as "Tea for Two" and Duke Ellington's "Sophisticated Lady." In early 1934, the duo moved from the relative backwater to the big time: WBBM in Chicago. There was less demand for hillbilly music at WBBM, and when a sponsor pulled out, the nineteen-year-old phenom and his partner were

Sunny Joe Wolverton (left) and Rhubarb Red (Les Paul) in Chicago in the mid-1930s. WAUKESHA COUNTY MUSEUM

back on the street—but not for long. They soon landed a job at the Chicago World's Fair. While exotic fan dancer Sally Rand was the star of the fair, the musicians did very well. However, Lester and Wolverton split after just a few months. Some sources suggest that Lester wanted to play jazz and experiment with electric guitar; others imply that perhaps he was no longer willing to do someone else's bidding.[5]

After a brief return to WLS, Lester landed a job at another of Chicago's prominent stations, WGN. He didn't take the job too seriously, however, and after vacating the deejay's chair on a late-night shift, he was fired. He tried out his skills as a jazz pianist at a strip club called the Sundodgers Rendezvous.[6] However, soon it was back to radio, with a revival of Rhubarb Red on WJJD. Once he'd been introduced to the dazzling recordings of jazz giant Art Tatum, Lester decided that he was never going to be a jazz pianist. But Tatum's recordings and those of Belgian gypsy guitarist Django Reinhardt inspired him to become even more serious about being a jazz guitarist.

Sometime in the mid-1930s, Lester Polfuss became Les Paul and began playing guitar in a jazz duo with organist Harry Zimmerman on WIND, the Gary, Indiana, sister station to WJJD. WIND catered to the South Side Chicago jazz crowd rather than the hillbilly market, which was still Paul's main audience on WJJD. Paul was also making the scene in Chicago, regularly attending the live performances of Louis Armstrong, Earl Hines, and other jazz stars, sitting in wherever he could. He appeared on a series of records with blues singer Georgia White. With guitarist George Barnes, Paul held jam sessions at a club called Barrel of Fun. He also formed a quartet, the Melody Kings, modeled on Reinhardt's famous Quintet of the Hot Club of France. During this time, Paul continued his instrumental innovating, designing a semi-solid-body guitar with two pickups so that he could be better heard both in live performances and on radio broadcasts.

Shortly after meeting Jimmy Atkins (the older half-brother of Chet), Paul formed a trio with Jimmy and bassist Ernie Newton. In 1937, the trio left town, playing gigs for a WLS touring group on the way to the new center of jazz, New York. The three young musicians joined a legion of other unemployed players in the Big Apple. Apparently, Les had sold the New York trip to his companions in part by pretending that he was close to Paul Whiteman, who led the most successful big music ensemble in the country. They pushed Les into taking them to Whiteman's office, where of course they were turned away, as Whiteman had no idea who they were. Incredibly, however, they ran into bandleader Fred Waring in the hallway, and an audition in the elevator led to Waring hiring the trio for his sixty-plus-member ensemble, the Pennsylvanians.

Having landed this new job, Paul brought his new bride Virginia (who he had met while working on the North Side of Chicago) out east, and they lived with Jimmy, Ernie, and many other musicians in a Queens apartment house called Electra Court. Waring's schedule was demanding, but the pay was good, and the three newcomers thrived. In addition to playing with the big orchestra, the trio was also featured on the Waring shows in its original format—and was a hit. Soon, the trio cut its first jazz records, which were favorably reviewed by *Down Beat*.

At night, Paul continued the routine he had established in Chicago, hanging out and sitting in at clubs with Tatum, Ben Webster, Stuff Smith, and Roy Eldridge. Everyone's idea of jazz guitar changed when Charlie Christian hit town; he played in a new style, influenced by the jazz of the Swing Era and the blues of what was then referred to as the Southwest (Christian grew up in Oklahoma City), which was a step in the direction of bebop. Paul and Christian sat in together at such spots as Minton's Playhouse, a birthplace of bebop.

In the meantime, Paul built a newfangled transmitter and set up a private radio station in the basement of Electra Court. The Booger Brothers Broadcasting Company broadcast all-night jam sessions that eventually included such notables as Lionel Hampton and singer Jo Stafford. The signal covered a several-mile radius in one of the most heavily populated areas in the country. But when the signal eventually interfered with that of the new North Beach Airport (now LaGuardia), the rogue station was forced to shut down.[7]

At the same time, Paul was experimenting with guitars. Although he had been playing a Gibson for some time and was listed as one of the company's endorsers in advertisements, the first legendary Paul guitar was conceived when he was trying out an Epiphone, a Gibson competitor. Trying to create sounds that he heard in his head, Paul put a second pickup on his guitars, which he often hid during performances and in photographs. His famous (or infamous) "Log" guitar was a section of four-by-four lumber with a neck attached, pickups, and, in at least one incarnation, a Kauffman Vibrola bar (for bending pitch). He later added the wings of an Epiphone to the "Log" so that it looked and felt more like a standard instrument.

In May 1941, a terrible accident occurred while some musicians were jamming in the Electra Court basement. Paul, his hands wet with perspiration, grabbed part of the transmission equipment and his electric guitar at the same time and suffered a serious electrocution, tearing muscles and ligaments in his chest and possibly developing neuropathy. Not knowing when he would be able to play again, he resigned from Waring's group and returned with Virginia to Chicago.

He returned to radio, but unable to play to his usual standard, Paul took over as musical director at WJJD and WIND. Confounding dire medical predictions, he soon regained the ability to play, at which time he moved back to WLS, then WBBM, where he was featured with the station's studio orchestra, conducted by Swing Era personality Ben Bernie. At the time of the musicians' union's first strike against recording companies in 1942, live music was still a viable option for city dwellers, but music lovers in the "boonies" could no longer buy new records. Radio became the only game in town in those communities, and Paul, who was frequently featured on one of the biggest radio stations in the area, became more popular than ever through this medium.

Bernie left the station for the West Coast, encouraging his young star to follow. But Paul was contracted for several more months to the studio orchestra, now led by the brother of musicians' union strongman James Petrillo. Through a convoluted series of shady maneuvers that involved underworld gang figures both in and out of the union, Paul was let go at the station to rejoin Fred Waring, then fired by the Waring organization immediately when the terms of the deal were understood. However, Paul got just what he wanted: the freedom to head west.

Paul arrived in southern California in 1943 and soon established a new Les Paul Trio, with pianist Joe Rann (later Paul Smith) and an old friend, Bob Meyer, on bass. The trio got work at the NBC studios making the transcription discs that were sent to troops overseas. They wrangled their way into a movie that was later released as *Sensations of '45*. In late 1943, with manpower running short during World War II, Paul was drafted into the service. However, when the music director at NBC, Meredith Willson (later famous for writing *The Music Man*), was designated to head what became the Armed Forces Radio Service (AFRS), he plucked Paul out to be a member of the unit's orchestra. With the AFRS, he formed a new trio and recorded with such famous entertainers as Jack Benny, Groucho Marx, and Kate Smith. Eventually, he was discharged on the basis of questionable health issues in 1944.

Over the next few years, Paul got the opportunity to work with some of the best musicians in the business. A call from Nat Cole in the summer of 1944 led to Paul being a part of the first of Norman Granz's groundbreaking Jazz at the Philharmonic concerts, the most famous and commercially successful "planned" jam sessions in the history of jazz.

After World War II, Paul returned to NBC. It had long been his dream to work with Bing Crosby, one of the biggest stars in American music, and Paul had discovered Crosby's favorite rehearsal room at NBC. One night, he slipped his trio into it just before Crosby's arrival. The trick audition worked, and Crosby invited the trio to play on his national radio show. Crosby sponsored recordings by the new "trio," which was actually a trio plus Paul. In 1945, Crosby recorded with the group, and "It's Been a Long, Long Time" went on to become the number one record in the country.

Later, Paul took his live show to Club Rounders, where he mixed his new jazz stylings with his old Rhubarb Red persona. He and his trio went on an exhausting but rewarding tour with another of the nation's top acts, serving as opening act and as backup band for the Andrews Sisters.

While Paul's performing and recording career was taking off, his experiments in the technical side of the music business also continued to develop. He appeared in advertisements for Gibson guitars yet could also be seen in photographs with an Epiphone.[8] He eventually owned three Epiphones that he continually experimented with, and recorded with; he called them Klunkers. He turned his little garage into a recording studio, and musicians who knew him began to sense that big things were about to happen. Word of what was going on in the studio got around town, and such diverse personalities as Perry Como, youngsters Andy Williams and André Previn, and comedian W. C. Fields visited the modest space.

In 1947 and 1948, Paul made important breakthroughs, perfecting an echo sound for recordings without an actual echo chamber and bringing the technique of overdubbing (and speeding up the recording to raise the pitch) to a new level, even for the big-name recording studios. These innovations led to the unique sound on Paul's early hit instrumental recordings "Lover" and "Brazil." Executives and engineers alike at Capitol Records were sold on Paul, and "Lover" received rave reviews from the public and the press.

In the meantime, as Paul's marriage with Virginia was failing, he met the bubbly, talented young country singer Iris Colleen Summers. When she later joined Paul under the stage name Mary Ford, they became one of the great successful duos of the 1950s. The sweet little singer from Pasadena may have seemed an odd match for the intense, hyperactive, and hyperambitious Midwestern redhead, but by all accounts, the two were madly in love.

But before they officially became a duo, in January 1948, Paul invited Ford to drive with him from California to Waukesha for a jam session celebrating the opening of his father's and brother's new tavern, the 400 Club. On the long drive back to California, the car skidded off the road and went down a steep embankment in Oklahoma. The injuries Paul suffered in this accident were even worse than those from his earlier electrocution. He lay in the hospital for months, his elbow completely shattered, and, for a time, he was reportedly near death. After long consideration, the elbow was repaired with bone from his leg, and the arm was permanently positioned bent into a ninety-degree angle, which allowed it to be in guitar-playing position. By summer, Virginia left California for the Midwest with their two children; though this was some time before their divorce, she was leaving for good.

During his long recovery, Paul determined that Ford's voice was the right one for his new musical direction. Although they cut a couple of unsuccessful records in the first part of 1949, magic didn't really happen until another visit to Waukesha later that year. With bassist Warren Downie, a partner from his early days, Paul went back to the 400 Club, and Ford evidently made her debut on rhythm guitar. A new trio was formed. (In time, Ford became a very accomplished guitarist, and she and Paul trading "hot licks" was an essential element of the live shows.) The group played around the Midwest, including the Stage Door in Milwaukee and the Blue Note in Chicago. Rather than returning to Los Angeles, where Paul was supposed to undergo another operation, the trio stayed on tour (the proceeds from which helped to defray his medical bills). Among their stops was Jimmy Fazio's Town Club in Milwaukee. During the engagement, Paul and Ford got married at the Milwaukee County Courthouse.

Finally returning to southern California, the pair started recording fifteen-minute radio shows for NBC, a combination of music, skits, and visits with guests.[9] Paul continued his studio experiments, and another instrumental, "Nola," became his next hit, climbing into the top ten in the summer of 1950.

To further his career, Paul took Ford and his gear and moved to New York. Trying to re-create the magic of his Electra Court days and home studio, the couple rented a small apartment in the same neighborhood and began recording there. Their homemade recordings, "Tennessee Waltz" and "Mockin' Bird Hill," hit the charts in late 1950 and early 1951. One more release secured Paul and Ford's success: by late April, "How High the Moon" was number one and "Mockin' Bird Hill" was number two on the pop charts.

Also in 1951, the Gibson company approached Paul with their new solid-body electric guitar, with the idea that one of the most popular guitarists in the country would be an ideal spokesman for their new line. Paul suggested a few minor modifications, and the Les Paul guitar went into production in 1952, followed later that year by a Les Paul amplifier. Boosted by the tremendous success of Paul and Ford's records, sales of the namesake guitars were immediately good.[10]

For the next several years, the couple's busy lives became even more hectic, turning into a whirlwind of activity. Paul was indefatigable, and besides playing live show after show, he felt the need to visit every possible radio station to push their records. It soon became clear to friends that Ford's constitution was no match for Paul's frenetic pace. However, she soldiered on, doing her best to keep up. The touring group became Paul; Ford; Ford's sister, Carol, singing harmony vocals backstage; Wally Kamin on bass; and all of Paul's magical electric gear. The records and performances garnered praise from many in the press and a large fan base but drew criticism from some quarters (*Down Beat*, for example) where more "pure" music making was the ideal.

Tickets and records continued to sell at a dizzying rate. According to Shaughnessy, "Les and Mary reportedly earned $500,000 by the end of 1951, roughly one hundred times more than they made the previous year."[11] Paul bought a big Cadillac and a home in a remote wooded area of Mahwah, New Jersey. The act went to England for a round of successful concerts, with a side trip to France, where Paul spent time with his hero, Django Reinhardt, whom he had met briefly in the United States in 1946. Upon their return, Paul went immediately to work in his new home

Mary Ford and Les Paul, 1955. WAUKESHA COUNTY MUSEUM

studio in Mahwah. According to a friend, for Paul "there was no separation between his work and pleasure."[12] Ford couldn't keep up and turned to alcohol.

But the hits kept coming. "I'm Sitting on Top of the World" became "the husband-and-wife team's thirteenth *consecutive* record to sell well over 500,000 copies, making them one of the country's most successful recording duos—and reinforcing Les's place in history as a guitarist."[13] Released in the summer of 1953, "Vaya con Dios," one of the most restrained records they ever made, eventually became their biggest all-time seller. In the fall, they started recording *The Les Paul and Mary Ford Show,* a five-minute segment that appeared five days a week on network TV and was edited for radio broadcast as well.

Ford gave birth to the couple's first child in November 1954, but the prematurely born girl died only days later, adding to Ford's misery. Not only was their marriage beginning to fall apart, but the musical act was never to be the same. This may have been in part because of Ford's internal personal strife (apparently she suffered from stage fright throughout her career), but much of it was due to changes taking place in American music and society. Bill Haley & His Comets released "Rock around the Clock" in May 1954, and American pop music was changed forever. No longer would the charts be dominated by the likes of Patti Page, Doris Day, Perry Como, or Les Paul and Mary Ford. Soon rock and roll took over the airwaves. As Shaughnessy astutely notes in her biography, "Ironically, the electric guitar that Les had done so much to popularize was becoming the instrument of his professional doom."[14] The duo's last hit record was 1955's "Hummingbird." Suddenly, people stopped buying the music Paul and Ford released.

Paul continued his experiments in sound, and he helped create the prototype of the first successful eight-track recording apparatus. Somehow, after their great success at Capitol Records had started to wind down, Paul and Ford managed to secure a contract with industry giant Columbia. In 1958, they adopted a daughter, and a short while later Ford gave birth to a son. They carried on for a few more years (making numerous appearances on Jack Paar's late-night television show), but the marriage was beyond saving. In the summer of 1963, Ford stole out of the house and flew back to southern California for good. She tried to resurrect her career, with only brief and modest success. Paul, too, tried to keep his act going with a couple of different singers (including buxom starlet Joi Lansing). But in 1965, he called it quits and never toured regularly again.

For a while, Paul was something of a recluse, hanging out in his home studio, occasionally entertaining friends with a jam session or stories from days gone by. In 1967, the children, who had been primarily cared for by a live-in German governess, went to live with their mother in California. The Gibson Les Paul model guitars had been discontinued for several years, but in the mid-1960s, Paul reconnected with the company, and in 1968, the line was renewed. Sales were initially slow, but eventually they picked up and remain strong to this day. In the meantime, Paul suffered a broken eardrum, and the onset of arthritis hampered his return to regular performing.

Surprisingly, an emergency call from jazz guitarist Bucky Pizzarelli in January of 1972 was the spark for Paul's unlikely comeback. The duo created a stir playing regularly in the St. Regis Hotel in New York City, with such musical celebrities as Count Basie, Doc Severinsen, and George Benson dropping by.[15] In 1974, Capitol issued a greatest hits album of Paul and Ford's best-known work. A concert with Pizzarelli at New York's Town Hall that year did not draw a huge crowd but brought attention, a rave review in the *Village Voice*, and a television appearance on ABC's morning show. Performances in San Francisco and London brought acclaim and the attention of young fans who knew that their rock heroes played guitars with Paul's name on them. Work on the first documentary film about Paul, *The Wizard of Waukesha*, began in 1975. In April, he took the stage in Carnegie Hall with Pizzarelli. Guitarists Benson and Laurindo Almeida were also on the bill; a jam session closed the show.

In May 1975, Paul went to Nashville to record the album that signaled his full return. Featuring the guitar duo of Paul and Nashville icon Chet Atkins, *Chester and Lester* was released in 1976 and earned a Grammy award for Best Country Instrumental Performance in 1977. Many did not consider it a country album, despite its country "glow." The tunes are standards largely associated with jazz, and even *Down Beat* published a rave review.

At the end of the 1970s, several aspects of Paul's life were looking up. The Paul–Ford recording of "How High the Moon" was inducted into the National Academy of Recording Arts and Sciences' Hall of Fame. Paul even made the mainstream media with an article in *People* magazine.

But life wasn't all good. Mary Ford died in relative obscurity in September 1977. *Guitar Monsters*, the follow-up to *Lester and Chester*, was not a hit. Atkins's first appearance in New York, with Paul at the Bottom Line, brought mixed reviews. In 1980, Paul was diagnosed with a serious heart ailment, and he underwent surgery that left him weak and upset. In business, Paul was unhappy with Gibson, whose products he started criticizing as they seemingly ignored him.

But things turned again. In early 1984, prodded by guitarist friend Wayne Wright, Paul played with Wright and bassist Gary Mazzaroppi at the lower Manhattan "quintessential jazz dive"[16] Fat Tuesday's for the first of what would turn out to be years of Monday nights in the club. He left Fat Tuesday's when the venue closed in 1995, but by the following year Paul had relocated to the somewhat glitzier Iridium Jazz Club. The Iridium trio initially included rhythm guitarist Lou Pallo and bassist Paul Nowinski and eventually grew to a quintet with Pallo, guitarist Frank Vignola, bassist Nicki Parrott, and pianist John Colianni.

The last two decades of Paul's life seemed almost charmed. Among guests who showed up at Fat Tuesday's (and later the Iridium) were jazzers Tal Farlow, George Benson, Larry Coryell, and Al Di Meola and rockers Keith Richards, Eddie Van Halen, Bob Dylan, Jeff Beck, Jimmy Page, Paul McCartney, and Milwaukeean Steve Miller. In 1985, Paul was inducted into the Hollywood Guitar Center's "Rock Walk." And after being feted by Gibson (the company and the legend had reconciled by then) with a star-studded birthday party at New York's Hard Rock Café in 1987, he was inducted into the Rock and Roll Hall of Fame in 1988. Later in 1988,

Les Paul in Waukesha in 1988, on the occasion of his mother's one hundredth birthday. WAUKESHA COUNTY MUSEUM

Paul returned to Waukesha to celebrate his mother Evelyn's one hundredth birthday. Her birthday was deemed Les Paul Day by the mayor and the governor, and the bandshell in Waukesha was renamed the Les Paul Performance Center. The party in the Pewaukee Country Inn lasted late into the night.

A permanent Les Paul exhibit opened at the Rock and Roll Hall of Fame and Museum in 2004. (Four years later, the Hall honored him with an all-star concert.) He was also presented with the first Lifetime Achievement Award from the Wisconsin Foundation for School Music in October 2004. In 2005, Paul's ninetieth year was celebrated with many events, including a concert at Carnegie Hall. The album *Les Paul & Friends: American Made, World Played*, recorded in 2005, won two Grammy Awards in 2006.

Paul returned to Waukesha to play a benefit concert in May 2007. Later that year, he received a National Medal of Arts from President George W. Bush. He was back in Milwaukee in June 2008 for a concert at the Pabst Theater and the opening of the "Les Paul House of Sound" exhibit at the Discovery World museum on the city's lakefront.

After one of the most celebrated careers in American music, Paul died in White Plains, New York, August 13, 2009, at the age of ninety-four. On August 21, his coffin lay in the theater of Discovery World, and fifteen hundred people paid their respects before he was buried in a private ceremony in the Prairie Home Cemetery in Waukesha. The December 2009 issue of *Down Beat*, finally acknowledging Paul's status as a jazz guitarist, included a feature article, "Les Paul: In Praise of a Master." On September 10, 2011, a "500-square-foot granite monument that recounts Paul's biography and a list of his most significant awards" was dedicated at the gravesite.[17]

In honor of what would have been Paul's ninety-sixth birthday, the Google "doodlers" put an interactive guitar-like version of their logo on the Google home page, which users could manipulate to make music.

In 2012, Paul's estate sold a number of his instruments; sixteen of them were purchased by a pool of contributors so the instruments could become a major part of the Les Paul Experience at the Waukesha County Museum. The exhibit opened to considerable fanfare in June 2013.[18]

There were numerous events associated with Paul's one hundredth birthday at Discovery World, the Waukesha County Museum, Prairie Home Cemetery, and, a month later, at Summerfest. The *Milwaukee Journal Sentinel* published a feature article, "Legacy of Les Paul: 70 Tidbits about Music Pioneer in Honor of His 100th Birthday." While Les Paul will probably always be best known for the instruments that bear his name, and secondarily for his innovations in recording technology, his status as a jazz musician should not be minimized or forgotten.

The Early Years

4

Early Jazz in Milwaukee

Two of early jazz's star trumpet players, though not born in Wisconsin, spent significant time in Milwaukee during their careers. The time that Jabbo Smith and "Wild Bill" Davison spent in the Cream City sheds some light on how Milwaukee, and Wisconsin, fit into the larger jazz scene during the 1930s and beyond.

Jabbo Smith

Jabbo Smith's brief stardom as a trumpeter came very early in jazz's history. His long connection with Milwaukee lasted decades after that early fame.

He was born Cladys Smith in Georgia in 1908. After the death of his father, Smith's mother left him at the Jenkins Orphanage (or Orphan Home) in Charleston, South Carolina, when he was only six years old.[1] From a musical standpoint, this placement was fortuitous, as the solid training offered at this institution also nurtured the development of later jazz stars Freddie Green, of Count Basie's groundbreaking All-American Rhythm Section, and Cat Anderson, trumpet star with Duke Ellington.

Smith apparently ran away from the orphanage at every opportunity, and at the age of twelve or thirteen, he played trumpet with a band in Jacksonville for several months before he was caught and sent back. He made his final escape at age sixteen, around the same time he was given the nickname Jabbo, and moved in with an aunt in Philadelphia. Before he was seventeen, he had joined Charlie Johnson's Paradise Ten, one of the top groups in New York. During his two and half years with this band, he made several notable recordings, including two well-known takes of "Black and Tan Fantasy" with the Paradise Ten's rival: Duke Ellington's band. Unfortunately for Smith, he turned down a job with Ellington, evidently thinking the pay would not be satisfactory. While still a teenager, he was let go by Johnson for excessive drinking and unreliability.

However, Smith landed on his feet, joining the pit band of the black musical revue *Keep Shufflin'*, a band that included early jazz giants James P. Johnson and Fats Waller. After the show closed, Smith was chosen to make a series of records for Brunswick Records as leader of the Rhythm Aces. According to historian Scott Yanow, "It was hoped that his record sales would compete favorably with Louis Armstrong's." Yanow describes the twenty-year-old Smith as "an erratic but very exciting trumpeter, overreaching at times and often on the edge of losing control, but far ahead of most of his contemporaries in terms of range, speed, and complexity of ideas."[2] Great swing trumpeter Roy Eldridge and bassist Milt Hinton were just two of the musicians who claimed that Smith was the one trumpeter in jazz at this time who could challenge the nonpariel Armstrong. And Benjamin Barbera describes an epic cutting contest in Milwaukee in 1930 when the up-and-coming Eldridge, known throughout his career for never backing down from such a challenge, was bested by the veteran Smith.[3]

But Smith's records were not a commercial success, and his drinking continued to be a problem. The Depression made life tough for most musicians, and for some reason Smith decided that he preferred working in the Midwest, leaving the spotlight of the East. He was comfortable spending much of the 1930s moving between Chicago and Milwaukee—according to some accounts, when he got in trouble in one city, he'd go to the other. But this transient lifestyle did not lead to a high profile in the jazz world. Smith told Yanow: "Milwaukee was a fine place. I played up there, got a steady gig, liked the city, and just chose to stay. I got married in 1932 and settled there for a long time."[4] He led an eight-piece group at the Wisconsin Roof off and on for about six years. During part of the decade, he worked with Claude Hopkins's respected Chicago-based band and recorded a few sides with Hopkins and as a leader.

Smith finally went back to the East Coast for the 1939 World's Fair in New York. Following that, he worked in relative obscurity in Newark,

Jabbo Smith during his late-career revival. NANCY MILLER ELLIOTT PHOTOGRAPH COLLECTION, INSTITUTE OF JAZZ STUDIES, RUTGERS UNIVERSITY—NEWARK

New Jersey, before returning to Milwaukee in 1944. He worked local music jobs at places like the Moon Glow and the Flame, while taking a day gig at Avis car rental company for many years. In a published photo possibly taken at the Flame, Smith appears with pianist Loretta White, saxophonist Bobby Burdette, reed player Buster Washington, bassist Pal Williams, and drummer P. G. Washington.[5]

According to Smith's papers at the University of South Carolina, he started a campaign in 1958 "to establish in Milwaukee an organization called 'Jabbo's Music Box Musicians and Entertainers Club, Inc.'—'The time has come . . . when we as a group of Negro's [*sic*] should—instead of depending solely on the white people of our community for our livelihood, to band together and create our own jobs and security—at least partially.' A sample blank letterhead with a Milwaukee address lists him as manager of the Sepia Music-Theatrical Talent Agency."[6] This was one of the earliest attempts to establish an African American organization for the promotion of Milwaukee jazz.

As Smith aged, he performed less and less frequently. However, he periodically resurfaced in the wider jazz world, and various attempts were made to "rediscover" him in the 1960s, 1970s, and 1980s. The most notable reappearance occurred in 1979, when he sang and played his own new songs in a vaudeville-jazz musical show called *One Mo' Time*. The show ran for two years in New York, Philadelphia, San Francisco, Houston, and Washington, DC. But after his brilliant early career, Smith never really hit the big time again. He died in New York in 1991.

Yanow's is a typical judgment on Smith's career: "He should have moved in 1930 to New York, where his impressive sight-reading abilities and exciting solo style might have led to fame or at least steady work."[7]

Yet in many ways, Smith seemed to prefer his predictable life in Milwaukee to life in an unpredictable spotlight in New York. Still, longtime Milwaukeean Smith will always hold a place in jazz history as one of the most exciting trumpeters of the early glory days of the late 1920s.

"Wild Bill" Davison

William Edward "Wild Bill" Davison was born in Defiance, Ohio, in 1906.[8] He went to Chicago in 1927 and made his mark on the jazz scene there during the next five years. He put together a big band with clarinetist Frank Teschemacher, but when Teschemacher unexpectedly died, Davison moved to Milwaukee, probably in 1933.

According to Hal Willard's detailed Davison biography, Carl Dunlap made Davison an offer to play in a band at the Wisconsin Roof, a dancehall on top of a building in downtown Milwaukee. Apparently Davison had already played in Milwaukee a number of times, at the club of John Mallio, a banana importer. The Roof band, built around Davison's talents, rehearsed for about a week before opening. On opening night, Davison became so ill that he had to be hospitalized (whether from pneumonia, intestinal flu, or a nervous breakdown remains unclear). He remained in the Belmont Hospital for about a month. But by the time he had recovered, there was no room for him in the band that had been supposedly built around him.

Looking for something new, he took a job with a band led by Al Sky, who had set up a tour through the Dakotas, Iowa, Nebraska, and Minnesota. Despite getting into a car accident on the way to the first gig he played with the band in Fond du Lac, Davison continued the tour with Sky through several states. According to Willard, though, Davison eventually left Sky in a huff in Grand Island, Nebraska, and returned to Milwaukee.

By this time, Dunlap had another gig for Davison, with a band at the Chateau Country Club in the Milwaukee suburbs. The band at the Chateau included several local musicians who remained on the scene for some years, including pianist Hilly Hansen and drummer Chick Hager; Bea Haven was vocalist. Davison, a great improviser, was not a strong reading musician, but he managed to learn the music for the club's floor shows adequately. He remained with the Chateau band for over a year, until the spring of 1935.

At that time, Davison finally joined the band at the Roof, a group that at times had as many as thirteen members. Among the other members of the band during Davison's time with it were Sammy Armato (see later in this chapter) and pianist Gene Schroeder (see chapter 5), who would go on to a notable career in New York. In fact, for many years, Schroeder played in a band at Eddie Condon's club in New York that also included Davison.

During this time, Davison lived up to one of the titles that had been given him, "the world's hottest trumpeter." He also lived up to his nickname, Wild Bill, due to his insatiable appetite for alcohol and women. Davison's mother moved to Milwaukee to be with him during this time, but she may not have seen a lot of him.

Willard reports that Davison also worked with a band at the Miami Club, which played for dancing and a show. From time to time, while in Milwaukee, Davison would show up for after-hours sessions at the Moon Glow,[9] an African American club in what later became known as the Bronzeville area of the city, where he would sit in with, among others, local saxophonist Jimmy Dudley. A famous session in 1936 included members of Ben Pollack's band and the celebrated trumpeter Harry James. Armato says that Davison "cut," or outplayed, James that night. Willard also tells of a night that Davison played with a seventeen-year-old pianist who had some talent but did not know how to play the blues. That pianist became the figure we now know as Liberace.

Davison played at the Club Metropole in 1937. At another well-known Milwaukee club, 26th and North, he led a band for some time; the emcee was comedian Morey Amsterdam, and well-known vocalist Helen Morgan sang there. With the exception of time off for a month-long gig in Colorado, Davison worked at the club until January 1938. For the next few years, Davison was back and forth between the Roof, the Chateau, the Alhambra Theater, the East Side Spa, Harry Lakota's restaurant and bar (from which radio broadcasts were aired), and occasional jobs out of town, such as at Sheboygan's Rathskeller. He may have been the first jazz musician, or at least big-name jazz musician, to play at the Blatz Palm Garden in the Blatz Hotel on City Hall Square. During the last eighteen

Wild Bill Davison, late in his career. This photo is rumored to have been taken by Lord Snowdon. COURTESY OF MARY LOU AND JERRY BARNES

months he was in Milwaukee, Davison worked a steady gig at Schmit's with a group called the Debonaires that included accordion, violin, and a female vocalist.

Davison's personal life was in upheaval much of this time. He went home to his native Ohio briefly; his wife had a miscarriage. While in Milwaukee, Davison met the woman who would become his second wife in 1943, Dianne Lee (born Lorraine O. Hansen), a singer from Wisconsin who was billed as "the Blonde Bombshell of Popular Song" and had become the new vocalist in the Debonaires. Davison also encountered "the world's oldest, and richest, groupie" at the Palm Garden, a Mrs. Robinson, who sent the trumpeter and his new wife to New York shortly after meeting Davison—with enough money to buy a house in New Jersey.[10]

Though Davison was in the service for part of World War II, he was essentially a New York resident for many years, playing regularly at Nick's and Eddie Condon's. In New York, he definitively established himself as one of the major voices of what is generally called Chicago jazz, although he had been respected for years already in places like New York and Milwaukee.

Davison moved to the West Coast in 1960 and spent much of the rest of his career touring not only in the United States but also in Europe, often as a single. (Wisconsin clarinetist Chuck Hedges toured with Davison on a number of occasions in the 1970s and 1980s; see chapter 10.) According to *The Biographical Encyclopedia of Jazz*, between 1965 and 1975, Davison recorded with more than one hundred bands in North America and Europe. He toured into his eighties, with an eightieth birthday concert at Town Hall in New York. He died in California in 1989 but will always be remembered for his brash, energetic, and unique version of Chicago jazz, and as a character who, by all accounts, earned his nickname Wild Bill.

Early Black Jazz Musicians

Sadly, much less is documented about early black jazz musicians in Milwaukee than their white counterparts, although there are names that always seem to come up in discussions of notable locals. Alto saxophonist Jimmy (sometimes seen as Jimmie) Dudley was born in Hattiesburg, Mississippi, in 1903, and after moving to St. Louis, he toured with such high-profile groups as Noble Sissle's band and McKinney's Cotton Pickers. Sometime in the 1930s, Dudley gave up travel when he fell in love with a Milwaukeean, moved to the city, and raised a family there.

Dudley, who was a favorite jamming partner of Wild Bill Davison, was mentioned by many musicians in this book, from Sam Armato and Joe Aaron (see later in this chapter), both of whom raved about Dudley's playing, to Chuck Hedges, who knew Dudley's music from a completely different era. Chick Hager said that Dudley sounded just like Duke Ellington's great alto saxophonist, Johnny Hodges. Art Dawson, who owned an after-hours club, was quoted in a *Milwaukee Journal* article from 1941 (unearthed by Benjamin Barbera) as saying that Dudley "could play with any colored band in the country, but he wants to stay around here till his daughter finishes high school."[11]

Other well-known early black jazz musicians from Milwaukee are tenor saxophonist Bert Bailey, bandleader Leonard Gay, and pianist Loretta White. Joe Aaron remembers that Bailey led a small band, and Willie Pickens recalled that Bailey was one of Bunky Green's teachers. Gay led a band that once included Milwaukee saxophone giant Berkeley Fudge. There is most certainly a rich history of the early black jazz scene in the city just waiting to be documented.

Sam Armato

Two emblematic jazz players on the Milwaukee scene—Sam Armato and Joe Aaron—had parallel careers. When they were interviewed for this book in July 2010, both were still actively performing at over ninety years of age (Armato appears in the photo that accompanies Joe Aaron's profile later in this chapter). While neither will ever be known widely, and neither was known strictly as a jazz player, both represent a vital part of what it meant to be a professional musician in Milwaukee.

Sam Armato was born in Rockford, Illinois, in 1916, and his family lived in both Rockford and Chicago during his youth.[12] As a ten-year-old violinist, he joined a group of kids that had established a band in Rockford some years earlier, the Ritz Vagabonds. Sam admired a C-melody saxophonist in the group, and in a couple of years he had saved up enough money to buy himself a saxophone. Frankie Trumbauer, the first and last great exponent of the C-melody instrument, became the young Armato's inspiration and model.

At age sixteen, Armato left school in order to play music, touring with an area band led by Joe Kayser. When Armato's father moved to Milwaukee to work with the Wisconsin Can Company, Armato was chosen to play in the band at the Wisconsin Roof featuring Wild Bill Davison. Armato played on and off in groups with Davison for the next several years at the Roof, the Miami Club, and 26th and North.[13] According to Wild Bill's biographer, Hal Willard, Davison's mother, who only periodically showed any maternal instincts toward her son, moved to Milwaukee for some months to be near him. But while Davison continued to lead the wild life that led to his nickname, his mother "may have seen more of Sammy Armato [than she did of Bill], the kid of the band and a skinny one at that. Momma decided [Armato] needed fattening up and invited him to have his meals with her and he accepted gladly."[14]

In 1935, at the tender age of nineteen, Armato left the Davison group at the Roof to return to the Miami Club as bandleader. His small unit played jazz but also backed up comedians, singers, and dancers for the shows that took place at the club seven nights a week. The young saxophonist remained active and flexible during the rest of the 1930s, returning to Chicago to work with the band of Maurie Sherman, which backed a vocal group that was just about to explode onto the national scene: the Andrews Sisters. In 1938, Armato accepted Milwaukeean Woody Herman's invitation to join his early band, the Band That Plays the Blues. After a few months with Herman, Armato decided that he didn't want to travel to the extent that Herman's band did. Furthermore, he wanted to get back to the girlfriend he'd left in Milwaukee, who was soon to become his wife. He returned to Milwaukee to lead a band that played every night of the week for the shows at the Chateau Country Club.

After working at the Empress Theater, Armato was drafted into the service during World War II. When it was discovered during his basic training that he was a musician, he was sent to Biloxi, Mississippi, to join a musical unit. Armato's Army Air Force group moved on to Denver, and then to the base at Pearl Harbor in Hawaii. From there, the group toured the Pacific, playing for troops wherever it was safe, with Armato playing both clarinet and saxophone.

Returning to Milwaukee after the war, Armato led the band the Hit Paraders at Tutz's bar but began working with orchestras and bands of all sizes that were employed by many of the radio stations in the city. For the next few years, he found work at WTMJ, WMLO, and WFOX. Armato primarily played saxophone and clarinet but also became a valued vocalist. He occasionally brought out his first instrument, violin, as well. Most radio work took place during the day, so Armato continued his jobbing in several of the clubs around the city. The Melody Room was a steady gig. His highest-profile jazz job during this part of his career was as clarinetist with Dick Ruedebusch's Underprivileged Five. Armato was with Ruedebusch when the band moved to its home at the Tunnel Inn, but he left before the Five's brush with national fame in 1962.

Armato ultimately left Ruedebusch because it was too much for him to play every night while working full days at WTMJ, the station that employed him at the time. His days were certainly full, as he was a member of virtually every band that the station used.

Alas, live music at WTMJ—and at virtually all other radio stations in the United States—was shortly to become only a memory. In the mid-1960s, as various radio bands at WTMJ broke up, Armato moved into the position of music librarian at the station. In this capacity, he affected the listening habits of Milwaukeeans for years, as he chose the music for most of WTMJ's music shows. He was not as active in Milwaukee's club scene as he once had been—and the clubs no longer employed as many musicians as they once had—but Armato continued to be a valuable sideman for decades. While he often played in "polite" bands for parties and weddings, Armato was usually hired for his abilities as a jazz player. He was often the "hot" player in the small bands in which he played, including some well-known and some long-forgotten but colorfully named groups: the bands of Steve Swedish and Bill Sargent, Bill Sanders's Basin Street Saloon Band, the Hot Shots (led by Joe Shotts), Grant Krueger and the Executives, Concertina Millie's polka band, and Johnny Zark's Miller Brewer Band.

In his interview for this book, Armato said that he was "ten going on ninety-five." The small number he used to remind himself and let others know that he was still young at heart and eager to learn; the large number reflected his true age. He has been quoted as saying that he was looking forward to a career as the "world's oldest performing jazz clarinetist." When he was age ninety-four, I heard him play fluently and convincingly with a group of seasoned Milwaukee musicians who were young enough to be his sons and grandsons. His obituary in the *Milwaukee Journal Sentinel* reported that he played his last "official" gig at age ninety-five in 2011, but despite suffering from Alzheimer's disease, he "continued to sit in with other performers—at the South Shore Farmers Market or a gospel brunch at the Riverwest Public House—as recently as 2012."[15]

Armato passed away on December 31, 2014, at the age of ninety-eight. According to the *Journal Sentinel*, appropriately, "He drifted off reading a book, a gift from his wife, on the famed jazz clarinetist Artie Shaw."[16]

Joe Aaron

Joe Aaron was a native of Milwaukee, growing up in a predominantly Jewish neighborhood around North Avenue and North Fifteenth Street in the 1920s.[17] He was the youngest of six children. An older brother, Alvin (better known as Abe), later became one of the city's accomplished jazz players (see chapter 5).

At age sixteen, Joe Aaron was talking his way into ballrooms and clubs so that he could listen to the resident or touring bands. Some club owners were sympathetic to the young music lover, but not to the extent that they would serve him alcohol. One of the players he was eager to hear was the young saxophonist Sam Armato, whose playing, Aaron says, "fractured" him. After he graduated from North Division High School, it wasn't long before Aaron developed into another of the city's respected reed players.

Aaron, like Armato, got a considerable amount of work in the studios of local radio. Aaron remembers three of the local stations in the 1930s and early 1940s—WTMJ, WEMP, and WMAW—having orchestras of some sort. For a while, Aaron toured with Clyde McCoy's band (whose hit "Sugar Blues" was on the charts three different times in the 1930s and 1940s).

Aaron also played in the orchestra at the Riverside Theater for a number of years, starting in the 1940s. He recalled,

> That was quite a run. It was a good job, I'll tell you. And I only toss this out to give you an idea: it was ninety dollars a week. And I think three dollars came off for Social Security and withholding. And a ninety-dollar check, this was in the Depression. . . . I would go home and give my mom the check, and she would give me five dollars spending money. That was nothing unusual then. I felt great about being able to do it; my dad was out of work, as were how many hundreds of thousands of people.

Joe Aaron is seated at the far left with his clarinet; Sammy Armato is playing. Both were over ninety years old at the time, which was at a memorial get-together for Chuck Hedges in 2010 at the Grove in Elm Grove. PHOTO BY LYNN LEW

Eventually, Aaron played for the WTMJ television orchestra. Like Armato, he also worked gigs at night and on weekends, many of them parties and weddings. Also like Armato, Aaron was frequently considered the "jazz guy" in the small groups in which he played.

But like so many musicians, he needed a day gig. Aaron completed a degree in music education at Milwaukee State Teachers College (which ultimately became the University of Wisconsin–Milwaukee). In 1952, he became an instructor of instrumental music at Juneau High School in the city. He taught there for thirty years, the last twenty-five in social studies.

In addition to all of his other work, Aaron played the entire twenty-four-year run of the Melody Top Theatre, the summer stock operation that brought Broadway shows to the Milwaukee area. Some of the city's finest players were members of the band, including members of the Milwaukee Symphony before the symphony became a year-round operation.

While Milwaukee Symphony concertmaster Ed Mumm was the contractor for the Melody Top's orchestra, Aaron was the "straw boss" of the group, responsible for the hiring of a fair number of the band's members. The symphony frequently hired Aaron for those rare orchestral pieces that require saxophone (Ravel's *Bolero*, for example).

Aaron also taught saxophone privately and at UW–Milwaukee. In fact, even if he had never played a note in public, he would be important for having taught some of Milwaukee's top saxophonists of later generations, including Warren Wiegratz, John Kirchberger, Tom Newburg, and Curt Hanrahan.

Into his nineties, Joe Aaron, like Sammy Armato, continued to be active as a musician. He played his last gig only a matter of weeks before his death on June 6, 2013, at the age of ninety-three.

5

Swing and Mainstream Figures

The Swing Era lasted from approximately 1930 through the end of World War II, roughly 1945. It was the one time in the history of American music when jazz or jazz-influenced music, largely through the medium of the big band, was the most popular music in the country. Wisconsin's most visible contributions to this movement were the two towering figures of Bunny Berigan and Woody Herman. But there were other notable Wisconsin contributors to swing and the music that followed it. A number of those musicians' stories are presented here.

Abe Aaron

Reed player Abe (born Alvin) Aaron, brother of Milwaukee saxophonist/clarinetist Joe Aaron (see chapter 4), was a longtime member of one of the longest-running and most popular big bands, Les Brown and His Band of Renown. Music writer Eugene Chadbourne has pointed out, presumably tongue in cheek, that Aaron "turned out to make one important contribution to jazz: his name would be the first one readers would come across in encyclopedias devoted to this genre."[1] Although Abe Aaron's name doesn't appear in all of those encyclopedias, he does appear in the first really popular one, Leonard Feather's *Encyclopedia of Jazz*.

Aaron was born in Toronto in 1910 but spent much of his youth in Milwaukee, like his brother Joe, gaining valuable experience in the theater orchestras of the city. The first name band he played in was Jack Teagarden's, which he joined in 1942. He toured with Teagarden only until the following year, however, when he settled in southern California. Once there, he became a member of Horace Heidt's and Skinnay Ennis's bands, evidently traveling some but also working radio broadcasts, and probably other jobs. But Aaron was certainly best known for his decades-long tenure with the Brown band, with which he made numerous recordings and toured internationally. Aaron died in 1970.

Freddie Slack

Pianist/bandleader Freddie Slack was born in La Crosse, Wisconsin, on August 7, 1910.[2] He spent most of his childhood in nearby Viroqua, where his father, Charles, was a businessman, at one time or another running Viroqua's first car dealership, its first gas station, and a successful insurance business. Slack was the last of four children by Charles's second wife (Charles sired four children by his first wife, his second wife's sister). Slack's brother, Graydon, was a drummer in Wisconsin's Third Regiment army band.

Slack started his musical career as a drummer but switched to xylophone, and then piano. Music aficionado Eddy Nix relates a story of Slack performing as a soloist at a state teachers' conference, probably on xylophone, and being brought back for two encores. As a youngster, Slack played in bands throughout his time in school, eventually working with the area group the Badger Serenaders.

While Slack was a teenager, his father was killed in downtown Viroqua in a freak accident; Slack's mother was struck on a sidewalk by a car, and she was thrown into Charles, who cracked his head on the sidewalk and died some days later.

The remaining family moved to Chicago shortly thereafter, where Slack took piano lessons at the American Conservatory. He was introduced to big-time jazz in the Windy City, where he was able to hear early jazz stalwarts Bix Beiderbecke and Earl Hines. He logged his first professional experience in the big city playing with Johnny Tobin at the Beach View Gardens. Slack moved to the West Coast and worked in several groups before landing his first job with a name band, Ben Pollack's, in 1934. According to music writer Mike Rowe, Slack had an "epiphany" while on tour with Pollack in Kansas City, where "he heard Pete Johnson playing boogie woogie."[3] He stayed with Pollack's band, which had nurtured jazz greats Benny Goodman and Jack Teagarden, until 1936, when he joined Jimmy Dorsey's outfit. He remained with Dorsey until 1939, when he moved into the new band of trombonist Will Bradley.

Slack came to the attention of the wider public shortly thereafter when the band recorded a huge hit, "Oh, Beat Me, Daddy, Eight to the Bar." The "eight to the bar" refers to the number of bass notes in a measure of boogie-woogie piano music. Boogie-woogie was a hot commodity on the scene at this time, with pianists Meade Lux Lewis, Albert Ammons, and Pete Johnson popularizing what was in some ways a simple, easy-to-follow formula, but with lots of energy, and sometimes real virtuosity. Transferring boogie-woogie to big band, the preferred medium of popular music, made plenty of commercial sense. According to drummer Ray McKinley (eventually coleader with Bradley), "We were playing one of [the new boogie-woogie arrangements] one night at the Famous Door. . . . There was one part where I had a drum break, and for some reason or other that night, instead of playing the break, I sang out, 'Oh, Beat Me, Daddy, Eight to the Bar!' "[4] Two songwriters at the club that night wrote a song using the break; it was an instant hit. Daddy, however, was not an anonymous father; Slack's nickname was "Daddy Slack." His skills were displayed again for two other hits that quickly followed—"Down the Road A-Piece" and "Scrub Me Mama with a Boogie Beat."

While known most widely for this moment of boogie-woogie fame, Slack gained further respect in the music community for his convincing blues playing on 1941 recordings with blues singer Joe Turner.

Like so many star instrumentalists in the bands of the Swing Era, Slack was eventually tapped to lead his own band, in 1941. Early in his relatively brief history as a leader, a Slack group (His Eight Beats) recorded a successful original, "Strange Cargo." Once the Slack band was established, "Cow Cow Boogie," featuring seventeen-year-old vocalist Ella Mae Morse, became a bona fide hit. The second single released by the brand new—and, within years, tremendously successful—record company, Capitol, "Cow Cow Boogie" reached number one on the best-seller charts and became Capitol's first gold record.[5] Slack's band appeared in a number of Hollywood motion pictures in the 1940s, mostly such forgettable releases as *Babes on Swing Street*, *Hat Check Honey*, and *Reveille with Beverly*.[6]

In addition to his work with Joe Turner, Slack established a connection with the blues world by employing later blues star T-Bone Walker as a member of his big band from 1942 to 1944.[7]

Publicity photo of Freddie Slack. ©RAY AVERY/ CTS IMAGES

Although Slack continued to record as a leader into the 1950s, it is not clear how much, if at all, the band toured or even played in public during those days after the demise of the Big Band Era. Accounts of Slack's activities during this time are sparse, but he continued to play in clubs in southern California.

The latter part of Slack's life was relatively undistinguished musically. He mostly played solo piano in a series of clubs and taverns, many of which were likely run by the mob. His name appeared with some frequency in the Los Angeles newspapers, usually for incidents involving alcohol: drunk driving and even an arrest for using salty language in a public place.

Noted big band historian George Simon was not kind in his evaluation of Slack, suggesting that "he never took his career as a leader seriously enough." Simon wrote,

> Slack, a pleasant, vague man muddled along in a boogie-woogie rut almost until his death in August, 1965. A clue to his apparent lack of enthusiasm for a commercial career: "You might not believe it," he said in 1941, "but writing boogie-woogie doesn't give me near the thrill that writing sweet stuff does." Apparently Freddy [*sic*], who made frequent attempts to reestablish himself, just kept barking up the wrong piano bench.[8]

Yet veteran musician Steve Jordan portrayed his good friend Slack as a "championship character" and related fond stories of his roommate from their days with the Bradley-McKinley band, and later on, when Slack led his own band.[9] While many of Slack's problems were created by his relationship to alcohol, he was a fascinating character. He had short romances with archery and darts, and famously owned a pet lion, which he named Buttercup. When Buttercup was shipped to the navy base where Slack was assigned for his first week in the service during World War II, it was soon decided that not only would Buttercup be shipped home, but that the navy would also be better off without Slack, who was already a nationally recognized figure thanks to "Cow Cow Boogie." Slack's second wife, Jean Ruth, played an "overseas disc jockey, Beverly, in the radio show 'Reveille with Beverly' that inspired [the movie of the same name]."[10]

Regardless of Simon's opinion, or Jordan's warm, yet bittersweet memories, Wisconsinite Freddie Slack obviously had a successful career. He was among the "famous musicians from Wisconsin" singled out by Duke Ellington in his autobiography when he wrote about his week-long residency in Madison in 1972, and Ellington's high regard seems appropriate for this distinctive pianist and bandleader of the Swing Era.

Heinie Beau

Clarinetist Heinrich (or Henry) "Heinie" Beau[11] was born in Calvary (referred to by many area natives as Calvary Station), Wisconsin, in Fond du Lac County, March 8, 1911.[12] He attended grade school in nearby Mount Calvary, and, after his family had moved the roughly fifteen miles to Fond du Lac, he graduated from Fond du Lac High School in 1929, having played in the high school band led by Joe Schmitz. Beau's professional career was launched in the family band nominally led by his brother Wally, a group that included at various times Wally; Heinie; brothers Harvey, Eddie, and Bill; and sister Marie.[13]

Wally, in 1965, recalled: The "first job we played was a barn dance at Chris Furman's place out near Wolf Lake. Then I remember there was a July 4 celebration at Marytown, . . . I think it was back in 1927." Harvey added, "It kept building and in 1929 we were playing three and four nights a week. We'd have trips as far as Rockford, Ill., and Iron Mountain, Mich. . . . Wally took care of the bookings, Heinie rehearsed the band, and I took care of the transportation problems."[14]

Heinie left the family band in 1939 to join the Nick Harper Orchestra (for which he had been already been writing arrangements), which was playing at the Wisconsin Roof Garden in Milwaukee. Beau told Ron Harvey, "While still with the Nick Harper band in 1940, the Red Nichols band was appearing across the street at the Schroeder Hotel and so I began writing arrangements for Red and was asked to sit in on a number of jam sessions with his band."[15] Nichols, a relative star in the jazz world at that time, left town for New York and soon asked Beau to join his group. Beau described this entry into the "big time":

> I joined Red Nichols at the Famous Door in New York. It was on [Fifty-Second Street, the center of jazz life in the city] and the place featured music from 10 p.m. until 4:30 a.m. As a result, many of the musicians from around town would come in after finishing their engagements. That's where I met people like Jimmy and Tommy Dorsey, Woody Herman, and others.[16]

After the Red Nichols Band, Beau played with one of the biggest stars in music at that time, Tommy Dorsey. He was with Dorsey from late 1940 until around 1943. An effervescent Beau clarinet solo can be heard on one of Dorsey's most exciting "flag-wavers," "Well, Git It!" Beau also arranged one of Frank Sinatra's early vocal hits with the Dorsey band, 1941's "Violets for Your Furs."[17] After several cross-country tours with Dorsey, Beau decided to stay in Hollywood following an engagement there with the band.

Beau and his wife, Grace (an Oakfield, Wisconsin, native), made southern California their home. Beau had no trouble finding work. He played with Alvino Rey's band, appeared with Benny Goodman's band in the film *Sweet and Low Down*, and regularly played and arranged for radio programs for such stars as Kate Smith, Fibber McGee and Molly, Eddie Cantor, and Bing Crosby. Starting in 1945, he wrote arrangements for a series of record sessions for singer Peggy Lee. He also recorded with such jazz luminaries as Louis Armstrong, Jack Teagarden, and Wisconsinite Woody Herman.

In the early 1950s, Beau began another notable association with Frank Sinatra. He wrote for a short-lived Sinatra television show and arranged

Record jacket from 1984. (Note the incorrect spelling of Beau's first name.) HENRI RECORDS

a number of Sinatra's records for over a decade, including the 1952 hit "The Birth of the Blues." He also arranged "Lean Baby" on *Swing Easy!*, Sinatra's first of a run of hit LPs on Capitol Records. And, often as a ghostwriter, he continued to do arrangements for Sinatra when either Billy May or Paul Weston, two of the singer's most favored arrangers, was unable to complete an assignment. Beau wrote many of the arrangements for Sinatra's last two Capitol albums (*Come Swing with Me* and *Point of No Return*, both 1961) before Sinatra started his own record label, Reprise.[18]

Beau also wrote for Eddie Fisher's television show. When Red Nichols's story was made into a film in 1958, as *The Five Pennies* (starring Danny Kaye), Beau wrote much of the score and played on the soundtrack. He also contributed significantly to the soundtrack to *The Gene Krupa Story*.

Beau had two long-running television gigs and worked for seven years each with two of the late 1950s' and early 1960s' most popular TV stars: Dinah Shore and Red Skelton. He had further stints writing and/or playing music for the shows of Danny Kaye, Jonathan Winters, Andy

Williams, Jim Nabors (who played the character of Gomer Pyle), Bing Crosby, and Bob Newhart. He wrote for the local Los Angeles television show of Ina Ray Hutton, who famously led an all-female band. On that show, only females were allowed to be on camera, and Beau claims that when the credits rolled at the end of the show, viewers saw "musical arrangements by Henrietta Beau."[19]

Beau retired from his busy career of incessant writing, claiming he "didn't feel like writing another note of music."[20] In the early 1980s, he reappeared on the music scene as a player, recording three records for his own label, Henri Records (see online discography).

In his later years, Beau returned to Fond du Lac on a regular basis and seemed to enjoy his visits there reconnecting with friends and family. He was interviewed by the *Fond du Lac Reporter* during visits in 1974, when he sat in at a jam session with local musicians, and in 1979, when he attended his fiftieth high school reunion. The Beaus established the Grace and Heinie Beau Music Scholarship at Goodrich High School in Fond du Lac in 1981 to help support Goodrich graduates going on to study music in college. In 1984, Beau told jazz writer Dave Dexter that the time he and Grace spent in Wisconsin each year was the highlight week of the year for them. Beau died in Santa Barbara, California, in 1987.

Gene Schroeder

Pianist Eugene Charles "Gene" Schroeder was born in Madison on February 5, 1915.[21] Schroeder's father was a trumpeter, and his mother played piano. Young Gene studied at the Wisconsin School of Music and started playing with his father's band at age eleven. In school he played clarinet, and he grew up with Frank Tifft, a local trumpet player who went on to play in a number of national big bands. According to Tifft, Schroeder lived on Dayton Street, right behind Washington School, where the two attended grammar school together. The pair started playing duets at a young age; they'd play "The Stars and Stripes Forever" and "On Wisconsin" at recess, as the other students marched outside. Schroeder also practiced at the Labor Temple on Johnson Street. The boys attended the now defunct Central High School, where, Tifft says, they "used to go across the street to the Methodist Church. . . . We'd sneak in through the side door, down through the furnace room, get into the band room at night, and have jam sessions."

Schroeder studied music at the University of Wisconsin for one year, beginning in 1932. He played in a band, probably both before and after he was at UW, led by bassist Norm Phelps and including Tifft and clarinetist/saxophonist Doc De Haven Sr., who later played in Bunny Berigan's big band. By sometime in 1933, Schroeder had moved to Milwaukee, where he remained for several years.

In Milwaukee, Schroeder led a quintet, playing at hotels and doing club dates, but he worked for other musicians as well, including Wild Bill Davison during Davison's residency in the city. He spent summer seasons back in Madison, at the Chanticleer. One day, while Schroeder was playing at a "bottle club" in Milwaukee, Benny Goodman's pianist Jess Stacy (who had wandered over from a Goodman concert at a theater) heard the young pianist and advised him to go to New York.[22]

Schroeder moved to New York City with Tifft in 1938 or 1939. Apparently he played "briefly with the Wes Westerfield Trio, then [with his] own group at Town Topics Club."[23] His break into a higher-profile position came when he joined reed player Joe Marsala's group at the well-known Hickory House in 1940. Schroeder moved over to Nick's with Joe's brother, the trumpeter Marty Marsala. In 1942, Schroeder reconnected with Wild Bill Davison, now back on the East Coast, and worked with him in Chicago, Boston, and New York. Schroeder went back to Nick's in 1943 to play in trombonist Miff Mole's band.

Schroeder would ultimately become most recognized for his membership in guitarist Eddie Condon's band. With Condon, he played a series of concerts at Town Hall, the Ritz Theater, and Carnegie Hall in 1944 and 1945. According to music writer James Doran, Schroeder worked with the bands of Mole, Condon, Davison, Joe Marsala, Muggsy Spanier, Pee Wee Russell, and Bud Freeman roughly during this same time.[24] This loosely knit group of players worked in various combinations together for years.

Condon was a jazz star—not for his playing (which some considered pedestrian), but for his quick wit, ease in front of a band, and especially his ability to organize groups of excellent players into working bands. This jazz entrepreneur opened his own club in New York in 1945 and, from its opening until about 1960, Schroeder was, effectively, the house band's

Gene Schroeder. WILLIAM P. GOTTLIEB/IRA AND LEONORE S. GERSHWIN FUND COLLECTION, MUSIC DIVISION, LIBRARY OF CONGRESS

pianist. His notable appearances with Condon's bands included the 1956 Newport Jazz Festival and a 1957 tour to Great Britain.

From 1961 to 1964, Schroeder was a member of the "retro" (and wildly popular) Dukes of Dixieland. In the second half of the decade, he worked with clarinetist Tony Parenti. He also freelanced in New York during this time.

Schroeder played at the Telemark Lodge in northern Wisconsin (near Cable) for one season, in 1967, and then suffered a stroke, the first of several that would eventually end his career. Unable to play at an acceptable level, he took over management of a motel not far from Telemark. But Schroeder's health worsened, and he was moved to a hospital and then a nursing home in Madison. When Duke Ellington's band was in residence at the University of Wisconsin in 1972, longtime public radio (WHA) personality and jazz show host Ken Ohst took Ellington's legendary baritone saxophonist Harry Carney on a tearful trip to visit Schroeder. Schroeder died in Madison in 1975.[25]

Gene Schroeder was largely overlooked by much of the jazz community during his prime. The Chicago jazz he made with Condon was hardly in the vanguard of 1950s jazz, despite its substantial audience and popularity. The style also tended to camouflage rhythm section players, with the "front line" horn players usually being the more prominent and featured players. Furthermore, according to friends and family, Schroeder chose to stay in the background. When soloing, he sometimes sounded like "an unequivocal stride man out of [James P.] Johnson and [Fats] Waller."[26] But he more frequently played a modern style, influenced not only by stride, but also by both boogie-woogie and Art Tatum, which is more in keeping with the "modern Chicago" style for which he is now remembered.

Billy Maxted

Billy Maxted was known and respected by many jazz musicians in the mid-twentieth century and recorded a number of albums under his own name, yet he never became a jazz star. His contribution to the genre could easily be overlooked in this age of information overload and overly simplified jazz histories. Maxted appears in this volume largely due to the efforts of fellow Racine native Ted Mesmer, who refused to let Maxted's memory disappear.

Maxted was born in Racine in 1917.[27] Very little about his youth in Wisconsin has been documented. He first surfaced on the national scene with Red Nichols's big band in 1937. He stayed with Nichols, who became a jazz star in the late 1920s, until 1940. Trumpeter Don Ingle said, "My friend, teacher, and mentor Red Nichols told me several times that Billy Maxted was the finest piano man and arranger that ever worked for him."[28] Maxted also worked for short periods with other well-known Swing Era leaders Ben Pollack, Teddy Powell, and Will Bradley (in whose band he followed Freddie Slack in the piano chair) before entering the service during World War II. He served as a navy fighter pilot, based on an aircraft carrier in the South Pacific, from 1942 to 1945.[29]

After the war, Maxted continued his career as a player and writer. He wrote arrangements for such luminaries as Benny Goodman and Claude

Thornhill. He co-led a band in 1947 and 1948 with Ray Eberle, who had become a star as a vocalist with Glenn Miller's band before the war. Soon Maxted became associated with the "traditional" jazz scene in New York, eventually becoming a virtual house pianist at Nick's, a bastion of the "trad" scene. Maxted performed there with the groups of Bobby Hackett, Phil Napoleon, Billy Butterfield, and Pee Wee Erwin as well as with his own band, which became known as the Manhattan Jazz Band. Maxted held forth at Nick's from 1949 to 1960, while Gene Schroeder was doing the same thing at Eddie Condon's club. The Manhattan Jazz Band cut a number of recordings, starting in 1955.

The Manhattan Jazz Band was usually six to seven members, and Maxted's arrangements for bands this size, often referred to as "little big bands," exhibited techniques that are still used in the jazz world today. Maxted and his band are intimately associated with New York, but in the 1950s, John Sheridan heard the band many times in Columbus, Ohio, where another big fan of the band was the legendary football coach at Ohio State University, Woody Hayes. Sheridan, who has written many arrangements for the Jim Cullum Jazz Band (on the long-running, nationally syndicated radio show *Riverwalk Jazz*), cites Maxted as one of his biggest influences and says that in his youth he was "the biggest fan imaginable."[30]

Maxted moved to South Florida in 1961. He played with Bill Thomas's Bourbon Street Jazz Band at the time, but his writing became better known in Florida (and later beyond) when Bill Allred's Classic Jazz Band, one of the most successful little big bands, formed in 1990 and played some of Maxted's old arrangements. When the band embarked on a more extensive touring schedule, Maxted contributed "quite a few of his great charts."[31]

Ted Mesmer has spoken to musicians from Racine who remember Maxted as generous with his time and advice to young musicians from the city, including a young Emil Pavlik, who arranged for Wes Adrian's Club Sahara Band,[32] a band similar in size to those for which Maxted is best known for writing.

Maxted led a life of relative obscurity in Florida until his death in Fort Lauderdale in 2011. But the legacy of this talented pianist lives on in his influential niche style of jazz arranging.

Cappy Lewis

Trumpeter Carroll "Cappy" Lewis (frequently listed as Carol in the local Wisconsin newspapers) was born in Brillion, Wisconsin, on May 18, 1917.[33] Lewis's father, Lawrence, was described by his grandson Mark as "a cigar maker and insurance salesman and whatever else." While Cappy was often considered to be self-taught, he was trained to some degree in his local high school band, and possibly in municipal groups, by Carl Wolf, one of the locally legendary music teachers who can be found in communities all over Wisconsin.

After graduating from Brillion High in 1935, Lewis started working in area "territory bands." Among these were the Beau brothers' band, which was well established in the region by this time, and the Nick Harper Orchestra. In newspaper ads for a show by Wally Beau's band at the Pla-Mor Bowling Lanes in Cedar Rapids, Iowa, Lewis is mentioned by name; in one, the band is said to feature "'Cap' Lewis and His Hot Trumpet." (Lewis claimed that he played cornet at this time, and the trumpet later when he joined Woody Herman.) Early in his career, Lewis always cited Bunny Berigan as a major influence and a favorite trumpet player.

In listings for the Harper band's appearances at the Wisconsin Roof in Milwaukee, Lewis was noted as one of the stars of the group, as "Cappy (Cave-in) Lewis." It was from the Harper orchestra that Heinie Beau jumped off to the big time. At just about the same time, in 1939, an arranger for Woody Herman's band, Jiggs Noble, heard Lewis play. Subsequently, Woody asked Lewis to join Herman's Band That Plays the Blues.

Sometime during his first six weeks with the band, Lewis was invited to Herman's hotel room to meet Herman and bassist Walt Yoder. Greeted with a bottle of Scotch, he felt officially welcomed to the big time. On his very first recording session with Herman, Lewis was a featured soloist on "It's My Turn Now" and "If I Knew Then." He was featured prominently and frequently with Herman during the next five years, although he spent six months with Tommy Dorsey's band in 1943. Lewis returned briefly to play in Herman's famed First Herd in 1946.

Cappy Lewis (right) with Woody Herman (see chapter 2), ca. 1941.
COURTESY OF MARK LEWIS

Tommy Linehan, who played piano in Herman's band when Cappy joined, said years later,

> When I first saw [Lewis], he reminded me of a young Scandinavian-type, with blond hair, very pale skin, and he looked like he just came off of somebody's back farm. . . . And yet, when he sat down and started playing he would almost 'lean into it,' like he was really getting into the thing. And you can play me any one of the Herman records or anyone's records, and you can tell it's Cappy![34]

At some point after his work touring, Lewis made the transition into the studio scene in southern California. He had considerable success in the studios, working on television shows and movie soundtracks. He was a favorite of the great arranger Nelson Riddle; Lewis played in his orchestra on television shows and on records, prominently those of Frank

Sinatra. On occasion, he also played with Benny Goodman. Lewis worked on *Hello, Dolly!* and *The Jungle Book*, among many other films. On the latter, a well-known Disney animated film, he played the trumpet solos throughout the catchy song "The Bare Necessities." Lewis made one jazz album as a leader, 1959's *Get Happy with Cappy*.

After a long, successful career, Lewis suffered a stroke in 1978 and was unable to continue playing. His son, Mark, followed his father into the Woody Herman band in the early 1980s and is still an active trumpeter on the West Coast. Cappy Lewis died in Los Angeles in 1992.

Beyond the State

6

Three Singers

Three singers from Milwaukee are among the best-known Wisconsin jazz musicians of any era. Milwaukeean Jackie Cain and her husband, Roy Kral, were a delightful, chic pair on the jazz scene from the late 1940s through the 1990s. Al Jarreau was arguably the most recognized musician from Milwaukee in any genre, with a remarkably successful career ranging from jazz to R&B to pop. And Tierney Sutton, who was influenced by Jarreau and recently recorded with him, is another highly respected singer performing first-rate jazz today.

Jackie Cain

Jackie Cain was a superb, stylish singer. When Michael Drew wrote about her and her husband, Roy Kral, in 1974 in the *Milwaukee Journal*, he quoted the *New Yorker* critic Whitney Balliett, who called the duo "extraordinary" and went on to describe Cain as "one of the best singers alive."[1] Drew also quoted a review that declared, "[Cain] possesses the jazz world's most underrated voice, pure liquid sound over voice."

I am grateful to jazz writer Marc Myers (contributor to jazzwax.com and the *Wall Street Journal*) for allowing me to quote liberally from his 2009 interview with Jackie Cain.[2] Many of the subjects of this book tell their stories in their own words, and I wanted to include Cain's version of her youth in Milwaukee in her story. The paragraphs below, and the quotes sprinkled throughout the rest of this profile, are excerpted from Myers's interview.

> I was born in Milwaukee in 1928. When I arrived my parents were already having financial problems. My dad sold office furniture and my mother didn't work. The Depression didn't help. They were unhappy, and they finally divorced when I was seven or eight years old.
>
> My mother and I lived with my grandmother until my mother finally landed a job with a photo imaging company. My mother went away for ten days to train on the company's equipment. When she returned, she went to work selling their services at the Boston Store.
>
> After my mother returned, she had to work to support us and was gone every day. When my mother made enough money, we moved to a rooming house in a big wonderful mansion that overlooked Lake Michigan, near where she worked. We had a big room in the front with French windows and a porch. It was a well-kept place. I was ten years old.

When Myers asked Cain about listening to music as a youth, she replied:

> We didn't have money for a phonograph or records. I always had been musical. From the time I was born, my mother played piano and used to learn songs off the radio and teach them to me. I could sing right away as a kid. I was always in the chorus at school, and in the a cappella choir in high school. I had a great ear.
>
> I wish I did read music, but I was never taught. I could follow music well, though. I was lucky. I soon was singing at small events around town that were pretty simple. Organizations always needed someone to entertain, and I had a good voice as a kid.
>
> When I was young I was on a [radio] show called *Cousin Betty*. It was a show for children. If people wanted someone remembered on their birthday, they'd send cards in or call the station with requests: "Please have Little Miss Cain sing this or that" [*laughter*]. It was a good experience.
>
> I also was singing with the Wurlitzer Melody Kids—a band that the local Wurlitzer music store had assembled. I sang *Rhythm Is My Business* and other hip stuff. My dad got me a job singing with a commercial band that had been traveling around the Midwest

> for proms and parties. It was a society band, and the leader played the violin. I sang with the band when it settled into a downtown Milwaukee club called Lakota's. This was roughly 1945.
>
> One night some people came into the club, and after I sang they asked me to come over to their table. There was a gentleman there who was visiting his family in Milwaukee. He said, "Gee, you're a very good singer. Would you be interested in singing with a band that I have in Chicago?"
>
> I said, "Gee, I'll have to ask my mother." I had just graduated high school and was seventeen years old at the time. When I asked my mother, she promptly said no. I kept begging her and carrying on. She still said no. So I disappeared into my room at home for a couple of days and didn't want to talk to her. I was angry. When the man called the house, I told him my mother wouldn't let me go alone to Chicago. I would have had to take a train down there, and I had never been out of Milwaukee.

Eventually, Cain's mother was talked into letting her daughter go, and Cain never looked back. In Chicago, she lived with a family and worked with bandleader Jay Burkhart. The unheralded Burkhart nurtured not only Cain in his band but also, later, future star vocalists Irene Kral (Roy's sister) and Joe Williams.

Wanting more experience, Cain started working in a small group with saxophonist Bob Anderson. Anderson took her to a club called Jump Town, where George Davis led a quartet. The band's pianist was Roy Kral. Cain described what happened next:

> Bob went up to Roy and said, "You ought to let Jackie sit in. She's a good singer." Roy said, "Nah, I don't like to play for girl singers." Bob said, "Why?" Roy said, "Well, because they never know what they want to sing, and when they tell you their key, it's usually in the key of Z."
>
> Bob came back and told me and we laughed about it. We went to the bar to have a drink with Roy, and Bob asked again. Well Roy and I got to talking and it just so happened that I knew a song that Roy knew. So suddenly he wasn't so negative about playing behind me.

She sang "Happiness Is a Thing Called Joe." Cain said, "When we finished the song, it broke up the place. The club went nuts. The reaction was great. The club owner was there and told George Davis, 'You need a singer.' George didn't resist [*laughter*]."

Cain was only seventeen, and Kral had a girlfriend, so there were no romantic sparks at that point. Dave Garroway, a big radio personality in Chicago, and later a television star as the founder and host of NBC's *Today Show*, heard Cain and became her champion.

At this time, Cain and Kral started working out a duo-vocal routine. Cain explained:

> I had listened to a lot of jazz records. You see, I had always tried to learn solos from musical instruments. . . . Listening to instrumental solos inspired us. Roy would write out a solo and I'd sing it. . . . So we'd take the first chorus straight. On the second chorus we'd use our voices as instruments, which is what vocalese is all about. Roy wrote all of that out. . . . He'd start by soloing on the song on the piano. Just blowing. When he found nice little phrases, he'd write them down. That's how we'd develop the things we sang.

Tenor saxophonist Charlie Ventura, fresh off Gene Krupa's big band and an attempt at starting his own, heard the pair and hired them for his small band that became known as Bop for the People. Cain and Kral were important to the success of the band, which also featured the top-notch instrumental work of Ventura, Conte Candoli, Boots Mussulli, and Bennie Green. Cain and Kral worked with Ventura for much of 1948 and 1949, coming to the attention of a much wider audience but also having to deal with the leader's jealousy.[3] During this time, they also became closer than just bandmates, and after leaving Ventura in 1949, they got married.

They continued to work in clubs, but when their daughter Niki was born in 1952, their career as a duo was compromised. However, in 1954 they recorded with former Woody Herman composer/arranger Neal Hefti for Coral Records. A year later, they were the first artists to record the Tommy Wolf/Fran Landesman classic, "Spring Can Really Hang You Up the Most," the first of a number of Wolf and Landesman's sophisticated songs that they popularized. By this time, they had moved

Jackie Cain and Roy Kral on the 1956 television show *Stars of Jazz*. ©RAY AVERY/CTS IMAGES

from vocalese (singing in an instrumental style, often without words) to hip interpretations of songs. Cain told Myers,

> The times were changing and we could hear that. There was only so much vocalese you could do before audience interest would wear thin. Audiences wanted to hear stories in the songs. . . . We started to shift into little-known songs and standards. We wanted to focus on an upbeat approach, with tight harmonies.

Myers colorfully described the next phase of Cain and Kral's career:

> The popularization of the 12-inch LP in 1956 boosted the fortunes of Jackie Cain and Roy Kral. On the larger color covers, the attractive duo was portrayed as hopelessly upbeat lovebirds, while their vocals inside sounded more like personal diary entries than the works of third-party songwriters. Producers and LP art directors cast Jackie and Roy as typical fun-loving suburbanites, but nothing could have been further from the truth.

In fact, the couple was working very hard on the club circuit and making records to support themselves and their two daughters. During the latter half of the 1950s, Cain and Kral's records appeared with regularity. For a few years, Las Vegas became their headquarters, as they found lots of work in the casinos, but the couple mostly resided near New York City.

By the 1970s, times were challenging for an act like Cain and Kral due to the continuing dominance of rock and roll. They adapted by judiciously choosing rock material (like Simon & Garfunkel, and the Beatles) and continuing to tour clubs that were still featuring music of their ilk. They even did jingles, advertising products such as Halo shampoo, Cheerios cereal, Plymouth automobiles, and Borden's products, which was lucrative work.[4] The duo signed with CTI Records and worked with producer Creed Taylor, with whom they had first worked in the 1950s at ABC-Paramount. They created successful records for CTI.

In 1973, their daughter Niki was killed in an automobile accident at age twenty. Cain says, "[Roy and I] were like zombies for years after that. We didn't work. We were stricken." Nonetheless, they resumed their performing and recording careers and continued to turn out albums throughout the 1970s and 1980s, and into the 1990s. Roy Kral died in 2002. Cain appeared on a 2004 album by saxophonist/composer/arranger Bill Kirchner but mostly lived in a quiet retirement until her death in 2014.

Jackie Cain and Roy Kral were never big stars in American music, but they were highly respected for the niche music they masterfully practiced for decades, to the delight of thousands of listeners.

Al Jarreau

Al Jarreau, like Les Paul before him, was a major figure in American popular music. Also like Paul, Jarreau was a figure that many do not think of as a jazz artist. Yet while hard-core jazz fans may have thought that Jarreau left the jazz realm many years before his death, ironically, the wider public, including the group that continued to buy his music, always considered Jarreau a jazz singer. Particularly in the early part of his career, there is no question that he was part of the jazz community.

Likewise, there is no question that Jarreau was a Wisconsin musician. His place in Wisconsin music history is not based solely on his place of birth. Although he lived in California for many years, his youth in Wisconsin and repeated visits back to the state kept him in touch with his Midwestern roots.

Alwin Lopez Jarreau was born in Milwaukee on March 12, 1940, the fifth of what would be six children, to Emile and Pearl Jarreau.[5] The Jarreaus lived in the central city, at 336 West Reservoir Avenue (they later moved to Capitol Drive), and their lives centered on family and the church. Pearl was a church organist, and Emile had been ordained and practiced as a minister, apparently until World War II, when he went to work in a munitions factory. Al claimed that he never heard his father preach in church, but that Emile "preached at home—he preached everywhere," although he made his living as a welder.[6] His father's influence was musical, too. In 1982, Al told *Down Beat* magazine, "My father was an incredible singer and also played the musical saw—with a bow!"[7] The family lived next door to a polka hall and Al recalled learning, like any good Wisconsin boy, all the polkas. He claimed to know "more polkas than Frankie Yankovic."[8]

A flyer lists Jarreau as having performed at age four as a "Boy Singer" for a "Garden Fair" at 1911 North Fifth Street, but he seems to have led a fairly normal childhood, without performing much until he was out of high school.[9] He listened to pioneering black deejay Daddy-O Daylie on Chicago radio, soaked up the music of his older siblings, who were also singers, and learned to harmonize with them while in grade school. The four Jarreau brothers, Emile Jr., Alphaeus, Alwin, and Marshall, harmonized in the family automobile.[10] Al sang doo-wop, a popular style of the day, but he said that "never was as exciting as singing 'How High the Moon' or 'Red Top' or something else that was just so much more consuming."[11] Jarreau recalled listening to such 1950s singers as Patti Page, Frankie Laine, and the Four Freshmen.

While he claimed to have been "a nerd of sorts" at Lincoln High School, he was by all accounts a serious and popular student.[12] A *Milwaukee Journal* photograph from 1958 shows him as one of the high school students who was approved for one day as a temporary legislator for the Milwaukee Common Council. During the summer before his senior year in high school he attended Badger Boys State, the American Legion's week of mock government for Wisconsin high school student leaders held

Governor of Badger Boys State Al Jarreau in a parade through downtown Ripon, 1957.
COURTESY OF RIPON COLLEGE

annually at Ripon College. There, his charisma led him to a leadership position, as he was elected governor. Jarreau was also a gifted athlete. He was a star high school basketball player, and a baseball player talented enough to be invited to a summer training camp by the Milwaukee Braves.

During high school, Jarreau sang in various locations around Milwaukee and got valuable training learning standard songs with respected local pianist Les (Lazlo) Czimber at venues like the Driftwood Lounge. Jarreau described himself as a "pup" at this time, a student that Czimber pushed into learning such challenging pieces as Dizzy Gillespie's "A Night in Tunisia."

Jarreau attended Ripon College on a scholarship that he won as a result of his state office at Boys State. The small liberal arts college was more challenging academically than Lincoln High, and poor grades caused Jarreau to lose his scholarship during his freshman year, even though he served as class president. (Years later, Jarreau said he not only "flagged" [flunked] two courses, but he "*red*-flagged" them.) He was able to remain in school when Doc Weiske, Ripon's basketball coach who would later become a coaching legend, finagled a basketball scholarship to take its place.[13]

While pursuing a major in psychology, Jarreau formed a popular student vocal quartet, the Indigos. On campus, the group sang at events like Night on the Town, Upperclass Stunt Night, Union Board gatherings, and Spring Sing; they also performed frequently off campus, including many weekend gigs at Green Lake's Tuscumbia Country Club.[14] In 1993, Indigos' member Peter Bock recalled those heady days: "At the peak of our career, after headlining the Notre Dame Collegiate Jazz Festival of 1962, we were offered a recording contract and a European tour."[15] But Bock and fellow Indigo Duffy Ashley-Farrand had plans for graduate school and real jobs, and the group broke up at graduation. As a soloist, Jarreau "thrilled the crowd" at the 1962 Miss Oshkosh Pageant, and he was hired to be the featured vocalist at the 1963 Miss Wisconsin Pageant, a real breakthrough for an African American in what was still largely a white pageant.[16]

The summer after his college graduation, with the help of Gus Azinger (editor of the entertainment magazine *Milwaukee Visitor*) as his manager, Jarreau worked seven weeks with Czimber at the Driftwood, with additional engagements at Milwaukee's Holiday House and the Columns in the Pfister Hotel. That same summer, he also volunteered through the Jewish Vocational Service in the city. Through the service, he met a University of Iowa psychologist who encouraged him to apply for a government grant. After receiving the grant, Jarreau moved to Iowa, where he continued to perform and eventually completed a master's degree.[17] A bootlegged recording of the Joe Abodeely Trio from 1965 proves that Jarreau performed with the group, possibly at the Tender Trap in Cedar Rapids.[18]

After six months in the Army Reserve, Jarreau set out for California and got a day gig as a rehabilitation counselor for the state of California in 1965. After several years of trying to juggle this job with the many club gigs he was working at night (he was sometimes billed as "the singing psychologist"), Jarreau decided to become a full-time musician. He worked for three years at the Half Note in San Francisco, backed by a trio led by pianist George Duke, who later became a star in the jazz and pop world.

In 1968, Jarreau started working with guitarist Julio Martinez—"just him and me and the cabasa [an African shaker-like gourd instrument]"—at Gatsby's in Sausalito.[19] The duo moved to Los Angeles and worked at clubs like the Troubadour, the Bitter End West, and Dino's but never got a big break. They went to New York for a year, where they were booked at the Improvisation and Rodney Dangerfield's club. Jarreau sang on the David Frost, Mike Douglas, and Johnny Carson shows and met other young entertainers including Bette Midler, comedians Richard Pryor and Robert Klein, and bandleader and film composer Quincy Jones. But life was tough in the Big Apple, too.

Jarreau's manager talked the duo into relocating to Minneapolis–St. Paul, where they lived for a year. They put together a band that played Jarreau's original material and opened a number of shows for big-name rock groups, including Steppenwolf, Canned Heat, and Three Dog Night. The band attempted to establish themselves in southern California, but lack of success there led all the Midwesterners except Jarreau to head back home.[20] Jarreau and Martinez took a weekend gig in North Hollywood at the Bla Bla Café, and Jarreau said, "After two years, I was able to pay my rent and all expenses with two nights' work a week."[21]

Jarreau's big break came in 1975. While opening at Hollywood's Troubadour Club for pianist/singer Les McCann, Jarreau impressed some executives from Warner Brothers Records, who, in short order, signed and recorded him. His 1975 major label debut album, *We Got By*, did well and was followed in 1976 by *Glow*, which contained the funky Jarreau original "Milwaukee." In it, Jarreau bluesily sings about his current life with regret, lamenting that he is two thousand miles from "my sweet home, Milwaukee." It is probably the only musical valentine to the city ever to gain national notoriety.

Jarreau was promoted by his record company in the United States, but his promotional tour through Europe reaped bigger rewards, including the German equivalent of a Grammy award for each of his first two albums. He performed at the Montreux Jazz Festival in Switzerland in 1976. His popularity on the continent led to his third album, *Look to the*

Rainbow, a double-LP set recorded live in Germany. It earned Jarreau his first American Grammy, in 1977, for Best Jazz Vocal Performance. The next album, 1978's *All Fly Home*, made it two Grammys in a row.

While some of the music on these albums could be categorized as light 1970s pop today, the singing is superb, sometimes spectacular. As early as 1970, when Jarreau returned to Milwaukee for a performance at the Pfister's Crown Room, *Milwaukee Journal* reporter Michael Drew wrote that Jarreau's vocal acrobatics included "imitations of flute, drum, and bass viol, simulated reverberation and frequent falsetto leaps."[22] His imitations of instruments (especially bass and percussion) in his improvisations kept him connected to jazz and led one critic to claim: "He has a whole orchestra in his throat."[23] Many of the songs were Jarreau's originals; their funky, soulful rhythms were prevalent in jazz at the time but were soon to be relegated to the categories of "fusion" and "smooth jazz." Jazz standards occasionally appeared on Jarreau's albums, and two of Dave Brubeck's early sixties hits—"Take Five" and "Blue Rondo a la Turk"—became evergreens for Jarreau, too, and were requested throughout his career. Chick Corea's "Spain" became another enduring fan favorite. In the late 1970s and early 1980s, Jarreau was a perennial winner in both *Down Beat*'s critics' and readers' polls.

A 1976 interview in *Down Beat* not only affirmed Jarreau's early standing in the jazz community but also managed to capture Jarreau's public persona. Lee Underwood observed, "In his music and conversation, Al Jarreau brims over with [a] spirit of affirmation." This was supported by Jarreau's quotes, such as: "Every thought, whether positive or negative, is creative thought. . . . So it is important to think positively and constructively about the things you want to unfold in your life."[24]

Jarreau continued to appear in Milwaukee almost every year as his career took off. In a review of a September 1980 concert at Milwaukee's Performing Arts Center, jazz writer Bill Milkowski colorfully described the Jarreau vocal arsenal.

> It's a wonder how this impassioned vocalist keeps from straining that wonderful instrument and blowing it out every night. He uses every little sigh and corner of sound that the larynx can possibly produce.

> Grunts, hisses, ahhhhhs. Outrageous, uninhibited scat-singing and heavy vocal coloring that goes well beyond the realm of conventional bebop.
>
> He imitates conga drums, flutes, cellos, trumpets, mandolins, electric guitars hooked up to wah-wah pedals. There is an endless supply of sounds in his throat, and each one comes forth as spontaneously as the next.[25]

As Jarreau's career progressed, the music did not change considerably, but its classification did. At the 1981 Grammys, Jarreau's "Blue Rondo a la Turk" won the award for Best Jazz Vocal Performance, and the album *Breakin' Away* won Best Pop Vocal Performance. Eventually it sold more than a million copies. In a 1982 *Down Beat* article, Steve Bloom wrote, "*Breakin' Away* broke through the Top-10 barrier this past fall and became the hands-down commercial jazz success story of 1981." But despite this commercial success, Bloom wrote,

> For those who must question, Jarreau had proven that he is more than just a vocal chameleon—he is a consummate jazz singer.... Jarreau is certainly neither Joe Williams nor Mel Torme, and few would argue that he has the scatting ability of the late Eddie Jefferson. He's more of a '70s creation; schooled in jazz but weaned on pop, Jarreau's your basic Top-40 radio baby.[26]

In the same article, Jarreau reflected, "The jazz character is always going to be in my music, but I'm kind of curious about how things are going and how my music is developing."[27]

By the early 1980s, Jarreau had reached a new level of popularity and a new audience. He was featured in *People* magazine, and when he appeared at Milwaukee's Summerfest in July 1982, he sang for a crowd of 17,900 at the main stage—not the jazz stage. In October, his alma mater lured him back to the Ripon campus for homecoming on the twentieth anniversary of his graduation. He did not perform on campus, spending most of his time with his former classmates, but a late-night session in the choir room of the fine arts building drew a capacity audience for a two-hour question-and-answer session. (A photograph from this session at Ripon later appeared in the music industry's biggest publication, *Billboard*.) He appeared at the homecoming football game on Saturday afternoon, then headed out to sing the national anthem for the World Series game between the Brewers and the St. Louis Cardinals in Milwaukee's County Stadium the next day.

Although he was approaching popular stardom by the mid-1980s, Jarreau had a unique distinction in the jazz community. Jazz immortal Miles Davis (who also was considered on the borderline between jazz and pop during this period) regularly played a tune called "Al Jarreau" while touring in 1986. Davis never recorded the work in the studio, but it was played on a performance that was recorded live at the 1986 Montreux Jazz Festival.[28]

Succeeding albums sold well, and Jarreau continued to tour both the United States and Europe. In 1987, Jarreau was heard weekly in homes all over America, singing the theme he composed for the hit television series *Moonlighting*. The next year brought another visit to Ripon, as he was presented with an honorary degree at the college.[29]

Jazziz magazine featured Jarreau in a cover article in their March 1989 issue and summed up his career to that point in the article's opening paragraph:

> Some people are born lucky, some good. Others, like Al Jarreau, seem to be both lucky and good. We know he's good because he's had a string of hits, awards and accolades longer than a waiting line at a Soviet potato sale. [His music] somehow, against all odds, [has] continued to earn the respect of both jazz and pop audiences.[30]

Jarreau's next album, *Heart's Horizon*, was nominated for a Grammy in the R&B category, and when 1992's *Heaven and Earth* won an R&B Grammy, Jarreau became one of the only artists ever to win Grammys in three different categories: jazz, pop, and R&B.

For the remainder of his career, Jarreau continued to straddle categories. Although he was rarely considered part of the jazz community after the early 1990s, a close inspection of his recordings reveals his continued ties to jazz. *Heaven and Earth*, the R&B album, concluded with a stunning two-part reworking of "Blue in Green," from Miles Davis's legendary *Kind of Blue*. Even the commercially oriented *Tomorrow Today* (2000), which is relatively generic pop and R&B, includes an infectious salsa romp and a faithful re-creation of the Josef Zawinul/Weather Report masterpiece, "A Remark You Made," retitled "Something You Said."

The year 2004 brought the release of *Accentuate the Positive*, which featured some of Jarreau's favorite standards ("The Nearness of You" and "My Foolish Heart"), as well as jazz tunes by Duke Ellington, Dizzy Gillespie, Eddie Harris, and Bill Evans. This album—with a title that could have been Jarreau's motto—with its sophisticated stylings of a classic repertoire would have to be considered a jazz album by almost any standard applied to vocalists.[31] From the 2006 album *Givin' It Up*, a collaborative album with George Benson, two singles copped Grammy wins: "God Bless the Child" (featuring Jill Scott as lead vocalist) for Best Traditional R&B Vocal Performance and "Mornin'" for Best Pop Instrumental (for Benson).

Jarreau did not restrict himself to any musical categories, and he also explored other artistic genres, appearing on Broadway for three months (as Teen Angel in *Grease*) and as an actor on two TV series: *Touched by an Angel* and *New York Undercover*. In 1999, he began performing with symphony orchestras. In addition to his Grammy awards and poll victories in *Down Beat*, he won election to the Wisconsin Performing Artist Hall of Fame; music awards from *Performance*, *Cashbox*, *Record World*, *Playboy*, and the NAACP Image Awards; a star on the Hollywood Walk of Fame; and an award from Verizon for his contribution to literacy through advertisements for reading, some of which were included in his CDs' cases.

Over the years, Jarreau continued to make appearances in Wisconsin, usually in Milwaukee. A particularly memorable performance occurred in 2006, back at Ripon College, where he performed a sold-out benefit to raise money for student scholarships. While in town for only about forty-eight hours, the energetic sixty-six-year-old also read to children at the Ripon Public Library; toured the campus; met with college students and with the alumni board; attended a dedication ceremony for the college's new baseball field; participated in the coin toss at the homecoming football game, where he also sang the national anthem; and filmed a segment of a cooking show for local cable television. After the concert, he spent several hours at a reception for friends and well-wishers.

Al Jarreau performing at Ripon College, 2006. COURTESY OF RIPON COLLEGE

Still active in his seventies, Jarreau produced one of the highlights of his recording career: 2012's *Live*, with the excellent Dutch Metropole Orkest. In 2014, after the death of George Duke, Jarreau's musical partner in San Francisco in the 1960s, Jarreau released *My Old Friend*, a collection of Duke compositions (with the exception of Jarreau's title track) fondly dedicated to his longtime pal.[32]

In October 2016, Jarreau returned to Milwaukee for a special event at the Pfister Hotel. He was presented with a Lifetime Achievement Award from the Wisconsin Foundation for School Music; it was just the fourth time the award was given. (Les Paul received the award in 2004.) At the same time, a scholarship fund in Jarreau's name was established for music students in the Milwaukee Public Schools.

In February 2017, Jarreau entered the hospital in Los Angeles, reportedly for exhaustion, and it was announced that he would no longer tour. But just a few days later, he died of heart failure. In September 2017,

Wisconsin Public Television broadcast a special, *Al Jarreau: Coming Home*, to honor this late great figure, a career retrospective that included his 2016 return to Milwaukee. Regardless of categories and classifications, Al Jarreau distinguished himself as one of the most popular and vital Wisconsin musicians of all time.

Tierney Sutton

When she was interviewed for this book in 2011, Tierney Sutton was one of the top jazz singers on the scene. Her most recent album, *American Road*, the ninth release by the Tierney Sutton Band, had just received a rare five-star review in *Down Beat*, and Sutton's career has only continued to grow and develop since.

Sutton was born in Milwaukee in 1963.[33] She has often stated that she had no exposure to jazz when she was a child. She did, however, sing a great deal, in school pageants and shows; she was in a musical version of Hansel and Gretel when she was only five. She took piano lessons from age six until twelve. But, she says, "Once it got to the point where I was going to have to read music and not play it by ear, . . . I didn't want to do it. I was lazy." She first lived on the west side of Milwaukee but then moved to the northeast side and went to high school at Nicolet. Sutton's father was a civil rights lawyer; among his clients was Milwaukee activist Father James Groppi.

After graduating from Nicolet, Sutton enrolled at Boston University. After freshman year, she returned to Wisconsin and got a summer job at the Heidel House resort in Green Lake. At the time, the Heidel House featured young women—the Heidel Honeys—who entertained guests with song and dance while doubling as waitresses. The women learned several different shows each summer, with different themes and songs. Sutton now looks back on those shows with distaste, which she felt to some degree even at the time. However, she would occasionally leave the Heidel House and cross the street to Tuscumbia Country Club, where the Mary Jaye Trio was playing. Mary Jaye (whose real last name was Jaber), from Fond du Lac, played piano and sang standards. While Sutton had little frame of reference to judge, she could tell that Jaber was performing good songs and doing them with integrity, in contrast to the shows at the Heidel House.[34]

After two years at Boston University, Sutton transferred to Wesleyan University in Connecticut. The jazz program there was being run by Bill Barron, brother of jazz pianist Kenny Barron. Barron brought top jazz performers to the campus, and when Sutton heard singer Betty Carter and her trio, her life was changed. She explained:

> I was very lucky, because the first month I was on campus, there was a jazz pianist who was a graduate who put up signs all over Wesleyan saying, "Jazz singer needed to sing bebop tunes and standards." I didn't know what a bebop tune was, but . . . I had a dim idea of what a jazz singer was. And I had a very dim idea of what a standard was.

The pianist took Sutton on and taught her lots of tunes; the very first was Billy Strayhorn's challenging classic, "Lush Life."

Another Wisconsin summer encounter was also influential for Sutton. She went to hear jazz pianist Lynn Bernstein (now known as Lynne Arriale; see chapter 7) perform with her trio. As Sutton described it:

> I was making my hipness known, by requesting good tunes; asking them to play "Lush Life." . . . I was just sitting there, and doing what I did in those days, which was taking notes on what they were playing. . . . I describe myself as sort of a jazz nun, . . . and [bassist Al Anderson] asked me to sing a song. So I sang something . . . and he said, "You sing pretty good. But you need to learn to swing. I want you to come to my house tomorrow, at noon." . . . So I go over to his house, and he puts a record on, and he says, "Guess who this is?" And it's this really swingin' voice, . . . and I'm guessing like, "Is that Carmen McRae?" . . . And I couldn't figure out who it was, and I said, "Are you sure I know this person?" He said, "I'm positive you know this person." . . . It was Al Jarreau.

The record was from Jarreau's time in Iowa, years before he became a national figure. Sutton did listen to this recording and learned a great deal about just how, precisely, eighth notes need to be swung. She says, "If I can swing, it's because of that record."

After graduating from Wesleyan with a degree in Russian language and literature, Sutton returned to Boston, where she studied with Jerry Bergonzi at the Berklee College of Music, working on improvisation and developing her piano skills. Sutton assumed that she would move to New York, because that is what jazz musicians on the East Coast did, and in fact, she was already spending a couple of weekends a month in the city. However, she got a call to join a vocal group that was being formed on the West Coast by Dash Crofts, who had briefly been a pop star in the 1970s with the group Seals & Crofts. The plan was to form an a cappella group, and Sutton went to Los Angeles to rehearse and test record. While there, she discovered that there were "a lot of great young players living in LA. . . . I didn't know that they had such a great scene there." Friends talked her into staying for a while; Sutton had "never lived anywhere with nice weather." As she recalled:

> For me, it turned out to be a really great move, because I was able to develop a lot because I made the choice to move to LA rather than New York for the following reason: . . . the scene in New York was actually a little less open to new players and singers than LA. I mean everyone wanted me to sit in in LA. All the bands. If I would go to see somebody, they'd always ask me to get up and sing a song, and there weren't that many serious jazz singers in town. So for the guys that were really jazz players, they were happy to see me, and very supportive.

Shortly thereafter, she met the rhythm section that was to become the Tierney Sutton Band: bassist Trey Henry and drummer Ray Brinker. They recommended pianist Christian Jacob to fill out the trio. Except for the addition of a second bassist, Kevin Axt, the band has maintained that same personnel since the mid-1990s.[35] Sutton feels so strongly about the group concept that pervades the band that she had the Tierney Sutton Band legally incorporated. All of the members are featured in performance, and the imaginative arrangements that are a hallmark of the group are the result of contributions from each member. Sutton partly

Tierney Sutton. PHOTO BY TATI SHOAN; COURTESY OF TIERNEY SUTTON

attributes the high level of collaboration in the band to the principles of consultation that are a part of the Bahá'í Faith that she openly practices.

Sutton's recordings reflect the seriousness with which she approaches the art of jazz singing. Following 1998's *Introducing Tierney Sutton* (which had been recorded three years earlier) came 2000's *Unsung Heroes*, a tribute to jazz instrumentalists, and 2001's *Blue in Green*, a tribute to jazz pianist Bill Evans. At that point, veteran bassist Ray Brown (once married to Ella Fitzgerald, and much later a mentor to singer Diana Krall) told Sutton, "Sweetheart, it's great that musicians love you, but you gotta find some songs that people have actually heard before."[36] *Something Cool* (2002) was something of a commercial breakthrough, including standards such as "Route 66" and "Crazy" and a medley of songs from *My Fair*

Lady. *Dancing in the Dark* (2004) was a tribute to Frank Sinatra, and *I'm with the Band* (2005), recorded live at Birdland in New York, conveys the tightness of this dynamic band, even in the looseness of club performances. Several theme albums followed: *On the Other Side*, which was intended to represent "the dark underbelly of the state of happiness,"[37] and *Desire*, a reflection on fame and material things through a variety of well-known and more obscure songs. *American Road* includes music from Gershwin's *Porgy and Bess*, Leonard Bernstein's *West Side Story*, and several doses of Americana.

Although she returns to Wisconsin frequently to visit her father in Milwaukee, Sutton doesn't often perform in her home state. Still, some notable recent appearances in the state include gigs in 2010 at Thiensville's Jazz on the Green series at Gathering on the Green and the Isthmus Jazz Festival in Madison, and in 2011 at Jazz Weekend at Lawrence University in Appleton. Wisconsin still feels like home to Sutton, and arriving in the Midwest in the fall of 2011, she expressed appreciation for the "smell of autumn" that one doesn't get in southern California.

At that time, Sutton was working in a duo with pianist Shelly Berg and a trio with flutist Hubert Laws and guitarist Larry Koonse, as well as continuing to tour with her longtime band. Her stunning 2013 album, *After Blue*, featured songs either written by or associated with Joni Mitchell and featured Sutton's onetime inspiration Al Jarreau. It received a rave review in *Down Beat* and, like several of her earlier albums, was nominated for a Grammy award. Its successor, *Paris Sessions* (2014), an intimate album with guitar and bass, was also nominated for a Grammy. In addition to her vast performing experience, Sutton was appointed to the faculty at Indiana University's Jacobs School of Music in 2017. Tierney Sutton is poised to remain an important figure in today's jazz scene.

7

Seven Pianists

Why have so many outstanding contemporary pianists come from Wisconsin? No one, including most of the musicians profiled in this chapter, seems to have a satisfactory answer. But these seven pianists—Lyle Mays, Lynne Arriale, David Hazeltine, Geoff Keezer, Rick Germanson, Ethan Iverson, and Dan Nimmer—are as distinguished a group of modern players active on the "big" jazz scene as one could imagine coming from the same state—especially one in the middle of the heartland, without a massive, jazz-filled metropolis.

Lyle Mays

Lyle Mays was born in 1953 in Wausaukee, Wisconsin, an extremely small village in Marinette County about sixty-five miles north of Green Bay.[1] Mays did not grow up in privileged circumstances (his father had dropped out of high school to drive a milk route), but his parents were musical. His mother was a pianist, and Mays says, "My father had taught himself to play guitar, couldn't read music at all, but he encouraged me to play along with him from when I was a very young kid." Together with his father, Mays played old tunes like "Ain't She Sweet" and "Bye Bye Blues." Mays started improvising early, without really knowing what he was doing. "[W]hen I got bored kind of picking out melodies," he says, "I'd start embellishing melodies. And eventually those embellishments didn't even resemble the melodies anymore. So effectively, I was improvising, but I just didn't know what that was called, . . . [and this was] before I even knew there was such a thing as jazz music."

Mays took piano lessons from a local teacher, Rose Barron. While she taught him in a fairly standard way, using the method books that were prevalent during that era, things changed at the end of the lessons. "My dad would wait in Rose's living room," Mays explains. "Rose would invite him in to the music room, I'd get on the organ, Rose would be on the piano, and my dad would be on guitar, and we'd just jam. . . . It wasn't called jazz, but it was playing music with some improvisational element with other people." And Mays knew that Rose treated him differently than her other students: "She discovered she couldn't play the piece of music that I was to practice for the next week in front of me at the end of the lesson, because I would kind of memorize it, instead of actually learning to play it myself."

Mays's high school band director, Dean Wheelock, was the first person Mays met who knew what jazz was. According to Mays, Wheelock "loved jazz, had albums, and he loaned things from his collection out." For Mays, hearing this music was "like a scene from a movie, you know, where the heavens open up and the light shines down." Furthermore, Wheelock told Mays about Darrell Aderman's Shell Lake jazz camps in northwest Wisconsin.

Mays attended Shell Lake the summer after eighth grade and auditioned for the stage bands on trumpet, which he also played in his school band. He was more comfortable reading music on trumpet than on piano. As he recalls:

> I sat in the last chair of the lowest band, . . . sputtering my way through these charts as best I could. And on one of the breaks, I started fooling around on piano, and I was playing "Take Five," [improvising]. One of the instructors came over and said, "What in the world are you doing playing trumpet here?" And he grabbed me and put me in the top band playing piano.

At this point in his life, Mays did not think of jazz as legitimate music. At Shell Lake, he discovered that perhaps jazz had some legitimacy. It did not in Wausaukee, because, as Mays explains, "You can't dance to it in a bar . . . [and] nobody requests it."

At Shell Lake, Mays realized that big band charts included parts for each player: "I kind of figured out that if I could write out the score and copy out the parts, I could hear my big band chart get played. . . . I think I wrote my first chart that summer."

Mays could not write for his own high school jazz band, because, as he says, the school had

> no swing band or combo of any sort. . . . [We] barely had enough to have a concert band. And our marching band was just tiny. And I used to tell people this joke that when we went out on the [football] field to spell Wausaukee, we'd lay down and move our arms and legs in shapes.
>
> I would live the whole year for those two weeks I could go to Shell Lake and be around other kids that were into jazz. There was nobody I could even talk music with in high school.
>
> So these heroes, like Darrell Aderman, Rose Barron, represent much more to me than [the] normal kind of person [who] had an influence when you were young. I mean these people were my *only* source of inspiration, about this music I loved. So they were huge; they were essential.

Several years later at Shell Lake, clinician Dan Haerle told Mays about a hot young improvisational guitarist named Pat Metheny, and encouraged the two to get together. Mays also met Rich Matteson, a prominent jazz educator, at Shell Lake, and Matteson encouraged him to consider going to North Texas State University (NTSU), the most prominent jazz school in the country in the early 1970s. But Mays didn't think he was ready:

> Not only was I from a backwards area of the country, I was also young for my age, and a little bit slow on the uptake, for social things. . . . And I think one of the reasons I ended up going to [UW–] Eau Claire is that I was terrified of making the plunge to a big school like North Texas, so many miles from home, at the maturity level I had.

However, NTSU's (temporary) loss was UW–Eau Claire's gain. UW–Eau Claire (UWEC) had a strong program at the time, during the Dominic

Spera era, with a number of other future jazz musicians there. Mays spent two years at UWEC, treating it almost like junior college while honing his skills as a player and writer. He could often be seen in local taverns, including the jazz club the Joynt, sitting in a corner booth, writing out big band charts. He joined area rock bands, sometimes playing trumpet and keyboard simultaneously.

During this time, he finally made a stab at connecting with Pat Metheny:

> I was just pulled inevitably toward hooking up with Pat, I guess. It took years. . . . We had talked on the phone once, but that was when I was in a rock band in Wisconsin. The guitar player had quit, and we had a gig out in California. On a whim, I called Pat up, to see if he wanted to do the gig, and he said, "Well, maybe it might be interesting, except I just got hired by [jazz star] Gary Burton." I felt like an idiot.

Mays dropped out of UWEC after two years to play in rock bands, largely to make money. Among the bands he played in were Community and the Vacant Lot. Of the latter, he says, "The [name] kind of gives you an indication of where [the band was] going . . . and what [its] prospects were. . . . I could see that I could keep doing that, maybe make connections, . . . get a reputation in bars in Wisconsin. . . . I kind of saw that that wasn't the way I wanted my life to go."

So he thought about his next step: "My plan was to go to North Texas and make a big splash. And I kind of figured I had to up my game a bit. The level of competition was going to be greater. So I spent about six months really trying to write some music that was more sophisticated than anything I'd ever done."

By this time, Rich Matteson was teaching at North Texas and was able to pull strings so that Mays could attend the institution on full scholarship. Upon arriving at North Texas, Mays made a big splash. It didn't take him long to get into the school's top band, the internationally famous One O'Clock Lab Band. Moreover, the several progressive original compositions that he had started in Wisconsin ended up on the One O'Clock band's annual record release, *Lab '74*. In his second year, Mays wrote all of the compositions that appeared on that year's *Lab '75*. Reportedly, this album was the first time a college big band had been nominated for a Grammy award.

In 1975, two huge events took place in Mays's life when he appeared at the Wichita Jazz Festival with a quartet from NTSU. First, legendary Wisconsin-born big band leader Woody Herman heard the group and told his manager to hire the pianist, bassist, and drummer for his band. The drummer was Wisconsin native Steve Houghton (see chapter 8). The bassist was Marc Johnson, who went on to play in the great pianist Bill Evans's last trio, as well as many other groups, and lived in Madison for some years in the 1990s. Mays accepted the offer and joined Herman on the road but remained with the Thundering Herd for only about nine months. "I could see how I could make a life being a big band piano player," he says. "Although I kind of saw that that scene was dying, . . . I purposefully didn't want to record with Woody. In my young, naïve, or superstitious way, I thought there was a chance I could be typecast as a big band piano player. And that wasn't the future I imagined for myself."

The second thing that happened at the Wichita festival was that Mays finally met Pat Metheny, who was performing there with Gary Burton's group. "We just kind of sought each other out," Mays recalls. "I think we even found an empty practice room somewhere and tried writing something together." On that day, Mays believes, they came up with the beginning of the piece "It's for You," which appeared later on their 1981 album, *As Wichita Falls, So Falls Wichita Falls*.

After his time on the road with the Herman band, Mays went back to Wisconsin but didn't know what he would do next. Out of the blue, he received a call from Betty Buckley, a singer who would soon be the lead in the Broadway hit *Cats*, who wanted him to do a couple of gigs with her. At about the same time, Metheny called Mays for a few more gigs in New York. As Mays recalls, "I thought, 'Well, that's it, I'm buying a car, and driving to New York, and I'm going to live there.' So, on the basis of two gigs that didn't pay much at all, I moved to New York City."

Mays's existence in New York was, as he describes it, "kind of week-to-week. I didn't have any money; I was really not getting anywhere on my own. Every once in a while I would sub for a society gig." Mays started jamming with musicians such as Randy and Michael Brecker and drummer Steve Jordan. Mays played some big band gigs with the Young Artists

Program, which performed for children in underprivileged parts of the city. His first "good money gig" was with singer Marlena Shaw. Metheny also did some work with Shaw and later told Mays that his intention was to convince Mays to quit and join him in a band.

"Pat's a very persuasive guy," Mays explains.

> After a couple weeks, he talked me into quitting, and moving to Boston, and putting together this band. We rented a house in Cambridge; rented a piano; Danny [Gottlieb]'s drums were set up all the time, and Pat and I started writing music, right off the bat. We were going to craft a new sound, and a new kind of band. The first thing we wrote, I think, was "San Lorenzo."

"San Lorenzo" was the opening track on their very successful first album, 1978's *Pat Metheny Group*, which eventually reached number five on *Billboard*'s jazz album charts.

After that, Mays says, "A lot of this is a bit of a blur, because, soon after we started doing gigs, word got out, and there was kind of a buzz, and we started working, almost constantly." It was the beginning of one of the most successful and longest-running groups in jazz. The collaboration between Mays and Metheny was remarkable. Three of the six tunes on their first album were cowritten by the two, and on the next two albums, *American Garage* (1980) and *Offramp* (1982), they were listed as co-composers on every track. The two also put out a co-led album, *As Falls Wichita, So Falls Wichita Falls*, in 1981. *American Garage* went to the top of the *Billboard* jazz charts, and other Metheny Group albums were to follow.

Offramp was the first Metheny Group album to win a Grammy, in 1983. The band went on to win Grammys in 1984, 1985, 1988, 1989, 1994, 1996, 1999, 2003, and 2006. In 1999, *Imaginary Day* won Best Contemporary Jazz Performance, and one of its tracks, "The Roots of Coincidence," won Best Rock Instrumental Performance. Of course, the band's commercial success, and the fact that it was not playing traditional jazz, led to critical backlash. But, as Mays puts it, "We were never that concerned with commercial success anyway. I mean, we never did anything . . . that was pandering. We tried to make it sophisticated, whatever we did." And the band's music lives on, not just with those who grew up with it, but with younger (and new, older) listeners as well. Pat Metheny's election to the *Down Beat* Hall of Fame in 2013 also reflects the quality and long-term viability of the work that Metheny and Mays created.

Despite the many albums with Metheny, Mays has not recorded many albums as a leader, but there are four significant entries in his recorded legacy (see online discography). Mays has also written music for films. He collaborated with Metheny on the music for the 1985 feature *The Falcon and the Snowman*. For productions in the Public Broadcasting System/ Rabbit Ears Productions children's series, Mays wrote the music for several classic children's tales, including Beatrix Potter's *The Tale of Peter Rabbit* and *The Tale of Jeremy Fisher*, both narrated by Meryl Streep.

In *The New Grove Dictionary of Jazz*, Patrick Will gives Mays credit for being "among the first keyboard players to employ polyphonic synthesizers in concert, which enabled him to provide a rich, complex backing to Metheny's playing."[2] Mays's ability to create lush textures with multiple keyboards brought him acclaim, though, not surprisingly, he was often disparaged by those opposed to electronics in jazz. He consistently ranked high in polls in *Down Beat* and *Keyboard* magazines for many years. The Alesis keyboard company even included sounds on a couple of its synthesizer models called "Maze Lead" and "Lyle" that approximated the sounds Mays made famous.

Mays has not been prominently visible since playing on the tour that backed up Metheny's 2005 album *The Way Up*. In August 2010, Mays performed at the Western Michigan University jazz club (and two theaters) as part of the Irving S. Gilmore International Keyboard Festival. He appeared with a quintet that included his niece, Aubrey Johnson, a Wisconsin native, vocalist, and Western Michigan alumna.

One little-known project that Mays took part in during 2011 renewed the application of the "mad scientist" and "genius" labels that some have applied to him for years. He collaborated with scientists from one of the country's most prestigious institutions, Cal Tech, to create a new piece of music "combining music composition, jazz improvisation, physics equations, algorithmic composition, speech patterns, live video mixing, and

Lyle Mays. PHOTO BY BETH HERZHAFT; COURTESY OF LYLE MAYS

a custom laptop linked network."[3] Regardless of the genesis and development of the music, Mays's fans would still easily recognize his style in the resulting music.

Many fans were gratified to see Mays return to the live jazz scene in 2014, appearing at the Montreal Jazz Festival with a quartet including his old colleague Marc Johnson on bass. From modest beginnings in small-town Wisconsin, Lyle Mays ascended to a very high-profile position in the jazz world, maintaining it for almost thirty years.

Lynne Arriale

Lynne Arriale was born in 1957 and grew up as Lynn Bernstein (she was adopted) in Fox Point, a northern suburb of Milwaukee. In Arriale's words:

> We had a little toy piano in our house, and it was about two feet wide, and plastic. And I started playing by ear when I was very young, I think before morning kindergarten. So I was playing songs I heard off the radio. . . . And I made a connection with music very quickly in terms of being able to hear the notes of a song and translating that into playing them on the piano. I had perfect pitch, which I think I inherited from my [biological] mom, because I guess it ran in our family.

Arriale started lessons at about age four with a local piano teacher and told a story almost identical to the one related earlier by Lyle Mays. She says: "[My teacher] would play the songs for me, and I would come back the next week and play them. And then I think she realized I was just learning them by ear, and not really learning to read the music. At that point, she refused to play them."

While still fairly young, Arriale began lessons with Sister Mary Romano, who taught at Cardinal Stritch College. According to Arriale: "She was a very fine musician, and I was probably a pretty poor student, because . . . she would circle the notes every week—this is wrong, this is wrong—and every week it was a different color pen, so my music looked kind of like a battleground. But I did study classical music with her for many years."

Although Arriale had not been introduced to improvisation, she says she would "make up little songs, or play songs [she'd] heard off the radio." While in secondary school, she began studying at the Wisconsin Conservatory with the legendary Adelaide Banaszynski, who taught classical pianist Ralph Votapek, gold medalist at the very first Van Cliburn International Piano Competition.

At age seventeen, Arriale met Rebecca Penneys, who also taught at the conservatory. Penneys eventually moved on to the Eastman School of Music, but Arriale spent crucial time with the woman she describes as "a brilliant concert pianist, instructor, and educator." Arriale recalls:

> Rebecca said to me, "We need to kind of work [on] your technique," because I had a lot of tension when I was playing. One of the things that was really remarkable about her as a teacher and as a pianist is that she used to be a ballet dancer. And she had learned how to use her body. . . . She had a beautiful, beautiful sound on the piano and really taught me how to sing everything.

After graduating from Nicolet High School, Arriale attended the University of Wisconsin–Madison. She earned a degree in music theory at UW but did not get a degree in piano, because she was driving back to Milwaukee every week to study piano with Penneys. After graduating, she moved back to Milwaukee, continuing study with Penneys, and earned a master's degree at the conservatory.

Arriale had just a slight connection with jazz at this time, having heard a little bit of Dave Brubeck and Paul Desmond, and a few hours of live jazz in Madison. "And even though I improvised," she says, "I was just playing by ear. I didn't really quite get that there was this whole language of bebop, and of jazz improvisation."

With a chuckle, she recalls that, about the time that she was finishing her master's program, she "was walking down the street, and I just had a passing thought: . . . 'You should do some jazz.'" So she began studying with her contemporary, David Hazeltine (see later in this chapter), already a jazz veteran, who taught at the conservatory. She studied with Hazeltine, who she calls "a wonderful teacher," for years.

After a couple of years of study with Hazeltine, Arriale began getting jazz and other professional jobs, even though she felt like a novice. The first group she played in was a trio, with Edie Harold on drums and Carol Seline on bass. She went on to work at several jazz venues in Milwaukee: Chip and Py's, the Bombay Bicycle Room at the Marc Plaza Hotel, and the Jazz Gallery (with Hattush Alexander). She also played a duo gig for some years with bassist Al Anderson at Snug's, in the Shorecrest Hotel. For a couple of years, she worked several nights a week at the Midway Motor Lodge in Glendale with singer Marcia Cunningham, Al Anderson, and drummer Randy Baugher. She learned valuable lessons working with a vocalist, as well as what was required of a leader, like calling the sets and learning the business aspects of the job.

"At some point," she says, "I thought, it would be good to move [to New York]. . . . That's another phase of one's growth, just to go to really the mecca of jazz in the world. And I went there [in the late 1980s], and I had my little demo tape that I made, and went door-to-door. Every club I could find."

It wasn't long before she got work at clubs—first at Garvin's and Café Lido. The first trio she worked with included Harvie Swartz (now known as Harvie S) on bass and Eliot Zigmund on drums. She soon played with other outstanding musicians such as bassists Rufus Reid and Bob Cranshaw and drummers Frank Gant and Lewis Nash. She recalls:

> I basically had to become a leader just by default, because I'd gotten the gig, and so I had to tell them, "Here's how we're going to do this tune," and "Here's what we're going to do on it." And there weren't any rehearsals, of course; it was just calling tunes. But I wanted the music to still have arrangements, or just a particular feel, so

> it wasn't just like . . . a jam session. . . . I just wanted to create something special.

Lynne Arriale. PHOTO BY R. ANDREW LEPLEY; COURTESY OF LYNNE ARRIALE

Arriale continued to work clubs, like Tavern on the Green, Sweet Basil, and Fat Tuesdays, where she held forth with her steady trio including Steve Davis on drums and Jay Anderson on bass. The trio began a series of recordings in 1994. Not long after, the group started touring in the United States and Europe.

In 1993, Arriale won the Great American Jazz Piano Competition. She also had what she called "a life-changing experience," substituting for Marian McPartland on a tour of Japan with a group known as 100 Golden Fingers. The other nine pianists on the tour included some of the most distinguished members of the jazz piano community: Hank Jones, Tommy Flanagan, Cedar Walton, Monty Alexander, Kenny Barron, Ray Bryant, Roger Kellaway, Junior Mance, and Harold Mabern.

Although already accomplished, Arriale took advantage of being in New York by studying with other pianists: Richie Beirach, Fred Hersch, Kenny Werner, and George Cables. Despite the steady work and recordings, Arriale was not particularly well known outside a relatively small circle in New York. She became more visible in 2009 with the release of her album *Nuance*. After the album earned a four-star review in the June issue of *Down Beat*, the magazine printed a feature article about Arriale in September. The November issue of *JAZZed*, "the Jazz Educator's Magazine," featured her on the cover and published an article that focused on her teaching philosophy and strategy. She later appeared as one of the featured performers in the April 2011 *Down Beat* article "Equal Time: On the Strength of Women in Jazz Today, Gender Lines Are Finally Being Erased."[4]

After living in New York for fourteen years, Arriale moved to Indiana, then to Jacksonville, Florida, when she was hired to the faculty of the jazz program at the University of North Florida, which was being led by Milwaukee native Bunky Green.

Arriale has thought carefully about her calling and made clear statements about how she thinks and feels about music, and how and why she plays it.

> I decided to make the transition from classical music to jazz because when I discovered jazz, it was like the whole world opened up. Not only do we have the opportunity to choose any tune we want to play, but how we play it. It can be fast, it can be slow, we can have different tempos, we can play it in any time signature, we can play with different feels—swing feel, or with a Latin feel, changing the character. We can change the key. We can arrange it in a way that it takes on a totally new light, reinvent the tune, which is one of the things I've tried to do when I arranged any tune.
>
> I think that the joy of music and the magic of improvisation is that . . . it can take us on a journey. And take us away from our stress, and whatever we're under during the day. . . . We never know who we're playing for. Meaning, we don't know if the person we're talking to on the street just found out they have cancer, or their mother just died, or their wife just left them, or they're depressed, . . . you just never know.
>
> The connection with the audience is really something very special. And I never forget . . . that they don't have to be there. They could be at home watching TV. . . . And for every audience that I play for, I'm very aware and appreciative of the fact that they took time out of their busy schedules to come, for a couple hours, and share sound, share the space with us. And, I feel an obligation . . . to bring my best to them, bring heart, and humor, and discovery, and all the things that we express when we're playing, to bring that to the audience.

Arriale's commitment to this philosophy of bringing her heart, humor, and musical skills to each performance certainly indicates that she will be a vital player for years to come.

David Hazeltine

David Hazeltine was born in Milwaukee in 1958 and grew up on Martin Drive, a little north of where Miller Park now stands. His siblings were much older than him, but his mother, who was a singer and guitarist, called David her "favorite mistake." His parents owned a club, the Corn Crib, that had live music, but when David was born, the Hazeltines were getting out of the club business.

His mother performed on a daily noontime television show on WTMJ that featured Joe Shott (real name Szot) and the Hot Shots. She also sang with her sister as part of a duo, the Winkert Sisters. David loved to hear them rehearse and vaguely remembers being at the TV station as a young child. He recalls: "The sisters were good at what they did. [My mother] had a beautiful voice. . . . Music, it just got me. I was just totally into it, from a very early age."

Hazeltine's musical training started a few years later. He explains: "I begged my parents to buy me an instrument when I was seven years old. . . . They finally got me an organ. And I started taking organ lessons from a local teacher that used to come around. I don't recall if I was really terrible, but I do recall that the organ teacher always asked for two aspirins when she'd show up."

A few years later, his mother took him to lessons with Archie Ulm, who Hazeltine referred to as a young "local celebrity" who was "big on the Hammond organ circuit." Ulm, who was only about twenty years old at the time, worked meticulously with Hazeltine for a couple of years before promptly dropping him as a student. His mother later said it was because the young boy "was getting too good."

Hazeltine remembers, "[My mother] came home one night from work with a Jimmy Smith record. . . . And I still have the record. And it completely changed my life." He had heard his older brother's jazz records around the house, but this one, featuring Smith on the Hammond B-3, was something different. Seeing the effect this had on her son, Hazeltine's mother found Will Green: a blind jazz organist who taught and played around town but made his living as an electronics technician.

"My mom and dad took me out to see him play," Hazeltine recalls.

"This was after the Jimmy Smith record, now I'm into it, and I was like, 'Oh, my God; I can take lessons with this guy?'"

So at age twelve, Hazeltine was dutifully driven by his mother to Will Green's house, at Seventeenth and Atkinson, for a lesson every Saturday. He remembers:

> [Green] had a little studio that he taught out of. . . . He was very popular in the neighborhood. People were always coming in and talking to him, . . . bringing in their stereos, or their TVs, for him to fix. And, they were always hitting on my mom. I'm taking my lesson; my mom's freaked out, you know, she's in the ghetto. This is when the race riots were going on. . . . But I have to tell you, kinder people I've never met; these people were so incredibly kind to me and my mother, and made us feel completely at home.

Hazeltine describes Green as being not only a great teacher, but a tremendously accomplished organist as well:

> He was amazing, and I was in love. I mean this guy was like my father. . . . Will smoked a pipe, and he was always suited up; even for lessons he'd have a suit and tie on. So when my mom and dad would go out, . . . I'd find a pipe, and actually sit at the organ, and put on one of [my dad's] suit coats and try to be this guy.

Green taught Hazeltine essentially by rote, telling his young student to play what he demonstrated. Hazeltine's ear allowed him to have immediate success following his teacher's models; later on, he could look back and analyze what he was doing. After a few years of lessons, Hazeltine started teaching for Green at his studio; Green was diagnosed with cancer and died just months later.

Hazeltine started jobbing at a young age. At thirteen, he played Friday and Saturday nights at Nicollo's on Mayfair Road. After he got his driver's license, he began playing at the Brother's Lounge, usually working with guitarist Charles Small, and club owner Lee Foster, on drums. Trumpeter Brian Lynch (see chapter 9) was a frequent guest. The talented keyboard player Marcus Robinson would sit in on organ and try to simultaneously intimidate and instruct young Hazeltine.

Hazeltine's early mentors included Manty Ellis and Berkeley Fudge (see chapter 11). "I can't say enough good things about those guys," Hazeltine says. When Hazeltine started working with Ellis at age sixteen, his mother told the veteran musician: "Take care of him. Don't let him do any of the things that musicians do."

After high school, Hazeltine enrolled at the Wisconsin Conservatory, where he continued to work with Ellis, Fudge, and bassist Skip Crumby-Bey. He had been prepared to attend the Milwaukee School of Engineering, because Will Green had told him: "Don't go into music as a profession—trust me." Hazeltine considered following in the footsteps of his mentor and going into electronics, but right before school began, he thought: "Wow, how much time am I going to be spending [studying] electronics, and it's not going to leave any time for music. I can't do this." At that point, Hazeltine made the decision to attend music school.

For a while he lived, and often worked, with Lynch and drummer Scott Napoli. While in school, he frequently worked at the Jazz Gallery backing up such prominent touring musicians as Chet Baker, Pepper Adams, Charles McPherson, Eddie Harris, and Sonny Stitt. He also worked a duo gig for some time with bassist Al Anderson at Snug's. After three years, he left school, at which time he began working six nights a week with vocalist Penny Goodwin at the Sheraton Mayfair. After about a year with Goodwin, Hazeltine got a call from legendary singer Jon Hendricks, who had recently picked up Skip Crumby-Bey for his band. Crumby-Bey suggested Hazeltine as a pianist for the group, so Hazeltine headed to New York.

At age nineteen, Hazeltine joined Hendricks's band, in a rhythm section with Crumby-Bey and a drummer who was even younger than Hazeltine, Marvin "Smitty" Smith, who went on to a distinguished career. When he wasn't touring with Hendricks, Hazeltine played whatever gigs he could get in New York, including some with Brian Lynch, who had also moved to the Big Apple. However, Hazeltine didn't like New York, and his wife had health issues, so after a year and a half, the couple decided to move back to Milwaukee. Hazeltine remembered veteran saxophonist Junior Cook asking him, "What are you going to do out in Milwaukee? Are you going to milk cows?"

Back in Milwaukee, Hazeltine went back to jobbing wherever he could, but after a time, he and drummer Scott Black (who Hazeltine had met in New York) founded the Jazz School, which they operated at the Jazz Gallery, a popular night club in Milwaukee. According to Hazeltine, "The [Wisconsin] Conservatory was really upset about the Jazz School. . . . It was so underground and so hip and cool, that we got much more of a response than we thought we were going to get. And people filled the place." But it was not easy running the new school, and Pat Jones at the conservatory kept after Hazeltine, eventually making him an offer to run the conservatory's jazz program that he couldn't pass up.

While at the conservatory from 1984 to 1992, Hazeltine rebuilt the jazz program but also became something of a victim of his own success, working four full days a week at the school in addition to a heavy performing schedule. During this time, he mentored such important up-and-coming pianists as Lynne (Bernstein) Arriale and Mark Davis. He started playing again (replacing Melvin Rhyne) with Al Anderson at Chip and Py's on the South Side. When Anderson left, he was replaced by Jeff Chambers, who had been playing with Buddy Montgomery. Eventually, Gerald Cannon took over the bass chair, and Cannon and Hazeltine worked together for several years at Chip and Py's, and later at Nance's on the near North Side.

Eventually, Hazeltine returned to New York. He has been busy—and successful—ever since. Back in the Big Apple, he played one of his first gigs with his old buddy Lynch on the late-night gig at the well-known Blue Note jazz club. Ira Gitler quotes Hazeltine as saying, in reference to that gig, "Those were my vampire days."[5] Some of his most important associations have been with singer Marlena Shaw, with whom he acted as musical director, and the collective sextet One for All. He has made numerous recordings with One for All and Shaw, as well as many, many others,[6] and has been leader on more than twenty-five albums.

Hazeltine prizes the associations he has had and recordings he has made with trombonist Slide Hampton (in his small group and the Jazz Masters) and bassist George Mraz. He also worked for some time with drummer Louis Hayes. Other important compatriots have been trumpeter Jon Faddis (in a small group with Hampton and Jimmy Heath, and with the Carnegie Hall Jazz Band); saxophone giant James Moody;

David Hazeltine. PHOTO BY JOHN ABBOTT; COURTESY OF DAVID HAZELTINE

vibraphonist Joe Locke; and drummer Killer Ray Appleton, with whom Hazeltine worked in Milwaukee.

In 2005, Ed Berger succinctly summed up Hazeltine's style in an article in *JazzTimes*: "No matter what the context, Hazeltine's playing is marked by its clarity, structure, and unerring sense of good taste. He has technique to spare but uses it only to serve the music, eschewing empty pyrotechnical displays."[7] While his clever compositions frequently appear in his recorded work, Hazeltine is perhaps better known for his meticulous yet creative arrangements of the works of others.

No other musician on the Wisconsin jazz scene has equaled Hazeltine's importance as a figure in jazz education in the state while also contributing so much to the Wisconsin, national, and international performance stages.

Geoffrey Keezer

Geoffrey Keezer was born November 20, 1970, in Eau Claire. His father, Ron, a percussionist, was a longtime member of the music faculty at UW–Eau Claire (see chapter 19). His mom taught music at Fall Creek Middle School, and Keezer says: "[She] played classical French horn and also taught piano at the house, so I grew up either with music in the house, or scampering around the university. . . . Between the two of [my parents], they had a pretty cool record collection: a lot of classical stuff, a lot of jazz stuff. I just listened to records all the time, and started up playing drums." Keezer's first piano teacher, Noreen Grey, then a student at UWEC and later a New York pro, taught him blues when he was just four.

According to Ron Keezer, "[Geoff] would always write music, from the year four on. He'd make up things at the piano, and then I had to write it down. Every day I'd come home, 'Dad, I got ten more tunes.' . . . After a while I said, 'Geoff, why don't you just learn how to write music?' So he did. I never showed him; he just knew what to do." Geoffrey, however, disputes this claim, saying that his parents taught him how to read and write music.

Keezer says the summers spent at Shell Lake music camps, where his father taught drums for years, helped him narrow his focus on jazz. "And that was my hang for three weeks every summer," he says. "When I was old enough, I was playing in the bands, and . . . pretty much grew up around that environment." At Shell Lake, he primarily studied with pianist John Radd, who was on the faculty of UW–River Falls, and then UW–Stevens Point. Keezer describes Radd as "an inspiring and fun guy to be around."

As Keezer continued through school, he says: "I just was really into Chick Corea and Weather Report. That was really my stuff. And Oscar Peterson a little bit. I was into jazz, but I was really into classical, too, and Dad [would] go to the music library in Eau Claire and get scores of Beethoven symphonies. And I would just sit with those records and look at these scores, and I think that helped me learn how to compose."

He took classical piano lessons with Don Patterson of the UWEC faculty. But Keezer's attention was not focused solely on jazz and Western classical music. He grew up listening to percussion ensemble music and percussion-heavy international music, like African music and Balinese gamelan. His early musical interests would eventually lead him to make music based on more distant cultures.

In the late 1970s, some UWEC students (aided by Ron Keezer) formed the Water Street Big Band, which played on Tuesday nights at the Joynt in downtown Eau Claire. Keezer started playing in the band (then led by saxophonist Greg Keel) around the time he was fourteen. According to Keezer, "We were playing lots of great stock arrangements and sometimes I would bring a new chart in to try. They were always very welcoming and receptive to playing new music."

As a student in the mid-1980s, Keezer won an award from the National Association of Jazz Educators. As part of his prize, he attended the association's convention in Atlanta, where he played in a band that included another young star in the making, trumpeter Roy Hargrove, who later became Keezer's roommate at the Berklee College of Music in Boston.

In Atlanta, Keezer also met pianist James Williams (already renowned for a ten-year tenure with Art Blakey's Jazz Messengers), with whom he had been corresponding and who became an important mentor and advocate in Keezer's career. Williams took Keezer around to play for, and with, jazz stars, including Dizzy Gillespie. Keezer later referred to Williams as "an exceptionally kind and generous human being."

Keezer was selected as a member of the McDonald's High School Jazz Band and toured with them in 1988. "We toured mostly in the deep South," Keezer explains, "very strange gigs. We played a lot of military installations and at McDonald's restaurants, and they fed us McDonald's [food] three times a day, every day. I gained forty pounds that summer."

Living with a musician of Keezer's talent and drive was not necessarily easy. His father, Ron, says,

> When [Geoff] was in high school, the last year he studied, he practiced eight hours *every day*. . . . Mary and I would go to the library. We'd say at midnight, . . . "That's it; you've got to stop; we've got to get some rest." [Geoff would say,] "Just one more thing." One time he was doing some lick, in all twelve keys and backwards and retrograde and . . . I said, "I think you have it, son." And he called up, "I don't have it yet, Dad. Don't bother me."

After graduating from high school, Keezer went east to Berklee. But one week after being at school, James Williams took Keezer to New York, where he auditioned for Art Blakey by sitting in with the band. After hearing him play, Blakey pledged to give Keezer the gig as soon as Benny Green, the current pianist, left the band.

And he did; Keezer was the last pianist to play in Blakey's Jazz Messengers, holding down the piano chair in the band until Blakey's death in 1990. Milwaukee native Brian Lynch (see chapter 9) was the trumpeter in the band at this time as well. The Jazz Messengers launched the careers of many young musicians, including Keezer.

While still with Blakey, Keezer was invited to the home of legendary master Miles Davis. Davis asked Keezer to join his band, but the young pianist decided to stay with Blakey.

After Blakey's death, Keezer returned to play at the Wisconsin State Music Convention in 1991 with a quartet that included a relative unknown but future star, saxophonist Joshua Redman. He also played with some of the most respected names in jazz during these years. In fairly quick succession, he worked with Art Farmer, Benny Golson, Jon Faddis, the Carnegie Hall Jazz Band (for which he also wrote), George Coleman, Gerry Mulligan, and the Mingus Dynasty. He spent an important stint with the trio of the great bass player Ray Brown. During the 1990s, he toured with veteran pianists James Williams, Mulgrew Miller, Donald Brown, and Harold Mabern in the Contemporary Piano Ensemble, and as a member of the "Three Musicians" with Joshua Redman and bassist Christian McBride. Another highlight of this era was Keezer's 1992 performance of George Gershwin's *Rhapsody in Blue* with the Hollywood Bowl Symphony.[8]

Eventually, Keezer went out on his own. He has been making albums under his own name since 1989, and they total more than twenty as of 2015. Notable among these is a recording of duets with piano stars Chick Corea, Kenny Barron, Mulgrew Miller, and Benny Green.

Keezer lived in Japan for a while before relocating to southern California. His many albums have crossed musical boundaries, incorporating classical music, rock, and a variety of world music traditions from the musical cultures of Hawaii, Okinawa, and Peru, the latter on his Grammy-nominated *Áurea* (2009).[9]

He is a sideman on many, many records, including the successful albums of vocalist Denise Donatelli. Three of the Donatelli albums have received Grammy nominations, and Keezer's arrangement of "Don't Explain" on *When Lights Are Low* received its own nomination for Best Arrangement Accompanying a Vocalist in 2010. Keezer played at the Fox

Geoffrey Keezer. PHOTO BY DAWN BOWERY; COURTESY OF GEOFFREY KEEZER

Jazz Fest in Menasha with Donatelli in the fall of 2014, after appearing there with his own trio in 2010.

It might seem odd that after coming up in bands led by some of the great mainstream figures of modern jazz, Keezer has recently appeared and recorded with not only Donatelli, but also such commercially successful leaders as saxophonist David Sanborn and trumpeter Chris Botti. Keezer explains this seeming dichotomy: "Art Blakey, Ray Brown, and Chris Botti, while drastically different musically, are all great bandleaders and great entertainers. They understand how to balance art with entertainment value, delivering quality music while making it fun and engaging for the audience as well."

Keezer does not take his upbringing at home or his Wisconsin education for granted. When questioned about the reason for Wisconsin's success at continuing to produce excellent jazz musicians, he speculates: "I think a big part of it is that there's music in the schools. You have access to it. You've got great band directors; there's so many great, inspiring, motivating band directors in Wisconsin. It's these kinds of programs [like the Wisconsin State Honors Jazz Ensemble] that encourage kids to be musicians and want to be good. That's the big one really. It's where you start. And maybe there's something in the water."

Rick Germanson

Rick Germanson was born in Milwaukee on May 29, 1972. Both parents, Ken and Ann, played piano, and Rick's oldest sister, Jill, played professionally, in wedding bands, and had "a really great classical repertoire." Rick began formal lessons at age six or seven but credits Jill as his first teacher. "[She] showed me how to mess around with the blues scale, and play a boogie-woogie bass line," he says, "so I really learned how to improvise first with her." (Jill died when Rick was just a teenager. His composition "Jill's Song," on his *Off the Cuff* album, is dedicated to her.) He took "standard" lessons with Laura Swenson, who was teaching at Alverno College, and Barbara Bunge, at Bob Kames Music.

Germanson went to Pius XI High School and was first exposed to big band charts when James Van Deusen became band director there. Van Deusen put his band to serious work immediately, as one of the first pieces Germanson remembers playing was the classic Count Basie/Frank Foster chart "Shiny Stockings."

When Germanson was looking for an instructor, one of his friends who studied guitar at the Wisconsin Conservatory recommended David Hazeltine. Germanson started private lessons with Hazeltine the summer before his senior year of high school and continued working with him every week for the next three years, until Hazeltine moved back to New York around 1992.

"The greatest thing he showed me to do," Germanson says, "was how to teach myself. . . . When he left, I thought, 'Well, what am I gonna do now?' [He told me,] 'You'll figure it out. I showed you everything that I can show you.' I wouldn't have known anything if it wasn't for Dave, because he showed me really what to do, and how to study, and how to go about learning this music."

Germanson sat in during this period on a couple of Hazeltine's gigs at either Chip and Py's or Nance's. "I used to go see [Hazeltine] play all the time," Germanson explains. "See him and Brian Lynch play, see Melvin Rhyne play. [I] went to the Jazz Oasis, the Jazz Estate. And eventually I got at least good enough to start working some gigs around town. A lot of older musicians really gave me a chance." And his opportunities grew after Hazeltine left town.

Among the musicians who gave him a chance, Germanson particularly singles out bassist Gerald Cannon and saxophonist Berkeley Fudge. Cannon, like Hazeltine, had come back to Milwaukee after spending some time in New York and later headed back to New York permanently.

Cannon led a band called the Jazz Elements, which played practically every weekend at the Jazz Estate. During that period, roughly between 1993 and 1995, Germanson also worked with Luis Diaz's Latin jazz quintet, which played there most Fridays. "I was there at the Estate every weekend," he says. "And that's how I learned, playing with those two groups. And there was another group on Thursdays that I was working with—the vocalist Billy Staffaroni. And we were doing a kind of 'Jump, Jive, and Wail' thing. . . . I'm indebted to all the older musicians that gave me a chance—and showed me how to play on the bandstand."

During this period in the early 1990s, Germanson attended the University of Wisconsin–Milwaukee. He graduated in 1995 with a degree in economics. While most of his music education occurred outside of school, he acknowledges the contributions to his education made by UWM jazz director Curt Hanrahan. After he graduated, Germanson did not directly use his degree but rather continued to play piano in Milwaukee, Chicago, and Madison. A milestone in his career came in 1996, when saxophonist Frank Morgan took him to a jazz festival in San Sebastian, Spain, to play duo. "I remember coming down to breakfast at the hotel," Germason says, "and there [were] Phil Woods, Ben Riley, Kenny Barron, Mulgrew Miller, . . . Eddie Palmieri. . . . I'm like, *What am I doing here?*" Later that year, he performed on a jazz cruise in the Caribbean with Morgan and bassist Jeff Hamann.

After returning to Milwaukee and winning the American Pianists Association competition in 1996, Germanson moved to New York, where he hung out at clubs like Bradley's, Zinno, Sweet Basil, and Visiones. He heard great piano players who were not well-known outside of the city—John Hicks, Ronnie Mathews, Harold Mabern—as well as some of the established masters like Cedar Walton, Hank Jones, Tommy Flanagan, and Barry Harris. He also recognized the prowess of pianists of his generation such as Eric Lewis, James Hurt, and Anthony Wonsey.

But after three months, feeling unprepared for New York both musically and maturity-wise, Germanson returned to Milwaukee. He knew what he had to do—practice. He was able to lead a good number of gigs in Milwaukee and structure what he was working on around those; many were trio jobs, which he usually played with bassists Jeff Hamann or Jim Paolo and drummers Brian Ritter or Dave Bayles. But he also

Rick Germanson (right) with bassist Gerald Cannon (see chapter 9). COURTESY OF GERALD CANNON

worked frequently with Berkeley Fudge. And for six months he worked with bassist (and legendary character) Skip Crumby-Bey. As a result of his winning the piano competition, Germanson was also able to record his first album, which eventually came out on the Fresh Sound New Talent label and included Milwaukeeans Brian Lynch and Luis Diaz.

Germanson moved to New York to stay in 1998. Since then, in addition to making his own albums, he has performed with a vast array of great jazz players, including Elvin Jones, George Coleman, Tom Harrell, Slide Hampton, Charles McPherson, Delfeayo Marsalis, Marlena Shaw, Jeremy Pelt, Papo Vazquez, and the Mingus Dynasty band. His most meaningful ongoing associations have been with two masters, Louis Hayes and Pat Martino. Drummer Hayes, who played with legendary small groups led by Cannonball Adderley and Oscar Peterson, has been leader of the Cannonball Legacy Band, with which Germanson has been playing since 2001. He also toured with Martino, one of the most important guitarists in jazz history, from 2003 to 2008, and his ongoing association with Vazquez has become increasingly important and fruitful. Rick Germanson's versatility, musicality, and professionalism make him a valuable member of the New York and wider jazz communities.

Ethan Iverson

Ethan Iverson was born in 1973 and spent his childhood and youth near Menomonie, much of it in a farmhouse several miles out of town in the area known as Irvington.[10] Iverson's parents, Minnesota natives of Scandinavian descent, moved to that part of the state when his father took a position in the art department at the University of Wisconsin–Stout.

"I think I was always interested in music," Iverson says, "and the first jazz I could get was just off the TV; stuff, frankly, from *Mr. Rogers* or *Sesame Street*. . . . As I got more interested in it, I started to play a little bit of boogie-woogie and music like that." As a youth, he built a huge record collection, initially ordering from Publisher's Clearing House.[11] "That was the way I got all the records, you know, in the pre-internet era," he says, "and there certainly weren't any record stores in Menomonie." By the time he graduated from high school in 1991, Iverson estimates that he owned a thousand records. By fifth or sixth grade, his favorite pianist (a "god" to him during this period) was the eccentric genius Thelonious Monk.

While listening to a wide variety of jazz, Iverson also played—a lot. He joined school band, playing saxophone, and eventually began to play piano, drums, and bass in high school jazz band. He loved drumming on a tune like "Johnny B. Goode" with the pep band. Marion Lang, who ran the Greenwood Players, a local theater group, hired Iverson to play and write music for some of the productions. And as just an eighth grader, he started playing Friday nights at the Creamery restaurant in nearby Downsville. Later, with the quartet of his high school band director Jim Borgaro ("a genuine jazz saxophone player," according to Iverson), he also started playing Saturday nights at the Creamery. It's fairly miraculous that a young pianist could get this sort of performance experience in a community like Menomonie in the 1980s and 1990s.

Iverson played two years in the Wisconsin High School Honors Jazz Ensemble, following fellow wunderkind Geoffrey Keezer in the group. And he had not only Keezer, from nearby Eau Claire, to look up to, but also slightly older Menomonie saxophonists Woody Mankowski and Sue Orfield (see chapters 18 and 19) as well. After Ron Keezer talked Iverson into auditioning for a competition held by the National Association of Jazz Educators, Iverson played at the NAJE's national convention with Ron and bassist Reid Anderson, who was then a student at UWEC, and would later become Iverson's bandmate in the Bad Plus.

Iverson attended summer jazz camp at Shell Lake in northwest Wisconsin, but the experiences that inspired him more were a session in Elmhurst, Illinois, at the Jamey Aebersold Workshops, and a camp at the Banff Centre in Alberta, Canada, where the faculty included such jazz luminaries as Steve Coleman, Kenny Wheeler, Rufus Reid, Marvin "Smitty" Smith, and Stanley Cowell. Among the other students at Banff with Iverson were Seamus Blake, George Colligan, and Ralph Alessi. Iverson would encounter these three again, years later, in New York.

In the meantime, he pursued his own musical goals. He recalls, "[In high school] I learned every single Monk tune. . . . I didn't learn them very well, but I learned them. And I actually look back on that with a certain amount of pride."

After high school, Iverson wanted to go to the jazz capital of the world, and so he enrolled in New York University. He dropped out after two years, in part because he was disappointed with the education he was receiving, in part because he saw massive school loans piling up, and in part because he was starting to get some work in town with groups like the New York Tango Trio.[12] Perhaps more importantly, he became music director of the Mark Morris Dance Group. In 2000, he told Howard Mandel: "After all, John Cage and Andrew Cyrille were among those who've played for dance classes. [Ballet star Mikhail] Barishnikov made a point of discussing with me how he enjoyed dancing to Cecil Taylor's music." A huge benefit of working with the Morris company was that world-renowned cellist Yo-Yo Ma also worked with the company. Iverson once said, "I've received about $1 million worth of chamber music lessons from Yo-Yo Ma."[13]

Iverson didn't play much jazz publicly while he was working with the tango band and the dance company. And that didn't bother him, because he felt that he wasn't yet ready to enter the tremendously competitive jazz scene in New York.

When he did feel ready, Iverson became part of what he has called the "late-'90s indie jazz scene." His first album, *School Work*, featured saxophone veteran Dewey Redman. Though Iverson later dismissed it as "not mature work,"[14] the album was reviewed not only in the jazz press, but in *Billboard* as well. Another trio album, with Reid Anderson and drummer Billy Hart, appeared in 1999. In 2000, a quartet led by Iverson and saxophonist Bill McHenry recorded live at Smalls nightclub in New York.

Iverson then worked with guitarist Kurt Rosenwinkel and saxophonist Mark Turner as a sideman in 2000 and 2001. When describing Iverson's compositions (although he could have been describing his playing) during this time, Howard Mandel said, "You'd think you're hearing a younger kinsman of Thelonious Monk, Herbie Nichols, and early Paul Bley."[15] Iverson told Mandel, "I hope to eventually make a good living through my music, with the most important thing [being] my growth and progress toward my Platonic ideal of playing, composing, and improvising. Getting close to that ideal is what I need to do."

Iverson worked on his growth and progress as he continued to study with jazz pianist Fred Hersch and the legendary, almost mythological Sophia Rosoff.[16] He formed the Bad Plus in 2001 with Minnesotans Reid Anderson on bass and David King on drums. Despite being an acoustic jazz trio, one of the most standard of all jazz configurations, it has been one of the most talked-about groups in all jazz in the 2000s.

Fresh Sound New Talent put out the first Bad Plus album, and the band was immediately noticed for its renditions of not only original compositions but covers of the 1930s standard "Blue Moon," a tune by the seventies pop band ABBA, and, most notoriously, Nirvana's "Smells Like Teen Spirit." The signing of the Bad Plus to the major record label Columbia made even more noise in the industry. Their first release for Columbia, *These Are the Vistas* (2003), included another version of "Teen Spirit" as well as covers of songs by Blondie and Aphex Twin. While it received a modestly positive review in *Down Beat*, it garnered a rave in *Jazziz*, and *Jazz Times* called it "one of the most important jazz albums to appear in more than a decade."[17]

Vistas and the following album, *Give*, led to even wider dissemination of the band's name, including into such venues as National Public Radio, which featured the band on its signature show *All Things Considered* in 2003. In that interview, the members of the band talked about their surprising success at the Village Vanguard, the world's most revered jazz club. Dave King later explained how the band played their usual repertoire at the Vanguard, expecting to be fired after one night. Instead, Lorraine Gordon, the owner of the club that symbolized the history of mainstream modern jazz, hired the trio to come back for a week.

The Bad Plus has been described as "a bare-knuckle piano trio," "the loudest piano trio ever," and "piano-trio gangstas."[18] Most famously (or infamously), in its August 2004 issue, *Down Beat* asked, "Is the Bad Plus Bad Ass or Just Plain Bad?" The responses ran the gamut. One musician said, "The Bad Plus finally convinces me that the downfall of civilized humanity is upon us." Guitarist Bill Frisell, on the other hand, responded, "What they're doing is the real deal; it's what music is all about. . . . They're just three guys trying to play good music. Totally honest and humble."[19] But for the band, this controversy was the kind of publicity that money can't buy.

The trio continued to experiment. On 2007's *Prog*, originals by each of the three band members are juxtaposed with covers of songs by Tears for Fears, Rush, David Bowie, and a pop classic, "This Guy's in Love with You." *For All I Care*, from 2009, contained tunes made popular by Nirvana, Pink Floyd, Wilco, Yes, Heart, the Flaming Lips, k.d. lang, and the Bee Gees. Sprinkled around these covers are arrangements of pieces by twentieth-century classical composers György Ligeti, Milton Babbitt, and Igor Stravinsky. On the strength of those interpretations, the Bad Plus was commissioned by Duke University to perform their own complete version of Stravinsky's most acclaimed work, *Le Sacre du Printemps*, which they played at Duke in 2011 and subsequently recorded.

Never Stop, from 2010, and 2012's *Made Possible* were comprised almost completely of originals by the band members. They also recorded the very successful collaboration *The Bad Plus Joshua Redman* in 2015.

Ethan Iverson. PHOTO BY CHRISTINA GUADALUPE; COURTESY OF ETHAN IVERSON

The Bad Plus remained a great success fifteen years after its founding, but it was not the only outlet for Iverson's creativity. He formed a quartet with Mark Turner in the early 2000s that later became the Billy Hart Quartet, in honor of their esteemed drummer. Iverson also continued working in a trio, which recorded an album of standards live at Smalls in 2009.

Different sides of this talented pianist can be heard in different settings. Iverson's style in the Bad Plus has been described as "a kind of straightened-out Cecil Taylor [famed avant-garde jazz pianist] by way of Vince Guaraldi [pianist best known for his music for the *Charlie Brown/Peanuts* cartoon specials] for the masses, his wall of sound generally two-fisted and furious when not contemplative."[20] In other settings, Iverson has been compared to "Lennie Tristano and Paul Bley and some Bud Powell for good measure."[21] The influence of Iverson's early model,

Monk, can also be detected in his style. With the Hart quartet, Iverson plays some of the atmospheric, almost classically oriented music for which the ECM record label is known.

Not completely content as just a performer and composer, Iverson is also prominent as a writer, penning reviews and feature articles for *Down Beat* as well as keeping up his prolific blog, Do the M@th, which is full of challenging, well-thought-out articles, interviews, reflections, and reviews. To the surprise of many, he announced in April 2017 that he would be leaving the Bad Plus at the end of the year. His provocative musical vision and breadth of interests promise to keep Iverson in the jazz forefront for the foreseeable future.

Dan Nimmer

Dan Nimmer is not a big name on the jazz scene, despite his being a longtime member of one of the most prominent bands in jazz, the Wynton Marsalis band. Nimmer is still young, however, and it seems likely that his career will grow and flourish in years to come.

Nimmer was born in Milwaukee in 1982. He started drums at an early age, playing rock and roll, as his dad had also done. He started on piano a little later than many pianists. As he recalls:

> We got a piano from my aunt when I was ten. And she didn't want it. . . . It was just an old upright. I just started playing by ear. And then I asked my parents for lessons. I studied classically with a lady named Barbara Bunge. And, after a few years, she noticed that I had a creative ability to improvise, because basically . . . I didn't have my lessons prepared, so I would come in and try to pretend like I knew this Bach or something, and put my own little thing on it. So she recommended that I listen [to and] study jazz music. She recommended that I look into the conservatory, and I got hooked up with Mark [Davis].

Davis (see chapter 11) suggested that Nimmer purchase some jazz recordings, and he ended up with his first two records, by Miles Davis and Oscar Peterson, and he was on his way. He studied with Davis for four years.

Nimmer went to Greenfield High School, and he attended summer jazz programs at the Wisconsin Conservatory, where he worked with Davis. The summer programs connected him with other talented young jazz students, including several at the Milwaukee High School of the Arts, where he often hung out. A group of them formed a band called Quarter After Nine, which worked occasionally at the Cigar Shop. The conservatory connection also led Nimmer to Berkeley Fudge and Manty Ellis. As a high schooler, he also subbed for veteran pianist Jerry Weitzer at Moe's Steak House, turning it into a trio job on weekends.

An important early gig that built Dan's confidence, and credibility, was when he subbed for pianist Dean Lea accompanying vocalist Adekola Adedapo at the Main Event. Nimmer can be heard on the CD that Adekola produced from that session.

Like others, including Geoff Keezer and Ethan Iverson, Nimmer played in the Wisconsin High School Honors Jazz Ensemble. There he met Ron Carter, head of the jazz program at Northern Illinois University (NIU). Carter convinced Nimmer that NIU would be a good choice for college, and for Dan, it was. For one thing, he studied piano there with Milwaukee native Willie Pickens (see chapter 11), perhaps the most respected jazz pianist on the Chicago scene. In addition, NIU hosted many special guests, including Benny Golson, Frank Wess, and Ed Thigpen, with whom Nimmer got to interact.

Nimmer dropped out of Northern Illinois during his third year at the school. He had made the decision to move to New York but had been advised that he needed to save some money before doing so. "So," he explains, "I took some time to work in Chicago. I was commuting back and forth. I was doing this steak house gig four nights a week, duo and trio. . . . And on Sundays I'd do Andy's [a top Chicago club]." He also started working with guitarist Fareed Haque, traveling "all over the country, in a van," in a fusion band.

Realizing that he knew a number of musicians in New York—David Hazeltine, Carl Allen, Rick Germanson, Brian Lynch, and Gerald Cannon—Nimmer was ready to make the move once he had saved enough money. "Actually," Nimmer admits, "I moved out there with my girlfriend at the time. She had a shock when she got there. She couldn't take it, so she left in two weeks." Faced with paying a full rent by himself, and without very good work prospects, he took a rather unusual step:

> I started going back and forth, and playing wedding gigs in Chicago, and still playing with Fareed, and kind of supplementing my rent money. I was actually driving back and forth. But I would try to make it so I would have like a week of gigs; some kind of gig that would supplement the whole trip.

When he finally got into the jam session scene in New York, at Smalls and at Cleopatra's Needle, he started making connections. One night in 2005, at Pumpkins, in Brooklyn, Wess Anderson, a longtime member of Wynton Marsalis's band, played with Nimmer and recommended him to Wynton. Shortly thereafter, Nimmer explains:

> I just went over to Wynton's apartment, played for a while, talked for a while. I didn't get the call for a couple of months. And then I got the call to go on the road with the small group. And then I joined the big band [Jazz at Lincoln Center]. . . . I was on edge the first couple years, because Wynton has a history of firing, especially piano players.

But Nimmer survived those times of insecurity, and years later is still working with Marsalis. He has played all over the world with Marsalis, including at many famous performance venues and jazz festivals. He has appeared on American late-night shows, network morning shows, and public television specials including *The Kennedy Center Honors* and *Live at Lincoln Center*.

When not working with Marsalis, Nimmer leads trio jobs in New York. He has recorded a number of trio albums, mostly for the Japanese label Venus (see online discography). He also has done interesting freelance jobs with artists as diverse as Celine Dion and opera legend Plácido Domingo.

About his Milwaukee mentors, Nimmer says that whenever he gets interviewed, he always says: "Without people like Berkeley or Manty, Mark Davis, . . . I wouldn't be sitting here, definitely. It's like they took me under their wing, helped me out, especially on gigs. I think number

Dan Nimmer with the Jazz at Lincoln Center Orchestra, 2009. PHOTO BY GOIO VILLANUEVA

one, Berkeley, because he was kind enough to hire me when I really couldn't play at all."

Dan Nimmer and Berkeley Fudge were together when they were interviewed for this book. Referring to Nimmer's time spent with Marsalis, Fudge said, "That turned out to be a pretty nice gig." Nimmer replied, "Yeah. I'm enjoying it. Keeps me busy. Traveling around the world, playing this music." And they both laughed, probably at the unlikelihood and good fortune that it happened at all.

Nimmer, like some other Milwaukee jazz luminaries, returns to the city from time to time and makes a point of working with younger musicians in addition to performing. In January 2012, he performed at the Eastside Jazz Festival, a day after participating in a workshop for students through the Milwaukee Youth Symphony Orchestra jazz program. He was the subject of a feature interview/article in the *Milwaukee Journal Sentinel* prior to his appearance with the Jazz at Lincoln Center Orchestra at the Marcus Center in December 2014.[22] Still in the early stages of a dynamic career, Nimmer should inspire even younger musicians for many years.

8

West Coast Players

Wisconsin musicians of several generations have made successful careers on the West Coast jazz scene in a variety of ways. Some of those stories are presented here.

Buddy Clark

Bassist Buddy Clark was born Walter Clark Jr. in Kenosha on July 10, 1929.[1] According to standard references, Clark first studied piano and trombone but switched to string bass in high school. He studied at the Chicago Musical College when he was about twenty years old. While in Chicago, he worked with two startlingly different jazz figures: the traditional Chicago-style saxophonist Bud Freeman, and Bill Russo, who made his name writing modern works for Stan Kenton's band in the early fifties before returning to Chicago in the mid-sixties and revitalizing the scene there.

Clark's versatility was clear in the fifties as he hit the road with the Tex Beneke band in 1950 and worked and/or recorded with Pete Jolly, Bob Brookmeyer, and the Les Brown big band before settling in Los Angeles in 1956. In southern California, he worked with many influential jazz figures of the West Coast, or "cool school," including Dave Pell, Jimmy Giuffre, Mel Lewis, and Bill Holman, all within a couple years of Clark's move to the area. He also recorded with film composer John Williams back when Williams was a jazz pianist. Additionally, Clark recorded with Red Norvo, pop singer Peggy Lee, and jazz singer Anita O'Day.

The early sixties were more of the same; although he spent much of his time as an active musician in the burgeoning Los Angeles studio

Buddy Clark. ©RAY AVERY/CTS IMAGES

scene, Clark also played and recorded with Gerry Mulligan and the Concert Jazz Band, and Mulligan's small group, as well as with Duke Ellington veteran Johnny Hodges. Yet he made very few jazz recordings during the second half of the decade.

Clark was most visible in his jazz career in the 1970s when he and saxophonist Med Flory transcribed and arranged the solos of Charlie Parker for five saxophones, and then assembled the group Supersax to play these arrangements. Supersax made a real splash on the jazz scene, opening at the famous North Hollywood club Donte's, which resulted in a rave review in *Down Beat* in 1973. With the impeccably rehearsed saxophones, a rhythm section, and at least one additional soloist, the band toured extensively for the next several years and recorded three very successful albums.

Clark returned to studio work in 1975. Unfortunately, he injured his hand in an accident in 1976 and could no longer play. He died in California in 1999, but he is remembered as one of the go-to bassists in southern California for two decades, as well as the founder of a true jazz phenomenon, Supersax.

Tommy Gumina

Another musical figure who made an impression on the West Coast jazz scene, Tommy Gumina, could only have come from the Midwest. Due to Wisconsin's large German and Polish populations, it is not surprising that the accordion has been a popular instrument in the state. In a 1955 *Milwaukee Journal* article, reporter Kevin Brown claimed that "Milwaukee's several thousand accordion students and devotees . . . have given it the reputation as the nation's accordion capital."[2] While many Wisconsinites immediately think of polka when they think of the accordion, Wisconsin's best-known jazz accordionist came out of a different tradition.

Born in 1931, Tommy Gumina was the oldest of three brothers who grew up on Milwaukee's south side.[3] In Gumina's own words, "When I was four, I had an uncle who played sax in a band. I used to get up and direct sometimes, at Italian weddings."[4] He knew by age ten that he wanted to play the accordion. In 1955, he told the *Milwaukee Journal* the story of how he got his first accordion.

> When I was 10 years old, my dad, who had a job at International Harvester Co., had been very ill with pneumonia. I wanted an accordion so bad that I was busting, but I knew we didn't have much money. . . . I told my dad how I wanted an accordion and he said, "Son, I'll rent one for you. I can't buy one. I haven't any money." Just renting seemed wonderful to me, but my dad, still too weak to go to work, went to a place to get an accordion—and he didn't rent it. He bought it—on time. Gosh. That's being fine to a kid.[5]

In an earlier interview, Gumina said his father had paid one hundred dollars for the instrument, when he was earning only eighteen dollars a week. "He sacrificed to send me to Chicago for lessons at a school connected with Loyola University," he remembered. "They cost five dollars apiece, and the fare for my mother and me was extra." By the time he was twelve, Tommy had become a teacher and had some students who were as much as four times his age.[6]

Gumina graduated from Don Bosco High School and got his big break shortly afterward. Jazz trumpet great Harry James was in Milwaukee, performing with his band at Devine's Ballroom. Somehow, Al Tusa, manager of the Tic Toc Club, talked James into coming over to hear the young player, despite James's antipathy toward the accordion. Gumina said, "I hit him with musician's music, jazz improvisations and a few classical numbers. No polkas, no 'Lady of Spain.'"[7]

James must have been tremendously impressed, because he hired Gumina to join his band, even though none of the other mainstream big bands in this era had an accordion player. (Lawrence Welk's "sweet band," most notably, did employ an accordionist.) According to prominent pianist Willie Pickens (see chapter 11), Gumina "changed the sound of the accordion, so he could kind of make it sound a little more jazzy."[8] James was quoted as saying, "I don't know how he does it but Tommy Gumina gets a tone and a style that I have never heard before from an accordion, . . . a real jazz feeling."[9] Gumina, whose playing earned him the nickname "Mr. Fingers," toured and recorded with James for several years, performing on early television shows hosted by Perry Como, Jackie Gleason, Arthur Godfrey, and Milwaukee's own Liberace. One set of Gumina with the James band, recorded at Chicago's Aragon Ballroom in 1952, is still available. In 1954, Gumina recorded two sides for Century Records, followed in 1956 by several sides for the Milwaukee-based Continental Records, a creation of Gumina and two area lawyers.

When James broke up his large band, he put together a seven-piece unit, which Gumina joined at least briefly.[10] But soon Gumina left James and began working as a single in clubs on the West Coast and in Las Vegas. In 1957, he released his new album for Decca Records, *Hi-Fi Accordion*, which included favorites like the feature from his James days, "Flight of the Bumble Bee," and an aria from the Italian opera *Pagliacci*. This release earned him a feature in Earl Wilson's nationally syndicated column, "It Happened Last Night."[11]

Tommy Gumina. COURTESY OF THE GUMINA FAMILY

A fascinating story from Gumina's early years in Los Angeles was recounted in a 1955 article in the *Milwaukee Journal*, "Squeeze Play by Sinatra Took Role from Milwaukee Accordion Player."[12] Gumina was under contract to Columbia Pictures and was evidently the studio's first choice to play the role of Italian soldier Maggio in the film *From Here to Eternity*. Sinatra, who was at a low point in his career, convinced the executives that he was perfect for the part, and Gumina was left out in the cold. Sinatra won an Academy Award, his career was revived, and Gumina remained a musician, not a movie star.

In 1956, it was reported that Gumina planned to write a column on accordion technique and related matters for *Down Beat*.[13] In 1958, having moved his family to the West Coast, he found financial security in the ABC television studios. Later on, Gumina did some teaching, including at one of Stan Kenton's early 1960s jazz education residencies.

Gumina next gained attention in the jazz community around 1960 when he left the security of the studios and formed a quartet with the outstanding clarinetist Buddy DeFranco.[14] One of the group's first dates away from California was at Curro's club in Milwaukee.[15] The quartet was successful enough to record five albums in five years, but the fan base they attracted was not large enough to sustain the group. Their music was straight-ahead jazz, with a slight West Coast flavor, but on a later album, the quartet caved in to commercial pressures and recorded a rock and roll tune called "The Monkey," which the *Milwaukee Sentinel* described as "a new dance which approximates what you might see if you taught the twist to King Kong."[16]

Gumina was always a tinkerer, frequently coming up with new twists for his instrument. In 1954, the *Milwaukee Sentinel* reported: "[Gumina's] fliers refer to 'Toner-amic Sounds.' The term, he says, is his name for an invention of his own, a different combination of reeds built into chambers to give the accordion a mellower sound and adapt it to a wider tonal range."[17]

In 1963, he was apparently playing "a unique instrument—the accordi-organ—invented and made in Milwaukee. It looks like an accordion but contains 200 transistors. They can reproduce the full range of a pipe organ but weigh only 18 ounces."[18] The instrument was invented by Fred Searles of West Allis. In the mid-seventies, when Gumina recorded with Art Pepper, the reviewer Keith Spore reported that he was playing "the polychord, which sounds like a combination of accordion and electric organ." Later on, while recording with Joe Pass, Spore noted that Gumina was at times playing "the polycorus, which includes synthesizing capabilities."[19]

Gumina moved into a new role in the music business in 1968, founding Polytone Musical Instruments, which manufactured amplifiers in California for decades. As late as the 2010s, the company boldly advertised its association with jazz legends Joe Pass and Ray Brown, the first endorsers of its guitar and bass amps, respectively, as well as other greats who endorsed Polytone's products. In an article on the website All About Jazz, critic Elliott Simon states, "When it comes to the accordion, Gumina's modifications and amplification development are on a par with Les Paul's guitar inventions."[20] This became the legacy of the latter part of Gumina's career, as his playing resurfaced only on occasion.

By the time of his death in 2013, Tommy Gumina had long since established himself as another unique figure in the music business, with roots in Wisconsin.

Mike Melvoin

Although few Wisconsinites have heard of pianist Mike Melvoin, a very large number of Wisconsin residents have undoubtedly heard his playing.

Melvoin was born in Oshkosh, began singing at age two, and started playing piano at age three.[21] He was quoted in a 2003 interview as saying, "[I thought] the alphabet ended at G."[22] When he was about five years old, his family moved to Milwaukee, where he spent the rest of his youth. Melvoin attended Dartmouth College in Hanover, New Hampshire, and graduated in 1959 with a degree in English. (At Dartmouth, he overlapped with another Wisconsin jazz musician, Chris Swansen; see chapter 18.)

Melvoin began his music career in New York after graduation but moved to Los Angeles in 1961 or 1962. Around this time, he developed the ability to play keyboards in just about any popular style. Carol Kaye, the legendary studio bassist, reported that shortly after Melvoin arrived on the West Coast, "You saw Mike *everywhere*," playing in recording studios for television and film.[23] During the next few decades, even a brief list of records featuring Melvoin on piano or organ boggles the mind: Frank Sinatra's "That's Life," the Jackson 5's "ABC," the Beach Boys' "Good Vibrations," Helen Reddy's "I Am Woman," Barbara Streisand's "Evergreen," Natalie Cole's "Unforgettable," John Lennon's "Stand by Me," and the Quincy Jones production "We Are the World." He also played on television shows ranging from *Mission: Impossible* to *Fame*, composing music for the latter and for the series *MacGyver*.

Melvoin was also known in the music community in southern California for his advocacy. He was president of the National Academy of Recording Arts and Sciences (NARAS), the organization that presents the Grammy Awards, but he didn't always agree with NARAS's policies. The *Los Angeles Times* reported,

> In 2011, when the Recording Academy made changes in the Grammy awards structure, Melvoin was in the vanguard of the movement to rescind the category changes. As a pianist whose career had touched every stylistic area, he was especially bothered by the effect of the changes upon instrumentalists.

"Everyone who has ever played an instrument," he said in a public statement, "has had the possibility of receiving recognition from the Grammys gutted. That cannot and will not stand."[24]

Melvoin's son, Jonathan, was a member of the popular rock group the Smashing Pumpkins. Sadly, Jonathan died of a drug overdose in 1996, at the young age of thirty-four. Mike's daughters also became musicians. Wendy and her twin sister, Susannah, were in rock superstar Prince's band the Revolution.

At heart, Mike Melvoin was a jazz pianist, and a very talented one. In one interview, he described his "successful work as an arranger and composer for pop and film music as 'what I do,' compared to jazz as being 'what I am.'"[25] When he first arrived in Los Angeles, he accompanied singers Peggy Lee and Joe Williams and also worked with jazz instrumentalists such as Frank Rosolino and Gerald Wilson. Don Heckman wrote, "Melvoin remained strongly linked to jazz, his first musical love, performing on a regular basis in local clubs, frequently touring internationally, and releasing numerous recordings of his own groups."[26]

On the jazz albums he released under his name later in his career, Melvoin displayed a wonderful touch and style in groups that included such jazz heavyweights as Charlie Haden and Phil Woods (see online discography). He was nominated for a Grammy for Best Jazz Instrumental Solo in 2003. Working almost completely in the background (almost anonymously), Wisconsin's Mike Melvoin made major contributions to some of the most iconic music of the twentieth century.

Steve Houghton

Drummer Steve Houghton was born in Kenosha in 1954.[27] His father, Ralph, was the longtime director of the Bradford High School band but became best-known as the supervisor of music in the Kenosha public schools. During his tenure as supervisor, Ralph brought the Kenosha system to the pinnacle of public school music education in the state of Wisconsin. Steve remembers his youth being filled with music:

> From as long as I can remember there was music around me. It sounds like a movie. . . . I was having ice cream socials with thousands of people in my yard, with bands in the front yard, and had marching bands marching down the street and stopping at my house. And we had parades, and it was just . . . kind of a real-life version of *The Music Man*. . . . I got to see all the instruments, and I got kind of a weird inside look at concert band, or just school music. And so it was early on, when I was five or six that I kept seeing the drum stuff, the young drum students, and . . . I really gravitated toward the drum section when they'd march by the house.

Once he got into school, Houghton had the luxury of playing in excellent bands, from junior high through high school. He came up in Kenosha with two other fine percussionists, Jeff Cesario and Jay Kennedy, as well as oboist Louis Covelli. (Cesario later became a prominent comedian and comedy writer on the national stage, Kennedy wrote hundreds of jingles for radio and television and is currently a vice president at the Berklee College of Music, and Covelli returned to Kenosha to serve as band director at Tremper High School for over thirty years.)

Houghton played in a jazz band in junior high, the existence of which was unusual at that time. In junior high and high school, his band director was Stanley DeRusha, who had quite a reputation as a classical and jazz player, and as a dynamic teacher. In high school jazz band, Steve and his buddies played the big band music of the day, from the bands of Maynard Ferguson, Stan Kenton, Buddy Rich, and Count Basie. "It wasn't the baby band stuff that students play now," Houghton recalls.

"By the time I was in junior high school," he says, "music was my life. [I] didn't really realize that it was going to be such a jazz-influenced thing." In high school he took part in the State Honors Band (before there was an Honors Jazz Ensemble), which had been established largely by Jack Pingel, Dick Gaarder, and Ralph Houghton. But after seeing Buddy Rich's band at the Playboy Club in Lake Geneva and the Kenton band (with young phenom Peter Erskine on drums) at a Milwaukee-area Holiday Inn, Houghton got hooked on jazz. And when his father brought the Woody Herman band to Bradford High, Houghton says, "That did it. So by my senior year I was ready to, well, get on Woody's band, that's what I wanted to do."

Houghton attended UW–Madison, on what he called a "nice" scholarship, and enjoyed working with percussion professor James Latimer and wind ensemble director Robert Reynolds. But, he discovered, "I couldn't really find my jazz dream there."

In the summer after his first year at UW, he played in the All-American College Band at Disneyland in California, where he got a first look at studio playing. Back at school, he did some jazz work in Madison with saxophonist Ray Rideout and pianist Barry Velleman, and sometimes with his old buddy Jeff Cesario. "At that point," he says, "oddly enough, the North Texas [State University] band came through and played a concert at UW. And I decided, 'Whoa, that's what it should sound like.'" Houghton had met North Texas faculty member Rich Matteson at a clinic in Kenosha, and he helped pave the way for Houghton's transfer in 1974, after only a year and a half at Madison.

Shortly after Houghton left Wisconsin for Texas, his friend and fellow UW student Beverly Dahlke (see later in this chapter) also made the move to NTSU. Lyle Mays (see chapter 7), who transferred to North Texas from UW–Eau Claire, also hit the Denton campus at the same time as Houghton. While they were there, the two of them played together almost every day. Bass trombonist Fred Sturm, a Lawrence University graduate and soon-to-be founding member of the band Matrix (the Appleton band; see chapter 18), was also at North Texas, in the famed One O'Clock jazz band that Houghton and Mays would soon join.

As related in chapter 7, Houghton and Mays got their first big break when they performed at the Wichita Jazz Festival in a small group with

Steve Houghton in the mid-1970s with Woody Herman's band (see chapter 2). COURTESY OF STEVE HOUGHTON

bassist Marc Johnson. Woody Herman was at a crossroads with his big band's rhythm section, and he hired Houghton, Mays, and Johnson as a unit. The three went on tour with Woody in the spring of 1975.

Houghton stayed in the Herman band for a year and a half. When he left Woody, he moved to New York, hoping to start a band with Mays. He moved into a building with Mays and Johnson, but it was not to be. Houghton says, "I didn't last very long in New York. I found out very quickly it wasn't my style." After only a few weeks, he left the city and returned to Texas, remaining there from 1976 to 1980. "Dallas was great for me," he says. "I played in a fusion band four nights a week, played in a big band every weekend, I did a [whole lot] of studio work." Occasionally he did gigs with vibraphonist Gary Burton.

"And then," he recalls, "it came to a point where [I thought], 'Okay, now it's time for a bigger stage.' So then I moved out to LA in 1980." His first important gig in Los Angeles was with Toshiko Akiyoshi's big band, and he played with them for four or five years. Given his experience at North Texas and with Woody Herman, Houghton was soon working with other great California big bands, including those of Bill Holman, Les Hooper, and Bob Florence. He also worked in a fusion-style band called Tribal Tech, the brainchild of guitarist Scott Henderson.

After meeting pianist Billy Childs, Houghton was asked to join star trumpeter Freddie Hubbard's band. He played with Hubbard for about five years, making five or six albums, and remained in California following his tenure with Hubbard. While he did a fair amount of studio work (including recording jingles with his old Kenosha buddy Jay Kennedy), Houghton was, in his own words, "really a jazz guy." Over the years, he worked with a huge list of jazz artists (see online discography). He also raised his family in Los Angeles.

It may have been a surprise when, in 2001, Houghton got a call from Indiana University, asking if he was interested in joining the jazz faculty there. He accepted the position and commuted back and forth from California to Bloomington for three years. "I still kept my work in LA," he says. "That was really fun to go be a professor for a minute, but then run back and be a musician." In 2005, he accepted the offer of a tenure-track position at IU.

In addition to being a world-class jazz drummer, Houghton has long been a versatile percussionist as well. He has commissioned percussion concertos from composers Les Hooper, Billy Childs, and Wisconsin's John Harmon. The Harmon concerto was premiered by the Chippewa Valley Symphony Orchestra in Eau Claire. Houghton has been active in the production of educational materials as well, putting out DVDs, play-along CD sets, and more than thirty books. His distinguished career as a player and educator continues in Bloomington and wherever his playing and teaching take him.

Beverly Dahlke

Beverly Dahlke was born in Wausau in 1954.[28] She grew up in the city and began to play the piano at the age of five, starting lessons at age seven. She claims, "We were all singers in my family," and describes her parents as the "best dancers in town." She went to parochial school, where the nuns occasionally rapped her fingers. Like many youngsters, Dahlke didn't particularly care for practicing, but she says: "[When] the band guy came through, we took that aptitude test and I had a very high score. And he said, 'You should be playing.' I picked the saxophone because my dad liked the saxophone. . . . I played saxophone from ten on, and . . . the piano kind of went away after that."

Dahlke attended Newman Catholic High School, where she worked with the talented director Richard Schroeder. Schroeder was especially interested in jazz and brought the Newman band to the jazz festival at UW–Eau Claire every year. The band even played a jazz mass at St. Anne's church in Wausau. Schroeder wrote arrangements for the school jazz band, including a memorable Beatles medley.

Dahlke, who started on alto saxophone, had switched to the larger baritone saxophone by high school—a rare instrument for a girl to be playing at that time. By her sophomore year, she successfully auditioned for the State Honors Band, and continued to play in it for three years. She also auditioned for Kids from Wisconsin in the early years of that celebrated group and became the first person from Wausau to be chosen for the ensemble. Dahlke soon earned the nickname "The Kid" and became a local celebrity, playing with the Kids for three years.

After graduating from high school in 1972, Dahlke enrolled in the University of Wisconsin–Madison's music program. She found a kindred spirit in drummer Steve Houghton, also in the program, whom Dahlke had already met in the State Honors Band. During her first year at Madison, the jazz program was run by Stan DeRusha; the next, it was taken over by Jimmy Cheatham. That year, Houghton left Madison for the jazz program at North Texas State. Dahlke remembers, "They were calling me up, [saying], 'Hey, if you're ever gonna do anything, you've gotta come down here.'" Since she applied late to NTSU for admission, Dahlke missed out on any scholarships, but somehow—through a mystery that she's never been able to explain—she qualified for in-state tuition. That tuition arrangement continued for the rest of her career at North Texas.

Her friend Houghton, who had made it into the One O'Clock jazz band, the best of NTSU's eight or nine jazz bands, was already off to Woody Herman's band by the time Dahlke entered the school.

After three years at North Texas, Dahlke earned a degree in classical baritone saxophone, the first one ever awarded at that school. More importantly, from the standpoint of her career, she became the first female member of the One O'Clock band. She worked her way up from the Five O'Clock band, to the Three O'Clock, and finally the One O'Clock. (The band names represent the time of day that they practiced, and the earlier a band met, the more advanced it was.)

After her audition for the One, Dahlke was told that she did not make the band. She later discovered that her audition had been the best, but that some people just didn't want a woman in the band. The decision did not last. Leon Breeden, head of the program, made a visit to Dahlke's house, where she lived with two other women. Dahlke recalls, "It's like the maestro has shown up at my door. And he goes, 'Well, after consideration we have decided that you should be in the One O'Clock.'" Upon receiving the news, Dahlke says, "I had to run over to some frat house or someplace where there was a phone, to call my parents."

The band traveled a lot, and some administrator may have anticipated that having a woman in the band would create logistical problems on the road. But with Breeden as her champion, Dahlke fit right in, and problems did not arise. The band went on a State Department tour of Russia and Portugal in the summer of 1976. Dahlke vividly remembers the band's receptions in Russia as the Cold War was raging. She played on the band's *Lab '76* album, which earned a nomination for a Grammy award (as did its predecessor, *Lab '75*, an entire program of compositions by Wisconsinite Lyle Mays).

In the fall of 1976, someone in the West Coast group Toshiko Akiyoshi-Lew Tabackin Big Band heard the One O'Clock band in concert, and not much later, Toshiko called Dahlke and asked if she could come to the coast and join their band for a tour of Japan. Her reaction was, "You've got to be kidding me." She was able to graduate early from NTSU to take the gig. When she moved out west, she lived with Toshiko and Tabackin. In addition to playing in Japan, she also appeared with the band at the 1977 Newport Jazz Festival in New York, performing in Carnegie Hall.

When the band's regular baritone player returned, Dahlke was told she wasn't needed anymore. She settled in southern California with her husband-to-be, Greg Smith, who had preceded Dahlke in the baritone chair in the One O'Clock band. In the interim, he had been on the road with Stan Kenton's band, and then Harry James's band. Shortly after Dahlke moved west, Smith joined the Buddy Rich band. While Smith was on the road, she started working hard on bassoon. She later picked up clarinet and flute as well, trying to make herself more marketable as a doubler. And she did what young players in big cities do: she played with rehearsal bands (bands that rehearse regularly but don't necessarily play many paying jobs).

One such band was led by Pat Longo. His band was rehearsing one night in a Los Angeles club, and representatives of Harry James's band came in to audition baritone saxophone players, using Longo's band as a platform for the auditioners. Drummer Sonny Payne, a member of the James band best known for his starring role in the great Count Basie bands of the fifties and sixties, was present that night. As the candidates played their auditions, Dahlke sat in a corner reading a book. When the auditions were over, Payne declared, "She [Dahlke] should be the one in the band!" He had heard her playing with Longo's group prior to the auditions, and felt that she was stronger than any of those auditioning.

Although James's manager expressed reservations about Dahlke touring with the other all-male band members, she was offered the job, and she joined the band in August 1977. It was another trailblazing moment: she was the first full-time female band member (not singer) with the James outfit. After a rocky first night, when Dahlke remembers James being "as drunk as a skunk," she ended up having a nice year-and-a-half run with the band. She was written up in *People* magazine for breaking the gender barrier with James. Dahlke left the band after playing New Year's Eve of 1978, as she and Greg Smith were engaged to be married in early 1979.

Dahlke had a moment of real, if brief, fame due to Greg's employer, Buddy Rich. Rich was good friends with Johnny Carson, and he appeared on *The Tonight Show* many, many times. On one show, during this era when issues of women's rights were big news, Rich was asked if he would hire a woman to join his band. He replied by saying something to the effect of "find me one." Someone at *Tonight* remembered seeing the article in *People*, and the show plucked Dahlke out of Arkansas, where she was touring with the James band, and flew her to Los Angeles. In March 1978, she appeared on the show, playing (and soloing) with the *Tonight Show* band, and even getting to sit in "the chair" for a short interview with Carson. Rich, regrettably, was not present.

Dahlke settled down with Smith in Studio City and entered the southern California music scene in earnest in 1979. With her skills at playing many woodwinds, Dahlke soon became a valued member of the community of musicians who play live shows (Broadway, live TV, and various others) and record music for television and movie scores.

In 1984, Dahlke frequently appeared on MTV and the few other outlets showing music videos at the time. She was presented with an exciting opportunity when Glenn Frey, a member of the popular band the Eagles, was tapped to sing a song for the Eddie Murphy feature film *Beverly Hills Cop*. "The Heat Is On" featured a repeated saxophone riff played by Dahlke's friend David Woodford. But because Frey had worked with Greg Smith's band Jack Mack and the Heart Attack and knew Dahlke, he hired her to appear as the saxophonist in the music video.[29] She appears in the video stylishly made up and dressed, but with what she refers to as her eighties "mullet" hairdo. The song rose to number two on the *Billboard* Hot 100 chart in early 1985.

Dahlke got another break in 1986 with Fox, a brand-new, struggling television network with only a few affiliate stations across the country. One of its first shows was the late-night entertainment show hosted by comedian Joan Rivers, who had become famous for her many appearances, including as a guest host, on *The Tonight Show*. Following the example set by Johnny Carson, Rivers planned to have a big jazz band on *The Late Show Starring Joan Rivers*. However, when the band started rehearsing, Rivers realized it was all men. Since she was breaking new ground as a female talk show host, she wanted to have a woman in the band as well. As Dahlke tells it, "The guys in the band of course all knew me because I'd already . . . been doing some shows around town. . . . A couple of the guys said, 'Well, if you're going to get somebody, call Bev Dahlke.'" She got the call, auditioned, and was hired.

Rivers wanted to develop a "personality" for the band, and eventually she began referring to the guys in the band as "the Party Boys." Then she decided she wanted Dahlke to stand out from the "Boys," so started referring to her as "the Tramp." The band was introduced in the show's

Beverly Dahlke-Smith (seated) from her days on the Joan Rivers TV show, with (left to right) orchestra director Mark Hudson, Rivers (and dog Spike), and announcer Clint Holmes. COURTESY OF BEVERLY DAHLKE-SMITH

opening as "Mark Hudson with the Party Boys and the Tramp." Dahlke became part of the act, in the way that saxophonist Tommy Newsom was part of the act on Carson's show (though in a completely different style). There was even one episode on the *Late Show* called "Who Killed the Tramp?" in which Dahlke was the victim of a fictitious murder involving the cast of the *Leave It to Beaver* TV show.

Dahlke staunchly defends Rivers—she says *tramp* was a term of endearment for Rivers—and she especially appreciates the way her exposure on Rivers's show furthered her career. *The Late Show Starring Joan Rivers* lasted less than a year, but Dahlke continued to play in the band of its successor, known simply as *The Late Show*, hosted by Arsenio Hall.[30] Dahlke's parents could not watch *The Late Show* in Wausau, as the nearest Fox channel at that time was probably in Milwaukee or Madison.[31] However, they eventually traveled to the West Coast to see the show live.

Another aspect of Dahlke's connection with Fox bears mention. One of the network's early successes, and now the longest-running sitcom in TV history, was *The Simpsons* (which grew out of a series of animated shorts for Fox's *Tracey Ullman Show*). Lisa Simpson, the daughter on the show, plays baritone saxophone. While Dahlke was never told that she was the inspiration for this aspect of Lisa's character, it seems likely, since she was the only prominent woman baritone saxophonist of the time and played in the band for *The Late Show*. Dahlke did not play Lisa's saxophone solos when the show debuted. However, just a few years later, she joined the band that recorded *The Simpsons'* soundtrack, and she played all of the baritone saxophone, bassoon, and contrabassoon parts on the soundtrack for years.

Out of the hundreds of live shows she's played over the course of her career in California, Dahlke has a number of favorites: the Mills Brothers, the Four Tops, the Temptations, and Johnny Mathis. She worked and recorded with such diverse musicians as Prince, the rock band Kansas (she played a bassoon solo on one of their records), Bette Midler, jazz singer Dianne Reeves, and jazz pianist Clare Fischer. Playing at ice-skating specials, she and Smith became friends with Olympic gold medalist and TV personality Scott Hamilton. Dahlke was often called to play with orchestras, including the Hollywood Bowl Orchestra and the Los Angeles Philharmonic. She's played on more than fifty movie soundtracks, appeared on camera in at least five films, and played for about twenty-five different TV series. She was in the band for many specials, including a tribute to Muhammad Ali; birthday specials for Frank Sinatra, Elizabeth Taylor, and Steve Allen; and *Comic Relief* with Whoopi Goldberg, Robin Williams, and Billy Crystal. She was also a "first call" for awards shows, including the Emmys.

Dahlke's playing career in Los Angeles came to a sudden and unexpected end in the early 2000s. She began to have difficulty playing. Her embouchure, the way a player uses facial muscles to play a wind instrument, was not functioning correctly. As she lost control, she practiced more than ever, and the more she practiced, the worse things got. The last couple of years of her full-time professional career in LA Dahlke describes as "a nightmare." She says, "I just thought, 'Why can't I play? What's wrong with me?' I thought I was nuts. . . . I did Alexander technique, I went to a psychiatrist, psychologist, I went everywhere." She was very busy at the time, playing in a production of *The Producers* (starring Jason Alexander and Martin Short), recording for *The Simpsons*, and playing with the big band institution Les Brown and His Band of Renown.

She was finally referred to a specialist, one of the few dystonia experts in the country, who determined that Dahlke had that serious neurological condition. She was told that if she got injections of Botox, she might be able to get 50 percent better. But she knew that the only thing that would do for her career was to get 100 percent better. She decided she had to call it quits and spent her last day as a southern California pro playing with the LA Philharmonic at the Hollywood Bowl.

Dahlke and Smith had already moved to California's Central Coast area, and after a period of playing a lot of golf, she started teaching in the area. She now teaches many students, from kids under ten to adults over eighty, and enjoys leading others to music.

Dahlke broke down many barriers in her career as the first woman to play in the North Texas One O'Clock band, in Harry James's band, in a late-night talk show band, and in the Les Brown band. She claims that there were some jobs she got because she was a woman (like the spot in the Rivers show band) and a lot of jobs that she did *not* get because she was a woman. But she was not on a pilgrimage or a mission. "I'm a stubborn German," she says. "When all these people said that [I couldn't do certain things because I was a girl, and later a woman], guess what I'm saying in my head? '[Expletive] you; I'm going to show you.'" Ever since she was in high school, she says, "I was a musician, and that's what I wanted to do for a living."

Tom Luer

Saxophonist Tom Luer was born in Chippewa Falls in 1974.[32] Luer's mother played guitar, and his sister took piano lessons, but his grandfather truly sparked his interest in music. According to Luer, "In addition to being a farmer, factory worker (Uniroyal tires), and veteran of World War II and the Korean War, [he] played the harmonica all his life." As recently as 2008, Luer says, his grandfather was still performing in a duo that played "what he called 'Old Timey' music, . . . polka, waltzes, schottisches, etc."

Luer joined his school band in Chippewa Falls, beginning on clarinet before switching to saxophone as a freshman in high school. He took lessons from local saxophonist Jeff Reitz. Luer can remember his high school director, Doug Greenhalgh, talking frequently about an "amazing" saxophonist who preceded Luer at Chippewa Falls High: Mike Walk, who remains an active player and teacher in the Twin Cities. (Tragically, Greenhalgh was killed, along with his wife and granddaughter and two others, when a bus returning the high school marching band from state competition crashed in October 2005.) Luer went on to take lessons with legendary area teacher (and now Twin Cities resident) Greg Keel. "When I heard Greg and started studying with Greg," Luer says, "that was my first role model."

Luer resisted advice to attend college at UW–Eau Claire, where Walk had done his studies, as he wanted to get farther than a twenty-minute drive away from home. He went to the big city, enrolling at the University of Minnesota. Although he transferred to UWEC after just two years in the Twin Cities, Luer remembers those years as valuable for the "city experience," and for getting "a sense of what it meant to be in a place where there was a 'scene'—a music scene, and an arts scene in general." He continued to job in the Twin Cities after returning to Wisconsin.

Luer graduated from Eau Claire in 1997, with a degree in classical saxophone. He didn't know what he wanted to do after school, but he didn't expect to stay in academia. Shortly before the next academic year started, however, UWEC jazz director Bob Baca connected Luer with Larry Panella, a "world-class jazz improviser and educator," according to Luer, who was teaching at Southern Mississippi University. Panella sent Luer to professional gigs in Gulf Coast casinos where he played with musicians like Frankie Valli and Fabian. After two years that Luer describes as "a really intense classical and jazz experience," he received a master's degree in classical saxophone.

That degree led to a three-year teaching stint at Bethel College in tiny North Newton, Kansas. Luer worked hard and turned a jazz artist-in-residence position into a full-time faculty position, while also teaching at a music store and a couple of area community colleges. He describes himself as being "fried" during this time, and he missed city life. He says, "[I was] at a place in my life where I felt all of this practicing and playing coming together in my improvising, and my saxophone abilities, and not having an outlet for it." He managed to land a teaching assistantship at the big jazz education school, the University of North Texas, although he had no intention of finishing another degree there. "I was really just intending to go there," he recalls, "be energized by a bunch of young saxophonists and young jazz musicians, and learn what I can from the program; spend a year, and then go to either New York or LA." He stayed in Texas for three years, in and out of school. He played in the One O'Clock Lab Band and taught a couple of classes at UNT, as well as taught part-time at both Texas Christian University and North Lake Community College. He also practiced a great deal.

In the summer of 2005, Luer decided to go for broke and headed for Los Angeles, which he thought would be a better match for him than New York. "I am passionate about jazz, and passionate about playing jazz," he says, "but I'm even more passionate about making a living as a musician." The day after moving to southern California, he drove to the musicians' union in Hollywood and ended up sitting in with one of the rehearsal bands that regularly operate there. So began his networking in the LA scene. One gig led to another, and two years later, he did a six-month tour, including appearances on television, with singer/songwriter, rapper, model, comedian, producer, and actor Queen Latifah. On a completely different end of the popular music spectrum, he also toured regularly with Engelbert Humperdinck.

While at home in LA, Luer does theater pit work and has made headway in the jazz scene, playing with his own quintet and subbing with the big bands of Bill Holman and (on a fairly regular basis) Gordon Goodwin. His regular gigs are with the big rehearsal bands of Mike Barone and Wayne Bergeron. Since recording his album *Project Popular* in 2009 (released in 2011), Luer has continued to play his material with a revolving cast known as Project Popular.

Tom Luer. PHOTO BY MIKE QUAIN; COURTESY OF TOM LUER

Luer also teaches private lessons and at Cal Poly–Pomona. He reconnected with the Wisconsin music scene when his old mentor Greg Keel invited him to join the faculty at the Shell Lake Jazz Camp. Luer was a featured guest artist at the UW–Eau Claire Jazz Festival in the spring of 2015 and also appeared on Sue Orfield's (see chapter 19) television show in Eau Claire in June of that year.

Luer says, "The idea of hopscotching around the United States and trying to make a living doing what I do in Los Angeles is quite a foreign idea to blue-collar folks in small-town Wisconsin, and [my family in Wisconsin has] been more supportive than I could have imagined."

9

New York Stars

Although many Wisconsinites have left their mark on the West Coast jazz scene, even more have made an impression in the most important jazz city in world, New York. A number of these musicians were discussed in chapter 7. Here are profiles of eight more.

Brian Lynch

Brian Lynch is, quite simply, one of the most celebrated jazz trumpeters of his generation. He has been a member of the bands of jazz greats Phil Woods, Horace Silver, and Art Blakey. He has been a prominent brass player in Latin jazz, often in association with his sidekick, trombonist Conrad Herwig, and the seminal Latin jazz pianist Eddie Palmieri. But Lynch continues to return "home" to Milwaukee on a regular basis, and he remains an influential figure in the city where he became a musician.

Lynch was born in Champaign, Illinois, in 1956 but moved to Milwaukee while still a boy.[1] He lived with his family in Glendale, and his mother shared his interest in music. "When I was growing up," Lynch remembered in a 2007 interview, "my mother sang in church choirs and occasionally in community operettas. In the last ten to fifteen years, she's pursued an avocation as a jazz singer and has actually recorded a couple of self-produced CDs, which is pretty amazing considering she's a lady in her mid-seventies."[2]

Lynch began playing trumpet at age eleven or twelve and continued through junior high. At Nicolet High School, he took part in school bands during only his senior year, by which time he was already quite serious about music. He had been playing in a concert band run by the local Elks organization, being the only "kid" in the group. "You play a trumpet," Lynch says, "you want to be in a rock band, so then you're listening to Buddy Miles and Sly [Stone] and Chicago and Blood, Sweat & Tears. . . . And so from there it was only a step from hearing Miles [Davis] and Freddie Hubbard and stuff like that. But I was [also] a big avant-garde jazz freak."

Lynch explains that he started paying closer attention to the jazz scene at age sixteen, when he would borrow his friend's driver's license to go to clubs. "I kind of came into the jazz scene straight from being a junior revolutionary," he says. "So it was doing things a little bit different, [which] was not unknown to me. You know, like going to the quote-unquote 'dangerous' neighborhoods and all that kind of stuff." The first time he sat in with musicians at a club, he played with Berkeley Fudge and Wendell Bond at Lloyd and David's on Green Bay Avenue.

In an interview with jazz writer Ted Panken in 2009, Lynch talked about working in a band with James Siegfried (later known as James Chance, and James White, of Contortions and James White and the Blacks), in what Lynch describes as an avant-garde jazz group. (Lynch and Siegfried still work together on occasion in New York.)

He frequently sat in with the Milwaukee group Matrix, which included Dave Phillips and Jack Grassel. "I knew very little about chords or anything like that," Lynch says of his time with Matrix, "but that was a great time not to know about chords!" He also had an unforgettable night sitting in with jazz great Sonny Stitt at Boatner's Lounge, which was owned by Stitt's cousin. Of that encounter, Lynch recalls: "As I'm playing, I forget what tune, all of a sudden, man, [Stitt's] like hitting me in the stomach. I'm like 'AAH!' [And he told me,] 'Use your diaphragm, use your diaphragm!'[3]

After graduating from high school, Lynch spent a few months in Chicago before returning to Milwaukee to attend the Wisconsin Conservatory, where he met Tony King (see chapter 11).[4] Lynch, like so many others, was inspired by King's attitude, and the way he saw jazz developing and being spread. King, in turn, must have seen Lynch as a part of his broad vision for dispersing the music wherever it might go.

At the conservatory, Lynch played in the Wisconsin Conservatory Jazz Combo that included saxophonist Rolla Armstead, trombonist Hary Kozlowski, pianist Marcus Robinson, guitarist Charles Small, bassist Jeff Chambers, and drummer Sam Belton. Mark Johnson also drummed in some editions of the group. The combo won contests, and particularly made a splash from 1977 to 1979 at the Notre Dame Jazz Festival in Indiana, one of the high-profile college jazz festivals of its era.

Around this time, Lynch also met David Hazeltine, who was still in high school. "He was an organist at the time," Lynch recalls, "[a] great, killing B-3 player. We used to play a lot in clubs like the Space Lounge and the Brother's Lounge, which was rechristened the Jazz Oasis. . . . We were very close through that whole period." Shortly thereafter, Lynch and Hazeltine formed a quartet along with drummer Scott Napoli and bassist Skip Crumby-Bey.

Lynch saw many visiting bands in Milwaukee during that time, at clubs like Teddy's and the Jazz Gallery. "It was great to play at [the Jazz Gallery]," he remembers, "and it was good for your morale that you could play one night with your group, and then the next night Woody Shaw would be there. I experienced a lot of stuff through being on that scene."

Another figure who made a big impression on Lynch and other young players in the city was Buddy Montgomery. "I played with him probably way before I even had a right to," Lynch says. "But he was very open to come down and sit in with him any time when his trio was playing. . . . I think one thing when I was growing up that was important and really shaped me was that . . . the scene that I was in was mostly African American musicians. . . . I mean it was on that turf. And the thing was, it was very welcoming. We never had any separation."

At age eighteen, Lynch moved to New York with his friend Jerry Weitzer and found the scene there to be quite different. He sat in at various places where he was occasionally frightened out of his wits, and soon realized that he needed to get his musical act together before trying to make a serious go of it in the Big Apple.

Lynch returned to Milwaukee where he worked with Sig Millonzi's big band and a large band that was contracted to play at Channel 10, the public television station. Though this band was paid to come to work every day, they only rarely made it on the air. However, this afforded

Lynch the opportunity to write for a large orchestra. The band eventually became the target of a protest because it consisted entirely of white musicians. A new, jazzier band formed when some prominent black musicians were hired, including Melvin Rhyne and Skip Crumby-Bey, and Lynch remained in the band. "That was like just getting paid to rehearse," he remembers. "We used to rehearse over at MATC [Milwaukee Area Technical College]. And we played some gigs. It was fun." Another experience in Milwaukee that helped prepare Lynch for his future musical life was working with the Latin jazz group La Chazz, led by Toty Ramos (see chapter 12). Lynch spent some time in San Diego, California, where his parents had moved and where he was mentored by the great saxophonist Charles McPherson.

When Lynch finally returned to New York in 1981, he was ready.[5] He would take any and all gigs that he could find. "Many's the time I would get a ride out to Jersey and play a wedding somewhere," he remembers, "and get dropped off somewhere in the Bronx at twelve-thirty in the morning to play the late set at a salsa gig until four."[6]

But the hustling soon paid off. In 1982, Lynch became a member of Horace Silver's storied quintet and remained in the group until 1985. He also became a member of Toshiko Akiyoshi's new East Coast big band and stayed with it until 1988. In late 1988, Lynch joined the classic jazz "finishing school," Art Blakey's Jazz Messengers, and remained with them until Blakey's death in 1990. (Geoffrey Keezer was the pianist in the band from 1989; see chapter 7 for Keezer's profile and see the book cover for a photo of Lynch and Blakey together.) It was a short but inspiring and fruitful collaboration.

Making it a trifecta of great jazz small groups, Lynch started working with Phil Woods's quintet in 1986. "He's a master, Phil Woods is," Lynch says, "and to be a part of his group is—it's not an apprenticeship situation. It's like becoming the second violin in the Juilliard String Quartet. . . . It's that sort of role as a collaborator in a great chamber jazz group. "[7] Lynch and Woods continued to work together from time to time until Woods's death in 2015.

Lynch is also a stalwart veteran in Latin jazz. He had been a part of the Latin scene in New York ever since his return to the city, but everything clicked when trumpeter Charlie Sepulveda took him to a rehearsal of

Brian Lynch. ©TOMOJI HIRAKATA; COURTESY OF BRIAN LYNCH

Eddie Palmieri's salsa band in 1987. Palmieri reportedly said, "Because of [Lynch], I really made my move into Latin jazz. I'm not a jazz pianist. But Brian was certainly a major part of me getting the confidence to go into Latin jazz."[8] A 1988 *Down Beat* article, one the earliest features on Lynch in the international press, described a typical Lynch performance: "When you attend a concert of Latin jazz, you expect the brass to be ablaze. Eddie Palmieri played the Blue Note one night a while ago but in the band was just one trumpet—and the one trumpet was fiery enough. Brian Lynch played as if a section unto himself, and added some of the brightest solos around."[9] Lynch continues to work with Palmieri today, and the Brian Lynch/Eddie Palmieri Project album *Simpático* won a Grammy award in 2005.

Although Lynch has never led a regular touring band, he has recorded twenty albums as leader or coleader and has been on more than one hundred records as a sideman. There are some surprises in that latter category. Lynch played on the albums of the Wisconsin band Mrs. Fun (see chapter 15), and those of fellow Milwaukee trumpeter Eric Jacobson long after he was already an established jazz star in New York. He also worked with rock superstar Prince.

In addition to his work as a musician, Lynch has taught extensively. He has been on the faculty of New York University and the Prince Claus Conservatory in the Netherlands and is currently an associate professor at the Frost School of Music at the University of Miami. He's also presented at workshops all over the world, and at some of the most prestigious music schools. Over the years, he has made numerous visits back to his alma mater, the Wisconsin Conservatory, to perform and work with young musicians.

Though he's a veteran of the scene, with an established reputation and musical identity, Lynch is not planning to stand still or rest on his laurels. As he said in an interview for *JazzTimes* magazine in 2013,

> I have a lot of these currents that swirl around me, even though from the outside it seems like I'm pretty neatly encapsulated into these little categories. . . . I'm going to be interested now in seeing how much I can maybe free myself up, extend myself a little bit more. My hope is to be able to surprise my listeners—and myself—with music that stretches and even violates the boundaries of what people have known me for up to now.[10]

Carl Allen

Drummer Carl Allen was born in Milwaukee in 1961.[11] According to the biography on his website, Allen "grew up on gospel, R&B, and funk, but later turned to jazz after hearing an LP by the legendary saxophonist Benny Carter." Allen's entry in *The New Grove Dictionary of Jazz* states that "his mother was a gospel singer and an elder brother also played drums." It should also be noted that another of Allen's older brothers, Eddie ("E. J."), became a successful jazz trumpeter in New York.

Allen attended Milwaukee Tech High School and says his band director, Robert Simiele, "was really the first one to expose me to jazz drummers. Because up until that point, I was really into fusion." The school's jazz band was active. "We'd go to these competitions," Allen recalls, "and I was fortunate and blessed to win these prizes and awards, and sometimes part of the award was that you got a chance to play with one of these guest artists. I got a chance to play with Sarah Vaughan when I was fifteen. Another time I got a chance to play with Maynard [Ferguson]. Another time I got to play with Woody Herman. Those things . . . were just big for me."

Allen was not particularly active in the music scene around Milwaukee while still in high school, but his percussion teacher occasionally called him to play gigs at a church for Christmas or Easter, and he played with the Community Civic Orchestra (sometimes on timpani). He also played "little funk gigs around town." He got his first jazz gig at age sixteen with Sonny Stitt and Red Holloway, which he described as "a huge moment." "The other thing that was very big for me while I was in Milwaukee," he says, "was getting the chance to play with people like Berkeley Fudge and Manty Ellis."

Particularly helpful to Allen's development was a band that he worked with during summers while he was in college. "The Wisconsin Connection," Allen remembers, "had Richard Davis, Manty, Berkeley, and there [was] a singer named Jessie Hauck. She since passed away. We would travel around—we would go up to Oconomowoc and Wausau and Eau Claire and Green Bay." The "elders" of that band taught him much about being a professional musician. In Milwaukee, eventually Allen played a steady gig with vocalist Penny Goodwin and future bass star Gerald Cannon (see later in this chapter) at the Bombay Bicycle Club at the Marc Plaza Hotel. He also worked at the Jazz Gallery with Melvin Rhyne and Skip Crumby-Bey, and at the Main Event.

Allen attributes much of his early interest and development in jazz to his connection with the University of Wisconsin–Green Bay (UWGB). He says:

> I often tell Lovell [Ives, who ran the program for years at UWGB] that a lot of who I am now had a lot to do with the time I spent [at Green Bay]. I started coming here when I was fifteen years old.
>
> It was really the first time that I was around people that I didn't

> know who also loved music. Because to be around people you know who love music, after a while you kind of take it for granted; that's just what people do. But when you're around other people who you don't know who love music, it's like, "This is kind of cool." That's when you start to see the big picture, and . . . how music affects other people.

Allen was also influenced by guest artists who came to the annual UWGB jazz festivals, including saxophone great James Moody. "When I was a freshman," Allen remembers, "Mel Lewis came, with Bob Brookmeyer. . . . And they were there for a couple of days. There was a residency and workshops. And Mel had taken a liking to me." Lewis was scouting for a drummer for the Count Basie band and eventually asked Allen to take the gig. But Allen replied, "I'm flattered, but first, I'm not ready. Two, I promised my mother I'd finish; she'd kill me if I left school." According to Allen, Lewis looked at him like he was crazy and said, "Well, man, if you don't want to do the gig, then you've got to get out of here. Man, because all you're going to do up here is play Dixieland, polka, and bar mitzvahs."

Taking this advice to heart, Allen took advantage of an exchange program his junior year at UWGB to go to William Paterson College, in New Jersey, just outside New York City. By the next year, 1982, he hit the big time, joining the great trumpeter Freddie Hubbard's band. This breakthrough job lasted on and off for eight years. With Hubbard, Allen played with such prominent jazz stars as Ron Carter, Buster Williams, and Kenny Barron as well as Milwaukee native Jeff Chambers, who briefly played bass in the band. Once established with Hubbard and living in New York, Allen was finally able to meet his drummer heroes: Art Blakey, Philly Joe Jones, Max Roach, Elvin Jones, Tony Williams, and Billy Higgins.

While with Hubbard, Allen also worked regularly with other high-profile musicians: Jackie McLean, the quintet of Donald Harrison and Terence Blanchard, and George Coleman. Along with his close friend and rhythm section soul mate, bassist Christian McBride, he worked for a few years in the early nineties with pianist Benny Green's trio, when Green was at the peak of his career. Allen has frequently led and recorded with groups under his own name, and the list of musicians with whom he has

Carl Allen. COURTESY OF CARL ALLEN

played on more than two hundred records is extraordinary. He connected with another Milwaukeean musician when he played with Frank Morgan (see chapter 11) at the Village Vanguard.

In 2001, Allen joined the faculty at the prestigious Juilliard School in New York, where he was the artistic director of jazz studies from 2008 to 2013. He continues to be active as an educator, conducting clinics all over the country, as well as remaining one of the busiest drummers in jazz. Allen returned to Milwaukee in January 2017 as the special guest artist for the Jazz Heritage Festival, where he worked with student groups and performed with Manty Ellis and the faculty of the Milwaukee Youth Symphony Orchestra Jazz Studies Combos. Like Brian Lynch, Allen is one of the most celebrated practitioners of his instrument in the business.

Gerald Cannon

Bassist Gerald Cannon was born in Racine in 1958. Cannon's story, like a few others in this book, will be related largely in his own words.

> [My father Benjamin was] a guitarist and a singer, a gospel singer. And my grandmother, my father's mother, was a pianist in Mississippi, and a really holy lady. And she taught my father all these hymns. [He was] one of thirteen brothers and sisters. So they moved to Wisconsin. He put together a singing quartet, which consisted of two of my uncles and some other guy that he had [grown] up with in the south. And my dad's job was that he worked at Racine Steel Castings, which is a foundry.

> There was always music in my house. Like every Tuesday night they rehearsed. . . . My dad had these guitars, and he would always tell me, "Don't touch my guitars when I'm at work." But as soon as he went to work the first thing I would do was go down there and start playing. But one day he caught me. He came home from work, and I was horsing around with one of those guitars, and he snuck out there. . . . "Didn't I tell you not to play my guitars?" And I was like, *Uh-oh. I'm in for it now.* . . . [He] said, "Well, play something; and it better be good." So I just basically played all the stuff that I always heard in church. . . . He was so impressed, he took me right away to a music store. And they gave me this music test, where I put these headphones on, and I would have to sing back whatever was playing through the headphones. I think I was . . . nine or ten. I got the highest score; I got a perfect score. And I sang back perfectly everything that I heard. I don't know how I did it. . . . So I got six months . . . free lessons, bass lessons. And my dad bought me my first bass that same day, a Lake Placid Blue Fender Jazz.

Cannon studied for some time at Pulice's music store, which was run by a fine drummer and pedagogue, Joe Pulice (who was also father to two outstanding drummers, Mark and Joe Pulice). Cannon also took lessons from Mel Lamar, a "big guitar guru in Racine," who, Cannon says, "pretty much taught all of the gospel guitar players the basic chords."

> A month later I was playing with this gospel quartet. My father was a real religious man, he was a deacon of [St. Paul Missionary] Baptist Church, and so he wouldn't allow me to play anywhere but in church, until I was eighteen. . . . And we traveled around . . . [to] different churches in Milwaukee, Chicago, Omaha, Nebraska. We would go to . . . Beloit, Wisconsin; Joliet, Illinois; Evanston, Illinois; all these different places, with my father on Sundays, playing with his quartet. . . . [This was] the best ear training that anyone could ever ask. Because my father didn't read any music, but he . . . played guitar. So he would play chords . . . and he would tell me to play these notes with that chord, which I found out later were . . . really the building blocks to my foundation to where I'm at now. . . . And

Gerald Cannon (back row, third from left) in his father's gospel band. COURTESY OF GERALD CANNON

> my father had a knack for playing not your normal chords, not your normal gospel progressions. He would always add alterations. And when I think about the way I play now, it's because [of] playing with him and hearing the way he voiced his chords.

Cannon went to Jerstad-Agerholm Elementary and Junior High, and then to Horlick High in Racine where he played football and basketball. About his musical experience in school, Cannon relates,

> It was really strange back then. . . . It was in the '70s, and I really wanted to play in the high school jazz band. And clearly I was a better bass player than any bass player they had, but I couldn't read any music. And so when I auditioned, and it was a different time, and there was some racism going on, you know. When I auditioned

for the band, the director told me no, because my reading wasn't good enough, and I should . . . just further my African tradition and play percussion, congas. . . . That really was a drag, because I really wanted to be in [the band], I really wanted to learn how to . . . play jazz.

My mom gave me my first Coltrane record when I was thirteen. . . . She worked at Dominican College. She worked in a boys' dormitory. And, after every spring semester, when everybody went home for the summer, they would leave things in their dorm rooms. And so, some guy left a stack of records. . . . And that was my first time listening to John Coltrane and Jimmy Garrison, of course my boss now McCoy Tyner, and my former boss, Elvin Jones.

I used to play in all these bands in Racine, but I could never do any gigs with them. But [my dad] would let me go to rehearsals. So I grew up playing in these funk bands, rock and roll bands. . . . Right after I turned eighteen, a guy's manager, a guy who'd been trying to get me to play with this band for years—my father kept telling him, "No, no, no"—he came by [and] my dad finally said, "Yeah." And my first gig was a battle of the bands at the Eagles Ballroom on Wisconsin Avenue. Wow! I was so excited. I got forty dollars, I remember.

After high school, Cannon attended UW–La Crosse and played on the basketball team. He intended to become a gym teacher, but music got in the way. "I was an electric [bass] player all my life," he remembers, but he really wanted to play acoustic bass.

[So] I started taking upright bass, and my teacher was a concert solo cellist; her name was Linda Brewer; and she just thought I was great. I didn't even think I was that good on it. . . . I just liked [it], and I practiced, I mean I skipped class and all I did was pretty much practice the thing all day [*laughter*]. And I missed basketball, I got kicked off the team, because I just spent all my time with the bass.

Cannon's life changed when the legendary bassist Milt Hinton came to the La Crosse campus.

> [Linda Brewer] invited me to go and see him play. . . . And I went to see him play, and it just blew me away. I sat there, [I had] never seen anybody play upright bass like that. . . . So I saw Milt Hinton play, and he was slapping the bass, and just having so much fun, and just making this incredible music. . . . And then I got a chance to talk to him, after his concert, in his dressing room. And he said some things to me that just inspired me. . . . And I played something for him. . . . He said, "Yeah, you should really keep [playing], because we need more young black bass players out here."

Inspired by the meeting with Hinton, Cannon decided to attend the Wisconsin Conservatory. He auditioned for Manty Ellis and, he thinks, Tony King and Berkeley Fudge. He remembers that David Hazeltine was in the audition band and was able to help Cannon through this trial by fire. "Next thing I knew," he says, "I was at the conservatory, and my first year, I was in six combos."

At the conservatory, Cannon says, "I thought I died and went to heaven. There's music everywhere, . . . everybody was bustling around, and serious about music." He studied piano with Martha Artis and aural skills with Joyce Altman. And like so many others, he was mentored in jazz and the jazz life by Fudge, Ellis, and King.

> There's Tony King, who just took me under his wing, and taught me all the things I needed to know that I still use today as a performer and as a teacher. Manty, you know he was hard on everybody, he was hard on me in the beginning, but he cared. Berkeley, . . . I thought, was the coolest guy I'd ever seen in my life, [or] been around. Beause he could play; he had a way of teaching.

Cannon studied with Milwaukee bassists George Welland and Harold Miller. "But, outside of those guys," he recalls, "I studied with Skip Crumby-Bey, who really taught me how to play some bass." Crumby-Bey made a huge impression on the Milwaukee scene in the few years he was in the city.

> Skip played at the Bombay Bicycle Club every Wednesday night with [pianist] Barry Velleman. And I would walk from Lyon Street, all the

> way to [the club], because I didn't have any money to get there any other way, and I was begging him for lessons. . . . Finally he said, "Yeah." And I studied with Skip all the way up until the time he left to go to Montreal.

In the summer break after his first year at the conservatory, Cannon toured the United States with a top-forty band. During the next year, he joined the Milwaukee fusion band Rainbow's End, which featured guitarist John Zaffiro, keyboard player Jerry Weitzer, and vocalist Marcia Cunningham. While at Zaffiro and Cunningham's house one day, Cannon was thrilled to meet a local jazz star, vocalist Penny Goodwin; but that day, she essentially ignored him. Not long after that meeting, however, David Hazeltine, Goodwin's pianist at the time, recommended Cannon for the newly vacated bass chair in Goodwin's band. "And that was it," Cannon says. "I worked with Penny for years after that . . . and that was serious baptism by fire."

Cannon started out on electric bass, but when Goodwin found out that he had an acoustic bass, she said, "Look, either you bring that g— d— bass to my gig tonight, or you're fired." He was barely getting started on the instrument, but he says: "I brought it anyways, and that was it, she made me play it. I learned how to play the bass, being in school, and playing six nights a week with her." He played a number of years with Goodwin, whom he calls "a Milwaukee institution," in the lounge at the top of the Pfister Hotel. Cannon says, "I'm forever in her debt."

But when it became time to move on, Cannon joined David Hazeltine in a duo at Chip and Py's. It was another learning experience, as Dave really opened up Cannon's ear. Unfortunately, Cannon says, "Around that time, I started getting really deep into drugs and alcohol. . . . I'd gotten married, my son was born, and things were just kind of crazy." Perhaps as an escape, in about 1983 Cannon made his first trip to New York. He went to visit with trumpeter Eddie "E. J." Allen (Carl's brother), and remembers: "I didn't even want to leave to come back, it was like a vacation."

He did come back to Milwaukee but moved to New York just six weeks later. This time in the Big Apple, he stayed with Brian Lynch. After struggling to make money playing in the subway (with such future jazz stars as Mark Whitfield and Cindy Blackman), doing a day job, and hanging out at jam sessions whenever possible, Cannon eventually landed in the late-night house band at the famous jazz club the Blue Note. He would go early to hear the headliners and soak up everything he could.

> And then I got the gig with Art Blakey [and the Jazz Messengers], for a minute. But around that time, my drug use had really escalated, and things were not really good, and I was still married, [but] separated from my wife. . . . So, I came home. Back to Milwaukee.

After about a year back in Wisconsin, Cannon recalls, "One night I just decided that was it. I had enough of this. If I didn't stop I was going to kill myself. . . . I just hated being back home, first of all. You know, Milwaukee's not a nice place in the winter. If you're from there or not, . . . it doesn't matter. It's winter, it's snow, I was homeless, I didn't have a bass, I was strung out on drugs, my life was just a drag, man." Thanks to interventions from his friends, including Berkeley Fudge, Cannon "checked into the county rehab, and . . . stayed thirty days, and I've been sober ever since."

When he got out of rehab, Cannon put together a band called the Jazz Elements. It included Rick Germanson (who was just a teenager) on piano, Berkeley Fudge, and drummer Robert Hobbs (who would later be replaced by Victor Soward). (Cannon appears in the photo that accompanies Rich Germanson's profile in chapter 7.)

Cannon returned to New York for a number of months, playing at Le Parker Meridien Hotel in a trio led by Milwaukee-based pianist Buddy Montgomery, who also encouraged drummer George Fludas to move from Milwaukee to New York. After two years of being clean, Cannon felt it was safe for him to go back to New York permanently.

Back in the city, he says, "It was amazing. No one remembered me. Oh, a few guys did." But he had to start "career building" all over again. The first one to offer him a gig was vocalist Andy Bey. Then he got the call that solidified his career, from young trumpet star Roy Hargrove. He worked with Hargrove for eight or nine years. One version of that band, with Larry Willis on piano, Sherman Irby on alto saxophone, and Willie Jones III on drums, was, Cannon says, "by far . . . *the* best band I've ever played [with] in my life." When he left Hargrove, he worked in a trio with veteran pianist Tommy Flanagan. But a great deal of planned work was canceled when the planes flew into the Twin Towers on September 11, 2001.

Getting by playing "local gigs," Cannon got his next break when he got the call from one of jazz's greatest drummers, Elvin Jones. About working with Jones, Cannon says, "Talk about going back to school, man, at [age] forty-something." And although a mix-up nearly led to his losing the Jones gig before he even started, Cannon ended up working with Jones for several years, almost up to Jones's death in 2004. Working with Elvin was so physically demanding that Cannon says, "I was lying in the bathtub the first year after every gig." Not long after Jones's death, Cannon got the call to play with another ex-member of John Coltrane's classic quartet, piano giant McCoy Tyner. He has been with McCoy's group ever since and is also a regular member of guitarist Russell Malone's trio.

Having worked with some of the most prominent mainstream small groups in jazz as well as leading his own projects, Gerald Cannon has carved out a significant niche for himself in the jazz scene.

Greg Tardy

Gregory Tardy (Greg to his friends) spent only a few years in Wisconsin, but they were important, formative years for him as a musician. Though he was based in New York for many years, he still feels a strong connection to Milwaukee.

Tardy was born in New Orleans in 1966. In his youth, his family moved around due to his father's job at American Can. From Indianapolis, the family moved to the Milwaukee area in the late seventies. Greg went to school in Brown Deer, Wisconsin. "My mother was a jazz vocalist in Milwaukee," he recalls. "She was very active on the Milwaukee jazz scene for a while." In fact, his mother, JoAnne Tardy, did an album that featured David Hazeltine and Berkeley Fudge called *Think of This* (1986).

In Milwaukee, young Tardy became a serious clarinetist and showed an early interest in having a career in classical music. After taking lessons with Carol Tilbury, he studied with Milwaukee Symphony Orchestra clarinetist Russell Dagon for a couple of years while attending Carroll

College (which is now Carroll University). Tardy transferred to UW–Milwaukee and continued his clarinet study there with Jack Snavely, with whom Tardy remains connected.

Tardy reports, "When I was at Carroll, . . . [band director Bob Halseth] got me a gig playing with a polka band [*laughter*], playing for tailgate parties around County Stadium." After transferring to UWM, he started playing saxophone with a local jazz fusion band known as Le Crew, which frequently played at Sardino's.

> We were playing Anita Baker songs and Spyro Gyra songs and stuff like that, and my brother, who had been studying with David Hazeltine, . . . told me I needed to check out some straight-ahead jazz . . . and turned me on to John Coltrane. And that just blew my mind.

So while at UWM, he says, "I also took a class at the Wisconsin Conservatory of Music with David Hazeltine. And that's when I started getting into jazz. And eventually I went from [Coltrane] . . . to Charlie Parker and Sonny Stitt, and then I was on my way."

Tardy had no intention of leaving the clarinet behind, but he was getting a lot of calls for work on saxophone. And he must have caught on to fusion sax playing quickly, because he went on to play, in short order, in Don Linke's band Cooler Near the Lake (which frequently played at Virginia's on the south side), and Paul Cebar's Milwaukeeans (which played not only in Milwaukee but in Chicago and Minneapolis/St. Paul as well). With Cooler, Tardy played on his first "real" record date, on the album *Knuckle Walking*, which included, in addition to Linke on guitar, Milwaukee veterans Dennis Klopfer, Michael Murphy, Tom McGirr, Eric Hervey, and Tom Newburg.

But, Tardy says, "At a certain point I just wanted to do jazz; like straight-ahead jazz. Well, those guys were all great musicians, and it had nothing to do with that, but I just wanted to focus on traditional jazz. But I wasn't ready for that scene yet, and . . . as a result I wasn't getting any work [*laughter*]. . . . [So] by the time I left Milwaukee [in 1990], I was almost homeless, because I couldn't get any work."

Of his time in Milwaukee, Tardy says, "[Brian Lynch] was always really supportive of me. When he would come to town he would never be disparaging toward me at all. He would always be complimentary and always encourage me to keep going." And when Tardy later moved to New York, Lynch was one of the people inviting him to sit in. Gerald Cannon also became one of Tardy's supporters during that time.

Drummer Vince Davis (who was then a member of Le Crew in Milwaukee but is now based in Chicago) also made a large contribution to Tardy's career. Tardy remembers: "[Davis] was a serious jazz musician at the time, and there was one point when he took me out in the car . . . and chewed me out, telling me that I needed to get my stuff together, and telling me about the scene in New York. . . . He lent me one time a whole lot of videotapes of all these great jazz musicians." Tardy is also grateful to Milwaukee keyboard player Jerry Weitzer. "[Weitzer] was a really big part of my life for the last year I was in Milwaukee," he says.

During his period of development in Milwaukee, Tardy's parents had moved to St. Louis.

> And so, I actually called my parents. . . . My dad came and got me. . . . And while I was in St. Louis I did a lot of blues gigs, and by then I started picking up some jazz gigs fairly quickly, and I started to get my stuff more together. And then from there I moved back to New Orleans for several years. It was a great time to be down there, because there were a lot of young jazz musicians that went on to be stars, such as Nicholas Payton and Brian Blade, and a whole lot of other ones. . . . And I also did some playing with Ellis Marsalis while I was down there, as well as some commercial work with Allen Toussaint and with the Neville Brothers.

Through his connection with Nicholas Payton, Tardy eventually ended up in legendary drummer Elvin Jones's band, at which point, Tardy's career was on its way.

He was a member of the Elvin Jones Jazz Machine, and then continued to play on the New York scene and, as Tardy describes it, "pretty much that whole scene at Smalls [jazz club]." His next big visible associations were in Tom Harrell's band, and working with Steve Coleman.

Somewhat to his surprise, Tardy was signed to a deal with the major jazz record label Impulse! In 1997 he cut an album as leader, *Serendipity*,

Joel Frahm (left; see next section in this chapter) and Gregory Tardy. COURTESY OF JOEL FRAHM

featuring the outstanding players Harrell, Mulgrew Miller, Aaron Goldberg, Reginald Veal, and Eric Harland. The band toured internationally. It seemed like Tardy was all set for a great recording run, but when Impulse! merged with Verve, many of its artists were dropped, including Tardy.

"But then I continued to make CDs for small labels," Tardy says. "Those [recording] dates have a lot of really . . . well-known musicians, and some lesser-known musicians, but they're all on a high level." Tardy also was a member of the last band of noted iconoclast Andrew Hill and played on Hill's last three CDs. At the same time, he worked frequently with Dave Douglas. A testament to Tardy's musical range is that he has recorded with Bill Frisell and Chris Potter (and with Potter, Tardy exclusively played the clarinet, his first love). He appeared on Brian Lynch's *Simpatico* and the young Milwaukee trumpeter Philip Dizack's inaugural album (see later in this chapter). Tardy's albums continue to appear with frequency; he had recorded ten by 2014.

In the mid-2000s, Tardy got a call to do an album with the Knoxville Jazz Orchestra in Tennessee, which included his friend Donald Brown. Between 2006 and 2010, he took some "time off" from his growing jazz career to follow his Christian beliefs and spend time playing for a mega church as his primary musical activity. At the very time he decided to leave his position at the church, he was offered a faculty jazz position at the University of Tennessee. So in the summer of 2010, he moved south. He continues to perform and tour with his peers, especially during summers, when he is not teaching at the university. He had a triumphant return to Milwaukee in June 2017 when he performed at the Jazz Estate with Brian Lynch, Mark Davis, Jeff Hamann, and Dave Bayles. Tardy's diverse career, in various locales and with a variety of important artists, is unique for an important Wisconsin musician.

Joel Frahm

Joel Frahm, another prominent New York saxophonist, was born in Racine in 1970 and spent his formative years in Wisconsin. Frahm's first music study was on piano, inspired by the music that Vince Guaraldi wrote for the TV special *A Charlie Brown Christmas*.[12] Frahm studied with a local legend named Grant Mahlme. "I would always play by ear," he remembers, "and [Mahlme] would put up with that basically, and chide me gently, 'You know you've really got to learn to read music.'"

In school, Frahm recalls,

> I played a bunch of instruments at first. I mean I played piano, and then I wanted to be in the band, so I played flute, not very seriously. I played bassoon, not very seriously, French horn, a little bit of guitar, kind of just messing around with stuff. I didn't really know what I liked. And then, my best friend [Giovanni Washington-Wright, now a musician in Texas], was playing alto saxophone in the wind ensemble and the jazz band . . . and I thought it was cool that he was playing saxophone. . . . That was when all the 1980s bands were out, and there were lots of rock and roll saxophone solos. . . . I didn't know anything about jazz at all, . . . but I was interested in just trying to play it. Because he played it. So I said, "I'd like to be in jazz

band." And I said I'd like to play soprano saxophone, because I heard a soprano solo on some rock tune. And [the band director] kind of laughed, and he said, "We don't really have parts for soprano saxophone in the jazz band, but we need a tenor player."

Young Frahm enjoyed one thing about his short time at Horlick High School: the jazz band, which was led at the time by John Dorsey. Frahm also studied saxophone at Stephen Bull Fine Arts School with Gary Mollenkopf.[13] He was one of several future jazz professionals who took lessons in Racine from Curt Hanrahan, who Frahm refers to as "a great guy, a great player, and a great educator."

Frahm's father, who worked for the *Racine Journal-Times*, took a job at the *Hartford Courant* in Connecticut. He went the extra mile and looked for a school in Connecticut where Joel could experience success, because, Joel says, "I really wasn't doing well at Horlick. I was a pretty oddball kid, and pretty uncomfortable in my own skin, and wasn't an athlete, and wasn't cool, and pizza face and the whole deal. I was really floundering, and failing out of school. And so [moving to Connecticut] was like a fresh start for me."

So Frahm ended up at West Hartford High School in 1985, in a jazz program that produced, among others, trombonist Pete McGuinness and jazz piano star Brad Mehldau. When his high school bandmates bought him six great jazz albums for his birthday, Frahm knew that he had found a home and discovered what he was meant to be: a jazz musician. He toured Europe three times with his high school jazz band.[14] And Frahm and Mehldau played a steady weekly club date while they were still high school students.

After high school, Frahm attended Rutgers University and then the Manhattan School of Music. After earning a bachelor of arts in jazz performance at Manhattan, he moved on to apprentice at Betty Carter's Jazz Ahead workshop. He joined Maynard Ferguson's big band and keyboardist Larry Goldings's band. He also spent time in a quartet with his old buddy Mehldau in the early 1990s. In 1996, Frahm was a semifinalist in the heralded Thelonious Monk Competition. In the late 1990s, he played often with drummer Matt Wilson. One of his most visible gigs in the early 2000s was with vocalist Jane Monheit, touring and recording. Since that time he has been all over the scene in New York, working with a wide variety of musicians, and has now recorded seven albums as leader. With a musical journey that began in Wisconsin, Frahm has become an important figure on the international jazz scene.

Ike Sturm

Ike Sturm, a jazz bass player and composer, is currently director of music for the jazz ministry at Saint Peter's Church in New York, also called the "jazz church." Like Joel Frahm, Sturm spent the first part of his childhood in Wisconsin, growing up in the town of Freedom in the Appleton area, where his father, Fred (see chapter 18), taught at Lawrence University. Young Ike started playing cello—standing up and plucking it like a bass—in the Suzuki string program led by Harry Hoecherl in Appleton. He played tuba in his school band in Freedom, continuing through high school. Early in Sturm's musical life, Rand Skelton, a local band director (and talented trumpet player), showed up at the Sturm home with a tuba and an electric bass, gifts for the young musician. Shortly thereafter, Sturm was thrown into jazz at a summer camp in Kaukauna. UW–La Crosse bass professor Karyn Quinn indoctrinated the young bass player into the world of walking bass lines. In Sturm's last year of school in Wisconsin, seventh grade, he started playing the acoustic bass.

Sturm attended many jazz concerts at Lawrence, where his father taught. He remembers meeting Dizzy Gillespie and Clark Terry when they visited Lawrence, and singer Dianne Reeves when she came to the Sturm home for dinner. The family moved to upstate New York in 1991 when Fred joined the faculty at the Eastman School of Music in Rochester. Neither one of his parents (both musicians) pushed him into pursuing music, and when the youngster talked about quitting band, his parents said "Okay," which caused Sturm to reconsider his threat. He went to high school in little Honeoye Falls, New York, which was blessed with a fine music program, including an award-winning jazz band.

Sturm studied bass with Eastman's Jeff Campbell during high school and for seven years as a student at Eastman, where he earned bachelor's and master's degrees. Sturm then moved to New York City with his wife, Misty, a singer from Eastman, and landed a teaching job on Long Island.

Ike Sturm. PHOTO BY MERRI CYR; COURTESY OF IKE STURM

After a self-described "austere" year out on the island, the young couple moved closer to some musician friends in Brooklyn. Sturm was hired at Saint Peter's Church in midtown Manhattan, where he has remained on staff ever since. He works at the church and elsewhere with some of the finest young musicians in New York. He has recorded four albums as leader, including *Jazz Mass*, which earned a rare four-and-a-half-star review from *Down Beat* in 2010 (see online discography).

Sturm returns to Wisconsin every summer to serve on the faculty at the Tritone Jazz Fantasy Camp in Door County. "[I appreciate the] great things about being [in New York]," he explains, "but I love . . . how people [in the Midwest] interact with each other; the kindness, and kind of informality, too. And it's just fun." Even though Sturm left the state while still a boy, Wisconsin will always feel like his home.

John Sullivan

Bassist John Sullivan, son of Wisconsin jazz guitarist Dave Sullivan (see chapter 18), was born in Sheboygan in 1978.[15] John became a major player on the jazz scene in New York, but at least as of 2015, his story has a different ending from others included here.

As far as his early interest in music, Sullivan says, "It didn't hurt having a pretty accomplished bebop guitar player as a father to segue into music." Dave was sizing up his son John's potential right from the beginning. "I know when I was born," John recalls, "my dad said that my fingers were too fat for piano, so he always figured that I would play bass, . . . [although] short, fat fingers [are] not good for bass either." Sullivan's earliest music-making memories are from the family kitchen, where he beat on pots and pans and where his dad hung out a lot and passed along his observations about music. By fourth grade, he was playing bass, accompanying his dad on electric.

By the time he was eight or nine, Sullivan began playing a half-size acoustic bass. Not many programs can supply young students with half-size basses, but Sullivan was afforded that opportunity at Jefferson Elementary School in Sheboygan. While he disliked the discipline of the practice schedule, he enjoyed the creative parts of the orchestra program. And by the time he was attending Horace Mann Middle School, he had cultivated these creative interests. Even at that age, he related to the electric bass playing of Jaco Pastorius, and so became very interested in the electric instrument. He began to play with rock bands in addition to orchestras.

By the age of ten or eleven, Sullivan was getting hooked on jazz. "The first time that I got into . . . pure, just straight jazz," he says, was when "[my dad] started showing me different interpretations of a major nine chord, you know, a chord with extensions." Needless to say, Sullivan was a somewhat precocious middle schooler. This intellectual interest in the inner workings of music led him away from rock and roll, and by the end of middle school, he was playing in the Sheboygan Symphony as one of its youngest members.

In his youth, Sullivan took lessons on both acoustic and electric bass from another Sheboygan native, John Gibson (see chapter 18). He would go to hear Gibson and pianist John Harmon play at the House of Lee in Appleton, and it wasn't long before the youngster started to sit in. By the time he was attending high school at Sheboygan South, Sullivan says, "I was pretty much deep into both jazz and classical music." He didn't find the high school orchestra program challenging, but he continued playing in the Sheboygan Symphony, and also the Milwaukee Youth Symphony. His father, Dave, got him on some jazz gigs, playing everything from Dixieland to bebop (including in trumpeter Brad Curran's group, Dig), but the younger Sullivan was already into the music of John Coltrane, and even the avant-garde.

Like a number of other prominent Wisconsin jazz musicians, Sullivan played in the state Honors Jazz Ensemble. And before he was even out of high school, he became friends with Lawrence University student Malcolm Martin, a trumpet player, and they traveled around the Fox Valley together, sitting in on the club scene. The guys would sit in with funk bands and jam for hours. They would also drive to Madison and go from bar to bar and party to party, playing wherever they could. Sullivan occasionally sat in with some of Milwaukee's top musicians, including Melvin Rhyne and Berkeley Fudge, as well as Madison's resident avant-garde saxophonist, Hanah Jon Taylor.

By the age of seventeen, John says he was practicing on the bass "six to eight hours a day." During the time, he won a concerto competition and performed with the Milwaukee Symphony. When Sullivan attended Lawrence University for a year, he thrived under the tutelage of jazz director Ken Schaphorst and Milwaukee Symphony Orchestra bassist Dave Stallsmith. Sullivan had already taken lessons from Stallsmith in high school, but he especially profited from Stallsmith's instruction in college. After only a year at Lawrence, Sullivan, with Schaphorst's blessing, transferred to the New England Conservatory. "I wanted something more challenging," he says. "I wanted people who played a lot better than me. And when you go to Boston, there's definitely people who play a lot better than you there. That was a really humbling experience, to be honest. I mean there's a lot of opportunity, but . . . [it was] competitive. I was behind the eight ball; I wasn't nearly as good as I thought I was."

At the conservatory, Sullivan first studied with veteran bassist Cecil McBee. Later, he studied with such varied jazz stars as Bob Brookmeyer, Danilo Perez, George Garzone, and "third stream" pianist Ran Blake. Despite all of this study, however, Sullivan says, "I probably should have gone to [the nearby Berklee College of Music] . . . because that's where the real strong, strong players were."

When he left Boston, around 2000, Sullivan was selected to go to the prestigious Thelonious Monk Institute, but he says he stayed only "for a brief minute." At that time, the institute was moving to southern California and was apparently in some disarray. Sullivan—along with saxophonists Walter Smith and Patrick Cornelius, and several others—decided to leave the school and move to New York. "And the people that [had been] at Berklee," Sullivan explains, "were my base. Because most all of them moved to New York."

Through his Boston connections, Sullivan ended up working with Robert Glasper, Marcus Strickland, David Sanchez, and R&B singer Bilal. At first, his jobs were low-paying or even no-paying, but Sullivan eventually worked with such musicians as Joanne Brackeen, Mark Whitfield, and Ravi Coltrane.

After he had been in New York for about a year, Sullivan got the job that established his reputation on the jazz scene: bassist in the band of legendary veteran drummer Roy Haynes. For some time, the Haynes quartet consisted of Haynes, Sullivan, saxophonist Marcus Strickland, and pianist Martin Bejerano. "And at that time," Sullivan recalls, "we were playing a lot." Getting the gig with Haynes was great for Sullivan's career, and financially it allowed him to do things that he might otherwise not have been able to do. But eventually, the opportunity almost turned into a double-edged sword. As Sullivan explains it,

> I was playing with Roy a lot. . . . When you get a [prestigious] gig like that, . . . you know that gig might sustain you financially somewhat, and allow you to be more selective about what gigs you take. . . . Maybe you don't have to take the $30 gig; maybe you can take the $75 gig. But the problem with that is that by not taking the $30 gig . . . when times are slow, [you may not get a gig]. As a hustler, I think the hustle part of it is difficult. And if you don't maintain a

John Sullivan in his early days in New York. COURTESY OF DAVE AND KAREN SULLIVAN

> consistent hustle, . . . then you have gaps. You have gaps; you have to figure out [how] to make money.

When work with Haynes began slowing down, Sullivan started looking elsewhere for a steady income. "I had never really thought about anything other than music," he says, "so [looking for a new job] was kind of refreshing." He briefly sold real estate. That made it tougher to go back to the music business, where, to further explain "the hustle," Sullivan says, you don't have to completely start "from scratch, but, you have to go out and basically reinvent yourself . . . every few months if you want to stay connected and have some kind of small, piecemeal income between these larger gigs."

Sullivan claims that his father felt the same way while playing jazz on the Wisconsin scene. He doesn't feel like he or his father is one of "these cats [who have] the ability to just constantly be hustling." So now Sullivan is a real estate agent who still spends time making music in a little home studio. His rise to the upper reaches of the jazz scene, followed by a complete change of direction, speaks to the vagaries of a tough business.

Joe Sanders

Bassist Joe Sanders was born in Milwaukee in 1984 and grew up at the intersection of Ninth and Locust Streets.[16] He first got the idea of playing bass when he was sitting in Ephesians Baptist Church, hearing the church band play but feeling that something—the bass sound—was missing. Some time after discussing this with his mother, she presented young Sanders with his first guitar, an electric bass, at Christmas. He was in fifth grade and attending Hopkins Elementary School. "My dad thought he could play a little bass," Sanders says, "so he'd teach me whatever he heard and thought he could play on the instrument."

After finishing fifth grade, Sanders was accepted at Roosevelt Middle School. He claims that if he had not gone to Roosevelt, he would not be a successful musician today. Because he expressed an interest in music, he was taken to the orchestra room on the first day of school, and he chose the acoustic bass (which he had never played) as his instrument for the school orchestra. Under the direction of respected jazz trumpeter Michael Betz, Sanders says that he "ate up" the music instruction at school. By his second semester, he had progressed through the beginning and intermediate groups into the advanced orchestra. "And that was just from me practicing six, seven hours a day," he says, "just because I had nothing else to do. . . . I had no siblings to bother me; the internet wasn't really around to distract me; obviously there was TV, but I was more interested in the bass."

The following year, Betz recommended Sanders for a "program through the Milwaukee Symphony Orchestra for 'inner-city children' to study with a person from the Symphony." Sanders was happy to participate but needed someone to drive him. So, every Saturday for three or four years, Tony Lucas, an employee at WTMJ, drove Sanders to his lessons with symphony bassist Catherine McGinn. And Sanders continued lessons with McGinn through high school, "Every Saturday, without fail, whether I wanted to or not," he says. "She became like my second mom." During those years of lessons, Sanders built a solid instrumental technique that has served as the backbone of his success ever since. And although he discovered jazz at just about the same time that he started studying with McGinn, he says that he was also "very interested in classical music" and played classical music in recital every year.

But jazz became his other musical love. Sanders claims that a fellow student talked him into skipping a class one day to go hear the jazz band, which was directed by jazz trumpeter Allen Johnson (see chapter 17). (Sanders suspects he skipped math class, which was taught by another well-known Milwaukee jazz musician, guitarist Steve Lewandowski.) On that day, as Sanders heard a "huge" jazz band playing Miles Davis's classic "So What," he was hooked. "From seventh grade until I graduated high school," he says, "I was always teetering [on] the line of whether I wanted to do classical or . . . jazz, and I was kind of thinking that I would do both, that it was a possibility." While continuing his jazz studies in and out of school and his classical studies with McGinn, he also played in the Milwaukee Youth Symphony Orchestra.

Sanders went on to the Milwaukee High School of the Arts (MHSA), finding himself in the excellent jazz program that had been developed by Cliff Gribble. Sanders remembers his audition for Gribble, when he didn't know what chord symbols meant. But he says, "I could play the hell out of the bass, I could solo, I could play really fast." Gribble was quick to admit him to the program, where Sanders started out in the beginning combo. By the second semester, Sanders had worked his way to the top combo, which included flutist Nick Cowles, saxophonist Paul Godin, award-winning trumpeter Tobias Kammerer, and the precocious drummer Romarcus Jones. Sanders says, "Everybody came up in a different part of Milwaukee, everybody had a different upbringing, so everybody had different perspectives of music. Everybody was listening to different types of jazz, different types of music, hip-hop, all this other stuff." Ironically, Sanders, from the "inner city," had more classical training than any of his bandmates.

In Sanders's sophomore year, his combo was invited to play at New York's JVC Jazz Festival. They played at Symphony Space in June 1999, opening for Donald Harrison (whose drummer at the time was Carl

Allen). While Sanders continued his classical studies, the pull of jazz was very strong; he says the experience at JVC "settled it."

Years later, in April 2013, when visiting the Jazz Estate in Milwaukee with his colleagues from the Gerald Clayton trio, Sanders said, "This is where it all began." He described his "first jazz gig ever," with Berkeley Fudge, like this: "I was fifteen years old. Smoke-filled jazz club. I got home, puked. . . . I wasn't drinking, obviously; my mom was there. But just the smell and the smoke, it was a surreal experience, but it was something I will never forget." Fudge hired Sanders to play with him after getting to know him at the Wisconsin Conservatory's summer jazz camp. While there, Sanders studied with Berkeley and other conservatory faculty members, drummer Dave Bayles and bassist Jeff Hamann. Sanders says, "I'm sure Berkeley and Manty [Ellis] saw us all the time, and they [thought], 'Let's hire these youngbloods for a gig.'" Sanders sometimes also worked with young pianist Dan Nimmer (see chapter 7) in the late 1990s and early 2000s.

While Sanders appreciates what he learned in school, he also highly values what he learned on these gigs. "When people talk about growing up in jazz," he says, "it's like, 'Where'd you learn jazz?' It's like, 'I learned jazz on the streets' [*laughter*]. Because playing with cats like Berkeley and Manty, that's like real, that's like the Art Blakey [Jazz] Messengers type vibe."

In Sanders's junior year at MHSA, the combo went to Europe and played at the North Sea Jazz Festival in the Netherlands. Romarcus Jones was the fearless member of the MHSA combo, unafraid to introduce himself to any jazz musician. It was a lesson Sanders eventually learned. When the combo played at a jazz festival in Stevens Point, Sanders's friends pushed him into sitting in at a clinic with prominent jazz guitarist John Scofield. And, sure enough, ten years later, Scofield called Sanders to do a session in New York.

In 2001, Sanders attended summer jazz camp at Vail, Colorado, where he studied with bassist John Clayton, who became an important mentor. In Sanders's senior year, he was selected as a member of the music industry-sponsored 2002 Grammy High School Jazz Band. While performing with the Grammy band, Sanders was heard and recruited by representatives of respected jazz schools from around the country, a process he likened to the recruitment of top high school athletes. And the opportunity Sanders saw was the same opportunity that many athletes see. He explains:

> You know, if you can get out of the ghetto [*laughter*], . . . do anything you can to get out of the ghetto. So I never really thought about it that way, but [music] was my ticket out, basically. It's not like it was hard, but . . . being confined, I mean the definition of the ghetto is just being in that one confined area, . . . and those exist everywhere. You know, whether it be black, white, Asian, . . . Jewish.

When Sanders found out that one of his bass idols, Christian McBride, was teaching at the Brubeck Institute, a new school in California, he applied, was accepted, and decided to attend. He had learned many of McBride's pet phrases and even some of his more challenging figures. After a few months, Sanders tried to match his teacher and played some of those things he had copied in his lesson with McBride. "Until one time," he remembers, "there's this one lick that I had been working on for weeks. You know, listening, transcribing. 'Okay, I'm gonna get him with this.'" But McBride was always able to outshine his student.

At that point, Sanders had what he calls his "epiphany moment": "First of all, why do I want to sound like somebody else? How is that going to get me gigs? . . . If they want Christian McBride, they're going to call Christian McBride." He had heard all the talk about "finding your own sound." And he says, "I knew that I would have to do that eventually, but that wasn't my goal." At that time, his only goal was to *not* sound like McBride.

At the Brubeck Institute, Sanders grew close to drummer Justin Brown. The two had met in high school, when both of their high school groups appeared at the Monterey Jazz Festival. They lived together for their two years at the institute and became musical companions, a partnership that continued for years in the Gerald Clayton Trio and other groups. Sanders also crossed paths at the institute with another successful Milwaukee bass player, Jeff Chambers, who was already well established in the Bay Area.

After the Brubeck Institute, Sanders moved to New York with Brown. He slept on the couch for a few months in the apartment of Milwaukee trumpeter Andy Neesley. In New York, he says, "I was just trying to get gigs, I was just trying to pay my rent, and I was just trying to eat." He would often play "stupid restaurant gigs," but after a while he was "gigging every day . . . [just trying] to play with everybody I could play with." Eventually he was sleeping on the couch of trumpeter Ambrose Akinmusire, another acquaintance from his high school days. Akinmusire was auditioning for the Thelonious Monk Institute and convinced Sanders that he should, too. Both young men were accepted to the selective school that year, as was Wisconsin drummer Zach Harmon (see chapter 18).

While the staff at the Monk Institute featured jazz legends Herbie Hancock and Wayne Shorter, the musician who Sanders says "completely messed up my head" was the leader of the program, trumpeter and composer Terence Blanchard. Blanchard's imaginative exercises and assignments caused Sanders to think conceptually and compositionally for the first time in his musical life. He also studied briefly with bass legend Charlie Haden, who in one memorable day, Sanders says, "got me *really* thinking about music, and [how] being socially conscious helps your music, and how the audience can tell." He studied two weeks with Ron Carter, whose repeated entreaty was, "Mr. Sanders: focus." Carter continues to be one of Sanders's mentors in New York. Sanders says, "You know, it's like everything that [Haden and Carter] do in music, it's not like they just do that there; it's all a part of their whole life, it's just, like, all encompassed into the music."

Sanders studied both semesters of his second year at the Monk Institute with John Clayton, who was his favorite teacher, and became a father figure as well. Like Sanders, Clayton was strongly grounded in both the classical and the jazz worlds and has proved that an African American player can live in both of those worlds. Over time, as Sanders has worked with Clayton's son Gerald, Sanders has said: "John calls me his adopted son."

After finishing his two years at the Monk Institute, Sanders moved back to New York in 2007. Since then, he has been in the bands of such established stars as saxophonist Jimmy Heath and the important trumpet

Joe Sanders, early 2010s. PHOTO BY EMRA ISLEK; COURTESY OF JOE SANDERS

player Roy Hargrove. Hargrove's pianist was Gerald Clayton, and when Clayton formed his own trio, Sanders was his bass man. It turned out to be a long-lasting and profitable musical pairing, rounded out by the drumming of Justin Brown.

Sanders also leads several different bands of his own and in October 2011 recorded his first album as leader, *Introducing Joe Sanders*, for the Criss Cross label. As of 2015, Sanders had recorded and was working with another great jazz veteran, saxophonist Charles Lloyd. Nurtured by the best Milwaukee had to offer, trained by giants of the jazz bass world, and now working with some of jazz's top artists, Joe Sanders should be a major player on the jazz scene for years to come.

Philip Dizack

Trumpeter Philip Dizack was born in Milwaukee in 1985. As a youth, Dizack "tried to play a number of different instruments," and, he recalls, "failed miserably" at drums, saxophone, and trombone. At his father's advice, finally he tried the trumpet. Dizack says,

> the trumpet was never anything that was difficult for me. I always was eager to practice it. But I had a knack, I obviously had some sort of natural ability. But looking back, I remember I could play the first day . . . and I think that really allowed me to be so interested in it so quickly.

Dizack's father, Bob, was an audio technician, and music was playing around their house "all the time." Dizack remembers his dad playing Oscar Peterson and Miles Davis, and even records of the younger Nicholas Payton.

Dizack attended Glen Hills Middle School in Glendale, where his band director, Tim McCarthy, quickly realized that he had a special student on his hands. Dizack says, "[McCarthy was] just a wonderful, wonderful teacher, and somebody that I still, anytime that I'm in Milwaukee, make sure that I at least let him know that I'm there." (Dizack also goes back to his old middle school to work with the students.) McCarthy told Dizack's parents about his gifts but never talked to Dizack about them. McCarthy had other lessons to impart on the young musician. As Dizack tells it,

> I heard a message, "Will Philip Dizack please go to Tim McCarthy's office." I'm like, "Okay, it's interesting; I've never been called to the music room before." And he said all these things . . . and I remember very specifically he was saying, "When somebody compliments you, you just say 'thank you.'" . . . Not realizing that he was telling me to not be egotistical and [*laughter*] shut my mouth, and he was putting me on the right path even though I didn't know it then.

Dizack went on to Nicolet High School, but he was already playing with students from the Milwaukee High School of the Arts, including Joe Sanders. Tobias Kaemmerer, an MHSA student who was a few years older than Dizack and already a very accomplished trumpeter, was an inspiration. Dizack also attended two well-known Wisconsin summer jazz camps: Birch Creek, in Door County, and Shell Lake, in northwestern Wisconsin.

Although Dizack appreciated the instruction he got from Doug Owens at Nicolet, he felt he needed more, so he transferred to the High School of the Arts for his senior year. Former MHSA jazz guru Cliff Gribble convinced Dizack to audition for the YoungArts Program of the National Foundation for the Advancement for the Arts. He made the cut and was chosen as one of just five students from around the country (and Europe) to represent the program and to attend Arts Week in Florida. (Wisconsin drummer Zach Harmon was also in the group that year.) The quintet, known as the Clifford Brown–Stan Getz Jazz All Stars, performed in Toronto and Japan.

Although Dizack had options for school at that point (including a full ride to the Berklee College of Music), he wanted to be in New York, the center of the jazz universe. He was recruited by Justin DiCioccio, director of the jazz program at the Manhattan School of Music, and, luckily, a generous scholarship allowed him to attend.

During his last years in high school, Dizack says, "Brian Lynch, being from Milwaukee, would come back to do clinics. And I would always get lessons from him, and from [the time I was] about sixteen, he became a mentor of mine, and was always eager to help me. . . . Anytime he was in town he would give me lessons." Lynch remained a mentor and advocate during Dizack's early days in New York.

At Manhattan, Dizack was immediately thrown in with some of the top young players in jazz: Ambrose Akinmusire, Walter Smith, Obed Calvaire, John Benitez, and Luis Bonilla. Smith suggested that Dizack should seek a recording opportunity, so he made a demo with Smith, Joe Sanders, pianist Gerald Clayton, and drummer Marcus Gilmore. Fresh Sound Records signed him to a deal. When the album was finally released—when Dizack was still only nineteen—it included Sanders and another part-time Milwaukeean, Greg Tardy.

Philip Dizack. PHOTO BY SASHA SLOAN; COURTESY OF PHILIP DIZACK

During this same early period of his career in New York, Dizack hunted down his hero, Nicholas Payton, and "hounded" him until he arranged a lesson, at which point the older man put the young Milwaukeean through his paces in a decidedly "old school" learning experience. But once he realized that Dizack could really play, Payton connected Dizack to Tim Warfield and Terrell Stafford. Stafford became another one of Dizack's important trumpet mentors. Eventually, Warfield started hiring Dizack, as did Latin jazz giant Eddie Palmieri, because of his connection with Brian Lynch. He also got the opportunity to play with another "living history" figure in jazz, organist Dr. Lonnie Smith.

Competitions were an integral part of Dizack's rise to recognition. He won third place at the International Trumpet Guild Jazz Competition in 2004 and was first place winner of the National Trumpet Competition in 2005. After Dizack won the prestigious Carmine Caruso Trumpet Competition in 2005, Stafford, who had been a judge at the competition, helped him get hooked up with another respected veteran of the scene, saxophonist Bobby Watson. Dizack ended up touring with Watson for a couple of years. Dizack also took part in the Thelonious Monk competition in 2007, which was won by Ambrose Akinmusire, whom Dizack describes as "my closest musical confidante."

Dizack worked with Greg Tardy's band for some months before Tardy left the scene to concentrate on church music. Work slowed down for Dizack, but he hung on in New York, eventually making his second and third albums as leader (see online discography), as well as playing on others' albums, including Greg Tardy's.

Around 2013, Dizack decided it was time for a change of scene, and he moved to the West Coast. He says,

> It's presented a different set of opportunities. I play more with Walter Smith. When I got out to LA, one of the first gigs I did was with Billy Childs. So, I have great opportunities out there. And then I also toured with the *American Idol* winner Philip Phillips for six months, opening for John Mayer.
>
> Moving to LA was such a great experience for me. Because I loved New York, loved it. But coming to LA, it's like you get to see . . . New York from the outside, and it gave me a new perspective of things.

By 2016, Dizack was back in New York. From the Midwest to the East Coast, the West Coast, and back east, Philip Dizack continues to make a name for himself in the jazz world.

Styles and Schools

10

Milwaukee Mainstream

By the late 1950s, parts of Milwaukee's jazz scene revolved around two local celebrities—Dick Ruedebusch and Sig Millonzi. A number of those who performed with these two musicians formed a core of outstanding players, some of whom have continued to work to this day.

Dick Ruedebusch

Dick Ruedebusch was a true Wisconsin phenomenon and became a legend. He displayed an outsized talent at an early age; became a local hero; made a splash on the national stage; gave up celebrity to return to his home state; and then, sadly, died young. He grew up in Mayville, only twenty-five miles from Bunny Berigan's hometown, Fox Lake. Ruedebusch played trumpet, Berigan's instrument, with Berigan-like technical ability, and his early death also mirrors that of Berigan. But except for their modest Wisconsin beginnings, exceptional talents, and early deaths, they are a study in contrast.

Born in 1924, sixteen years after Berigan, Ruedebusch grew up in a world not much different from that of the previous generation.[1] He showed an early interest in music, and his jazz education received a great boost from Mayville resident and jazz fan Winfred Herberg. Herberg frequently traveled to Milwaukee for jazz events and, after recognizing serious talent in the young Ruedebusch, got the family's permission to take the kid along on some of his outings. This odd couple went to hear Bob Crosby's well-known band at the Modernistic Ballroom when Ruedebusch was twelve years old. Apparently, Ruedebusch was invited to come onstage to play with the trumpet section—a tremendous thrill for a young kid. On another of their Mayville-Milwaukee jazz adventures, story has it that outsized jazz character Fats Waller offered the youngster a drink.[2]

For the most part, Ruedebusch led a typical small-town, all-American childhood. His family owned a Ford dealership, which sold farm equipment. Ruedebusch played in the Mayville High School band and a smaller "dance unit" at school, but he also played football and basketball and was a conference champion in tennis. He was coeditor of the school's yearbook and was elected senior class president. At his high school graduation ceremony, not only did Ruedebusch give the "Address of Welcome," but he also played Herbert Clarke's classic variations on "Carnival of Venice" and, with a brass quartet, selections by Richard Wagner.[3]

Ruedebusch graduated from high school in 1943, and, at the height of World War II, entered military service. His musical talent was recognized, however, and rather than being sent into combat, he played with service bands at Fort Slocum, New Jersey, and Fort Hamilton, New York. His proximity to New York City allowed him, while on leaves, to sit in with some of the great big bands of the day—Gene Krupa, both Jimmy and Tommy Dorsey, and Wisconsinite Woody Herman, who later became an important figure in Ruedebusch's life.[4] His army unit was one of many that contributed to the war effort musically by broadcasting over the radio, and playing for servicemen and women in a variety of venues.

After his discharge from the service, Ruedebusch joined the family business. But his attraction to music was very strong. His father's attempt to keep Ruedebusch home by adding cars to the dealership proved unsuccessful.

At first, Ruedebusch played with area groups, including Earl Youngbeck and the Midnight Ramblers. With Winfred Herberg, he heard Eddie Getz's small group at the Stage Door in Milwaukee, and after sitting in for a set, Ruedebusch was invited to join the group anytime he was in town. Soon thereafter, the young trumpeter began attending the Dixie Bash sessions at Club Hollywood in Madison. He made his first record, a 45-rpm single, as Dick Ruedebusch and his State Street Ramblers for the Andoll Record Company in Baraboo.[5] His other workplaces in Madison included the French Villa and the Paladium Supper Club's Gold Room, which presented to its bands and audiences the competition of the loud racket from an upstairs bowling alley.[6] Ruedebusch's active group competed with rival groups on the UW campus including that of Dominic Spera (see chapter 17).[7]

Ruedebusch moved to "the big city," Milwaukee, and worked with Joe Gumin's band prior to bringing his own group to the Club Everleigh, on Center Street. When the Everleigh was damaged by fire, Dr. Keith Epperson, who had become an avid fan, bought and opened the Tunnel Inn on Front Street, across from the Pabst Theater. The club opened in 1959 specifically to provide Ruedebusch and his Underprivileged Five a home base. The band worked five nights a week at the club for years. At the club's opening, the band included Sammy Armato on clarinet, Bill Johnson on trombone, Orv Ehlenfelt on piano, Lee Burrows on bass, and Clyde Hornburg on drums.[8]

Armato (see chapter 4) was working days at WTMJ and decided to leave the band because he felt he couldn't keep his day gig and continue to work nights with Ruedebusch. The personnel eventually settled in with Chuck Hedges on clarinet, Sonny Sievert on trombone, Ron Martinson on piano, Burrows on bass, and Al Praefke on drums. Sievert put together many of the crowd-pleasing arrangements. At the Tunnel Inn, according to Hedges, "We were kings; no question about it. We could do no wrong; but we took care of business, too. And it was incredible."[9] Woody Herman, back in his hometown, stopped in at the club in 1961 and was knocked out by what he heard. With his long-standing clout in the business, Herman took on Ruedebusch as a project.

Herman made arrangements to bring the Underprivileged Five to New York. It worked for several weeks opposite Woody's Swingin' Herd at the Metropole jazz club. An even bigger coup was an appearance on Ed Sullivan's popular Sunday night television show in January 1962 (guest hosted by comedian Sid Caesar). According to Jack Baker, a telegram sent to Sullivan in appreciation for having Ruedebusch on the show contained 1,244 signatures.[10] Ruedebusch and the band received glowing reviews from the *New York Herald* and *Down Beat*. *New York Times* critic John Wilson wrote a favorable review of the band, but it was largely the personal story of a Midwestern boy breaking out of the family business and making it in the jazz world.[11]

Dick Ruedebusch. COURTESY OF THE MAYVILLE LIMESTONE SCHOOL MUSEUM

The band traveled cross-country from New York, playing Reno, Las Vegas, and Lake Tahoe, and back to Columbus and Pittsburgh. It even appeared at President John Kennedy's "winter White House" in Palm Beach, Florida.[12]

Hedges spoke of Ruedebusch as being "a very unsophisticated guy," but noted that "he had a tremendous, tremendous talent and an incredible work ethic, which is what led to his great playing."[13] People around the country seemed to relate to his clean-cut, "aw, shucks" personality: Baker quotes a reviewer who said that "Dick should have come out of the Midwest riding a white charger."[14] Ruedebusch was quoted in the family-oriented *Saturday Evening Post* as saying, "When we swing, we're swinging straight. Nobody's got a pill in him or a drink. It's a funny band—like a bunch of Boy Scouts." He went on, "I guess the reason I don't drink . . . is that my dad expects that's what I'd do, and I'm not going to give that to him!"[15]

Ruedebusch missed his family and the Midwest and returned later in 1962 to Milwaukee and the Tunnel Inn, where he and the band played for another three years, a residency interrupted only occasionally by trips to festivals and club dates out of town. In 1965, the Tunnel Inn was sold, and suddenly, but only briefly, the band had no home base. The group eventually settled at the Sheraton-Schroeder Hotel's Black Knight Room, where they also were broadcast on a weekly radio show.[16]

The Underprivileged Five disbanded on New Year's Eve in 1965. An announcement in the December 29, 1965, edition of the *Milwaukee Journal* reported that Ruedebusch went to Cocoa Beach, Florida, in January to join a newly formed band. It said that Ruedebusch "lost out to clarinetist Buddy De Franco for the job of front man for the new Glenn Miller Orchestra."[17]

But at about this same time, Woody Herman reappeared in Ruedebusch's life and career and evidently made him an offer he couldn't refuse. Sometime in 1966, Dick joined Woody's big band for a year of touring,[18] including three weeks in England, where Ruedebusch was hailed as "a magnificent find" and lauded for his "phenomenal technique and marvelous purity of tone."[19] However, he was not heard as a soloist on the records Woody made during Ruedebusch's time with the band. Additionally, Chuck Hedges said that Ruedebusch's playing was too "traditional" for the mostly young players then in the Herd, and that his superb abilities were appreciated by only a few who "knew."[20]

Ruedebusch returned to Milwaukee in 1967, but during the year he had been gone things had changed. With the Tunnel Inn and the Black Night Room no longer available, he ended up at the Tumblebrook Country Club in Waukesha County with a quartet. In 1968, Ruedebusch suffered a heart attack, and a day before he was to have bypass surgery, a massive coronary ended his life at age forty-four.[21]

One might argue, as many do in the cases of other jazz figures who have died young, that Ruedebusch had already outlived his time musically. Jazz-rock fusion was just about to take over as the dominant genre in jazz, and Ruedebusch's style was far removed from that trend. Yet had he lived longer, he likely would have reaped the benefits of musical "survivors" whose music reached a considerable audience later on, when audiences rediscovered the merits of more traditionally based styles. But this enormously talented musician will be remembered for years as a Wisconsin jazz legend.

Chuck Hedges

Happily, rediscovery was the fate that awaited clarinetist Chuck Hedges, who ended up leading the most distinguished career of any of the Underprivileged Five. Hedges (born in 1932) grew up in Chicago, and after attending a military academy for high school returned to his home city and became part of the music scene there in the mid-1950s.[22] Having been influenced by New Orleans clarinetists such as Alphonse Picou and Larry Shields, Hedges began his career working with some of the "names" of traditional jazz who were living and playing in Chicago, including trombonist George Brunies and cornetist Muggsy Spanier. Brunies was on location at the 1111 Club (where the band competed with the noise of the "L" trains overhead), and Hedges had many stories about just what made Brunies a legendary jazz character, besides his exceptional playing—putting Limburger cheese in others' instruments, setting fires under musicians' chairs, and playing many other practical jokes.

After scrambling for work, which included some "record turning," Hedges finally hooked up with trombonist Dave Remington when Remington took a band to the Wagon Wheel Resort in Rockton, Illinois, just south of Beloit, Wisconsin, in the late 1950s.[23] The traditional jazz group was one of several bands employed on the grounds. According to Hedges, the band played "six or seven hours a night" for a year and "tore the place up." It made a couple of records during that time. For a while, the trumpet player in the group was Oshkosh native Bobby Lewis, fresh out of high school, before he was drafted into military service. Disagreements with management led the group back to Chicago's Rush Street, but shortly thereafter Hedges, looking for a change of scenery, auditioned for Ruedebusch and joined the Underprivileged Five.

This was not Hedges's first time to Milwaukee, however. He recalled working in Milwaukee some years earlier with Wingy Manone (the "court jester" of Bing Crosby's radio show) at the Brass Rail, an "awful" club, according to Hedges, at Third and Wells. The club was run by Izzy Pogrob, a three-hundred-pound character with probable connections to the underworld, who disappeared one day in 1960 and whose body was discovered the next day in a Mequon field, an apparent robbery victim.[24]

Hedges had fond memories of his time with Ruedebusch and the Tunnel Inn. He had a great deal of respect and admiration for his colleagues in the Underprivileged Five, asserting that the group was not only a collection of talented individuals, but a real band. As he described it, "You'd [have to] be willing to take six men and be able to improvise, for the most part, ensemble, and give it a band sound. That took experience, years, knowledge; it took everything to get that whole ensemble and creative sound." Mixing the influence of his early heroes from New Orleans, the great Edmond Hall and swing giants Benny Goodman and Artie Shaw, Hedges developed a fluent style that was perfect for this band and, later, for other groups.

Around the same time that Ruedebusch went with Woody Herman in 1966, Hedges returned to the Wagon Wheel with a different band. While working there five nights a week, he learned instrument repair in an apprenticeship in nearby Rockford. Hedges quit playing for most of the next decade; repairing instruments (primarily at Cascio Music in Milwaukee) was his principal occupation.

In the late 1970s, Bobby Lewis convinced Hedges that it would be rewarding—both musically and financially—to reenter the scene on the festival circuit. By this time, many jazz festivals had been established across the United States, and they catered to the tastes of a wide range of jazz fans. Hedges usually played traditional jazz festivals, including the La Crosse Great River Jazz Festival in Wisconsin, now one of the top festivals of its kind. He played at La Crosse for years, often as part of the festival's house band.

These festival appearances revived Hedges's career not only in the United States, but internationally, as well; he toured Europe on a number of occasions, usually with trumpeter Wild Bill Davison (see chapter 4), whom Hedges met early in his career renaissance. Davison's biographer, Hal Willard, wrote, "Hedges could have played head-to-head with Benny Goodman on Goodman's best days and never missed a beat, and he could blow the well-known and much admired Pete Fountain down the road like a piece of chaff, which is only a little bit of hyperbole."[25] Hyperbole or not, Willard's praise is a good indication of the respect that Hedges had earned in his musical community.

While he often played with Davison, Hedges also played with some other fine jazz musicians over the years. Among hundreds, he developed meaningful relationships with drummers Barrett Deems, Ed Shaughnessy, and Butch Miles; bassists George Duvivier and Milt Hinton; and trombonist Bill Allred.

Starting in the 1980s, Hedges led a group on Monday nights at the Chicago jazz hot spot Andy's. When he established his Swingtet, little did anyone know that it would play those Monday nights for the next twenty years.

In the early 2000s, Hedges started up a Wisconsin group much like his Chicago Swingtet. The Wisconsin Connection recorded in 2001 with personnel that included Sheboygan guitarist Dave Sullivan (see chapter 18)

Chuck Hedges in the early 2000s. PHOTO BY JOE TONDU

and the Milwaukee-based trio of Gary Meisner on piano, Mike Britz on bass, and Andy LoDuca on drums. A 2007 album featured Hedges with what was, by then, the Milwaukee Connection: Sullivan, LoDuca, Bob Maynard on vibes, and George Welland on bass. When Hedges was forced to leave the band because of health problems in 2009, he was succeeded by John Blegen; Maynard and Welland remained, and new additions included Jack Carr on drums and Steve Lewandowski on guitar. That band worked a regular Thursday-night gig at the Grove in Elm Grove.

Hedges died on June 24, 2010, after a long battle with cancer. In July, a memorial party held in his honor at the Grove was attended by many musicians who had worked with him. A variety of combinations jammed over a long afternoon and evening for a large and enthusiastic audience of Hedges's admirers. The Milwaukee Connection, led by Lewandowski with Maynard, Welland, and Carr, continued to work (although the Grove closed in 2011).

As further proof of Hedges's legacy, Milwaukee's Jazz Unlimited jazz society has held annual memorial concerts in his honor. The MC Swingtet (as it was then known) performed at the 2012 Hedges Memorial Concert at Serb Hall at Oklahoma and Fifty-First Streets. The 2017 Hedges Memorial Concert, featuring the Milwaukee Connection and other musicians from Milwaukee and elsewhere, was held at the Sharon Lynne Wilson Center for the Arts in Brookfield. The memorials seem an appropriate way to honor one of the great contributors to jazz in Wisconsin, in Chicago, and even internationally.

Sig Millonzi

Outside of Dick Ruedebusch, probably the most visible jazz musician on the Milwaukee scene in the 1950s, 1960s, and into the 1970s was pianist Sigmund "Siggy" (or "Sig") Millonzi. Millonzi was born in Milwaukee on August 8, 1924, and grew up in the Bay View neighborhood.[26] Young Sig apparently began playing piano at the age of three and, according to a 1975 profile in *The Entertainer*, was "motivated by a close-knit and highly musical family that included a musician father, brother, uncles, and cousins."[27] By age thirteen, he led a big band that played for dances and social gatherings. The youngster studied classical piano at what was then known as the Wisconsin College of Music (which later merged with the Wisconsin Conservatory of Music). Millonzi went on to become one of Milwaukee's most celebrated jazzmen for much of his fairly short life.

After a stint in the service during World War II, Millonzi came back to Milwaukee and married his childhood sweetheart, Eileen, in 1946. He had a day job doing cement work, but both he and Eileen were constantly worried about the likelihood of his injuring his hands, so he soon became a full-time musician. By the early 1950s, Millonzi—whose name then usually appeared as Ziggy or Ziggie—was playing in a variety of venues in both Milwaukee and Chicago. One notice lists the duo of Millonzi and bassist Bill Erni featured at Michaelangelo's on Fond du Lac Avenue at Sixty-Second Street in Milwaukee. An ad for the Joker Club, at 1111 West Vliet Street, lists Ziggie Malonzi [*sic*] at the piano, perhaps with, or perhaps trading off with, Jerry King and His Famous Swing Combination.

Millonzi made his first real impression, however, playing in a trio with bassist Connie Milano and guitarist Don Momblow. Usually listed as the Mil-Con-Bo Trio (with or without the hyphens), the trio worked at the Streamliner and the Blue Note in Chicago, and the Towne Room ("Where Food Is King") in Milwaukee. Millonzi also appeared at Jimmy Fazio's, the Tic Toc Tap in Sheboygan, and the Tree Top Room in distant Moorhead, Minnesota. Although Milano's singing was one of the big selling points for the group, the band's first LP, released in 1955 under the name the Mil-Combo, was all instrumental. This was not just a local production, as it was released by the fairly new, important, and ambitious label Capitol Records. It was also reviewed in the *Chicago Daily Tribune* as well as in national publications *Billboard* and *Down Beat*, where it received a four-star review. *Billboard* reported, "Here comes a Milwaukee threesome to prove that accomplished practioners [*sic*] of modern jazz are not confined to the East and West coasts," and noted, "From the outset, pianist Ziggy Millonzi's fast fingerwork at the keyboard attracts attention."[28] The trio even went to New York, playing two weeks at Birdland ("the Jazz Corner of the World") opposite the Stan Kenton Orchestra.

The Mil-Con-Bo Trio. From top, Sig Millonzi, Don Momblow, Connie Milano. COURTESY OF THE SIG MILLONZI FAMILY

For whatever reasons, the trio decided not to go national and commit to an exhausting touring schedule, and eventually Millonzi began working as a single again, at such spots as the Top of the Marine on East Wisconsin Avenue in Milwaukee. In 1958, the local entertainment magazine *Going Places* ran a photo of Millonzi at Curro's (one of his steady gigs) on a page that also spotlighted Bill Otten at Blue Dahlia, Jean Carlton at Old Heidelberg, Gene Krupa at the Brass Rail, and a number of exotic dancers at some of Milwaukee's steamier entertainment venues.

By the mid- to late 1960s, Millonzi began performing as part of a trio again, and for a number of years the trio included bassist Lee Burrows and drummer Jack Carr. This group recorded the LP *Three Times Over* for

Millonzi's private label, Stacey Records, named for his young daughter. The album's liner notes were written by Harry John Brown, then conductor of the Milwaukee Symphony Orchestra. At this time, the trio was playing two nights a week at Ciro's in Brookfield while serving as the core for a larger Dixieland band at the new Someplace Else on Water Street downtown.

Around the mid-1960s, Millonzi also began leading a sextet, which continued for much of the rest of his life. This group was the trio plus, usually, trumpeter Walt Ketchum, clarinetist Chuck Hedges on saxophone, and trombonist Ted Torcivia. Hattush Alexander and Tony Pagano sometimes took the saxophone chair, and Kaye Berigan sometimes played trumpet.

Millonzi's bands contributed to the changing music scene in Milwaukee. An article for the *Journal* in January 1970 titled "Jazz Fights for Place in Rock 'n' Roll Town" quoted Millonzi as saying, "We have a minority audience that puts us on a pedestal. . . . Good music is at a premium and that's fine with me."[29] At the time the trio was working at Brothers Two on North Downer.

Over the years, Millonzi's groups played at the Pabst Theater, Lakefront Festival of the Arts, Cardinal Stritch College, and Enderis Playfield as part of the Municipal Recreation Department's summer evening concert series. A more sophisticated setting was one of the Milwaukee Symphony's early "Dimensions in Music" concerts, in the 1971–1972 season; Millonzi's composition "'Clairaudience,' for Jazz Trio and Orchestra" was premiered.

Millonzi had several periods of inactivity due to health problems. A photo of him appeared in the paper in 1967 with the caption "Splint at the Keyboard," showing Millonzi playing with a huge bandage covering his left hand. Apparently he had "jammed a screwdriver into his left hand," and the article explained that for his daily lunch hour gig at Frenchy's restaurant on North Avenue and his nighttime gig at the Grove on North Water Street, bassist Art Koenig had "assumed the duties of Millonzi's left hand." Additionally, in 1969, as he was working on remodeling the old Lake Theater on South Delaware into a recording studio, he developed pain in his left hand that led to surgery on his hand and elbow. Last, in October 1972, Millonzi suffered a serious heart attack. Six groups performed a benefit at the Imperial Ballroom two months later to help cover expenses while he was unable to work.

Millonzi did not appear as a performer again until the following summer at Summerfest, at the Miller Jazz Oasis. In a 1973 newspaper article by Rod French titled "You Would Hardly Know Sig Millonzi's Been Away," attention was drawn to the other members of the occasion's quintet—guitarist Manty Ellis, saxophonist Berkeley Fudge, drummer Carr, and an unidentified bassist. However, it is noteworthy that Millonzi was working with Ellis and Fudge, two of the most prominent members of Milwaukee's African American jazz community. These three had certainly known each other for years, but evidence suggests they rarely worked together until about this time.

One of Millonzi's most visible musical aggregations in Milwaukee was his big band. He initially formed the group for the first annual Dick Ruedebusch Memorial Concert in 1968. At various times, the band included such Milwaukee stalwarts as trumpeters Kaye Berigan, Ron DeVillers, and Tom Baker; trombonists Ralph Hutchinson, Bill Schaefgen, Herb Draeger, and Hary Kozlowski; saxophonists Ben Baldewitz, Hattush Alexander, Berkeley Fudge, John Kirchberger, Larry Lange, Tom Newburg, and Ray Rideout; and, in addition to Millonzi's normal trio as the rhythm section, Don Momblow on guitar.

In 1975, the band began playing every Monday night at Club Garibaldi, on the south side. It was a club where Millonzi had played when he was just thirteen years old. He called the big band venture "one of the best things I've ever been into."[30] Many other Milwaukee musicians would have agreed. Eventually, the band played some Friday nights at Pal Joey's in the Brownport shopping center, as well as at Brothers Two. It also made appearances at festivals, schools, and special occasions.

Upon Millonzi's death in 1977, a memorial concert was held in his honor at the Grand Ballroom of the Pfister Hotel. It was a massive affair, with many of Milwaukee's most prominent jazz groups performing. These included the Sig Millonzi Memorial Sextet, pianist Claude Dorsey, the Don Momblow & George Pritchett Duo, the Ray Tabs Trio & Penny Goodwin, the Manty Ellis Quintet with Berkeley Fudge, the Sig Millonzi Memorial Big Band, the Buddy Montgomery Septet, the Will Green Jam

Session, the Wisconsin Conservatory Jazz Ensemble No. 8, and the Beverly Pitts Trio with Mary White. In a lengthy article in the *Journal* in 1977, Bill Milkowski called the concert "Jazz at Its Best." Among the highlights was the premiere of "Song for Sig," written by Art Koenig, who by this time had moved to New York, often backing up singer Morgana King. Appropriately, it was played by the Millonzi big band. This great pianist, a Milwaukee icon, will live on in the city's memory.

Jack Carr

Jack Carr was born in 1940 in Indianapolis, where he attended grade school and learned to play drums.[31] He recalls,

> I guess I was always excited about playing drums, beating on things, taking knives and kitchen things and beating on the bottom of pots and pans in my mom's kitchen. When I was ten years old I had a paper route. . . . And there was an organization, the Indianapolis Newsboys Band, that you could join, and they would teach you how to play, and you could march in parades with the Newsboys Band. So I started doing that. And I had lessons once a week, and I learned to do all the basic rudiments, and they gave me a pair of sticks, and [I learned] how to read.

The following year Carr's father, who worked for General Motors, was transferred to Dayton, Ohio. "I continued taking lessons there," Carr says, "and just tried to play in all the bands I could, . . . whether it was an accordion band or a polka band or a neighborhood small band—just to play. And, finally the guy that was giving lessons to me, he said, essentially . . . 'Listen, you've learned about all you need to know to go out there; just go out there and play.'"

Carr attended Notre Dame University, where he says he was in almost every band there: "The marching band, the concert band, the pep band, the jazz band, the dance band." During his freshman year, in 1959, he was able to join a Dixieland band and travel with them on a nine-week tour of Europe. "That was a good summer," he recalls.

After another year of college, Carr's family moved to the Milwaukee area. He had two years left in college, but in the summers, he would play with dance bands and party bands in Waukesha County.

The summer of 1962, after Carr's senior year of college, while he waited to join the army that fall, he met and began to play with pianist Les Czimber (known in the music community by the nickname "Tarzan"). That summer, Carr joined Czimber and young bassist George Welland at the Driftwood Inn, on Capitol Drive, where young Al Jarreau often sat in. Later the trio moved to the Columns, inside the Pfister Hotel.

Once in the army, Carr was stationed in his hometown of Indianapolis. There was plenty of family around (think Sunday dinner with Grandma), but there was an amazing music scene as well. Notably, guitarist Wes Montgomery was still in town, just before he hit the national scene in a very big way. At jam sessions, Carr occasionally got to sit in with the great guitarist, as well as returning local heroes Freddie Hubbard, Slide Hampton, and David Baker when they were back in town.

Out of the service in the fall of 1964, Carr returned to Milwaukee. He remembers, "I decided, 'Well, before I put my education to work, I think I'll see what would happen if I tried to make a living playing.'" Carr quickly hooked up with Sig Millonzi (with Lee Burrows on bass) and played in Millonzi's small groups for five years. In addition to the venues mentioned earlier, Carr recalls the band having residencies at Someplace Else and Naughty Gal.

By the late 1960s, he realized that freelance musicians could not get insurance or credit, so he "got a legitimate job, if you call advertising a legitimate job." Carr kept his hand in music by playing weekend gigs when he could. After Millonzi died in 1977, Carr and trumpeter Ron DeVillers took over the Millonzi big band. For many years, this band doubled as the Packers band at County Stadium. The band also appeared at Summerfest, Jazz in the Park, and other special gigs. But interest in big bands "dwindled," and in 2014, Carr claimed that the remnants of this band had not had a big band gig in five years. "I got to be sixty-two years of age," he remembers, "and my wife said to me, God bless her, 'Why don't you retire early, and play more music?' 'Damn, woman, that's a good idea.' So I did."

And in fact, Carr did begin playing more. He played with the new big band of Gary Christensen and, separately, with clarinetist Chuck

From left to right: George Welland (see next section in this chapter), Dave Sullivan (see chapter 18), Jack Carr, and Chuck Hedges (see earlier in this chapter). COURTESY OF CAROLE HEDGES

Hedges. Since Hedges's passing in 2010, Carr has continued to work with the same band, the Milwaukee Connection. For a number of years, he has worked once a week with vocalist Jackson Dordel (with Ray Tabs on piano and keyboards) and frequently plays with groups led by trumpeter Kaye Berigan. Like other top Milwaukee pros, Carr has backed up many touring singers, comedians, and musical acts. He has been respected as one of the finest straight-ahead drummers in Milwaukee for decades and will be for years to come.

George Welland

Bassist George Welland (born in 1942) grew up in Appleton. In high school, he played in a good high school jazz band led by Russell Thorne, and he later attended UW–Milwaukee, where he earned a degree in music. During the summer of 1962, after his freshman year, Welland got a call to come down from Appleton to Milwaukee to play with Les Czimber and Jack Carr at the Driftwood. They played there six nights a week before moving downtown to the Columns in the Pfister Hotel. Welland also started working occasionally with Berkeley Fudge and Manty Ellis, and he had a gig of some length at Alfie's, at Teutonia and Atkinson. He worked enough to essentially pay his way through school. He even played in Dick Ruedebusch's band, before it left the Tunnel Inn.

Welland stayed at the Pfister for the better part of ten years, playing six nights a week for most of that time. From the Columns, he moved upstairs to the Crown Room, where he was leader of the house band for six years. For much of that time, the pianist in the trio was Santo Malio; Ronnie Martinson also played. Drummers who joined Welland during the period included Lou Lalli and Bob Budny.

At the Crown, Welland played with many touring greats, including Mel Tormé and Rosemary Clooney. He remembers especially clearly and fondly working with the singer Billy Eckstine. When Eckstine came to the Crown, he would bring with him a superb drummer, Charli Persip, and an excellent pianist, Bobby Tucker (who Welland knew as Bobby Thompson), but would not bring a bass player. Welland would play with them every time they came to town. In contrast, he regrets never being able to play with Sarah Vaughan, who always brought a complete rhythm section with her. It speaks to the vagaries of the business that jazz great Vaughan might be in for two weeks, only to be followed for two weeks by Frankie Avalon.

After graduation from UW–Milwaukee, Welland taught for many years in the Milwaukee public schools. First, he taught orchestra; later on, he was an early computer educator. He says, "I taught myself computers. I did that for a couple years, and I got a master's degree in educational psychology." Welland spent the latter part of his career in the school system as a guidance counselor at Juneau High School.

For two or three years in the 1970s, Welland taught at the Wisconsin Conservatory, playing in the faculty jazz group with Fudge, Ellis, Budny, and pianist Eddie Baker, who came up from Chicago. A feature on this group ("5 Jazz Teachers Help Weave Art from Chaos") appeared in the *Milwaukee Sentinel* in 1977, reporting on their collective work at the conservatory and publicizing a series of concerts that the combo would be performing over several months at the Skylight Theatre.

When the Grove in Elm Grove closed in 2011, Welland was playing there seventy nights a year. Like Jack Carr, Welland has been a prized commodity in Milwaukee for decades, not just for his excellent musicianship, but also for his ability to play in a variety of styles—with shows, with Kaye Berigan and other modern players, but also in the more traditional style of someone like Chuck Hedges.

Steve Lewandowski

Guitarist Steve Lewandowski, like Carr and Welland, has led a varied career in Milwaukee jazz. He was probably first recognized on the scene for his work with the fusion band Opus beginning in 1979 (see chapter 12). But Lewandowski branched out into other styles and has, as he says, "stayed alive" through a range of projects and gigs.

Born in 1954 and raised in Milwaukee, Lewandowski says he "learned how to play music from the very beginning as a drummer." He studied with Al Praefke, a famous Milwaukee drummer who also worked with Dick Ruedebusch at that time. Lewandowski remembers:

> At about eleven years of age, I decided to switch to guitar. So I stopped taking lessons with Al, and I basically was self-taught on the guitar from that time on. I did take lessons from Donnie Momblow. . . . I went to hear Donnie and George Pritchett, and [a] couple other guys in town—Dick Eliott was in Las Vegas at the time, but he was around, as well; he would come back to town. . . . But I learned to play guitar, self-taught, mostly through the rock music of the time in the 1960s.

Lewandowski attended Hamilton High School. He grew up in the neighborhood where the Dominguez family lived (see chapter 12), and he would work out with future professional bassists Peter and John Dominguez in his parents' basement. Lewandowski spent some years as a student at UW-Milwaukee, where he hooked up with the other members of Opus, and like so many others, he also attended the Wisconsin Conservatory for several years.

Like George Welland, Lewandowski also had a career in the Milwaukee Public Schools, teaching both mathematics and music. Incidentally, Lewandowski did his student teaching with Frank Dominguez (Frank DeMiles) as supervising teacher. Starting as a substitute teacher, Lewandowski eventually took a band position at Fulton Middle School (which was later renamed Malcolm X Academy). In 1991, he moved on to Lincoln Middle School of the Arts, where he did an administrative practicum that led him down a different path. He tried his hand at administration for a little while, but ultimately decided to return to teaching. At Milwaukee High School of the Arts, he led a dual life, teaching mathematics and leading a jazz guitar ensemble. He finished his teaching career (2004–2011) at the New School for Community Service.

After the heyday of Opus, Lewandowski worked, as he says, "a gajillion" jazz jobs all over the city with a variety of people. His longest-lasting job may have been at the Clock Steakhouse, where he played for something on the order of ten years. He also worked for many years with Chuck Hedges at the Grove in Elm Grove. In 2015, Lewandowski began a long-standing solo guitar gig at Ally's Bistro in Menomonee Falls. Similar to Carr, Welland, and others, Lewandowski has been a core rhythm player on the mainstream Milwaukee jazz scene for years, making many groups sound their best.

11

Modern Jazz in Milwaukee and the Wisconsin Conservatory

This chapter is about the standard-bearers of so-called "modern jazz" in Milwaukee. Modern jazz is the music that emerged in the 1940s as part of the revolution fomented by Charlie Parker, Dizzy Gillespie, Thelonious Monk, and others, and which is still central to much of today's jazz. There have been many prominent jazz musicians in and from Milwaukee since the 1940s, but two names tend to surface in any conversation about modern jazz in the city: Manty Ellis and Berkeley Fudge.

Manty Ellis

Manty (pronounced Man-*tee*) Ellis was born in the city on January 16, 1933.[1] "My old man [Grover Edwin Ellis] was [a] piano player," he says. "And Milwaukee, in the community where we came up, there was a lot of parties, house parties of people. And he was entertaining. He would go to a house party, and he played piano, and he'd sing, danced, did all that." Young Manty and many of his musical buddies lived in the Sixth Ward, where most families knew each other and the kids all went to Lincoln High School. One of those kids was Bunky Green (see later in this chapter), who left Milwaukee when he was fairly young and eventually gained a national reputation.

Ellis's first instrument was piano, and he started his playing career at age nine.[2] A big influence on his early playing was Carmen Cavallaro, who was known for his flashy technique but was hardly considered a jazz pianist. Willie Pickens, another up-and-coming Milwaukee pianist, told Ellis to start listening to bebop pianist Bud Powell. Ellis says he and Pickens (who was two years his elder) were "inseparable" as teenagers. The young musicians became ardent followers of Bud Powell, Parker, Gillespie, and then-lesser-known moderns such as Miles Davis, Fats Navarro, and Wardell Gray.

"Around here," Ellis recalls, "we had Billy Wallace, who was probably the best overall musician [among the younger set in Milwaukee]." Wallace eventually left Milwaukee with saxophonist Illinois Jacquet and went on to establish himself in Chicago, Seattle, Las Vegas, and Denver. The highlight of Wallace's jazz career may have been recording with Max Roach in 1957 (see online discography).

Pickens worked a lot of piano gigs as a teenager, and if a gig came up that he couldn't play, he would usually give it to Ellis. Many young players in the city performed with a big band called the Rhythm Kings, including Pickens and saxophonists Green and Frank Morgan. "I was the sub for piano," Ellis remembers, "because . . . reading was one of the things I wouldn't spend time on, because I knew so much about basic chords and things like that. You never called it theory in those days. And so Willie would learn the charts, and then he'd show them to me, and I could play them all."

As a teenager, Ellis took up guitar, which he would take to his piano gigs. He told journalist Aaron Cohen in 1997:

> Once I got the guitar, I spent all my time trying to learn it. . . . I'd take the guitar and amp to gigs when I was playing the piano and would practice before gigs and during the intermission. I was working with a saxophone player, drummer, and bass player. One night, I was practicing and when he went back onstage, I plugged my guitar in and the saxophonist didn't pay any attention. He just counted off the tune and I played the guitar. From that day forward, I never had to play any more piano.[3]

Ellis thought of the guitar as a keyboard, not as "strings," until he met Wes Montgomery in Chicago in 1961. "Now, I'm telling you, this was as amateurish as you could be," Ellis recalls, "and here's Wes Montgomery handing you his guitar. Man, that guitar weighed about 1,000 pounds. They talk about plans. A fighter talks about fight plans until he gets hit. Then the plan goes out the window. Oh man, that was the lesson of my life."[4] The lesson with Montgomery changed Ellis's conception of the guitar—how to play it, and how it could be used—and Ellis went on to become not only one of the top local guitarists in Milwaukee, but a backup "musician of choice" for touring musicians who came through the city.

One of Ellis's more notable jazz jobs was the long run he played with jazz legend Sonny Stitt in 1974. Stitt's uncle, whose surname was Boatner, ran a barbecue joint in Milwaukee with his wife, Jeanette, to whom Stitt was much closer than he was with his uncle. "Sonny, being the doper he was, was scheduled for hospitalization," Ellis explains.

> And we had to clean him up, to get him in the hospital. So he came [to Milwaukee] to stay with Jeanette [his aunt]. And on Richards and Burleigh was a place . . . called the Most. It had a stage in it. And Sonny came and looked at the stage and said, "I can stay here; give me a band, I'll play every night." So he's playing for nothing. He got ahold of me. [Organist] Will Green worked with him for a while. Melvin Rhyne worked with him for a while. And several drummers worked with him. And we stayed over there forty-nine straight nights, every night.

Ellis spent a short time in Oakland, California, but hated it and returned to Milwaukee in the early 1970s. At that time, jazz pianist Ray Tabs was working at Noll Piano, on Muskego Avenue, and got Ellis a job there tuning pianos. Shortly thereafter, a guy who moved pianos into the store rented Ellis a space for a brand-new music store at 1912 West Hampton Street. Ellis built a stage in the store and set up a piano, a drum set, and a bass amp. The store, called Ellis Music, would become part of his legacy.

The store opened during the heyday of the Jazz Gallery, a Milwaukee venue that hosted first-rate touring jazz artists. Many artists who came through town to play at the Gallery spent parts of their days at Ellis Music. Among those who spent time there were Lou Donaldson, Freddie Hubbard, George Benson, Mulgrew Miller, Frank Foster, Stanley Turrentine, and, according to Ellis, "the whole Duke Ellington band." Musicians would practice, hang out, or even sleep on the couch in the store's office. But Ellis says, "I never sold nothing," and eventually he had to close the store. Nevertheless, Manty Ellis and Ellis Music earned their place in the annals of Milwaukee's modern jazz history. Ellis's contribution to the Wisconsin Conservatory jazz program is discussed in Tony King's profile later in this chapter.

Berkeley Fudge

The other Milwaukee modern jazz icon, saxophonist Berkeley Fudge, was born in the city in November 1937 on Summer Street, a street that no longer exists.[5] His family moved to Ninth Street, and young Berkeley attended Lloyd Street School, followed by Lincoln Junior High and North Division High School, from which he graduated in 1956. Fudge grew up with his mother, as his parents split up when he was young. He took piano lessons as a youth but didn't enjoy them. He got back to music in high school in the early 1950s.

Besides playing in school, he played in the big band of Leonard Gay, eventually getting his chance to play one solo a night. After high school, he moved on to perform in the small group of a man known as "Little Bo." At that time, Fudge was playing alto saxophone. Soon, he started getting calls from a variety of groups and began playing in the numerous clubs in the neighborhood: the Flame, the Seville, the Rio, the Celebrity Club, Rancho's. Some of the musicians Fudge remembers from those days were tenor saxophonist Bobby Burdette, who worked at the Polka Dot, and organist/vocalist Mary White, who held forth at the 20-42 Club. Drummer Jimmy Duncan was also active on the scene. In addition to hosting jazz performances, these clubs had floor shows. Fudge formed a four-piece group that worked with singers, dancers, impersonators, and an emcee.

Fudge worked with Gay and was aware of some of the older musicians in the city, but, like Ellis, he was also interested in the music of Charlie Parker and his followers. Fudge pursued his interest in this music by studying with Bunky Green (only two years his senior) for

From left to right: Berkeley Fudge, Manty Ellis (see previous section in this chapter), and Jessie Hauck. COURTESY OF THE WISCONSIN CONSERVATORY OF MUSIC

several years. Surely he did not play bebop in the shows for which his band supplied music, but it's a pretty good bet that he did play bebop at times in those clubs.

While active in the music scene, Fudge, like so many musicians, had a series of day jobs; the longest lasting was with American Motors, where he worked for about five years. Finally, in the 1970s, Ellis connected Fudge with the Changing Education through the Arts (CETA) program that was associated with the Wisconsin Conservatory. Besides their association at the conservatory, Ellis and Fudge worked in a group together for twenty years, starting at the Hut on Twelfth Street and North Avenue.

Practically every Milwaukee musician that I've spoken with who was born in the 1950s or later and who plays modern jazz cites Fudge as one of their most important influences. While they marvel at his musicianship, and especially his ability to play long solos in which he never repeated himself, they rarely speak of a direct musical influence. Rather, they say something similar to what bassist Jim Paolo says:

> I owe everything to Berkeley about knowing how to . . . not just play jazz; it's not that he would tell you stuff. . . . He just kinda led by example. And he showed me how to relax with the music. There was never any stress or strain on his gigs. If I didn't know the tune, he'd do a different tune. . . . I mean he was just so generous. . . . I learned how to play jazz, how to listen, and how to do everything from him.

After being the dominant saxophonist on Milwaukee's scene for years, Fudge suffered a stroke in November 2010. A benefit to help with his medical expenses was held at the Jazz Estate shortly afterward by vocalist Adekola Adedapo, pianist Barry Velleman, trumpeter Allen Johnson, bassist John Price, and drummer Sam Belton, along with many other guest musicians.[6] In January 2011, the Wisconsin Conservatory put on another benefit featuring his faculty colleagues, including drummer Dave Bayles, trumpeter Jamie Breiwick, pianist Mark Davis, pianist/trombonist John Foshager, bassist Jim Paolo, singers Robin Pluer and Adekola Adedapo, guitarist Paul Silbergleit, and others.[7] Fudge has not returned to active playing but will always remain a revered figure in Milwaukee jazz.

Willie Pickens

Willie Pickens followed a different path. Born in Milwaukee in 1931, Pickens grew up in what is now known as the Bronzeville neighborhood, near Sixth and Walnut Streets. His mother was a pianist who taught Willie's older sister how to play classical music. Young Willie listened to piano in his house, but he also listened to the bands whose records and broadcasts were on the radio—Duke Ellington, Lionel Hampton, the Dorsey brothers, Artie Shaw, Benny Goodman, and even (as Willie described them) "Horace Heidt and his triple-tonguing trumpeters," and the "un-jazzy" band of Blue Barron.

The neighborhood, which is considered historically black, was ethnically diverse during Pickens's upbringing. "I lived next to a Jewish family," he remembered. "The other side of me was an Irish man that owned the laundry; my mother worked there and my aunt worked there. Up the street was an Italian family. And then in the back was a Czechoslovakian school, and church and all that. So I had all those influences in my development." And he was inspired by the variety of music in the neighborhood as well. "I liked the polkas," he said, "because I could hear them cats noodling in there."

Pickens got a taste of show business at a young age. Some of his earliest memories, even before he played the piano, involved him dancing. "This woman had a dance group," he remembered. "Her name was Mabel. And she had a revue where she had a chorus line, she had somebody playing spoons, somebody playing banjo, somebody playing a string in a tub, a guitar player, a saxophone player, a comedian, and I was the song and dance man. I had [a] little girl partner that I would waltz around with and sing to her." The revue performed in the Milwaukee suburbs, including Shorewood, and at clubs like the well-known Moon Glow. "I guess you would have to call it vaudeville," Pickens remembered with a laugh, "because I had . . . tails, a top hat and everything. So, I looked real professional."

Unlike his sister, Willie had no formal musical training until he reached high school; he had been playing piano at home by ear. As Pickens entered Lincoln High School, his sister was just finishing up there. She talked their mother into letting him take lessons from a now-forgotten instrumentalist who played classical piano and bass. Willie was very motivated, and after two years of study, he was already playing George Gershwin's formidable *Rhapsody in Blue*. From a mail order book that he purchased for a dollar forty-nine, Pickens learned basic harmony. In high school, he discovered the music of Parker, Gillespie, Powell, and Monk, and he listened to the more progressive big bands of Stan Kenton and Milwaukee's Woody Herman.

Pickens began working with bands as a teenager, including a band of mostly older players led by Bernie Young that played in the suburbs. Pickens claimed that at this time he "wasn't really good at improvising," but he could read the notes in the stock arrangements played by bands during this era. He also played with the aforementioned Rhythm Kings, led by trumpet player Russell Ennols. Pickens remembered playing gigs with other youngsters in such places as Lapham Park.[8] "We would play for those dances," he said, "and a lot of times it wasn't really [the Rhythm Kings], it was more or less a little five- or six-piece combo that we got to play. And we'd play . . . I think either Friday or Saturday night at the social center from maybe about . . . seven to nine, or seven to ten. . . . I think we were making six dollars apiece." They even played on an early television show, a Saturday afternoon show for young people on WTMJ. Pickens was also friends with Al Jarreau's older brother Emile, who, he said, "always used to be singing."

During this time, the only member of this young crowd who was officially studying jazz was Bunky Green; he studied saxophone and harmony, perhaps with Bert Bailey. For the others, Pickens remembered, "Training at that time came from listening, and from playing with older musicians [who] knew more."

In Pickens's mind, one particular gig stood out as an indicator of the climate of the times.

> We were booked up into Burlington, Wisconsin, for some kind of affair. And the racism at that time was of such a nature that there was no place for us to stay, even high school kids. So they put us in . . . the city jail or whatever it was. Nobody was in there; all these empty cells and all. So it was a ball for us, because we were playing around, having water fights and all that. . . . But I mean, just to think of the nature [of that]. . . . They couldn't put us up in the hotel or somewhere else; they put us in the city jail.

Pickens was not particularly influenced by any of the pianists in Milwaukee, but he was aware of Billy Wallace, who he considered the "most advanced" pianist in the city. He also remembered learning one lesson in his youth from an unnamed pianist, which he was able to relate with relish sixty-five years later:

> I was in high school, and he used to ask me to sit down and play, and I remember playing a tune, "Body and Soul." After I got through, he said, "Man, pump that left hand!" . . . Because you know, at that time, [playing] bebop, we weren't playing . . . stride stuff. He said, "Pump that," and it stuck in my mind for a long time. He said, "What do you want to be? A flunky for a horn player all your life?"

Pickens continued his classical studies, doing two years with Otho Tankersley, whose playing Pickens called "very sophisticated and effeminate." Then he went to the Wisconsin Conservatory, where he studied for a number of years, first with Nita Raschig and later Queron Doyster.

Pickens then went into military service. He spent his two-year stint in San Francisco, where he played a lot of clarinet (which he had picked up at the conservatory) as well as piano.

Returning home, Pickens learned of the opportunity he had to go to school with financing from the GI Bill. He entered what was then Wisconsin State College–Milwaukee, which became the University of Wisconsin–Milwaukee before he graduated. Pickens still aspired to become a classical musician, but his teachers warned him that it would be a difficult way to make a living. "So they counseled me to get a degree in music education," he said, "which I did. I wound up with a degree [in 1958] in . . . vocal and instrumental music."

Pickens's life took another turn when he took a duo gig at a Chicago club, the Domino, with Milwaukee bassist Connie Milano (who was working mostly with Siggy Millonzi and Don Momblow at the time). Having found what he called a "fertile area" for jazz, playing with locals such as drummer Wilbur Campbell, bassist Victor Sproles, multi-instrumentalist Ira Sullivan, and the superb pianist Andrew Hill, Pickens decided to stay in Chicago.

Pickens came to national attention in 1961 with the recording of Chicago saxophonist Eddie Harris's album *Exodus to Jazz*. The theme from the then-current hit movie *Exodus* may have seemed an unlikely jazz vehicle, but Harris's recording made a splash. The band appeared that summer at the Newport Jazz Festival in Rhode Island.

Pickens was making a go of it as a freelance pianist, but as his family grew, he realized that he needed a steady source of income. After he applied for all sorts of day gigs, and often was told that he was overqualified for the positions, a fellow musician suggested that he go to the Chicago school board and inquire about a teaching position. When Pickens went to Lindbloom High School to see about the band director position, he was offered the job and told to start work the next day. He went on to lead the Lindbloom band to a superior rating at contest that year, something they

Willie Pickens, 1988. PHOTO BY DENNIS OWSLEY

had not accomplished in years. However, as the most recent hire, he was let go at the end of the year when someone with seniority from another school moved in. After being hired and similarly dumped by the brand-new Kenwood High, Pickens went on to Wendell Phillips High School, where he remained as band director until 1990.

In the meantime, Pickens became the house pianist at Chicago's most famous and long-lived jazz club, the Jazz Showcase. Many featured performers came to the Showcase as "singles," soloists who would play their engagement with a local rhythm section. More often than not, the rhythm section included Pickens on piano. Over his decades spent at the Showcase, Pickens played with Gene Ammons, Sonny Stitt, Zoot Sims,

Lee Konitz, Art Farmer, Slide Hampton, and Dexter Gordon, to name just a few. In other venues, he accompanied such singers as Sammy Davis Jr. and Johnny Hartman.

During the 1970s and 1980s, having established himself in Chicago with both a full-time teaching position and a tremendous amount of jazz playing, Pickens was able to spend time with his family, including attending the recitals and performances of his talented daughter, Bethany. But in 1990, when offered a chance to tour with jazz drumming legend Elvin Jones, Pickens retired from his teaching position and hit the road. He toured with Jones for about five years, playing in clubs, at festivals, at Carnegie Hall, and in Europe and Japan. (Gregory Tardy worked in Jones's band with Pickens and later wrote and recorded a piece in Willie's honor, "Blues to Professor Pickens"; see chapter 9.)

Back in Chicago after leaving Jones's group, Pickens continued work at the Showcase, also bringing jazz into church services (see online discography) and initiating a "Jazz Christmas" program at his church, the Hyde Park Union Church, that ran from 1995 to 2012 and brought in such guest artists as Branford Marsalis, Pickens's childhood friend Bunky Green, Charles McPherson, and Michael Brecker. In the 1990s, Pickens also began teaching at Northern Illinois University, where Milwaukee piano phenom Dan Nimmer (see chapter 7) became one of his students.

Milwaukeean Willie Pickens's contributions to jazz life in his hometown, his adopted hometown, and the wider jazz community made him one of Wisconsin's most important jazz figures. In what was a fitting capstone to Pickens's career, the Jazz Education Network presented him with its Donald Meade Legacy Jazz Griot Award at its annual conference in New Orleans in January 2017. Pickens died while practicing before a gig at Jazz at Lincoln Center in December 2017.

Bunky Green

Vernice "Bunky" Green was born in Milwaukee in 1935.[9] Some of his early work in the city has already been mentioned in the sections on Manty Ellis and Willie Pickens. In 2011, he recalled working with Billy Wallace and Willie Pickens while still in Milwaukee in the mid-1950s, perhaps while he attended what was reported in *Down Beat* as Milwaukee Teachers

College (probably what became UW–Milwaukee). Green played in New York on a short tour with jazz giant Charles Mingus by late 1956. But he moved back to the Midwest, to Chicago, around 1960, when he led his first recording session as a leader. He returned to school at Wright Junior College and won awards at the Notre Dame Collegiate Jazz Festival. In 1965 and 1966 he recorded two more albums as a leader (see online discography).

While several of Green's albums garnered national notice and he was respected regionally, he was primarily known as a jazz educator. He taught at Chicago State University from 1972 until 1989. Occasionally the wider jazz world was reminded of his unique voice, as upon the release of his 1990 album, *Healing the Pain*, which received a five-star review in *Down Beat*. Green moved to teach at the University of North Florida in 1990 and served as head of that distinguished program until his retirement in 2011, upon which he received considerable acclaim and several honors for his educational work. (For several years at North Florida, Green was a colleague of Lynne Arriale; see chapter 7.)

Later in his career, Green was rediscovered by younger generations of saxophonists, and he performed with such well-known figures as Steve Coleman and Greg Osby (in the 1970s) and Rudresh Mahanthappa (in the 1990s). Upon the release of one collaborative album, Green and Mahanthappa appeared on the cover, and in the accompanying cover story, of the February 2011 issue of *Down Beat*.

Frank Morgan

Saxophonist Frank Morgan was born in Minneapolis in 1933. His father was Stanley Morgan, the guitarist with the popular 1930s and 1940s vocal group the Ink Spots, which was inducted into the Rock and Roll Hall of Fame in 1989.[10] According to Manty Ellis, Morgan moved to Milwaukee at the age of five or six to live with his grandmother. He spent a good bit of his youth in Milwaukee while he was developing as a musician. In an interview late in his life, Morgan recalled studying with "the great saxophonist" Leonard Gay.[11] Ellis says that Morgan was already smoking dope by the time he was twelve or thirteen, an ominous omen of what was to come in his later life.

Morgan moved to the West Coast with his family in 1947 and came of age in the post–World War II jazz scene in southern California. Through his father, Morgan met many musicians, including Charlie Parker, with whom he hung out a number of times. The same year that Morgan recorded his first album as leader and was hailed as a successor to the recently deceased Parker (1955), he was incarcerated for drug possession. Morgan's drug use has been attributed to his desire to emulate Parker and copy his musical lead.

Morgan spent much of the next three decades in prison for drug offenses. Miraculously, he reemerged in the mid-1980s and went on to lead a highly successful jazz career until his death. During the 1990s, he moved back to Milwaukee and spent some time living with Manty Ellis. He also worked with a number of younger Milwaukee musicians, including Jeff Hamann, Dave Bayles, Rick Germanson, and former Milwaukeean Skip Crumby-Bey. In 1998, Morgan suffered a stroke and was largely inactive until 2003, when he made another successful comeback. He recorded numerous albums from 1985 until his death in 2007, some of which are listed in the discography. In the mid-2010s, detective novelist Michael Connelly, who referenced Morgan's music in a number of his popular Harry Bosch novels, was the moving force behind a well-received documentary on Morgan, *Sound of Redemption: The Frank Morgan Story.*

Tony King

The Wisconsin Conservatory of Music has been important in the continuity of the modern jazz tradition in Milwaukee for decades. Although Manty Ellis is respected as one of the finest players in Milwaukee, his legendary status has resulted at least as much from his role in jazz education as from his playing. Along with Tony King, Manty established the jazz program at the Wisconsin Conservatory that became the breeding ground for many of Milwaukee's best jazz artists of the next several generations.

King was a larger-than-life figure who was the brains behind the new program, and Ellis calls him a genius. While the details of his life are hard to pin down, Ellis remembers King being from Springfield, Illinois, and studying music in college, perhaps at Tennessee State University. Ellis laughingly recalls King's modus operandi as a pianist who worked as a single: "He'd sit down at the piano, play a couple chords and start talking, and people sitting around the piano, man, he'd have people crowded around, and he don't play another note. He'd just talk, you know?"

A road warrior, King eventually came to Wisconsin and worked all over the state. "He bought a home here," Ellis remembers, "and when I was a little kid, we used to go by; my buddies lived right next door to him. He was always on the road, but when his car was there we knew he was home, and he had to sleep. So we'd heckle him."

"Wisconsin's such a horrible state," King once told Ellis. "When I come here, I was working in Green Bay, and every night, when I finished the gig, I couldn't stay in town. I had to get out of town to sleep in my car on the highway. . . . I was six or seven weeks doing that."

Ellis continues the story: "I said, 'Man, that must have been horrible.' He says, 'It worked to my advantage.' I said, 'Why?' He said, 'I just had to buy car batteries.' I said, 'Why?' He said, ''Cause I kept the lights on and I read all night.' "

King attributed his lifelong love of reading and learning to the Jim Crow discrimination he faced as a kid in Springfield. He wanted to pass along his love of learning and to teach Milwaukee jazz musicians their craft. In our interview, Ellis described the genesis of the program at the conservatory:

> Matter of fact, that jazz program from the conservatory was constructed right there [in his living room] where that grand [piano] is sitting. We sat there, day after day, for years, like these three years, with him writing up the program and everything. When we got it all set, he said, "Now I'm gonna present this." He says, "We should shake up the world." [*Laughter*] And honestly, I didn't believe what he was doing. When he got through, and wrote all this up, he said, "I'm getting old. . . . I don't have no legs. Man," he says, "you put it in action." And he hands me this program, point blank. I'm reading this program, reading, reading; man, I gotta go out. I gotta . . . come up with a budget, for equipment that we need. I'm gonna have to formulate a faculty that will be conducive to what Tony King and I

Wisconsin Conservatory's award-winning combo in the early 1980s. Standing from left to right: Manty Ellis (see earlier in this chapter), Brian Lynch (see chapter 9), Charles Small, Marcus Robinson, Hary Kozlowski, Rolla Armstead, and Jeff Chambers. Seated: Sam Belton (see later in this chapter). COURTESY OF THE WISCONSIN CONSERVATORY OF MUSIC

> [had conceived]. . . . He's a genius, and I'm trying to satisfy him. But he taught me every day for twenty years, man.

Early in the program's existence, it was blessed with a brilliant group of students who could carry out King and Ellis's vision. Ellis worked with a combo that included trumpeter Brian Lynch, saxophonist Rolla Armstead, trombonist Hary Kozlowski, pianist Marcus Robinson, bassist Jeff Chambers, drummer Sam Belton, and, later, guitarist Charles Small. This group had tremendous success on the college festival circuit, especially at the Notre Dame Collegiate Jazz Festival, one of the country's largest and most prestigious festivals for college groups in the late 1970s. The group was recognized, and Robinson, Lynch, and Small won individual awards as well. In Ellis's words, "We wiped that out three times in a row, and the third time, Father Wiskirchen, who was in charge down there, invited Tony and myself to breakfast the next morning, after . . . we had all these awards. . . . And in so many words, he asked us not to come back down there."

Tony King teaching at the Wisconsin Conservatory. COURTESY OF THE WISCONSIN CONSERVATORY OF MUSIC

Brian Lynch says, "When I got to the conservatory . . . I met Tony King. And he was a very inspiring person in terms of his attitude and . . . the vision that he had about the music. And I think he knew where it was going and he couldn't keep the music. . . . It was black music, but you couldn't hold it there."

Tony King, Manty Ellis, and Berkeley Fudge influenced a host of younger musicians. Two of those, Brian Lynch and David Hazeltine, went on to international prominence and are discussed in earlier chapters.

From the first combos that Ellis led at the Wisconsin Conservatory, several other players went on to careers in music. Guitarist Charles Small has lived in southern California for many years and is best known for his work with vocalist Barbara Morrison. Bassist Jeff Chambers, after leaving Buddy Montgomery's trio in Milwaukee, has had a tremendously successful career. He has worked with a long list of important jazz musicians and recorded with Buddy Montgomery, Marlena Shaw (along with David Hazeltine), Ahmad Jamal, Charlie Rouse, Freddie Hubbard, and many others.[12] He resides in the San Francisco Bay area, where he performs, records, and teaches extensively.

After twelve years of success, mixed with some frustration, Ellis left the conservatory in 1984; he was still an active player in 2017. King died in 1990. He will never be forgotten by the musicians he mentored, and for the program he masterminded.

Buddy Montgomery

A significant chapter in the story of modern jazz in Milwaukee was the roughly twelve-year residence of Indianapolis native Buddy Montgomery.[13] Montgomery was a member of a musically accomplished family. His oldest brother, Monk (1921–1982), was best known as a pioneer of the electric bass, and his middle brother, Wes (1923–1968), is almost universally considered the most important jazz guitarist of his generation.

Buddy was born in 1930. Influenced by his sister Lena, Buddy took up piano as a youth, and at age eighteen, he went on the road with blues singer Big Joe Turner. He returned to Indianapolis to play with his brothers and other local musicians. Buddy entered the service but could not play in a service band because of his inability to read music. Upon discharge, in 1951, he joined another Indianapolis family band, the Hamptons (which included future trombone great Slide Hampton). Shortly thereafter, the Montgomery Johnson Quintet was established, including Buddy, brothers Monk and Wes, Robert "Sonny" Johnson, and Alonzo "Pookie" Johnson. In the mid-1950s, Buddy took up vibraphone as well.

Buddy formed the Mastersounds in Seattle in 1957, with brother Monk on bass, Richie Crabtree on piano, and Benny Barth on drums. The band moved to San Francisco and became one of the hottest groups in the country. Their first album, *Introducing the Mastersounds*, became a best seller. Their second album, *The King and I*, a jazz version of the musical, was another jazz hit. In 1958, Buddy and the Mastersounds made a splash in *Down Beat*'s polls. Crabtree later moved to Milwaukee and became an important pianist on the scene there.

After the Mastersounds disbanded in 1960, Montgomery was briefly with Miles Davis's group. But he spent much of the 1960s working and recording with his brothers until Wes's death in 1968.

In 1969, Buddy moved to Milwaukee.[14] According to Manty Ellis, the Montgomery Brothers band played a gig at one of the city's Mafia-run

Buddy Montgomery. ©RAY AVERY/CTS IMAGES

restaurants, and one of the younger female members of the "family" took a liking to Buddy, and he to her. Not long afterward, he moved in with the woman, named Rosie, in Milwaukee.[15]

Montgomery remained in the city for about twelve years and was a major musical force for most of that time. He was probably best known for his long residencies at the Bombay Bicycle Club in the Marc Plaza Hotel and at the Pfister Hotel. He often worked as a solo pianist, but the trio of Montgomery and two young Milwaukeeans, bassist Jeff Chambers and drummer Sam Belton, was an important group. Later versions of the small group included percussionist Dumah Safir, local drummer Andy LoDuca, and another Indianapolis transplant, drummer "Killer Ray" Appleton.

Brian Lynch, who lived in Milwaukee during Montgomery's residency, says: "Buddy was a super-big influence on all of us [younger players]. I mean, David [Hazeltine] and myself, and other people, especially. I played with him probably way before I even had a right to. But he was very open to [having us] come down and sit in with him any time."

Montgomery was not just a local player, however. Journalist Michael Drew recalled, in a memorial piece on Buddy, that a "concert he promoted in 1971 at the old Palace Theater attracted some of the music's biggest names at the time: the Freddie Hubbard Quintet, singer Joe Williams, and groups fronted by McCoy Tyner and Eddie Harris."[16]

Montgomery taught for a time at the conservatory, and he also formed the Milwaukee Jazz Alliance. According to Ben Barbera's master's thesis, Montgomery formed the Milwaukee Jazz Alliance "with the goal of creating a larger audience and fostering growth in the jazz community." During its short life, it sponsored performances in clubs in black neighborhoods, the Upper East Side, and downtown.[17]

Shortly after taking up residence in Milwaukee, Montgomery recorded an album for what was then the hottest label in jazz, Impulse! *This Rather Than That*, recorded in Chicago in September 1969, included Manty Ellis on guitar and Melvin Rhyne on keyboards (see online discography).[18]

Early in the 1980s, Montgomery went to Las Vegas, where his brother Monk was suffering from cancer. After Monk's death, Buddy moved on to California. In 1989, he went to New York and held a "house" job at the Hotel Parker Meridien for four years. He then moved to southern California, where he lived and worked until his death in 2009. His last trip to Wisconsin was for an appearance at Mequon's Gathering on the Green in 2006.

Melvin Rhyne

Born in 1936 in Indianapolis, keyboard player Melvin Rhyne, like the Montgomery Brothers, developed on the fertile club scene in "Nap Town" and is widely reported as working with a young Roland (later Rahsaan Roland) Kirk by 1955. When Wes Montgomery was "discovered" by the larger jazz community, he made his first recording as leader in the format with which he was comfortable, a traditional organ trio. This trio was comprised of Montgomery; Paul Parker on drums; and on organ, Rhyne, with whom Montgomery had played and worked for years (see online discography). Rhyne toured with Montgomery off and on between 1959 and 1964.[19]

According to Manty Ellis, Rhyne made the move to Wisconsin because of the rampant Jim Crow discrimination that existed at that time in Indianapolis. Others have speculated that the jazz scene in Indianapolis was just closing down. Although the documentation is sketchy, sources suggest that Rhyne moved to Madison around 1969 and worked with his brother Ron (a drummer) and guitarist Johnny Shacklett (see chapter 14). Guitarist Jack Grassel, one of Rhyne's frequent musical companions, estimates that Rhyne lived in Milwaukee for twenty-five years after spending a few years in Madison.[20] Other sources claim Rhyne moved to Milwaukee in 1973.

Rhyne played organ on Buddy Montgomery's 1969 record *This Rather Than That*. Occasionally they would collaborate, with Montgomery on vibes, but the two keyboard players rarely performed together. Rhyne's exceptional musical abilities made him a valued player in Milwaukee, and he worked with most of the city's "usual suspects," including, of course, Ellis and Fudge. Working with Rhyne, however, could present challenges. Jack Grassel remembers:

> I used to play with Mel occasionally at after-hours ghetto bars with almost no audience. Each tune would be about an hour long. We'd play two to three tunes on a whole gig. He has the capability of playing anything in all twelve keys. He has no song list and can learn any song instantly upon one hearing. So if he heard something on his car radio on the way to the gig, he would play it on the gig. He never told us what key, the name of the song, tempo, or counted anything off. There were no charts. He would just start to play. I had to memorize the entire tune in whatever key it was in upon one hearing in case he had me play the first

> solo. It raised the skills of anyone who played with him to a very high level.

In a much different setting, Rhyne worked with vocalist Jackie Allen when she landed the house job at the Wyndham Hotel in the late 1980s. (Rhyne appears in the photo that accompanies Jackie Allen's profile in chapter 13.) "I learned so much from him," Allen wrote in the liner notes of her 1999 album, *Which?*, "like how to swing, how to develop a repertoire. He is a master."[21] Rhyne also worked with singer Adekola Adedapo off and on during the 1990s and into the early 2000s at the Wyndham, the Jazz Estate, and the Main Event. Brian Lynch refers to Rhyne as "another fantastic influence" on his development.

While still in Milwaukee, Rhyne began to return to national prominence in the 1990s with a series of albums that continued well into the 2000s. After he played on an album by guitarist Herb Ellis, Brian Lynch asked Rhyne to appear on his album *At the Main Event*, recorded in December 1991. The head of Criss Cross Records was so pleased with what he heard on the Lynch session that he asked Rhyne to record a full session as leader the next day. That resulted in *The Legend*, which, incidentally, was issued two years before the Lynch disc.

Rhyne continued to record through the 2000s while living mostly in Indianapolis. He died there in 2013, having made a lasting mark in the world of modern jazz.

Sam Belton

One of the most interesting of those careers to emerge from the conservatory has been that of drummer Sam Belton. He was born in Milwaukee in 1952 and grew up there; for many years, his parents ran the Vine Street Tap, at Fourth and Vine Streets. He attended Keefe Avenue Elementary School, then E. L. Philipp Junior High. "I started to teach myself drums in the middle school," Belton recalls, "[in] about seventh or eighth grade. I just got interested in playing drums, after playing clarinet. Then I studied with Roy Schneider, the drum instructor in the Milwaukee public schools." Sam went on to Rufus King High School, where he played in marching band and orchestra; the school had no jazz band. He was inspired by an older drummer at King, future Milwaukee music professional Victor Soward.

One of Belton's most memorable experiences at this time was backing up Milwaukee legend Satin Doll at her lounge on West Fond du Lac Avenue, after sneaking in because he was underage. All high school students had out-of-school bands in the late 1960s, Belton remembers. "And so I played with several different bands at that time," he says. "I'm playing Chicago, and Sly and the Family Stone, and all of that. But the first tune I learned to play, what inspired me really to play drums, was Brubeck's 'Take Five.'"

One of those bands, the Showstoppers, went on the road as Our Father's Children; Belton traveled with them for about a year, until he discovered his partner was pregnant. "I was on the road," he recalls, "and I had a little girl on the way, so I decided I was coming back home. So I left the group, came back home. And that's when I made the decision to go to the conservatory. And it was the very earliest part of [the jazz program's] beginning."

At the conservatory, Belton took lessons with Vic Soward, and with Tele Lesbines, timpanist with the Milwaukee Symphony Orchestra. Like so many others, he was inspired by Tony King, "not just musically, but lifewise." Belton and bassist Jeff Chambers were tapped to play in Buddy Montgomery's trio at the Bombay Bicycle Club, which Belton did for about a year. During that period, he says he was "at the top of my game" as a drummer.

Around this time, Belton says, "I got saved; I got born again." And his new Christian faith made him increasingly uncomfortable in nightclub life:

> I just made a decision; I didn't want to be bothered with the clubs anymore. That's when I left the group. And . . . most people, they kind of thought I had stopped playing; but I hadn't really stopped playing. I was playing a lot of gospel and really getting my spiritual act together; my relationship with God. . . . I was ordained in the ministry in 1979.

Belton has continued his ministry to this day. He is a senior pastor at Spirit of World Truth Ministries and has had the opportunity to travel all over the world, primarily to various destinations in Africa as well as Russia and Central America.

The ministry remained Belton's primary career for quite some time. But around 1990, he had the urge to do something different. "I had basically finished my performance degree at the Wisconsin Conservatory," he says, but he needed certification in order to teach in public schools. "I decided that I wanted to go get my papers; so I went to Alverno [College]. I was the only male going there at that time, to be certified. I got certified [in] K–12 instrumental, general music, and choral." He taught in the Milwaukee public schools at Burroughs Elementary and Alexander Mitchell Integrated Arts Elementary School, and for nine years at the MacDowell Montessori School. At McDowell, Belton led choral groups, started bands, and even launched a recorder ensemble. He also gained some notoriety for writing a rap for the school system, "Be Cool, Stay in School." Over the years, he also taught at Alverno and at the conservatory. Cliff Gribble hired Belton onto the staff of the Milwaukee Youth Symphony Orchestra jazz program in 2006.

In the early 2000s, Belton explains, "I started getting involved in the coffee industry. So we have a place up on Seventy-Second and Burleigh that we opened up some years back." That establishment, CITY.NET Café, has become so successful that as of 2015, it had four Milwaukee locations. Jazz artwork decorates the downtown location; jazz plays over the sound system, and there is frequent live jazz as well.

As if he weren't busy enough, lately Sam has been more active on Milwaukee's jazz scene than he was for years. He led a band on the Milwaukee Jazz Visions' Visions on the Lake concert at the Summerfest grounds in August 2015. Belton and the jazz that he has played, promoted, and inspired will continue to influence the city of Milwaukee for years to come.

Mark Davis

While David Hazeltine (see chapter 7) revived the conservatory jazz program and became its moving force for a number of years, pianist Mark Davis took over the program in 1993. Along with bassist Jeff Hamann and drummer David Bayles, Davis also became a core member of the important rhythm section that spearheaded the next generation of modern jazz in Milwaukee. All three are on staff at the conservatory and form the backbone of the conservatory's performing faculty jazz groups, We Six and the We Six Trio (Davis appears in the photo that accompanies David Bayles's profile later in this chapter).

Davis was born in 1969 and grew up in Wauwautosa. His father, a campus minister at Marquette University, was instrumental in setting up the Coffee House, a "folksy hangout" in the basement of Redeemer Lutheran Church in downtown Milwaukee (Nineteenth and Wisconsin). The many nights Mark spent listening to music there when he was young probably had something to do with his future. "I was hanging out at music clubs," he remembers, "and around musicians, and we had folk musicians staying at our house." Davis also heard his first jazz pianist there, Milwaukeean Claude Dorsey, who attended the church and occasionally played at the coffee house.

Davis started piano lessons in third grade and was an enthusiastic student, in part because he was allowed to improvise right away. While a middle school student (in the early 1980s), he began lessons at the Wisconsin Conservatory with a Milwaukee legend, Adelaide Banaszynski. "Miss B," as she was called, was an "old school" classical teacher. Davis's time at the conservatory stirred up his interest in jazz, and he began to check out records of such pianists as Erroll Garner and Oscar Peterson from the library.

Around this time, someone encouraged Davis to study with David Hazeltine, who had recently returned from his first foray into the New York City scene. Davis began lessons with Hazeltine in 1984. A year later, he joined a combo at the conservatory and was in classes led by Manty Ellis and Berkeley Fudge.

Davis studied with Hazeltine through high school, and Hazeltine introduced him to the local jazz scene. By the time he was sixteen, Davis was working in clubs, notably, the Jazz Oasis and the Jazz Estate. He spent many nights at Chip and Py's, on Fifth and National, where Hazeltine had a duo with bassist Gerald Cannon. Occasionally Davis was able to play with Cannon, Fudge, and Hattush Alexander. Hazeltine, however, was the big influence. "My dad passed away when I was a junior in high school," Davis says. "Dave really kind of took me under his wing at that point, and we hung out a lot together, and he'd take me around to record stores and clubs. And you know, we just did a lot of stuff together. He was definitely just an enormous influence on me."

After graduating from high school in 1987, Davis went east to Skidmore College in Saratoga Springs, New York, to study visual art. But once he got there, he says, "I just practiced like a maniac." He often played with saxophonist Mark Vinci, who taught at Skidmore and was also (and remains) an active player in New York City. Davis played a few gigs in the Big Apple during this time.

After graduating in only three years, he returned to Milwaukee in 1990. He played gigs at the Oasis and elsewhere and started teaching private lessons. In 1992, when Hazeltine went back to New York, he recommended Davis to replace him at the conservatory. Since that time, Davis has been, arguably, Milwaukee's most important pianist.

At the conservatory, Davis connected with saxophonist Charles McPherson, perhaps best-known for his work with Charles Mingus. McPherson had been a mentor for Brian Lynch in San Diego and was invited by Lynch to visit the conservatory. McPherson enjoyed the conservatory rhythm section so much that he hired Davis, Jeff Hamann, and former Milwaukeean Brian Ritter to accompany him on various dates in the Midwest, especially for his visits to the Jazz Showcase in Chicago.

After shoring up the jazz program at the conservatory, Davis also built what is now known as the Jazz Institute (at the conservatory) into a much healthier program. In the last several years, the institute's Batterman student ensemble has been selected twice to perform at the Charles Mingus Festival and Competition in New York (winning the Spirit Award in 2013), received an outstanding performance award from *Down Beat* magazine, and was invited to perform at the Jazz Education Network's 2016 convention. Just as David Hazeltine passed the jazz mantle on to Davis, Davis is passing it on to future generations of Milwaukee musicians.

Jeff Hamann

Bassist Jeff Hamann was born in 1968 and grew up in the Milwaukee suburbs of Elm Grove and Brookfield. At the recommendation of a friend, he began attending the Wisconsin Conservatory in the early

1980s, as a junior high student. In that environment, he was heavily influenced by Berkeley Fudge, Manty Ellis, and David Hazeltine. Hamann started playing the drums and was skilled enough to be selected to play in the State Honors Jazz Ensemble in 1985 (along with Geoffrey Keezer), but after switching to bass, Jeff took lessons from Gerald Cannon. He was also motivated by other students who attended the conservatory or were working around town: Mark Davis, David Bayles, saxophonist Juli Wood, and pianist/trombonist John Foshager. Describing his time at the conservatory, Hamann says, "Not only do you get to meet the great players [his teachers], but you meet people of your age that are going to pursue it also; a group of friends that you can have a group with and go from there."

Once he switched instruments, Hamann found himself in an ideal situation. "I got a gig right when I started playing bass," he remembers, "in Embassy Suites with a piano player, and that was my first year of college at the conservatory. . . . And that was six nights a week. . . . I'd just go to school, I'd do the gig at night, practice in the day; that really helped me, too, working that many nights a week, just doing it." He started gigging with his contemporaries, but it wasn't long before he moved on to working with such advanced players as saxophonist Charles Davis Jr. and pianist Neal Chandek. Shortly thereafter, he moved on to the "big leagues," working with Hazeltine and Milwaukee icon Hattush Alexander. Hamann often worked with Frank Morgan when he came back to Milwaukee in the 1990s, as did David Bayles.

Once he was established on the scene, Hamann could work enough to make a living. He became something of a celebrity when in 2000 he took over the bass chair on Michael Feldman's nationally syndicated radio show, *Whad'Ya Know?*, working with pianist John Thulin until the show closed in 2016. Hamann also took several international trips with Madison pianist/vocalist Ben Sidran. For some time he had a steady trio gig at the North Shore Bistro in Milwaukee.

David Bayles

Drummer David Bayles was born in Skokie, Illinois, in 1964, but he moved to the Milwaukee area while still in grade school. In middle school, he

We Six in 2015. From left to right: Jeff Hamann, Eric Jacobson, Eric Schoor, David Bayles, Mark Davis, and Paul Silbergleit. (With the exception of Eric Jacobson, whose profile appears in chapter 17, and Paul Silbergleit, profiles of these musicians appear elsewhere in this chapter.) COURTESY OF THE WISCONSIN CONSERVATORY OF MUSIC

heard a group from the conservatory play at a free concert; it included guitarist Jack Grassel, bassist Harold Miller, and drummer Bob Budny. Although somewhat baffled by the music of a group that he sensed as being avant-garde, Bayles was convinced to study drum set with Budny.

In 1982, Bayles went off to Northern Colorado University, a perennially strong jazz school, but after a year he decided to return to Milwaukee. Eventually, he enrolled at UW–Milwaukee, in music education. What he was doing nights, however, was probably a more important educational experience than the formal one he was getting during the day. He recalls:

> Almost the whole time I was going to school there, I had a seven-night-a-week gig playing jazz. Five to nine at the Hyatt, playing with Manty Ellis and Berkeley Fudge and Charles Ledvina and Dave Stoler. [Jeff] Pietrangelo did some of them, and Jackie Allen. So it was like just getting thrown in there. It was a great learning experience. During the day I was doing my legit stuff. And eventually, at some point, it was more jazz, obviously.

> Actually that gig [at the Hyatt] lasted at least ten years. It went from seven nights to four then three then one and then gone. You know that story. But playing every night, and then Jeff [Hamann] and I would do another gig Sunday night, and then another one, at the Estate.

Like Davis and Hamann, Bayles established himself as a go-to player in the city in the mid-1980s and remains one of the busiest drummers not only in Milwaukee, but around Wisconsin, working in just about any kind of group in any jazz style. For almost three years in the mid-2010s, he played a steady trio gig in Lake Geneva with the excellent pianist/organist Dan Trudell. In addition to teaching at the conservatory, Bayles is on the faculty at UW–Milwaukee and University of Wisconsin–Parkside in Kenosha.

Adekola Adedapo

Vocalist Adekola Adedapo was born in the late 1940s in Chicago and lived there as a young girl. "My grandfather was part owner of the 411 [on the South Side]," she explains, "which was the bar the greats frequented before they got great, and they would have a lot of jam sessions and things." She also heard black and white singers on the jukebox: Billie Holiday and Sarah Vaughan, but also Jo Stafford. Home was in the Altgeld Gardens housing project on the far south side. "My father was a record company owner and entrepreneur," she says. "But he also played piano every night."

Life changed, though, when Adedapo's family moved to Muskegon, Michigan. After high school, she attended Michigan State University. When she auditioned for the Miss Michigan pageant, she remembers the leader of the MSU jazz ensemble telling her, "You should sing jazz; you shouldn't do anything in your whole life but sing jazz." She began studying the jazz greats and, as she says, "just started working."

Adedapo moved to Milwaukee in 1973, became engaged in the civil rights struggle, and joined the Republic of New Africa.

> I was in the RNA, and the whole thing went sour, and I realized I didn't want to be a rifle revolutionary. . . . I left that segment of the

> revolution and went into the spiritual side, and that's what led me to the Village. . . . I went to South Carolina when I was twenty-eight to be initiated into the rites of African indigenous religion. While I was there, I had to sing over drums, in the woods. . . . The sound of the woods . . . is like a natural amplification; but you have to learn . . . to lead the chant and be heard over the drums. And I did that for two and a half years. And so when I came back to Milwaukee [in 1978] I was really ready to be a solo singer, which I never imagined myself to be.

After her return, on a dare, Adedapo sang at a jam session at the Jazz Gallery. Her story of struggle to gain jazz credibility is told in detail in Derek Pinkham's *Milwaukee Jazz Profiles*, including a description of her first connection with Buddy Montgomery. Adedapo explains that, after hearing her at a jam,

> Buddy took me on the road for a year, to prisons, and hospitals. I was with other African-centered artists in his band, and Puerto Rican, all the instrumentation you could want to do African music: timbales, conga, djembe . . . [with] bassist Jeff Chambers and [drummer] Killer Ray [Appleton]. . . . [Buddy] wouldn't let me sing for a year; he had all these other singers singing. . . . But I had to attend all the band rehearsals. And so he trained me, is what he did. And finally we were in Indianapolis and he said, "Okay, suit up, you're singing tonight."

After Montgomery left Milwaukee in the early 1980s, Adedapo moved back to Chicago for over a decade. She says she "got married [and] started having kids, so the next thirteen years, fourteen years, was devoted to that." She did, though, make a connection with Von Freeman during that time, frequenting his south side club. Milwaukee transplant Willie Pickens was also a major influence during those years.

Returning to Milwaukee in the early 1990s, Adedapo established herself in the local jazz community, largely through working with Melvin Rhyne. Vic Soward was also an early ally. Eventually, Adedapo began working regularly at the Jazz Estate, usually with Rhyne, Soward, and

Berkeley Fudge. She also worked with pianist Dean Lea and had a steady one night a week at the Main Event as well.

Adedapo also contributed to a milestone in the chronicling of Milwaukee history: the 1998 Theatre X production of local playwright John Schneider's drama *Jazz*, which is essentially the story of the post–World War II Walnut Street, or Bronzeville area, entertainment scene. Evidently, Adedapo was asked to get together a band for the production. Overcoming trepidation about asking Fudge and Rhyne, and motivated by her belief in the project, she talked the two musicians into forming the core of the band. They brought on drummer Robert "Bob" Hobbs and pianist Dean Lea. After assembling the band, however, things turned out a little differently than she anticipated:

> We get to the first rehearsal, I got the musicians lined up, the director brings out the actors, and all the actors telling these black stories are white. And I'm saying, "I'm dead . . . I'm going to be burned [at the] stake" [*laughter*]. But it turned out beautifully, because this Milwaukee is Main Street. And had it not been those white actors that Milwaukee was familiar with telling the story it may not have been received; we were playing the music, because we're the children.

There was a great deal of music throughout the show; the band played music of the period—"Tuxedo Junction," "In a Sentimental Mood," and "Caravan"—and the big production numbers. The show has had several runs over the years, most recently in 2003.

Adedapo worked for sixteen years in Milwaukee's public schools, beginning in the mid-1990s at Lloyd Street School. At Lloyd Street, she remembers, "I was an assistant, and I did reading classes. But then when I started writing and producing the black history program, that became mine." She says, "I was able to take music and start [my students] in basic note reading and also . . . teach them that all songs are a poem, and take the song lines and teach poetry." After retiring from teaching, she became program coordinator for the Cultural Education Center at Alverno College.

In 2011, Adedapo basked in some parental glory when her daughter, Naima, made it to the top eleven of the tenth season of the hit series *Amer-*

Adekola Adedapo. PHOTO BY LEIKO NAPOLI

ican Idol. That led to a tour with the other top contestants from July to September of that year. Naima earned a bachelor of fine arts degree in dance from UW–Milwaukee and continues an active music career.

Adedapo worked at the Packing House with pianist Jeff Stoll in the 2010s, recording there live in November 2015. In the mid-2010s, she also solidified her position on the Milwaukee scene with a long-standing association with the Paul Spencer Band at Caroline's club. After the premature death of Jessie Hauck, and excluding the more independent path taken by Penny Goodwin, Adedapo is the one singer associated with the modern jazz scene described in this chapter who has had a long, ongoing career.

12

Jazz Rock

In Milwaukee, the rest of Wisconsin, and, in fact, most of the United States, many jazz musicians who came to prominence in the late 1960s and the 1970s grew up, in the words of Milwaukee saxophonist Warren Wiegratz, "listening to more rock and roll and rhythm and blues" than to jazz.[1] The music that these musicians played in their early years has often been categorized as something other than jazz, or at least as a subset of jazz, such as "jazz rock" or "fusion."

"That was the popular music of the day," Wiegratz continues, "and it was from that that you expand out . . . to listening to jazz and whatever. I always had that feeling that the rock music, or the rhythm and blues music could take elements of jazz and the freedom of that kind of music [jazz], but in that R&B context, and the rock context."

Some of the most successful jazz and jazz-oriented groups in Wisconsin history were born at that intersection. When they were developing as young players, these musicians listened to James Brown; Blood, Sweat & Tears; Chicago; "electric" Miles Davis; and such jazz artists as Jimmy Smith and Kenny Burrell.

Sweetbottom

Warren Wiegratz was born in 1948 and grew up in New Berlin. He says,

> I kinda knew what I always wanted to do, from when I was in kindergarten, when they had the music teacher come in for the very first day. She got on the piano and started singing, and then they passed

> out little percussion instruments. And I got the sandpaper blocks. I'm five years old, [so you just] put your hands together and go "shhew!" And I was just enthralled.

According to Wiegratz, his family was "completely nonmusical," not even owning a radio or record player. When they got a television, Warren was immediately drawn to the musical programs, and when he heard a saxophonist on *American Bandstand* at age nine, he knew that's what he wanted to do.

One of Wiegratz's first bands was the Mustard Men. When he was in high school, the Mustard Men won a couple battles of the bands and even cut a single on a 45-rpm record.[2] After high school, Wiegratz enrolled at the University of Wisconsin–Milwaukee in the music education program. At UWM, he studied with Joe Aaron (see chapter 4) and became one of many Milwaukee-area saxophonists of his generation to profit from Aaron's tutelage.

In 1967, Wiegratz joined Freddie and the Freeloaders, a group that the Mustard Men had beaten in a battle of the bands only a short time earlier. He describes the Freeloaders as "a complete R&B band" with horns. (The bandleader, Fred Bliffert, who is currently still active on the Milwaukee music scene with Fred Bliffert and the Blifftones, came from the family that ran Bliffert Lumber Company.)

Daryl Stuermer, a Milwaukee native born in 1952, got into music at the age of about four. "My father got me a snare drum," Stuermer recalls, "because he played drums in the navy." In third grade, when he could sign up for school band at Thompson School, he expressed his interest in drums. But because there were enough drummers already, his director talked him into beginning on trumpet, which he continued to play when he entered St. Francis High School.

Stuermer was inspired to take up guitar at age eleven because his older brother, Duane, was playing it. Stuermer remembers getting his first guitar, a Kingston, from Sears: "When you're just starting out, you have some buddies, and you say, 'Let's start a band.' And that means you've had a guitar for three months." He and several friends did just that, and the Sultans played at eighth grade promotion day. The boys made ten dollars—two dollars each. "So that was my first gig," says Stuermer, "and it was a dance. And right at that point I think I was hooked, because it was so much fun."

Some years later, when Stuermer was about seventeen, he and his brother Duane started a band called Burtram Grimm. Influenced by Blood, Sweat & Tears; Chicago; and bands such as Electric Flag and Lighthouse, the brothers incorporated horns into their sound. The members of Burtram Grimm, including trumpeter Mike Betz and drummer Mike "Ding" Lorenz, eventually moved on to Warren Wiegratz's band, Yesterday's Children, which then morphed into a noted rhythm-and-blues band that spawned many jazz players: Family at Max. (Before Yesterday's Children, Wiegratz and Betz briefly joined Freddie and the Freeloaders.)

In addition to Wiegratz, Family at Max included vocalists Sylvia St. James and Charlie Brooks, Lorenz (replacing Sheldon Brady) on drums, Betz and Jim Salamone on trumpets, bassist Gary Christensen, and Daryl on guitar. Trumpeter Mike Drake, a unique figure in the Milwaukee music scene, later joined the band. Eventually, Wiegratz engineered getting Michael Murphy into the drum chair. The band was initially named after one of Stuermer's compositions, "Family at Mac's," but the spelling was soon changed. Although the band played covers of popular tunes on the radio, Stuermer says they also had "a set and a half of all original stuff, and it was vocals and things with odd time signatures, and open sections, arranged, unarranged." Despite their experimental nature, Wiegratz says, "For some reason, people would still hire us." Surely, this was partly due to the radio hits they played, like so many other horn bands of the time.

Stuermer's brother Duane, just returned from a tour of duty in Vietnam, eventually joined Family at Max as a vocalist. According to Daryl,

> Duane was driving a truck in Vietnam, and he was frisking people at the border; that's kind of the work he was doing. He saw on a bulletin board: "Bass guitarist, guitarist, keyboardist wanted." He went for it. Now, being a guitar player he could sort of dabble in bass playing. . . . But he wasn't yet a "bass player" bass player. So then he started playing bass with a band over in Vietnam that just played on a flatbed truck; they would go to the different infantry areas

Members of the short-lived band Transatlantic, probably in the early 1980s. It included former Sweetbottom members (left to right) Mark Torroll, Daryl Stuermer, Warren Wiegratz, Duane Stuermer, and Michael Murphy. COURTESY OF WARREN WIEGRATZ

> and play for the guys, and then move on, go on a helicopter, and somewhere else.

The Stuermer brothers left Family at Max in 1972 and formed the first edition of what was to become the wildly successful Sweetbottom. After the Stuermers and, later, Sylvia St. James left Family at Max, Madison singer Jeffrey Stoner took over as Max's featured vocalist, bringing piano player Harris Lemberg with him. The band took a new direction into funk and soul, featuring the music of such artists as Marvin Gaye and War.

According to Daryl Stuermer, they formed Sweetbottom because "we were just a little more interested in some other kind of music as well. We were getting into the progressive rock thing . . . getting a little away from the standard R&B and pop kind of thing. I liked Jethro Tull, and bands like King Crimson. We weren't doing that kind of stuff in Family at Max."

Sweetbottom started out as a trio: the Stuermers with drummer Mike Kowaleski, known professionally as Mike Kowal. Soon they were joined by saxophonist John Kirchberger and Stanley Palkowitz, who played organ. (Daryl had met Palkowitz at a polka gig, where he was playing accordion.) When Sylvia St. James joined Sweetbottom in 1974, the band worked for some time at Vitucci's on North Avenue. Wiegratz frequently came to the club and sat in, and he eventually moved into the band, taking over saxophone and keyboards, replacing Kirchberger and Palkowitz. John Ricco briefly played percussion in the band. It wasn't long before Kowal was replaced by Murphy in the drum chair.

Michael Murphy was born in 1951 and raised in the Milwaukee area. His music career started when he was a student at Mary Queen of Heaven School in West Allis. He wanted to play in the percussion ensemble at school, but remembered, "They had enough snare drum players, so they talked me into playing my very first instrument: tuba." The boy faced grammar-school humiliation. "I'm taking a little red wagon to school, with a tuba in it," he recalled, "and my lessons were at lunchtime, in the principal's office. And as I would walk to the principal's office with this tuba, people would dunk their milk cartons, banana peels [right into the tuba]." After that experience, he never again took part in formal school music.

In the 1960s, Murphy became infatuated with the British Invasion of the Beatles, Rolling Stones, and other groups. He was determined to become a drummer, so he started taking lessons at Cascio Music store.

> I had a teacher named Donnie Lang; his real name was Donnie Langlois. His claim to fame was he played for Steve Allen. He was very high-strung; we were in this four-by-six room, and if I didn't know my lesson, he would throw the sticks and lose his temper. . . . And he scared the crap out of me, so I practiced. . . . I studied with him for about six months and then I got a letter from Mr. Cascio, "Mr. Langlois won't be with us anymore."

Despite a lack of encouragement from his parents, Murphy kept working on his instrument. The store sponsored a percussion ensemble, and, inspired by listening to jazz great Max Roach's experiments with percussion, in about eighth grade Murphy wrote a piece for the group for a composition competition. "I won third place," he remembered. "I got this little ribbon; I still have the piece of music." Around 1965, Murphy formed a band with Mike Cascio, son of the owners of Cascio Music, on guitar; Tom

Zeitlow on guitar; and Joe Turano on keyboards. (Turano went on to a successful career on the West Coast, recording with quite a few artists as a vocalist before becoming known as a saxophonist. He sang and played saxophone with Milwaukee's Al Jarreau and was Jarreau's musical director for many years.) When the band played a school dance as freshmen at Pius IX High School, Bruce Dentice heard them. Murphy said, "I started playing every Italian wedding when I was sixteen with Bruce Dentice and his father, Carl. We worked for Frank Balistreri, [who] was at every wedding I played. I played every Saturday when I was sixteen; I was making fifty bucks."

Murphy heard Wiegratz's Mustard Men in the brief time that he was a student at the University of Wisconsin–Oshkosh. After returning to Milwaukee, "Murph," like so many of his contemporaries, studied for a while at the Wisconsin Conservatory of Music when Tony King and Manty Ellis were running the program. He and Mike Cascio would visit Sardino's Bull Ring (a club tucked into a residential neighborhood on the east side, at Bellevue and Newhall) to hear Sweetbottom. Things had started slowly at the Bull Ring, but owner Jimmy Sardino stuck with the band, and it turned into a five-night-a-week house gig that lasted from 1973 to 1975. Word of mouth was a powerful force in those days, and before long, the club was packed, first on weekends and eventually on Wednesdays, Thursdays, and Sundays as well. Murphy would sit in whenever he could.

When Murphy finally took over the drum chair in Sweetbottom, the "classic" and hugely successful edition of the band was set: the Stuermers, Weigratz, Murphy, and St. James on vocals. Musicians passing through town would often stop by the club and sit in with the band, including members of Frank Zappa's band; John McLaughlin's Mahavishnu Orchestra; and Woody Herman's big band, including pianist Lyle Mays (see chapter 7). Sweetbottom established a relationship with the Zappa band, particularly keyboard player George Duke and drummer Chester Thompson, when they had a chance encounter with Thompson before a Zappa concert in Chicago.

During this period, Sylvia St. James occasionally left the band to go to California. As a child of the 1970s, she followed the Guru Maharaj Ji. She eventually stayed on the West Coast and had some success as a vocalist there, recording with George Duke after he left Zappa's band and started a solo career. Sweetbottom auditioned a number of possible replacements and worked with singer Donna Renée for a short period, but eventually they decided to play as a strictly instrumental band.[3]

After a year and a half of success in Milwaukee, and following St. James's lead, the guys in the band decided to take a week off from their residency at Sardino's and go to California, and, as long as they were going to be there, they naïvely thought they'd pitch the band to national record labels. While they were in California, French jazz-rock violinist Jean-Luc Ponty (then working with Zappa) was looking for a guitarist for his new band. Tipped off by George Duke, Ponty called Daryl Stuermer, who just happened to be in California. A quick audition led to a firm offer two months later, bringing Stuermer back to California. For the next three years, Stuermer worked with Ponty, who became a major force in jazz-rock fusion, and made a name for himself on tours and on Ponty's albums.

Stuermer went on to a high-profile career in the music business, though not in jazz. At the end of a tour with Ponty, the tour manager of one of progressive rock's biggest groups, Genesis, called Stuermer looking for a guitarist for the touring band. Genesis had been founded in 1967 by superstar vocalist Peter Gabriel, and when Gabriel left in the mid-1970s, after reportedly trying out four hundred singers, the band decided that Phil Collins, the band's drummer, would become lead vocalist. When guitarist Steve Hackett decided to leave, Stuermer, after a most interesting audition in New York, was hired to replace him on tours. Stuermer was not a member of Genesis—which officially included just guitarist Mike Rutherford, keyboardist Tony Banks, and Collins—but he played in the Genesis touring band from 1978 through 2007.

In between Genesis tours, Stuermer played a memorable tour with 1970s star Gino Vannelli's band. In 1980, when Phil Collins decided to branch out from Genesis into a solo career, Stuermer played on Collins's first album, *Face Value*, with its huge hit "In the Air Tonight," and he has continued to tour and record with megastar Collins ever since. Since Stuermer would be flown to England to rehearse with Genesis and Collins before their tours, it didn't matter where he lived in the United States. He decided to move back to his hometown in 1980 and has lived in the

Milwaukee area ever since. When not otherwise occupied, he frequently leads a local band. For some time, that group has included keyboard player Kostia (Efimov), bassist Eric Hervey, and drummer Al Arber. Vocalist and saxophonist Woody Mankowski joined in the 2010s. The Daryl Stuermer band plays major venues in Wisconsin and the Midwest on a somewhat regular basis.

Desperate for a replacement for Stuermer, Sweetbottom approached local guitarist Jack Grassel. He was not interested but suggested one of his students, Martin "Marty" Appel, who joined the band in the 1970s. Though many feared that Stuermer's departure would be a heavy blow to the band, instead the band's local popularity continued to grow, and it even took on another night a week at Jimmy's brother Joe Sardino's club on Farwell: Sardino's East.

Around this time, businessmen (and brothers) Perri and Marco Giorgi decided to open a new Milwaukee club, but in an area that did not seem promising for drawing traditional Milwaukee club-goers—Sixty-Eighth and Forest Home, on the southwest side. Sweetbottom played the opening of the club, on one of the few nights the band was off at the Bull Ring, and the Giorgis made the band a very attractive financial offer to become the house band at the new club. The guys went to Joe Sardino and asked for a small raise, not even close to the Giorgis' offer. When he held firm to what he was already paying, Sweetbottom picked up and moved to the new spot. And, as Murphy remembers, "Giorgi's exploded." The band's popularity had never been higher, and their house gig remained the local spot for touring musicians to sit in. Musicians who sat in during one Sweetbottom era or another include bassist Jaco Pastorius of Weather Report and guitarist Al DiMeola of Chick Corea's Return to Forever, as well as drummers Chester Thompson, Alphonse Mouzon, and Ralph Humphrey, and bassist Alphonso Johnson.

In 1976, at the peak of this success, Murphy got a call from the band Matrix (the Appleton band; see later in this chapter), which was playing at the famed West Coast club Concerts by the Sea in Redondo Beach, California, after having just played the Monterey Jazz Festival. Matrix was looking for a new drummer. When the band returned to Wisconsin at the end of their road trip, Murphy auditioned for the drum chair and eventually took it, leaving Sweetbottom with another big hole to fill.

Again, Sweetbottom found a most suitable replacement with a young powerhouse, Mark Torroll. With Torroll on board, the band cut its first album, *Angels of the Deep*, with the financial help of the Giorgi brothers and Marty Appel's parents. Through tireless self-promotion, primarily by Wiegratz, the album became a local hit. According to Wiegratz, at one point it was the best-selling album in Wisconsin, beating out the national bestseller, *Saturday Night Fever*.[4]

After this regional success, Elektra/Asylum, a giant record label at the time, picked up the album, and Sweetbottom had its first national release. This led to Sweetbottom opening concerts in the Midwest for some of the biggest names in the music business at that time—Kenny Loggins, Jefferson Starship, Blue Oyster Cult, and Toto. They cut their second album, *Turn Me Loose*, in Los Angeles in 1979.[5] The record was delayed a few months, and the week it was released, the jazz-fusion division of Elektra/Asylum was shut down.

In 1980, Sweetbottom put out another album on their own, *Double Motion*, but Wiegratz says, "It didn't sell as well, and Marty's parents were pressuring him to drop music, and so, [the band] just folded."

But Wiegratz, although burned out and ready to lie low for a while, was hardly done performing. His next band, Oceans, started with him sitting in with a group led by Pete Safir and eventually included Sweetbottom veterans Mark Torroll (Ernie Adams also drummed) and Duane Stuermer.

Oceans got its biggest boost after Wiegratz was asked by a former buddy, John Steinmiller, who had moved into the front office of the Milwaukee Bucks basketball team, to play the national anthem at a Bucks game. Further discussion with Steinmiller led to the idea of Oceans replacing the somewhat tired and out-of-date Bucks band led by veteran contractor Steve Swedish. One afternoon, Steinmiller brought Bucks owner (but not yet US Senator) Herb Kohl to Sardino's East to hear Oceans. Kohl was not exactly on top of current trends in music, but he was convinced that the Bucks needed something more contemporary to excite the audience at games. Oceans became the Bucks' house band for the 1984–1985 season, and Wiegratz played the national anthem at almost every game thereafter, becoming a local legend for that alone.[6]

Thanks to the Bucks gig, Oceans was heard by thousands on a regular basis, and eventually they were invited to play at the National Basketball

Association All-Star Game. After releasing a locally made album, they were signed by the Pro Jazz label. The release *Ridin' the Tide* was a commercial success, and the band played at various spots around the country. But after a time, it became clear that other members of the group had a different vision of the band than that of Wiegratz, who felt he had to walk away from the group.

However, he didn't want to lose the lucrative and rewarding Bucks gig. At the 1990 Summerfest, he heard a fine band from the Fox Valley called Streetlife. Streetlife was on the verge of breaking up, but after some negotiation between leader/drummer Tony Wagner and Weigratz, and the reaffirmation from Steinmiller that the Bucks contract was still in play, Weigratz joined Wagner, bassist Kevin Allen, and keyboardist Kurt Cowling and brought Streetlife to the Bradley Center in 1990. In 2015, Streetlife (with completely different personnel from the original band) played their last game as the Bucks' house band.

Wiegratz, who has won a dozen Best Reed/Brass Player awards from the Wisconsin Area Music Industry (WAMI) over the years, was inducted into the WAMI Hall of Fame in the spring of 2014. In the mid-2010s, he works often with guitarist Tim Stemper and vocalist Pam Duronio in the trio VIVO.

September and La Chazz

Sometime after John Kirchberger left Sweetbottom, around 1974, he started a new band called September with guitarist Toty Ramos and bassist Jim Paolo.[7] When they started September, all three were playing in Family at Max. Also in the new band were drummer Paul Redmann and percussionist Dave Newson. According to Kirchberger in 1976, though Family at Max was making money, "There were too many nights when it was especially nonrewarding to stand up there and do one repetitious song after another. I didn't feel the kind of fulfillment after a while that I knew music had to offer."[8]

September's first gig was at the Mine Shaft; they also played at the Kenwood Inn in the Union at UW–Milwaukee, but they really established themselves when they took over the house gig at the Bull Ring after Sweetbottom left to go to Giorgi's. The instrumentation was essentially

September. Left to right, back row: Paul Redmann, John Kirchberger, Dave Newsome, and Toty Ramos; front row: Michaela Carey and Jim Paolo. COURTESY OF TOTY RAMOS

the same as Sweetbottom (right down to Kirchberger doubling on keyboards and saxophone), but one thing that distinguished September from other bands was Ramos's writing. His original compositions were unlike anyone else's in Milwaukee.

Bassist Jim Paolo was born in 1950 and grew up on the east side of Milwaukee, attending St. John's Cathedral High School. After those days of fusion in the 1970s, Paolo branched out, playing with a wide cross-section of Milwaukee's jazz community. For some years, he was local saxophone legend Berkeley Fudge's first-call bassist. He has appeared weekly (or even more frequently) at the Jazz Estate, with one group or another, often as leader. At the time of this writing, he is probably the busiest bassist in jazz in Milwaukee. He is also an instructor in the jazz program at the Wisconsin Conservatory.

John Kirchberger was born in 1951, lived in Menomonee Falls from the age of five on, and graduated from Menomonee Falls High School. He attended UW–Milwaukee, where he, like Warren Wiegratz, studied saxophone with Joe Aaron. Kirchberger left September in late 1976 to join Matrix (the Appleton band) along with Michael Murphy. When Matrix quit traveling, Kirchberger took a day job in Milwaukee's northern suburbs and was not often seen performing in the city, although he played for years with George Busateri's band, where he retained his unique, powerful musical voice.

Toty Ramos was born in 1950 and moved with his family to Milwaukee from his hometown, Eagle Pass, Texas, in 1962. Ramos started playing guitar when he was seven or eight years old, with his father as his first guitar teacher. He played trumpet in the band at Lincoln High School, where his band director was jazz trumpeter Kaye Berigan. Ramos really emerged on the Milwaukee scene with Family at Max and September, but prior to that, he had played many gigs in different styles with groups of diverse sizes. After September dissolved, he went back to widespread jobbing, including a few duo-guitar performances with Manty Ellis. Ramos remembers rehearsing for those gigs at Ellis's music store.

Ramos will probably be best known in Milwaukee music history for his founding of the Latin jazz band La Chazz. The band was formed in 1978 to open a show in Milwaukee by the legendary Puerto Rican singer Celia Cruz, and then they decided to keep it going.[9] Early in the band's history, Ramos told Bill Milkowski of the *Milwaukee Journal*, "I've done stints with a lot of Latin bands in the community—I've done the wedding scene, the rock scene, the heavy metal scene; I touched on mainstream jazz. The next move for me was to come back and incorporate everything I've gone through."

Talking with Milkowski about what he wanted to accomplish with the new band, Ramos said, "We do have musicians who are oriented to a

La Chazz in 1979. Left to right: Wally Robles, Neil Chandek, Paul Sorensen, Mike Betz, Stu Melis, Leo Tato, Edgar Martinez, Albert Rivera, Toty Ramos, Miguel Gonzalez, and Cecil Negron. COURTESY OF TOTY RAMOS

fusion style. I know I am. But we want to make it true Latin music. We want the Latin feel to be the heart of the music instead of using it as an exotic touch." From the very beginning, although the band performed the music of many Latin artists, its identity was distinguished by the compositions of Ramos, which remained the core of its library.

While the personnel changed over the years, La Chazz held together for an amazingly long time. In its early days, the band performed at the Jazz Gallery and the Jazz Estate and did a concert in conjunction with the Milwaukee Symphony Orchestra in 1981. Almost ten years after its founding in 1978, it became the house band at the Café Melange in the Hotel Wisconsin, performing once a week. It remained there until 1999, when the hotel was closed for renovation. During this time, the café became the place for visiting bands to sit in, and La Chazz began filling the role that Sweetbottom had held at the Bull Ring and Giorgi's in the late 1970s and early 1980s.

Bands whose members dropped in to play with La Chazz included those of Grover Washington Jr., Branford Marsalis, Harry Connick Jr., Santana, the Philip Glass Ensemble, and Roy Hargrove. Some of Milwaukee's finest jazz players have had associations with La Chazz, including trumpeters Allen Johnson, Jeff Pietrangelo, and Mike Betz; trombonist Michael Franceschi; pianist Neal Chandek; drummers Dave Bayles and Jeno Somlai; and bassist Jim Paolo. Betz (see earlier in this chapter) was an award-winning teacher for many years at Roosevelt Middle School for the Arts and played in many bands and for many touring shows.

La Chazz reunited in the early 2010s, and with Ramos's original music still serving as the backbone of its repertoire, the band played around Wisconsin to considerable acclaim.

Montage

Montage was another Milwaukee fusion band from this era.[10] The prime musical forces in Montage were keyboard player Tom Sandquist, saxophonist Bob Rebholz, and later, singer Marcia Cunningham. Sandquist came to Milwaukee from Long Island, New York, as a student at Marquette University, where he graduated with an anthropology major in 1972. While at Marquette, Sandquist took some courses at the Wisconsin Conservatory, through what he calls "some kind of exchange program." After Marquette, he tried unsuccessfully to get into the music program at UW–Milwaukee. However, the conservatory accepted him, offered him a teaching position, helped him get student loans, and generally made him feel welcome. He studied one summer with Buddy Montgomery, but Tony King was his longtime mentor. Sandquist believes that he was the first graduate of the jazz program at the conservatory in 1975.

Rebholz, who played a variety of woodwinds with Montage, earned a music degree at UWM.

Sometime late in his schooling at the conservatory, Sandquist (playing Hammond organ) and Rebholz started a trio with drummer Paul Redmann, who was also drumming with September around this time. One of their first steady gigs was at a place called Julie's, where they were billed as the Tom Sandquist Trio. The band grew and evolved into Montage. Three bassists who would later become important players in Milwaukee played at some point with the band: Harold Miller, Tom McGirr, and Al Anderson. Joe Dolister played bass on the band's 1978 album, *Project One*. Drummers Mike Kowal, who had been with Sweetbottom, and Dave Krohl put in time with Montage as well. After a time, guitarist John Zaffiro and percussionist John Seydewitz joined the group. While Marcia Cunningham is usually remembered as the band's main vocalist, Michaela Carey, Suzanne (Sue) Falcone, and Pam Duronio also spent time with Montage. A young Peter Dominguez, a bassist who would go on to prominence elsewhere, played for a while near the end of the group's run, as did guitarist John Northrup.

In the summer of 1976, Montage played a couple of nights a week at the Kenwood Inn, on the UWM campus, while Matrix (the Appleton band) played the weekends. Montage was the house band at Sam and Sons in West Allis for a while, and then followed Sweetbottom and September into Jimmy Sardino's Bull Ring, where they were in residence for a year and a half, as Sandquist recalls.

A highlight of the band's career was a 1977 performance with the Milwaukee Symphony. Montage performed Rebholz's "Sundip" and Sandquist's arrangement of Earl Klugh's "Vonetta" with the symphony, and then did a second set of their own music, featuring Sue Falcone. Not long after, a second performance with the symphony featured Cunningham. Montage recorded an album of their original music in 1978, *Project One*, which featured the compositions of Cunningham, Sandquist, Rebholz, and Zaffiro.

Sandquist had a side music career in Milwaukee as the first contractor for the Alpine Valley Music Theater. In this capacity, he booked local musicians who were needed to back up the headliners, ranging from Frank Sinatra to Sonny and Cher to Bobby Vinton. He also contracted musicians to back up Aretha Franklin in concert at County Stadium.

The beginning of the end of Montage came when Cunningham, Zaffiro, and Redmann left to start the group Rainbow's End, which also at times included keyboardist Jerry Weitzer and a young bassist who would go on to big things in jazz, Gerald Cannon (see chapter 9). Rebholz moved to Denver, Colorado, in 1979, followed shortly thereafter by Sandquist; they remain active on the music scene there. Cunningham has remained in Milwaukee and most recently has been heard with Wicked Long Day, which also features her husband, Jerry Weitzer.

Matrix (Milwaukee)

Before leaving the Milwaukee fusion scene, another band with the name Matrix (not part of the interrelated groups previously discussed) needs to be mentioned. In 1971, a jazz-rock band was formed that had an unorthodox membership.[11] Two of the band members were also members of the Milwaukee Symphony Orchestra. The senior member of the group, bassist David Phillips, then in his early thirties, had received traditional classical training at two of the country's leading music schools, the Eastman School and Indiana University. The *Milwaukee Sentinel* described Phillips in 1972 as "an Oklahoman with a penchant for headbands and heavy chords on his electric bass guitar." Five years younger was MSO flutist David Shostac, who boasted a degree from Juilliard. In Matrix, he played flute and saxophones. The rest of the band was still younger, mostly in their early to mid-twenties. Jack Grassel (see chapter 15) was a fire-breathing local jazz guitarist who also had strong roots in rock and roll.

Drummer Andy LoDuca—who, like Grassel, was still active on the Milwaukee scene in 2017—is a native of Dousman. He joined Matrix after the departure of Mike Rosen, drummer during the first part of the band's existence. LoDuca, according to the *Sentinel*, "started his career by playing his father's imported accordions." In the early 1970s, he "double[d] as a part time commercial artist, winning the 1972 Brady Street Fall Festival poster contest." And he had spent a year in Costa Rica with the Peace Corps around the same time. The keyboardist was Dennis Klopfer, who had studied architecture at the University of Illinois but left school to perform with bandleader Manty Ellis. However, he was drafted into the army and spent three years in Germany "playing piano in officers' clubs." Klopfer and LoDuca had played jazz together as teenagers.

The music Matrix played was an eclectic mix. Phillips was quoted in 1972 as saying, "Some of the younger heads consider us heavy rock, others think of us as sophisticated jazz. The pure boogie freaks don't dig us because we don't play that music exclusively. I guess it's a mixture." Martin

Hintz of the *Sentinel* described what he heard from the band: "The quintet's philosophies have jelled to a common purpose: to experiment with new sounds through original compositions. Matrix might be one of the few jazz-rock-classical-boogie-folk-and, etc., groups to use sheet music as a takeoff for its improvisations. It allows discipline tempered with individual expression."

When Grassel reissued the band's 1973 album on CD in 2003, he wrote in the liner notes: "The idea was to play only music composed by band members and attempt to explore anything that was interesting with no holds barred: unusual time signatures, song forms, melodies, and harmonies." One can hear all of these strains, influences, techniques, and styles on that album, which was titled *(stimulus for the auditory nerve)*.

The band played clubs in the city and, not surprisingly, played at least two performances with the Milwaukee Symphony. It lasted three years, disbanding when Shostac moved to California. Phillips, a colorful and unique member of Milwaukee's musical community, died of cancer at the age of forty-three in 1981. His obituary in the *Milwaukee Sentinel* noted that his "lifestyle embraced many creative facets of life. . . . As a high school student Phillips excelled in the low hurdles. He taught in the Milwaukee public school system. He loved sports of all kinds and was enthusiastic about sports cars. . . . Spiritual cultures were of special interest to Phillips. He was a proponent of the Eastern philosophy of life, although he was raised as a Southern Baptist."[12] Bassist Roger Ruggeri wrote a special arrangement to feature the MSO bass section that the orchestra performed in two concerts following Phillips's death. Phillips willed his beautiful seventeenth-century string bass to his symphony section mate Laura Snyder, who said she was "completely blindsided" by the gesture. She plays the instrument with the orchestra to this day.[13]

Matrix (Appleton)

The later, and ultimately better-known, band Matrix was the brainchild of John Harmon, who was teaching jazz in the early 1970s at Lawrence University in Appleton.[14] Sitting in J. W. Puddy's bar one night in 1974, Harmon was musing about the outstanding core of students in the program at Lawrence, yet, due to less-than-ideal working conditions, he knew he would soon leave the faculty. He wanted to take a big band on the road, but once he realized the financial impracticality of that plan, he looked at his available players and ended up forming an only slightly more manageable nine-piece group.

The band debuted in the late spring of 1974 in Appleton, consisting primarily of Harmon's students from Lawrence. The original personnel included trombonists Kurt Dietrich and Fred Sturm, who had both graduated from Lawrence in 1973 and spent the previous year in graduate school—Dietrich at Northwestern University and Sturm at North Texas State University; 1974 Lawrence grads Mike Hale and Jeff Pietrangelo on trumpet; undergrads (and soon to be dropouts) Michael Bard on reeds and Larry Darling on trumpet; drummer Tony Wagner, an Appleton native who was the Lawrence University Jazz Ensemble drummer, but not an enrolled student; Fox Valley bassist Randal Fird, best known at the time for having played with the hard rock band Tailor; and, of course, Harmon on piano. Darling and Fird were excellent lead vocalists, an important commodity in any band of this type.

The band settled in for a residency at the nightclub at Appleton's Embassy Motor Lodge and learned a library of music that ranged from Chicago, Tower of Power, and Blood, Sweat & Tears to Stevie Wonder, Carole King, and the Beatles, as well as jazz from standards to Gil Evans to Herbie Hancock. From the very beginning, the band's book included original compositions; Harmon was the group's most prolific composer, but Fred Sturm also contributed strong personal works and was particularly inventive in his arrangements of pop and rock material. Bard, Darling, and Hale later contributed originals as well.

The early days of Matrix featured club dates around Wisconsin (including two monthlong stays at the new Sir Thomas Lounge in Racine), at ski lodges in Michigan's Upper Peninsula, and, even in the fairly early days, some concert dates, which often included clinics at schools. After all, in addition to Harmon, the former college instructor, four members of the group had music education degrees from Lawrence. The band took their first long road trip in November 1974 to a jazz festival in Rochester, New York. A highlight from the spring of 1975 was a performance with the Milwaukee Symphony Orchestra, which featured major three-movement works for the band and the orchestra, written by Harmon and Sturm. In the summer of 1975, Matrix made the first of numerous appearances at Summerfest on the Milwaukee lakefront.

In the second half of 1975 and into 1976, Matrix started playing in the Chicago area, including a number of gigs at Poor Richard's in Skokie, Illinois. In May, the band, now with Gary Miller on drums, recorded an album at Vern Castle's studio in Lake Geneva. During the summer of 1976, the band played Friday and Saturday nights at the Kenwood Inn, on the UW–Milwaukee campus. In these early years, the band worked practically without a break, as nine mouths were a lot to feed.

At Poor Richard's, a distinguished elderly gentleman came to hear the group several times and eventually spoke with the band about having an old friend come to hear them. It turned out that the man was Fred Wacker, of the family for whom Wacker Drive in downtown Chicago is named, and his friend was Willard Alexander. At that time, Alexander, whose career as a booking agent started in the 1930s with bands such as Count Basie and Benny Goodman, was the dean of jazz booking agents. In the mid-1970s, he was still booking most of the remaining big bands, including those of Basie, Buddy Rich, Woody Herman, and Maynard Ferguson as well as such jazz stars as Dizzy Gillespie and Ella Fitzgerald.

Alexander extricated the band from an unfortunate management contract and in the fall of 1976 sent the Midwesterners west. He booked a tour that not only included colleges and high schools in California (including a gig, which would not be the band's last, opening for Dizzy Gillespie), but, even more importantly, booked Matrix in a prime spot at the Monterey Jazz Festival. Leonard Feather, jazz critic for the *Los Angeles Times*, wrote a rave about the band's Monterey performance, followed by another great review when the band played at Concerts by the Sea in Redondo Beach, a top jazz venue on the coast.

After this heady experience, Matrix returned to Wisconsin, playing some school dates but mostly clubs (including Giorgi's in Milwaukee). It was time for a change, and Bard and Miller left the band, replaced by two important Milwaukee players, John Kirchberger and Mike Murphy.

Alexander sent the band on the road again in January 1977. A series of dates in California concluded with a week at the Playboy Club in Century City, after which the band drove straight across the country,

Matrix at La Bastille in Houston, Texas, 1977. Left to right, standing: Randal Fird, Fred Sturm, Mike Hale, John Harmon, Jeff Pietrangelo, Larry Darling, and Kurt Dietrich; kneeling: Mike Murphy and John Kirchberger. COURTESY OF KURT DIETRICH

not stopping except to eat and change drivers, to open a weeklong gig in Miami. Dates followed in Atlanta, Birmingham, Houston, Reno, several cities in California, some of the band's old Wisconsin haunts, and gigs up and down the East Coast.

Alexander sold Matrix's self-produced album to the record giant RCA, and the eponymous album was newly released under the name *Matrix IX* (a name the band used briefly for legal reasons) in August 1977. Almost simultaneously, Elvis Presley died, and RCA spent most of its energies selling Presley records for the next year or two. A new jazz band from Wisconsin was not high on the label's priority list.

The touring pattern established in 1976 remained Matrix's way of life until the end of 1979. Alexander's agency would book a tour of several weeks, the band would travel (sometimes with ridiculously demanding itineraries), then return home to Wisconsin to play whatever gigs it could in nearby environs. Summerfest was a constant in the summers, and Matrix opened at different times for Ramsey Lewis, Les McCann, Sonny Rollins, the Brecker Brothers, and Maynard Ferguson at the late, lamented Miller Jazz Oasis. Fred Sturm left the band in 1977, to be replaced by Brad McDougall (from Rockton, Illinois), whom the band had met and auditioned in Miami. Sturm began his legendary teaching career back at his alma mater, Lawrence. Randal Fird left and was replaced by a young virtuoso bassist from Santa Barbara, California: Randy Tico. (Tico has had a significant career and now tours regularly with Jeff Bridges's band.)

Eventually, Alexander finagled another record contract for the group, this one with the hottest label in the United States at that time, Warner Brothers. For Warner Brothers, Matrix recorded *Wizard* (1978) and *Tale of the Whale* (1979), both at the new Shade Tree Studio in Lake Geneva.

In those years of almost constant touring, the band continued to have great success on the West Coast; it played the new Telluride Jazz Festival in Colorado twice and it cracked into New York with a performance at Lincoln Center's Alice Tully Hall as part of the Newport–New York Jazz Festival, returning for a week at the Other End (previously known as the Bitter End). Interestingly, Milwaukee's Sweetbottom was booked to play the Bottom Line in New York at the very same time but had to cancel due to Warren Wiegratz's illness. Matrix played all over the country for over three years.

Back in Wisconsin, some of the gigs were at places best left unmentioned, but among the better-known venues were the vital 1970s clubs Teddy's (Milwaukee), Bunky's (Madison), and the Joynt (Eau Claire). The band also played a second concert with the Milwaukee Symphony.

Matrix's last big tour occurred in the fall of 1979. Brazilian jazz star vocalist Flora Purim had been looking for a new band while at the Telluride Festival that August. Hearing Matrix, she found what she was after. She came to Wisconsin for a week of rehearsals in Harmon's hometown of Winneconne; the band played a concert with her in Neenah and then headed west. With Purim, the band played colleges and prime club dates in Seattle, San Francisco (the Great American Music Hall), Hollywood (the Roxy), and San Diego. After a couple of dates back in the Midwest, the band decided to go on a "sabbatical." There had been too much traveling, not enough money, and not enough time with families, and there was an unclear outlook for the future. Alexander negotiated one last record contract for the band, with Pablo Records, which resulted in 1980's *Harvest*. But the band never toured to back up the new album.

A reunion took place in the summer of 1992 for a concert for the Green Lake Festival of Music. During the same week, the band played in the noon outdoor series at the Performing Arts Center in Milwaukee and a concert at the Pabst Theater, with opening act Random Walk. Milwaukee trumpeter Allen Johnson helped out in the horn section.

In 2000, the band again reunited for a performance at the Neenah Jazz Festival. Fox Valley saxophonist Tom Washatka filled in for John Kirchberger. Spurred on by this performance, the band recorded another album in 2001–2002, *Proud Flesh: A Matrix Reunion*. In June 2002, Matrix played at the one and only Northern Aire Jazz Festival in Lake Arrowhead, Wisconsin (near Wisconsin Rapids). The band's last hurrah was on Labor Day weekend in 2009, when its members got together one last time to perform at the Thrasher Opera House in Green Lake and the Fox Jazz Fest in Menasha.

Several of the musicians in Matrix have already been noted in this chapter. John Harmon and Fred Sturm, two very important figures in Wisconsin jazz, are further discussed in chapter 18; Jeff Pietrangelo is featured in chapter 15. Drummer Michael Murphy, after a distinguished career in both jazz and more popular styles in Milwaukee, died of a heart attack in 2014. He battled the demon of alcoholism for years but remained not only a respected player, but also an infectious, entertaining personality who could light up a room—or a bandstand.

Larry Darling was born in 1952 and grew up in Rochester, Minnesota. He began playing trumpet in 1960, playing in school band programs and a few rock/dance groups until 1972. "I jumped from nineteenth chair as a sophomore to fourth chair as a junior," he recalls, "not because I practiced, but because I played in rock groups and made meaningful, personal music connections that school programs didn't provide me." Darling played and sang in a band called Therica (which included future Matrix sound engineer Peter "Herb" Butler on bass) following his graduation from high school until he enrolled at Lawrence in 1972.

After touring with Matrix, Darling pursued his passion for recording and worked at Irish-Saxe Studios, a commercial music production studio in Appleton. "My primary role began as a singer, [and] trumpet and keyboard player," he says, "but evolved into writing/arranging as well as audio engineering."

Darling continues, "[I] started my own production studio in 1986 with my partner [and later wife] Patricia Schultz. I bought a farm [outside Dale, Wisconsin] in 1989 and relocated the studio there to focus on original music production for commercial/corporate applications." The couple founded Impact Music Library, which created music that was used in commercials and industrial films throughout the Midwest. After some freelancing, Darling was offered a part-time position in the Lawrence Conservatory's audio recording department in 1996, which developed into a full-time job in 2000. He continued to play trumpet as a member, at various times, of the Fox Valley Symphony, the Lawrence Brass Quintet, and the Appleton-based Big Band Reunion.

Darling is responsible for the recording of the hundreds of music events that take place at Lawrence every year. He teaches courses in recording and has recorded and/or produced a number of albums at Lawrence over the years, including Matrix's *Proud Flesh* and albums by Wisconsin jazz artists Dane Richeson, Mark Urness, and John Harmon.

Opus

Only a couple of years behind the groups mentioned earlier in this chapter, the group Opus was formed at UW–Milwaukee by musicians from the Racine–Kenosha area: saxophonist Curt Hanrahan, keyboardist Jim Sodke, bassist Larry Tresp, and drummer Brian Ford. Later, the band added guitarist Steve Lewandowski (see chapter 10). While Opus's bread and butter was fusion, the players also developed their traditional jazz chops doing Thursday nights at the Riverboat Lounge, where it was understood that fusion would not be played. Opus, like Sweetbottom and Matrix, has had periodic reunions with the original personnel. The band

Steve Lewandowski (left, see chapter 10) and Curt Hanrahan play at a reunion of Opus in Milwaukee, 2015. PHOTO BY LYNN LEW; COURTESY OF STEVE LEWANDOWSKI

recorded a new album in 2015, *Definition*, and was a headlining act on the Jazz Visions on the Lake program (hosted by Milwaukee Jazz Visions) in August 2015.

Curt Hanrahan was born in Kenosha in 1953. His dad was a freelance tool and die machinist and his mother, Ruth, was an impressive piano player who had something of a music career going before marrying and ultimately raising five children.

Hanrahan went to Catholic schools and got involved with the Catholic Youth Organization band program. Early musical influences were some records that his older brother turned him onto, and others that he bought from Columbia Record Club. His mother's influence was strong, too; Hanrahan remembers that she "would play three hours a night . . . just for her own enjoyment." In a tiny house with seven occupants, she essentially gave "a little concert every night," Hanrahan says. He found out much later that his mother played in the first all-female swing band in southeast Wisconsin, which performed in his grandfather's tavern in Kenosha.

Hanrahan took saxophone lessons from area teacher Reno Fillippi. His school band program was weak, but he began to play in urban soul groups around age thirteen or fourteen. One of these was the Kenosha group Yesterday's Children, which moved north to Milwaukee and eventually became Family at Max. While in high school, Hanrahan studied with the respected teacher and saxophonist Stanley DeRusha, who was the band director at Bradford High School in Kenosha at that time.

After graduation, Hanrahan enrolled at UWM, where he studied with Joe Aaron, who he remembers as "an amazing player." But Hanrahan's first year of classical saxophone study was not a success, and he decided to try jazz instead. He left Milwaukee and went to Boston to study at the Berklee College of Music. Instruction at Berklee was world-class, but the school was expensive, and his money ran out. He joined a show band, which eventually ran out of gigs and money in Sault Ste. Marie, Michigan. Hanrahan had to have money wired to him to return home.

He returned to Milwaukee and UWM, from which he earned a music education degree in 1978, studying with Jack Snavely, whom Hanrahan calls "an incredible musician and teacher." The UWM practice area was full of activity at that time, as musicians from the conservatory (such as Brian Lynch and Hary Kozlowski) played there; John Kirchberger was also around, as was Joe Aaron's son Rick, a fine jazz flutist. During this time, Hanrahan formed Opus. When not playing with the band, he taught at Joe Pulice's music store in Racine and built up a significant studio of saxophone students. In the early 1980s, Hanrahan decided to go back to school and was accepted at the Eastman School of Music. But when his wife became pregnant, the timing was no longer right for him to attend school. Hanrahan remained in Racine, continuing to play and teach around southeastern Wisconsin.

Around 1990, Snavely, who was then leading the jazz band at UWM, managed to talk Hanrahan into taking it over. At that point in the UWM program's history, Hanrahan says, there was "not much happening." But he worked hard to make the band more visible. When Snavely retired from teaching saxophone at the school, Hanrahan took over that position as well.

Through Hanrahan's foresight and efforts, a jazz major (which had been lying dormant for decades) was reestablished in 2005 or 2006, and by 2013 there were about twenty jazz majors in the program. Unfortunately, the state legislature passed massive cuts to the UW system in 2015, and the jazz major at UWM was disbanded, with several adjunct jazz faculty let go.

Hanrahan has played with many bands over the years, and also with the Milwaukee Symphony Orchestra for both pops concerts and classical programs. He has appreciated working with Milwaukee veterans from Frank DeMiles, George Pritchett, Manty Ellis, and Berkeley Fudge to his near contemporaries Jack Grassel, Allen Johnson, Tom Newburg, Tim Bell, and others, as well as in the big bands of Nick Contorno, Ron DeVillers, and Chuck Howard.

Hanrahan and Jim Sodke eventually bought Joe Pulice's music store in Racine and turned it into the Lakeshore Conservatory (the small retail part of the operation had mainly been serving the large number of students who came there). Among Hanrahan's outstanding students to come out of Racine are New York jazz star Joel Frahm (see chapter 9); Bill Nelson, an outstanding saxophonist and longtime teacher in Ripon, Wisconsin; Dan Kinzelman, who is now having a solid jazz career in Italy; David Bixler (see chapter 17); and West Coast saxophonist Eric Morones.

13

Madison Loves Its Singers

Sometime early in my interviews with jazz musicians in Madison, someone told me, "Madison loves its singers." And it does seem that singers in Madison have been more prominent and present on the scene than singers in, for example, Milwaukee. The stories of a number of these musicians follow.

Jan Wheaton

One of Madison's prominent singers, Jan Wheaton is a native of Kansas.[1] She was born in 1943 and raised in the small town of Cherryvale, a predominantly white community but one with a vital and active black community. She grew up, musically speaking, in the local black Baptist church where her mother was pianist and organist. Wheaton was in the church choir from the time she was about eight years old.

A seminal moment for Wheaton occurred when she was a senior in high school, and she was chosen to be part of the "entertainment" at the state convention of the Future Homemakers of America. She remembers:

> There was this audience of about three thousand kids, which I hadn't really seen until I got out there [on stage]. And I freaked out. . . . I did the first song, and [the audience] jumped up and down, and they screamed and they hollered and they made an encore thing happen. So we came back, and I did "Blue Moon." . . . And when I started singing it, they all went, "AAAAHHHH." I thought, *Oh, my God, what's*

going on? So that was the really first time that I realized . . . that's what I did.

Upon graduation from high school, Wheaton attended the University of Kansas. "I ran into some jazz musicians there on campus," she says, "and actually started hanging out with them in bars, and singing." She worked with those musicians for several years, getting as far as Kansas City to perform. In the city, she performed with jazz trumpeter Carmell Jones.

Wheaton earned a BA in microbiology, and at its completion she was interviewed by someone from Wisconsin's State Laboratory of Hygiene and offered a job. Her first reaction was: "I'm not going up there. Jesus Christ, it's cold." She also had some concern that, compared to the predominantly white world that she had grown up in, Wisconsin would be even more homogenous. But when she expressed her reservations, her mother replied, "Well, if you want to keep eating, you will." Wheaton arrived in Madison in June 1964.

The State Lab job was the first in a series of public sector jobs that defined Wheaton's career outside of music. She earned a degree in bacteriology at the University of Wisconsin, and when she began to get bored after thirteen and a half years at the lab, she was able to take a position in the office of the dean of the Agriculture School. The job was "to do recruitment and counseling and retention . . . for students of color," Wheaton recalls. She remained at the Ag School for ten years, eventually becoming an assistant dean. During that time, she earned a master's degree in 1984.

Wheaton's next move was to the Athletic Department, where she became an academic advisor for the department. Her experience in the world of big-time college athletics was a real eye-opener. "When I got there," she says, "the offices for the academic advisors looked like . . . a slum compared to the offices of everybody else. And I started raising a bunch of hell about it, because I'm thinking, 'You're bringing parents in here . . . okay? And you want me to tell them how important academics are, and this place looks like this?' " Her hell raising had the desired effect, and soon the offices looked much better.

Wheaton worked hard at her job, trying to give the best academic advice she could to student athletes. But those recommendations were often ignored by others in athletics, close to the students. After a while, Wheaton feared that the powers-that-be in the department were probably going to get her fired. But Dean of Students Mary Rouse initiated a review of the academic side of the Athletic Department and shortly afterward offered Wheaton a job in the Dean of Students' office, which she was happy to accept. Soon, she became the director of the Campus Assistance Center, where she stayed until she retired.

Throughout her academic career in Madison, Wheaton also pursued music. When she first lived in Madison, a cousin visiting from Kansas City connected her with guitarist Johnny Shacklett (see chapter 14), who asked her to join his band. "They used me," she says, "when the audience would get restless and get tired of hearing improvisational crazy stuff. And then they'd bring me in and I could sing something and calm them down." She worked music gigs both in Madison and out of town with Shacklett until he left the area.

At that point, Wheaton ran into another legendary Madison jazz musician, Ted Jackson. "Ted was a piano man," she recalls, "and he played like my mom had played. So it was very comfortable to work with him. And he gave me a little more freedom. Like I would get to do a whole set, instead of one or two songs." They worked together in Madison, but also frequently at the Spring Green Restaurant (which is now the Frank Lloyd Wright Visitor Center).

Jackson passed away in the 1970s, and Wheaton went on to work with many of Madison's best-known jazz musicians, including pianists Harris Lemberg, John Thulin, Joan Wildman, Dave Stoler, and Jane Reynolds; bassists Johnny Widdecombe, John Schaffer, John Christensen, and Hans Sturm; saxophonist Hanah John Taylor; and guitarist Cliff Frederickson. Wheaton worked all over town, including at hotels. Special in that regard was the Concourse, where Cal Worrell kept good musicians working for many years. Wheaton cut two albums: *Small World (Isn't It?)* in 1989 with Peter Lundberg on piano, Richard Davis on bass, and Jim Latimer and Michael Weiss splitting the drum duties; and *Love's 3 Faces* in 2000 with pianist Harris Lemberg (see online discography.) In the late 1980s, Davis and Wheaton went to New York for a week, where she sang

Record jacket from 1989 featuring Jan Wheaton, Jim Latimer, Richard Davis (see chapter 14), and Peter Lundberg. COURTESY OF PETER LUNDBERG

several numbers each night with an all-star New York band at the jazz club Sweet Basil.

In the early 2000s, she found a new musical partner: Israeli-born and classically trained pianist Matan Rubenstein, who was then a graduate student at UW. She remembers him serving as her "anchor" for almost ten years, until he left town. They made a record, *Expressions of Love*, in 2005. Although Wheaton still works when she can, she is not actively seeking music jobs, and many of her gigs are private parties and fund-raisers. While she enjoys singing for many occasions, including events like Live at Five on Capitol Square, she says, "[I miss] the club atmosphere. Because then I can really reach out and grab you . . . and establish some kind of connection." Wheaton has appreciated her career in music. "It kept me out of jail," she says, "it gave me some play money, it made me some pretty good friends, and it gave me the opportunity to work with some really special people—which everybody doesn't get."

Gerri DiMaggio

Gerri DiMaggio is a Madison native who came from a big, musical Italian family. Her grandfather Rucci played accordion and guitar, and she remembers he "literally would pack the boys in and they'd go off and play weddings." Her uncle, Joe Rucci, a guitarist, made a name for himself in the clubs of St. Paul, Minnesota. The DiMaggio family moved to Madison after Grandfather DiMaggio, who owned a speakeasy, was arrested and spent almost two years in prison. In Madison, an aunt and uncle owned the White Front Grocery Store, which later became the Mifflin Street Co-op.[2] DiMaggio doesn't remember a time when she didn't sing: "I was always in the choir when I was a kid."[3] In her youth, her mother dragged her to the Hoffman House, to hear guitarist Johnny Shacklett; and in the late-1960s, she heard pianist Ted Jackson.

When DiMaggio was in high school in the late 1960s, she heard Ben Sidran in Madison clubs. She also listened to organist Melvin Rhyne at the Jazz Showcase with drummer George Brown.[4]

While a student at Madison's Central High School, DiMaggio was inspired by an older student performing during a seventh-hour school showcase: "There was Tracy Nelson," she recalls, "she was a bohemian before anyone used the term hippie, . . . playing this great guitar. . . . That was it for me. And then I started playing guitar." (Nelson went on to a major career as a blues and country singer.)

After high school graduation, DiMaggio left Madison for Colorado, where she became a ski bum, teaching skiing in Aspen for seven or eight years. She worked on her music, too, singing and playing some country blues. A pianist introduced DiMaggio to the music of Ma Rainey and Bessie Smith during this time. She also became interested in her mom's records, which included vocalists Sarah Vaughan, Billy Eckstine, and Italian American heroes Frank Sinatra and Tony Bennett.

On a visit home to Madison in the mid-1970s during the off-season in Aspen, DiMaggio and a friend went to the State Street "hippie hangout,"

Good Karma. A trio known as Mills Street Foundation was playing there: Bob Pesselman on guitar, Jeff Ernstoff on flute, and Ira Sussman on bass. (They jokingly referred to themselves as the Jewish Crosby, Stills, and Nash.) The band played standards and tunes ranging from Billie Holiday to Wes Montgomery. Pesselman was a student of celebrated Madison guitar teacher Roy Plum (as was Roger Brotherhood, who also became an important Madison guitarist). Some weeks later, DiMaggio learned that the band was looking for a vocalist and successfully auditioned. Soon thereafter, she moved into what she remembers as a "little hippie house" on Mills Street with other members of the band. Many jam sessions were held there, occasionally attended by luminaries like Ted Jackson.

DiMaggio's jazz education continued as she sat in on Pesselman's lessons with Roy Plum. She says, simply, "I fell in love with this music." The young musicians made trips to Milwaukee and Chicago, seeing performances by such musicians as Carmen McRae, James Moody, and (at the Marc Plaza in Milwaukee) Buddy Montgomery.

Mills Street Foundation landed a house gig at the Edgewater Hotel, which continued for about five years. The band also went on the road, especially during summers. Besides standards, they did the more contemporary music of artists like Chick Corea and Flora Purim, and strayed into R&B-influenced music. Musicians who played in later incarnations of the band included Hans Zermuehlan on keyboards, saxophonist Mark Johnson, bassist David Davenport, and bassist/vocalist Woo May. Eventually the band moved from the Edgewater to Inn on the Park. The band performed at Summerfest in Milwaukee and opened shows for saxophonists Stanley Turrentine and Charles Lloyd.

Like other musicians in Madison who had house gigs, DiMaggio has fond memories of some of the noted visitors who showed up to listen over the years. Two standouts include blues violin legend Papa John Creach (who was then touring with Jefferson Starship) and the enormously influential Joni Mitchell.[5]

DiMaggio and Pesselman were married in 1983. On a whim, they asked Buddy Montgomery to play at their wedding, and to their great surprise, he accepted.

For a semester during this time, DiMaggio attended Richard Davis's Black Music Ensemble meetings at the University of Wisconsin. Pesselman studied privately with Davis for a while, and DiMaggio also studied briefly with Davis, receiving both musical and life lessons. The two were connected further through their practice of Buddhism.

By around 1984, DiMaggio says, "We had been on the road for like ten [years]. . . . We'd been on and off, doing all kinds of gigs, and we were getting into our thirties and it was like, 'Are we ever gonna have any money to do anything that [normal people our age do]?' " Another consideration for leaving the performing life was the prevalence of drug use. One notable victim of that culture was area guitarist Junior Olson, who died in his early forties. Some other members of the scene ended up with hepatitis later in life.

Off the road and out of the clubs, DiMaggio joined the furniture business of her sister and brother-in-law. In 1986, she opened her own business, DiMaggio's Euro Design, and says, "I really kind of stopped doing music for about five years."[6] Pesselman, who had a degree in chemistry, went to work for Covance Industries. After concentrating on her business career for several years, DiMaggio began playing again in the early 1990s.

Only a couple of years later, DiMaggio got a call from Mary Lang Sollinger, a onetime candidate for mayor in Madison, who was running the Greater State Street Business Associates (GSSBA). The GSSBA was thinking of establishing a music festival, which DiMaggio pushed into becoming a jazz festival. With the help of Cal Worrell and Cathy Sullivan, Jazz at Five was born. Over the years, Jazz at Five has hosted the best of not only Madison's jazz community, but the wider jazz world as well.

After eight or nine years booking the musicians for the series, DiMaggio says, "I was getting more serious about my own music. Here I was thinking, 'I'm getting older; I don't have anything on record. This is silly, I should really start doing some stuff.' "

In the late 1990s, Pesselman and DiMaggio checked out a trio at the Concourse.[7] She immediately took to Paul Hastil's piano playing, and years later they are still making music together. Since 2001, DiMaggio has cut several albums (see online discography).

In 2007, DiMaggio and Hastil performed at the Telluride Jazz Festival in Colorado. They had a two-year engagement at the Edgewater, and then at Otto's. More recently, they have worked sporadically at the Cardinal, the Fountain, Otto's, Capitol ChopHouse, and Heritage Tavern

Gerri DiMaggio with Paul Hastil (see chapter 16) on piano and John Mesoloras on bass.
PHOTO BY BOB PESSELMAN

as a duo or a trio (usually with bassist John Mesoloras) and occasionally as a quartet.

Lynette Margulies

Lynette Margulies, known professionally as just Lynette, grew up in an Orthodox Jewish home in Washington, DC, in the 1950s and 1960s. As a young girl, she took piano lessons. Every week, the *Washington Post* printed a popular song's melody and chords. "And so I was performing at a very young age," Margulies says, "because I'd figure out the song, and then I'd call all my friends up . . . and I'd say, 'Listen to this.'" By age fourteen, she played her first paying gig, on guitar. She participated in school choirs, but because of her family's religious practice, she rarely could take part in concerts, which took place on Fridays or Saturdays.

In 1970, Margulies went to New York to attend Stern College. "I lived in an eighteen-story building a block away from the Empire State Building," she says. "And I would sit in the elevator or in the lobby and serenade everybody who got in the elevator . . . I just couldn't help myself." After a year at Stern, she went to Israel for a year, where she attended Hebrew University in Jerusalem. She remembers, "I hooked up with this guy who played guitar and this woman who played harmonica. And we did many gigs in Jerusalem and surrounding areas," playing the music of Bob Dylan, the Beatles, and Smokey Robinson. Margulies started writing tunes she described as "pretty dark" while in Israel, and started scat singing before she even knew what scatting was. When she dropped out of school and returned to the United States, she waitressed and took piano lessons in DC. Desperate to escape home, she applied to and was accepted at the University of Wisconsin.

Margulies arrived in Madison on New Year's Day in 1972. She went to hear music at the Brat House on State Street, where Ira Sussman, Jeff Cesario, Michael Weiss, and Jeffrey Ernstoff were playing. Although she was a Hebrew major in school, she took music courses, including music theory, and joined Jimmy Cheatham's Black Music Ensemble. She also hooked up with UW Music School faculty member Joan Wildman. Margulies graduated with her degree, but she had the music bug.

She was doing a solo gig—singing and playing her little blond Wurlitzer piano—at the Cardinal Bar, where she also tended bar, when she was heard by one of the partners of the new Full Compass studio in Madison. He asked Margulies to come to the studio to record. The session sidemen included members of the local band Regalia. With Margulies, they started a new band, Four Chairs No Waiting. With Joe Wickham on guitar, Duane Freeman on saxophone, Andy Feldman on harmonica and percussion, Ira Sussman (and later David Davenport) on bass, and Michael Weiss on drums, this band, like Gerri DiMaggio's Mills Street Foundation, became one of the area's most popular groups.

Doing music ranging from Chaka Khan to the Yellowjackets, or as Margulies describes it, "funk-blues-jazz-etc.," the band played constantly and to packed houses. "[It was] my true, love-of-my-life band," says Margulies."We're still married to each other in our sixties." But, as sometimes happened in the 1970s, "Some guy was talking about making us famous and all that, and I was not very stable at the time, and I turned it down, and kinda ended Four Chairs No Waiting."

Margulies had a desire to get closer to jazz, so she went back to school for more music study. Through Joan Wildman, Margulies met pianist

Three members of Four Chairs No Waiting setting up for a gig in the late 1970s. Left to right: Duane Freeman, Lynette, and David Davenport. PHOTO BY KEITH ROBERT WESSEL

Jane Reynolds, and the two have been making music together off and on since 1979. They have done hundreds of gigs together, as just a duo or with larger groups.

An invitation from singer/songwriter/pianist Ben Sidran changed Margulies's life in the early 1980s. He invited her to take part in what she remembers as "these alternative services for Jewish high holy days: Rosh Hashanah, the New Year, and Yom Kippur. And I had already practically turned anti-Semitic by that time. I had a lot of issues with . . . a lot of stuff." She told Sidran, " 'No way; absolutely no way.' He said, 'Just try it.' So I did it, and as soon as I sang that stuff, it brought me back to my childhood. And when I sing this Hebrew stuff, . . . it taps into a place . . . beyond what I already tap into." Although Sidran talked about doing a Jewish album at this time, Margulies became ill and left Madison for six years.

Finally, around 1990, when Margulies was in Washington, Sidran called and told her it was time to make the Jewish album. Margulies remembers, "I said, 'There's no way I can make it.' And he said, 'No, you can do it, you can do it.' " A plane ticket and reservation got her to Minneapolis.

"I was not well," she says, "and I was really thin. . . . I was frail, fragile; and I went into the studio. And we laid down pretty much just the vocal track. And when I started singing, I'm telling you, the very first measure, [I] started singing this Hebrew song, and my grandmother, who was already gone many years, was holding my hand. I mean it still gives me chills." The album, *Life's a Lesson*, was released in 1994. Over a period of years, Margulies did thirty to forty gigs with some of the great musicians who are on the album—Phil Woods, Rufus Reid, Steve Khan, Howard Levy, Mike Manieri, and others. She performed in venues ranging from the Tolerance Center in Los Angeles to the Orpheum Theater in Vienna, Austria.

Shortly after the recording of *Life's a Lesson*, when Margulies returned to Madison, she went back to activity on the local scene. Over the years, she has played with many jazz musicians in the city, in a variety of combinations. Pianists that she worked with (besides Jane Reynolds) ran the gamut from John Thulin to Joan Wildman. In the early days of the Madison Music Collective, Margulies and Eliza Lightfoot sponsored one of the earliest regular jam sessions in Madison, at O'Cayz Corral. One of Margulies's later career highlights was doing a short bit with the great vocalist Bobby McFerrin during a performance at the Overture Center.

To pay the bills, Margulies, like so many other musicians, has had a series of alternate jobs. She drove for Union Cab for about ten years, and recently, she worked for an alternative health care organization. The only time she made a living making music was during the Four Chairs era.

While less active on the scene in the 2010s, Margulies continues to explore musical possibilities as well as new ways to contribute to the wider local jazz scene.

Jackie Allen

Many consider Jackie Allen to be a Madison singer, but others consider her a Milwaukee singer, and others yet a Chicago singer.

Allen was born in 1959 in Brown Deer, near Milwaukee. Her family moved to the Madison area—McFarland—when Allen was nine or ten years old. Her father, Louis, was a Dixieland and polka tuba player (often with the Mississippi Valley Dutchmen); he was known as Lou in the polka world, and as Gene in the jazz world. Louis played professionally into the 2010s, and in 2013 was presented with the Distinguished Service Award by the Wisconsin Polka Hall of Fame.

Allen's mother, Fern, sang at funerals and weddings, and played piano. Allen grew up in a household where music was playing constantly, and like her four siblings and father, Allen took up a brass instrument—the French horn. Her high school band director was Tom Dvorak, son of the legendary University of Wisconsin band director Ray Dvorak; Tom went on to lead bands at UW–Milwaukee. At McFarland High, Allen also sang in the choirs and took part in the theater program, which was led by a local icon, Gene Olson. At times, about a quarter of the school's students were participating in the theater program, for which Olson wrote scripts and music until his death at age eighty-seven.

As Allen remembers, UW–Madison "didn't have a jazz vocal major, so I auditioned in the classical area—performance. And for some reason, I got in [*laughter*]. What a joke. Because I had no knowledge, no interest in classical music." Entering UW in 1978, she immediately became involved with jazz, joining Richard Davis's Black Music Ensemble and taking Joan Wildman's improvisation class. She was the only singer in the improvisation class, "where [she] began to meet all the other musicians and interact with them." She also sang with the jazz ensemble, led at that time by Les Thimmig. Her interest led to private lessons with Davis, who eventually set up a jazz vocal class, which Allen occasionally led.

A transforming experience took place when, as Allen remembers, "My brother took me to [the] Kool Jazz Festival in Milwaukee, and back-to-back, Friday night, Saturday night . . . was Ella Fitzgerald and Sarah Vaughan. . . . We sat out there and watched them singing, and I remember thinking, 'This is what I'm gonna do.'"

"While I was in college," Allen says, "I already had started playing out with groups around town. And I never finished my degree. . . . I was already out doing what I wanted to do, [and] teaching other students." One of these groups was the band Java, which frequently worked at the Church Key in Madison and Milwaukee's Summerfest. Of her studies outside jazz, Allen says, "I remember going to my classical voice lessons, and my teacher was just like, trying to strangle me. . . . At one point she said,

'You think you can do it all.' Because here I am, a classical voice major, but I would have to leave master class early with my microphone in hand to go and sing with the jazz ensemble."

Allen recalls one of the first jobs she did with her future husband, bassist Hans Sturm, in the Hotel Washington. Sturm remembers that the hotel "had a disco upstairs; it had a restaurant and rock and roll on the first floor, and in the basement, [which] was also split in two, there was a private gay bar in the back . . . called the Barber's Closet." (The space functioned as a barbershop by day.) Allen says, "[Singing with a bassist] was such a challenge for my ear. . . . But that really helped develop me as a singer."

At one point while Allen was performing around Madison, she was hired for a gig in Milwaukee and immediately called Melvin Rhyne. The two worked together briefly at the Hilton Hotel and then moved to the Wyndham Hotel downtown, where they worked four to five nights a week as a duo for several years. Despite being in the lobby lounge of a major hotel, Allen remembers Rhyne played "the crappiest piano there, it was just awful." Due to the Wyndham's proximity to the city's downtown theaters and what was then called the Performing Arts Center, theater people and performers from the center would frequently stop in. Allen has vivid memories of interacting with the Modern Jazz Quartet, and even with pop singer Frankie Valli.

Allen moved to Milwaukee in 1989 and taught at the Wisconsin Conservatory. She took part in jam sessions at the Jazz Estate and the Jazz Gallery, where she met many of the veterans of the Milwaukee scene. During part of this time, she dated a blues guitarist; she says, "After my gig would get done at midnight, I would go to the blues clubs, and oftentimes they would let me sit in." She worked back in Madison from time to time.

After this apprenticeship with Rhyne, Allen moved to Chicago. "It was easy to get into the scene down there," she remembers. "People were very inviting, and within a year I convinced a club owner to give me ten grand to . . . pay for my first CD, and then—boom, boom, boom." Allen was over thirty and hardly a novice at this time. She worked many rooms in Chicago, including the Jazz Showcase and the Green Mill. She had a steady gig at the Pops for Champagne downtown. After a time, Allen began working regularly with the gifted pianist and vocalist Judy

Jackie Allen with Melvin Rhyne (see chapter 11) at Jackson's Supper Club in Milwaukee, ca. 1990. COURTESY OF JACKIE ALLEN

Roberts. The two did a steady one-night-a-week job at Philander's in suburban Oak Park. Allen maintained a decent income with her club work and a busy schedule recording jingles in the Chicago studios.

After her premiere album, Allen recorded two albums with Roberts, then a duo album with Hans Sturm, and an album with prominent West Coast musicians for the Naxos label. Then she became something of a flagship artist for the Chicago label A440 records, cutting two albums that included the nucleus of a band that still performs today—Sturm, percussionist Dane Richeson, and Chicago guitarist John Moulder. Just as A440 was about to go bust, Allen was signed to the major label Blue

Note. But she made only one album for the label, which then dropped her, along with many other artists, in one of its periodic resizings (see online discography).

Allen's life changed in 2003 when Sturm, now her husband, was hired to the faculty at Ball State University, and the two of them moved to Indiana. Eventually, they put together an album with members of the Muncie Symphony Orchestra. After eight years in Indiana, in 2011, Sturm and Allen moved to Lincoln, Nebraska, when Sturm got a position at the University of Nebraska. Allen recently released two albums—*My Favorite Color* in 2014 and *Rose Fingered Dawn* in 2017—and she and her band played gigs in Wisconsin and Chicago after both releases.

Allen attributes her easy assimilation into the jazz world to the atmosphere around her home growing up—"hearing my father doing the Dixieland [thing]." This early exposure to jazz, combined with her immersion in the jazz scene at UW and in Madison in the early 1980s, followed by her invaluable time with Melvin Rhyne, resulted in one of Madison's most successful and talented jazz singers.

Kelly De Haven

Kelly De Haven was born in 1957 and grew up in a musical family—in fact, a family that, because of her father, Doc (see chapter 14), was considered jazz royalty in Madison. De Haven took piano lessons in elementary school and fell in love with music listening to her dad, her AM transistor radio, and her grandparents' record collection. She grew up singing along to everything. Her other passion as a child was ballet, and by fifth grade she was taking ballet classes. At age ten, her first performance onstage was as Clara in a production of *The Nutcracker* at the UW Union Theater. She continued dancing with the Wisconsin Ballet Company (now the Madison Ballet) through high school. When De Haven went to college at UW–Madison, she majored in communications but also continued studying dance at the university.

About this time, her father, Doc, told her she could make some extra money singing. De Haven's first public vocal performance was onstage with her father. She recalls her dad's bandmates were "old school" musicians; trained in the aural tradition, they could play a huge array of songs in any key, and were also storytellers and jokesters. With them, she says, “Sometimes I felt like I was in a Marx Brothers’ movie. . . . That time performing with my dad and his band was a gift to me on many, many levels.” The inexperienced and shy De Haven was almost the opposite of her father’s wry, sometimes cantankerous stage persona, and this contrast became part of their onstage banter.

But De Haven also wanted to sing with musicians of her generation. She worked briefly with a Madison band, the Cheeters, performing 1960s rock covers regionally. The rock and roll scene involved booking agents, sound and light crews, and incredible volume—as De Haven remembers, “Nothing like the jazz scene.”

She wanted to get back to jazz and create original music. De Haven occasionally worked with her father, including a regular Tuesday night gig at the Inn on the Park, and at the post–UW football game gigs at Union South. “This was back in the 1980s,” De Haven says, “when the Badgers rarely won a football game. But the fans didn’t seem to mind—drinking beer and dancing to Dixieland.”

Around 1985, longtime Madison guitarist Cliff Frederickson told De Haven about an opportunity to audition for a gig at the Concourse Hotel downtown. Cal Worrell hired De Haven and Jeff Eckels, a bassist who was a dynamic presence on the Madison jazz scene for years. They pulled in pianist Harris Lemberg and drummer Todd Steward, and the band landed a six-night-a-week gig at the Concourse, billed as Kelly De Haven and the MisbeHaven Band. The band had steady work and the budget to bring in guest musicians.

Cal Worrell, general manager of the hotel, was a pivotal figure for Madison jazz and was named Jazz Personality of the Year by the Isthmus Jazz Festival in 2005. De Haven received this award in 2000.

When Lemberg left the band after about three years, Eckels talked Philadelphia pianist Dan Kleiman into moving to Madison to start a new band performing original music. The MisbeHaven band performed mostly originals and was renamed NEO in the mid-1980s. Eckels and Kleiman wrote the much of the music; De Haven wrote the lyrics. During this time, she was named Best New Regional Vocalist by Arts Midwest, and NEO won second-place honors in a national competition sponsored by *Down Beat* magazine in 1987.

Kelly De Haven. PHOTO BY JOE TONDU

In 1990, Kleiman moved back east, and Vince Fuh and Paul Hastil shared the role of NEO's pianist. Dane Richeson frequently drummed with the band, as did Clyde Stubblefield. The core of the group was a quartet, but a fifth instrumentalist was often incorporated—over the years these included Jeff's brother, guitarist Steven Eckels; acclaimed saxophonist Ernie Watts; pianist Arman Donelian; saxophonist Rick Hirsch; and violinist Randy Sabien (see chapter 19). The group also appeared from time to time as a trio and as a vocal-bass duo. De Haven frequently worked in duos with Fuh, Hastil, and Dave Stoler. She made recordings under her own name as well as with her father, Doc (see online discography).

De Haven's regular Madison gigs in the 1990s took place at Fyfe's Bistro, Café Montmartre, and the Mendota Beach Club (for Tuesday night jazz), as well as a Wednesday night summer gig at the Great Dane following Concerts on the Square. Tours and corporate gigs took the group to Las Vegas and college football bowl games; they also played regional orchestra pops performances. De Haven enjoyed collaborating with other singers in the Madison music community as well (see other profiles in this chapter).

Another of De Haven's varied professional associations was with singer/songwriter Ken Lonnquist. Lonnquist's musicals for children were performed by the Children's Theater of Madison, but he often utilized a small troupe of four or five singers, which included De Haven, for his entertaining educational programs. His Christmas program, *Old Befana*, has enjoyed long-running success. De Haven enjoyed bringing singing, dancing, and acting together. Her multiple talents were a perfect fit for Lonnquist's programs, which took place in schools, libraries, and community centers around the Midwest.

De Haven and trumpeter David Cooper (see chapter 16) worked together and eventually married. Her musical career gradually took a backseat while she raised their daughter and traveled for the University of Wisconsin and the UW Foundation.

De Haven describes her twenty-plus-year musical career in glowing terms: "I was like the luckiest girl in the world, just being able to be onstage, and performing, and [to] be amidst people that were far better musicians than myself. It was really wonderful."

Harmonious Wail

Harmonious Wail, one of Madison's longest-running groups, was founded in 1987. Although it started as a mostly instrumental group, it has always included vocals, and when Maggie Delaney-Potthoff became a member of the group in the late 1980s, vocals became a different kind of mix. Since then, Maggie has become one of Madison's best-known singers.

The band was founded by Sims Delaney-Potthoff, who was born in 1954 and raised in Racine. He began playing trumpet in a marching band, the Racine Saints Band, which was made up of students from the city's Catholic schools. Sims went to grade school at St. Rita's and high school at St. Catherine's. Though he played the cornet, he wanted to be a drummer. Coming up in Racine, which he called "the drum and bugle capital of the world," Sims says he "started leaning toward jazz, right away, as a youngster."

After Sims graduated from high school in 1972, he began playing the guitar, and what he called "cowboy songs." Then, in the mid-1970s, he says he "discovered the mandolin, went to Chicago to buy a mandolin, and was given a business card for a fellow named Jethro Burns. And that changed everything." Burns, a legendary country musician, best known as half of the duo Homer and Jethro, had another life as an extremely influential mandolin player who played country, bluegrass, popular tunes, and jazz. To Sims, Burns took on the role of a father figure. Maggie says, "He was our mentor for living a musician's life. . . . He taught us all we needed to know to . . . stay the course."

Maggie was also born in 1954 and grew up in Hartford, Wisconsin. She claims, "I was kind of a little dork. But my big brothers always had jazz on, [and] the Kingston Trio, a lot of folk stuff. Peter, Paul, and Mary. My mom had 101 Strings." But Maggie listened to Barbra Streisand and the Beatles. In school, she had an influential choir director, Ruth Knoll, who built such a legacy that a theater in the Schauer Arts and Entertainment Center in Hartford was named in her honor.

During her senior year in high school, Maggie auditioned and was accepted for a new program called America's Youth in Concert, which included two kids from every state in the country. With the group, Maggie performed in Carnegie Hall and the Kennedy Center for the Performing Arts. The group also toured Europe, including a performance at the Mozart Festival in Salzburg. Maggie went on to attend college at St. Norbert College in De Pere, Wisconsin.

Maggie and Sims both moved to Madison in 1978, although they did not know each other at the time. Maggie auditioned for music theater, what she called her "little hobby." After studying mandolin with Burns, Sims played three or four years with a Madison bluegrass band, Stone Oak. Maggie came to hear the band at its very first performance, at Stillwaters bar. She says, "I went up and introduced myself [to Sims] and talked to him about bluegrass music." Almost exactly one year later, they ran into each other at the same bar. "He went, 'Oh, it's you!' " she remembers. "We've never been apart since then."

When Stone Oak broke up, Sims and Maggie considered their options. Sims decided to attend the Berklee College of Music in Boston, and he and Maggie moved there in 1984. Sims entered Berklee as a violin player;

he says, "I was terrible. . . . [But] they didn't know what to do with a mandolin player."

The couple and their new baby moved back to Madison in 1986. Sims secured health insurance for the young family by driving a cab. When he ran into John Cooper, a guitarist who also had attended Berklee, the two became charter members of the band Harmonious Wail. The other members of the quartet were violinist Chris Wagoner and bassist Laurie Lang. "The notion was to put the violin and mandolin out front," Sims remembers, "and guitar and walking bass as the rhythm section, . . . but to approach it like a jazz band, [a] string jazz band."

After two or three years, Cooper decided to go back to Boston, and Lang had some issues with travel, so the band changed. It was made over with Maggie, who had been sitting in for a tune or two ever since the earliest days, becoming a full-time member of the group. The band had always included vocals, as Sims, Lang, and Wagoner all sang. "And so it was songs, . . . bebop tunes, and Django Reinhardt, gypsy jazz instrumentals," Sims recalls. "We had a violin player who got hired by the symphony, and he did a last-minute bail on a gig, and I turned to Maggie and said, 'Can you sing these lines?' So she looked at all these violin lines and sat down at the piano and worked them out, and that was her entrance to the band." Sims says, "The concept has always remained the same, and the music has not changed, really." Although Maggie's training and experience had mainly been in classical music and music theater, she had little trouble adjusting to Harmonious Wail's music.

The band first toured Europe in 1994, where on the streets of Amsterdam they first heard what Sims calls "authentic Django Reinhardt gypsy jazz." That group was the Robin Nolan Quartet, which Harmonious Wail later brought to the United States for some shows. That success laid the groundwork for Harmonious Wail's gypsy jazz festival, now known as the Midwest Gypsy Swing Festival, which began in the early 2000s.

Significant contributors to Harmonious Wail throughout the band's over twenty-five-year history have been guitarists Doug Brown and Tom Waselchuk and bassists Henry Boehm and Jon Cristensen. "The original band was really full of Louis Jordan, Nat King Cole, really swingy, swingy, swingy stuff; kinda pop music," Sims says. After being approached by the

Harmonious Wail (left to right): Sims Delaney-Potthoff, Jeff Weiss, and Maggie Delaney-Potthoff. COURTESY OF HARMONIOUS WAIL

record label Naxos World Music in the early 2000s, the band moved toward so-called gypsy jazz. More recently, their sound includes a strain of Americana. Now, says Sims, "We can play [a] folk festival, jazz festival, blues festival, gypsy jazz festival, . . . the whole . . . shebang."

While Wail sometimes works as a quartet, the basic group is now a trio: Sims on mandolin and guitar; Maggie on vocals, in addition to playing brushes on a cardboard box (like a drummer on a snare drum); and, since 2011, Jeff "Jeffo" Weiss on bass. Weiss grew up in Middleton. His first instrument was saxophone, but he switched to bass in order to play in a rock band with other kids. He played in his high school orchestra, then went to UW–Madison to study bass with Richard Davis. Weiss was a serious classical player, even auditioning for an opening in the Chicago Symphony after graduating from UW. He still has an interest in classical music but is currently so busy with Harmonious Wail that he can't find the time to do that kind of playing.

Sims says that Harmonious Wail led a "first fun-filled group tour along the west coast of Ireland" in 2015, with a group of more than twenty people. He philosophizes about the band, and the music of Django and jazz standards. "To kids," he explains, "that's old guy music, or it's old-fashioned music. Well, it never hit us as that way, because it's so smokin', it's just so happenin'. And we've never really cottoned to whether something's in style or out of style or old or not. It's just: where's the groove? [We] could do this for another fifty, seventy, hundred years."

Ben Sidran

Unlike the other singers in this chapter, Ben Sidran, who didn't think of himself as a singer for years, became a national figure. In 2003, he wrote a detailed autobiography, *Ben Sidran: A Life in the Music*, which fans and interested readers will want to consult. The following is a brief account of his life but focuses mostly on his career, based largely on what he wrote in that book.[8]

Sidran was born in 1943 in Chicago, but after his father, Louis (born Sidransky), enlisted in the army during the latter stages of World War II, Ben's mother, Shirley, took Ben and his sister and moved in with her parents in Racine, Wisconsin. Sidran remembers music from his very earliest days, and when his father returned from the war, that music included Benny Goodman, Nat Cole, Erroll Garner, and Pine Top Smith. The piano in the living room of their home on Carmel Avenue became the center of his universe. He says, "In general, I lived a pretty normal life for a Jewish kid growing up in a small Midwestern town." (However, this "normal life" did include some incidents of anti-Semitism.)

His father worked for a small advertising firm in Racine, but by the time Ben was a teenager, Louis had taken a job in Chicago and was gone most of every weekday. As a student at McKinley Junior High School and Washington Park High, Ben worked a variety of jobs and spent most of his money on jazz records. After a failed round of piano lessons when he was younger, he had success in high school lessons with Milwaukee teacher Milton Mieritz.

At the end of his first year of high school, Sidran played his first gig with a small band led by a senior at the school. Before graduation, he was recruited by University of Wisconsin student J. C. Holly to play in the Natural Five, which worked on a somewhat steady basis, mostly for college parties.

Sidran entered UW as a student in 1961. He lived on North Henry Street and frequently practiced on the piano in Lowell Hall, a girls' dormitory, while studying in the Integrated Liberal Studies Program. He played jazz gigs in fraternity houses and hung out at the Pad with early members of the counterculture.[9] Drugs, music, and cultural and political awareness led Sidran to more actively pursue what he called "the Integrated Liberal Studies Program of the streets." He and his fellow seekers were hungering for knowledge where, as he recalls, "learning was the key. We were on fire. We kept stoned to keep cool."

He spent most of the next summer in Racine working at Young Radiator Company. Back at school, he encountered the Ardells, a rock band that included lead vocalist and guitarist Steve Miller (a Milwaukeean) and bassist Boz Scaggs, both of whom were headed for eventual stardom. Not long afterward, Sidran left his jazz gigs to make significantly more money with this band, working on campus and traveling around southern Wisconsin. Sidran also connected with storied UW history professor Harvey Goldberg, and he started writing a column for the campus newspaper, the *Daily Cardinal*. In the spring of 1963 he stumbled into the not-yet-open Discount Records on State Street, was offered a job, and dropped out of school.

Sidran says, "Working at Discount Records was a graduate education in music and the record business," which was exploding at this time. At the store, he had immediate access to all the new records in every genre of America's music industry. In Sidran's new residence on Mifflin Street, George Brown, a new drummer in town, preached the gospel of John Coltrane.

By early 1964, President John Kennedy had been assassinated, and Sidran was back in school. The quest for knowledge continued, the drugs became more exotic, and suddenly Sidran found himself in California, living in Berkeley with a female friend and working in another Discount Records. He returned to school in Madison after a few months but struggled. Drugs were a part of everyday life, and of special occasions, such as when George Brown brought the band of (Rahsaan) Roland Kirk to Madison. In early 1965, Sidran returned to Berkeley, where LSD was prevalent, and started class at San Francisco State, where S. I. Hayakawa was becoming famous. Sidran worked at yet another Discount Records in San Francisco, and his landlord was jazz saxophonist John Handy.

Eventually, Sidran decided to return to Wisconsin and school. "By the fall of 1965," he remembers, "what had once been a relatively small counterculture was becoming a major movement." Sidran, though, retreated into himself, reading and listening to music incessantly. As the era of "flower power" burgeoned, the specter of the Vietnam War hung over the heads of Americans, especially draft-age men. A bright spot in his turmoil was the appearance of Judy Lutrin, with whom Sidran has remained to this day.

Sidran says, "A crystallizing event [in Madison and "the movement"] came that spring [1966] during the occupation of the university's administration building," as protesters borrowed the tactics of the civil rights movement to resist the draft and protest the war.

Instead of going to California with Steve Miller, Sidran finally finished his degree at UW. Then he decided to attend graduate school in England. His studies, the absence of a regular performing outlet or practice venue, and the intimidating musical presence of pianist McCoy Tyner caused Sidran to quit playing piano for the first time since he was a child. But a stray piano on campus led to some quality time rediscovering the joys of playing. Furthermore, he discovered, "I didn't sound like anybody else. I sounded like me, for better or worse."[10] When Steve Miller came to London to record, Sidran ended up alone in the recording room with Boz Scaggs late one night, and their duet, with Sidran on harpsichord, ended up on the new Miller album. Sidran continued to be present during historic political moments; a trip to visit Harvey Goldberg in Paris landed him in the middle of the 1968 student protests that led to the general strike that almost brought down the government of Charles de Gaulle.

Later in 1968, Sidran returned to the United States as his father's health deteriorated. "Pop" died in September. A short while later, Sidran spent an emotional afternoon with his father's childhood friend, Nobel Prize–winning author Saul Bellow. When Sidran was called for his preinduction physical exam for the draft, he visited a psychiatrist who had been recommended to him by the Grateful Dead's Jerry Garcia. He never read the letter the psychiatrist wrote for him, but he was dismissed at his exam as unfit for the armed services.

Sidran stayed in Madison and worked on his doctoral dissertation. A spring break trip to California led to an offer to join the staff of the new magazine *Rolling Stone*, but after serious consideration, he turned it down. He returned to California later to help on Steve Miller's new album, and one wild late-night session led to Miller and Sidran creating the song "Space Cowboy." The royalties, according to Sidran, eventually "paid for my graduate education."

Judy and Sidran married in 1969, and the couple returned to England. He recorded a marathon session with the Rolling Stones, but none of the material was ever released. Renowned recording engineer Glyn Johns brought Sidran into the famous Olympic Studios to record a demo of his original material just before he defended his dissertation.

Returning to the States, Ben and Judy eventually made it to Los Angeles. Holt, Rinehart, and Winston decided to publish Sidran's dissertation, which became *Black Talk, or How the Music of Black America Created a Radical Alternative to the Values of Western Literary Tradition*. Some months later, he had a record deal with Capitol Records.

The record deal was contingent, however, on Sidran singing on the album. He had never sung in public. When the album was completed, Sidran says, "[It] mixed jazz, pop, and blues in a way that I had not heard before, and which, a few years later, might have been called 'fusion' music." Sidran's vocals have been an integral part of his live and recorded work ever since.

Largely because Judy was miserable in California, Ben turned down an offer from Capitol to be a producer, and the couple returned to Madison. They arrived in the wake of the bombing of Sterling Hall on the UW campus, a turning point in the public's perception of the antiwar movement. Ben's record, *Feel Your Groove*, was released but poorly supported by Capitol. In Madison, the Jazz Workshop had opened, and Sidran remembers, "Wild sessions were taking place there every night." George Brown was back in Madison, and when the James Brown band came through town, drummer Clyde Stubblefield decided to stay.

Although he is not profiled in this book, Clyde Stubblefield was a real presence in Madison for decades, mostly on the jazz scene. But his revered place in American music is in funk and soul. As James Brown's drummer from 1965–1970, Stubblefield created some of the signature drum feels for a whole genre of music. His rhythm pattern on Brown's "Funky Drummer" is one of the most sampled musical segments ever, having been used on at least a thousand recordings, according to Rolling Stone. He died in 2017.[11]

Sidran signed a new record deal with Blue Thumb Records in late 1971. Hearing his new album, *I Lead a Life*, jazz great Tony Williams asked Sidran to produce his next album. Sidran supplemented his income by teaching at UW. He hosted a weekly late-night talk and movie show on local television, *The Weekend Starts Now*, that drew guests ranging from Jane Fonda and Kinky Friedman to the Firesign Theater, pianist McCoy Tyner, and Madison's mayor, Paul Soglin. The Good Karma Restaurant in Madison started a jazz policy, hiring jazz acts over other styles, and hosted jazz artists Mose Allison and Charles Mingus.[12]

While Sidran was touring to support his second Blue Thumb album, the record company suddenly folded. But Sidran wrote an article on the current state of the record industry for *Rolling Stone* and produced an album by jazz vocalist Jon Hendricks.

Shortly thereafter, Sidran was signed to the new Arista label; *Free in America* (1976), his first album on the label, included all-star sidemen David "Fathead" Newman and Woody Shaw. Among the selections was the first recording of Billy Joel's "New York State of Mind."

Later in 1976, Sidran got a steady trio gig at La Creperie in Madison (with bassist Dennis Oliver and Clyde Stubblefield) and continued to work on other projects. For Chicago Public Television's *Soundstage* series, Sidran put together two successful jazz shows: a Dizzy Gillespie reunion, and a jazz vocal summit with Jon Hendricks, Annie Ross, Eddie Jefferson, and Leon Thomas. Sidran's son, Leo, was born that November.

Sidran had also become deeply involved with the National Organization to Reform Marijuana Laws, and he spent some unforgettable times with gonzo journalist Hunter Thompson at the organization's national convention.

In 1977, Sidran recorded another album, much of it with Richard Davis (who had recently moved to Wisconsin) and Tony Williams. An unfulfilling European tour did not give him any reason to hope for more support from Arista, but he hung on with the label through 1978, recording two albums on which, he says, he was "determined to find a new way to combine bebop and dance music."

In 1979, Sidran recorded what he considered his breakthrough album for Horizon, *The Cat in the Hat*. He calls it "a first-class example of bebop songs captured with a funk attitude—the marriage of the past and the present, of classic jazz and contemporary dance grooves." But the label folded the week before the record was scheduled to be released.

The next year, Sidran led a band that included saxophonist Bunky Green (a Milwaukee native), Richard Davis, and drummer Wendell Bond for the opening of the new Civic Center in downtown Madison. In July, he was part of a Carnegie Hall tribute to jazz vocalese pioneer Eddie Jefferson.

To welcome 1981, Sidran served as the New York anchor for National Public Radio's *Jazz Alive!* broadcast on New Year's Eve. Later in the year, he was hired to produce a series of programs called *The Jazz Life* for a Japanese company. The shows were filmed at the Village Vanguard in New York, and the first set of shows featured top jazz artists.

In the fall, Sidran toured as an opening act for another Milwaukee native, Al Jarreau, who was playing in large arenas around the country. Sidran's new album, *Old Songs for the New Depression*, went all the way to number one on the jazz sales charts in 1982, a year in which he took over the regular hosting of *Jazz Alive!* from Billy Taylor, spending three days a week in Washington, DC, putting the show together. A summer tour promoting *Old Songs* stretched across the continental United States and to Hawaii, Australia, and New Zealand.

There was a new album in 1983, and a duo concert with Richard Davis at the Elvehjem Museum in Madison was recorded and became yet another album. *Jazz Alive!* was canceled at NPR, but not long afterward Sidran was brought on to do jazz segments for *All Things Considered*, the network's flagship news program.

In 1985, a new NPR radio program, *Sidran on Record*, made its first appearance. For the next few years, Sidran produced more than one hundred episodes of the show, interviewing a who's who of the jazz world. His monthly commute from Madison to New York City for about five years was part of what Sidran describes as "[continuing] my musical and spiritual education."

Around this time, Sidran reconnected with his old friend Steve Miller, who was now a bona fide rock star. That led to Sidran's band becoming Steve's band for his next record, *Born to Be Blue*.

Sidran continued to expand his activities, becoming host of the VH1 network's successful *New Visions* program. Sidran hosted artists ranging from Al Jarreau to Sun Ra and from Don Cherry to Philip Glass. The show won an Ace Award for the best music series on cable television, but an ill-advised expansion to five nights a week led to its cancellation. The late 1980s offered opportunities in Spain, Italy, and in Cannes, France, where Sidran produced two shows.

In the summer of 1988, a Sidran tour stretched from New York to Paris and around the United States, ending with a concert on the lakefront at the zoo in Racine. Late in the year, the Sidran band went on tour with Steve Miller, but Sidran felt that their style was not a good match for Miller's *Greatest Hits* or the audiences on the tour. Yet Miller hired them for more summer tours, and in 1993 Miller recorded several songs written by Sidran's teenage son, Leo. Disagreements over publishing the songs, however, led to Sidran ending his thirty-year relationship with Miller.

In 1989, *Cool Paradise* was the first release from the new label Sidran founded, Go Jazz. Go Jazz went on to release albums by Mose Allison, British singer Georgie Fame, and others. Go Jazz projects that were especially meaningful to Sidran included the music he composed for the soundtrack to the acclaimed documentary film *Hoop Dreams* (with Milwaukee's Carl Allen drumming) and his album of Jewish songs, *Life's a Lesson*, recorded over a period of several years with a long list of collaborators such as Carole King and jazz stars Dave Liebman, Steve Khan, Lee Konitz, Randy Brecker, and Mike Mainieri. Madison's own Lynette (Margulies) supplied many of the vocals (see earlier in this chapter), as did the Gates of Heaven Children's Choir from the local synagogue. Despite the presence of big names, no major label would touch the album. But an appearance on CBS television's *Sunday Morning* show led to an explosion of interest in the project. Sidran initially had five hundred copies made, which he sold out of his basement for years; after the show aired, other media outlets ran with the story, and eventually more than twenty-five thousand copies were sold.

Ben Sidran at Facteur Chavel Palace in France, 2011. COURTESY OF BEN SIDRAN

Other interesting highlights from Sidran's career included recording the legendary Peggy Lee with jazz singer Michael Franks, and producing Diana Ross's gala concert featuring the music of Billie Holiday. In 1992, forty-three interviews derived from the *Sidran on Record* radio series were published in book form as *Talking Jazz: An Illustrated Oral History*.[13]

Although by 1993 he had reached the point in his career where he thought he never wanted to play in little nightclubs again, Sidran started working in a small Madison club called Mr. P's Place; he wanted to play in public with his son, Leo, by then an accomplished drummer.

Sidran's autobiography includes less about his career after 1994 and more of his reflections on his Jewish and family heritage, including his pride in the growth of Leo's career. Despite some serious health issues, Sidran continued a record career and some performance and production work, including a concert of Jewish music in Vienna, Austria, in 1997 on the anniversary of Kristallnacht, and a concert in Spain in 1998 celebrating the one hundredth anniversary of the birth of poet Federico Garcia Lorca. At home in 1997, Sidran put together a "dream concert" at UW's

Union Theater and performed with many of his closest musical friends, including Phil Woods, Richard Davis, Leo on drums, and Lynette.

He continued to work in the 2000s, frequently returning to perform in Europe and Japan. He released small group albums and a bilingual children's CD (cowritten and coproduced by Leo), which won a 2003 Parents' Choice Award. As an artist in residence at UW, he taught a class called "Jewish Popular Music in America: Irving Berlin to Lenny Kravitz." During summers in the 2010s, Sidran could be heard on Tuesday nights in a trio with Nick Moran and Louka Patenoude at Madison's Cardinal Bar on Wilson Street.

Sidran has accumulated many honors over the years. In 1995, he was appointed a Wisconsin Academy of Sciences, Arts and Letters Fellow and received a UW Distinguished Alumnus Award. In 2006, he received the Madison Area Music Awards Lifetime Achievement Award.[14] In his autobiography, he explains the decision he made to live in Madison long ago: "To this day, when people ask me how I can live in such a small town, I just smile and think, 'The road leads from New York City to Madison, not the other way around.'"

Elaborating on that point in 2014, Sidran told me:

> Moving back to Wisconsin forced me to invent myself (or reinvent myself) as a viable commodity. If I had stayed in LA, I would have had a career as a producer, perhaps, but the teaching, the writing, and much of the solo performing would probably not have happened. At first it was difficult—I heard a lot of "area code 608, where's that?"—but, eventually, it became part of a good life rather than a struggling career.[15]

14

In and Around the University of Wisconsin–Madison

The discussion of Bunny Berigan in chapter 1 contains a bit of the jazz history of Wisconsin's capital. The variety of venues in Madison—clubs, theaters, bars, restaurants, and other performance spaces—appear in Berigan's chapter and elsewhere in this book, but this chapter focuses on the University of Wisconsin–Madison campus and the musicians who spent time playing in and around the school.

UW–Madison is one of the great educational institutions in the United States. Its importance to the state of Wisconsin, not only educationally but also culturally, can hardly be overstated. Jazz has been associated with the university probably since the earliest days of jazz—if not as part of the curriculum, at least as part of the entertainment that emerges in communities with major universities.

As part of the curriculum, jazz at UW–Madison has had a somewhat checkered history. The program has never been as musically unified as those of Lawrence University and UW–Eau Claire, or produced the highly skilled and award-winning ensembles that have been the long-time standards at those institutions. While UW–Madison jazz faculty members have tended to operate independently rather than as a group, a significant number of widely differing students have found inspiration in the program as a result.

Doster "Doc" De Haven

Madison's "longest-running" and in some ways most successful jazz artist was Doster "Doc" De Haven.[1] De Haven was born in 1931. His father, also Doc De Haven, was a jobbing musician in Madison who spent a few weeks on the road with Bunny Berigan's ill-fated big band in 1939. The elder De Haven spent much of his youth in Baraboo; he and his seven siblings had a family band, largely a vocal group, and they performed vaudeville acts when they were young.

Young Doc was raised on the popular big band music of the day. He said, "As a result of being with my dad, and listening to recordings with him as a youngster and growing up, I learned a lot of tunes, by ear." He was inspired in his early playing days by Frank Tifft, a veteran trumpeter in the city. De Haven's earliest memory of playing a professional job was when then-president Harry Truman came to Madison to dedicate a building while on a campaign trip. While in high school, De Haven played with local bands led by Al Alverson, Eddy Lawrence, and Benny Her as well as his father. After graduating from Central High in 1949, De Haven attended UW–Madison for a year before entering the service during the Korean War.

In the service, De Haven played in a Special Services band at Lackland Air Force Base in San Antonio, Texas, and the 512th Air Force Band at Tinker Field in Oklahoma City. (One of his bandmates was West Coast trumpeter Jack Sheldon, who later became the comic musician in the band on Merv Griffin's popular afternoon variety television show.)

After a few years in the service, De Haven returned to Madison and UW. One of his closest friends at this time was fellow trumpeter and Oshkosh native Bobby Lewis, who would go on to play with jazz trombone great Jack Teagarden, and then to a long and successful career in jazz and commercial music in Chicago. Teagarden asked De Haven to join his band during the 1950s, but as he was in college and married, with one child and another on the way, De Haven turned down the offer.

Another running mate was trombonist Jim Beebe. After spending much of his childhood in Sparta, Wisconsin, Beebe attended Beloit College for a year before he joined the service during the Korean War.[2] Beebe became a service musician and, while stationed in California, sat in with the famed traditional jazz band led by Bob Scobey. After a couple of years, Beebe returned to Madison and enrolled at UW. Scobey hired him in the late 1950s, and Beebe went on to play with the famous Dukes of Dixieland before settling in Chicago for many years of band leading.

Another member of this core of Madison players was Jim Godfriaux, a trombonist who played piano on the Madison jazz scene for many years. While in college, various combinations of these musicians and others played frequently for fraternity parties on campus, as local musicians had already been doing for several decades.

Following De Haven's career is like taking a tour of Madison-area nightspots—a nostalgic journey for those who lived through these eras. Starting in college, De Haven worked with Johnny Salerno's band in such clubs as Three Bells Bar on University Avenue, the Kollege Klub on State Street, and the Pirate Ship on Fairchild Street, just off State, which later became Dotty Dumpling's Dowry. In the summer of 1954, he worked in Wisconsin Dells at the Dell View and the Purple Grackle.

He started a band in 1955 that included, at times, his college friends Lewis, Beebe, and Godfriaux. They played at the Campus Inn on State Street, the French Villa and the Shuffle Inn on South Park Street, and Mallards Bar on Wilson Street. When Salerno left town to relocate to Manitowoc, De Haven moved in and started a residency at the Pirate Ship that became the longest-running in Wisconsin history. Beginning in the fall of 1956, the six-piece band played Wednesday, Friday, and Saturday nights at the club for fourteen years. This longevity was due to steady support from not only university students, but an older crowd as well. Obviously, the music had a wide appeal. The band started making records in 1962 and continued into the compact disc era (see online discography).

Besides De Haven, the one constant member of the band was clarinetist Erle Smith. Smith had been coleader of a small band with Bunny Berigan's uncle Bob in the 1920s. (Bunny worked with the Smith-Berigan band around Madison for a couple of years in the mid-1920s; see chapter 1.) Once in a great while, the elder Doc De Haven would sub for Smith when Erle couldn't play with young Doc at the Pirate Ship. Other members of the band over the years included Harry Sharp (a sociology professor) on bass, Gene Herritz and Jim Godfriaux on piano, Eddie Stein and Bob

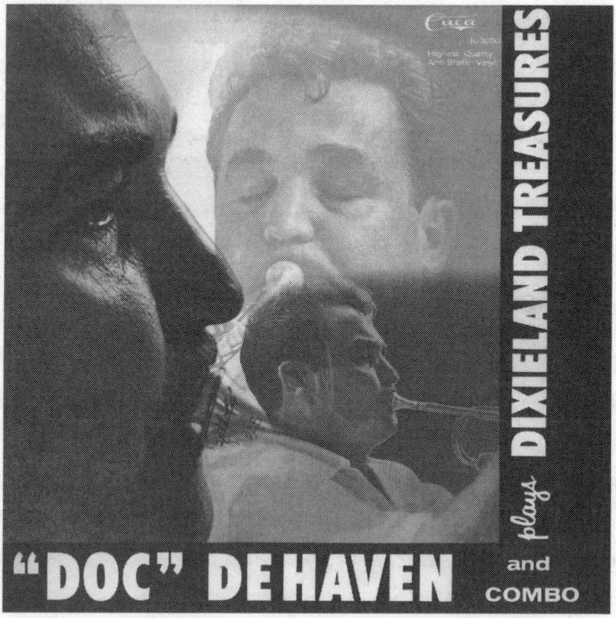

Doc De Haven's album on Cuca Records, ca. 1963. COURTESY OF JIM KIRCHSTEIN, PRESIDENT OF CUCA RECORDS

Russell on drums, and Jack Gehrken on trombone. Saxophonist Bill Grahn, who had played with De Haven at UW in the 1950s, was a frequent collaborator, often substituting for a trombonist, playing baritone saxophone. After Smith died in 1982, Grahn took his place in De Haven's band.

Once the band finally left the Pirate Ship in the early 1970s, De Haven played just about everywhere one could play jazz in and around Madison: Maxine's French Quarter on East Washington, the Top Hat in Middleton, the Edgewater Hotel on Wisconsin Avenue, the Seven E Supper Club in DeForest, the Athens Restaurant on State, the Westside Business Men's Association (Westsider Business Club), the New Orleans Chart House on University Avenue, the Signature Lounge at the Inn on the Park, Union South on North Randall Avenue, Hansen's Jazz Restaurant in Monona, Nakoma Golf Club, and the Madison Club. These were only the public venues; like most jobbing groups, De Haven's band also played many, many private parties. The band won the Best of Madison award for top local jazz band practically every year in the 1980s and early 1990s. De Haven was honored as Jazz Personality of the Year at the 1990 Isthmus

Jazz Festival and in 2012 was presented with a lifetime achievement award by the Madison Area Music Association.

In the mid-1990s, once De Haven quit leading his own band on a regular basis, he played with the Brad Pregeant Jazz Band at the Crowne Plaza Hotel for eight years. He would also go out with the Dick Jurgens Orchestra, a ghost band left over from the Swing Era, then led by Don Ring and headquartered in Madison. De Haven also played in the Madison Jazz Orchestra in its early days, when it was led by bassist Dennis Oliver.

It should be noted that during all this time, De Haven also had a day job—he taught school music in the Deerfield and Monona Grove public schools. But perhaps De Haven's most visible job was at the UW's Union South, where he played the Badger Bash parties after the UW football games for over two decades. Later, in the 1990s, he had a band in the bar at the Concourse Hotel on West Dayton after the games. Doc De Haven died in 2016. Thousands of UW alumni and jazz enthusiasts in Madison remember him fondly.

Johnny Shacklett

Definitive information about guitarist Johnny Shacklett is difficult to find. Though he didn't have a direct connection to UW–Madison, he spent much of his time in Madison near campus at his club, the Tuxedo Lounge, on Beld Street east of the Arboretum. The following is what I have been able to piece together about this legendary figure.[3]

Shacklett was reportedly a native of Indianapolis—the city that also sent Buddy Montgomery to Milwaukee, and Melvin Rhyne to Madison and Milwaukee (see chapter 11). As an adult, he worked a day gig at Oscar Mayer in Madison. He is always described as an inventor, and his so-called "jazz harp" was apparently constructed by welding four or five electric guitars together. The instrument is pictured on the cover of the LP he recorded in 1969 at Madison's Hoffman House with brothers Melvin and Ronnie Rhyne. Shacklett also referred to this instrument as a baraka.

Ben Sidran recalls working with Shacklett at the Tuxedo Lounge. According to Sidran, Shacklett "played guitar upside down without a pick and used octaves and block chords." Vocalist Jan Wheaton also remem-

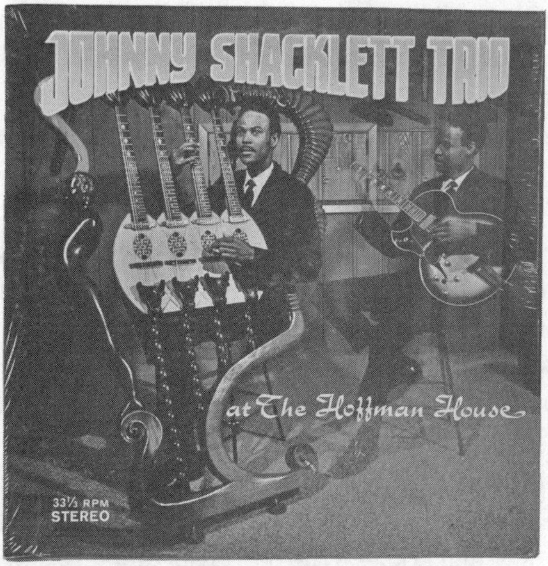

Johnny Shacklett Trio album cover featuring his "jazz harp." COURTESY OF JOHN NONDORF

bers Shacklett playing upside down and backward. During a time when Shacklett was having trouble making ends meet, he hired Sidran (on organ) and Ronnie Rhyne (on drums) to play at the Tuxedo Lounge six nights a week.[4]

Singer Gerri DiMaggio recalls being "dragged" by her mother to hear Shacklett in the late 1960s at the Hoffman House, where Shacklett cut the previously mentioned album. She remembers him as a "really beautiful player." Wheaton worked with Shacklett at times, both in Madison and out of town. "I was a girl singer," she says, "that was attached to a bigger entity [Shacklett's trio]." And she remembers being used when the audience got tired of the "improvisational crazy stuff." Shacklett appears to have left Madison shortly after his residency at the Hoffman House.

The Duke Ellington Orchestra in Madison

A signal event in Wisconsin jazz history took place when the maestro Duke Ellington and his legendary orchestra held a residency at UW–Madison in the summer of 1972.[5]

The occasion was accompanied by the appropriate official bluster as Governor Patrick Lucey declared July 17–21 to be Duke Ellington Week. The proclamation specified Ellington's importance to American culture, stating that "his name alone is synonymous with the cultural core of twentieth-century American music" and that "he continues to enrich the lives of the citizens of Wisconsin, America, indeed the world." Profits from the weeklong Duke Ellington Festival would be, the program book read, "Used to Establish the Duke Ellington Fellow Program for the Study, Research, and Performance of American Music—Popularly Known as Jazz at the School of Music, University of Wisconsin–Madison."

Clinic/workshops were scheduled on Monday, Tuesday, Thursday, and Friday with members of the Ellington orchestra, and master classes with Ellington himself were offered on Thursday and Friday. Concerts were scheduled every night of the week, and each had a different theme: Monday, Wednesday, and Friday at the Wisconsin Union Theater; Tuesday at Camp Randall Stadium; Thursday as part of UW–Milwaukee's School of Fine Arts Summer Arts Festival. Friday night's concert, Night of Suites, included the *UWIS Suite*, which the program described as an "entirely new work, especially written for this festival. . . . Inspired by people met in Wisconsin, from Wisconsin. The many joys experience[d] throughout the years from Wisconsin. His indebtedness to the beautiful people."

While the *UWIS Suite* is generally considered one of Ellington's lesser works, it holds interest for Wisconsinites.[6] The titles of the three movements, "Uwis," "Klop," and "Loco Madi," reflect Ellington's practice of assigning four-letter codes to his new compositions. The first movement is the longest and richest, and while congenial, it also contains some of the unpredictable and progressive music that Ellington was writing at this stage of his career. "Klop" refers to a particular part of Wisconsin's musical heritage, the polka, with the first four letters reversed, and can be heard as an affectionate parody of the genre. "Loco Madi" refers to Ellington's longtime fascination with trains, which is reflected in other outstanding works from throughout his career. Ellington wrote, "I first went to Milwaukee by train from Chicago—ninety miles in ninety minutes. I remembered the railroad dining car at Hayward, and the circus train (which had already inspired one composition) at Baraboo." At the premiere performance, Duke performed what Ellington historian Stanley Dance called an "improvised musical bouquet" solo prior to the written movements, which he later referred to as "solo reflections . . . on the beautiful people he had met from or in Wisconsin." *UWIS Suite* was recorded in October 1972 (see online discography) and released by Pablo Records in 1976, two years after the Duke's death.

In his memoir *Music Is My Mistress*, Ellington was extravagantly generous in his comments about his hosts—James "Jim" Latimer, professor of percussion at UW, and his wife—during Madison's Duke Ellington Week in 1972. Dance wrote that during the week "there were hilarious complications during the festival, arising from the fact that Ellington's lady admirers from all parts of the United States had descended on Madison."

According to Dance, "The composer had a genuine affection for Wisconsin"; in addition to trains, and his Wisconsin friends, he remembered "the state's famous cheese and its ubiquitous beer." In his autobiography, Ellington mentioned "the famous musicians from Wisconsin: Woody Herman, Bunny Berigan, Gene Schroeder, Dick Ruedebusch, Freddie Slack, Les Paul, and last but not least, Hilly Edelstein, the man who wrote the fanfare we still use at the beginning of the [greatest hits] medley." Edelstein is all but unknown to the jazz community.

Ellington also recalled places that he had played over the years, some of them long gone by the 1970s, including "the Wisconsin Theatre, the Wisconsin Roof, the State Fair Park, and the Modernistic Ballroom." He also fondly remembered playing his first piano recital in Wisconsin: "The time I had my name in lights on Milwaukee City Hall."

Early UW–Madison Jazz Faculty

The highly regarded (if not universally loved) avant-garde pianist Cecil Taylor was hired to teach at UW–Madison in 1971. However, Taylor's stay at the university was brief, and apparently not happy. Reports suggest that Taylor was not a good match for the academic and student climate at UW at that time. There are varying (and disagreeing) stories about what transpired. The following is Jeannie Cheatham's account.

> Cecil had come to Madison to teach black studies, and he had come with his mind made up and his heart set to teach the truth. He warned

> the huge class that gathered to view this jazz giant that he would be giving them lessons, lectures, and examples, just as in any other subject. He also warned them that they would have to take an exam.
>
> Somehow, despite Cecil's warnings, the students thought, and bought into the myth, that the presence of a jazz musician meant that they could come to class in droves, party, get stoned, and say "Right on!" Well, "Right on!" became "Right off!" when at least two-thirds of the class flunked Cecil's extensive exam. The shocked university muckety-mucks tried to force Cecil to reverse the failing grades. Of course, being a man of integrity, he refused and resigned.[7]

When Taylor left, he was replaced for a semester by another respected, although less prominent, avant-garde musician, Bill Dixon.

After Dixon's one semester at UW in the early 1970s, trombonist Jimmy Cheatham was the next appointee to teach jazz at UW. His tenure was also fairly short, as he left in 1978. Cheatham apparently held positions in both the music department and in Afro-American Studies. He established the Experimental Improvisational Black Music Ensemble, which has continued into 2017 as the Black Music Ensemble. After being led for many years by Richard Davis, the group became student led upon his retirement in 2016.

While at UW–Madison, Cheatham brought both the Count Basie band and the Thad Jones–Mel Lewis orchestra to town. A mayoral proclamation issued in 2010 credits both Cheatham and his wife, Jeannie, a noted vocalist who was also a vibrant presence in Madison, with "providing opportunities for UW jazz students to perform with professional musicians in local commercial venues, [and] performing extensively around the city and region with their own outstanding band."[8]

In her autobiography, *Meet Me with Your Black Drawers On*, Jeannie describes how her first gig in Wisconsin was for a meeting of the Ku Klux Klan.[9] But the Cheathams went on during their time in Madison to perform regularly at the Park Motor Inn (Inn on the Park) on Capitol Square and at the Church Key on University. They played in a regular group with local musicians Dennis Oliver (bass); Stefan Sylvander (drums); and Bob Leyson, a saxophonist whom Jeannie refers to only as "Bob the booking agent." In the Church Key band, they played with Oliver, drummer Clyde Stubblefield, saxophonist "Fat" Richard Drake, and trumpeter Bob McCurdy.

The Cheathams often allowed others, including UW students, to sit in with their bands. Jeannie became close with Ruth Harris, who had once been a pianist and organist for gospel singer Mahalia Jackson. In the late 1970s, Jeannie and Ruth were hired to teach eurhythmics at UW–Baraboo. Jimmy and Jeannie, later joined by Ruth, also taught a course for some time at the Oxford Federal Correctional Institution in central Wisconsin.

When "Cheatham Day" was proclaimed in October 2010 (three years after Jimmy's death), Jeannie returned to Madison and the university for a day of celebration.

Les Thimmig

Les Thimmig has been a presence at UW–Madison since 1971. He was born in 1943 in Santa Maria, California, but moved as a young child to Joliet, Illinois. "I started playing the clarinet at six," he remembers, "was in the union at thirteen, [and] made my first jazz recording session at fifteen." The school music program in Joliet was world famous; according to Thimmig, it was the first clarinet player, rather than the quarterback of the football team, who commanded the attention of female admirers in the school.

Thimmig took saxophone lessons in downtown Chicago with an important teacher of that era, Santy Runyon, and began studying jazz composition with Chicagoan Bill Russo, who had come to fame as an arranger for the Stan Kenton band in the 1950s. Also while in high school, Thimmig drove into the city for jam sessions that often included prominent young Chicago musicians like saxophonist Joe Firrantello (who later became known as Joe Farrell), drummer Maurice White (who later became the famed leader of the band Earth, Wind & Fire), pianists Denny Zeitlen and Herbie Hancock, and Jack DeJohnette (who was known as a pianist before becoming one of the most respected drummers in jazz).

Thimmig went to college at the Eastman School of Music in Rochester, New York, between 1961 and 1965. He immediately became friends with trumpeter Lew Soloff (who later became famous as a member of Blood,

Sweat & Tears and then as an important freelancer in New York). Soloff helped connect Thimmig with the summer music scene in the Catskill Mountains, where resorts hired bands to cater to the tastes of thousands of vacationing New Yorkers. Thimmig played there each summer he was in school and continued to play the Catskills until 1969. He recalls those summer jobs as consisting of "three acts a night, six nights a week . . . usually, no rehearsal. Talk over, sight-read, boom, bang, play. And you got done with that, you could sight-read a piece of used flypaper." On off nights, the resort musicians would go to the city, where Thimmig rubbed elbows with great young saxophonists of his generation.

A highlight of this period of his career was a seven-week tour with Woody Herman's band. Herman was not at one of the heights of his career, but he was about to reenter the consciousness of a wider jazz public with one of his greatest bands (see chapter 2). It was pretty heady stuff for a twenty-year-old, but Thimmig knew the value of completing his degree at Eastman.

Thimmig went to graduate school at Yale University, where he earned two master's degrees and did some teaching. The short hop from New Haven, Connecticut, to New York City allowed him to stay connected not only to the Catskills, but to the city jazz scene as well. In 1969, he accepted a teaching job at the University of Victoria in British Columbia, where he headed up the music composition program at the practically new university. He had no qualms about leaving the East Coast, but the jazz scene in western Canada was extremely tame compared to that of the Big Apple. Connections in nearby Vancouver afforded some playing opportunities, and he ended up recording for the Canadian Broadcasting Company.

After a couple of years in Victoria, Thimmig began feeling that the West Coast, as he says, "just wasn't me." A phone call from UW–Madison led to an Easter weekend interview and the job offer that brought Thimmig back to the Midwest. He was hired to teach composition and advanced theory courses; later he picked up jazz composition. He led the UW jazz ensemble from 1982 to 1988 and took over the Jazz Improvisation class when Joan Wildman retired in the early 2000s.

In his second year at Madison, Thimmig began subbing with the Milwaukee Symphony, the state's largest and best-known orchestra; he knew

Les Thimmig. PHOTO BY AMELIA JOHN; COURTESY OF THE UNIVERSITY OF WISCONSIN–MADISON

both of the regular symphony clarinetists from his time at Joliet and Eastman. He also did big band work in Milwaukee and collaborated with guitarist Jack Grassel. Over the years, Thimmig built up his connections. By 2002, he claimed eighty-eight trips to Milwaukee on his tax return, performing in public, outside of UW, 208 times that year. He also maintained connections on the East Coast, doing residencies at the New England Conservatory and subbing occasionally in New York groups.

One of Thimmig's most memorable jobs in the Midwest was with the Duke Ellington band in the 2000s. Although this was years after Ellington's death, playing with the band was still a significant musical credential, especially sitting in the baritone saxophone chair, as Thimmig did, which had been held for almost fifty years by jazz icon Harry Carney.

Thimmig led several jazz groups in Madison. He had a trio that played at the world-class Madison restaurant L'Étoile, beginning in the 1970s, when the establishment was listed in the phone book as L'Étoile Restaurant and Jazz Club. The drummer was Thimmig's saxophone student Jeffrey Ernstoff, who later became a music producer for such events as the Super Bowl. Another Thimmig-led band was Crosscurrent (1982–1988), which included pianist Jim Erickson, bassist Jeff Eckels, and drummer Dave Stanoch—all students at UW who would later become professionals. In the 1990s, Thimming led the Les Thimmig Seven, which has recently resurfaced in a somewhat different manifestation on campus as the Jazz Composers Group. He was also a member of Madison's preeminent Latin jazz group, Madisalsa. As of 2017, Thimmig continues what must be one of the longest-running faculty careers in the history of UW's School of Music.

Joan Wildman

Joan Wildman was born in 1938 and grew up on a cattle ranch in Nebraska. The nearest town was Spalding, a town of fewer than a thousand residents. "Our mailbox was two miles away," she recalls, "and I rode my horse to a country school." Being isolated in a rural area, Wildman says, "was good and bad. . . . The good part of it was that I was able to do my own thing and to use my own imagination and try things. So I played by ear, even though I was studying piano when I was six." She first played with other musicians at age twelve, with a nearby family who eventually became Tompall and the Glaser Brothers, a prominent Nashville act.

At age sixteen, Wildman went to college at Mount St. Scholastica College in Kansas, where she planned to be a piano major. The summer after her sophomore year at school, she went to the "big city" of Topeka, where she played in a club and on a local television show. A mentor in a music store in the city assigned Wildman to learn one new tune every day and supplied her with the place to do it—the store. The summer before her junior year, Wildman got a six-night-a-week solo piano gig.

When she returned to school in the fall, she decided she had to play more jazz, so she moved to Boston to attend the Berklee College of Music (then called the Berklee School of Music). But at Berklee, she says, "I missed Beethoven." So she moved to Minneapolis–St. Paul, where she attended MacPhail School of Music. In her short version of the story, Wildman says, "[I] met my husband, got married, had four kids, moved out to . . . western Minnesota, and then to Idaho, and then got into the doctoral program at the University of Oregon." Her husband was a trumpet and bass player, and they played together in groups in all three states.

Around 1970, Wildman got a teaching job at Central Michigan University and spent several years there, including one unforgettable night. Duke Ellington, who was in the throes of cancer, played with his band for the last time in Sturgis, Michigan, on March 22, 1974. On March 23, the band played at CMU without Ellington, who had been sent back to New York, where he would die on May 24. At CMU, the band needed a piano player and it was determined that Joan could fill in. "I said I would love to do it," Wildman remembers. "And being the . . . very innocent naïve person I was back then, the only question I had was, 'What should I wear?'" Duke had no written or printed music for himself, so of course neither did Joan. "So the bass player's standing right next to me," she recalls, "[telling me] what tune and what key."

Wildman got her first full-time teaching job at the University of Maine in 1975. She stayed two years, simultaneously completing her doctorate at Oregon, and then joined the UW–Madison faculty in 1977. She taught music theory and for many years a popular course in jazz improvisation. Area musicians interviewed for this book who spoke about working with Wildman at UW include Lynette Margulies, Chris Washburne, Jackie Allen, Jeff Erickson, and Vince Fuh.

Besides teaching at the university, Wildman quickly became an important member of the Madison jazz scene. When she first moved to town, she brought along her trio from Maine; the members soon found that they could not survive on gigs in Madison and left town. Next, she worked with bassist Karen Horner and drummer Tom Crosby. Eventually, Hans Sturm became her bassist, and Dane Richeson became the "permanent" drummer of the trio, which worked extensively and recorded. Wildman became friends with the avant-garde giant Roscoe Mitchell, best known as one of the saxophonists with the Art Ensemble of Chicago, who lived for some years in Madison.

Wildman considers it "an important thing" that she was a founder of the Madison Music Collective (MMC). Her desire to establish a support group for musicians to strengthen their position in the workplace was fueled by her group having been shut out of a mid-1980s gig. The band showed up at the job only to find that the club had closed indefinitely. When the place reopened, she says, "I booked another gig there, stupidly; they did it again."

The Joan Wildman Trio from the 1980s (left to right): Hans Sturm (see later in this chapter), Joan Wildman, and Dane Richeson (see chapter 18). PHOTO BY JOSEPH BLOUGH; COURTESY OF JOAN WILDMAN

"I just thought about that for a long time," she says, "thinking that something has to happen here. This is not right. And it wasn't just my group that had trouble. . . . [So had] a lot of the musicians in town . . . and there was nobody to stand up for them." In 1985, with the help of Hans Sturm, bassist Dennis Oliver, and singer Liza Lightfoot, among others, Wildman says, the Madison Music Collective "was born under the maple tree in my front yard." In April 2015, she performed at the Brink Lounge on the occasion of the thirtieth anniversary of the MMC.

In her retirement, Wildman occasionally performs in public (as at the 2014 Isthmus Jazz Festival), and she continues to write and play in private settings. She speaks enthusiastically of her weekly Wednesday sessions with retired UW professors Dick Lottridge (bassoon), Doug Hill (who taught horn at UW but plays bass in this group), Diedre Buckley (viola), and Willy Walter (bassoon). Wildman refers to their music as "orphan folk music."

While active and visible for many years, Wildman was always seen as a fringe artist, usually labeled an avant-garde player and bandleader. She certainly energized the experimental part of the Madison music scene. Listening to and enjoying her trio's recordings is not easy; it is challenging, forward-looking music. As large numbers of repertoire ensembles have formed and historically reworked jazz classics have become prevalent during the last thirty or more years, Wildman has thought deeply about jazz's current state. "The idea of looking back to see where we've been is very, very important," she says. "But it's how you use that that is the important thing. . . . And if you only use it to keep yourself back there, . . . it is not productive. It's so important that we find ways to move the music forward. . . . You go to these older guys for inspiration as to how they said it, and then you develop your own voice out of that."

Richard Davis

Richard Davis moved to Wisconsin in 1977 to teach at UW–Madison. He had lived in New York for over twenty years, and he left the city at the height of a remarkable career, in which he was recognized as one of the two or three top jazz bassists in the city. He has lived in Wisconsin ever since.

Davis was born in Chicago in 1930.[10] In 2000, he told interviewer Sara Freeman,

> I came up in a neighborhood where all the music was there. I was raised in a black ghetto in Chicago. Even when I was a kid, we were singing all the time, imitating the Ink Spots and all those people. Trying out for talent shows. I got a bass. I used a broomstick at first because I didn't own an instrument. Then I got one that first Christmas, after I started playing, six months later. I guess the first person I played with was a guy who lived in my mother's apartment, in the basement. There was a piano down in the basement, and we used to jam, play boogie-woogie bass lines, stuff like that. One thing led to another. I was turning out for the high school band, and then I started to get gigs.[11]

Playing string bass in high school, Davis studied with legendary band director Captain Walter Dyett. Among the legion of important musicians who worked with Dyett at DuSable High School were vocalists Dinah

Washington, Johnny Hartman, and Nat "King" Cole (also a superb jazz pianist); saxophonists Gene Ammons, Von Freeman, Johnny Griffin, Eddie Harris, and Clifford Jordan; and trombonist Julian Priester. Dyett was also associated with two other renowned jazz bassists, Wilbur Ware and Milt Hinton, who worked with Dyett in his earlier position at Phillips High School.

Davis also took lessons from Chicago Symphony Orchestra bassist Rudolf Fahsbender for ten years. He went on to Chicago's VanderCook College of Music, earning a degree in music education in 1952. While still in the Windy City, Davis worked with other up-and-coming jazz artists such as Andrew Hill and Ahmad Jamal. Eventually, he joined pianist Don Shirley, whose group moved to New York in 1956. In New York, Davis played briefly with the Sauter-Finnegan Orchestra and Charlie Ventura before embarking on the job that established his reputation—six years with jazz vocal star Sarah Vaughan's trio.

When not traveling with Vaughan, Davis began freelancing with a vengeance, playing with symphony orchestras and Broadway pit orchestras, and in the studio with a variety of artists. Davis is proud of his work in the classical area. A film clip shown at the 2014 ceremony at which Davis received his National Endowment of the Arts Jazz Masters award showed him playing with the New York Philharmonic under the direction of Leonard Bernstein. Davis frequently mentions his working with twentieth-century musical giant Igor Stravinsky, and he has worked with other distinguished conductors ranging from Leopold Stokowski to Pierre Boulez. Among the popular singers he eventually worked with were Frank Sinatra, Barbra Streisand, Van Morrison (on whose monster hit "Moondance" Davis played), and Bruce Springsteen.

Davis did graduate study at the Manhattan School of Music. His most notable jazz association of the era was in 1961 with the Eric Dolphy–Booker Little Quintet, one of the most acclaimed progressive combos of the era, and he played on Dolphy's seminal album *Out to Lunch*. During the 1960s, Davis recorded with a virtual who's who of jazz across a wide stylistic spectrum, including J. J. Johnson, Ben Webster, Milt Jackson, Stan Getz, Bill Evans, Joe Henderson, Tony Williams, Johnny Hodges, Rahsaan Roland Kirk, and Earl Hines.[12]

In 1965, Davis was a charter member of the great Thad Jones–Mel Lewis Orchestra, and his playing on the band's early albums demonstrated a new and different way for bass to function in the big band context. Work with Dizzy Gillespie and Chick Corea at the Village Vanguard followed, as did more recordings. Davis was voted top bassist in the *Down Beat* Critics' Poll every year between 1967 and 1974.

Davis claims that he moved to Wisconsin not because he chose it, but because, as he says, "Wisconsin chose me." While early in his time at UW, Davis led the jazz band. Soon he was teaching only "classical" string bass (although many of his students played jazz) and leading the Black Music Ensemble in the music department. For years, he also taught Black Music History, until his retirement in 2016.

Davis's work with prominent jazz musicians hardly ended with his move to the Madison area, but it did slow down. However, in the late 1970s and 1980s, he recorded in New York, Europe, and Japan with former associates and others, including Elvin Jones, McCoy Tyner, David Murray, and Mal Waldron.

In the early 1980s, Davis worked in a short-lived group known as the Wisconsin Connection, with Milwaukee jazz stars Manty Ellis and Berkeley Fudge; vocalist Jessie Hauck; and a young star in the making, Carl Allen, who was still a college student. Davis also played and recorded in duo with Madison pianist Ben Sidran. Davis continued to work in New York into the 1990s, especially with pianist Roland Hanna. Davis recorded a dozen albums under his own name from the late 1960s through two independently produced efforts in the 2000s. He has reportedly performed on three thousand recordings and/or jingles as a sideman.[13]

In 1993, Davis founded the Richard Davis Foundation for Young Bassists, Inc., which annually provides masterful bass instructors/performers to teach young bassists ranging in age from three to eighteen. (The program is now run in large part by Davis's protégé, Wisconsin born and raised bassist Peter Dominguez; see chapter 15.) In 1998, Davis created the Retention Action Project, which focuses on opening up lines of dialogue about multicultural differences. He also initiated a Madison chapter of the Institutes for the Healing of Racism, Inc.[14]

The listing of awards he has received is impressive, demonstrating his wide influence in the community.[15] Davis was profiled on the Wisconsin Public Television program *Wisconsin Life* in the spring of 2014, shortly after he received the NEA Jazz Masters Award, perhaps the capstone of his career.

Richard Davis. PHOTO BY BOB PESSELMAN

Davis cares deeply about his work and legacy in Madison.

> The history class I teach, Black Music History, relates to the role of black people in a white society. So I teach it with that in mind, and the result I get is the white students are gathering information that they have not gathered in any other classes on the campus. Because I talk about the racial issues that [make] the music happen—the exploitation of the black artist. And, comparatively speaking, not enough credit is given to the black artists for the contribution made in this country, of jazz.

Davis also taught a course at UW for first-year students called the Oneness of Humankind. "I teach that class with a passion," he said, prior to his retirement in 2016.

> It is very, very personal. I have [the students] to my house; and they say, after four years of being [here at UW], . . . "Man, am I glad I took YOUR class." Because they have not had something that penetrates their remoteness as much as that class does. And I make sure that they keep journals of everything that they experi-

> ence during the day. And they say, "Without your class, I would never have recognized what was going on. But you made me aware of so many things."

While he continued to challenge his students about race and racial issues, Davis also says, "As much as I am a promoter of what I'm talking about, I am still a student, wanting to know more, and how to say it better, and to live it."

Chris Washburne

Trombonist Chris Washburne was born in Akron, Ohio, in 1963 and grew up in nearby Bath.[16] Washburne claims that he came to UW–Madison as an undergraduate without much musical training. "My stepfather was an amateur Dixieland drummer," he says, "so I was exposed to it. He was a big band fanatic. And back in those days, the big bands were still coming around. . . . So I saw Lionel Hampton's band, Count Basie's band a number of times, Gerry Mulligan, Woody Herman. . . . I played in the high school concert band, and the jazz band. The first band I ever played in was a Led Zeppelin cover band." He admits, "It was a bit difficult to sound like [Zeppelin guitarist] Jimmy Page on the trombone. I'm still trying to sound like him today."[17]

Washburne decided to attend UW–Madison for several reasons.

> I was looking for a school of music where I could expand my horizons. . . . Madison had a good philosophy department, a good forestry department. The campus was beautiful, close to farmland and natural spaces. It was also real funky. . . . It didn't hurt that the day I visited with my mother, there was a huge rally on the mall with a killer reggae band.[18]

But when he arrived at UW, he says, "I was not a very good trombone player." By dint of hard work and the constant pushing of his trombone professor Bill Richardson, Washburne eventually made his way through the system and graduated in 1986 as a trombone performance major.

Washburne often worked in an unconventional way.

> I realized if I became the person that looked after the [practice] cards and [practice room] keys, that they would give me a set of keys to the [UW Humanities Building]. . . . I had access to the entire building, so I would spend all night long in the big concert hall spaces, practicing and jamming with my friends. And that's how I learned how to play music.

He was also encouraged by School of Music faculty members. "Most music programs have a divide: you're either jazz or you're 'legit,'" Washburne says. "But Richard Davis and Les Thimmig helped me. They said you can do both—just go for it."[19] So Washburne practiced hard in his classical training and eventually played with almost every instrumental ensemble at the school.

Other unexpected musical opportunities emerged from the School of Music. Washburne recalls that Karlos Moser, head of the opera program, also loved early jazz and Jelly Roll Morton. "He had made a bunch of transcriptions," Washburne says, "and every once in a while he would put together a big band in a restaurant or a bar, and we would play those charts." Gary Fagin directed the UW orchestra at that time and transcribed Ellington tunes as a hobby, which Washburne played at UW. He also became a member of Joan Wildman's Improvisational Quintet in 1985.

Washburne remembers the early years of playing jazz off campus in Madison in the 1980s.

> I had a quintet first. It was kind of a collective with a bass player named Tim Goss. [We] started a band, and we approached the Madison Inn [now the Graduate]. . . . And they had a little tiny bar there, and we went in there and said, "Could we play jazz here?" And they said, "Yes." They gave us Thursday nights. I think we got paid fifteen dollars each, and maybe like a free beer.

Later on, bassists Hans Sturm and Jeff Eckels spent time with the band, as did trumpeter Grant Manhart. JoAnn Funk became the pianist, and eventually Les Thimmig joined the group.

Chris Washburne. PHOTO BY LENA ADASHEVA; COURTESY OF CHRIS WASHBURNE

> And to be a trombone player, and to have to be the only melodic instrument, and solo for three hours on jazz standards, I learned a ton of tunes, and my chops got strong. . . . I couldn't have done this anywhere else. At the same time, I was playing at the Rathskeller of the Union, once a week, doing small jazz trio things, or a variety of stuff. I think it's the reason I'm a professional musician.

Washburne will also never forget playing in the backup band of Madison blues singer Robert J, and being blown away by legendary drummer Clyde Stubblefield on Washburne's first gig with Robert J's band.

Washburne left Madison and eventually earned a master's degree at the New England Conservatory. He earned his PhD in ethnomusicology at Columbia University and built a performing career in New York, playing and recording with groups as diverse as the Manhattan Chamber Orchestra, pop stars Björk and Justin Timberlake, and the Duke Ellington Orchestra. He gravitated to the Latin jazz scene in New York and has played with the biggest names in the business—Tito Puente, Eddie Palmieri, Celia Cruz, and Ray Barretto—as well as the younger pop-oriented Latin artists Gloria Estefan and Marc Anthony.

Washburne's book, *Sounding Salsa*, a study of New York's salsa scene, earned critical acclaim upon its publication in 2008. In 1992, he founded the band SYOTOS (See You on the Other Side), named when Washburne wasn't sure if he had long to live because of a health crisis. It is a Latin-oriented progressive band that employs a wide variety of musical influences. SYOTOS continues to play and record in 2017. While remaining busy with performances, Washburne is also a committed academic and is established as an associate professor of music and the director of the Louis Armstrong Jazz Performance Program at Columbia University.

Hans Sturm

Hans Sturm was born in 1960 and raised in Pennsylvania, where his father taught at Bucknell University. His dad had been a trombonist but played piano in Sturm's youth; his mother, a high school English teacher, was a singer. Sturm's first instrument was violin, but he began playing string bass in high school while also playing drums in marching band. He played bass in concert band and jazz ensemble and studied with symphony bass players in both Philadelphia and Pittsburgh during high school. Hans attended Middlebury College in Vermont, where he did not study music but realized that he wanted to pursue music as a career. He transferred to the Cincinnati College-Conservatory of Music, where he studied with Bill Grimes.

But when Grimes decided to leave Cincinnati, Hans says, "My father actually turned me on to an article about Richard Davis in the *New York Times*. And so I went out and took a lesson with Richard. And he was the right teacher for me at that time." Sturm came to UW–Madison in 1981 and studied with Davis and with violinists Lowell Creitz and Tyrone Grieve. Sturm began working with a band called Ultra Blue, which included saxophonist Paul Harper; keyboardist Phil Kellman; and drummer Kim Zick, who later became well known in Wisconsin playing in the band Mrs. Fun. Another group included Harper, vibraphonist Mark Johnson, and drummer Michael Weiss. Not much later, on the recommendation of Weiss, Hans joined the trio of Joan Wildman.

While in Madison, Sturm worked with many of the prominent figures on the scene at that time, including drummer Dave Stanoch; violinist

Randy Sabien; and pianists Jane Reynolds, Dave Stoler, and John Thulin (Sturm's roommate for a time). Sturm occasionally played at the Concourse Hotel. For a while, he and Thulin played alternating weeks (five nights a week) with singer Lynette (Margulies) at the Sheraton Hotel from about 1983 to 1985. Sturm also played for a while with Thulin on Michael Feldman's radio show *Whad'ya Know?* Sturm worked frequently with guitarist Jack Grassel, and a few times with Madison star Ben Sidran and with Milwaukee saxophonist Berkeley Fudge.

Through Joan Wildman, Sturm met the world-famous avant-garde saxophonist Roscoe Mitchell, who lived in Madison for most of the 1990s and 2000s. Mitchell, who became a major jazz figure through his solo saxophone work and his longtime membership in the Art Ensemble of Chicago, rarely performed publicly in Madison, though he did play in the city. Sturm describes some of Mitchell's life in Madison:

> He moved out [of Chicago] because Madison was a very beautiful place to live. . . . He loved Madison. He would do small gigs, and we had a trio. . . . I worked with him; we were like hitting partners. We would get together, five mornings a week, Monday through Friday. . . . This went on for maybe four years. His favorite soap opera was *The Young and the Restless*. The greatest avant-garde saxophonist in the world, watching [a soap opera]. . . . So we would get together about 8:30, 9 in the morning, and play until the soap came on [at 11]. And then he would watch his soap and I would go. And [we] would do a huge range of material. So we would do Bach. . . . He did the top tones for saxophone, long tones, we would do Galamian violin arpeggios together. . . . We would work on Coltrane transcriptions.

When asked about living in Madison in a 1998 interview, Mitchell was quoted as saying, "What's most interesting to me right now is time to study. I could be anywhere right now. I like Madison because you really don't have the hustle and bustle that you have in the big cities, getting around and so forth."[20]

Mitchell composed music while in Madison, including a work for a chamber orchestra, *Sketches from the Bamboo Terrace*, that featured UW violin faculty member Vartan Manoogian, soprano Mimi Fulmer, and

Sturm. Years later, the piece was recorded in different form, with Joan Wildman on piano. Mitchell left Madison in 2007 and moved to California upon being appointed Darius Milhaud Chair in Composition at Mills College in California.

When Hans Sturm joined Joan Wildman's group in 1982, Michael Weiss was drumming. When Weiss left town, John Becker took over as drummer, while also playing vibes. He was followed briefly by Dave Stanoch. But the long-term solution for the drum chair was Dane Richeson, who was living in Appleton and teaching at Lawrence University at the time. Wildman, Sturm, and Richeson worked together for a number of years, producing some of the most challenging music in Wisconsin. Richeson and Sturm recorded an album in the mid-1980s with guitarist Carl Michel called *Food of Love* that drew national notice.

Sturm completed a master's degree at UW in 1990 and took a one-year teaching position at Augustana College in Rock Island, Illinois. He moved back to Madison briefly but in 1992 moved to Evanston, Illinois, to attend Northwestern University for doctoral study. Sturm was hired to the faculty at Ball State University in Indiana in 1994, where he taught for seventeen years. He then took the position as head of jazz studies at the University of Nebraska–Lincoln, where he teaches now. (He followed former Madison jazz bassist Jeff Eckels into the position.)

Sturm's longest-standing association musically, and the one of most interest to Wisconsinites, has been with his wife, singer Jackie Allen, whose career is recounted in chapter 13. The two have made eight albums together in a variety of combinations, from playing as a duo to participating in a project with a symphony orchestra (see online discography).

Stanley Jordan

A short-term resident in Madison was the mercurial guitarist Stanley Jordan. Busking, or street performing, is a long-lived tradition on Madison's State Street mall, from UW to the Capitol. Few of Madison's buskers have ever approached the level of Jordan's talent, however.

Jordan was born in Chicago in 1959. He attended Princeton University, where he studied music theory and composition with avant-garde composer Milton Babbitt. He played with some noted jazz figures while in college and developed a guitar-playing technique that, while not completely new, made a splash on the jazz and pop scene as something new. Usually referred to as "tapping" (playing on the guitar's fretboard without strumming or picking), Jordan's method became known as "touch technique" or, as one person described it, "an advanced form of two-handed tapping."

Jordan, who did not drive, was brought to Madison by his manager, Don Dickson, and eventually found Hans Sturm and John Thulin, who were living on Edgewater Court. According to Sturm, "[Dickson would organize and Jordan would play] these guerilla concerts where they would, just because [Jordan] had the tapping technique on the guitar—he could busk anywhere." Remembering Jordan, Sturm also identified him as "a genius" and described some of the devilishly complex theoretical musical models that Jordan worked on while in Madison. "He had three-ring notebooks of everything," Sturm said. "He had considered everything: how, if he's playing two guitars separately, all the voicings, all the possibilities, how he could move his body."

Shortly after his Madison residency, in 1985, Jordan was "discovered" by record executive Bruce Lundvall, who was blown away by the young guitarist's ability. Lundvall was just about to launch the new version of the venerable Blue Note record label and chose Jordan's album *Magic Touch* for the label's first release. Jordan's career took off from there.

Jazz around the State

15

More Milwaukeeans

Many fine Milwaukee jazz musicians were not core members of the scenes discussed in chapters 11 and 12, although at times they very probably made music with a number of the figures discussed there. Some of those musicians' stories are related here.

Kaye Berigan

Trumpeter Kaye Berigan has been a prominent jazz musician in Milwaukee for decades. He is a tall man and stands out in a crowd—or a band. His healthy shock of hair has been gray for some time, and he is immediately recognizable at music venues throughout the city.

Berigan, in his inimitable style, says he "was born in July of 1939 in St. Joseph's hospital in Beaver Dam because I wanted to be near my mother."[1] His father, Don, was the brother of trumpet legend Bunny Berigan, and the young family lived in the Berigans' hometown of Fox Lake until Kaye was three years old. They moved to Chicago, then to Milwaukee, where Don was a barber and Kaye's mother, Loretta, progressed from maid to seamstress to interior decorator to interior designer and furniture buyer at the Boston Store. Kaye claims that he "walked to grade school, high school, and college."

He says, "I always wanted to be a jazz trumpet player, as a kid; and I always wanted to play tunes," but also, "I didn't want to practice my teacher's lesson of exercises." That teacher, Sam Holdorf, who eventually became Kaye's band director at Riverside High, was inspirational to Berigan. "It's probably why I became a high school band director," he says.

At roughly the age of seventeen, Berigan was told that he sounded like Miles Davis—a musician he had never heard of before. When he discovered Davis, it was a true awakening, as he was used to hearing the music of Benny Goodman and Tommy Dorsey at home. At college at UW–Milwaukee in 1957, Berigan says, "I was one of a handful of, quote, 'jazzers,' who were in ill repute, because jazz was the devil's music." There was no jazz program at UWM, nor had there been one at his high school. "And kind of all I did was practice improvisation," he says. "I listened to a lot of recordings, and friends of mine turned me on to other people who I would not have come across."

Around the age of eighteen, Berigan recalls, "A trombone player friend told me there was a 'Blue Monday' session at a club on Walnut and maybe Eighth, Eleventh—it's all freeway now. And that's basically what was Bronzeville, I guess, which I didn't know." The club was the Lounge, where trumpeter Billy Howell told him he could play any time.[2] "So I played six to seven nights a week at that club," Berigan says. "I got my degree from UWM, but I got my jazz degree from being able to play at the club." Among the players Berigan sat in with during those days were prominent African American musicians Bobby Burdette, Loretta White, and Jimmy Duncan at the Lounge, the Rag Doll, and other spots.

Milwaukee jazz icon Berkeley Fudge, who was two years older than Berigan, came up at the same time, and Berigan worked with him occasionally. While the scene was (and continues to be) racially mixed, over time Berigan began working more frequently with white players such as drummer Bob Budny and keyboard players Frank Vlasis, Les Czimber, and Frank DeMiles at clubs like Dmitri's and the Driftwood. "And most of the repertoire I learned working with Tommy Sheridan and Siggy Millonzi, . . . two wonderful jazz pianists," Berigan recalls.

After finishing at UWM, Berigan was drafted into the service in 1962. Following basic training, he spent about six months at the Naval School of Music before being assigned to the Forty-Ninth Army Band, with which he was stationed in Verona, Italy, until his discharge in 1964.

Back in Milwaukee during the late 1960s and early 1970s, along with guitarist Don Linke and drummer Budny, Berigan would spend summers working on the music of various jazz artists; they had a Thelonious Monk summer, a Cecil Taylor summer, and so forth.

Berigan was also in an avant-garde band that was initially called Laverne and ended up being called What on Earth. Amid a revolving cast, the mainstays of the band were trombonist Bill Schaefgen, pianist Leigh Cowen, Budny, and guitarist Jack Grassel. Berigan says,

> We played free improvisations that were amazing in their cohesiveness . . . and original tunes by [Schaefgen]. . . . We also did a lot of standards, much to the disappointment of those coming to hear us play wild things. The band was an amazing source of expanding thinking for me and an important source of my development.[3]

But Berigan played all sorts of jobs. Once he became established in town, he remembers, "I played a lot of weddings and parties, in downtown hotels and North Shore country clubs, and some jazz clubs. . . . I was working 90 to 120 gigs a year for decades, until [the mid-2000s]."

One of the prominent bands Berigan worked with was what musicians refer to as a "kicks" band—one that musicians play in just for the fun of it, for kicks, not for the money. That was Siggy Millonzi's big band (see chapter 10). Berigan also played with Millonzi in quartets, quintets, and sextets. He believes that a Millonzi group played the first Summerfest gig in 1969. "We played at noon on the first jazz stage," Berigan remembers, "the [Miller] Jazz Oasis." Millonzi's band routinely opened for the night's headliner at the Oasis.

As related in chapter 10, when Sig Millonzi died in 1977, his big band was taken over by trumpeter Ron DeVillers and drummer Jack Carr. Jazz gigs were becoming scarce in those years, so the band played dances until even that market dried up. A pair of articles in the *Milwaukee Journal* from May 3, 1988, lamented the dwindling jazz clubs in Milwaukee, due to a lack of demand for the music.[4] Michael Drew's article referred to Berigan as a "tall, dark, and attractive smooth talker" and a "gifted soloist," and he described Berigan and pianist Rudy Moroder as "the odd couple of jazz." Drew reported that the two had been playing together for about twenty years, including a recently terminated thirteen-month engagement at the club Chelsea.[5]

Berigan formed the All-Star Superband in 2000 (fronted by bassist Gary Christensen) and suggests that it is the successor to the Millonzi

Kaye Berigan. COURTESY OF KAYE BERIGAN

band and the DeVillers/Carr band. The Superband has managed to stay alive for years, moving from one home to another around the city and suburbs, playing one night a week.

Over the years, Berigan played many venues in Milwaukee, including the Lounge, the Rag Doll, Dmitri's, the Driftwood, Club Garibaldi, Chelsea, the Jazz Oasis, the Jazz Gallery, the Celebrity Club, Basin Street, the Speakeasy, Mr. Ricky's, Brothers Two, Pzazz, the Packing House, Mr. Henry's, the Brass Rail, and the Kenwood Inn at the UW–Milwaukee Union.[6]

The other side of Berigan's music career was teaching, which began when he was a student at UWM and taught in the Milwaukee public schools' Saturday music lesson program. He did his student teaching at the all-white Nicolet High School. After being discharged from the service in 1964 and spending a year substitute teaching, Berigan started his full-time career at the all-black Lincoln Junior-Senior High, on the east side. He was transferred a couple of years later to Burroughs Junior High on the west side. The elementary school that fed into Burroughs was very strong, and Berigan says his junior high band there "rivaled many of the high school bands." He taught private lessons at home throughout this time and eventually taught summer school, as he says, "to make a buck." He eventually moved to Madison High School and describes his situation there like this:

> That first season we had 160 kids in the marching band—and me, I was the only adult. Four yellow school buses and me; and I'm not a marching band fan. I always said the marching band was to education as the trumpet player at a bullfight was to animal husbandry.
>
> But . . . they allowed me to divide that band into two. So I had a ninety-some-piece symphonic band and a forty-some-piece wind ensemble.

Those groups enjoyed tremendous success at contest in his first year, but not long thereafter, the school changed.

> What happened through the years was busing came in, specialty schools came in—there was a school for fine arts, college bound; we were given the school for agriculture. And I said, "Are you going to grow corn? Plow the athletic field and grow corn?" So they changed, not because of me, to electronics. The neighborhood schools dissipated; nobody was sending anybody to [Madison]; I was fighting. . . . I was trying to make a music department happen. I was pulling rabbits out of a hat, and I looked in the hat and there were no more rabbits, and I retired [in 1994, after twenty-nine years].

Throughout his career as a jazz musician, Berigan has made an effort not to benefit from the fame of his uncle, Bunny Berigan.

> I didn't know anybody really knew who [Bunny] was—even though at home I heard him with Benny Goodman and Tommy Dorsey—until I got in the army, and guys came up to me and wanted to know if I was a relation. And then they would take me out for drinks or a

> meal. . . . It began to sink in that he was an important jazz player. . . . I never played off of it, and sometimes bandleaders would want to use that—announce that I was the nephew. . . . There was some band guy . . . and he called me up to play at a place . . . in a northwestern suburb of Chicago. [He] had a white tux, and a baton and everything. . . . He wanted to introduce me to the audience as the nephew of Bunny Berigan, and I said, "No, I don't do that." And I never got hired back.

In the mid-2000s, Berigan became ill with Guillain-Barré Syndrome. He says, "My immune system attacked my nervous system, and I was paralyzed. And I was in the hospital for thirteen days, and I did not eat for eighteen weeks." He has never completely recovered, but he has improved to the point where he can play again, and play well.

As Bunny's nephew, Kaye is invited every year to play at the Bunny Berigan Jazz Jubilee in Bunny's hometown of Fox Lake. Despite the fact that Bunny played swing his whole career, the music at the Jubilee is all Dixieland (or traditional) jazz, which, Kaye says, "I could never understand." The band Kaye brings to the jubilee each year is the one band there that plays bebop-based mainstream jazz.

In Milwaukee in the mid-2010s, Berigan frequently plays with sympathetic musical companions Steve Lewandowski, George Welland, and Jack Carr (often at Ally's Bistro in Menomonee Falls).

Berigan succinctly sums up his life in jazz into these three points: "1. There are two parts to being able to play jazz: having the chops and technique, and learning the repertoire; 2. It's been a great road; 3. I've always been lucky."[7]

Frank DeMiles

Pianist Frank DeMiles is about a foot shorter than his sometime musical foil Kaye Berigan. DeMiles was born Francisco Dominguez in Waukesha in 1931. He describes his early music education as follows.

> [I] went to a teacher to continue my lessons when I was eleven years old on the Hawaiian guitar; she said she didn't teach that string

> instrument. She says, "Let me see your hands." And I held out my hands, and she said to my dad, "He should play the piano." So when I was twelve to fifteen, when we were still in Waukesha, I took lessons from this Blanche Wilson, who came to the door when we first met her with a wig as white as could [be, and] teeth I swear belonged to George Washington, because they sounded like wood. Anyway, but that's where I started; classical training. And we came to Milwaukee, and . . . I still studied a little classical music at Wisconsin College of Music, [with] Irma Habeck Dufenhorst.

Frank attended Marquette High School, where he played in the orchestra and sang in the choir. He says, "[I] never picked up any jazz music in school; it was all on my own."

Next, he went on to Marquette University.

> My dad wanted me to be a doctor; he worked in a foundry all his life. And he wanted me to not have any worry about money when I grew up. So I was in premed. . . . After my two years [in premed], I said, "Dad, I don't want to be a doctor." I said, "The sciences and I don't agree."

Frank tried dental school for two weeks, but it was clearly another bad match. At the instigation of his young wife, Nancy, he decided to do what made him happy, which was to study music. He went to UW–Milwaukee, got a degree in teaching, and started teaching choral music in 1956 in Greenfield. Despite all the playing that Frank ended up doing in Milwaukee, he needed a steady-paying day job, as he and Nancy ultimately had eleven children.

Frank got his first professional job in 1950 at the Italian Village, in a small band of musicians led by Honey Trent. "It was not a jazz band," he remembers. "It was there for dancing." At this time, he changed his professional name from Dominguez to DeMiles. His heritage is half Italian and half Mexican; he decided that his Hispanic surname did not fit the Italian setting, so he changed it.

Around 1954, DeMiles began playing with Zeb Billings, a saxophonist at that time. Billings went on to found a successful piano and organ store and eventually came up with innovative organ lessons on cassette, which were, according to a *Journal Sentinel* article, "popular enough that some organ manufacturers built cassette players into their instruments."[8]

After several years with Billings, DeMiles landed a plum job at the Holiday House. He describes the Holiday House as a "showcase lounge" located at Clybourn and Van Buren that brought in name performers. DeMiles played in the house band, which also played for many headliners over the years. But his encounter with Tony Bennett, one of America's revered entertainers, was one of the most meaningful of DeMiles's life.

> I'll never forget the night that Tony Bennett, who used to, on his breaks, go back in the corner of the barroom, where a table was nice and dark; nobody could bother him . . . but the waitress came over and said, "Tony wants to talk to you, Frank." So I went over. He says, "Frank, I've been listening to you guys." He says, "You're great, I love your music." I said, "Thank you, Mr. Bennett." He says, "I would give my right arm to trade places with you." 'Cause he had heard about the family. . . . I said, "What do you mean?" He says, "You can go home to your wife and kids every night."

On the jacket of his 1959 album (and 1994 CD re-release), *Live at Stefano's*, DeMiles listed Milwaukee-area clubs where he had played. The list included a wealth of names that will resonate with Milwaukee jazz fans of a certain era: the Italian Village, Kodric's, Lakeside, the Blackamor Room, Stefano's, Gallagher's, Curro's, Sardino's, the Holiday House, De Salvo's, the Layton Place, Bobby's Lounge, Pal Joey's, Tonight Milwaukee, Ma's, Hanon's, Aladdin's, Richard's Retreat, Andy's Tap, Tumblebrook Country Club, the Red Garter, Pitch's, Columns of Tuckaway, Alexander's, Hoffman's East, Gritz's Pzazz, Edelweiss Cruises, Cathedral Square, the Red Mill, and the Cigar X Change.

DeMiles told me flatly, "I was not jazz like Siggy Millonzi was." When playing with his own groups, especially earlier in his career, the songs would emphasize DeMiles's skilled and attractive vocals. However, DeMiles's piano playing in the trio was tasty—and jazzy. And many agree that his later recordings and performances display a true jazz player—quirky, demonstrating an original synthesis of a variety of influences,

From left to right: Tom, James, Frank (DeMiles), and Peter Dominguez (see next section in this chapter) at Milwaukee's Italian Community Center, 2013. PHOTO BY SUSAN ROSE DOMINGUEZ; COURTESY OF PETER DOMINGUEZ

and with a remarkable ability to quote from a dazzling spectrum of tunes (see online discography).

In the 2010s, DeMiles's public performances have become infrequent. But he plays private parties, works occasionally at the Italian Community Center, and makes a yearly appearance at the Bunny Berigan Jazz Jubilee with Kaye Berigan's group.

Of DeMiles's eleven children, two—John and Peter, both string bassists—have distinguished themselves in the jazz world. (His daughter Susan, who plays and teaches violin in New York, is married to Milwaukee-born New York pianist Rick Germanson (see chapter 7), and his son James plays drums in a Milwaukee firefighters' band.) John Dominguez was a prominent bassist on the Milwaukee scene for years before heading for California in the early 2000s. Better known on the national scene is son Peter Dominguez, whose story follows.

Peter Dominguez

Peter Dominguez was born in 1956 and was inspired by his father, jazz pianist and singer Frank DeMiles, from his earliest days. Dominguez remembers hearing his father sing in church: "His clear tenor voice soared above the choir and organ and reverberated throughout the church. I think I was around four or five years old and hearing his heart through my ears was an awakening."[9] As a youth, Dominguez took lessons on piano and, later, clarinet. He began playing with his dad's trio when he was sixteen and continued to do so for five years—performing as Peter DeMiles. The father and son also played with Milwaukee professionals Hattush Alexander and Kaye Berigan, among others.

Dominguez attended Hamilton High School. "I was playing bass in orchestras and jazz ensembles," he remembers, "and singing in the public schools, which were rich in talent and programs. I was playing bass in Music for Youth and jamming rock and blues on the electric bass with friends." He also has fond memories of meeting other local jazz musicians: "Ken Schermerhorn and the Milwaukee Symphony were thriving and I got the chance to meet [several of the MSO bassists]. I also knew jazz bassist . . . Skip Crumby-Bey. Dad took me around town and introduced me to guitarist George Pritchett and pianist Buddy Montgomery."

Dominguez became a fan and friend of the jazz fusion bands Sweetbottom and Matrix (with John Harmon and Fred Sturm). He was a member of the last edition of Montage, with Tom Sandquist and Bob Rebholz (see chapter 12), and he remembers watching two other superb bassists, Gerald Cannon and Jeff Chambers, coming up on the Milwaukee scene.

Dominguez went to college at the University of Wisconsin–Madison, where he first studied jazz with Jimmy Cheatham. In 1977, Richard Davis came to Madison, and it changed Dominguez's musical life and career. "Richard kicked my butt and transformed me in many ways," he says. Davis's mentorship continued when Dominguez became his graduate assistant in 1980. "We joke now that he taught me about the street and I taught him about the academy," Dominguez says. "He remains a close confidant and mentor." In 1993, the two of them started the Richard Davis Foundation for the Young Bassist, Inc., and Dominguez has organized

Peter Dominguez and Richard Davis (see chapter 14). PHOTO BY SUSAN ROSE DOMINGUEZ

the foundation's annual conference ever since. Before leaving Madison upon the completion of his master's degree in 1982, Dominguez was a major presence on the jazz scene in the city.

Later that year, he went to the University of Miami to work on his doctorate. While he primarily studied classical bass, he spent a good deal of time in Miami's renowned jazz program, where he played with such legendary jazz musicians as Ira Sullivan, Tommy Flanagan, Paquito D'Rivera, and Bobby McFerrin.

In 1984, Dominguez won an audition to join the Florida Philharmonic Orchestra but chose instead to take a teaching job at Michigan State University. His twelve years in East Lansing led him to playing opportunities in Detroit and more jazz as well as classical encounters. He left MSU in 1996 to take a similar position at Oberlin College in Ohio. A major coup for Dominguez and Oberlin's conservatory occurred when legendary jazz bassist Milt Hinton left a variety of papers, his jazz photographs, and four basses to the institution upon his death. That included the bass that Hinton played for the vast majority of his long and storied career, which is now available for students to play. Dominguez also runs Oberlin's biennial Milt Hinton Institute for Studio Bass—an honor that is particularly meaningful to Dominguez, who won the first-ever Milton J. Hinton Scholarship in 1980.[10]

Jack Grassel

Guitarist Jack Grassel was born in Milwaukee in 1948. "When I was two years old," he remembers, "I used to reach my hands over my head and play my mother's piano. And I realized that I could play melodies that I heard on the radio." Not long afterward, he says, "My dad took me to the music store and said, 'We'd like to start my son on music lessons, but he's got these little fingers, 'cause he's only three years old.' So they came out with this teeny little accordion." On accordion, Grassel learned how to play melody and chords together at an early age.

He first performed in public in a show run by his aunt, Adeline Grassel.

> [She] had a touring group called Bar O Ranch; it was like a Lawrence Welk show, or an Ed Sullivan show, where there'd be all these people on the show. You know, a ventriloquist, the dancer. . . . And [my aunt] said, "Well, we'll give Jack ten dollars a gig, if he comes out and plays a song." So I did that. . . . I was four years old. And since Hopalong Cassidy and Roy Rogers were popular, I would dress like a cowboy and walk out and sing and play these things.

In his preteens, he played accordion for weddings and baby showers. "I was gigging a lot," he remembers. Grassel won the Wisconsin State Music Festival, an accordion competition, three times starting in 1958. One of his early inspirations was Milwaukeean Kenny Kotwitz, the longtime accordionist with Lawrence Welk, who Grassel calls "the best accordion player in the world."

But then new music caught Jack's attention.

> When I turned twelve, I was tired of gigging so much on accordion, and rock and roll started, so I said, "I'm gonna do this." So I went to the music store, and I told Frank Cascio, "Frank, I need this equipment to play this gig with this rock band [the Triumphs]."

Cascio outfitted Grassel with a bass guitar and an amp. "I played rock and roll and R&B all through high school," he says, often in a band called the Rivieras. He wound up playing six or seven nights a week while in high school—"Not getting much education in high school, obviously," he admits. By age seventeen, Grassel was already burned out from performing so much. But after quitting playing and enrolling in school at UW–Madison, he quickly realized that he missed music. Inspired by such guitarists as Howard Roberts and Wes Montgomery, Grassel switched to guitar during this time and worked the "teen bar" circuit with a band called the Chevrons.

Grassel briefly enrolled at UW–Waukesha, having been told that he should go to music school and get a degree. Jack Whitney, who ran the jazz band there, introduced Grassel to more jazz as well as twentieth-century classical music. But Grassel was playing so many gigs, and was by then getting noticed by recording studios as well, that he dropped out of school. "I was making so much money," he says. "[During] the whole decade of the 1970s, I did thousands of gigs." His peak year for working was 1982, when he claims that he played 522 gigs.

He recalls, "I was doing school concerts [for the Young Audiences program] during the day, recording sessions, playing in bars, and doing shows. One day in 1982, I did seven gigs in one day. Started early in the morning at 9 a.m., and I ended at 1 a.m." One of Grassel's regular gigs during the early 1970s was with the band Matrix (the Milwaukee band; see chapter 12). He played with touring artists who performed in Milwaukee and also with such diverse groups as the Barnum and Bailey Circus band and the Holiday on Ice orchestra. For some time, he was playing six nights a week at the Pfister Hotel downtown.

Around the same time, Grassel became interested in applying to the Wisconsin Conservatory. Milwaukee Symphony bassist Dave Phillips told him that the school was looking for a guitar teacher, and Grassel quickly went from student applicant to instructor. "So I got the gig teaching the jazz guitar program," he remembers, "and I didn't know what I was doing. So I had to learn real quick. 'Cause the students came in and they were better than me." In order to deal with the situation, Grassel says, "I started writing my own stuff, because at that time there weren't any guitar books in print to do what I wanted to do. So that's how *Guitar Seeds*, my first book, came into print." Grassel has now written eleven books of instructional material.

After the banner year of 1982, the work scene in Milwaukee suddenly dried up. Disco eclipsed live music in the clubs; studios and shows started using prerecorded music rather than live musicians. Grassel says,

> I didn't know what else to do. And we were scuffling, and I had children, and a wife and a house and we had no money, and our refrigerator was broken. I needed a car. I started to sell my equipment, to buy food. All my guitars and mandolin and banjo that I used for studio work. I had to sell it to put food on the table, buy my kids shoes.

Around this time, Grassel got a six-week job in the pit orchestra for a touring company of *Annie*. He was on the verge of a mental breakdown while playing the show eight times a week; he was burned out on the show's music, and there were no prospects for future work. But on a tip from saxophonist/music educator Nick Contorno, Grassel heard about a teaching job at Milwaukee Area Technical College, and he was able to secure the position. He eventually designed the jazz program there, and taught at MATC for over twenty years.

Grassel was hardly done performing, however. By the 1990s, he was back to performing frequently—sometimes seven nights a week—with small groups and Chuck Howard's twelve-piece band. Grassel regularly recorded under his own name, especially after establishing his own record label, Frozen Sky Records. He developed an instrument he called the SuperAx, which basically combined a bass with a guitar. With fellow guitarist Kirk Tatnall on the same instrument, the two worked many years at Uptowner in Milwaukee and recorded albums with drummers Dane Richeson and Ernie Adams.

Throughout his career, Grassel continued to learn from others. Early in his guitar career, local guitar legend George Pritchett showed Grassel what he called some "really advanced techniques of the guitar that only [Pritchett] had." And Grassel also learned some chord technique from Don Momblow. From 1990 to 1993, Grassel studied with jazz guitarist George Van Epps in California. Over a period of four years, starting in 1994, Grassel regularly drove sixteen hours one-way to take lessons with jazz guitar icon Tal Farlow at his home in New Jersey. Grassel claims it was his most rewarding association.

In 1998, Farlow was quite sick with the cancer that eventually killed him, and he had a performance scheduled at the National Guitar Workshop. He was supposed to play solo but didn't feel up to it. Grassel helped Farlow get to the venue, hauled his equipment in, and then played along with him. "He knew this was his last time out," Grassel remembers, "and we played two hours. And when we finished, all the people jumped to their feet, and they're screaming and yelling." Farlow died a short time later.

Since then, Grassel has studied with Jimmy Wyble in California and Lloyd Garber in Toronto; Grassel calls Garber "the most advanced guitar player on the planet."

In 1999, Grassel met singer Jill Jensen in the Yardarm Bar in Racine. They quickly connected, both personally and musically, and have worked together now for many years.

In 2004, Grassel suffered from a serious staph infection, which resulted in damage to his body, brain, and nervous system. For many years he was unable to play music. However, he eventually recovered, left his teaching position at MATC, and devoted himself to full-time playing again.[11]

In the 2010s, Grassel and Jensen primarily perform as a duo—Jack and Jill Jazz. Grassel claims that he wasn't happy when he was playing on a standard guitar, so he devised another instrument, which has three necks. On one neck, he establishes a bass line as Jensen sings the first chorus, which is then looped to create subsequent choruses. The second time around, Grassel plays chordal accompaniment, which he also loops. Then he solos on the third neck over the two layers already created. Besides gigs in the Milwaukee area, Grassel and Jensen spend several weeks a year playing at a resort in Mexico.

Jack Grassel, with his three-necked guitar, and Jill Jensen.
COURTESY OF JACK GRASSEL AND JILL JENSEN

Grassel believes that he has now played almost fourteen thousand gigs in his career. He has continued to play and has changed gears so many times because, he says, "I have a really short attention span, so I have to constantly change what I'm doing. And now . . . Jill and I are married; our whole band fits in the car."

Grassel has won multiple WAMI (Wisconsin Area Music Industry) jazz awards and was recognized as one of the country's top guitarists by *Guitar One* magazine in the early 2000s. As of the writing of this book, he has recorded at least eighteen albums as a leader.

Jeffrey Pietrangelo

Jeffrey Pietrangelo was born in Milwaukee in 1952. At the age of eight, according to family legend, he became fascinated with the bugle that his father had played in the service and still pulled out and played on Sundays and special occasions. When Pietrangelo was given a trumpet for Christmas, he said, "I was real disappointed when I got this thing that had buttons on it, you know?"

In fourth grade, he started taking lessons from a Mr. Seewus. "He was a real old guy," Pietrangelo remembered, "and he used to schedule me last, . . . but I'd have these hour and a half lessons that were supposed to be a half hour. . . . He used to write out my lessons by hand, and he put a date on everything. And I've got a couple that I'm going up to Ds, Es, and Fs [very high pitches] in my second year of playing!"

In his school music program, Jeff was once introduced as a member of a small group called the Musical Toads, the name of which he joked about years later.[12] One of his first jobs was playing "Taps" at a cemetery after a funeral.[13] In junior high school, Pietrangelo studied with local trumpet player Bob Dominiak, and later with Wayne Cook at UW–Milwaukee. He participated in Milwaukee's Music for Youth orchestra program, and the Wisconsin State Honors band and orchestra, and when the family moved to the Chicago area for his last two years of high school, he became a member of the Chicago Youth Symphony—one of the top ensembles of its kind in the country.

The family returned to Wisconsin in 1970, and Pietrangelo's father, Patrick, opened Pat Long Chevrolet in West Allis. Pietrangelo headed north to Appleton to attend Lawrence University, where he continued to hone his remarkable trumpet skills, both in classical ensembles (he was the principal trumpet in both the Lawrence Symphonic Band and the Lawrence Orchestra for his four years at school) and in the jazz program that took off under the new leadership of John Harmon (see chapter 18). Pietrangelo also spent time at school displaying what one of his classmates described as "some of his other specialized skills: Frisbee-throwing, kicking a football, foosball, ping-pong, standing with a trumpet on his head."[14]

During summers while Pietrangelo was in college, he spent days working at his father's car dealership while working at night in the pit orchestra at the popular Melody Top Theatre, which put on summer stock musicals at Seventy-Sixth Street and Good Hope Road for twenty years. This was Pietrangelo's first professional music work in the city, and he made friends with such local stalwarts as Joe Aaron (see chapter 4), drummer Roy Schneider, bassist Tom McGirr, and the legendary "summer only" lead trumpet player Vic Knutzen.

During the spring of Pietrangelo's senior year at Lawrence, he was among the group of students who, with the leadership and vision of Harmon, formed the new band Matrix (the Appleton band; see chapter 12). The band served as Pietrangelo's home—a musical home on the road—for the next five and half years. From the very beginning, Pietrangelo's dazzling trumpet playing was a hallmark of the band, and his technical capabilities inspired the group's principal composers, Harmon and Fred Sturm, to craft some of the virtuosic horn writing that earned the band its following.

Once Matrix quit traveling in 1979, Pietrangelo returned to Milwaukee. "I basically didn't get a job for six months," he said. The locals expected him to head out on the road again, and they wouldn't hire him for anything long-term. "Finally," Pietrangelo said, "I convinced everybody I was going to stay and started working. Around that time I met Chuck Hedges, and Hedges and [Bill Sargent] told me, 'You could make a lot of money if you'd learn to play the Dixie book.'" And that's exactly what he did. With Hedges, one of the most respected musicians in Milwaukee history, Pietrangelo rounded out his musical education.

Pietrangelo's big fat tone, superb reading skills, and impeccable tuning soon led to his being hired to play in the backup orchestras for touring shows that came through Milwaukee—the Temptations, the Four Tops, Aretha Franklin, Henry Mancini, and many others. He taught trumpet and led combos at the Wisconsin Conservatory, where he met up with Manty Ellis and Berkeley Fudge.

Over the next three decades, Pietrangelo became one of the few jazz musicians in the city to play with just about every different clique in the jazz sector. He worked with Hedges, with Ellis and Fudge, and the late Hattush Alexander, and, on another end of the spectrum, with bands such as Cavalcade of Swing and George Busateri's Society Band. He connected

Jeff Pietrangelo. PHOTO BY JOE TONDU

with his ethnic heritage playing at Milwaukee's annual Festa Italiana for years. He also played with George Pritchett before the guitarist's death in 1987.

Pietrangelo frequently played at Caroline's club, and recorded with Caroline's house drummer, Paul Spencer, and his band. Pietrangelo recorded several times with guitarist Jack Grassel (see online discography), and he also worked in the World Jazz Band of drummer Andy LoDuca. At times, Pietrangelo also played with the "newer" conservatory faculty—Mark Davis, Jeff Hamann, and David Bayles.

In the early 1980s, Pietrangelo was a member of Toty Ramos's Latin jazz band La Chazz. Later, in that setting, he created musical sparks with his longtime playing partner and friend Allen Johnson. By the 2010s, Pietrangelo was playing not only in La Chazz, but also in Madison's Latin band Madisalsa, and the Milwaukee band Clave y Afinque. At the same time, Pietrangelo worked in Wicked Long Day, with outstanding keyboardist Jerry Weitzer; his wife, vocalist Marcia Cunningham; and young saxophonist Eric Schoor.

In addition to teaching at the conservatory, Pietrangelo taught briefly at UWM, and for a number of years he was a "traveling" teacher who went from school to school for Milwaukee Public Schools. Late in his career, Pietrangelo was hired by Cliff Gribble to teach in the Milwaukee Youth Symphony Jazz program. He also won the outstanding reed/brass player award from WAMI (Wisconsin Area Music Industry) in 1999 and 2007.

Pietrangelo's friends considered him one of the funniest people they knew. He was a master of physical comedy, especially adept at using his face, which led to friends affectionately calling him "Chimp." He was also known for his musical humor. On a club gig, when a non-native speaker requested the popular Frank Sinatra tune "Strangers in the Night" by calling it "Strangers in Night," Jeff played the song and omitted the missing word by leaving out the note that represented it every time. He invented hilarious "short versions" of countless tunes—a two- to four-measure version of virtually any song, with a beginning and an end, that summed up the entire song. He was also known to play solos that wound through all twelve major or minor keys.

Unfortunately, Pietrangelo also battled substance abuse at times during his career. While he sometimes had difficulty getting to gigs, his playing never seemed to suffer once he was on the job, and he maintained his friendliness, good nature, and modesty through the worst times. Despite compromised health, he was able to put those problems behind him toward the end of his career and was playing at his usual high level just days before his death.

When he passed away in December 2012, there was a swift and strong reaction from the Wisconsin musical community. Pietrangelo's Facebook page was flooded with comments from colleagues, friends, and fans. They acknowledged his abilities and prowess as a musician, his modesty, and his friendliness and sweetness of character.

Musicians of all stripes who worked with him consider Pietrangelo one of the finest players ever on the Milwaukee scene.

Tom Newburg

Saxophonist Tom Newburg is the kind of professional that a small city's jazz scene is dependent on. He has, in his own words, "never had a day gig," and over a period of almost forty years has continued to work and to contribute to the local scene.

Newburg was born in 1950 and grew up on a farm outside Oconomowoc. His mother brought home an instrument from the area music store's band promotion night so that he could start band at the same time as his younger brother, and shortly thereafter he joined the band at his Catholic grade school. The next year, Newburg entered public school with his sidekick Fred Sturm (see chapter 18), and they eventually thrived in the school music program. Like many Milwaukee saxophonists, Newburg studied in his early years with Joe Aaron, who gave him a firm grasp on playing the instrument correctly. Newburg found his way to North Texas State University for college, when NTSU was the largest and most successful university jazz program in the country.

During the summer following his freshman year in college, Newburg played with the new Kids from Wisconsin, a dazzling summer show band made up of top young musicians from around the state. When the NTSU schedule threatened to end Newburg's summer early, Kids' founder, Colonel Mark Azzolina, suggested that perhaps Newburg should transfer to a school closer by with a more flexible schedule. So without any real planning, Newburg ended up transferring to the University of Wisconsin–Eau Claire. It was a good time to be in jazz at Eau Claire, with Dominic Spera heading up a program that included future professionals Allen Johnson and Steve Zenz and would soon include star pianist Lyle Mays. While at Eau Claire, Newburg was part of several of the jazz-rock bands that proliferated during this era.

After graduating with a music education degree, Newburg followed the path of others of his generation and, with fellow Wisconsinite Bob McCurdy, joined a rock band in Florida. McCurdy, a fine trumpet player from Brookfield, was one of the few jazzers to attend UW–Madison at that time and had also been in Kids from Wisconsin. In addition to playing five-and-a-half-hour gigs at night, Newburg also helped paint the motel where they stayed for extra money.

When Newburg returned to Milwaukee in the mid-1970s, he was able to work right away because his buddy Keith Sarnow had more jobs than he could play. Newburg briefly took classes at the Wisconsin Conservatory with Tony King. Over a number of years, he worked with a big band that Azzolina booked for the State Fair, and later another Azzolina-led band, the Cavalcade of Swing. Newburg relates that although Azzolina "was real corny with his baton," it was "a killer band" that included many of the finest players in the city. Newburg also was a member of the Sig Millonzi big band during this time.

Eventually Newburg went out on the road for over a year with the Tommy Dorsey Band, led during that time first by multi-instrumentalist Murray McEachern and then trombonist Buddy Morrow.

When Newburg returned to Milwaukee, he played in the "staff band" at the local public television station (Channel 10) for two years—a group that included Brian Lynch, Tom Fabre, Scott Napoli, and other good jazz musicians. If he ever had a "day gig," this was it. He also took a job playing on a cruise ship for several months a couple of times in the early 1980s.

In the glory days of the mid-1980s, when Newburg was back in Milwaukee, married and somewhat settled down, he also played in a quartet with pianist Rich Crabtree, bassist Harold Miller, and drummer Rich Krause six nights a week at the Bombay Bicycle Club. At the same time, he played two afternoons a week at the Pfister Hotel, which simultaneously employed a "small big band" several nights a week.

Since the 1980s, Newburg has played more gigs than he could possibly remember with dance bands, show bands, party bands, fusion bands (including Don Linke's Cooler Near the Lake), and yes, even jazz bands. Why did he stay in Milwaukee? He says he had a "big jazz epiphany" early on, when he asked himself, "Well, are you going to try to do this, and practice and go to New York? Like, wow, you're going to go to New York, live like an animal; even if you're really good. . . . And they don't pay anything, and if you're really, really great, [you get] to where you've got to practice eight hours a day, to get these [expletive] gigs."

After forty years in the business, he says, "I just want to be able to make a couple bucks in this, because I'm already kind of into it now. . . . I'd rather play a bad gig with a bunch of guys I like . . . than play in this really great group [with] a bunch of jackasses. . . . I'll take that bad gig any day of the week. What's the point? This is supposed to be fun. Otherwise you get a real job."

Luis Diaz

Percussionist Luis Diaz was born in Puerto Rico in 1957 and grew up in the small town of Dominguito, outside of the city of Arecibo, on the northern coast of the island. Interestingly, Diaz remembers listening to American music in Puerto Rico, largely the popular soul music of Motown. He says, "I used to see all these salsa major acts on TV—[but] I didn't pay much attention to them." At a certain point, however, he says, "[My class] went on a field trip to one of the TV stations in San Juan to see one of the big bands that played at noon. . . . And it was mind-blowing. Oh, and I wanted to be a drummer from that day on."

As a child, Diaz followed other members of his family to Milwaukee—first his mother's cousin, then an aunt, then his mother, his stepfather, and finally Diaz's grandmother and his siblings. His aunt got a job at Gimbels department store, and the family chose to settle in Milwaukee over other cities due to the job opportunities that they found there. His mother worked for Florsheim Shoes, and his stepfather worked at the infamous Peter Cooper Glue Factory in Oak Creek.

Twelve years old when he came to the United States, Diaz first attended Vieau School, on the south side at Fourth Street and National Avenue. He says it was "a blessing" that he landed in that school, with its "excellent teachers." The school reflected the ethnic diversity of that part of the city in 1970; Diaz describes it as "really integrated, with Mexicans and Puerto Ricans, and Polish, German, Native Americans, African Americans. So it was like a real melting pot." The next year he was at Kosciuszko School and the following year, he moved on to South Division High School.

In Milwaukee, Diaz started buying albums of Puerto Rican and Cuban music. "With some friends at South Division," he says,

> we formed a little [musical] group to play school functions—parent-teacher conferences and assemblies—and sometimes when we had the cultural programs, we would represent, obviously, Puerto Rico, and we played typical music from Puerto Rico.

Diaz began on the guiro, then moved up the ladder of instruments (maracas, bongos, etc.) on his way to timbales and congas. "I used to go and audition every Friday and Saturday at [a band] rehearsal," he remembers, "and they would fire me and tell me to go home. The next week they would call me and say, 'We need you.' [*Laughter*] Because there was no one else to fill in."

> I actually took lessons with a gentleman named Victor Narvaez, who had a group in town.[15] And, he took me under his wing. And he would let me take his bongos home to practice, and he would say, "Bring it back on Saturday, we're going to be playing at such-and-such club." And then I could sneak in and watch them. So that was part of the entire education for me.

Another important mentor was Ismael Ortiz, who, Diaz says, "was a Puerto Rican gentleman when I wasn't."

> Even though [Ortiz] didn't know how to read or write music, . . . sometimes he would play bass, sometimes he would play guitar, sometimes he would play timbales. He sang; he directed the band. . . . He would come and ask my mother if I could go and play with him. . . . He never sat me down and said, "This [is] what you gotta play," but by his actions and by his guidance onstage, I knew what he wanted played.

Early music making for Diaz also involved jamming at the Milwaukee lakefront, as it did for well-known local percussionists Dumah Safir and Mack Perkins. Many ethnic groups and musical styles were represented in this gathering place, including American rock musicians with their guitars.

Diaz did not complete high school at South Division, dropping out in the middle of his senior year. However, he did earn his GED through a program at UWM and studied for an additional year at MATC afterward.

Diaz first really connected with the Latin jazz scene in Milwaukee when he joined Toty Ramos's band La Chazz (see chapter 12). Diaz joined the group in the late 1980s, when its first conguero left, and remained during its long stay at the Café Melange in the Hotel Wisconsin. La Chazz was not exactly a salsa band, and its music was not traditional Afro-Cuban or Puerto Rican. It was really a reflection of the unique synthesis of styles found in Ramos's original compositions. It was great experience for Diaz, and he made a significant contribution to the group. La Chazz also brought him into contact with some of the city's finest jazz players.

The next step in Diaz's development, and his immersion into Milwaukee's jazz community, was when pianist David Hazeltine decided to form a Latin jazz group. Hazeltine was well known for his formidable straight-ahead jazz skills, but he had decided that it was time for something new. He simply added Diaz to his working trio at the time, with Gerald Cannon on bass and Mike Schlick on drums. When it came to music, Hazeltine didn't do anything halfway, and he dove into Latin music with a passion. And due to Hazeltine's perfectionism, Diaz felt that he was constantly on the spot in the group and always needing to improve. Diaz recalls,

> That was another step into playing at another level. . . . I had to sharpen up. . . . The format was: [Hazeltine] would take a solo, Gerald would take a solo, and then either they would vamp behind me in a solo, or sometimes they would leave me freeform, myself and Mike Schlick. And that was like, [*laughter*] where do I stop? Whcrc do I come back in?

Diaz played with Hazeltine for about two and half years before Hazeltine headed back to New York in 1992. But when Hazeltine left town, the Jazz Estate wanted to keep Latin jazz going at the club, since they'd done such good business with the Hazeltine group. Diaz was tapped to be the leader of a new band. He brought together his two old friends, drummer David Bayles and bassist Jim Paolo; trumpeter Mike Plog, fresh from the Berklee College of Music; and pianist Rick Germanson, who as a teenager had occasionally sat in with Hazeltine's Latin group. Nominally, it was Diaz's band, although he says, "They allowed me to be the leader of the band, even though any one of them could have been . . . or should have been the leader of the band." The other members of the Luis Diaz Quintet

The Luis Diaz Quintet (left to right): Steve Einerson, Mike Plog, Luis Diaz, Jim Paolo (see chapter 12), and David Bayles (see chapter 11). COURTESY OF LUIS DIAZ MUSIC PRODUCTIONS

wrote the arrangements, but clearly Diaz was an indispensable member of the group.

The band played at Summerfest, Jazz in the Park, and most Fridays at the Estate. Brian Lynch, who was by then ensconced in the band of Latin jazz giant Eddie Palmieri in New York, would sit in when he came back to Milwaukee. The group made an album in 1996 with Lynch as guest soloist (see online discography). When Germanson moved to New York in the late 1990s, the band again had a big hole to fill; a strong replacement was found in pianist Steve Einerson.

Eventually, the group disbanded. Diaz, in the meantime, had started playing with Madisalsa, usually in that band's hometown, Madison. In another arena, Diaz was brought in by Dave Bayles—after some serious grilling by the administrators and the development of a curriculum—to teach at the Wisconsin Conservatory from 1999 to 2006. Diaz initiated a class in Latin percussion for adults and many outreach programs and clinics in the Milwaukee schools.

Diaz returns to Puerto Rico from time to time, and he has done a percussion clinic there. For a number of reasons, with the other percussionists there, he found himself "doing the clinic, and apologizing to them at the same time," but it was a good experience nonetheless.

Diaz says that a "dream come true" was playing with the heralded Ko-Thi Dance Company in Milwaukee, one of the city's revered cultural institutions, for many years. Playing percussion with Ko-Thi was extremely demanding, as what the percussionists did was totally dictated by the dance. Diaz recalls, "You had to be mentally and physically fit."

Having frequented the Bombay Bicycle Club in the Marc Plaza Hotel to hear Buddy Montgomery's group in the 1970s, Diaz calls playing and recording with Montgomery the "greatest thrill in my musical career." This took place near the end of Montgomery's life, when he was living in southern California. Montgomery began to call Diaz periodically, asking him to come out to Los Angeles and play a few gigs—an invitation impossible to refuse. On one of those occasions, the band recorded the album *Remembering Wes* (see online discography). The last time Diaz played with Montgomery was shortly after Montgomery suffered a stroke and couldn't play piano as he wished. He switched to his other instrument, vibraphone, and hired Melvin Rhyne to play piano.

Diaz is not very active on the Milwaukee scene today, and there is not as much work as there once was. He has moved to Waukegan, Illinois, but still appears from time to time in his home city, particularly with the groups Clave y Afinque and Rumbrava—the latter a collaboration with Connie Grauer and Kim Zick of the band Mrs. Fun.

Juli Wood

Saxophonist and singer Juli Wood was born in 1959 and grew up in Muskego, west of Milwaukee. One of her brothers was a rock and roll drummer, another brother played twelve-string guitar, and her sister played in the school band. Wood began playing the saxophone in her school band in sixth grade. She found out years later that it had been her mother's dream to play saxophone, a dream that was partly lived out through Juli.

In Bay Lane Junior High (where her dad taught industrial arts), Wood obtained a very fine saxophone after an area professional passed away. She proceeded to play in the school concert, marching, and jazz bands through high school. In her high school jazz band, led by Kenneth Olson, she recalls being introduced to some "nice [Count] Basie charts."

After graduating in 1977, Wood went to UW–Milwaukee. She attended for only a year before dropping out to become an active member of the Milwaukee music scene. Shortly she was playing with the R&B Cadets, which featured John and Mike Sieger (who later played with another popular Milwaukee band, Semi-Twang), and singer Robin Pluer. A later version of the R&B Cadets featured Paul Cebar. Wood clearly remembers one of her first gigs with the band, at a rural bar outside Racine. "We made thirty-five dollars apiece," she recalls; "I thought that was great."

Next, Wood played in Hot Canary, another primarily R&B band, featuring Ellen Dearing on vocals and fiddle, and guitarist Mike Judy (who's now known as a visual artist). Both of these bands played around Milwaukee—especially at Shank Hall, Century Hall, and Teddy's—and in Racine.

Wood returned to UWM in 1983, where she pursued a degree in classical saxophone. Many students were being advised to be prudent and get a degree in music education so they could get a job after school, but Wood remembers being told, "Well, you'll just get married anyway, so it won't matter." She gained some valuable experience playing in the concert band under Stanley DeRusha, and the jazz band, led for a while by Tim Bell, whose regular teaching job was at UW–Parkside.

In 1985 and 1986, Wood started working on her jazz chops. She sat in with Melvin Rhyne when he was playing with singer Adekola Adedapo at the Wyndham Hotel. She would also sit in with Rhyne and Hattush Alexander when they played at Eddie Jackson's on the south side, in Bay View. She participated in the jams at the Jazz Estate and Jazz Oasis.

From about 1987 to 1993, Wood was not actively working in jazz but was playing with the very successful blues band Paul Cebar and the Milwaukeeans. Cebar leads popular bands to this day. During that period, the band toured around the Midwest, primarily in Chicago, the Twin Cities, and Milwaukee, where their most common haunt was Shank Hall. Of her time in Cebar's band, Wood says, "It showed me that you can make a living, not a lot of money, but you can pay your rent and have a good time, and save some money [in the music business]. . . . It was fun." She remembers, "We had a lot of fun, fun gigs. And traveling, I love to travel,

Juli Wood. COURTESY OF JULI WOOD

so . . . even though sometimes the travel's not optimum, you're kind of crammed together in the van. . . . It was always fun to go to different cities." Wood also enjoyed the other members of the band, including several other saxophonists during her run (during which she played baritone and alto saxophones)—Rip Tenor, Paul Scher, Tony Jarvis (briefly), and Greg Tardy (see chapter 9).

During some of this time, Wood also worked one night a week at the Café Melange in the Hotel Wisconsin with the band Rhythm Club, with singer Robin Pluer and the duo of Mrs. Fun (Connie Grauer and Kim Zick); Duane Stuermer played bass for a while.

Wood also taught saxophone lessons at Melk Music, Hartland Music Academy, and the Brass Bell. At one time, she was teaching as many as forty students a week. "I can't imagine how I did that," she now says.

After a good run with Cebar, though, Wood says, "It just got kind of loud for me. That's why I turned to jazz," which held her interest. Much of her time during the next three years was spent developing the Juli Wood Quartet. The other members of the band were pianist John Foshager, bassist Bob Siegel, and drummer Mike Schlick. In the quartet, Wood also started singing jazz. She began doing programs in the Milwaukee public schools for the Milwaukee Symphony Orchestra's ACE (Arts in Community Education) program. Wood and Schlick still present these programs, usually with Foshager and bassist Jeff Hamann. The quartet eventually won a Wisconsin Area Music Industry award in the mid-1990s.

Wood and Schlick moved to Chicago together in 1996 to pursue new musical opportunities. Wood made her first album in 1998, with Milwaukee musicians Melvin Rhyne, Mike Plog, Dave Bayles, and Dumah Safir (see online discography). In Chicago, she got a fair amount of work at a top jazz club, the Green Mill, because, she claims, "They wanted to hire Melvin."

During her time in Chicago, Wood has worked a variety of jobs and developed a working relationship with Chicago pianist Earma Thompson. She worked for a while with one of the top "jobbing" big bands in the city, the Orchestra of the Americas. She has also established an interesting steady job with the band at the Christ Universal Temple, where she is the only female and only white member of the temple's band. She has played touring shows in the city, including *Cabaret* (several times), which has an all-female band onstage. And she currently leads the band Chicago Calling, a quartet that plays music by Chicago jazz legends such as Eddie Harris and Johnny Griffin, and vocalists Dinah Washington and Joe Williams. Another of Wood's groups, Natalies Wood, plays the music of Rahsaan Roland Kirk.

In 1993, Wood traveled to Finland, where she says she "bummed around" for a couple of months and "met some musicians." For a number of years, she returned to Finland every other year for fun and did gigs at clubs and festivals. Eventually, she started going back every year, and in 2015 she also played in Estonia. She has learned to sing some jazz standards in Finnish, and a recording project based on Finnish folk tunes has grown out of these visits (see online discography).

Wood is known for her unfettered, joyous, bluesy style, both playing and singing. She returns to Wisconsin frequently, continuing work with the ACE program, playing occasional club gigs, and for special projects such as Valley of the Dolls, with singer Janet Planet and the duo Mrs. Fun.

Mrs. Fun

The duo Mrs. Fun consists of multi-instrumentalist Connie Grauer (who mostly plays keyboards and sings in this group) and drummer Kim Zick. When I contacted Grauer in the summer of 2015, she told me, "I have done all the interviews for Mrs. Fun throughout the years, am used to speaking for Kim and she is more than happy with that arrangement." The following, mostly about Grauer, is based on our interview.

Both Grauer and Zick grew up in Waukesha, a small city that Grauer calls "rich" in arts and music programs. As a youth, Grauer learned many instruments and sang. She remembers the first time she met Zick.

> Our original meeting was in middle school, in the summer, between seventh and eighth grade in a summer drum program. I was in the program, and she came in a couple weeks after it started. And I was the only girl in the class, so the teacher, automatically, when Kim came in [said], "Go stand next to her." And Kim's very quiet; she doesn't really talk, she's never really spoken on the mike in our twenty-eight-year career. After she got started, we had to follow an order of drum patterns, starting with number one, and going to twenty-five, to see how much we had accomplished, . . . and within the first couple weeks, she said one thing to me the whole time. . . . She said, "Let's skip to number fourteen."

Grauer and Zick started high school at the same school, but when Waukesha North was completed, Grauer went to the new school while Zick stayed at Waukesha South. Grauer won music awards in junior high and high school, which supported her playing. Despite playing a variety of instruments, Grauer was not a "band kid" in school but rather participated in choirs. She often played guitar with the choirs, and when she obtained a banjo during eighth grade, her music teacher, Ginny Lighte, pushed her into learning enough in a month to play with the choir for a concert. The instruments—various guitars, banjo, mandolin, bass, drums—kept piling up.

Grauer had one music gig while in high school—playing banjo at Shakey's Pizza Parlor in Waukesha. Many of the Shakey's restaurants of that time featured music, usually with banjo at its core, complete with the vest and straw hat. Grauer was younger than the Shakey's musicians were supposed to be, but she says, "They let me slide on that."

Grauer and Zick graduated in the late 1970s. Subsequently, both were enshrined in their respective high schools' halls of fame.

Grauer went to college at UW–Oshkosh. It might have seemed a strange choice, as UWO was not known as one of the top music schools in the state system. But it was just what Grauer was looking for. "I just couldn't be away from my family," she says. She was afraid of the bigger, more high-powered, and more distant schools.

Grauer had taken music theory in high school, and when she arrived at Oshkosh, she was moved out of the basic theory classes into more advanced work. Theory professor Roger Dennis gave her considerable personal instruction in advanced theory. Grauer was studying to be a choral director and says, "I never wavered from that as my goal—until I had my first interview. And then I knew that wasn't for me, and I should be a performing musician. . . . I totally made sure that I didn't get that job, deliberately."

Outside of school, during her Oshkosh days, Grauer was turned in a new direction when she began to play the piano. On the recommendation of a friend, she sought out lessons with pianist John Harmon (see chapter 18). For ten months, Grauer drove from Oshkosh to nearby Winneconne to study with Harmon. Over time, Grauer has become something of a keyboard virtuoso, playing intricate bass lines with her left hand, simultaneously doing all the things that the right hand traditionally does—soloing and comping—and frequently singing on top of it all.

After graduating from Oshkosh, Grauer moved back in with her parents and began pursuing a music career. Zick remembered their shared past and recruited Grauer for the 1980s fusion band Side Street. Although the band didn't last long, it was an important milestone. Grauer says that when they played their very first job together, "I looked over at Kim, and honest to God, I said, . . . 'I'm going to be performing with that person for the rest of my life.'"

For about a year, Grauer moved on to a big band that played dinner theaters around the country. Then, both Zick and Grauer were recruited

Mrs. Fun: Kim Zick (left) and Connie Grauer.
PHOTO BY DEONE JAHNKE; COURTESY OF MRS. FUN

to play in a Nashville-based band, backing up the singer Tracy Peel. Grauer and Zick soon tired of playing country music covers, but they moved to Nashville during this period, and while they were there, around 1987, they formed Mrs. Fun. The new band received valuable career advice from veteran producer Jim Rooney, who produced Mrs. Fun's first album and passed along excellent insight into how the business worked and how to handle publishing. Eventually, this led to the establishment of the companies Funtime Records and Black Sky Publishing—one to be their record label and the other to publish their music.

Grauer and Zick met and worked with big-time vocalists k.d. lang and Indigo Girls, acoustic bassist Edgar Meyer, and electric bass star Victor Wooten. These connections led to Mrs. Fun opening shows for lang, jazz drummer Billy Cobham, guitarist John Scofield, and others; and they toured all over the United States with Indigo Girls in the 1990s and 2000s.

Grauer and Zick moved back to the Milwaukee area after only five years in Nashville, and when the recession of 2008 hit, it was no longer profitable to do the kind of touring that they had become accustomed to. According to Grauer, "Things were too tight . . . so we just decided . . . it was a little more beneficial for us to stay closer to home and do shorter trips. And so it's been more regional now."

After they moved back to Wisconsin, they became involved in projects with Victor DeLorenzo, drummer with the alternative rock band the Violent Femmes.

Mrs. Fun's music is difficult to categorize. Grauer doesn't consider their music jazz, but she says that Zick does. On their website, the top line of the home page reads, "MRS. FUN PLAYS NU JAZZ." It continues: "Complex, sophisticated, and adventurous, their music is a unique blend of off-center jazz, ultra-funk, spoken word, and their own brand of neo-cabaret." Journalist Dave Luhrssen says Mrs. Fun "work[s] intuitively from a jazz base, spinning out funky but thorny rhythms and memorable but subtle melodies from disparate threads of rock, pop, tango, and the most venturesome explorations of avant-garde '60s jazz."[16]

Mrs. Fun has won a Wisconsin Area Music Industry award for Best Contemporary Jazz Group; Zick and Grauer have also won multiple individual awards from WAMI. In 2015, in addition to working as a duo, they worked with Luis Diaz in the Latin group Rumbrava, and with vocalists Janet Planet and Juli Wood in a group known as Valley of the Dolls.

Eric Schoor

Saxophonist Eric Schoor was born in 1990 at St. Luke's Hospital in Racine, where his mother was a dietetic technician, and he was raised in Kenosha. He claims, "I didn't see a whole lot of any other part of the country or the world; I wasn't exposed to a lot of music." Like many other musicians of his generation, he says, "The influences that I had were from a small CD collection and a few very key educators." Forced by his parents to get involved with music, he began piano lessons in about second grade. He didn't want to join band when that opportunity was presented in fifth grade. He says he "just wanted to go to school and then come home and veg."

However, when a friend joined band, Schoor decided to give it a try, expecting to quit after a year. He thought he was going to play cornet, but his mother made a mistake filling out a form, so he began on clarinet instead. He experienced early success because of his piano training but was frustrated with the instrument's limitation of playing only one note at a time. Still, his early success got him hooked. "I liked knowing I was making progress in something," he says, "and that I was getting good, and it was fun to excel."

Before he entered Lincoln Middle School, where Ken Wiele led a strong jazz program, Schoor was trying to figure out how to play clarinet in jazz band. When it was pointed out to him that tenor saxophone used many of the same fingerings as clarinet, and the same transposition, he switched. Ironically, though, when he finally joined the jazz band at Lincoln, he spent his first year playing piano, not saxophone.

The jazz band at Lincoln was not typical for a middle school.

> Ken Wiele was such an inspiring band director, because he was so positive, and he would do all kinds of stuff that you wouldn't get from an average band director that wasn't hip to the jazz language. He would do call-and-response and ear training with us, . . . get [us] going on the blues scale, and he was always talking about improvisation. I didn't realize how valuable that was at the time, but it just kind of made it fun, and the band sounded good, and when we played concerts everybody was yelling and screaming. . . . All these external rewards sort of started piling up around music.

Schoor also took up electric bass during middle school, playing it mostly in garage-type bands, thus becoming something of a triple threat. Eventually, he learned guitar as well. He took private saxophone lessons from Garrett Kornman, assistant director of the Kenosha Pops Band.

When Schoor moved to Tremper High School, Ken Wiele had preceded him there by a couple of years. He joined a core of talented young jazz players there—Ken Wiele (son of the band director), Dan Meinhart, Carl Kennedy, Tim Ipsen, Dustin Laurenzi, Nick Croyder, and Alex Mariani. (Chris Misch-Bloxdorf followed Schoor.) These young musicians, who were older than Schoor, had a profound effect on him. "I was inspired by those guys," he remembers, "because they were playing, and sometimes they were actually gigging and making money, and that's kinda where the big turning point happened." When Schoor played a gig and earned seventy-five dollars, he says, "It was more money than I ever thought possible"—eye-opening to a kid who had been working at Goodwill and Pick 'n Save for minimum wage.

He decided to become a professional musician, which led to the issue that so many young musicians face—parental disapproval of a profession that can be hard, unforgiving, and dicey. But Schoor was determined, and he stepped up his music work. In his senior year, he made the decision to focus primarily on saxophone, and he began lessons with Curt Hanrahan, who was also head of the UW–Milwaukee jazz program. Hanrahan realized the young saxophonist's promise and pushed Schoor to do some very serious woodshedding, or heavy practicing. Schoor also took part in the UWM program of jazz for high school students.

When it came time for college, Schoor checked out high-profile programs at Lawrence University, Indiana University, and Northern Illinois University. A straight-A student in high school, he was offered considerable academic scholarships at several schools. Musically, he claims, "I didn't really have it together very much, even for a high school student going to pursue music. I guess I was still an advanced high school student, but not really like some of the other guys" who had come out of Kenosha. At the last minute, Hanrahan pushed Schoor into applying at UWM, and the school made him an offer that he couldn't turn down. "I was getting paid to go to school," he says. "They paid for my housing for four years, paid for all my books, all of my tuition, and then I'd get a stipend each semester." There was also the appeal of being close to the jazz scene of a large city.

Schoor connected with the larger jazz community in Milwaukee. Early on, he sat in with guitarists Neil Davis and Steve Peplin at the Lemon Lounge, a tiny hole-in-the-wall on Oakland Avenue. Soon he was joining the two guitarists for their monthly gig at the Jazz Estate, which continued for a couple of years. Schoor practiced for hours a day at school (unlike most of his peers there).

Hanrahan gave Schoor the opportunity to sub in the band Wicked Long Day with Milwaukee veterans Jerry Weitzer on piano and Jeff Pietrangelo on trumpet. About Pietrangelo, Schoor says, "I had never heard anybody play the trumpet like that in my life. It was . . . life changing to hear something like that." Wicked Long Day played various venues, including Caroline's on Florida and Second, where for some time the band held a weekly jam session.

At this time, around 2010, Schoor says he was still "completely oblivious to the [Wisconsin] Conservatory" and the jazz tradition that surrounded it. Then drummer Dave Bayles, who was associated with both UWM and the conservatory, asked Schoor to play on a job at the Estate. Mark Davis and Jeff Hamann, stalwarts at the conservatory and on the Milwaukee scene, were soon calling Schoor for gigs as well. When Berkeley Fudge suffered a stroke and became unavailable for the many jobs that he was playing, Schoor was in the right place at the right time. Eventually, that led to his joining the conservatory's faculty jazz group, We Six. (Schoor appears in the photo that accompanies David Bayles's profile in chapter 11.) This band led to further connections, with trumpeter Eric Jacobson, who joined We Six at about the same time; guitarist Paul Sibergleit; drummer Todd Howell; bassist Jim Paolo; pianist Mike Kubicki; trumpeter Allen Johnson; and others, who became young Schoor's colleagues around the city and beyond. Collectively, all these experiences and players, Schoor says, "molded me from somebody that could maybe play the instrument, to actually developing a concept of what I want my style to be." He got back to studying piano in order to learn how to arrange tunes for small groups and big bands. His harmonic ideas were enriched by playing with such advanced pianists as Dan Trudell and Barry Velleman.

In 2012, Schoor and Jacobson, with the help and blessing of trumpet superstar Brian Lynch, recorded an album live at the Estate. Schoor also began teaching at the conservatory in 2012, giving saxophone lessons and leading combos. Through the conservatory's Connections program, Schoor works with high school and middle school big bands in afterschool programs. In 2014, he was working once a month at Transfer Pizzeria with Jeff Hamann and veteran Manty Ellis. At the ripe old age of twenty-seven (at the time of this book's publication), Eric Schoor is probably the busiest saxophonist in mainstream jazz in Milwaukee today.

Andy Schumm

Unlike the vast majority of his peers, who are usually placed in a general category of "modern mainstream" jazz, Andy Schumm is decidedly not a mainstream musician. Schumm primarily plays traditional jazz (not to be confused with Dixieland); musicians such as Schumm may necessarily be serious students of this older music that is largely out of current style. In a city as large as Chicago, there is a critical mass of these musicians, and a viable audience for the music, so that a musician like Schumm can make a reasonable living playing jazz.

Schumm was born in 1985 in Waukesha and grew up in nearby West Allis. There was a radio on top of the old Wurlitzer spinet piano in his home. "I used to play along with the radio," he says. "[I was] real young. That's the first thing I remember doing." He began piano lessons at about age seven with Tom Brown, music director at the Schumms' church. "I took that pretty seriously, but, like every kid, didn't want to practice," he recalls. But Schumm kept up with piano, and occasionally organ, lessons through high school. He started trumpet in grade school, having discovered his dad's old trumpet in the basement.

Schumm attended Nathan Hale High School in West Allis, where he remembers band director Kelly Schultz as a motivational jazz teacher. Schumm became infatuated with the recording of Benny Goodman's famous 1938 Carnegie Hall concert. Soon, he dug into Richard Sudhalter's study of early white jazzmen, *Lost Chords*, moving beyond Goodman to Red Nichols and Bix Beiderbecke. He became serious about trumpet in high school, and in his junior year started taking lessons from Milwaukee trumpeter Mike Plog. Schumm worked hard, and says, "[Plog] really did get me ready for college."

Schumm played his first real gig on piano, at a wedding, when he was still quite young. At age sixteen, he played his first gig on trumpet in Milwaukee with the New South Rampart Street Paraders (the band had previously been the North Water Street Tavern Band); Schumm describes them as a "kind of novelty Dixieland band." At the Organ Piper (on South 108th Street), trumpeter "Mild Bill" (not Wild Bill) Davison, who had played in the Riverboat Ramblers with Wisconsin's other top traditional cornet player Bob Schulz, let the youngster sit in. The packed house and the music that he heard turned Schumm around: "I've been kind of chasing that excitement ever since," he says. He decided to start playing guitar as well; when that was not a great success, he switched to the more traditional banjo.

In college, at the University of Illinois, Schumm went back to arranging and playing contemporary big band music. "I got into the top band," he recalls, "squeaked in, the fifth trumpet chair, and I shouldn't have been in there, it was a bunch of . . . recovering alcoholic guys off the road. I said, 'What is this? This wasn't in the brochure.'" Early on, Schumm says, "I was equally into Coltrane as I was to . . . [traditional jazzer] Turk

Murphy. . . . I liked them both. But it was kind of two lives. I'd go to school, and it would be modern jazz time; I totally got into it. And then I'd go home for the summer, and I'd play Dixieland jobs on banjo."

Eventually, he admits,

> I found every time I went back to school, I liked the modern stuff a little bit less. . . . By the last year, I couldn't stand it. Not that I disliked the music. . . . I wasn't getting any better; I probably wasn't practicing it. . . . And I've always had a streak of . . . contrarian.

While in college, Schumm had the chutzpah to contact Vince Giordano, a New York City saxophonist, bandleader, and expert on jazz of the 1920s and 1930s. They had a four-hour phone conversation, and later, when the U of I jazz band went to the city, Schumm spent a day with Giordano. "It was neat to see a guy who was so serious about [this music] and was not affected at all by what other people thought about it," Schumm says. "And obviously he was successful." Some years later, when Schumm had his own band and was playing at festivals, he says Giordano was "gracious enough to come out and play with me."

During his time in school, Schumm got a few jobs playing mainstream jazz, for low pay (and sometimes a few Old Styles), and he occasionally played with blues bands. But, he says, "I was working a lot playing Dixieland things, and slowly getting more into the 1920s," mostly playing in Milwaukee, sometimes in Illinois.

After college, Schumm moved back to Milwaukee. Besides the Paraders, he worked with the Dixie Doodlers, mostly playing bass saxophone. Bands found out that he could play various instruments because, he says, "I was obnoxious about it . . . [and] probably a really annoying teenager." Schumm also worked with the Rhythm Aces (and continues to in 2017), playing cornet and piano, frequently at the Bavarian Inn in Glendale.

This led to work in Illinois, and eventually to a Chicago group, the West End Jazz Band, with which he started playing drums. For almost a year, Schumm would play a steady job in St. Charles on Saturday night, then sleep in his car before driving a few miles down the road for the West End's Sunday brunch job. He switched from drums to trumpet with

Andy Schumm. PHOTO BY JOHN FORTIER

West End. He was barely getting by but was buoyed by his family and his girlfriend.

With the West End Jazz Band, Schumm's name started to become better known. "[The band played] these festival circuits, these Dixieland and twenties things, swing festivals," he says. And he didn't play exclusively traditional jazz. For several years, he played swing Thursday nights at the Green Mill in Chicago with Alan Gresik's Swing Shift.

By 2014, Schumm had moved to Chicago and was making a living playing "old" jazz. He played two nights a week at Chicago clubs with the Fat Babies. The band was also popular on the party circuit, so he was often playing four to five nights a week. There are gigs, many back in Wisconsin, with the Rhythm Aces, and another group, the Vagabond Reeds.

Schumm has also been a part of the Archipelago Project, an advocacy group that does short, intensive residencies with groups of (mostly) young musicians, outside of school. He has made trips with the project to Venezuela, Peru, Austria (where part of the group is from), and around the United States, including an annual summer camp in Traverse City, Michigan.

Schumm has toured Australia twice with the Hot Jazz Alliance, a group of traditional musicians; on one tour, they played about twenty-six jobs in twenty-eight days. This group toured in the summer of 2015, starting in the United Kingdom, playing in New York, Chicago, and many cities in between, before ending up at the Bix Beiderbecke Festival in Davenport, Iowa.

Schumm is a deep thinker when it comes to the music that he plays and arranges. He has chosen a path less traveled, and he is having considerable success.

16

More Madison Scenes

Madison is home to many jazz musicians with diverse styles. Since the 1990s, in addition to those discussed in chapters 13 and 14, there has been a core of active, visible performers in the city. Some of the musicians in that group are profiled in this chapter.

Vincent Fuh

Vincent Fuh was one of the most active musicians on the jazz scene in Madison for almost two decades. Some might find it odd, then, that Fuh says he never felt comfortable as a jazz pianist and was thinking about, in his words, "divorcing" himself from jazz when he was being interviewed for this book.[1]

Fuh was born in 1965, and when he was very young he lived just blocks away from old County Stadium in Milwaukee. After a few years in Kentucky, his family moved back to the Milwaukee area, and Fuh attended junior high and high school in Brookfield. He started piano lessons at a very young age and was expected to practice every day. In junior high, he joined what was called show band, which played arrangements of pop tunes. Because his father listened to classical music exclusively, show band was Vince's first real encounter with pop music. "I'd heard pop music before," he says, "but . . . I had no performing experience with it, so it was really foreign to me."

Fuh's horizons were expanded when he got to Brookfield Central High School and joined the jazz band. While he could figure out chord symbols, he didn't know what a pianist should do in a jazz band. He took classical lessons at the Wisconsin Conservatory one summer, and took a few jazz lessons at his parents' urging. But there was too much to learn in a short amount of time.

Shortly after high school graduation, in the summer of 1983, Fuh entered the University of Wisconsin–Madison on scholarship in an accelerated premed program. He stayed in this program for about two years, and says he "was just miserable." In the meantime, he took piano lessons at the School of Music. "I just went through a really, really rebellious period," Fuh says, "and part of that involved me being somewhat involved in the music scene here. I was studying piano—classical piano; then I was taking part in the jazz ensemble here, [and] Black Music Ensemble." He also took improvisation class with Joan Wildman.

> Even going through college, I can't say that I had a good understanding . . . of what I needed to do. And it wasn't just music, it was life in general; it was a very difficult time for me. . . . And then I was really testing the waters, because I didn't know whether I wanted to be a jazz musician or a classical musician.

Fuh's skills developed further when he was hired by Al Chase, who for many years led a "society" band in Madison. Fuh says,

> He got my name somehow. . . . I really wasn't in the market. But we had to wear tuxedos, and all that. . . . It sure beat working for minimum wage. . . . And that was really sort of like baptism by fire, because playing in jazz ensemble [at UW], if you didn't get something right away, you can get away with murder practically. But out on a gig, you really had to deliver.
>
> There was actually a pretty decent scene, relatively, back in the 1980s, compared to now. I mean, you had gigs. And that's how I met Kelly De Haven, Jeff Eckels, . . . and of course Kelly's dad, Doc. . . . And so I got sort of absorbed into that circle, never ever feeling like I deserved to be.

Fuh switched to the School of Music, although he lost the support of his parents when he left the premed program. He eventually earned a degree in classical piano. When he finished school, he says, "I just tried to stay afloat. I took day jobs. And I was actually doing okay. I got a job within the university system that actually paid well and that I actually enjoyed doing. It had nothing to do with music." After a short stint in a clerical job with WHA radio, he worked as a technical typist in the physics department. Fuh remained in this job for years, making decent money, with benefits, and working as a jazz pianist nights and weekends, most often with Kelly De Haven and Eckels.

Fuh continued to play jazz steadily through the 1980s and 1990s and into the 2000s. In the mid-1990s, he quit his day job and became a full-time musician. Although he was playing jazz a lot, he wasn't sure that was the way for him to go. He says,

> I never really took [jazz] that seriously. I never considered myself really a jazz musician. I begrudgingly admitted that I could get by; I could fake my way through a gig. The real reason why I have a reluctance to describe myself as a jazz musician [is that] I wasn't brought up listening to the music. I didn't receive an education in it, in terms of knowing the historical context of this music. I feel like an imposter.

Since the mid-1990s, Fuh has managed to make a living as a pianist, largely through his work as a collaborative pianist. At UW–Madison, a major university with a large music school, Fuh has had no trouble finding this sort of work. Now, in the 2010s, he has as much accompanying as he can handle. He is an important presence at UW, accompanying many recitals by students and faculty alike. He also appears with other ensembles, such as the Bach Dancing and Dynamite Society, and he has a long-standing relationship with Madison's Opera for the Young. Fuh feels a sense of purpose in his educational mission—teaching music students what it's like to work with a professional—and he also feels rewarded when he sees children who attend Opera for the Young performances "getting into it."

Outside classical music, Fuh enjoyed playing with Madison's best-known salsa band, Madisalsa, of which he was a founding member, and with El Clan Destino, a group he started with bassist Nick Moran.

El Clan Destino (left to right): Yorel Lashley, Francisco Martinez, Vincent Fuh, Nick Moran (see later in this chapter), and Juan Tomas Martinez. COURTESY OF NICK MORAN

> [El Clan Destino] was like a further extension of my interest in Cuban [music]. . . . But it was also an opportunity for me to involve other musical interests. Because there's a lot of other popular music that I really enjoy that I can't play because there's no acceptable type of ensemble that would play this type of music. So El Clan Destino was kind of a petri dish for that. We'd start with this Afro-Cuban center, and then expand from there, and experiment with more aggressive types of popular music, like rock and funk, eventually heavy metal.

Almost anyone who has heard Fuh play jazz would be surprised to learn that he considers himself a jazz "imposter." He certainly does not sound like one. Fuh remains humble about the music he plays and grateful for the career path he has followed. "I'm terribly indebted to all the jazz musicians that I've worked with in the jazz scene here in Madison," he says, "because I picked up so much about how to perform from them that I wouldn't have had as a classical musician."

David Stoler

Pianist David Stoler, known as Dave to his friends, was born May 7, 1962, in Madison. He grew up on the city's west side, and one of his earliest memories is of being in a playpen in his living room, at the age of two or three, hearing music from his father's vintage Norelco Continental 400 tape deck. Music of different styles was played in his household; one memorable album in the rotation was Miles Davis's *Green Haze*.

When he turned seven, Stoler started piano lessons with Mrs. Yoder, who lived down the street. He mostly worked on classical music, but after about a year he found himself drawn to exercises that had boogie-woogie bass lines, with independent melodic lines, which, Stoler says, "helped get my ear moving in the direction of the [jazz] idiom."

His next teacher was Jerry Borsuk, a former child prodigy who had a piano studio in the area of Regent and Allen Streets. "[Borsuk] was very proactive about showing me how to read chords for the first time," Stoler says. "This is when I was eleven. And also, I think he made it a point to give me music that was really above my ability." So Stoler began learning such works as Beethoven's *Pathétique* sonata and Richard Rodgers's *Slaughter on Tenth Avenue* at an age at which many teachers would have opted for something easier. Borsuk also ran off mimeographed lead sheets for pop tunes, including standards that Stoler believes he may still be playing today. However, by the age of thirteen, Stoler felt he had "hit a wall," and quit lessons.

In high school at Madison Memorial, Stoler wanted to play in the jazz band, a high-achieving group led by one of Wisconsin's jazz education pioneers, Bill Endle. Stoler describes Endle as "old school," with motivational methods that might be questioned in today's educational climate, but he developed a prize-winning ensemble at Memorial, known around the state for its outstanding performances. Lead trumpeter in the band at the time was John Ahern, who went on to the powerhouse program at North Texas State University and is still an active musician in Minneapolis–St. Paul.

Stoler wanted to improve his piano fundamentals, so he started taking lessons again with another classically trained pianist. Occasionally he would hear jazz artists live, including Maynard Ferguson's band at Verona High School and guest artists at the Eau Claire Jazz Festival. He was a member of the 1979 State Honors Jazz Ensemble, which included his schoolmate, trombonist Joel Adams. Stoler's disciplined study with pianist (and fine trombonist) Randy Tomasello, who was in residence in Madison at the time, was important to his development during his high school years. A clinic with UW–River Falls faculty member John Radd was also influential.

After high school graduation, Stoler enrolled at the University of Wisconsin–Madison in 1980. He did not begin his college career in the School of Music, although he auditioned for the jazz ensemble, led at the time by Richard Davis. Stoler describes Davis as a "very strong music presence" for him, another veteran with an old-fashioned teaching approach. Stoler learned many lessons from Davis, including the basic "always be prepared" lesson that is so easily forgotten, especially by confident, or overconfident, young players. Davis brought some of his old cronies from New York to UW during those years; Stoler particularly remembers the visit of Elvin Jones.

During the five years that Stoler was at UW–Madison, there was much jazz activity in the city. Two clubs, Bunky's and Merlyn's, were catalysts in that activity and were where Stoler heard Dizzy Gillespie; Art Blakey and the Jazz Messengers, with its young star, Wynton Marsalis; and the bands of Dexter Gordon and Woody Shaw, the latter featuring pianist Mulgrew Miller. Unfortunately for the community, both clubs were closed by the mid-1980s. Stoler was also greatly influenced by seeing Miles Davis and his band four times during the 1980s.

The first significant long-term engagement in Stoler's performing career was a three-year stay at the Ovens of Brittany in Shorewood, playing Saturday nights with bassist Leon Dorsey.

In part because of the example set by bassist Peter Dominguez, Stoler pursued graduate study at the excellent program at the University of Miami. As he describes it, "The level of musicianship [at Miami] at that time, I mean, what I witnessed at that time, . . . it's hard for me not to be biased, but it sort of dwarfs even what's expected now." In Miami, he met and heard saxophonist Bob Mintzer and trumpeters Clark Terry, Tom Harrell, and the great Thad Jones.

David Stoler. COURTESY OF DAVID STOLER

After earning his master's degree, Stoler moved back to Madison briefly before taking up residence in Milwaukee. But when the opportunity arose to move to New York City in 1989, he could not resist, and he lived there for about two years. "That ended up being a really great experience," he says, "because it was really at a time when the original jazz masters who were still living were still active." While working a day job, Stoler says he "was playing at certain rooms that didn't have much visibility, but hanging out at the higher-visibility places." At those higher-visibility places, he was hearing jazz masters Gil Evans, Hank Jones, Tommy Flanagan, Kenny Barron, Cedar Walton, and even the teenaged Wisconsin phenom Geoff Keezer.

Stoler moved back to Madison in 1991. Musically, it was a stark contrast, but he says staying in New York "would have been just a much greater compromise in terms of my lifestyle than I was willing to [make] at that time."

Stoler's career in the wider jazz scene benefited from his success at three different jazz piano competitions. He was a semifinalist in the very first Thelonious Monk International Piano Competition in 1987. Several years later, he was a semifinalist at the 1992 American Pianists Association Jazz Piano Competition, held in Indianapolis, where he competed against Brad Mehldau, among others. Last, he was a finalist in what is now the Great American Jazz Piano Competition in Jacksonville, Florida. But Stoler's life and career have been in Madison for the last twenty-plus years, although he does make periodic trips to New York, where he not only visits but plays in venues such as the jazz club Smalls. He performs in Madison with the Tony Castaneda Latin Jazz Sextet and with his own

Ad for the New Breed's Jazz Jam at the Cardinal Bar, ca. 2014. Front (left to right): Paul Hastil, Nick Moran, and Louka Patenaude. Back: Michael Brenneis. COURTESY OF NICK MORAN

trio. Stoler was voted the 2009 Isthmus Jazz Personality of the Year. He is glad to have moved back to Madison to be with his folks, and he believes that the quality of life in Madison, "arguably, is the best in the country."

In 2014, Stoler said, "My basic philosophy now with music is that it has to be honest, and you have to be very clear about what your expectations are in advance." He could have made a career in New York, but, he says, "I felt like I could still develop as a musician here [in Madison], and I feel like I have."

The New Breed

The New Breed originated in the early 2000s, the brainchild of pianist Tim Whalen. The original members were Whalen, drummer Leo Sidran, and bassist Nick Moran. At times, the group has included trumpeter David Cooper; pianist Paul Hastil; trombonist Joel Adams; saxophonists Paul Daugherty, Anders Svanoe, Patrick Breiner, and John Keech; guitarist Louka Patenaude; and drummers Jamie Ryan, Michael Brenneis, Dane Richeson, and Kyle Hernandez. It was designed as a group to perform new, original music but also as a vehicle to spearhead local jam sessions.

In 2011, the New Breed began conducting an open jam session every Tuesday night at the Cardinal Bar (now Nomad World Pub) on Wilson Street (see photo on previous page). By this time, the band's personnel was Patrick Breiner on saxophone, Paul Hastil on piano, Nick Moran on bass, and Michael Brenneis on drums. When Breiner left town, guitarist Louka Patenaude took his place. The mission of this new edition of the New Breed is not just to give young (and old) players a place where they can play, but also to make that space welcoming. In Hastil's words, the members "really want a sense of friendliness, and an unthreatening atmosphere for those who come down and are going to sit in. And our mission is to make everyone sound as best as they can sound."

David Cooper

Early New Breed member David Cooper was born in St. Charles, Illinois, in 1963. The family moved to Columbus, Ohio, then on to Cleveland before landing in Green Bay, Wisconsin, when Cooper was a sophomore in high school. By this time he had become interested in music, where he had success; he says he was a "very middle-of-the-road student in every other subject." Cooper attended Southwest High School and was a top player in his high school band. He attended jazz camp at UW–Green Bay, where he met Lovell Ives, head of the jazz program at the school. But, he says, "Things didn't really get interesting until I got in the State Honors [Jazz Ensemble]." He was in an edition of the band that starred saxophonist David Bixler and drummer Steve Godfrey; future jazz figure Pete McCann was playing guitar. Indiana University's Dominic Spera (see chapter 17), formerly at UW–Eau Claire, led the band with an iron fist, old-style discipline, and the tactics of fear. Cooper met a lot of talented young players who loved to play jazz, which led him to take trumpet lessons with Ives.

Cooper's college odyssey began with a two-year stay at UW–Green Bay. He left Green Bay, he says, because "in my mind I was trying to just look to improve, . . . not necessarily to get a degree. I really wanted just to be . . . a good trumpet player. I didn't love orchestra playing, and I didn't love jazz playing—I just loved trumpet playing." His next stop was Indiana University, where he studied with the fabled trumpet pedagogue Bill Adam. Dominic Spera was there, of course; at that age, Cooper says, he was able "to deal with him on a little bit more adult level."

After hearing a great big band from Ohio State University, Cooper went there for a year, studying with another excellent trumpet teacher, Tom Battenberg, who also ran OSU's award-winning jazz band. Cooper ran out of money, so he returned to Green Bay, where he lived with saxophonist Woody Mankowski (see chapter 18) and played in a couple of rock bands. Cooper remembers, "[I was] trying to figure out what to do next. Fred [Sturm] actually called my house. And said, 'Well, if you're not doing anything, you might want to check out Lawrence.'" Lawrence University proved to be a great match for Cooper, and he remembers it as "the best place" that he ever went.

Cooper earned a degree after two and a half years at Lawrence, then went to graduate school at the University of Akron, where he played in an excellent graduate brass quintet. Inspired by a performance of the Chicago Symphony at Akron, he devoted himself to orchestral playing, studying with great orchestral players in Cleveland, Cincinnati, and Columbus. He says, "[I was] just trying to immerse myself, because I felt so far behind. . . . There's just more of a concrete lifestyle in the classical world [as compared to jazz]." He found some good musical opportunities, with freelance work in the Cleveland area, playing in brass groups and orchestras.

Around 1989, Cooper heard about an open doctoral assistantship in trumpet at the University of Wisconsin–Madison, which included playing in the faculty ensemble, the Wisconsin Brass Quintet. His audition failed. But a year later, the job opened again, and Cooper was determined to prove to the quintet that they had been wrong the previous year. The second time around, in 1990, Cooper got the chair. In the quintet, he recalls, "Nine hours a week, we rehearsed the hardest brass quintet literature that anybody could think of." He describes it as both "amazing, and . . . somewhat unrealistic from a musical standpoint."

In his third and last year in the program, Cooper began moving back into jazz. He worked a variety of jazz jobs in and around Madison, and after finishing his assistantship at UW, he met Kelly De Haven (see

David Cooper. PHOTO BY JOE TONDU

chapter 13) at the Mendota Beach Club. The two felt an immediate connection and began working together a lot, although Cooper was also playing with the Madison Symphony and the Wisconsin Chamber Orchestra at the time. A few years later, after the couple got married and had a child, Cooper says, "We thought, 'Well, shoot, one of us should probably have insurance.' And so we started trading day jobs so that we could have insurance." Cooper did computer programming; De Haven worked at a photo studio.

Cooper was still freelancing in both jazz and classical music (playing simultaneously in the Fox Valley, La Crosse, and Dubuque Symphonies) when the trumpet position at UW–La Crosse opened up in 2000. Cooper quickly finished up the requirements for his doctorate and secured the position at La Crosse, where the young family then moved. That situation was not without its challenges, as Cooper was largely teaching music appreciation rather than trumpet, and De Haven was having to make a lengthy commute to continue her music career in Madison. When a job opened at UW–Platteville in 2005, Cooper jumped at the opportunity.

When he got the position, the family moved back near Madison, where Cooper could easily commute to Platteville.

Getting back into the jazz scene in Madison was not as easy as the couple had hoped, however. De Haven's steady engagements were long gone, and both she and Cooper were much less excited about taking low-paying late-night jobs while keeping their family together.

In addition to his many jobs with De Haven, Cooper was a member of the New Breed from 2000 to 2007 and played in Tim Whalen's Nonet. He was the go-to jazz trumpet player in Madison for many years, and it could be argued that he retains that title in 2017. He is one of those rare individuals who is not only a very fine jazz player but a superb classical player as well. Faced with a daunting round of treatments for a serious cancer in the summer of 2014, Cooper thought, "Well, you know, this is a bucket list; what I've always wanted to do was make a jazz quartet recording. Now's the time. Why not?" So he wrote original melodies to the chord changes of classic jazz themes and recorded the album with pianist Johannes Wallman, bassist Mark Urness, and drummer Ernie Adams (see online discography).

Paul Hastil

Paul Hastil established himself in Madison shortly after moving to the Midwest from New York City in 1992. He was born in 1956, had grown up in the Big Apple, and started playing the piano at a young age. Originally playing by ear, he was drawn in two musical directions as a young teen—toward blues on the one hand, and the music of Claude Debussy on the other. Eventually, he heard pianist Wynton Kelly as an intersection of those two styles. Hastil attended Hampshire College in Massachusetts; supposedly on a science track, he says, "[The intersection of blues and classical] music didn't leave me alone, and I knew I wanted to be a jazz player." Home in New York City, Hastil heard Jaki Byard at Bradley's, and he began commuting to Boston for lessons with the iconoclastic pianist.

After college, in the mid-1970s, Hastil moved back to New York to try out the life of a jazz musician. A key event in this journey was his attendance at a symposium led by David Liebman and Richie Beirach, where Hastil met important new music scene saxophonists David Binney and

Ellery Eskelin. This led to Hastil's collaboration with both musicians. To keep afloat, he played piano for the Dance Theater of Harlem, and played and composed for the National Dance Institute, which he describes as "a city-wide program that basically brought dance as a disciplined growth opportunity for inner-city schoolkids."

Hastil says, "[Although] I swore I'd never leave New York City, my wife and I had a son. [And] due to our values, he was kind of a feral child in New York City." Eventually they moved to his wife Camille's native Wisconsin, which they saw as a healthier place to raise a family. They ended up in a rural area south of Madison with chickens and a garden, where they still live today. "Nature predominates," Hastil says, "and somehow I [have] managed to walk a tightrope but survive as a musician."

For a while, Hastil wrote music for Spring Green's American Players Theater. He also met bassist Jeff Eckels and started working a lot with Kelly De Haven, playing every Friday and Saturday night at the Concourse Hotel in downtown Madison. A few years after he started working with De Haven, Hastil formed a musical association with vocalist Gerri DiMaggio, which continues to this day. (Hastil appears in the photo that accompanies Gerri DiMaggio's profile in chapter 13.) Eventually, he became an important member of the Madison Music Collective.

In 2001, Hastil landed a dream job at the new Hilton Hotel in Madison, playing solo piano five nights a week on a nice new instrument for a manager and staff who appreciated what he was doing. He even got regular raises in this job—a rarity for musicians any time, but especially in the twenty-first-century economy. However, he was eventually cut back to fewer nights, and later on, nights weren't even guaranteed—he'd get a call only on nights when the hotel was doing good business. The job ended in 2007.

From 2001 to 2003, Hastil also played in Capital Line Investment, with Louka Patenaude, bassist John Mesoloras, and drummer Dane Richeson, and another band with saxophonist Ray Rideout. He played original music in a trio with bassist John Christensen and drummer Devin Drobka.

Another meaningful engagement for Hastil has been his involvement with Madison Music Makers. Founded by retired music teacher Bonnie

Green, the organization brings musical opportunities, Hastil says, "to marginalized kids, particularly in the immigrant community." In Madison, Hastil has worked through the Music Makers with children "from Nigeria, from Central America, but there are [also] Hmong, and also Chinese." And since 2010, Hastil has been a member of the New Breed.

Making it as a musician in Madison is not easy; Hastil is used to getting paid very little, and on a sporadic basis. "That's the thing," he says. "Ultimately it's the unfortunate plight. And, I have to say, the anxiety about money never goes away, and it's been the trade-off [for doing what he loves]." Hastil keeps fighting the good fight, teaching disadvantaged youth, supplying a forum for young musicians to test their wings, writing compositions (sometimes with titles like "The Tyranny of Dead Ideas"), and playing the music that he loves.

Nick Moran

Bassist Nick Moran is a musical omnivore. While he is recognized as one of the strongest and finest jazz bass players in Wisconsin, jazz bass is only one aspect of Moran's playing career.

Moran was born in Madison in 1978. He claims that he was "discovered musically" in the third grade by a teacher who "saw a spark . . . and got me into children's theater," where he first performed—singing. His parents, who he describes as "really cool," let him take lessons in classical guitar. "And then," he says, "I started playing cello in third grade."

At Van Hise (now Velma Bell Hamilton) Middle School, as he prepared to join the orchestra, the school ran out of cellos before they got to Moran in the alphabetical sign-up. He switched to bass and fell in love with the instrument. Moran started on electric and upright bass, playing acoustic at school and practicing on electric at home. He listened to his parents' music—the Police, Primus, reggae, and punk-oriented rock. When he began attending Madison West High, Moran joined other talented music students, including Leo Sidran. Tim Gruber ran the jazz band at West, but Moran was also inspired by legendary West band director John Rafoth, who established a culture that encouraged young musicians to immerse themselves in music.

In the Madison jazz community at this time, there was a dearth of bass players, with Jeff Eckels seemingly playing in just about every band. But he couldn't play everything, so Moran became a working professional at the age of fifteen. Avant-garde saxophonist Hanah John Taylor hired the young bassist, and soon Moran was performing not only in Madison but in Chicago as well, at such important clubs as Hot House and the Velvet Lounge. Moran learned lessons on those gigs, too, finding that audience members knew tunes that he did not.

Moran's professional jobbing caused issues at school, as his mother let him skip first period on days after he had played a gig the evening before. In a meeting with him and his parents, the school principal warned Moran that he wouldn't be able to make a living as a performer. But after coming to an agreement about attendance, Moran says, "The next week he was at my show, on a school night, paying a cover to see me." Moran also recalls getting to work with Doc De Haven, who required that he wear a blue blazer, the uniform of the day in that jazz sector.

Moran went to college at UW–Eau Claire, in the thriving program run by Bob Baca. While a student at Eau Claire, he studied classical bass with James Clute of the Minnesota Orchestra. By this time, Moran was doing even more jobbing, often with Harmonious Wail, spending most weekends working with them and other bands. He enjoyed his time at UWEC, but when his parents' marriage dissolved, Moran came home to, as he says, "mediate." He transferred to UW–Madison, but he knew that he didn't want to continue in the jazz program there, and decided to become a Latin American Studies major.

After earning his degree, Moran set out to prove his high school principal wrong. "It was my great experiment," he says. "Can I do music full-time in this town and not only survive, but be able to save money and do the things I want to do?" Working with Harmonious Wail, and then getting tapped to play in the Latin band Madisalsa, Moran met some of Madison's best jazz musicians. He moved away from playing with Hanah Jon Taylor, but not before learning one of his "biggest musical lessons": "How to make something happen. Because you know sometimes people think the answer's on the page; it's not. You just have to work together as musicians and make an event." Moran was inspired by other Madison musicians including vocalist Jan Wheaton (who, when Moran was underage, would sneak him and his friends into clubs where she was working) and the powerful bassist Dennis Oliver, who Moran remembers as "a major figure in Madison."

Moran's musical education continued, sometimes in unexpected ways. When his dad fulfilled a lifelong dream of going to Cuba, Moran went along and ended up studying with Orlando "Cachaito" Lopez, the bass player with the heralded Buena Vista Social Club. For two weeks, Moran spent four hours a day with Lopez, and he returned to Wisconsin with a good understanding of the bassist's primary function in Afro-Cuban music. The Morans' home served as host to Peruvian *cajon* (a box-shaped drum) player Juan "Cotito" Medrano. Moran later traveled to Lima, Peru, his father's hometown, and made music there.

Since that time, Moran's talent and versatility have catapulted him into the role of Madison's most prominent bassist. Although he could not have made a living in Madison as strictly a jazz bassist, he says, "I always consider myself coming from a jazz school." In the jazz scene, Moran has held down the crucial bottom end of the New Breed, the Tim Whalen Nonet, Whalen's Tribute to Art Blakey band, and other groups. (Moran appears in the photo that accompanies the New Breed profile earlier in this chapter.) He has played with jazz singers Ben Sidran, Gerri DiMaggio, and Joy Dragland (in Dragland and Leo Sidran's band Joy and the Boy). Besides Madisalsa, Moran founded the experimental Latin band El Clan Destino with Vince Fuh. This was followed by a trio with guitarist Richard Hildner and Peruvian *cajon* player Juan Daniel Pastor.

Expanding into other genres, Moran has played with the Madison-based reggae band Natty Nation. He was a fixture in the popular funk band Phat Phunktion, which was founded in 1996 by a group of UW students including Whalen and saxophonist/vocalist Al Falaschi. The band made an unlikely musical splash in Japan, which led to touring there. Not least of Moran's musical ventures has been dumate, a hip-hop band that has opened in Madison for such acts as Digible Planets and DJ Cool Herc.

Furthermore, Moran does studio work, recording in Madison studios for the libraries of such computer programs as Apple's GarageBand. When Moran was presented with the Jazz Personality of the Year award at the 2014 Isthmus Jazz Festival, his involvement with Madison Jazz Consortium was noted (he is now in charge of program development and production), as was his membership in the bands mentioned previously and many others: Son Contrabando, Golpe Tierra, Tani Diakite and the AfroFunkStars, the Goodie Two-Shoes (with his vocalist wife, Megan), and his newest band, Sinister Resonance (with UW–Madison trombone professor Mark Hetzler, Vince Fuh, and percussionist Todd Hammes).

Moran is very much aware that in today's world, jazz players must be not only talented and versatile, but also, as he says, "scene makers"—people who get out and push their projects, much in the way that singer/songwriters do. As far as the music business goes, Moran says, "I see the change, . . . I see what you can do with it, so I'm excited for my students; they're going to capitalize on the newer culture model. But I just wish it was supported by our media and the powers that be."

Moran has the ability and drive to survive musically in a much bigger city than Madison. However, he is happy in his hometown, from which he can tour Wisconsin, the Midwest, and the world, and pursue his wide musical interests. "That's always one of the things I feel fortunate for," he says, "is being a Madison musician."

Louka Patenaude

Guitarist Louka Patenaude was born in 1977 and grew up in the Madison area. His name comes from his Greek mother and his father, a Wisconsinite of French Canadian, German, Irish, and Spanish heritage. Patenaude got turned on to music through rock and roll, making music at home with brothers who played drums and piano. He loved the music of Eddie Van Halen and other so-called "shredder metal."

Patenaude began studying guitar at the age of twelve or thirteen with local professional Roger Brotherhood. Brotherhood, he says, "gave me all the foundations in order for me to be able to interpret and to be able to play; to be able to have something to say and make it a coherent statement." Through Brotherhood and his dad's record collection, which included jazz, Patenaude started expanding his musical outlook. He went to high school in Middleton and played in the high school jazz band led by Brad Schneider. Although still drawn to rock's power players, he also began to appreciate Wes Montgomery, Stan Getz, and Miles Davis.

After high school graduation in 1995, Patenaude attended the University of Wisconsin–Madison. Like Nick Moran, Patenaude did not study music at UW, majoring in anthropology with an emphasis on archaeology. He did, however, take part in Richard Davis's Black Music Ensemble. He appreciated the looseness of this ensemble, where the emphasis was on learning tunes and improvising. Patenaude remembers, "[Davis] had a presence that made everyone want to get it done, and do it. . . . [But] most important for me was the people I met in that group."

One of those people was vocalist Amelia Royko, with whom Patenaude and others in the Black Music Ensemble started performing in the late 1990s in Madison clubs, particularly at the Monastery on East Washington. Royko then formed a trio with Patenaude and Paul Hastil. Patenaude recognizes Hastil as another important person to his development, saying that for him, "[Paul] just cracked the nut wide open."

Patenaude got to know Ben Sidran through Sidran's son, Leo. Leo set up a situation in the New Breed jams in which Patenaude played along with Ben, and eventually Ben invited Patenaude to tour with him in Europe. For a while, Ben Sidran (on his Hammond B-3 organ) worked Tuesday nights at Café Montmartre with Leo, Patenaude, and saxophonist Paul Daugherty. Eventually, this gig migrated to Thursday nights, and Patenaude started working Friday nights there with his country group, the Fingers. When Ben Sidran had the opportunity to play in a trio at the Cardinal Bar, he elected to work with Patenaude and Nick Moran. (Patenaude appears in the photo that accompanies the New Breed profile earlier in this chapter.)

Patenaude, like Paul Hastil and Nick Moran, is one of the relatively few musicians in Madison who is able to make a living in music. To do so, he has found that he just needs to "expand, expand, expand." While acknowledging the vagaries of the music business and its focus on the almighty dollar, Patenaude believes that good music will survive.

> I've been pretty happy. And I think it just has to do with doing, just doing it, and sticking with it. And you probably have to go through all that psychological baggage to be able to get past that you're not very secure. . . . But then you become secure. . . . I think it just has

> to do with having all your bases covered. Are you fulfilling yourself in all the ways you need to be fulfilling yourself?

Between the variety of gigs that he plays and the teaching that he does (including his job teaching jazz guitar at UW–Madison that he started in 2016), Louka Patenaude has found that security.

Hanah Jon Taylor

Hanah Jon Taylor does not comfortably fit in a category with the other musicians in this chapter, although several of them have worked with him. He occupies a unique niche in Madison's music scene.

Taylor grew up in Chicago in the 1950s. His father was a Pullman porter, and his aunt was one of the first black women to sing at Chicago's Lyric Opera. Her sister, Taylor's mother, hoped that her son would also take up music. The music he related to, however, was what he called the "screamin' blues"—the music he heard from the guys sitting around the taxi stand across the street.

Taylor was initially more interested in sports than music. In school, he played football and basketball but became a standout in track, as a mile runner. While in school at Southern Illinois University, he went to the 1969 Amateur Atheltic Union trials. Taylor was also active in the Black Student Union and the Panther Party, and he eventually became student body president. But by that time, Taylor had already been bitten by the music bug, listening seriously to Miles Davis and John Coltrane. A friend loaned him a flute, which led to his taking up soprano saxophone at the age of twenty.

Taylor's musical ignorance was tolerated by other musicians for a while, perhaps because of his personality or involvement in other activities. But finally, a musician on the bandstand told him, "And now, if you don't mind, we'd like you playing some real music." His roommate, the well-known French horn player Vincent Chancey, taught Taylor some music basics and pointed him in the right direction.

While at SIU, Taylor had the opportunity to play with touring musicians including Richie Havens and Nina Simone. His later interaction with South American students in a group called Hermanos de Amoures led to tours in the West Indies and Venezuela.

In 1974, Taylor earned a bachelor's degree in design, studying with the world-famous Buckminster Fuller. He went on to do graduate work in music therapy, a field so new that there wasn't a standard term for it. Taylor coined the term *musonics* to describe the preventive therapy that he was studying. He earned a Master of Science degree in 1976.

After graduate school he returned to Chicago, where he got a job as a social worker with Methodist Youth Centers. In 1977, Taylor suffered the onset of Bell's palsy, the result being that he lost the ability to control half his face. One doctor told him he would never play saxophone again. In the depths of despair, Taylor remembers, "I said to God, . . . 'I don't know why this is happening to me. But if I were ever to get my strength back and my ability to play again, I would promise to play every gig as if it were my last [expletive] gig.'" He tried alternative medicine, working with a naprapath (a doctor who uses a hands-on, holistic approach when working with connective tissue) who later became his fiancée. After a year and half, one night at dinner Taylor was able to blink his eyes at his mother. He ran home and pulled his horn out of the closet. When he finally recovered over a year later, he left his day job to focus on music.

In 1977, Taylor had become a member of Chicago's Association for the Advancement of Creative Musicians. He had gone through what he called a "spiritual kind of metamorphosis" in Islam and took the name Alkhaitt Hanah. (In 2015, Taylor said he considers himself to be "more of a universalist.") A two-week trip to Europe in 1979 turned into three months in Amsterdam, during which he played with a number of musicians, including drummer Sunny Murray, and studied with saxophonist Steve Lacy.

Back in Chicago in the 1980s, Taylor became active in the new avant-garde music, playing with the Colson Unity Troupe and Kahil El'Zabar and the Ethnic Heritage Ensemble. He also had a group called Everyday Heroes with bassist (Donald) Rafael Garrett and drummer Steve McCall (both freshly back from New York). For a time, he studied with Pharaoh Sanders. Despite playing the challenging music that these musicians were known for, Taylor was able to make a living in the 1980s, working seasonally, taking trips to Europe (sometimes with the Hanah Jon Taylor European Ensemble), and filling in dry periods at home and work through Urban Gateways, an organization that hired musicians to work in the Chicago public schools. Taylor also served as jazz band director

Hanah Jon Taylor. PHOTO BY PAUL S HOWELL; COURTESY OF HANAH JON TAYLOR

at the University of Chicago for several years. In 1986, he was with the first avant-garde jazz band to visit Cuba.

In 1985, Taylor's mother died, his son was born, and he lost his home to, as he says, "a profiteering loan shark." He says he found himself "couch surfing" at friends' places for a year while continuing to work every day. Hardly anyone knew that he was, in effect, homeless.

In 1993, Taylor changed his life, leaving his situation in Chicago and, on the advice of photographer Charlie Behnke, moving with his son to the relative safety of Madison, where they still reside. They return to Chicago on a fairly regular basis, however, as Taylor says, "to get that cultural inspiration."

Taylor has had to endure what he calls "cultural misunderstandings" as an African American in Wisconsin. One of those has to do with assumptions people make when meeting Taylor. "Maybe because I wear a fedora," he says, "if they've never heard the music before, immediately they think it's blues."

Taylor has worked a variety of jobs to support himself and his son over the years—instructor at Ward-Brodt Music, school security officer, substitute teacher. In 1994, he founded and became the sole proprietor of the House of Sound, on Williamson Street, where he taught and performed; high school groups also came in and played there. But Taylor says, "I got my horns ripped off—twice. The landlord then decided that it was prone to burglaries, so for that reason he wouldn't renew the lease." Following that, Taylor and Susan Fox established the Center for Creative and Cultural Arts. For three and a half years, they ran the center on Dayton Street, downtown. Taylor says they served "about 350 people a week, with classes, workshops, and performances." For eight years after that, Taylor taught a variety of courses at the Madison Media Institute. He now runs his music therapy practice, Musonics. In March 2017, Taylor and Susan Fox opened a new jazz venue, Café CODA in Madison, in what was formerly the Fountain, on Dayton Street.

Through everything, as of 2017, Taylor has continued to play his uncompromising music in Madison, Chicago, Detroit, and elsewhere. I have heard stories of Taylor surprising unsuspecting audiences in various Wisconsin cities with music that is more radically progressive than anything they've previously heard. In contrast, I also witnessed his engaging presentation of a short history of jazz to a rapt audience of largely jazz neophytes at a small-town library. Hanah Jon Taylor remains a singular figure in Wisconsin jazz.

17

Racine–Kenosha

Over the years, the Racine–Kenosha area has produced outstanding jazz musicians. For more than a generation, some of the most prominent of these musicians were brass players and saxophonists, a number of whom are profiled here.

Dominic Spera

Trumpeter, composer, and jazz educator Dominic Spera was born in Kenosha in 1932.[1] His father worked for American Motors, at that time a major employer in Kenosha. Spera grew up mostly with aunts and uncles, as his parents had marital issues. He started on trumpet as a kid because he had pronounced buckteeth. Given the choice between a cheap trumpet or expensive orthodontia, his family chose the former. The youngster took to trumpet, and also began writing music while a student at Bradford High School, where his band director, Mr. Dunham, encouraged him. At school, Spera says, they had "a wonderful jazz band—stage band, they called it then."

Outside of school, when he was fifteen, Spera joined the trio of Raoul "Frenchy" Boutan, who played accordion and, according to Spera, "sang like an angel."[2] The young trumpeter also sang and occasionally played bass. A group of young people in the area that included Spike Robinson (see later in this chapter) and Frank Bencriscutto (who would later become the director of bands at the University of Minnesota) was also interested in playing jazz. Spera says of others in the group, "Two died of overdoses, and the bass player, he got eighteen years for dealing [drugs]."

Spera claims, "They let me out of high school and said, 'Don't ever come back.'" He briefly attended Chicago Musical College before transferring to the University of Wisconsin–Madison. Spera says Raymond Dvorak, director of bands at UW, "was like a father to me." Dvorak let Spera write arrangements for the marching band, and Spera wrote "St. Louis Blues," based on the Glenn Miller arrangement, for the band's appearance at the 1953 Rose Bowl. (The Wisconsin team's star was Kenosha native Alan Ameche, who won the Heisman Trophy in 1954.) Even more impressively, Spera did an arrangement of Mahler's Fifth Symphony for the finale of the show.

While on campus, Spera was a member of one of the active jazz bands that played on campus and around town; Dick Ruedebusch (see chapter 10) led another. For Spera, "There was too much jazz on campus to go to class. . . . [I] came back from the Rose Bowl, and there was greetings from the United States government; I was going to be drafted. So I went to the Fifth Army Band." He was stationed at Fort Sheridan, north of Chicago. Once when Spera soloed with the band, he was heard by Don Jacoby, the top studio trumpeter in Chicago. Jacoby sent word to the young trumpeter that he would be willing to give him lessons, and, Spera says, the month and a half that he lived and studied with Jacoby "was the beginning of my life as a professional trumpet player."

Around 1956, Spera was transferred to the Thirty-Fifth Army Band in Indianapolis and assigned the task of reviving their finance center choir. "So when I got there," he says, "I figure[d], 'Well, if I have really good-looking sopranos and altos, [getting men to join will be] easy, because I'm on an army base.'" Indianapolis turned out to be great for Spera; he met Al Cobine and David Baker—two people who became very important to his career—and his future wife, Patty. While still in the army, he played in the Indianapolis Philharmonic and studied with Indiana University trumpet professor William Adam. In one week in 1956, Spera was discharged from the service, got married, and enrolled at Indiana University as a full-time student.

While Spera was at IU, the third trumpet position opened in the Indianapolis Symphony, and Spera won the audition. While he was opening the envelope that held the offer of the symphony position, the phone rang. Don Jacoby was on the other end, and Spera remembers that he said, "Go to New York, Fred Waring is looking for a lead trumpet player." "So I thanked the people in Indianapolis," says Spera, "and went to New York, [still] needing fifteen credits to graduate." The Speras stayed in New York for ten years.

In the Big Apple, Spera says he "did a little bit of everything." He studied with William Vacchiano, principal trumpet in the New York Philharmonic. He played gigs with Lester Lanin, the busiest "society" bandleader in the city. He taught parochial school. His sons were born in New York. Eventually, he played Broadway shows for four years. "I enjoyed that immensely," he recalls. "[But] it was very hard work." He played in the pit for the Pulitzer Prize–winning show *How to Succeed in Business Without Really Trying*, and the two Anthony Newley showcases, *The Roar of the Grease Paint—the Smell of the Crowd*, and *Stop the World—I Want to Get Off*.

Ten years was enough time in the rat race for Spera, and after cutting his lip in another show, he decided to return to Indiana to finish his degree. David Baker, then head of the jazz program at IU, got Spera a graduate assistantship, even though he had not yet earned a degree. In his first week back, Al Cobine, one of the most important band contractors in the country, hired Spera to play four days with the touring band of Henry Mancini. While playing many shows for Cobine, Spera earned both bachelor's and master's degrees. He also became the head of instrumental music at the University School, a private high school in Bloomington. When the school went public, Spera's routine of teaching and touring would no longer work. So with his new master's degree in hand, he looked for college teaching jobs.

Trumpet jobs were open at both UW–Whitewater and UW–Eau Claire, but Dominic decided to try Eau Claire. After a grueling audition, he was offered the job in 1968.

Spera's hiring changed things at UWEC. According to Spera's colleague Ron Keezer,

> Dominic was a professional, jazz-oriented person, and he had all that background and his personality on top of everything else. And he just yanked [the students] up from being what he called "jackpine savages" into just crazy people—they would do anything for him.

From left to right: Ron Keezer (see chapter 19), Lyle Mays (see chapter 7), Dominic Spera, and Jerry Way, 1973. COURTESY OF SPECIAL COLLECTIONS AND ARCHIVES, W. D. MCINTYRE LIBRARY, UW–EAU CLAIRE

In his nine years at UWEC, Spera built the program into a powerhouse. From his earliest days, he taught musicians who have gone on to long and distinguished careers in Wisconsin—Allen Johnson, Steve Zenz, Tom Newburg, and Bill Buchholtz, to name a few. The biggest name of all arrived in 1971—pianist Lyle Mays (see chapter 7). The band attended and won big competitions and played at the State Music Convention in Madison and the Midwest Band Clinic in Chicago. The Eau Claire Jazz Festival became a huge regional event thanks to Spera's influence. Spera was also writing prolifically at this time. While many of his compositions and arrangements were created for the newly established educational market, he also wrote music specifically tailored for bands he was leading at school.

"What I'm most proud of, of my teaching at Eau Claire," Spera says, "is that . . . the majority of my jazz students [and] my trumpet students stayed in Wisconsin and taught public school."

In addition to his success at UWEC, Spera also was active as a player, especially in the Twin Cities, backing up such touring artists as Johnny Mathis, Andy Williams, and (again) Henry Mancini.

Spera left Eau Claire in 1977 to return to Indiana University, where he was hired as the right-hand man to his old friend David Baker. Although Spera says that the first band he led at Indiana (the school's number-two jazz band) "was a mere shadow of my Eau Claire band," the program at Indiana steadily grew in size and stature, and Spera remained there until his retirement in 1997. After leaving full-time teaching, Spera remained active composing, performing, and conducting clinics—but at a much slower pace than previously.

Allen Johnson

Allen Johnson was raised in Racine (except for a brief sojourn to Pittsburgh) in the 1950s. He was the third of eleven children. At Garfield Elementary School, like many students of his generation, Johnson started playing trumpet in band in fifth grade. Why trumpet? Johnson says, "Louis Armstrong got me into the trumpet," in an era when one could see Armstrong on television. Johnson also recalls hearing Cat Anderson, the "screech" trumpet player with Duke Ellington's band.

Johnson moved on to Washington Junior High School, but in the summer, he would ride his bicycle out to Jerstad-Agerholm Junior High for lessons. When his bike broke down, he would walk the three- to four-mile trek to Jerstad. For a while in junior high, he didn't have a trumpet to play, so played baritone horn instead. Then his dad bought him a new trumpet.

Johnson went to high school at Horlick. He was constantly pushed by another trumpeter in his class, Terry Andrag, who introduced Johnson to triple tonguing. Johnson remembers, "[I asked,] 'Where'd you learn that?' He said, 'I learned it from Johnny Hemkes, my teacher.' I said, 'Well, I'd like to study with him, too.'" During his junior year in high school, Johnson started lessons with Hemkes, a local legend.

Many of Kenosha's brass players spent some of their formative years studying with Hemkes.[3] He was not just a run-of-the-mill local guy teaching trumpet lessons. He had a reputation around the Midwest as a soloist, in the tradition of famous cornet soloist Herbert Clarke, and he became known for the "Hemkes Singing Sound," eventually laid out in his book, the *Singing Brass Manual*. Hemkes taught for over seventy years, mostly in his own studio, before his death in 2006. "Things got a little bit better, you know?" Johnson recalls, jokingly understating Hemkes's influence on his own playing. "I got a scholarship to [UW] Eau Claire."

Johnson graduated from Horlick in 1969 and entered UWEC just as Dominic Spera was building a formidable jazz program there. The small scholarship he earned was from a local music store, Johnson's Music (no relation), but with the cost of UW schools for state residents in that era, the scholarship was enough to make college possible. Spera was the trumpet teacher as well as the jazz program director, and he was known as a strict taskmaster. According to Johnson, "[Spera] kicked me in the ass so hard!"

After college, Johnson went on the road briefly with the Tommy Dorsey band. Tom Baker, another Milwaukee-area trumpeter, was in the band at the same time. (And Tom Newburg's first night with the Dorsey band was Johnson's last.)

After a few weeks on the road with the Dorsey band, Johnson went into education; his first teaching job was at Regis School in Eau Claire. But he heard the call of the road again, and in 1975, he left school to do a two-month stint with a jazz institution, the Count Basie Band. Decades after its founding, the band was still great, and it featured such celebrated soloists as trombonists Al Grey and Curtis Fuller and saxophonist Jimmy Forrest, as well as younger stars: drummer Butch Miles and trumpeter Pete Minger. After that experience, Johnson went back to the Eau Claire area, and although he played in some different local groups during that time, he says, "That [soon] got old." Dominic Spera had moved to Indiana University, and he talked Johnson into coming to school there. Johnson's mentors at IU included David Baker in jazz and trumpet professor Bill Adam.

Baker took the IU jazz band to New York for a performance or two, and as Johnson says, "Next thing I know, I got a call," asking if he wanted to join the Maynard Ferguson band. In 1979, Johnson toured with the Ferguson band for several months, during which the band recorded the album *Hot*. Johnson says, "I hated to leave the band, but I had to go back

Allen Johnson. COURTESY OF ALLEN JOHNSON

and get that master's degree." After completing the degree, he hit the road for several more months with the Glenn Miller band.

Back in Wisconsin, Johnson settled in, playing touring shows and whatever jazz gigs he could get. For two years, he taught jazz and trumpet at UW–Oshkosh. But he says, "That wasn't the best place [for me] to be." He moved to the Milwaukee area, where there were more gigs available, and took a job teaching lessons at Kosciuszko Middle School. Johnson decided to go back to school to work on a doctorate, but during a visit to Milwaukee Public Schools' central office, he was offered a job as band director at the middle-level arts school, Roosevelt. He describes the school as "right down in the hood," at Eighth and Walnut. At Roosevelt, he led three concert bands and two jazz bands for eighteen years before retiring.

During all of that time, Johnson worked extensively on the Milwaukee scene. Two of his most important associations were with La Chazz and the George Busateri band. He also played in Bill Sargent's midsized band. In those instances, Johnson crossed horns with his close friend Jeff Pietrangelo. Both were outstanding players, and over the years they borrowed from each other, with each man's style in some way beginning to resemble that of the other, while they retained their individual voices. In a band like La Chazz, their musical exchanges were dynamite. Johnson also played many small-band jazz dates with the city's established jazz figures—Manty Ellis, Berkeley Fudge, Melvin Rhyne, Buddy Montgomery, drummer Robert Hobbs, and vocalist Adekola Adedapo. In retirement, Johnson practices every day and remains active on the music scene.

Mike Hale

Mike Hale was born in 1951 in Oklahoma; his family moved to Texas when he was three (thus his nickname, Tex). The Hales moved to Racine in 1960, and eventually Hale's father moved into the highest executive levels of Racine-based Walker Muffler. Hale started playing music the summer before sixth grade, on a Thor-model trumpet his family bought from Montgomery Ward. He had picked up a fingering chart for trumpet and learned his C scale—an octave higher than he was supposed to. He attended Jerstad-Agerholm Junior High, where he worked with band director Robert Gish, an important figure in his musical development. He went on to high school at Horlick, where he played with fellow trumpeter Allen Johnson. And like Johnson, Hale studied with Johnny Hemkes.

Hale was also involved with drum and bugle corps, first with the Racine Junior Scouts and then the Racine Kilties, which went to the VFW national championship in Philadelphia when Hale was in high school. His father took him east a day early for that trip, and they went to hear Duke Ellington and his band at the Rainbow Room in New York. In high school, Hale also met Joe Pulice, a drummer who ran a music store, and the father of future jazz drummers Mark and young Joe Pulice. The elder Joe got Hale into the local big band led by John Bunic and also intensified Hale's interest in drum set, which became a valuable second instrument for Hale.

Hale entered Lawrence University in 1970, along with fellow trumpeter Jeff Pietrangelo, with whom he shared a multitude of musical (and nonmusical) adventures. The band Matrix (the Appleton band; see chapter 12) started up a couple of weeks before Hale and Pietrangelo graduated. Hale was the lead trumpet player in Matrix, and every night he powerfully delivered the challenging parts at the top of the dazzling horn arrangements fashioned for the band by John Harmon and Fred Sturm. But he was also a unique lyrical soloist who enriched many of Matrix's charts.

After Matrix disbanded, Hale moved back in with his parents, who then lived in the northern Chicago suburbs because his father had become president of the national chain Car-X Muffler. Hale gigged in Chicago, almost exclusively on drums. But soon he took a job as band director at St. Mary Central High School in Menasha. He decided to get a master's degree, which he did at the University of Northern Colorado (he was there at the same time as John and Chris Salerno; see chapter 18). Upon finishing the degree, Hale became a teaching assistant at the University of Wyoming, as well as teaching at Laramie High School. For a while, he returned to the Fox Valley, substitute teaching in the area schools, playing gigs, and holding down a day job at a local business.

In the mid-1990s, Fred Sturm connected Hale with a cruise ship opportunity, and Hale played trumpet in the house band on the Royal Viking Sun. It circled the globe, leaving from Ft. Lauderdale, stopping at various ports in the Caribbean, traveling through the Panama Canal and across the Pacific to Australia, Southeast and South Asia, and Africa before striking a coral reef in the Red Sea in the spring of 1996. The ship was towed to Sharm el-Sheik, Egypt, where it became a political volleyball, with Egypt demanding a huge fine for its release. The passengers, and the band, had to be removed from the vessel and flown home.

Hale worked as a salesman for Larry and Patty Darling's Impact Music Library before returning to teach music in the Appleton school system, which he did from 2001 until his retirement in 2017.

Claude Cailliet

Trombonist Claude Cailliet grew up in Kenosha, the son of world-famous musician Lucien Cailliet.[4] Lucien had moved to the United States in 1918 and become a member of the Philadelphia Orchestra. In his twenty years playing and arranging for the orchestra, he also taught at universities in the Philadelphia area. He moved to the West Coast and composed, arranged, and orchestrated film music in the 1940s and 1950s. Lucien moved to Wisconsin in the late 1950s to begin an association with the G. Leblanc musical instrument company, overseeing publications and leading school bands all over the country. Claude remembers his father being away from home many weekends when Claude was young, off to Texas or Kansas to work with an all-state band or orchestra. The elder Cailliet also conducted the Kenosha Symphony Orchestra.

Claude Cailliet was born in 1959 in Kenosha. Not surprisingly, he took up music at a young age. His first instrument was euphonium (baritone horn), and he joined school bands in early grade school, a year or two before kids were normally in the school groups. Cailliet explains, "I played euphonium, [and the junior high school band teachers said,] 'Hey, we need euphoniums.'" So by the time he reached Lance Junior High, Cailliet was able to join the good band right away. He took up trombone about a year and a half after he started euphonium, and he played it in the school jazz groups. He also studied privately with Johnny Hemkes. Cailliet went on to high school at Tremper High in Kenosha, which in the 1970s had probably the most outstanding high school music program in Wisconsin. As he remembers it, in the mid-1970s, Tremper had "two jazz bands, full orchestra, chamber orchestra, wind ensemble, three other concert bands, [and] I think, three or four choirs."

Cailliet went to college at Indiana University, which was one of the largest music schools in the country at that time. Its jazz program, led by David Baker (assisted by Dominic Spera), was well known and well respected. But Cailliet's parents, after his father's retirement, had moved back to southern California, and Cailliet also thought, "Gee, it's probably good to wind up getting the degree somewhere where there's [musical] activity, as opposed to Bloomington." So he transferred to the University of Southern California, where he earned a bachelor's degree. At USC, he studied trombone with Terry Cravens and euphonium with studio musician Jim Self (the tuba "voice" of the mother ship in Stephen Spielberg's *Close Encounters of the Third Kind*). While Cailliet did complete his degree, he was not solely focused on his work during the time he was in school. A year or two into his program at USC, he auditioned, successfully, for a Latin band called Tipica Antillana that worked five nights a week at the Candilejas Club on Sunset in Los Angeles. He played with the band for over two years. Cailliet also got Wisconsin trumpeter Dan Fornero into the band.

Cailliet graduated from USC in 1982 and entered the music profession full-time. He continued to work with Latin bands and some blues and R&B bands as well until, in 1987, he joined the band of rock star Neil Young, who was adding horns to his working band. "It turned out to be [the] greatest gig ever," Cailliet says, "because we were part of the writing of all the stuff, and [Young] was a great guy. And [we were] making more money than we could have imagined."

Joining Cailliet in this band was fellow Kenoshan John Fumo, a trumpeter who was a couple of years ahead of Cailliet at Tremper High. At that time, Fumo was recently divorced and living with Cailliet. Fumo has continued to make a living playing music in Los Angeles for many years now.

Cailliet's gig with Young lasted for about two and a half years, and it led to other short engagements and recordings with the likes of Crosby, Stills, and Nash; U2; David Lee Roth; Joe Jackson; the Tower of Power horns; and others. Eventually, one of Cailliet's projects with a backing band for Delaney Bramlett (half of Delaney and Bonnie), for an Australian and US tour with Fleetwood Mac, fell apart, and it was time for a change. Cailliet had plans to get married, and he had been busy enough in Los Angeles that he could leave, he says, "without feeling like I never did anything."

Cailliet moved back to Wisconsin, but one last connection in Los Angeles led to Cailliet's joining Brian Setzer's band, at the forefront of the swing revival movement in 1991. He played tours with the Setzer band for the next five years, usually in the company of old friends from LA.

Besides starting married life, Cailliet had arranged to go back to school at UW–Madison. He became a teaching assistant and led UW's big jazz band through his graduate school career, which resulted in master's and doctoral degrees by 1997. After his assistantship ended, he was hired as a lecturer and kept on as jazz bandleader. During his time with the band, Cailliet rebuilt the group into an ensemble of music majors, which it had not been for years, if ever. In the meantime, he picked up a part-time position at nearby UW–Baraboo. In 2001, when the position at Baraboo became tenure track, Cailliet left UW–Madison to pursue the lower-profile (and lower-pressure) full-time job at the two-year school. As of 2013, when he was still happily employed there, he said he found the job, in some ways, "more gratifying than . . . what was happening in Madison."

Madisalsa in 2012. Left to right: José J. Madera, Jesús Burgos, Richard Larson, Claude Cailliet, Michelle De La Rosa, Jon Schipper, Junior Rivera, Nick Moran (see chapter 16), Vincent Fuh (see chapter 16), Jim Doherty, Tony Ayala, and Jeff Pietrangelo (see chapter 15). PHOTO BY ARMANDO S. VERA (MANDO PHOTOGRAPHY); COURTESY OF JOSÉ MADERA

As a freelancer, Cailliet has played hundreds of jobs in Wisconsin—he's been part of backup bands for visiting shows in Milwaukee (including the Temptations, the Four Tops, Johnny Mathis, and many others), the society band of George Busateri (in which other fine jazz players also worked), the band for the Fireside Dinner Theater in Fort Atkinson, and others. His connection with saxophonist Tom Washatka led to Cailliet performing and recording with singer Janet Planet.

But probably Cailliet's most lasting and visible contribution to the Wisconsin music scene was his founding of the Madison-based Latin jazz band Madisalsa. The origin of the band is somewhat curious. While Cailliet was at UW, his faculty colleague Joan Wildman, knowing of Cailliet's experience in southern California, asked if he might be willing to put together a Latin jazz band for Madison's 1992 Isthmus Jazz Festival. Cailliet had brought a small library of Latin jazz charts with him from California and was up to the task. He knew plenty of horn players but had to do some serious legwork to find appropriate percussionists in southern Wisconsin.

Originally a mostly instrumental Latin jazz band featuring some of Wisconsin's fine horn players, Madisalsa slowly transformed into a vocal-based salsa band over the years. In the mid-2010s, one of the vocalists was Cailliet's daughter Michelle. Founding members Cailliet, who continued to write charts for the band, and pianist Vince Fuh remained with this Madison institution until it disbanded, after twenty-four years, in 2016. Cailliet then left Wisconsin to begin a new phase of his career in Nashville.

Dan Fornero

Trumpeter Dan Fornero was born in 1959 and raised in Kenosha. His musical career started as the result of an agreement his father Robert, "Bob," made with his friend John Vagnoni while in military service in Korea in the 1950s. Fornero explains, "[My father said to John,] 'Hey, if we make it out of here alive, let's start a drum and bugle corps.' So they did, and in the mid-1950s, they started a drum and bugle corps called the Kenosha Kingsmen." The fledgling corps rehearsed in such places as the Danish Brotherhood hall and Eagles Club. Fornero remembers sitting "in front of thirty horn players, . . . just wanting to be those guys so bad."

Occasionally, at outdoor rehearsals at the now defunct Lakefront Stadium, the little boy would fill in a spot marching for a missing member of the group. When Fornero was eligible to join a drum corps, at age ten, he joined Kiltie Kadets, the junior division of the Racine Kilties. While playing bugle in the corps, Fornero also learned trumpet and played in school. His first trumpet teacher was Al Sabo, band director at Bradford High. Fornero left Catholic school for public school, in some measure so that he could continue with music. He went on to study trumpet with Joe Bolyard, and for some years with Jack Yorton, a prominent jazz trumpeter in the Racine–Kenosha area.

For five years, Fornero's parents dutifully drove him to Racine several times a week for drum corps rehearsals. But he had a big decision to make in his sophomore year at Tremper High School. He had moved up to the Kilties, but he wanted to be able to play jazz, like senior trumpeter John Fumo. Fumo advised him to go to one of Jamey Aebersold's summer jazz camps, but the camp met at the same time in August that the Kilties would

Dan Fornero is playing; to his left is West Coast trumpet star Wayne Bergeron.
COURTESY OF DAN FORNERO

be taking part in the big Drum Corps International contest. As much as he had loved being in the corps, jazz won out; Fornero left the Kilties and began studying jazz seriously.

Fornero went from Kenosha to the jazz "factory" that was North Texas State University in the late 1970s. When he arrived in Denton, he was placed fourth chair (out of five) in the eighth of the school's nine jazz bands. By his last two years at NTSU, he played lead trumpet in the famed One O'Clock Lab Band. During that time, he studied with Don "Jake" Jacoby. After four years in Texas, Fornero returned home and toured the country for six months with the Al Pierson Big Band USA. (The running joke about the band was, Fornero says, that "it paid $350 a week and all the pride you could swallow.") Although he was young and was eventually fired for thinking he was "way too hip to be in that band," Fornero learned valuable lessons about music and life on the road.

Fornero returned home again, but he and his parents, Bob and Teresa, mutually decided that his living in their basement was not ideal, so in

1982 he moved to Los Angeles and slept on Claude Cailliet's couch for about a year. After that year was up, Fornero became lead trumpeter in Woody Herman's great band and stayed with Herman for about a year. When he left Herman, he joined Cailliet in Tipica Antillana. Fornero has remained active on the southern California music scene ever since.

Fornero's list of credits includes tours with such stars as Tom Jones and Neil Diamond, and with Phil Collins as a member of the Vine Street Horns. He has performed on a huge number of film scores and television shows—the TV work ranging from talk shows (Jay Leno, David Letterman, Conan O'Brien, Jon Stewart) to entertainment shows like American Idol, America's Got Talent, and the Grammy and Emmy awards shows. In jazz, Fornero has been a member of the Gordon Goodwin Big Phat Band and the Bob Mintzer Big Band. In April 2014, he returned to Wisconsin to be a guest artist and clinician at the University of Wisconsin–Milwaukee, hosted by his childhood friend Curt Hanrahan. In 2017, Dan Fornero remains one of the most in-demand trumpet players in one of America's biggest and most competitive music scenes.

Russ Johnson

Trumpeter Russ Johnson was born in 1965 in Racine. He went through the public schools in Racine, attending McKinley Junior High School and Washington Park High School. Neither of Johnson's parents were musical, but his older brother Dale played trumpet, and Russ listened to Dale's jazz records by Miles Davis, the Brecker Brothers, and Chick Corea. Dale took lessons with Johnny Hemkes, and although Hemkes normally would not take on students until they had reached tenth grade, he agreed to teach Russ as a seventh grader when Dale decided that he was not going to be a musician. Johnson says, "I was able to . . . have incredible fundamental trumpet lessons from a very young age." Although most of Hemkes's students had to work their way through the fabled Arban's book, Hemkes did not teach everyone exactly the same way, and Johnson says he "played music the whole time."

In junior high, Johnson adopted the school's flugelhorn and kept it for the rest of his school career. As his interest in jazz grew, he stayed up late nights trying to figure out what Freddie Hubbard was doing on an album that Johnson had on eight-track tape. He also started working with the Jamey Aebersold Play-A-Long jazz records and attended one of Aebersold's summer jazz camps. Johnson says, "It was just amazing being surrounded by people that were like me, and that liked the music [jazz]." While at camp, he encountered New York drummer Adam Nussbaum in the camp record store, and Nussbaum persuaded Johnson to buy classic Miles Davis albums. "That moment changed my life," Johnson says. "That [music] spoke to me in a way that was crystal clear; that's what I wanted to do. So my parents never had to ask me to practice ever again."

In his high school, Johnson was inspired by saxophonist Bill Nelson, who was a couple of years ahead of him at Park.[5] Johnson says, "[Nelson had a] work ethic and . . . dedication, 'cause he could really play, and I saw how hard he worked at school." Johnson put together a band that played a few gigs, including his high school prom (which he remembers as "a miserable thing"). He played in the State Honors Jazz Ensemble in 1982, along with Eau Claire guitarist Pete McCann, who, like Johnson, would go on to a successful jazz career in New York, where the two played together frequently. He also became friends with saxophonist Dave Bixler and drummer Peter Buck—other Racine natives who went on to jazz careers.

After high school, Johnson dreamed of attending one of the big jazz schools, but he ended up at nearby University of Wisconsin–Parkside instead. The years 1983 and 1984 were a good time to be at Parkside. Tim Bell had built a strong band, one that freshmen normally could not get into, but Johnson made it. He remembers, "We just sight read chart after chart after chart," a skill that would serve him well later on. When Johnson realized his dream and attended the Berklee College of Music in Boston the following year, he says, "There was literally nothing they put in front of me in the audition that I couldn't read." At Berklee, he joined an outstanding group of students (such as saxophonist Donny McCaslin) and studied with trumpeter Tim Hagans and other excellent faculty. However, Johnson's student loan money did not come through after his first year, and he was devastated not to be able to continue there. Not knowing what else to do, he returned to Racine and Parkside.

Outside of school, Johnson often played with Bill Nelson and occasionally played with young Milwaukee players such as Mark Davis, Jeff Hamann, and Dave Bayles. At the time, David Hazeltine was playing a steady duo gig at Chip and Py's with Gerald Cannon, and they frequently let Johnson sit in with them; he says, "[They] were very good to me." But Johnson says, "I was so upset that I was not where I wanted to be [that it] drove me even further into the practice room."

He ended up landing a job playing with a cruise ship band for most of the next two years, interrupted by a romantic sojourn in London for some months.

In 1988, at age twenty-three, Johnson took the plunge and moved to New York. He stayed until 2011, and Johnson says, "From age nineteen until forty-four or forty-five, . . . I never had a day job; I only played my trumpet."

The adventure started with Johnson living in the apartment of an old friend, Dave Bixler. "I basically went out there to sublet his apartment for two months," Johnson says, "and then never came back." During the early part of his career in New York, he remembers, "You're just trying to work, you're just trying to make money." Johnson did that by playing in Latin bands and the bands of touring shows. He also played on Broadway and on tours of shows that went to Europe. Also, he says, "[I] spent two years in my basement in Astoria, Queens, learning . . . to play bebop."

A visit to the hotbed club of new music, the Knitting Factory, changed Johnson's life. He was captivated by the music of Tim Berne's group and developed a new passion for the music of what became known as "the downtown scene." Trombonist Curtis Fowlkes became his gateway to that scene. The Knitting Factory became world renowned during this time, and Johnson was able to work there steadily (in the Tap Bar) for about two and a half years. He also went back to school at the Manhattan School of Music, where such players as Jason Moran and Eric Harland were his fellow students. Johnson earned both bachelor's and master's degrees while becoming serious about composing as well as playing.

Another of Johnson's companions at Manhattan was Israeli-born saxophonist Ohad Talmor, and the two became fast friends and musical associates. They formed the Other Quartet, a new music group that recorded two albums. Talmor also connected Johnson with legendary saxophonist Lee Konitz, who hired Johnson in the late 1990s to join his nonet. Later on, Johnson was hired to work for some years with another legendary jazz figure, bassist Steve Swallow.

Russ Johnson. PHOTO BY YVES DORISON; COURTESY OF RUSS JOHNSON

The great success of the Knitting Factory in the 1990s came to an abrupt halt on September 11, 2001. With the destruction of the World Trade Center, a great deal of commerce in that part of the city shut down. "It reopened," Johnson says, "but it wasn't the same; people stopped going down there." But the Knitting Factory had established Johnson's name, not just in New York but also in Europe, and from the mid-1990s until his move back to Wisconsin in 2011, he played four or five months of every year on the other side of the Atlantic.

Johnson's versatility and range of interest was such that shortly before his return to the Midwest, he realized that he was playing in bands led by musicians who were in their twenties, thirties, forties, fifties, sixties, seventies (Steve Swallow), and even eighties (Lee Konitz). A consummate sideman, Johnson worked with a variety of groups and leaders—including non-jazz stars like Elvis Costello and Kelly Clarkson—and at the time of this book's publication, he has been on seventy-five to eighty albums.

Johnson moved back to Wisconsin when Tim Bell retired from UW–Parkside. Johnson had reached a point in his life where a number of things came to a head—he and his wife were not sure they wanted their daughter growing up in the city and attending the Brooklyn schools, and Johnson could also see that the Konitz nonet and Swallow's chamber music group had just about run their course. He applied for Bell's position—a year-and-a-half appointment—and got the job. He commuted to Parkside from New York while his family stayed out east.

When the job turned into a tenure-track position, the Johnsons moved to southeastern Wisconsin in 2011. After resettling, Johnson continued to make frequent trips back to New York to perform, reversing the commute he had been making for the previous year and a half. He also started working in Chicago, eventually putting together a band of Chicago musicians. He connected with such Wisconsin musicians as Jamie Breiwick and Devin Drobka and has performed at Sugar Maple, a bar in Bay View that books Chicago avant-garde acts. Along with Drobka, Johnson organized a once-a-month jam session at Sugar Maple for those interested in this experimental music. The musical attitude and outlook that Johnson brought back from the East Coast have helped him land many gigs, record several CDs, and establish a vital progressive connection from Chicago to Milwaukee and Madison (see online discography).

Eric Jacobson

Yet another distinguished player from the area is trumpeter Eric Jacobson. Jacobson was born in Racine in 1975 into a family of trumpeters. "My mom, my dad, and my uncle all played trumpet," he says, and his mother was the most serious. Jacobson says, when he was in fourth grade, "I picked up the trumpet and never let go." He had two influential teachers; the first was Johnny Hemkes. "[Hemkes] was such an influence," Jacobson recalls. "You know, not only just getting to play the trumpet better, . . . [but something] that really always [is] still [in] my head is that . . . he always said, 'Sing through your horn.'" Hemkes also made an impression on Jacobson because he learned that teaching lessons could be lucrative. Jacobson remembers, "[Hemkes] would just say that he paid [for] his house in cash from teaching lessons."

The other memorable teacher was Norm Lanning, Jacobson's band director at Washington Park High School. Jacobson remembers Lanning as a "very strict, stern guy," but also says, "[He was] exactly what I needed. . . . I developed a lot of responsibility as a musician [because of Lanning]."

Another influence was Russ Johnson, though Jacobson didn't meet Russ until after high school. Jacobson's high school jazz band leader, Doug Johnson, gave him a cassette tape of Russ Johnson—this very successful Park High School graduate—and it made a big impression on Jacobson. When Russ returned to play at the Yardarm Bar in the city and Jacobson heard him play, he remembers thinking, "That's exactly what I want to do."

UW–Whitewater jazz program director Steve Wiest served as a guest artist at Jacobson's high school, and their meeting eventually led Jacobson to UWW for college. He had considered attending the University of North Texas with a couple of his high school buddies, but not only did he feel unprepared for that, he also wanted to pursue soccer, and Whitewater expressed an interest in his athletic skills. It was an opportune time to go to Whitewater. Wiest had the program operating in high gear, and the group of students included other outstanding young musicians: pianist Steve Einerson (now a successful professional in New York), saxophonist Eric Morones (now a southern California pro), Milwaukee-area saxophonist Sam Fettig, and trombonist Matt Faytle. "We just had this group of four or five guys that were so serious into studying jazz," Jacobson remembers, "and we would stay up all night in the music center transcribing solos for each other, and performing them . . . for a good four years."

Milwaukee trumpeter Mike Plog, who commuted to Whitewater to teach jazz trumpet, was a strong influence on Jacobson during this time. Jacobson started attending Monday night jam sessions at the Jazz Estate, which were led by pianist Rick Germanson (see chapter 7). Whitewater trumpet professor Frank Hanson also influenced Jacobson, even though the student and teacher often butted heads. Jacobson also spent time studying with Madison-based trumpeter David Cooper and Milwaukee veteran Allen Johnson. Jacobson says that Steve Wiest was "an amazing role model, and such a huge motivator," and he became "a father figure" for the aspiring young jazzer.

Jacobson made another connection, while only a college freshman, with trumpet star Brian Lynch. Jacobson was fascinated by Lynch's abilities, and he took advantage of Lynch's visits to Milwaukee by listening to him play, taking lessons from him, and picking his brain. Years later, Lynch was a guest on Jacobson's 2001 CD *Inspiration*. He considers Lynch not only his mentor but also "a really good friend."

Jacobson earned his degree at Whitewater and took a day job as an instrument tester at the Getzen Company in nearby Elkhorn. After a while, he says, "[I] started to finally get a couple gigs here and there, and then I started teaching lessons at Cascio Music Store." Shortly thereafter, he dove headfirst into Milwaukee's jazz scene, attending the standard jam sessions and eventually working his way into the modern jazz crowd discussed in chapter 11.

These days, in addition to the playing that he does around town, Jacobson teaches a lot. He hasn't been at Cascio for years, but he teaches many students at his Wauwautosa studio, which he has set up just like Johnny Hemkes's old studio. (Jacobson doesn't expect to pay off his house with lesson money for a while, however.) Around 2001, he began teaching lessons at the Wisconsin Conservatory. A few years later, the conservatory received a significant grant and used it to found the Jazz Institute. Soon Jacobson was leading combos and teaching lessons and at the institute's summer jazz camp. Eventually, Jacobson took over the trumpet chair in the faculty group We Six. In 2015, he was into his seventh year in the sextet. (He appears in the picture of this group in chapter 11.)

Jacobson says, "It's funny how being a musician—it's like you have to be everything. You've got to be a teacher, you've got to be a great musician, you've got to be a promoter, you've got to be able to be a businessperson." He hopes to improve in the latter field, as he wants to continue making more albums (see online discography), and to get a band together to work cities other than Milwaukee. But he also intends to become a teacher who might have the same kind of influence on others that his distinguished mentors had on him.

Jamie Breiwick

Trumpeter Jamie Breiwick, born in 1978, grew up in Racine but did not study with Johnny Hemkes. Breiwick's family was not a family of musicians, but, he says, "My dad was definitely a music fan and had a lot of different styles of music [in his music collection]." Breiwick began playing trumpet in fifth grade and joined the Mitchell Middle School jazz band in seventh grade. Thanks to his enlightened teachers, he played in a combo that listened to and performed music by Charlie Parker, Duke Ellington, and Herbie Hancock.

At about that time, Breiwick started trumpet lessons with local band director Eric Weiss. They would play with the Jamey Aebersold Play-A-Long recordings, and soon Breiwick started listening seriously to Miles Davis. Breiwick went on to Washington Park High School, where fellow trumpeter Eric Jacobson had recently attended, as had West Coast saxophonist Eric Morones. Breiwick was in school with guitarist Jay Mollerskov.

Breiwick was already considering going into music as a career when he attended the summer jazz camp at UW–Whitewater. He joined the youth jazz ensemble that Curt Hanrahan had put together at UW–Milwaukee and was also a member of the State Honors Jazz Ensemble in the summer of 1995, a band that included future New York professionals John Sullivan, Andrew Neesley, and Pete Zimmer.

Breiwick enrolled at UW–Milwaukee in 1996. He knew from the beginning that he wanted to be in the music education program. While he appreciated the security (relative to a performing career) that a teaching career offered, he also wanted to do it because, he says, "That was where I got hooked." He studied trumpet with classical teachers Wayne Cook and Kevin Hartman. While the big band at UWM was good, Breiwick felt that the jazz program was marginalized within the institution.

Breiwick's jazz education was profoundly linked to that of his high school buddy Jay Mollerskov.

> We went to high school together, and then we went to college together . . . and hung out, practiced together, learned tunes together, and eventually started gigging together. . . . A couple years into school, we started to get gigs. So if one of us got a gig, we would use the other and vice versa. And we started playing a little bit, going to the jam session at the Jazz Estate on Monday nights. I look to that as probably as important an educational experience as any. . . . Ricky Germanson [had] moved to New York, . . . but there was a great rhythm section. Brian Ritter was the drummer at the time—him or

> Jeno Somlai; Doug Ebert was the bassist usually. . . . That was where it was really inspiring, and where I look to as where I really started to learn a lot.

Fellow trumpeters Eric Jacobson and Andrew Neesley would show up at these jams, as would core Milwaukee rhythm players Jeff Hamann and Dave Bayles, and veteran pianist Jerry Weitzer.

Some lessons with UWM music theory professor Steve Nelson-Raney and a single trumpet lesson with Mike Plog began what Breiwick calls the "turning on of the light bulb," and Breiwick began to put in the work to develop bebop vocabulary. Another single lesson, with Milwaukee's legendary trumpeter Brian Lynch, pushed Breiwick further down the road. Nonetheless, years later, he admits that for the most part, "I've gotten to where I am now just from playing and listening a lot."

Around 1998, Breiwick started playing with the local band Clamnation. The other horn players in the group were trombonist Max Day and saxophonist Mike Pauers.

> I would call it a jazz group, but we played Afro-Cuban-influenced music. . . . We would play these gigs, and play this totally out-there material, but it was very danceable, because we kind of filtered it through an Afro-Cuban kind of a vibe, so people really dug it and would dance. . . . But at the same time, we would be able to stretch out and take these huge solos, . . . long solos.

While at UWM, Breiwick also played in a band called Hudson that was doing similar music—groove-based, with a lot of improvisation—but playing original compositions. Playing with these bands, he says, "really helped my development."

When Milwaukee drummer Carl Allen was brought back to UWM as a guest clinician one year, Breiwick, a student at the time, and Dan Kinzelman, another Racine native who was then in the high school youth band, were chosen to play in a combo with the visiting artist. Years later, Kinzelman, who now has a successful career in Italy, came back for a visit and asked Breiwick to play some gigs with him.

Breiwick taught at the Wisconsin Conservatory between 2005 and 2010, which brought with it membership in the faculty jazz group We Six. When he left the conservatory, he taught jazz trumpet at UW–Milwaukee, a position that lasted until 2015, when the state legislature made drastic cuts to the entire UW system.

These days, besides playing frequent special events, Breiwick appears with pianist Mark Davis two nights a week at the Mason Street Grill in the Pfister Hotel complex in downtown Milwaukee, a long-standing steady gig. His other active groups are Dreamland (the Music of Thelonious Monk), Choir Fight, the SPIRITS Quartet (with Tony Barba, Tim Ipsen, and Andrew Green), and the Lesser Lakes Trio (with John Christensen and Devin Drobka). (See online discography for recorded work by these groups.)

Breiwick has also been important on the Milwaukee scene as an advocate for jazz. After a gig at the Jazz Estate one night with guitarist Neil Davis and drummer Kevin Hayden, the three got into an interesting conversation. Breiwick explains,

> The MO of a lot of the musicians in [Milwaukee] was to kind of complain about the state of the scene, and the amount of gigs, and why is jazz not presented here anymore, and this gig is stopped, and this club closed, and this series is done, and all that. . . . Rather than complaining and bitching about it, we decided to do a concert.

With some serious organization and promotion work, the three, with a group eventually known as Milwaukee Jazz Vision (MJV), put together the first Eastside Jazz Festival. The festival occurred six times between 2010 and 2012, featuring local acts and such guests as David Hazeltine and Dan Nimmer. (North Coast Brewing Company, which brews Brother Thelonious Beer in honor of Thelonious Monk, donated products to the cause.) MJV also established a website that lists local jazz events, and a series of weekly jam sessions at the original Jazz Gallery, so that young musicians could profit from that experience. MJV also pulled off 2013's Visions on the Lake, a jazz event sponsored by the group and Milwaukee World Festival, Inc., the parent organization of Summerfest. The event was repeated in 2015. Milwaukee Jazz Vision has been a sponsor of the

Jamie Breiwick. PHOTO BY STEPHEN KALLAO; COURTESY OF JAMIE BREIWICK

annual Bay View Jazz Festival, which was inaugurated in 2014 and takes place in several venues in the Bay View neighborhood.

Not least, Breiwick is another significant Milwaukee jazz figure who spends his days teaching music as a public school teacher. After many years at Maple Dale Middle School in Fox Point, Breiwick took a position in his hometown at Racine's Prairie School in 2015.

Spike Robinson

Racine and Kenosha have not produced jazz brass players exclusively. Saxophonist Spike Robinson was one of those unique figures who seemed to appear with some frequency in jazz. Growing up in Kenosha, he played music in his youth, then embarked on a long professional life outside of music, only to return to music upon his retirement. He then became something of a jazz star, especially in Great Britain, where he frequently worked and was held in high esteem until his death in 2001.

He was born Henry Robinson in 1930.[6] According to his obituary in the *Scotsman*, he

> showed an early interest in music, playing the once fashionable C-melody saxophone in the first instance, then clarinet. His father encouraged his interest, but was a stern taskmaster. Robinson recalled being rapped on the knuckles with a fly-swatter if he played wrong notes in his reading exercises. . . . He aspired to a classical career as a young teenager, but gradually shifted his focus to jazz, and was playing professionally while still too young to join the union, having lied about his age in order to do so. He claimed to have gone to the lengths of drawing on a fake moustache in order to get into some of the jobs he was hired to play.

Robinson moved to Chicago in the late 1940s, but soon thereafter, perhaps because of a lack of playing opportunities, joined the navy. Fortuitously, he ended up in London, England. He was a member of an American service band, and various reports have him spending time in jazz clubs such as the Club Eleven in Soho, with well-known British players Johnny Dankworth and Ronnie Scott, and at the Eleven and Feldman Clubs with Victor Feldman and others. Robinson recorded with Feldman in 1951, which, like his sitting in with British musicians, was "in defiance of Musicians' Union rules prohibiting foreign players."[7] Peter Vacher reported in the *Guardian*, "By the time his national service ended later that year, he had built up a lucrative circuit of London engagements."[8] But according to one report, when booked as a guest soloist for a gig, the British union complained to American authorities, and Robinson was transferred to "jazzless" Naples, Italy, for the rest of his stint.[9]

Robinson returned to the States and studied mechanical engineering in Colorado, and then in the Detroit area. He worked in the aerospace industry, mostly in the Denver area, for years. "But throughout this 30-year period," Vacher claims, "Robinson played jazz gigs—now exclusively on tenor-saxophone—becoming something of a local treasure, largely unknown elsewhere."[10]

Robinson recorded his first album under his own name in 1981; on it, he was reunited with Feldman, who had by then been in America for years. The album led to tours back to the UK in 1984 and 1986. Once he retired from his day gig, Robinson soon built a career around regular work in the United States, England, and the European continent. He

Spike Robinson at the Guinness Cork Jazz Festival in Ireland, 1994. PHOTO BY TONY RODGERS

moved to London in 1989 but experienced several serious health crises, including meningitis, tuberculosis, and a bad fall that resulted in broken ribs and a damaged lung. However, he rallied, married his agent, and experienced a career revival for the rest of his life. Many references are made to his being a serious Anglophile, and especially to his love of, as Vacher calls it, "that most un-American game," cricket. He died in Essex in 2001.[11]

After his death, this succinct description of Robinson's style appeared in the *Scotsman*: "Robinson's elegant, light-hued, deftly swinging tenor playing drew on a lineage that ran from Lester Young through Zoot Sims to Stan Getz, although Charlie Parker was a crucial formative influence on his style when he was still a teenager. . . . He developed a refined tenor style close to that of Stan Getz, but with a sinewy elegance which was all his own."[12]

David Bixler

David Bixler was born in 1964 in Indiana. His connection to saxophone started with his family there. As Bixler explains,

> My grandmother grew up in the Depression on a farm, very poor, in southern Indiana; she wanted to have a saxophone. And evidently my great-grandmother . . . thought that she could make the payments on a saxophone, the monthly payments, if she could get the money together for a down payment. So they went to town [Vincennes] and went from house to house with bushels of corn to try to come up

with that down payment, and they never could. So my grandmother never had a saxophone, but she vowed that one of her children would. And my mother had a saxophone.

Bixler's family moved to Racine when he was three years old. He began music instruction on piano, but when he reached fifth grade, old enough to play in school band, he said, "My choice was made for me because there was a saxophone at my grandmother's house." He took lessons from Lee Will, a teacher at Washington Park High School.

Will eventually sent young Bixler to the go-to saxophone teacher in the area, Curt Hanrahan. "And he was very influential [in] a couple things," Bixler remembers. "One was just instilling in me the need to 'shed' [a common jazz expression meaning to go to the woodshed for serious, extended practice]. . . . And [he] turned me on to a lot of music; he was giving me LPs to take home." Soon Bixler was going to the Jamey Aebersold summer jazz camps and, as he says, "doing whatever I could do that smelled of jazz." Bixler attended Case High. His father was into jazz, and when Bixler was about fifteen, his dad took him to a concert at Milwaukee's Pabst Theater that featured two titans of jazz saxophone, Dexter Gordon and Johnny Griffin. Seeing Gordon, in particular, Bixler says, "[was] kind of a monumental point in my development. . . . It was just 'that moment.'"

As a high school student, Bixler drove to downtown Milwaukee to the Jazz Gallery and heard such visiting artists as Sonny Stitt, McCoy Tyner, and Horace Silver, as well as many local players.

Partly because of the family connection to the state and the university, but also because he had met Dominic Spera at the 1981 State Honors Jazz Ensemble, Bixler enrolled at Indiana University in 1982. He studied jazz with David Baker and classical saxophone with world-renowned pedagogue Eugene Rousseau. When living at home during summers, he attended jams at the Gallery, where Hattush Alexander was running the sessions. He also frequented the Jazz Estate, the Jazz Oasis, and the Space Lounge. The summer before his senior year at Indiana, Bixler received a National Endowment for the Arts grant to study in New York with saxophone master George Coleman.

By 1987, Bixler had graduated from Indiana, gotten married, and moved out to New York, because he says he believed, "This is where I have to be to attempt to learn to play this music." The next year, he was hired on the Lionel Hampton band; he toured Europe with the band and played off and on with them for some years.

David Bixler. PHOTO BY JON MACAPODI; COURTESY OF DAVID BIXLER

While in the city, Bixler made a living in part by playing shows. Bixler has always composed, and since the late 1990s, he has led a quintet to showcase his compositions. "That's been an important thing to me," he says. "And, so [I] always had this quintet going, and finally, made my first recording in 1998." He has now recorded six of his own albums. In New York, Bixler also did club dates and taught part-time at Montclair State University in New Jersey.

Around 2000, he got a call to play a rehearsal with a re-formed Chico O'Farrill Afro Cuban Orchestra, led by one of the seminal figures in New York Latin jazz. Bixler played over ten years with O'Farrill's band. This turned into a relationship with O'Farrill's son Arturo, a respected pianist, and Bixler played in Arturo's small group for several years as well.

By the mid-2000s, however, the scene was drying up in New York, and many of Bixler's gigs were not musically satisfying to him. He earned a master's degree studying composition at Montclair with Robert Aldridge (whose opera *Elmer Gantry*, as recorded by Milwaukee's Florentine Opera Company, won a Grammy in 2012). And in 2007, Bixler took a teaching job at Bowling Green State University in Ohio, at one of the biggest music schools in the country. He still tours with his quintet, but without the pressure of having to make a living playing music in New York.

Bixler's Auction Project, a band he formed in 2004, got its name from Bixler's wife, violinist Heather Martin Bixler. She too attended Indiana University, then went on to the Juilliard School and became interested in Irish music. The Bixlers formed the band for (and named it after) the annual auction that raised money for a music program at their children's school in New York. The band played its first real gig (outside of the auction) in 2006. Eventually the band recorded an album in 2010, with Bixler and Arturo O'Farrill as coleaders.

Bixler returns to Wisconsin every summer to teach at the Birch Creek Jazz Camp in Door County. He has forged a musical relationship with Milwaukee trumpeter Jamie Breiwick, and they frequently do gigs together when Bixler is in the area—a combination of two excellent horn players to come out of the Racine–Kenosha area.

18

The Fox Valley

Musically, if not strictly geographically, the Fox Valley stretches from Green Bay through Appleton and Oshkosh, and even to Fond du Lac. Additionally, many musicians from the Lake Michigan cities of Manitowoc and Sheboygan have, over the years, become part of this scene. A number of the important figures from this area are profiled here.

John Harmon

John Harmon is one of the most respected jazz musicians in Wisconsin. A superb pianist, a composer of wide scope, and an influential teacher, Harmon has been a major figure on the Wisconsin scene since he returned to his home state from the East Coast around 1970.

Harmon was born in 1935 and grew up in Oshkosh.[1] His mother was an "ear" piano player, and his father had a large collection of piano records—largely boogie-woogie. At age six or seven, Harmon was imitating these records and had absorbed twelve-bar blues form. Soon he was listening to Duke Ellington, Count Basie, Fats Waller, and Mary Lou Williams. One of his early heroes was Teddy Wilson, for what Harmon calls his "seemingly effortless touch and style." Harmon took music lessons, but without much success. He figured out how to play "Sweet Georgia Brown," and it became the signature tune for him and his mother when they played piano together at parties and family gatherings.

Harmon followed his brothers to high school at Culver Military Academy in Indiana. Once, while he was home on a break from school, he discovered an Art Tatum record in his dad's collection; it was a musical turning point for him. Back at Culver, Harmon remembers playing cat and mouse with the night hall monitor: "As soon as he departed, I would put the [Art Tatum record] back on. I just could not get enough of this. All night long I listened to the damn thing, and it became obsessive." Harmon says, "I would "re-create even tiny bits of what I was hearing," figuring out some "jazzy, sophisticated chords, without having a clue as to what they were."

At about the same time that Harmon accepted that his dream of becoming a professional baseball player was unrealistic, a family friend convinced the Harmons that he should go to music school, despite his lack of formal musical training and his virtual inability to read music. Despite these setbacks, Harmon was admitted to Lawrence College (now called Lawrence University) based on his ability to play by ear.

While immersed in what Harmon considered musical "basic training" at Lawrence, he played gigs at fraternity parties, and dances and engagements off campus as well. He went to a memorable Dave Brubeck concert in the Chicago area and later became a student of the music of Charlie Parker, Sonny Rollins, and Miles Davis.

During 1957, Harmon's senior year at Lawrence, someone gave him a brochure for the new School of Jazz, organized by Modern Jazz Quartet pianist John Lewis, in Massachusetts. Harmon was accepted on the basis of a taped audition and went to Lenox for eight weeks with an amazing faculty that included the complete Modern Jazz Quartet, the Oscar Peterson Trio, and the Jimmy Giuffre Trio. Max Roach and Dizzy Gillespie were there, as were guests such as Rex Stewart, Coleman Hawkins, and Sonny Stitt. Harmon studied piano with Peterson and played in a combo five days a week with Ray Brown and Milt Jackson. Peterson's warmth and encouragement toward Harmon led to a lifelong friendship.

On the way home from Massachusetts, John visited New York City. He went to the Village Vanguard to hear the Modern Jazz Quartet, but what turned him around that night was the relatively unknown intermission pianist, Bill Evans. Transformed by the performance, Harmon dove into Evans's music.

Harmon entered the army in 1958 and was eventually stationed at Fort Leonard Wood, in Missouri. He played in the band, where he says he "was exposed to a lot of new concepts, and got to meet a lot of St. Louis players, . . . fabulous players."

Upon discharge from the service in 1960, Harmon decided to move to New York and try to make it as a jazz musician. While establishing residence to gain his musicians' union card, he worked for months in the resorts of the Pocono Mountains. Back in the city, Harmon struggled to stay alive in the business. He was hired for a monthlong engagement in Bermuda but ended up staying for six or seven months, playing solo piano at a small club for mostly New York patrons. But, he says, "At midnight the hotels closed, and I would inherit a rhythm section from one of the hotels, and there was a jam until 3 [a.m.]." Over the next few years, he had three separate residencies in Bermuda, ultimately spending about two years on the island. He established two steady gigs and recalls, "[I] couldn't spend the money (which was tax-free), I made so much."

In between Bermuda trips, Harmon's army buddy Vincent Pitts arranged a record date with Yusef Lateef in August 1961. On the resulting album, *Lost in Sound*, Harmon's mature style is already recognizable. Unfortunately, while the record and the piano player were very favorably reviewed (four stars in *Down Beat*), Harmon's name was misspelled as Hormon on the jacket; only those who already knew him understood that Harmon was the album's pianist.[2]

After misconnecting on an engagement possibility in New Delhi, India, Harmon's wanderlust was next satisfied by a USO (United Service Organizations) tour of Europe. Playing at military bases around the continent, the troupe consisted of a magician, a dancer (Harmon's future wife, Wende Pollock), Harmon's trio (the Harmon-ies), and Jerry and Myrna Music, who did a music and comedy act.[3]

Back in the States in April 1963, Harmon visited Wende's family in Buffalo. When he landed a steady gig at an area pizza joint, he decided to stay. After a few months, he entered the State University of New York at Buffalo in a graduate program where he studied with noted twentieth-century composer Henri Pousseur.

At SUNY Buffalo, Harmon met a young bassist, Joel DiBartolo, who had obvious ability, if little experience. DiBartolo, who went on to become the bass player in Doc Severinsen's house band for Johnny Carson's *Tonight Show* for years, worked with Harmon in a trio during a crucial time in DiBartolo's development

Degree in hand, Harmon moved back to Wisconsin in 1969, having been told a job at Lawrence University might materialize. With the money he'd saved from his time in Bermuda, he built a house by Lake Butte des Morts.

But Lawrence was not ready to hire Harmon, and he failed to secure a day gig in the area. He started a trio, with Dan Peterson on drums and Lee Kusserow on bass, that held forth at the Town House in Oshkosh. Soon singer Kathy Law joined and added commercial appeal. Gigs "for the money" included playing in the house bands for two local television series that featured area country musicians Glenn Cass and April Walker. Harmon wore sunglasses on the set in hopes that no one would recognize him.

Finally, Lawrence called, and Harmon was hired to a new part-time position at the conservatory in 1971. Harmon led the big band, wrote many of the ensemble's charts, and taught improvisation, jazz, and composition and arranging. In his time at Lawrence, the university's jazz ensemble won the college competition at the University of Wisconsin–Eau Claire Jazz Festival and took first place at the Elmhurst Jazz Festival in Illinois, securing an invitation to the National College Jazz Festival.

During Harmon's third year at the conservatory, things were not as happy at home (he and Wende got divorced) or at school as they might have been, and Harmon decided to move in a different direction. As the driving force behind the formation of the band Matrix (the Appleton band; see chapter 12), Harmon left Lawrence in the spring of 1974.

Matrix toured for years, but after they quit traveling, in late 1979, Harmon returned home to Winneconne. Not long afterward, Brazilian jazz singer Flora Purim, who had performed with Matrix on the band's final tour, provided Harmon with a new opportunity. Thanks to her connections, Los Angeles's famed the Orchestra commissioned Harmon to create a major work for her and the star-studded group.

Harmon played odd jobs around the area until he was hired to play in a quartet for a one-night-a-week job at Arbuckle's in Fond du Lac in 1980; that band became Fire and Ice (see later in this chapter).

Harmon helped support his growing family (with his new wife, Linda, a popular area piano bar player) by securing other work. Leroy Wolter, a

John Harmon and Janet Planet (see later in this chapter) performing in Kurgan, Russia, 2012. PHOTO BY MATTHEW STRAUB; COURTESY OF JANET PLANET

longtime Oshkosh band director, encouraged the district to hire Harmon as composer in residence for the school music program in the early 1980s. During those two years, Harmon wrote for bands, choirs, orchestras, and combinations of these, at levels from elementary school through high school. He and Wolter also gave presentations to the general music classes in the lower grades.

The Oshkosh residency led to a similar two-year appointment in Appleton. Harmon was later hired for a variety of tasks at the University of Wisconsin–Oshkosh, and at Lawrence, where he served on the staff from time to time in various capacities.

In California for a residency around 1982, Harmon met Los Angeles studio trumpet stalwart Bobby Shew, and a firm friendship was formed. Shew commissioned Harmon to write a concerto, *Wolf River*, that he performed with the Duluth Symphony Orchestra and elsewhere. Shew has played numerous gigs with Harmon in the Midwest. In 2001, Sea Breeze Records issued a double-CD set under Shew's name, *The Music of John Harmon*, featuring Shew with four different Lawrence groups and in a set of duets with Harmon.

After being with the band Fire and Ice from 1980 until mid-1986, Harmon never played in a steady band again. He often worked solo, or in a duo with bass. For nine years he played solo, in duo with John Gibson, and in trio with Gibson and Dane Richeson at the House of Lee in Appleton. In the 2000s, Harmon played in Green Lake at the Heidel House Resort and Two Chez, with bassist Charles Ledvina.

Although Harmon and Janet Planet (see later in this chapter) parted ways when Fire and Ice broke up, they did not stay apart. Duo gigs led to their 1995 album, *More Beautiful Than Planned*, and Harmon has appeared on many Planet albums. They also did gigs together with orchestras, with Harmon writing some of the pieces and arrangements and Maury Laws writing others. A culmination of Harmon and Planet's work together came in 2006, when the pair premiered *Ava*, a Harmon opera written for Planet and to be accompanied by Harmon. Harmon has worked with Planet in New York as well, sometimes with veteran New York guitarist Gene Bertoncini. Harmon, Planet, Tom Washatka, and Tom Theabo also did a short tour of Japan in 2004. In the spring of 2012, Harmon and Planet performed in Russia as part of Appleton's sister city program.

One of Harmon's most valuable contributions to jazz life in the Midwest (and elsewhere) has been his teaching. A short list of his former piano students includes many musicians profiled in this book: Matt Turner, Mathew Buchman, Patty Darling, Mary Louise Knutson, and Connie Grauer, as well other professionals—Laura Caviani, Stephen Edwards, and Connie Olivera. Harmon's former composition students include Fred Sturm and Patty Darling.

Harmon has taught at summer camps for years—most recently at the Tritone Jazz Fantasy Camp at Lawrence University's Bjorklunden campus in Door County. He has been composer in residence for years at the Red Lodge Music Festival in Montana, writing chamber music and orchestral music, as well as teaching and playing jazz. His symphony *Crazy Horse* (named in honor of the great Native American figure) was premiered and recorded by the Oshkosh Symphony Orchestra in 2016.

Harmon has also had a significant impact on Wisconsin jazz in his role as artistic director of the Fox Jazz Fest (originally the Neenah Jazz Festival). He has booked all of the acts for the festival for over twenty years. In 2010, Harmon took on the same position for the new series, Jazz at the Trout, at Appleton's downtown art museum.

John Harmon is among the most modest of men, and I had to sneak into a cabinet in his home to find some of the many recognitions that he has received over the years: distinguished service awards from both the International Association of Jazz Educators–Wisconsin (2006) and the Wisconsin Music Educators Association (1999), and a 2005 honorary doctor of fine arts degree from his alma mater, Lawrence University. He was named a Fellow of the Wisconsin Academy of Sciences, Arts and Letters in 2005. And last but not least, in 2011 he was named to the Hall of Fame of the Wisconsin Area Music Industry.

Zach Harmon

John Harmon's son Zach, a drummer, has also experienced considerable success in the wider jazz world. Zach was born in Neenah in 1985 and grew up in Winneconne. At age three, he started studying piano with local teacher Hildegard Peterman; he also sang in the Appleton Boychoir. He didn't start on drums until eighth grade, at which point he played mallet percussion and timpani solos, and in various percussion ensembles at solo and ensemble festivals. He also played in the Oshkosh Youth Symphony. At home, he was surrounded by music with two extremely talented parents and older brother Noah, a budding jazz pianist. Eventually, Zach took lessons from drummers Dane Richeson and Ryan Korb.

Zach's skills improved in high school. In 2001, he got into the honors program of the National Foundation for Advancement in the Arts, first regionally, in Madison, and then at the national level. He was selected to play with the Clifford Brown–Stan Getz All Stars, which included Milwaukee trumpeter Philip Dizack (see chapter 9), Chicago bassist Gabe Noel, and pianist Mahesh Balasooriya. This group performed at the foundation's summit in Miami, and then the International Association for Jazz Education conference in Toronto in 2003. They later played at the Monterey Jazz Festival and did a brief tour of Japan.

Zach went to college at the University of Southern California, where he was happy to learn that Noel and Balasooriya were also enrolled. While there, Zach studied with Terri Lynne Carrington, who encouraged

Zach Harmon. PHOTO BY ZIGGY SPIZ; COURTESY OF ZACH HARMON

him to apply for the Thelonious Monk Institute, which was housed on the USC campus. Zach was accepted at the institute, in a distinguished class with Walter Smith, Ambrose Akinmusire, Tim Green, Chris Dingman, Romain Collin, and Milwaukeean Joe Sanders (see chapter 9), all of whom now enjoy significant jazz careers. Among other experiences, this class toured Vietnam and India with jazz greats Herbie Hancock and Wayne Shorter. On another occasion, after the Monk students had rehearsed at the Kennedy Center in Washington, DC, Zach had the opportunity to sub for Carrington in a rehearsal with Hancock, Ron Carter, Terence Blanchard, and Stevie Wonder.

Since his completion of the Monk program, Zach has recorded with Romain Collin, veteran Terence Blanchard, and the up-and-coming vocalist Sara Gazarek (see online discography). He has also toured with Collin (to South America and Europe, among other places), and with the young jazz star Tigran Hamasyan.

Zach always enjoys coming back to Wisconsin. He brought a trio to the 2013 Fox Jazz Fest that played his compositions exclusively. He looks forward to possibly working more with his brother Noah, who has forged a successful career in the Fox Valley, some of it playing a very personal combination of his classical and jazz influences.

Janet Planet

Jazz singer Janet Planet was born Janet Heimerman and grew up in Appleton in the 1950s and 1960s. Her childhood was not happy; her father was rarely home. But she does remember him playing music. "When my dad was home," she recalls, "he worked two jobs; one was in a paper mill in Menasha, and at night he'd go to the bowling alley and bartend. We lived in an eight-hundred-square-foot home on Christine Street in Appleton, . . . just newly developed. So it was us, a couple more houses, and a lot of fields. Dad would come home between jobs, and he'd go down in the basement . . . and he'd sit at this piano we had, and he'd play to unwind."

Eventually, Planet's father disappeared for good, leaving her mother with six children to raise. "We kind of raised ourselves," she says, "because my mom would be working two or three jobs. We were on welfare, and [there was] just a lot of turbulence. . . . She didn't have a lot of time to spend explaining things. A lot of things were learned from neighbors. . . . The neighbors on either side had the mom, and the dad, and the vacations and so forth."

Planet's interest in music began when her best friend started taking piano lessons. "I wanted piano lessons so bad," she remembers. "So when [my friend] was in having her piano lessons, which she hated, I'd go down in our basement and make believe I was having a piano lesson."

In first grade, Planet became convinced that she would grow up to be a singer with long blond hair. "That was always in my head," she says. "And I used to make believe that I was onstage. . . . I was singing all the time. . . . I'd do dishes for four hours, and I'd just sing and sing and sing and sing."

By sixth grade, she started playing trombone. It was, she says,

> the only instrument that was available, because my uncle had one. My mom couldn't [afford an instrument]. . . . I was good at memorizing the lessons and would never read the music. [Once,] I was in

> class, and doing just fine, and the teacher came up behind me, and he says, "What are you playing?" And I say, "I'm playing what everyone else is playing." And he goes, "You're on the wrong page, Janet."

Planet picked up guitar and had a few lessons at the YMCA until she could no longer afford them. Still, she remembers that her house was always full of music:

> My mom was working at a bowling alley, and every six months or so the jukebox guy would come and give my mom all the 45 [rpm] records and put the new ones in. And so she'd come home with these boxes, and it was like Christmas Day. We were listening to music all the time in that little house. Really, that was our savior. . . . And then as we got older it was albums. . . . My sister was listening to It's a Beautiful Day, Janis Joplin, Neil Young. I was listening to Frank Zappa, Cat Stevens, and Frank Zappa [*laughter*]. And my brother was listening to Yes and the Doobie Brothers. . . . My mom would come home and put on Tom Jones and the New Christy Minstrels and the Ray Coniff Singers.

But the family never listened to jazz, other than the times when Louis Armstrong came on the television, and her father would say, " 'Satchmo's on; be quiet, Satchmo's on.' "

At age twelve or thirteen, she says, "still dreaming about singing, . . . I wrote my own songs and played guitar, until the day that my mom got mad at me and banged me over the butt with the guitar and broke it, and that was it."

Planet's teenage years were filled with anguish. "I was very angry," she remembers, "and mad that I wasn't going to be able to go to [college or] to follow my dream and be this singer with long blond hair." Coming up through school, she says, "I hung out with the druggies. They were either pregnant, dropped out, or were in institutions, or arrested." But by the time she was a senior, most of her friends were gone, and she decided to try something totally different: she got involved in music.

"Fran Bubolz was the teacher at Appleton East at the time," Planet recalls.

> And I'll tell you, you know that show *Glee*? Okay, that was my life. . . . [On audition day for choir,] I go to the piano, and [Ms. Bubolz] starts playing the pitches. And then she goes up, midlevel, and then she's up—and now I'm way up here. . . . And at this point she's looking, "Well, how high? What is your range?" And at this point all the talking is quieting down. And that's when my life became hell.

Planet's impressive singing skills caused her to be ostracized by her peers. She often came home from school crying, but her mother encouraged her to ignore the teasing and keep trying. Planet continued to try out for talent shows, solos, and ensembles, and she earned a spot in the choir for the traveling show *Amahl and the Night Visitors* when it came through town.

Planet was the first person in her family to graduate from high school, and she eventually got an associate degree in early childhood education from Fox Valley Technical College, but her life was primarily focused on music. "The whole group of people who [I hung out with]," she remembers, "were very bohemian-esque, if that's a word. I listened to a lot of different music; had a lot of creative and innovative gatherings; and [my friend] had a huge record collection, thousands. . . . I'd just listen to [everything]."

Around 1979, while Planet was attending school for early childhood education, she was also bartending at the Paradise Club (a strip club) and gigging on the weekends. She joined the Blue Collar Blues Band and played some weekends with them. At Champagne Charlie's, she'd watch Dave Jahnke and Tom Theabo in a duo called Two Much. "And that really changed my life," she says. "They were doing Eddie Jefferson, Jon Hendricks, Joe Williams, George Benson." Eventually, she got the opportunity to sit in.

> [Dave Jahnke's] singing "Going Back to Chicago," and I'm improvising my whole part, and I'm coming back with this sass. . . . So that's how we got together then. And then I was in another group with him, Theabo, and another rhythm section . . . called Sweet Davy J's Body Talk, featuring Janet Planet. So that's kind of that transition from a blues band and then into this kind of jazz, and then an R&B mode.

Janet's intersection with Tom Theabo was one of the most important of her musical career.

At this time, Janet says, "I was in a group called Fun Time, which eventually became Lifetime. And Tony Wagner pretty much threw it together. And Matt Kahovec was on bass, and Tom Theabo on guitar, and I sang; just a quartet. Eventually we had Jeff Pietrangelo come on board. And he was playing trumpet and percussion, and we were doing pretty well. And doing things from Nancy Wilson to Stevie Wonder." Then, in 1984, Janet joined Fire and Ice. (The band is described in more detail later in this chapter.)

After the demise of Fire and Ice, Planet, Tom Washatka, and Theabo started what Washatka calls "one of the first karaoke bands." Washatka learned how to use a sequencer, and they recorded rhythm section tracks and played them back at their gigs on cassette tape. Washatka says, "With three of us, we were making three hundred bucks a gig, man, and if we worked six gigs in a month, that's six hundred dollars. That was more money than I had ever been making up to that point." In 1990, booked six nights a week at the upscale Fox Hills Resort near Manitowoc, the trio finally figured out that the musical magic was coming from the three of them, not the recorded tracks. Focusing on that, they created arrangements that are still in use in different contexts twenty-five years later.

In 1992, Planet signed with Gerard Entertainment in Milwaukee. "They were turning out all these pop stars," she says—most famously, the band Gerard and R&B singer Eric Benét. The band Gerard had a brief period of considerable fame; Benét has had a significant career in the business.

Planet spent hours a day, for weeks, in the studio under contract to Gerard, mostly doing demos of material that the Gerard team was pitching to big-time singers. She received very little financial reward but learned valuable lessons about how to sing and produce pop music.

Planet and Washatka started a romantic relationship in 1994. The following year marked the public revelation of Stellar Records, which has been primarily an outlet for Planet's many recordings, although the label has featured other artists including Washatka, Theabo, John Harmon, Matt Turner, Madisalsa, and cult figure Nancy King. In addition to extensive recording, Planet continues to perform around Wisconsin, with regular jaunts to New York (where she has been highly praised in the national press), as well as private commercial gigs around the country. She has performed internationally in Japan and Europe.

Tom Washatka

Saxophonist Tom Washatka was born in 1956 and grew up in Milwaukee in a family of twelve children. Washatka relates,

> One of my earliest memories was sitting on the couch between my mom and dad, watching Lawrence Welk [*laughter*]. I was probably five or six, and Mom noticed I was kind of keeping rhythm and time while I watched. My mother was a piano player; she started teaching me piano lessons when I was nine. I studied with her for three or four years. Picked up clarinet in seventh grade. . . . In eighth grade I had the opportunity to play saxophone, so I did, and the rest was history. I didn't really listen to much jazz in school. I was into more progressive rock. . . . Brothers and sisters of course listened to Motown, and the Beatles, Stones, Kinks, Turtles, all those. So I got an earful of all that stuff. [We played] some Basie stuff. . . . I wasn't really sure what I was listening to, what I was playing.

After the lessons with his mother, Washatka studied with a nun at his local Catholic school, and then briefly at John Marshall High School. When his family moved to Appleton, he attended Appleton West High School, where he played in the jazz band, which Ike Spangenberg was directing at the time, for two years.

Washatka went to college at UW–Oshkosh. His roommate, he says, "had a bunch of Blue Note stuff [and] Paul Desmond, Gerry Mulligan. But . . . it still didn't trip my trigger." When Washatka turned twenty, though, he made a life-altering discovery:

> I was kind of a late bloomer to the bebop thing, but checked out an album, when you could still check out vinyl at the library, and it was *Supersax Plays Bird*. And I'm not ashamed to admit I did not know who Supersax was, and more importantly, didn't know who Bird

> was. So I took it home, put it on; within thirty seconds it changed my life. I really dropped all my academics, switched my major from education to performance and just started hitting the horn. That was 1976.

Studying with John Harmon at Oshkosh made a lasting impression on Washatka as well. "[Harmon's] the one that really got me inside the music," Washatka recalls.

> I started listening to everything I could get my hands on. I think I listened to every album that was at the library. And I started reading [a] huge number of jazz history [books]. And discovered that I needed to go all the way back to the turn of the twentieth century—Sidney Bechet, Frankie Trumbauer—and then work my way through, up to the post-bop players and contemporary players. . . . That's where I fell in love with those guys—Sonny Rollins, Wayne Shorter, . . . John Coltrane, Harold Land.

Washatka graduated from college and began playing with bands of different genres: big bands, polka bands, a jump-swing band. "The 1980s was really my decade for hitting the horn—a lot," he says. "Punched the clock, put in my time."

In 1980, he started playing with the group that would later be called Fire and Ice and ended up staying with the band for six years. "[Fire and Ice] was actually started by Eric Late, bass player in Fond du Lac," says Washatka. "And he landed Harmon on piano, and [drummer] Tony Wagner." The band had a weekly gig at Arbuckle's in Fond du Lac, and after John Gibson replaced Late, and Tony Taylor replaced Wagner, they eventually moved to Fred's Bar in Oshkosh. "We wanted to try to make a living with this band," Washatka remembers. "And we knew we couldn't keep doing what we were doing. So we thought we could maybe stretch out a little bit and go a little more commercial."

The band cut a record, *Island Dancer*, and became very active, working four or five nights a week, though not on particularly high-paying gigs. Washatka and especially Harmon were composing at a furious clip in the so-called fusion style of the times. The band traveled to Minnesota and

Fire and Ice performing at Milwaukee's Summerfest in the mid-1980s. From left to right: Tom Theabo, Janet Planet, Tony Taylor, Tom Washatka, John Gibson, Chris Swansen, and John Harmon. COURTESY OF JANET PLANET

Michigan but mostly played around Wisconsin. When trumpeter Jeff Pietrangelo left Lifetime in early 1983, he joined Fire and Ice, starting what Gibson remembers as the most fun period of the band's history. After about a year, Pietrangelo left, but Janet Planet and Tom Theabo, a package deal, took his place.

Washatka had known Tom Theabo since around 1978, when they'd played together in Big City Bob and Ballroom Gliders. "Fortunately," Washatka says, "all these musicians were in this big music loop. All different styles, very eclectic; and that was where Tom [Theabo] came in. Because he grew up with a lot of these folks, and he has such a diverse range and expanse of influences and styles. . . . We gigged now and again; so we'd always kept in contact."

At this time, Harmon and Washatka began to write material to fit the band's new personality, now strongly defined by the dynamic vocalist Planet. One night at the Blue Moon in Oshkosh, Chris Swansen heard the band play, and its direction was about to change again.

When Swansen joined Fire and Ice as a second keyboard player in early 1985, the band had a steady gig at the Blue Moon (now Peabody's) in Oshkosh. Swansen had a three-record deal with Sea Breeze Records. The first record, *Piper at the Gates of Dawn*, featured Phil Woods's quartet and vocalist Kim Parker (daughter of Charlie Parker), with Swansen on synthesizers. For the second album of his contract, Swansen recorded *Sweet Thunder* at his studio at Cary Bluff (outside Pittsville). Janet Planet's name is listed first, and in the largest lettering on the record jacket, followed by the line, "Featuring John Harmon/Chris Swansen." When Harmon left the band in mid-1986, those remaining worked on the third album in Swansen's contract, but according to Gibson, "We just couldn't hold it together. It just completely disintegrated, and halfway through the second recording project, it just fell apart." Within a few months, the group disbanded.

After playing a variety of gigs, in early 1990 Washatka tried life in a top-forty band, but after about eight months, he couldn't stand it. He returned to the Fox Valley area, hooked up with the Madison Latin band Madisalsa, and founded the business Narrator Tracks with Mark Gungor, a videographer from Marshfield. The idea was to create music that clients could use for commercials, videos, and other professional projects. Clients could buy the music outright and not have to pay royalties. Much of what Washatka wrote, he calls "music by the pound." He was paid a salary ("a jazz musician on salary!" he exclaims) to create between four and six CDs a year. He has written hundreds of tracks, some of which he and Planet turned "into real music." He now owns the business himself.

Washatka continues to be one of the most active players in the Fox Valley and beyond, working most often with Planet's various bands and his friends from over the years. He joined Matrix (the Appleton band; see chapter 12) at their reunion in 2000 and subsequent gatherings, becoming the honorary tenth member of the band. Washatka taught jazz saxophone at Lawrence University as well as private lessons

John Gibson

Bassist John Gibson was born in 1957 and grew up in Sheboygan. His father, Rodney, was band director at Sheboygan North High School for over thirty years and played bass; Gibson started on the instrument in about fourth grade. He also took up trumpet in school band, then switched to tuba.

By his mid-teens, Gibson began subbing for his dad on gigs. Shortly thereafter, his dad gave up playing, freeing up more jobs for Gibson at establishments like the Riverdale and Pine Hills Country Clubs, and the Sky Garden on the top floor of the Security First Bank of Sheboygan. He played for weddings, but mostly in establishments for dining crowds that would get up and dance—a common practice in Wisconsin well into the 1970s. The polka bands Gibson played with (such as the Reggie Barber Orchestra) performed traditional pieces but also more contemporary pieces that they referred to as "the moderns." Although Gibson started on acoustic bass, he began playing primarily electric in the 1970s, under the influence of Stanley Clarke, Jaco Pastorius, and Verdine White of Earth, Wind & Fire. He played bass guitar even in the polka bands, trading off with tuba on the old standards.

Gibson went to college at UW–Madison. He played in the jazz band led by Richard Davis but did not take lessons from him. Gibson was a tuba major and intended to become a band director like his father. He enjoyed his studies with tubists Jeff Hoard and Mitch Gershenfeld (who was well known around the state as a classical music host on Wisconsin Public Radio) but eventually dropped the idea of becoming a band director. Looking for a different direction, he transferred to UW–Oshkosh in 1979 to enter its brand-new recording engineering program. In time he finished the program, despite his constant gigging outside of school. His first steady gig was with Fire and Ice.

After Gibson joined the band in late 1980, it remained a quartet—Gibson, Harmon, Washatka, and Wagner—for some time. Gibson remembers the band's steady gig moving from Arbuckle's to Pirates Cove in Appleton and Fred's Bar in Oshkosh. Fred's was a particularly colorful dive bar. According to Gibson, "[Fred, the owner] played the piano. He had a piano up in the window. Up high, like at bar height. . . . [And] when it got real cold in the winter, the bathroom would freeze up and he'd just put a bucket in there." The band played for the proceeds of the door. Gibson says, "We took turns on breaks, walking the bar, . . . passing the hat. And tapping these guys on the shoulder who were facedown on the bar. You could say, 'Hey, it's a dollar cover charge,' and some of them would tell you to go to hell, and others would just pony up . . . and we'd end up with, you know, twelve bucks."[4]

After Fire and Ice fell apart, John Gibson reconnected with John Harmon, and they ended up playing a duo gig at Appleton's House of Lee for about six years. Eventually they were joined by drummer Dane Richeson. Another long-standing gig included Harmon; Mike Hale, who played trumpet, flugelhorn, and drums; and cellist Matt Turner. They supported vocalist Mary Catterton in a seasonal series of performances at an Appleton church, and the band was known as Surprised by Grace. Gibson worked days as an engineer with Larry and Patty Darling at MIDI West Studios, where they recorded a large number of commercials, jingles, and industrial film tracks. He also worked a couple of days a week with the Green Bay recording firm Made Ya Look.

He got out of recording for a while, but there were a lot of gigging opportunities in the 1990s and 2000s, much of it with the Janet Planet Band (with Theabo and drummers James Levre and Danny Lueck). Gibson also worked in Green Bay with guitarist Phil Nelson, saxophonist/vocalist Woody Mankowski, vocalist Todd Buffa, and pianist/vocalist Christine Salerno; and in Stevens Point with pianist Mathew Buchman, drummer Ryan Korb, and saxophonist John Greiner. "For a few years," Gibson says, "I was playing almost every day with somebody." This activity continued until the crash of the economy in 2007 and 2008. Gibson had, in the meantime, gotten back into the recording scene with Tom Washatka's Narrator Tracks Music Library, but that too was scaled back following the economy's collapse.

With so many gigs dried up, Gibson went back to part-time work at Made Ya Look. By 2013 he was working there almost full-time. The studio mostly produces corporate videos, with Gibson doing much of the audio portions. For some years, the Green Bay Packers were a major client. Area giants Schreiber Foods (one of the largest cheese companies in the world) and Kimberly-Clark are also important to the studio's success. In 2015, Gibson became owner and head of the recording operation.

Gibson continues to play around the Fox Valley, with many of the area's best musicians—Harmon, Planet, vocalist Steve March Tormé,

Christine Salerno, Woody Mankowski, and, occasionally, western Wisconsin's violinist Randy Sabien.

Chris Swansen

Chris Swansen came to Fire and Ice by a completely different route than any of its other members. He was born in 1939 and grew up in Milwaukee, attending Shorewood High School.[5] According to a tribute produced by a college classmate, Swansen had been vice president of his high school class, belonged to an honor society, and worked on the school newspaper. Besides participating in band and orchestra, he also played on his school's football, tennis, and track teams.

Swansen attended Dartmouth College in New Hampshire from 1957 to 1961. He made a big impression on his musical classmates with his perfect pitch and a remarkable ear—a friend recalled Swansen's ability to tell the speed of a car they rented one summer by the pitch of the engine. He played trombone in a small jazz group on campus as well as the Barbary Coast (Big) Band, which still exists in 2017. He led both groups during his last two years at school. Interestingly, future star pianist Mike Melvoin (see chapter 8), another Milwaukee native, was the leader of the Barbary Coast Band when Swansen arrived at school.

Following graduation from Dartmouth, Swansen attended the Berklee School of Music in Boston for two years. While there, he played trombone and wrote for Herb Pomeroy's big band, a Boston institution. In 1963, Swansen attended Tanglewood—the summer home of the Boston Symphony Orchestra, which offered advanced study for highly qualified students—and he studied with Gunther Schuller, Aaron Copland, and Iannis Xenakis. He was the director and conductor of the New York Improvisational Ensemble from 1964 to 1968.

In the late 1960s, Swansen's playing career took off. He played with the big bands of Stan Kenton and Maynard Ferguson, eventually playing with other jazz greats such as Phil Woods, Gary Burton, Eddie Gomez, and Joe Henderson. He recorded with Burton in 1962 and Woods in 1969 (see online discography). He composed works on commission from the Canadian Broadcasting Company, the National Educational Television Network, Stan Getz, Burton, and other groups.

The year 1968 marked a change in direction as Swansen became interested in synthesizers; the following year, he became composer in residence and musical director at synthesizer pioneer Bob Moog's company in upstate New York. In the summer of 1969, under the direction of Swansen and Herbert Deutsch, the Moog synthesizer made its live performance debut at the Museum of Modern Art in New York.[6] Bob Moog reports that Swansen played at this concert with a group that included guitar god John McLaughlin, pianist Hal Galper, and drummer Bob Moses.[7]

Although still connected with the East Coast music scene, Swansen moved to little Pittsville, Wisconsin (near Wisconsin Rapids), in 1974 and founded Badger Music Company. He had recorded two albums of synthesizer music in the mid-1970s (see online discography), but he also recorded two albums with Phil Woods, in 1979 and 1984, after moving back to Wisconsin.

Swansen lived in Pittsville until he died from brain cancer at the age of fifty-six, in 1995. In 2010, Planet's Stellar Records released an album of Swansen's songs; Planet sang most of them, supported by several different configurations of Fox Valley musicians, with many of the arrangements by Washatka.

Dane Richeson

Since moving to Wisconsin in 1984 to teach percussion at Lawrence University, Dane Richeson has been an important member of Wisconsin's jazz community.

Richeson was born in Columbus, Ohio, in 1957 and grew up in nearby Bremen. The youngest of seven children, he grew up hearing his older brothers' rock bands rehearsing in the basement. Richeson played piano and French horn. But the drum parts in his brothers' bands were too fascinating to resist, and Richeson switched to the set. By the end of eighth grade, he was proficient enough to play in what he calls a "Holiday Inn circuit" top-forty band. But his interest soon turned toward the music of Weather Report and Miles Davis's 1960s quintet (with Tony Williams).

> My brother came back from Boston; we started up this fusion band, and actually we created this nice little studio space, bought

> a reel-to-reel recorder. . . . And we just started playing and playing and playing, and rehearsing and rehearsing, and recording all these jam sessions, and making tunes. . . . And then my brother got us some gigs up in Columbus, and we started playing out.

Richeson quit school band but stayed in choir, played football, and made music outside of school. His parents allowed him to drop out of high school to join his brothers in Boston in a band. Things did not work out for the band, but Richeson hung out in the practice rooms of the Berklee College of Music, played for a jazz dance company, and heard great live jazz in the city.

When he returned to Ohio, Richeson got regular work in Columbus, as did his brother Doug, who went on to play for years in Ralph Sharon's trio backing up the great Tony Bennett. Richeson finished high school through special programs and enrolled at Ohio State University. He transferred to Indiana University of Pennsylvania, then back to OSU. After completing a degree, he went to Ithaca College in New York for graduate work, and then came to Lawrence directly from Ithaca.

Richeson is an inveterate jobbing musician and has played just about every kind of gig available on Wisconsin's music scene. In his first year in Wisconsin, he played a weekend of polkas in Wisconsin Rapids with two accordion players and reed man Don Chesebro. One of the accordion players was talented teenager Brian Erickson, with whom Richeson later recorded a jazz album.

Another of Richeson's early connections in Wisconsin was Joan Wildman (see chapter 14), who was then conducting jam sessions at her home. Bassist Hans Sturm was at one of those sessions; Richeson and Sturm went on to play many jobs and make recordings together, with Wildman and others. Richeson also worked in Madison with a much different trio that included pianist Tim Whalen and bassist Jeff Eckels. Richeson was an early member of the New Breed, with Whalen, Eckels, and David Cooper, and he continued with the group as its personnel turned over to include Paul Hastil, Nick Moran, and Louka Patenaude (see chapter 16). Through his connection with Wildman, Richeson had the opportunity to play with Roscoe Mitchell, once in Madison and another time with the contemporary chamber ensemble CUBE. Richeson has long performed

Lawrence University Faculty Jazz Quartet in 2015 (left to right): Bill Carrothers, José Encarnacion, Mark Urness (see chapter 19), and Dane Richeson. COURTESY OF DANE RICHESON

with Madison's Bach Dancing and Dynamite Ensemble. He has also worked frequently with piano/harmonica virtuoso Howard Levy.

Richeson has not been quite as active in Milwaukee as he has been in Madison, but he did have a long-standing musical partnership with Jack Grassel and often played with him in a trio format with Kirk Tatnall. Over the years, he played with Melvin Rhyne, Gerald Cannon, and Milwaukee icons Manty Ellis and Berkeley Fudge.

In the Fox Valley, Richeson's longest-running steady job was probably at the House of Lee in Appleton, with John Harmon and John Gibson. He has played all over the state with jazz violinist Randy Sabien and has worked with some of Wisconsin's best singers, including Jackie Allen (Richeson played on more than four of her albums), Janet Planet, Gerri DiMaggio, Lynette, Zara Enzekian, and Ben Sidran.

While Richeson is known as a drummer, those who know his playing realize he is more than "just a drummer." In his recorded work, he plays instruments not associated with the traditional drum set. His intense interest in many types of world music has led to significant residencies in Brazil, Cuba, and Ghana. He has performed in Europe and China. At Lawrence University, Richeson has collaborated with such visiting artists as Bobby McFerrin and Kenny Wheeler. Richeson finally released an album as leader in 2013 (see online discography). He continues to perform in groups across the stylistic spectrum while introducing his students to worlds of percussion.

Brad Curran

Trumpeter Brad Curran grew up in Fond du Lac in the 1950s and 1960s. As a student at Goodrich High School, Curran began studying trumpet with Paul Smoker, who was then teaching at UW–Oshkosh. Thanks to Smoker's influence, Curran went from listening to Herb Alpert and the Tijuana Brass to Nat Adderley, Freddie Hubbard, and Miles Davis.

When it was time for Curran to attend college in 1970, he joined Smoker, his mentor, in Oshkosh. But after a year, Smoker left, and Curran began studying with Allen Butcher, the new trumpet professor, who also took over the jazz band. Butcher served UWO in a variety of capacities over many years and was an active classical and jazz trumpeter in the Fox Valley as well as a member, for many years, of the Green Bay Packers band.

Upon reaching what should have been his last semester in college, Curran, disillusioned with the music education program, dropped out of school to join the band Funky Norman. Funky Norman was fronted by a talented singer, Dave Jahnke, and included trombonist Tim George (Curran's high school and college classmate), saxophonist Michael Bard, bassist Wilbur Vandenberg, pianist Dave Evans, drummer Neil Herwey, and guitarist Tom Theabo. Fans were drawn to the band for its combination of rock, blues, and funk, and it experienced considerable regional success.

After quitting Funky Norman, Curran became a clerk and bookkeeper at Oshkosh's Plaza Motor Inn. When his wife left him, Curran took custody of his two children and raised them alone for five years. To support his family, he worked for a radio station, an insulation company, and, for eleven years, a towel and uniform company.

Curran remained involved in music, particularly after meeting his second wife, Bonnie. He returned to UW–Oshkosh in 1988 and fought

Left to right, front row: Brad Curran, Father Joe Mattern, and Dave Dunning; back row: Andy Mertens and James LeFevre. PHOTO BY JOE TONDU

his way through a troubling piano requirement to finally complete the degree. He taught English at Webster Stanley Middle School in Oshkosh before taking on the band director position at Seton Catholic Middle School in Menasha in 1990, where he built a model jazz program. In 2015, he went back to Webster Stanley as band director.

Curran has been active in a variety of groups in the area over his many years on the scene. He worked extensively with big bands led by Don DeLapp and Howard Schneider and eventually became the musical director for the Ron Harvey Orchestra, a successful society band that worked around the Midwest. He also worked with the ghost band that played the book of Swing Era leader Jan Garber, eventually becoming musical director of that group as well. He even worked for a year with a polka band, the Bill Tull Recording Orchestra.

Curran founded the jazz quartet Dig, which explored the music of Chet Baker and Gerry Mulligan. Originally, the band featured Sandy Schaeffer on vibes, guitarist Dave Sullivan, and bassist Denny Wiarsky;

later editions featured bassist John Sullivan, baritone saxophonist Simon Weller, and pianist Noah Harmon. Curran played with Green Bay big band Bay City Swing and other area groups as well. In 2009, Curran reunited with other UW–Oshkosh alumni from his era—drummer Jim Frakes, Chicago pianist Marshall Vente, bassist Al Zuberbuehler, trombonist Tom Perry, and others—to form the Mohawk Avenue Jazz Band.

Curran served a term as president of the Wisconsin chapter of the International Association for Jazz Education and continues to be recognized for his accomplishments in jazz education.

Lovell Ives

Much of the jazz scene in Green Bay has revolved around the activity at the University of Wisconsin–Green Bay. The jazz program there was established and carried on for decades by trumpeter and composer/arranger Lovell Ives.

Almost always referred to by his first name, even by his students after he became a venerable figure, Lovell Ives was born in Marshfield on August 13, 1928. (The nickname "Oodie" is used by his closest friends.) Lovell's older brother Wally was an accomplished cornet player, and Lovell followed him on the same instrument. Wally played in Marshfield and Stevens Point dance bands from 1939 until the United States entered World War II. Then he went to Los Angeles to work at Douglas Aircraft, but he missed the Midwest and returned to work in the munitions industry closer to home.

In the mid-1940s, Wally took a job in a band in Winona, Minnesota, and brought his little brother Lovell to live with him for the summer. Lovell played his first dance job in Caledonia, Minnesota, and despite Wally's help, Lovell says, "I was terrible." He went back to Marshfield to finish high school, but when he was offered a spot in another band in Winona in the spring of 1946, he took the job and never finished school. This band was led by brothers Harold and Leonard Edstrom and named after them: the Hal Leonard Band. After the band broke up, the Edstrom brothers went on to establish a music store and publishing business, and the Hal Leonard Company, now headquartered in Milwaukee, is a giant of the music publishing industry.

Lovell returned to Marshfield and started writing arrangements for a band his brother was starting, but Wally, in order to make some money, joined Lawrence Duchow's band instead. (The hugely successful Duchow band, apparently based in the Appleton area at that time, made three hundred records and were known as second only to Lawrence Welk's band in their niche in dance music.[8]) Eventually, Wally returned to Marshfield and started Wally Ives and His Jolly Dutchmen, for which Lovell says he wrote "tons of stuff," while also writing for other bands. A largely self-taught writer, Lovell did get a few pointers from area musician Duke Duvall.

Lovell was then offered a job with a new band at WKOW radio in Madison. The band was to play a popular noon-hour program of German music, mostly polkas, hosted by the on-air character Uncle Julius (Ross Gordon). Lovell was supposed to play in the band, but as it turned out, he just wrote—constantly. The band not only played at the station, but it also played jobs around southeastern Wisconsin. During this time, Lovell played in another band next to saxophonist John Salerno, who Lovell calls "the best damn jazz saxophone player I ever heard." They were working together the night that Salerno's son, John, was born. (Lovell appears in the photo that accompanies John and Christine Salerno's profile later in this chapter.)

At age twenty-five, after his two-and-a-half-year-old daughter died, Lovell decided to make a change in his life. Although he had not finished high school, he had eventually been awarded a diploma. So he applied for school at Wisconsin State University at Stevens Point. He had never been a good student, and the dean at Stevens Point was hesitant to admit Lovell. With a promise to work hard, he was admitted on "final probation." Lovell did work hard and was one of the first students to graduate from the school with a music major.

In 1957, Lovell was hired as band director in Colby, Wisconsin. He attended Indiana University during the summers, working on an advanced degree in trumpet, and rubbed elbows with Dominic Spera, the soon-to-be jazz guru at UW–Eau Claire, and David Baker, who would later become the leader of IU's jazz program. Despite these connections, Lovell left Indiana and enrolled at Vander Cook College in Chicago, where he earned a master's degree.

After four years at Colby, Lovell moved to take a job at Medford High School that had been turned down by his future UW–Green Bay colleague Robert Bauer. While at Medford, Lovell continued his summer studies, at the Eastman School of Music—the only formal training in jazz Lovell ever received. According to New York composer/arranger Manny Albam, the folks at Eastman wanted "to see this guy that wrote all these polkas and waltzes and stuff."

In 1969, Lovell was hired at UWGB. His new jazz program hit the ground running. In the first few years, the group included such strong players as pianist Pete Polzak (who had been recruited from the local Pink Panther bar), drummer Dave Charles, trumpeter Terry Winch, trombonists John Hinckley, Dan Gould, and John Davies, and Lovell's eventual successor at UWGB, John Salerno. By Lovell's second year, the university was hosting a jazz festival that brought in high school jazz bands for competition and hosted great guest artists. The festival's guests have included Randy Brecker, Allen Vizzutti, Kenny Werner, David Liebman, Ingrid Jensen, and—Lovell's personal favorite—jazz icon James Moody. Over the years, the GB band also became known for its library, much of which was written by Lovell.

When Lovell was hired at the university, he was offered the leadership of the UWGB marching band, which had received a big start-up donation from the Green Bay Packers. Lovell didn't feel that he was best suited to lead that band, which his UWGB colleague Robert Bauer led the previous year while teaching at the Marinette UW Center. However, Lovell wrote arrangements for this band, which went on to play at many Packers games, starting in the fall of 1970.[9] Pretty soon, Lovell became a member of the official Packers band.

Around 1982, Lovell was approached by Packers board member John Torinus (publisher of the Appleton *Post Crescent*). According to Lovell, Torinus said, "Would you be interested in taking over the Packers band? Because [the fans] don't like that military thing; it's old-fashioned." The official Packers band at this time was the Lumberjack Band; despite its name, it was a military-style band. After expressing interest, Lovell was officially offered the job by Judge Robert Parins, then president of the team. Lovell made it clear what he would need—new music and music stands—and the new version of the Green Bay Packers Band, a swinging big band, was born.

For years, Lovell also played with the River City Six, a popular Dixieland band in the Fox Valley. His longtime teaching companion at UWGB, Wayne "Jake" Jaeckel, was the band's clarinetist. The two met when they were in high school and Jaeckel was playing oboe; they started a little band together in which Jaeckel played piano and saxophone and Lovell played either cornet or trumpet. Once the music program at UWGB had started, Lovell sought out Jake, who was teaching in the Chicago area, to join the faculty.

Later members of the UWGB program who have made names for themselves in Wisconsin jazz are drummer Danny Lueck; saxophonists Woody Mankowski, Kevin Van Ess (also an accomplished clarinetist), and Marc Jimos; and trumpeters Kevin Short and Nathan Behling. Schoolmates Mark Israel (trumpet) and Mark Burditt (trombone) went on to successful careers in military service, playing for years in one of the country's top service jazz bands, the United States Air Force Academy Band Falconaires.[10] Brothers Eddie "E. J." Allen, a trumpeter, and drummer Carl Allen (see chapter 9) made it to the New York stage after going through UWGB's program, as well. All of these players reflect Lovell Ives's legacy as one of the most important jazz educators in Wisconsin history.

John and Christine Salerno

John Salerno was born on June 8, 1951, in Madison, where his father was jobbing as well as repairing instruments at Ward-Brodt music store. Impulsively, his father moved their family to Manitowoc when young Salerno was in first grade, casting his lot with his wife's family, the Bilottis, who ran a successful pizza business. Salerno went to Lincoln High in Manitowoc, where he was a bassoonist in the band. In college, he spent a year at the UW two-year campus in Manitowoc. He thought he was destined to attend UW–Madison but instead ended up at the practically new UW–Green Bay campus after auditioning for the music program on piano. "Over the summer," Salerno remembers, "I started

Christine Paquin (Salerno), John Salerno, and Lovell Ives (see previous section in this chapter) in the 1980s. COURTESY OF JOHN SALERNO

to play saxophone before I came [to UWGB] . . . and I was terrible, but Lovell kept me in the band anyway."

After earning his bachelor's degree, Salerno was one of the few students to earn a master's degree in UWGB's short-lived music program in the Environmental Arts and Sciences. Then he went to the University of Northern Colorado, where he worked on a doctor of musical arts degree while leading the university's second jazz band. With only his final composition left to complete the degree, Salerno moved back to Wisconsin along with his future wife, Christine Paquin (whom he had met at UNC), to lead the music for a summer theater group in Superior. The couple moved to Green Bay for a year, then to Allegan, Michigan, where Paquin had been hired to teach music. Salerno finished his doctoral composition, and in 1986 the couple went back to Colorado for another year. After receiving his doctorate, Salerno was hired to teach core music courses and saxophone at Florida Atlantic University in 1987. After four years in Florida, Salerno was offered the opportunity to teach at UWGB in 1991, which he happily accepted, returning to his family and roots.

Christine "Chris" Paquin was born on November 5, 1960, in Kalamazoo, Michigan. She attended Western Michigan University, where she became one of the school's first jazz performance majors. She participated in the famed Gold Company jazz vocal group at WMU and did lots of jobbing as a pianist. A few years later, while working as an assistant at Northern Colorado in vocal jazz, she began playing piano in the jazz band that John Salerno was leading, and their collective fate was sealed. As the couple moved to Green Bay, then Michigan, then back to Colorado, and finally to Florida, jazz piano jobs were a constant for Chris. She also led the vocal jazz group at Florida Atlantic.

John has been at the helm of the Green Bay program for years, and Chris taught there starting in 1992, with classes in vocal jazz, private jazz voice and piano, choral arranging, keyboard class, and jazz history. She also taught for seven years at Lawrence University in Appleton. She says, "[I taught] their jazz singers, and also private jazz voice; [I] taught keyboard, and . . . vocal jazz techniques class."

As a performer, Chris has been seen and heard over the years with big bands; as a single pianist, vocalist, or both; and with her group ZIJI, which focuses on Brazilian-influenced music, mostly originals composed by Chris. The band has featured area musicians such as woodwind player John Croarkin, bassist John Gibson, and drummer Danny Lueck.

John Salerno shows up on an occasional track on the ZIJI recordings (see online discography) playing flute, as he usually does at live gigs. Notoriously self-deprecating about his abilities, John is known around the area as an outstanding saxophonist and flutist. Besides leading the big band at UWGB, he leads a "Tribute to Sinatra" band, featuring the vocals of his cousin, Dino Bilotti. Together and separately, John and Christine Salerno have been a major presence in the Green Bay scene, as both performers and educators, for over twenty-five years.

Woody Mankowski

Arguably, the best-known UWGB jazz graduate around Wisconsin and beyond is Forrest "Woody" Mankowski. Born in 1966, Mankowski grew up in western Wisconsin. His family lived in Rice Lake until he attened junior high and started playing saxophone. Then they moved to Menomonie, where Mankowski's dad worked for Santa Dairies making Swiss Miss products. "By the time I got to Menomonie," Mankowski says, "I was already . . . a little ahead of the game . . . because I practiced a lot. My mom and dad made sure of that." In high school, Mankowski says, "[Band director Jim Borgaro] gave me a cassette tape with some Charlie Parker on it, and . . . [I] just couldn't believe that anybody could actually do that. And then I found out that he was actually making it all up on the spot." He decided, "I *have* to be able to do that."

Mankowski entered UWGB in 1983 and immediately began playing in both school and area bands, including, briefly, Streetlife. For a year he lived with David Cooper (see chapter 16), and the two listened to jazz and practiced constantly. Mankowski attended school with two others who would go on to become significant players and teachers on the local scene—trombonist Bill Dennee and fellow Menomonie saxophonist Marc Jimos. Mankowski studied with Wayne Jaeckel until Jaeckel's untimely death.

After graduating from GB, Mankowski stayed in the area, playing and singing with such area bands as Charisma, Project '60s, and the high-powered but short-lived fusion band Ripped Tissue and the Wastepaper Products. He eventually took his vocal skills to the local studios, and although lately the jingle business has largely dried up, Mankowski's voice can still be heard on radio and television ads all over local airwaves. He made most of his income from studio work in the late 1990s and early 2000s.

In the early 1990s, Mankowski introduced his vocal work to the public when he started working with the band that would become Big Mouth. "And that ended up being a really popular band in Door County," he remembers. "And it was more fun than I'd had with . . . any rock band that I'd played with, . . . [but] I still considered myself strictly a jazz musician." A horn section, with Nathan Behling, Marc Jimos, and Bill Dennee, was added to Big Mouth a couple of years later. The band continued playing into the 2010s as an area favorite.

Mankowski had in the meantime firmly established himself as one of the finest jazz saxophonists in Wisconsin. He became active in Madison, playing with Tim Whalen's Tribute to Art Blakey band, the New Breed (see chapter 16), Kelly De Haven, and his old buddy David Cooper. While

Woody Mankowski (left) and David Cooper (see chapter 16). PHOTO BY JOE TONDU

true jazz gigs are hard to find, Mankowski was a memorable leader at the late, lamented Fox Note jazz club in Princeton, Wisconsin, and on the Jazz at the Trout series in Appleton. He played a series of duo jobs in the early 2010s with Christine Salerno at the Black Boot in De Pere. In 2012 he was voted Wisconsin Area Music Industry Reeds/Brass Player of the Year.

Mankowski joined the Daryl Stuermer Band in 2011. Stuermer's (see chapter 12) top-notch band played the music of, and music that was reminiscent of, his two superstar pop employers, Genesis and Phil Collins. Mankowski is primarily a vocalist in the band but occasionally gets in a few licks on saxophone. He also has performed with orchestras around the country as lead vocalist in Fred Sturm's *Baseball Project*.

In the spring of 2012, Mankowski took the trip of a lifetime, performing in Cannes, France, with Microsoft cofounder Paul Allen's rock band.

Much of the trip was spent on Allen's yacht, but the band also traveled by helicopter and Allen's private jet to London to record.[11]

Another aspect of Mankowski's career has been his life as a transcriber, largely for Wisconsin's Hal Leonard Company. He has transcribed books of jazz solos by artists ranging from Louis Armstrong and Lester Young to Oscar Peterson and John Coltrane, and many singers, including Frank Sinatra, Diana Krall, and Norah Jones.[12] This transcription work became the source of a major portion of Mankowski's income.

In the fall of 2015, with the security of periodic work with Paul Allen's band, Mankowski moved to southern California to test the scene there. He continues to play with Allen and on some jazz gigs, many with an organ trio called Rumproller.

Dave Sullivan

Guitarist Dave Sullivan has been an important player on the Wisconsin jazz scene—in his hometown of Sheboygan, the Fox Valley, Milwaukee, and even Chicago—ever since he moved to the state in 1971. His route to Wisconsin was circuitous and fascinating.

Sullivan was born in Hot Springs, Arkansas, in 1939. His father was in the service, and his family lived in Germany (for about three years right after World War II), San Antonio, and Oklahoma. For his first instrument, Sullivan says he "found a little ukulele in the trash, and put some nylon fishing line on it, and started plunking around." But his mother thought he might appreciate a guitar, and he got a Gene Autry model that his brother had earned by selling seeds from a catalog. When Sullivan was about twelve years old, he and his brother played guitar and accordion on a San Antonio street corner for tips.

In Hot Springs, Sullivan had played country and western music with local musicians. But in San Antonio, he says, "I started hanging out with people that listened to jazz, and rock and roll was coming in." As a teenager he played with a band that did pop hits, rock and roll, and R&B. The band opened for Elvis Presley at a handful of concerts when he was still up-and-coming. The band traveled around the Southwest but eventually ended up in San Jose, California, where Sullivan stayed for a while.

He was back playing in La Porte, Texas, with this same group when rhythm and blues pioneer Louis Jordan came through town with his Tympany Five. Jordan hired Sullivan's buddy Sammy J. to play bass and Sullivan to play guitar (even though well-known jazz guitarist Teddy Bunn was already in the band). While touring in Florida with Jordan's band, Sullivan remembers that, despite the leader's fame and despite the fact that sit-ins for civil rights were taking place there, "The black guys in the group couldn't go out in the crowd, [and] talk to customers, or anything like that."

Back in California, Sullivan played in the Ajax Club in the Tenderloin neighborhood of San Francisco, and at Henry's Whip in Long Beach. Later, he went on the road with the Hollywood Argyles, the one-hit wonder that was famous for the 1960 song "Alley Oop." But making a living as a musician was challenging, and Sullivan says he "can remember trying to play for tips . . . [to] get enough money for a hamburger."

One of Sullivan's steadiest gigs was with the Bumblebees. When threatened with a lawsuit for violation of copyright, the band changed its name to the Flintstones and briefly dressed up like the characters in the famous Hanna-Barbera cartoon. The band settled in at the Condor Club in San Francisco, which featured topless dancers and the silicone-augmented Carol Doda as its star. Guests and celebrities came in from all over the country; Sammy Davis Jr. even sang with the band one night. "It was like New Year's Eve every night," Sullivan remembers. The house band parlayed this notoriety into an appearance in the film *Dr. Goldfoot and the Bikini Machine*, the James Bond and beach movie spoof. After about a year and a half with the Flintstones, Sullivan moved on.

In the mid-1960s, Sullivan decided to try Las Vegas. He couldn't get a high-paying gig in the show bands at the big casinos, but he was able to land some work touring with the band of Lou Sino (trombonist with Louis Prima), playing popular tunes and old jazz favorites. Sullivan also went on the road for a while with Susie Arden, a country-western artist who sang, played fiddle and guitar, and yodeled. Arden's band went to Jackson Hole, Wyoming, for a summerlong gig at the Cowboy Bar, where country music greats Homer and Jethro, also in town during the summers, would drop in. On a lark, Sullivan decided to take part in a play performed nightly in the town square during the summer, *The Hanging of Clover the Killer*, in which his character was shot and killed every night on a rooftop.[13]

When Arden's regular guitarist was released from jail, Sullivan returned to Las Vegas. He joined the trio of Mary Kaye (a Hawaiian singer whose real name was Mary Ka'aihue); in the late 1940s, she had been one of the earliest musical acts to work steadily in the Vegas lounges. The trio played music and did comedy, and they had a number of hit records prior to Sullivan's time in the group. Sullivan traveled all over the map with the trio—from the Nevada circuit to Anchorage, Alaska, to southern California, and to Kentucky.

When that tour broke up, Sullivan moved to Minnesota's Twin Cities, took up the banjo, and joined the Banjo Brass. That band was in residence for some time at Bulldog Pub, downstairs at Frenchy's Restaurant on North Avenue in Milwaukee.[14]

Around 1969, Sullivan decided to go out on his own, and he developed a solo act where he sang, played guitar, and emphasized the beat with a pair of hi-hat cymbals. When he got booked for a summer at the Flame Supper Club in Brainerd, Minnesota, his rhythm section evolved into a rhythm machine and a set of bass pedals. More importantly, the gig introduced him to his future wife, Karen.

When Karen was hired to teach home arts at Kohler High School in Wisconsin in 1971, the couple moved to Sheboygan.[15] Sullivan was still doing his one-man band, but through drummer Tony Wagner he met pianist John Harmon. Harmon was working with a trio at that time, but Sullivan began playing with him some, occasionally on bass. For a brief time, Sullivan ran a music store in Sheboygan, but the well-established Goodell Music convinced him that he'd be better off teaching for them than running his own business. Sullivan also taught jazz guitar for some years at Lawrence University.

Sullivan played in Sheboygan at the Executive Inn, but there was not much of a scene in the area for someone of his interest and ability. He worked wedding receptions and parties in the 1980s with the area band Patchwork, which included fine jazz saxophonist Gene Hunn. Sullivan also played with the Green Bay Packers Tailgate Band at Lambeau Field.

Sullivan most visibly displayed his jazz skills in groups led by Chuck Hedges (see chapter 10). (Sullivan appears with Hedges in the photo that accompanies Jack Carr's profile in chapter 10.) Hedges first hired Sullivan to play in the Milwaukee Connection in the early 2000s; the band played weekends at Selen's, on Layton Avenue near the airport. Also, after the guitarist in Hedges's Swingtet became ill, Sullivan played with that group weekly at Andy's in Chicago until Hedges's long tenure there ended. After several changes of ownership and a fire, the job at Selen's ended, but by then Sullivan had joined the Hedges group that played at the Grove in Elm Grove. Sullivan also played at jazz festivals with Hedges, including one memorable trip to Scotland, and he appears on four of Hedges's albums (see online discography).

In the Fox Valley, Sullivan played for some time with Brad Curran's group Dig, and for a while his son John (see chapter 9) joined the group on bass. After undertaking a true musical odyssey before landing in Sheboygan, Sullivan remains a vital player on the Wisconsin scene.

Marty Robinson

Marty Robinson and Matt Buchman grew up as contemporaries in the Fox Valley, attended Lawrence University together, left the area, but eventually returned to lead the jazz programs at UW–Oshkosh and UW–Stevens Point, respectively. Both are important Wisconsin jazz players.

Robinson was born in 1969 and grew up in Neenah. He started trumpet in school band in fifth grade. He had taken piano lessons, but as he notes, "[My teacher] probably didn't celebrate my creativity and . . . [my] not wanting to practice."

What drew Robinson deeper into music, and jazz, in particular, is a uniquely Wisconsin story.

> My family had the fortune of going to Packer games all the time. . . . And, my parents' tickets were literally right across the field from this amazing big band, led by Lovell Ives, with some of the best jazz musicians in the state playing great big band charts. . . . I really remember listening to them, and as a trumpet player, just being blown away by these amazing, screaming trumpet players, and . . . all the great charts . . . arranged for big band by Lovell.
>
> I think when I was in eighth grade I went down there and sat next to the band before the game. And I met this trumpet player, Al Butcher, who played second, and some of the solos in the band. . . .

I thought, "Hm. Maybe I should take lessons with this guy, 'cause he's really cool, and plays in this great jazz big band."

So in high school, Robinson studied with Butcher at UW–Oshkosh. Robinson also attended the UW–Green Bay jazz camp, where he says Lovell Ives "lit a fire" under him to write jazz. Lovell also suggested that Robinson get in touch with John Harmon. Soon enough, Robinson was driving to Winneconne for lessons with Harmon that combined improvisation, composing, arranging, and jazz piano.

The jazz program at Neenah High School had been established by one of the giants of Wisconsin jazz education, Dave Kiepert, some years earlier. But the program was still very strong when Robinson was there in the mid- to late 1980s, when it was being run by Gary Neustadter. Besides playing in the expected school groups, Robinson also started working with the Neenah Pop Strings, playing piano (with an occasional solo on trumpet), along with his buddy David Dunning, who played bass. (Dunning went on to become a fine trombonist, playing with many area jazz and classical groups, and has taught in the Neenah school district for years.) Robinson was not even thinking about attending Lawrence University until Fred Sturm heard the Neenah string group with Robinson soloing. Sturm's charisma won Robinson over, and he enrolled at Lawrence in 1987.

After a rewarding four years at Lawrence, Robinson was accepted into graduate school at the Eastman School of Music. Little did he know that Sturm would be offered a position at Eastman that same year, and the two began there at the same time. Robinson earned his master's in jazz studies in 1993. He moved to New York City, where he had success freelancing, often with the funk band Peanut Funker and Jam. He was also writing, composing, and teaching during that time. Despite his freelancing success, Robinson always thought he would be a teacher, and in 1994 he took a position at Florida A&M University, a historically black institution, where he taught trumpet and jazz studies for ten years. While at A&M, he earned a doctorate in composition at Florida State University.

Despite the excellent program and some very high-profile students who went through A&M (including trombonist Wycliffe Gordon and trumpeter Scotty Barnhart), Robinson jumped at the chance to return to

Mathew Buchman (left; see next section in this chapter) and Marty Robinson. COURTESY OF MARTY ROBINSON

his home state, near both his and his wife Anne's families, when the trumpet/jazz job opened up at Oshkosh. Since his return in 2004, Robinson has been a visible presence in the music scene in northeast Wisconsin, and he has strengthened the UWO jazz program. He has also been a member of the faculty at the Birch Creek Music Academy summer camps in Door County. Robinson is grateful to all of his teachers, but like many others, he feels most indebted to the mentorship he received from Fred Sturm and John Harmon.

Mathew Buchman

Mathew "Matt" Buchman, like his friend Marty Robinson, was born in 1969. Buchman grew up in Appleton. He began playing piano when he was four and took classical lessons into high school, when one of the most pivotal moments in his early musical life occurred.

> The first big fire that was lit under my butt was when John Harmon was commissioned to write a big piece [for band, orchestra, and choir] for Appleton High School West, . . . and he included a jazz quintet as well. . . . John was asked to conduct the piece . . . [so] the part that I think he had envisioned himself playing, which was piano in this quintet, . . . they pointed to me. I was so far out of my league. . . . [I was] scared out of my wits; but it was one of the most electrifying moments in my musical life, . . . playing in this quintet with Tom Washatka, John Gibson, Dane Richeson, and Jeff Pietrangelo.

After the performance, Buchman took lessons from Harmon before going on to attend Lawrence in 1987, where he followed a different path. Buchman started out as a composition major but spent most of his time in the jazz program. During his junior year at Lawrence, he says, "My grades took a nosedive." He was in a band called Nearvana, with Tom Washatka, guitarist Scott Dercks, bassist Ken Skitch, and drummer Brian Brinkman, that had steady work. Buchman took a temporary leave from Lawrence and began studying regularly with John Harmon. Around this time, a meeting with Lyle Mays (see chapter 7) at the UW–Stevens Point jazz festival led Buchman to study with this great keyboard artist sporadically over a period of years; Buchman would try to line up a lesson whenever Mays was staying at his farm outside of Columbus between tours with Pat Metheny. Before the last two of Buchman's six years in and out of Lawrence, Fred Sturm left and Ken Schaphorst took over the jazz program, so, as Buchman says, he got the "best of both worlds" working with the two of them.

After graduation, Buchman hit the road for a year with the show band Circus, playing all over the United States and Canada. When he returned to Wisconsin in 1994, he taught at the Arts World summer camp in Stevens Point and was recommended for a UWSP position when it was vacated by Laura Caviani. (Caviani, also a Lawrence grad and former student of John Harmon, has since become a prominent jazz pianist in Minneapolis–St. Paul.) Buchman was slowly and methodically promoted from a half-time position to head of the UWSP jazz program. In 2015, as he worked toward his doctorate in composition at UW–Madison, he was certainly one of the most in-demand pianists in the state, playing with Randy Sabien, Tom Washatka, Tom Gullion, and others. Buchman also runs the UW–Stevens Point Jazz Festival and has been the artistic director of the Riverfront Jazz Festival in Stevens Point since 2007.

Fred Sturm

Fred Sturm—who was the face of jazz studies at Lawrence University from the late 1970s to the early 1980s, and from 2002 to his death in 2014—was born in 1951 in Woodstock, Illinois, and spent his first twelve years in nearby Algonquin. Fred's grandfather was a string instrument maker and repairman in Chicago, and his father, Harry, grew up in the city playing cello. At age eighteen, Harry moved to Kansas City to be the principal cellist with the symphony there. After other stops on the symphonic circuit, he returned to his hometown as principal cellist with the NBC orchestra in Chicago, when the big radio stations still had staff orchestras. Later, Harry became associate principal cellist in the Chicago Symphony. Fred Sturm's mother, Kay, was a staff singer for a Chicago radio station and sang on records with comedy bandleader Spike Jones and others. Fred grew up hearing symphonic excerpts, solo cello works, and the string quartet that often rehearsed at their home. His mother also taught voice lessons at home and pursued an interest in American folk/pop. Fred's sisters Carolyn (a horn player) and Marina (a clarinetist) became professional symphonic players. Young Fred tried, but eventually resisted, lessons on voice, piano, cello, and violin.

After Harry Sturm became principal cellist and personnel manager for the new Milwaukee Symphony, the family moved to Oconomowoc. In eighth grade, Fred was strongly impressed by the playing of symphony principal trumpeter Charles Schlueter. Harry enlisted Schlueter (who went on to play in the Cleveland Orchestra and Boston Symphony) to teach Fred, who managed to catch up to the other local band kids, who had a two- or three-year head start on him, over the summer. Fred entered the Oconomowoc program, one of the strongest in the state, and began playing under junior high band director David Reul. Sitting in front of him was tenor saxophonist Tom Newburg (see chapter 15), who quickly became Sturm's best friend, musical partner, and later, a respected saxophonist in Milwaukee. Newburg already knew the music of Zoot Sims, Al Cohn, and the Woody Herman band, and he introduced Sturm to the music of those players. A summer visit to Fred's uncle Egon (a jobbing pianist and Hammond B-3 organist who Fred says was considered the "black sheep" of the family) led Sturm further into the music of Louis Armstrong and the jazz trumpet tradition.

At Oconomowoc High, Sturm and Newburg entered another top-notch program, led by the jazz-savvy Roger Gard. Gard would pack his most interested students into his car to go hear big bands, such as those led by Maynard Ferguson and Buddy Rich. A close encounter with Woody Herman's band fueled Sturm's interest in the genre.

> [My parents] gave me the keys to the station wagon. . . . [I] was the first guy [to McHenry, Illinois], and was far and away the youngest person in the room. . . . I sat about five feet from [pianist] Alan Broadbent in the rhythm section. . . . I don't think I picked my jaw up off the ground until about the end of the first set. I thought, "This is the greatest thing I've ever heard in my life."

Before he graduated from high school, Sturm had written his first big band arrangement.

Sturm entered Lawrence University in 1969, where he studied brass with Derald DeYoung and played in the concert bands of Fred "Prof" Schroeder. During Sturm's freshman year, as the jazz band prepared for its one concert of the year, Sturm remembered a senior trumpet player saying:

> "Hey man, the music that we play in the jazz band is such crap, why don't you write something?" I did an arrangement of "Watermelon Man." . . . And I remember the reaction of the guys when we were done reading it the first time. . . . It was the first, real musical pat on the back I got at Lawrence. . . . I felt like, "Wow, maybe I am going to amount to something after all."

At the end of his freshman year, Sturm confronted the fact that his embouchure was not well suited to the trumpet and switched to trombone, beginning study with his father's old Chicago Symphony friend, Frank Crisafulli. Sturm played euphonium and even tuba in the band at Lawrence but evolved into an accomplished bass trombonist.

Sturm became a prime contributor to the development of the jazz program at Lawrence. As a sophomore, he instigated the movement to get jazz band officially recognized and considered worthy of academic credit, even though the group was student run. Sturm's experience as the student leader of the jazz band was invaluable to his later career, both as a composer/arranger and a jazz educator. He connected with John Harmon, who took over the Lawrence program, and Harmon introduced Sturm to the music of Gil Evans, Clare Fischer, Thad Jones, and others outside the big band mainstream.

Sturm got valuable playing experience at the Melody Top dinner theater during the summers of his college years, sitting next to Milwaukee Symphony principal trombonist Don Haack and working with Vic Knutzen, Joe Aaron, and other top Milwaukee professionals.

Sturm went to graduate school at North Texas State University, which was the hottest big band jazz school in the country at that time. To his surprise, he ended up in the famous One O'Clock Band, a group filled with future jazz professionals. But Sturm wasn't completely happy with the cutthroat atmosphere at North Texas, and when the call came from Wisconsin that his old buddies were going to start a band in the summer of 1974, it was easy for Sturm to leave Texas behind.

The story of Matrix the Appleton band is told in chapter 12, but it must be mentioned here that Sturm's experience as a writer was crucial to the band's early success. He would write a medley of Beatles or Stevie Wonder tunes so that everyone in the club could recognize them, but the arrangement would be so sophisticated and artistic that it drew raves from the more hip members of the audience, and it would keep the players in the band challenged and happy. When Matrix performed in the spring of 1975 with the Milwaukee Symphony Orchestra, members of the orchestra (Sturm's father's peers) were amazed at the artistry of both Sturm's and Harmon's original works.

Sturm tired of life on the road before most of his Matrix colleagues did. After an unsettled period, he accepted an offer to teach at his alma mater, Lawrence. Without any formal teaching experience, Sturm quickly rebuilt the jazz program that Harmon had developed. Sturm stayed for fourteen years, and the Lawrence program became a significant player on the national scene. During his time teaching at Lawrence, Sturm had embarked upon a master's program at the Eastman School of Music in Rochester, New York, and become the teaching assistant to Rayburn Wright, head of the jazz program. After Wright died in 1990, Sturm was chosen to take over some of Wright's duties.

Shortly thereafter, Sturm left Lawrence and became the head of the program at Eastman, and the prominent position opened doors for him. He became an in-demand clinician all over the country, working in Europe and eventually writing extended works for jazz orchestras in Germany, Sweden, Scotland, and Norway. Sturm's students at Eastman went on to prominent careers as performers and writers in New York and southern California and as leading jazz educators throughout the country.

When Sturm left the program in Appleton, Ken Schaphorst, a composer/arranger of considerable originality, took over and kept Lawrence in the vanguard of college jazz education until he was tapped to lead the jazz program at the New England Conservatory. But when Schaphorst left and Lawrence began looking for his replacement, Sturm went from being a consultant for the position to a candidate. He decided that eleven years at Eastman was enough, and he returned home to Wisconsin in 2002, where he maintained Lawrence's position as a nationally recognized program.

Sturm was known as a "gold standard" jazz clinician from his earliest days at Lawrence. His irresistible personality, knowledge of literature, and pedagogical gifts led him to direct all-state groups and high school and college clinics all over the country (often writing commissioned compositions for the occasions). *Down Beat* magazine recognized Sturm with one of its prestigious Jazz Education Achievement Awards in 2010.

Sturm wrote works for Wynton Marsalis, Bob Brookmeyer, Clark Terry, Phil Woods, Gary Burton, Arild Andersen, Kurt Elling, and John Scofield, although they have not been released on commercial recordings. His theme albums with the hr-Bigband of Cologne, Germany, are available. His major project for Bobby McFerrin and the NDR Big Band, *Migrations: One World, Many Musics*, based on folk music from all over the world, premiered in 2007 and toured Europe the following summer.

Fred Sturm in the Lawrence University Chapel. COURTESY OF LAWRENCE UNIVERSITY

(McFerrin performed *Migrations* with the ensembles at Lawrence in 2010.) Sturm also created *The Baseball Music Project*, a program of music about our national pastime for symphony orchestra (written in part by Wisconsin transplant Maury Laws), which includes Sturm's nine-movement ode to the game, *Forever Spring*. The *Project* has been performed by the Boston Pops Orchestra and the Detroit and Chicago Symphonies, among others, including Wisconsin's Fox Valley Symphony, and often features Baseball Hall of Famer Dave Winfield as narrator.

In 2011, Sturm spearheaded the *Radiohead Jazz Project*—a collection of the progressive rock band's works arranged by many of Sturm's favorite writers. Three books by Sturm have also been published: *Changes over Time: The Evolution of Jazz Arranging*; *Kenny Wheeler: Collected Works on ECM*; and *Maria Schneider: Evanescence*.

After a decadelong battle with cancer, during which he continued to teach almost throughout, Sturm died at home on August 24, 2014. A memorial service held at the Lawrence University Chapel in November drew a huge crowd from all over the country, that included old friends, hundreds of Sturm's former students, and a wide swath of jazz educators and players who had been influenced by Sturm.

Patty Darling

Patricia Darling, known by her friends as Patty, was born Patty Schultz in Milwaukee in the 1960s. Her family moved to Manitowoc when she was a toddler, and she started piano lessons when she was six. She had already been playing around on an instrument at home: she describes it as "one of those little keyboards on a stand, . . . almost like a little accordion." She took formal lessons at Holy Family Conservatory of Music, where her teacher was Sister Alberta, who, Patty says, "was about . . . four feet tall, . . . about 120 years old, and stern as stern gets." For positive rewards at lessons, Sister Alberta would give away candies; for punishment, a student might receive a rap on the knuckles with a ruler. But Patty says the sister was "an excellent teacher" who gave her "a really good foundation in classical piano." During this time, Patty also played in the Holy Family Conservatory Orchestra.

She went to school at Washington Junior High and Lincoln High in Manitowoc. In junior high, Patty played with a little band that learned tunes by Chicago and other current rock bands. In high school, the young, ambitious band director John Greene was making a name for the Lincoln jazz band. At this time, a jazz festival experience made a profound difference in Patty's life.

> We're going to all the jazz fests every year. . . . [They] were very competitive. . . . I knew nothing about jazz, because I was only studying classical. . . . We get done, and the bands are tied; and the clinician came up onstage, and he said, "Well, the bands are really both good. You guys both deserve first, but I'm going to give it to [the other school]," and he said, "Here's why: because [Lincoln's] piano player doesn't know what she's doing."

Directing such an insult to an individual student would, it is hoped, never occur today. It could have destroyed Patty's desire to continue playing jazz. However, after getting over the initial mortification of causing her band to lose the contest, she transformed the experience into motivation. Greene steered Patty into private study with John Harmon.

Patty skipped out of school to drive to Harmon's home in Winneconne for her supposedly hourlong lessons, which usually stretched to two hours. In addition to piano and theory, she quickly moved into composition as well. She had already transcribed TV themes of the day—"Taxi" and "The Muppet Show"—for her school jazz band, and had even done some original composing. Harmon introduced her to a new world; he also wrote a piece for Patty to play with her school band.

During these years, Harmon introduced her to Fred Sturm; Patty also was deeply affected by seeing the band Matrix (the Appleton band, which included her future husband, Larry Darling). By her last year in high school, Patty was selected for the State Honors Jazz Ensemble, led that year by Sturm. That experience could have led Patty right to Lawrence for college, but, unsure about her educational path, she enrolled at UW–Green Bay in 1981.

Green Bay could have been a good choice. Patty studied composition there with Lovell Ives, and at the time Green Bay's jazz band was full of excellent players, including saxophonist Brian Simonds, trumpeter Mark Israel, and trombonist Mark Burditt. But Patty was strongly drawn to Lawrence, in part because of the studio orchestra program Sturm had established, with its exceptional opportunities for writing.

After a semester, with Lovell Ives's blessing, Patty transferred to Lawrence. Still hedging her bets, she briefly pursued a biology major in addition to her music major. She found another outstanding group of students at Lawrence, including trombonist John Caviani, trumpeter John Carlson, and fellow pianist Connie Trok. Besides studying with Sturm, she studied composition with Rodney Rogers.

Patty connected with Larry Darling when she wrote an arrangement for one of Sturm's classes that was recorded at Irish-Saxe Studios, where Larry was employed. They worked together in a local band that Larry led, and soon connected professionally and romantically.

Larry began recording on his own, first in his home on Packard Street

Patty Darling. COURTESY OF SEIZE THE MOMENT PHOTOGRAPHY

in Appleton and later on the farm that he and Patty bought outside of Dale, Wisconsin, with a newly outfitted basement studio. The Darlings ran a successful business producing jingles and advertisements. Patty wrote most of the material, and with the help of area musicians, Larry recorded it. The recordings produced in their studio, MIDI West, were heard on local airwaves for years. Eventually they moved from the world of fifteen- to thirty-second ad spots to background music for documentaries and training films. They established the Impact Music Library as a repository for much of Patty's music.

Things were going along very well until a variety of changes in the business and technology led to an industry bust. Larry started working part-time at Lawrence, in a new recording department; Patty held down the fort at the studio, and the couple raised their two sons. Eventually, the marriage broke up. Patty increased her private teaching load, helped out with her kids' music activities at school, and led music at their church. At one point, Fred Sturm asked Patty if she would be interested in leading the second jazz band at Lawrence. But, as she recalls, "The boys were struggling; it was a very, very hard transition for them, to have us split up, . . . and I turned it down."

In 2008, the Darlings' boys were better settled, in school and personally, and when Sturm offered Patty the job again, she accepted. "The learning curve was tough," she says, "because I was going into [the job] as a writer, but not really with a lot of chops as far as rehearsing large ensembles." Soon, however, Patty's gifts as an ensemble director became evident, and she has experienced great success in her work at Lawrence. She has also continued to write, and a number of her unique and very personal compositions and arrangements for big band have been published. When Sturm died, Patty took over the direction of the Lawrence University Jazz Ensemble as well as some of Sturm's other teaching duties. She has obvious gifts as an educator, which she attributes to the examples of her mentors John Harmon and Fred Sturm.

19

Outliers

Most of this book relates the stories of jazz musicians from southern, southeastern, and northeastern Wisconsin. This chapter focuses on musicians whose roots lie outside those areas in the state.

Bob Schulz

"Traditional jazz" cornet player Bob Schulz was born in Reedsburg, Wisconsin, July 1, 1938, and grew up in nearby Wonewoc (pronounced Wone-ee-walk), between Wisconsin Dells and La Crosse, in Juneau County.[1] The population of the village was about eight hundred when Schulz was a youth, and his father ran a local hardware store for many years. Schulz followed his older brother and sister to the local piano teacher, but, he says, "I got yelled at by the teacher, and I guess I cried." His mother told him he didn't have to take lessons, but of the four siblings, he was the only one who went on to play. The family trumpet was passed down from his sister to his brother and finally to Schulz.

Schulz began playing in school band in fifth grade and soon joined the local American Legion band, which turned into a city band that played outdoor summer concerts. Since there was no city park in town, the band set up in an empty lot between the post office and the bakery. In this band, Schulz played trumpet trios with his brother Bud as well as Norm Kingsley, a former member of Horace Heidt's Swing Era dance band.[2]

The summer after his high school graduation, Schulz played with his high school band director, Jerry Bernard, in a quintet that played pop tunes of the 1930s and 1940s at the Crystal Bar in Mauston. Schulz recalls being paid nine dollars a night for the four-hour jobs that became his introduction to professional life.

In the mid-1950s, Schulz enrolled at what was then Wisconsin State College–La Crosse. He told music writer Rosemary Hallum that he went to college with the intention of becoming an athletic coach. But, he says,

> after the first semester I changed my mind, deciding I'd rather work with kids in music. I lettered in track (high and low hurdles) as well as being in the band, chorus, and symphonia. There was no music major at La Crosse, so my major was social studies with music and biology minors.

One summer during his college years, Schulz went back to playing with Jerry Bernard at the Valley Inn Country Club in Elroy. During college, Schulz put together the Four Sophs, a band that mostly played for high school homecomings and proms. He recalls that the band members wore "Bermuda shorts and white shirts and ties and blazers."

After finishing college, Schulz joined the Wisconsin National Guard. In the service, he remembers,

> I went to basic training in Fort Leonard Wood, Missouri, and from there I went to Fort Knox, Kentucky, where I was schooling as a track-vehicle mechanic [*laughter*]. And I'd no sooner joined that and finished my training, [than I] came back in December and couldn't get a teaching job at the time, so I went back to college and took another semester.

Finally out of school, Schulz got a teaching job in little Reeseville, in Dodge County. He says, "I was the band director for the high school, the chorus director, and I had general music in first through eighth grade in one school, music lessons in [nearby town] Lowell, and music lessons and choir in Reeseville." For good measure, Schulz also taught world history and supervised study hall. Despite the huge teaching load, he was young and energetic, and he loved the job. However, after one semester, the National Guard came calling.

Upon moving to Reeseville, Schulz transferred to the Guard's Thirty-Second Division Band. In early 1962, the division was called to active duty, which turned out to be a good thing for Schulz. The division was sent to Fort Lewis in Washington State, where he says "they needed music for all these little special things, and [the division] formed a little Dixieland band." The band also played every Sunday night at the non-commissioned officers' club. The group was stationed at Fort Lewis only between January and August of 1962, after which Schulz returned to Reeseville. But most of the service band members, including Schultz, continued to play together in Wisconsin as the Riverboat Ramblers.

Schulz started a family and continued teaching in Reeseville until 1968, when he moved to Lake Mills, in Jefferson County, for a position in the local schools. At Lake Mills, he was responsible for junior high band and lessons at the high school, where he also helped out with marching band and started a jazz ensemble. After the high school band director Franklin Else retired, Schulz took over his duties and began working full-time at the high school. Schulz particularly enjoyed taking the school band as Wisconsin's representative to Disney World's Bicentennial Parade in 1976.

In the meantime, the Riverboat Ramblers remained active, playing all over southern Wisconsin and beyond. The band played on the Mississippi River in St. Louis at the 1979 Ragtime Festival, and, as luck would have it, they were heard by trombonist Turk Murphy, one of the biggest names in traditional jazz. Murphy liked what he heard and asked Schulz to join his world-famous band in San Francisco. Having just gone through a divorce, Schulz was ready for a change in his life and career and jumped at the chance.

Schulz played at Murphy's San Francisco club, Earthquake McGoon's, until it closed in 1984. He began singing with Murphy early on and to this day remains an engaging vocalist. Schulz and Murphy continued to make many records together until Murphy's death in 1987. Not long after that, Schulz began recording and working with a band he called the Frisco Band, the name of a band led by Bob Scobey years earlier. Scobey had spent most of his career in San Francisco and had appeared with Murphy over the years, in addition to leading his own band—he was one of Schulz's early cornet heroes.

While he has had a long, profitable, and rewarding career in California, and his Frisco Band remains his primary music vehicle, Schulz also

Bob Schulz. PHOTO BY JOHN FORTIER

makes appearances all over the country in various combinations. He appears virtually every year at the Bunny Berigan Jazz Jubilee in Fox Lake and elsewhere in the Midwest, often billed with his Mid-West All Stars. Bob Schulz may have lived in California for decades, but he remains close to his Wisconsin roots.

Steve Zenz

Drummer Steve Zenz was born in Chippewa Falls in 1949.[3] He says,

> I got into the music field, because I was always in trouble in junior high, . . . and I decided I wanted to learn how to play drums . . . just because I thought it would be pretty easy, and it would be fun; it would be something I could do. And I found that as I took a lesson, and especially got into eighth grade band, that I really liked this. . . . It was something I wasn't getting into trouble with; it was productive.

Zenz's first music job was in 1963 with a band called the Auroras that played at his junior high graduation dance. The band knew only three tunes (including the drum feature "Wipeout"), which they played over and over. At the end of the dance, each member was paid around two dollars. Zenz's high school rock band, the Matchmen, played tunes by bands like the Ventures; when the Beatles hit the United States, suddenly vocals became a necessity for a rock and roll band, as well as a sound system, which the Matchmen constructed with cardboard boxes and an old jukebox amplifier.

Bill Hoppe, the owner of a Chippewa Falls music store, let kids come into his store and listen to his jazz records—that's where Zenz got the jazz itch. At age sixteen he accepted an offer from an area bandleader, Conrad Johns (given name, Johnstad), to play Dixieland and swing with his band. Subbing for the regular drummer, young Zenz sometimes played six nights a week, often at Eau Claire's Yardfor Supper Club. Eventually strippers became part of the entertainment, and Zenz had to sit in the cloakroom between sets as he was underage and not allowed in the area where alcohol was served.

Upon high school graduation, Zenz attended nearby UW–Eau Claire. In his first year there, the 1967–1968 school year, Zenz says, "I got an inkling of what an aesthetic experience was like. . . . I went, 'Oh, man! This is better than just fun.'" Dominic Spera came to Eau Claire the next year, and the jazz program took off. Zenz was not just playing at school, however. He played in blues bands with pianist Chuck Solberg, including the Last Fair Deal, which played Monday nights at the Joynt in Eau Claire, for which Zenz was paid ten dollars a night. He played a show for George Hamilton IV (a country artist famous for the 1963 hit "Abilene") at Turtle Lake High School and made sixty dollars, a pretty penny in those days. Music seemed to Zenz like a possible a way to make a living.

Zenz claims to have flunked out of school at UWEC twice, as he was almost exclusively interested in Spera's jazz band and nothing else academically. In 1972 he left school of his own volition to tour with the Count Three Road Show, what he called a "Holiday Inn band," for $150 a week. Having played mostly in country and polka bands until that time, Zenz says he enjoyed the "twelve different colored tuxedos and all that." He was on the road for about a year, but, newly married and with a child on the way, he realized that he needed a college degree.

After completing a music education degree at UW–Eau Claire, Zenz took a three-day-a-week position teaching elementary music in Augusta (southeast of Eau Claire) and taught percussion at UW–La Crosse one day a week. In the meantime he played constantly with big bands that toured through the area—including those of Les and Larry Elgart, Blue Barron, and Bob Crosby—as well as small bands. He worked for years with musicians from Lawrence Welk's band when they toured, especially accordion player Myron Floren and vocalist Dick Dale. Zenz was playing so much during this time that he quit the job at Augusta.

Besides teaching at La Crosse, he also taught for a while at Luther College in Iowa and at Mount Senario College in northern Wisconsin at Ladysmith. He eventually joined an Eau Claire group that performed for young audiences all over the state, especially in Milwaukee elementary schools (up to four performances a day). Zenz replaced Ron Keezer in the group, joining Dominic Spera, Lyle Mays, and Jerry Way on bass, but in the "heyday" period a few years later, Noreen Grey was on piano and Bob Sutherland on trumpet. (An early photograph of this group before Zenz replaced Keezer appears in Dominic Spera's profile in chapter 17). Zenz also taught at jazz camps around the state, beginning at Shell Lake in the early 1970s.

After a summer spent touring with his old rock band, Zenz and his family moved to Fond du Lac in 1979. "I started to get entrenched, be it ever so slowly, in the Milwaukee music scene, and in Madison," he says. "Essentially I'd go to Madison and play jazz gigs for . . . little or no money. But I was getting calls in Milwaukee to play some commercial gigs, and those paid more money." In Milwaukee, he played with a show band in La Playa, the nightclub on the top floor of the Pfister Hotel (now called Blu), first led by Chuck Howard, then by Dennis Klopfer. On off nights, he would job, often at Hooligan's, with a bluesy band called the Strokes, with his old boss, Chuck Solberg; Chuck's brother, blues guitarist Jimmy Solberg; and jazz horn players Tom Newburg and Tom Baker. After that period, Zenz made good money playing casuals with the society band of Ernie Brusubardis, largely in the prosperous northern suburbs of Milwaukee.

Veteran Milwaukee musicians at Allen Johnson's retirement party. Left to right, back row: Bill Stone, Tom Newburg, and Ernie Brusubardis; front row: Duane Stuermer, Allen Johnson, and Steve Zenz. COURTESY OF STEVE ZENZ

In 1983, Zenz and Mike Irish were hired to run the new jazz program at UW–Stevens Point. In order to maintain the position, Zenz was told that he needed a master's degree. He earned that degree at Stevens Point in jazz studies—a degree program that he helped write—studying with his friends Irish, Bob Kase, and John Radd, who was hired a few years after Zenz. Throughout this time, Zenz was still jobbing heavily in Milwaukee and doing clinics and concerts around the state.

Zenz's marriage broke up in 1988, and he took a leave from UWSP and worked for a semester playing on cruise ships. When he returned, he worked at music camps at Stevens Point, UW–Green Bay, and Birch Creek in Door County, and he met the woman who became his second wife.

But driving around the state was becoming exhausting, and Zenz's job in Stevens Point was still part-time. In 1991, he officially left UWSP to go back into public school teaching. He substituted for a year at Hamilton High in Milwaukee, then landed a full-time job in Slinger.

In the mid-2000s, through a program at UW–River Falls, Zenz was placed in an exchange program in Argentina. While spending four weeks in Cordoba observing, taking notes, giving clinics, and doing in-service programs, Zenz met German Siman, who ran a small conservatory in the area. Using Shell Lake as a model, Zenz helped Siman start a jazz camp in a monastery in Jesús María, Argentina. Zenz worked there for three years. When he returned from the United States around 2010, the camp had grown to include more than one hundred students, not only Argentines but also students from Chile and Brazil, with a crackerjack teaching staff of young professional musicians mostly from Buenos Aires. Siman made a connection with New York's Jazz at Lincoln Center, and the future of the camp seems bright.

Though Zenz has retired from full-time teaching, he still teaches at Shell Lake and at the camp in Argentina, and he is still a presence on the jazz scene in Wisconsin.

Randy Sabien

Randy Sabien was born in Rockford, Illinois, in 1956. He didn't move to Wisconsin until the 1970s, but his connection to Wisconsin began at an early age. Sabien's great-grandparents had settled near Shell Lake, north of Eau Claire, and his family visited there in Randy's youth. "I just loved being on a lake in northern Wisconsin," he says. "My earliest childhood memories are from being put in the backseat of the car, early in the morning, and driving up."

From the time he was very young, Sabien says, "I wanted to be a rock and roll drummer, because of the Beatles, basically." He started drums in fourth grade, but his teacher was the high school orchestra conductor, who soon talked young Sabien into taking up violin. He took classical lessons throughout school, but Sabien retained an interest in rock and roll, blues, and folk music.

> I learned to play the guitar; writing songs and being in a rock band was all part of my scheme. . . . Little by little, that music started leaking onto the violin, . . . first through some fiddling, and then, there were some rock bands in the 1960s that had violin players: Hot Tuna, Jefferson Airplane, and Dan Hicks and His Hot Licks.

Sabien enrolled at the University of Illinois at Champaign-Urbana in 1974. At a concert by Asleep at the Wheel, which had two violinists, he spoke to one who turned him on to jazz violin pioneers Joe Venuti and Stephane Grappelli. Excited by this music, Sabien joined a jazz band at the U of I, where John Garvey's jazz program was one of the strongest in the country. Sabien also played in Garvey's balalaika orchestra, in which he played the Russian folk instrument. In 1977, he went to Boston to attend the Berklee College of Music. By the spring of 1978, Sabien had transferred to the University of Wisconsin–Eau Claire. That summer he started a string camp at the Shell Lake Arts Center, which was a top summer destination for jazz students and educators at the time.

But in the fall of 1978, Berklee determined that it was time to have a string department, and they hired Sabien to start it. According to Sabien, it was the "first string department where you could get a degree in what would be called jazz or contemporary music on the violin, viola, and cello." He ran the program for three years, interacting with great faculty colleagues and jobbing in a duo with faculty guitarist Larry Baione.

Sabien was playing and teaching, but the pay at Berklee was very low, he wanted to perform full-time, and he didn't particularly like living on the East Coast. He returned to Wisconsin (living near Madison) in 1981 and toured as a duo with folk singer Jim Post, playing violin, mandolin, guitar, and some piano. Sabien really wanted to lead his own jazz group, and in 1982 he put together a band called the Randy Sabien Jazz Quintet that included Wisconsinites Mike Dowling, Peter Dominguez, and Steve Zenz, and recorded his first album as leader, *In a Fog*, which was released in 1983.

Sabien moved to Eau Claire in 1983. In a simplified summing up of his career since that time, he says,

> That was the start of me putting rhythm sections together and living in Wisconsin, where I felt comfortable living. . . . Basically, since 1983 I've been doing the same thing. . . . I go off by myself and meet up with the band and play the gig, and spend the night and go on to the next gig or go home. And do some workshops along the way, with high school orchestras, or . . . public school string programs, from fourth grade through high school.

Randy Sabien. PHOTO BY ALICE GEBURA; COURTESY OF RANDY SABIEN

Sabien has continued on that path for over three decades now. The band for his second record, *Fiddlehead Blues* (1988), was a group of Madison-based players: drummer Clyde Stubblefield, bassist Jeff Eckels, keyboard player Dan Kleiman, and Mike Dowling. Sabien frequently performed live with this band, driving from his home (eventually in Hayward) to meet them wherever the gig might be.

A residency in Colorado led to Sabien's third record. His wife was training as a competitive cyclist in Colorado, and Sabien tagged along, playing gigs and making connections. He became an artist in residence in Crested Butte, near Aspen. The album, *The Sound of Fish Dreaming*, was written in Colorado but recorded by Wisconsin musicians, including his frequent companions from the Fox Valley: John Harmon, John Gibson, and Dane Richeson.

Two other jazz albums under Sabien's name have followed (see online discography). Besides his jazz gigs, he performs frequently at the Big Top Chautauqua in Bayfield. He enjoys working at the nationally known Café Carpe in Fort Atkinson (run by singer/songwriter Bill Camplin). Sabien performs with orchestras using some arrangements that were used by the great Joe Venuti.

In 2009, Sabien founded the alternative string department at McNally Smith College in St. Paul, Minnesota, where he has a home, while also maintaining his home in Hayward. He admits to being stunned that he has been able to lead this successful career in the Midwest.

> [Musicians] who come to the Midwest have this idea that somehow an audience in New York is going to be different; they're the same. . . . I talk to my friends in New York, or Chicago even. They're envious of me; I live in Wisconsin and I have gigs. I hire some of these people to play with me; [they say], "God, I don't make this much money when I go play a club [in the big city]." So I'm just thrilled . . . to continue to live in a beautiful place . . . and travel through Wisconsin and the Upper Midwest playing music that I love to play with people that I love to hang out with. What could be better than that?

Matt Turner

Matt Turner might not call himself a jazz musician, but he has been a vital member of a number of different jazz scenes in Wisconsin. At Lawrence University, where he has taught off and on for many years, he leads the Improvisation Group of Lawrence University, which reflects the diverse musical interests of its leader.

Turner was born in Platteville in 1966. Both of his parents were music teachers in the public schools there. His father was an orchestra director—originally a saxophonist, he played the music of Charlie Parker and John Coltrane at home—and he enjoyed the music of such experimental composers as Morton Feldman and George Crumb. Matt Turner didn't love his early violin lessons, but when he started piano lessons at age eight and cello lessons at age nine, his fate was sealed. By fifth grade, he had formed a rock band with some of his buddies; they played blues, Beatles, and even originals. As a teenager, Turner met Randy Sabien at the Shell Lake music camp, which opened Turner's eyes to the possibility of improvising jazz on a stringed instrument.

Continued classical studies on both cello and piano led Turner to consider Lawrence University for college. While he planned to be a classical cello major, the jazz program was a strong selling point. Besides working with John Harmon and Fred Sturm (playing piano in the jazz ensembles), Turner studied composition at the college with Rodney Rogers.

After Lawrence, Turner went to graduate school at the New England Conservatory, where he was in the Third Stream Studies program. He studied piano with Geri Allen and cello with bassist Dave Holland. A bigger influence on Turner, however, was the unsung Joe Maneri, a saxophonist. After school, Turner spent a year in Indiana, where his wife was teaching before they returned to Wisconsin in 1993.

Turner soon became active in several different scenes. He frequently worked in Madison, often in the musical situations created by guitarist Scott Fields, who put together projects with improvisers of different stripes, mostly cutting-edge experimentalists. Through Fields, Turner worked and recorded (almost exclusively on cello) with such musicians as Art Ensemble of Chicago saxophonist Joseph Jarman, pianists Myra Melford and Marilyn Crispell, and European artists as well. Turner developed a unique, progressive voice on electric cello.

In the Fox Valley, Turner performed on cello and piano. He worked with a trio that included Dane Richeson and multi-instrumentalist/composer Ken Schaphorst. He played piano with what he calls the Valley's "usual suspects": Janet Planet, Tom Washatka, John Gibson, and drummer Ryan Korb. For a while, Turner the pianist was frequently in the company of bassist Charles "Chuck" Ledvina, during Ledvina's residency "up

Matt Turner, with Bill Carrothers behind him on piano. PHOTO BY JOE TONDU

north" in Appleton. (Ledvina moved there from Milwaukee, and some years later moved back.)

Turner has worked in Milwaukee and Chicago with musicians who are improvisers but not jazz players, such as Steve Nelson-Raney and Hal Rammell. Turner has also worked with folk musician L. J. Booth and singer/songwriter Keller Mason.

A more recent collaboration that has borne much musical fruit is Turner's association with pianist Bill Carrothers. Carrothers, who developed a sterling reputation in New York in the late 1980s and early 1990s, moved to Michigan's Upper Peninsula in the 2000s and joined the Lawrence faculty in 2013. Turner has recorded several fascinating albums of improvised music with Carrothers, and a trio album of improvisations with Carrothers and French clarinetist Jean-Marc Foltz (see online discography for these and other albums on which Turner plays). Turner's constant exploration of improvisation, jazz, and other music styles has made him a significant and singular figure on the Wisconsin music scene.

Mark Urness

Bassist Mark Urness was born in Platteville in 1971. His high school orchestra director was Matt Turner's father, Bill, whose teaching methods were unorthodox to say the least. Urness remembers,

> [At] my very first lesson, you're sitting with a bunch of young bass players, and instead of saying, "Here's how to hold [the instrument], you have to make sure to do this; do that," [Mr. Turner] says, "Here's how you make all these crazy sounds." And he showed us, . . . banging on the bridge, and percussion sounds, and how to make it sound like a barking dog. He said, "Okay, take these things home, and see how many crazy sounds you can make."

Soon, Urness thought it was normal that all the violinists in his fifth-grade orchestra lined up to take improvised blues choruses. "I didn't find out until much later that that was unique and innovative," he says. Through middle and high school, Urness took lessons with Mr. Turner, studying jazz theory and improvisation concepts.

In high school, Urness was selected to play in the State Honors Jazz Ensemble (Ethan Iverson was also in the band; see chapter 7). Bob Washut, director of the jazz program at the University of Northern Iowa, led that year's band, and his influence steered Urness to Cedar Falls for college, and eventually a degree from UNI. Besides playing in a strong jazz program, Urness had the opportunity in college to spend time with master bassists Drew Gress and John Clayton.

Urness went to graduate school at the University of Cincinnati College-Conservatory, studying classical bass. Upon finishing his master's degree, he was hired to teach bass at his alma mater (UNI) as well as to serve as principal bass in the Cedar Rapids Symphony. "But I always wanted to be in New York," he says. So after two years, he and his wife moved to the big city. As a freelancer, Urness played whatever gigs came his way. He worked at the world-famous Knitting Factory, in the band of trombonist Curtis Fowlkes. While playing whenever possible, Urness also went to school to study computers and got a day gig in the IT field. Not feeling completely comfortable in New York, the Urnesses moved back to Iowa when the internet bubble burst. Urness was able to return to his position in the Cedar Rapids Symphony and taught in Iowa City while beginning more graduate work at the University of Iowa. He taught an interdisciplinary program, combining music studies with computer science.

In 2003, Matt Turner called Urness to let him know of a bass opening at Lawrence University. Urness secured the job and intended to continue the music-computer combination at his new school. However, his bass duties—in both the classical and jazz areas—and other teaching commitments quickly filled his teaching load.

At Lawrence, Urness has worked with outstanding guest artists such as Benny Golson, Danilo Perez, and Kenny Wheeler. He has become the first-call bassist in the area and plays with many bands, local and national, in the Jazz at the Trout series and at the Fox Jazz Festival. (Urness appears in the photo that accompanies Tom Gullion's profile later in this chapter.) However, Urness values his experience with his Lawrence colleague Bill Carrothers as much as any other he has had.

At Lawrence, Urness has been heavily involved as a mentor to students whom he describes as "of different cultural and racial backgrounds" (largely from New York City) who have been brought to campus in the Lawrence Posse Foundation program. Urness continues to contribute to the richness of jazz in Wisconsin while serving a broader purpose as a mentor.

Greg Balfany

Two prime movers of jazz in La Crosse during the past several decades are longtime University of Wisconsin–La Crosse faculty members Greg Balfany and Karyn Quinn. Greg Balfany was born in La Crosse in 1949. He grew up in the city and attended Emerson Elementary School and Lincoln Junior High. He joined his elementary band on clarinet and made quick progress, but he eventually quit because of boredom, since his elementary director had to deal with fifty kids all at once.

At Lincoln, band director Don Hoffmeister made a big impression on young Balfany, but he also remembers, "[Hoffmeister] made me promise every lesson that I would not go into music." At Central High, band director Bill Baker was a biology teacher, and the band program was lacking in many respects. Yet, Balfany says, "Bill Baker was a very inspirational person and a lot of people became music teachers and directors and performers because of him." Dave Seiler, a La Crosse native who later became an important jazz educator, moved back to town before Balfany's senior year and gave him clarinet lessons.

Upon graduation from Central, Balfany passed up a small scholarship to study science at the University of Chicago and went to the University of Idaho instead. He initially intended to become a nuclear physicist but decided to study music, and became a clarinet major while getting a music education degree. Though Balfany has been known during his professional career as a jazz saxophonist, he never studied saxophone formally until working on his doctorate. He was a member of the first band of college students to play the summer season at Disneyland, in 1971, and calls it the "best job I ever had." (The students were paid union wages and made more money than some of the regular Disney workers.) After college graduation, Balfany turned down a junior high teaching job in Bountiful, Utah, choosing to go on the road for a couple of years instead.

In the early 1970s, he played in one band that was led by a former high school mate who, Balfany says, "fancied himself an entertainer . . . in a Liberace mode. And he played really nice cocktail, effervescent, fluorescent piano. . . . We played the Left Guards [a restaurant chain run by Green Bay Packers Fuzzy Thurston and Max McGee]. Places like that." Another of Balfany's bands, Good and Plenty, worked out of Milwaukee. A third group was led by Duilio Mordini, who Balfany remembers as "a phenom enal singer."

When his father died in 1974, Balfany returned to La Crosse to run his dad's tavern, the Buckhorn, until the estate was liquidated. Realizing that he was not going to make a living on the road, Balfany reconnected with Dave Seiler, who led him to a graduate assistantship at the University of New Hampshire. While there, Balfany got quite a bit of jobbing work in New England, often with a jazz quartet that included keyboard player Gregg Mangiafico (who later became a successful "jingles" player in New York) and guitarist Brian Rolland (who went on to fame in the New Age market). In 1976, Balfany played in a big band put together by Seiler that toured Europe with jazz great Clark Terry.

Greg Balfany and Karyn Quinn (see next section in this chapter).
COURTESY OF GREG BALFANY

After leaving New Hampshire, Balfany taught high school in Maine, still doing a lot of playing in the Northeast. In the summer of 1978, he was faced with a few options: stay in Maine, take a sabbatical replacement job back at UNH, or travel to Reno to play with a show band at the brand-new MGM. He chose New Hampshire, and married Martha that year.

A job at UW–La Crosse opened in 1979, and Balfany was offered the position. Though they did not plan to stay long in his hometown, Balfany and Martha are still in La Crosse more than thirty-five years later.

Despite challenges achieving balance among different instruments in the band, Balfany was leading three jazz bands by his second year at UWL. A few years later, his position became tenure track, at which time he began work on a doctoral degree at UW–Madison. He completed the degree in the late 1980s; his dissertation was a study of popular jazz saxophonists David Sanborn and Stanley Turrentine. At one point, Sanborn flew Balfany out to New York, where he spent three days with the blues/jazz icon while Sanborn recorded an album. Balfany had arranged a similar meeting with Turrentine, but the drug-addicted saxophonist made one of his periodic disappearances, and it didn't happen.

In addition to his other professional activities, Balfany taught for twenty years at the New Hampshire summer camps. In La Crosse, Balfany founded the Great River Band in 1972 (now known as the La Crosse Jazz Orchestra).[4] It features some of the finest players in the western part of the state, including saxophonists Jeff Erickson (from Stevens Point) and Jeff Reitz, lead trumpeter "Bucky" Buchholtz, bassist Karyn Quinn, and drummers Tim Henke and Rich MacDonald. It has backed up all sorts of entertainers, including jazz musicians Ed Shaughnessy, Bob Mintzer, Curtis Fuller, Kurt Elling, and Clark Terry. Besides other performances in a variety of venues, the band has played a summer series of concerts in La Crosse area parks for over thirty-five years.

Balfany retired from full-time teaching in 2012 but remains active around the state.

Karyn Quinn

Karyn Quinn was born in La Crosse in 1962 but grew up in Ellsworth, Wisconsin. She took piano lessons while in elementary school. Before starting school music, she played in the neighborhood with the children of one of Wisconsin's top jazz educators, Dave Kiepert, who was her band director when she started percussion in sixth grade. She took summer lessons from celebrated pedagogue Harvey Halpaus, her junior high band director. In seventh grade, Quinn joined choir when an inspiring teacher, Mary Lee Huber, returned from the Fox Valley to teach in her hometown. Working with Huber and Halpaus, Quinn says, "You couldn't help but love music."

Quinn took up the challenge of learning bass guitar so that she could play in the new junior high jazz band. Soon she was playing not only in a big band, but in a combo as well. Partway through her seventh-grade year, she was also in a ninth-grade small group. (Halpaus says, "She was a fast learner.") The pianist in the combo was Connie Trok, who has gone on to a successful music career in Washington, DC, under the name Connie Olivera. Halpaus got Quinn to write out bass lines for blues and sent her home with recordings by Woody Herman, Art Blakey, and other jazz greats. Quinn says she thought, "Well, electric bass is cool, but I need to learn how to play the string bass; I'm going to be a jazz bass player." She also decided to be a music teacher. She had played ice hockey in sixth grade, but once she fell in love with music, Quinn decided to quit hockey for fear of hurting her fingers. The junior and senior high jazz bands from Ellsworth competed at the UW–Eau Claire and UW–Green Bay festivals, where they excelled.

By the time Quinn got to high school, Kiepert had left town. But Halpaus continued to develop the jazz program that he and Kiepert had established at Ellsworth. John Lingenfelder capably continued the band program, but Halpaus remained Quinn's mentor, and this somewhat odd couple attended jazz events together all over the country, including at the National Association of Jazz Educators conference in Dallas in January 1978, where they heard the Wisconsin group Matrix (the Appleton band) perform. After that, Quinn and Halpaus would go see Matrix anytime the band was in the area. They heard many other jazz bands, especially at the Prom Center in St. Paul. Quinn profited during high school from the frequent visits to Ellsworth of pianist John Radd, who was teaching at nearby UW–River Falls.

Quinn played for three years in the Kids from Wisconsin and was a member of the very first two State Honors Jazz Ensembles, in 1978 and 1979. (The pianists in those bands were Radd's son Peter and David Stoler, respectively; see chapter 16.) Quinn played in student jazz recitals at River Falls. She also took lessons from the Twin Cities bassist Billy Peterson. While Quinn was still in high school, a couple of lessons with Minnesota Orchestra bassist James Klute made her realize how much work she had to do in the classical world. During her senior year, renowned vocal jazz arranger Phil Mattson brought his college group to Ellsworth, and upon hearing Quinn, asked her to join a combo and play with the jazz vocal groups at Shell Lake Camp in northern Wisconsin and at a Western Michigan University camp the following summer. She did both.

In 1980 Quinn entered the University of Wisconsin–La Crosse. "I got in [to school] more as a percussionist than as a bassist," she says, since she played snare drum in La Crosse's marching band. She studied hard and played in the school's big bands on acoustic and electric bass. After her freshman year, Quinn got a call from John Radd to play a six-week engagement in South Haven, Michigan, with a combo led by Don Greene, who was on the music faculty at UW–Stevens Point. When she got back to La Crosse in the fall, Quinn played with drummer Mike Sturgis, who has since gone on to a notable career in rock and roll and now lives in London. There was substantial musical activity in the city during this time, and while she was a student, Quinn played in small city bands led by John Alexander, Greg Balfany, and trumpeter Dick Chaffee. Quinn completed her music education degree in 1985.

After finishing at La Crosse, she went to graduate school at the University of Northern Colorado with an assistantship in vocal jazz. Two Wisconsin trumpeters were there as graduate students: Mark Israel, who ended up having a long career as a jazz player in the armed forces, and Mike Hale (see chapter 17), who led the big band at UNC during Quinn's first year there. Two years later, Quinn returned to La Crosse and taught at Central High School and Lincoln Middle School, filling in for Martha Balfany, who was on maternity leave. Quinn taught as a substitute in the city system for the rest of the year. Next, she taught jazz for a year at Michigan Tech University in Houghton. Quinn brought legendary jazz trumpeter Clark Terry to Houghton, where he played in a combo with Quinn, John Radd, guitarist Mike Irish, and Steve Zenz. This led to Quinn being hired to work at Terry's Summer Big Band Camp in Le Mars, Iowa.

In 1989, Quinn returned to UW–La Crosse in a part-time position. Coincidentally, just a couple of years later, Clark Terry's camp moved to the La Crosse campus. During one wildly successful summer, the faculty included jazz greats Snooky Young, Marshall Royal, Al Grey, Red Holloway, and Ed Shaughnessy. That year Terry was filmed for the *Sunday*

Morning with Charles Kuralt television show. But for reasons that neither Balfany nor Quinn understand, they were not able to recruit enough students to hold the camp the next year.

For many years, Quinn led the vocal jazz program and the second jazz band and taught jazz history at UWL; she eventually substituted music theory for vocal jazz. She was the recipient of a National Endowment for the Arts Jazz Fellowship to study with eminent jazz bassist Rufus Reid, and was a finalist in the 1997 International Association of Bassists Jazz Bass Competition. Quinn became active in the Wisconsin Music Educators Association and the International Association of Jazz Educators and served as president of the state chapter of the latter. She has been in constant demand as a bass player all over the state as well as in Minnesota and Iowa. In the fall of 2014, Quinn went to China for a week with an exclusive group of Western jazz musicians, including international stars Eric Alexander and Swedish trombonist Nils Landgren, as well as Wisconsinite Mark Israel, for the second annual China (Shanghai) Jazz Festival and Competition.

When Greg Balfany retired from full-time teaching in 2014, Quinn took over as director of jazz studies at UW–La Crosse. She retired in the spring of 2017.

Jeff Erickson

Saxophonist Jeff Erickson is another important jazz educator and player in Wisconsin. He was born in Appleton in 1962. He began his music studies in the successful instrumental program that Sam Ostwald led at Einstein Junior High. Erickson had a rocky start in junior high band thanks to his self-proclaimed "bad attitude," and he tried hard to quit during his first year. But in his second year, he was bumped up a level musically and responded to the challenge with great improvement.

Erickson's interest in jazz was sparked during his high school years at Appleton West, in Ike Spangenberg's program. Spangenberg kept jazz albums at school, and students were encouraged to take them home for listening. Erickson was attracted to Sonny Fortune, and then the albums of the 1950s Miles Davis quintet. By the time he graduated from West in 1980, he says, the jazz ensemble was "kind of my identity."

Jeff Erickson. PHOTO BY PAULA DEHART; COURTESY OF JEFF ERICKSON

That summer, when Erickson went to the University of Wisconsin–Madison for new student orientation, the barrage of music requirements that he would face as a music major made him decide to go into business. But, he says, "I took as many things out of business as I could," including courses in acting, philosophy, and women's studies.

After his UW graduation, following in the footsteps of his CPA father, Erickson went to Minneapolis–St. Paul to start a job at an accounting firm. He says that's when "I found out what I *really* didn't want to do." He took saxophone lessons at the University of Minnesota, and after working all day he would practice late into the night. After a year, Erickson moved back to Madison. He taught at Madison Business College and reentered

UW as a "special student." He met (and soon married) Paula DeHart, continued teaching, and entered the jazz studies program at UW, where he studied with Les Thimmig, Richard Davis, and Joan Wildman. He finished his degree in music, and DeHart took a job in the education department at the University of Florida.

The move to Florida was not happy for DeHart, who disliked living in Gainesville, but led to four great years of further musical education for Erickson—not in school but on the job. There were excellent jazz musicians in Gainesville, some of them musical refugees from Miami who had left the dissolute South Florida lifestyle that threatened to destroy them. Besides playing jazz, Erickson also worked extensively with Puerto Rican and Cuban bands.

After four years, DeHart wanted to leave Florida, and she encouraged Erickson to look at graduate programs. When he was accepted into the jazz program at DePaul University in Chicago, the couple moved back to the Midwest. Shortly afterward, DeHart was hired to the UW–Stevens Point faculty. Erickson studied at DePaul with Mark Colby and worked with Rob Parton's Jazz Tech Big Band, the Big Band of Chicago, Barrett Deems's big band, and the 911 Mambo Orchestra. He taught at the American Conservatory and Naperville High School while trying to get to Stevens Point to be with his wife on the weekends. In Stevens Point, he met UWSP faculty member Bob Kase and started playing in Kase's group (co-led by George Bures), Full Speed. He also played with blues band the Common Faces, which played in Madison and at the House of Blues in Chicago.

Eventually, Erickson's schedule and traveling itinerary became unmanageable, something he starkly realized when, after playing with Janet Planet's band at the Dubuque Jazz Festival in Iowa, he drove off the road late at night and had a frightening accident that landed him in the hospital. The car was totaled, but fortunately Erickson was not badly injured.

Not long afterward, Erickson got a call from the dean at the UW–Marathon County campus, asking if he might be interested in leading the concert band at the two-year college. While Erickson's training in conducting was almost nonexistent, his musicality and work ethic carried him through. From the late 1990s on, Erickson went on to teach a variety of courses and lead groups at Marathon and at the UW–Marshfield/Wood

County campus. He continues to be an active player; he's a regular with the La Crosse Jazz Orchestra and plays small band jobs at such diverse venues as the Amherst Coffee Company, Consolidated Paper, Wausau's Grand Theater, and Marshfield's Chestnut Center. Erickson led the Wisconsin Jazz Orchestra for several years, during which time the band played gigs and sponsored a jazz festival for area schools. He has played numerous shows at Green Bay's Widener Center for the Performing Arts.

Erickson decided in 2011 to pursue a doctoral degree in jazz, focusing on playing and writing. At the University of Illinois, he researched rhetorical devices in jazz. In the fall of 2017, Erickson became director of jazz studies at UW–La Crosse, succeeding Karyn Quinn.

Ron Keezer

Ron Keezer was born in Eau Claire in 1940 and grew up in nearby Chippewa Falls. In his youth, he was immediately drawn to drums from hearing concerts and parades in Eau Claire. When he was very young, he remembers,

> My mother thought I was going to be the next Fred Astaire, so she turned me into a dancer. . . . [She] would send me around the neighborhood during World War II. . . . I had a little navy outfit and a little army outfit, and she taught me how to sing "Praise the Lord and Pass the Ammunition" and a couple of other songs. . . . I'd get money for that, and I [would say], "Whoa, a penny!"

Keezer joined school band in fifth grade, on drums. About three years later, with several schoolmates, he formed a polka band called Wiggy's Wizards. After the band learned a few swing charts, Keezer says, "We played dances at the local Knights of Columbus hall, or wherever they'd hire us, ten cents a person or something. But we did it because we loved it, and we just went crazy."

When he was a teenager, his interest in jazz was piqued when he was in the hospital with pneumonia. In the bed next to him was Dennis Oliver, who would later become a prominent bassist in Madison. Oliver had a recording of Louis Armstrong singing "Now You Has Jazz" with Bing

From left to right: Geoffrey Keezer (see chapter 7), Al Hager, Ron Keezer, and Bob Baca (see next section in this chapter), 1987. COURTESY OF SPECIAL COLLECTIONS AND ARCHIVES, W. D. MCINTYRE LIBRARY, UW–EAU CLAIRE

Crosby that struck Keezer as "pretty neat." Shortly thereafter, Keezer went to music camp in Madison, where he played big jazz band charts.

A friend convinced him to attend Winona State College (now University) in Minnesota, which Keezer did for two years. The jazzers at Winona recorded and made regular trips to the Prom Ballroom in St. Paul to hear bands like Stan Kenton's.

After a couple years at Winona, Keezer decided to attend the Berklee School of Music in Boston, one of the few schools then teaching jazz. After working for a year to save up money, Keezer went east in 1961. Musically, his experience at Berklee was overwhelming. At one point, Keezer's lessons with drummer Alan Dawson were preceded by Dawson's lessons with Gary Burton and followed by lessons with Tony Williams (then a high school student), two future greats.

Money was tight, and Keezer recalls, "I'd play gigs in strip clubs, and whatever I could, and half the money would go to school, and half to try to live on." Unfortunately, after two years, the money ran out, and Keezer came back to Wisconsin State University–Eau Claire. Many of his Berklee courses would not transfer, but his training there facilitated

Keezer's accelerated path to a music education degree from Eau Claire in 1965.

After his graduation, Keezer and his new wife, Mary (a pianist and horn player), moved to Monroe, Wisconsin, where Mary taught school and Keezer commuted to UW–Madison to work on a master's degree, though he did not finish the degree. The Keezers moved to Muskego, where both taught, and Keezer also wrote music for school bands.

In 1968, Keezer and Mary each secured a graduate assistantship at Eau Claire, and they moved back. After a year and a half, the percussion position opened in the music department, and Keezer was a logical choice for the job. He held the position for thirty-three years. Keezer was valuable to the jazz program for keeping well-trained drummers (including future pros Mark Pulice, who was Carmen McRae's drummer for fifteen years; Randy Richter; and Larry Lelli) in the bands, as well as leading a jazz band for many years.

Keezer was on the faculty at Shell Lake Camp for many years and served an important role as an officer in the state chapter of the National Association for Jazz Educators (later IAJE) for another long tenure. Not least, Keezer and Mary raised their son, Geoff Keezer, who has become one of the top jazz pianists on today's scene (see chapter 7).

Bob Baca

Bob Baca was born in 1958 and grew up in Lockport, Illinois. In blue-collar Lockport, many men, including Baca's father, worked at the Texaco refinery, and the school band program was a matter of tremendous local civic pride. Baca's junior high band director, Pete Pappas, made a deal with the school administration that he would produce the high-level program that they were looking for as long as they didn't ask any questions. All of the band students were required to take private lessons; Baca says the thinking was, "Well, that's what the director said, so that's what we have to do."

After graduating from high school, Baca attended Joliet Junior College. He transferred to Indiana University in 1979, where he was in and out of school for a number of years. In pursuit of his desire to teach music in Chicago's inner city, Baca earned a bachelor's degree in music education.

He became a graduate assistant to renowned IU trumpet professor William Adam and was principal trumpet in the university's outstanding top orchestra, challenged by the most demanding symphonic literature.

Once out of school, Baca finally became a jazz player in 1983, when he postponed his marriage in order to join the band of mercurial hall of fame drummer Buddy Rich. Professional trumpet players from all over the country stopped in Bloomington for remedial work with Bill Adam, or to help correct bad trumpet habits they had developed on the road. One of the trumpeters working with Rich was Doug Clark. Clark and Baca became friends, and at some point, Baca said, "You know, if there's ever an opening on the Buddy Rich band, I'd love to do that." Sure enough, a chair opened up, and Clark sent for Baca. Clark knew how well Baca played trumpet but had never heard him play jazz.

Baca had not immersed himself deeply in Indiana's jazz program and was something of a novice when he joined one of the top jazz bands in the world, led by one of the most notoriously impatient and merciless bandleaders in the business.

> All [Clark] had to do [to find out if I could play jazz] was say, "Let me hear you play [this figure]." And that would have been it right there. But he didn't. And so he said, "You're sure you can do this?" And I said, "Yeah, I'm sure I can do it."
>
> The first night that I got on the band, . . . the bass trombone player turned around and said, "In all due respect, have you ever played this kind of music before?"
>
> [Clark] found out after about two or three measures, and so after a huge verbal whipping, he said, "You can't get fired from this band . . . because if you get fired from this band, my reputation is going to be really bad. . . . You're going to have to learn this music." So we spent every night after the gig, and he went through the entire book, from the left to the right, and he basically said, "This is how it goes."

For weeks, Baca and Clark practiced two to three hours a night after the jobs were over, and somehow they escaped the wrath of Rich; Baca went on to a successful run with the band.

In 1984, Baca left the Rich band and toured with American icon Frank Sinatra's band through part of the year. But soon, Baca left the road and moved with his new bride from Bloomington to Indianapolis, where Baca led the tenuous life of a freelance musician. That life was made easier with the mentorship of trumpeter Larry Wiseman, and the fact that Al Cobine was in the city. Contractor Cobine sent Baca out on national tours with Mel Tormé, Tony Bennett, and the 1980s celebrity Pia Zadora. Around 1985, Baca toured again with Sinatra, on one of Sinatra's last tours. Years later, when Sinatra was celebrating his seventy-fifth birthday, Baca and Dominic Spera (see chapter 17) played together in a band backing him up in Las Vegas.

Spera, who had been at Indiana since he left Wisconsin, told Baca in 1986 that the open position at UW–Eau Claire would be a really good job for him. Baca thought of Wisconsin as a great place to fish. He applied for the job, thinking that might allow him to "be able to be in paradise, and be able to teach at the same time." And that's how it turned out—he remains an avid fisherman to this day.

Baca has maintained Eau Claire's tremendous record of excellence ever since. A raft of awards from *Down Beat* magazine over the years for outstanding big bands and individuals, and two of those big bands' albums' nominations for Grammy awards, have just confirmed nationally what Wisconsinites already knew about the program. Eau Claire bands have taken tours to Europe and China. Under Baca's leadership, the UWEC Jazz Festival has become one of the most successful festivals in the country (and one of the longest running). (Baca appears in the photo that accompanies Ron Keezer's profile earlier in this chapter.)

Baca can cite a number of his students who have gone on to professional success: Jeremy Miloszewicz, from little Cameron, Wisconsin, who is a top trumpeter in the theaters of Broadway in New York (as is another UWEC trumpet graduate, Platteville native Dan Urness); New York jazz trumpeter John Raymond (who is now on the faculty at Indiana University); and Scott Pingel, who, after a most promising start in jazz, became principal double bassist in the San Francisco Symphony Orchestra in 2004.

Baca has remained active as a player, like his predecessor Dominic Spera, playing shows in the Twin Cities and with both the Milwaukee Symphony and the Minnesota Orchestra in addition to jazz gigs.

Mary Louise Knutson

Pianist Mary Louise Knutson was born in Madison in 1966. Adopted by Barbara and Kenneth Knutson, she grew up in Wausau. She started taking piano lessons at the age of four, from a fourteen-year-old friend of the family. Knutson loved playing and continued her piano study with several teachers while also taking up violin and playing in school groups from grade school through high school.

While she studied and played mostly classical music, she did play in the Wausau East High jazz band, which she describes as more of a "stage band." Several experiences led Knutson to jazz. First, she met John Harmon and Fred Sturm when she was in high school. Harmon's piano playing made a strong impression on her, as did Sturm's infectious personality. Second, she spent one summer during high school attending a program at the Eastman School of Music in Rochester, New York. Knutson was there to study classical music, but she says,

> At the same time there were all these jazz kids there. And we're all in the same dorm, and . . . it was the best summer of my life. First time away from home . . . [and] I got to go hear these jazz kids play. And I was like, "Oh, my gosh! What is this music? I have to find it when I get back to Wausau."

Knutson's band director put her in touch with another talented young Wausau musician, bassist Laurie Lang, from across town. "Probably once every other week, . . . we got together and played," Knutson remembers. "And she knew more than I did about playing." Laurie Lang Croasdale was a student of Richard Davis at UW–Madison. She was a founding member of Harmonious Wail (see chapter 13), and has played with a wide range of artists in Madison, from Doc De Haven to Joel Adams, as well as her close collaborator in her Improv Music Workshop, John Becker. She is an important player, music educator, and advocate in Madison. "[She] was great at booking," Knutson says. "She booked us a gig, a little duo gig, . . . at the Peking Restaurant in Wausau. . . . That was one of my first jazz gigs."

Knutson went to Lawrence University, not to study jazz, but to study classical piano, which became her major. But she played in the excellent jazz groups at Lawrence, although she always felt like she was behind the other students in the jazz program. "It was just a foreign world," she recalls.

> But I was trying to get into it. . . . I was just so afraid to improvise, and coming from a classical background, where every note was expected to be perfect. . . . That's a great, wonderful background to have, but it was really difficult for me to make that transition, . . . for me to hear notes come out of my fingers that I didn't want. . . . Everything sounded wrong to me, and that was so painful to hear what I thought was wrong music coming out.

For a couple of summers, she drove regularly from Wausau to Winneconne to study jazz piano with John Harmon, who introduced her to chord voicings, improvisation, and the role of a pianist in the rhythm section. On the drive, she would listen repeatedly to a cassette recording of Bill Evans on her car's tape player.

> By the time I was a senior, . . . I knew that I wanted to be a jazz pianist. Classical music was wonderful, but something about jazz was just [doing] it for me emotionally. And so I was like, "Soon as I get out of here, I'm just going to dig right in and figure out how to play this music."

In 1988, Knutson went to Minneapolis–St. Paul to pursue this dream. She taught students at Schmitt Music and worked part time at the Institute of Arts (now Institute of Art). She found out about jam sessions at the Artists Quarter and, despite being terrified, made herself take part. "Even though I was scared to death of soloing, [people noticed me,]" she says, "because I knew my chords, I could accompany, and I was sensitive, probably because of my classical background." These abilities led her to an all-female trio, Naima, which worked frequently for a couple of years and recorded an album. By the mid-1990s, Knutson moved on to accompanying singers. "My calling card really was that I was a good accompanist,"

Mary Louise Knutson, 2011. PHOTO BY DIETRICH GESK; COURTESY OF MARY LOUISE KNUTSON

she says, "and was willing and able to meet with the singer, and go over their tunes, find their keys, probably write out a ton of charts for them." She worked with such local favorites as Debbie Duncan (touring with her in Italy in 2007) and Connie Evingson.

But Knutson wanted to be an independent instrumentalist. She was chosen in 2005 as a finalist for the national Mary Lou Williams Women in Jazz competition at the Kennedy Center in Washington, DC. For years now, she has been the pianist with the JazzMN Orchestra, the Twin Cities' premiere big band. Knutson also realized her dream of organizing a working trio. The Mary Louise Knutson Trio, featuring Gordon Johnson on bass and several of the area's best drummers, has released two well-received CDs (see online discography). The trio toured California, the Plains, and the Midwest in 2007, fulfilling Knutson's long-standing desire to take her music on the road. Two compositions from the first album won awards from *Billboard* magazine.

Knutson has become a first-call pianist in the Twin Cities for a dazzling assortment of big-name visiting jazz artists, pop artists, and even symphony concerts that require pop or jazz accompanists.[5] At a Christmas program with the Minnesota Orchestra in 2010, she says she was "discovered" by Doc Severinsen, longtime leader of the band on Johnny Carson's *Tonight Show*. Severinsen enlisted Knutson to organize a band of Twin Cities players who have joined him on a number of tours since 2012.

In recent years, Knutson has led her groups in concerts at Lawrence, at Ripon College, and at the Fox Jazz Fest in Menasha. She has also performed in Wisconsin with UW–River Falls jazz program director David Milne's One World Consort, which often performs the music of Fred Sturm. The Twin Cities have long been a destination for Wisconsin jazz musicians, and Knutson has been one of the most successful in this field.

Sue Orfield

Saxophonist Sue Orfield was born in 1967 in Menomonie, in western Wisconsin. She says she started playing music as a "wee child." Since her older brother was taking piano lessons, and she wanted to be like him, her parents (both teachers) allowed her to start lessons in kindergarten. She loved playing and never had to be told to practice, but as was the case with other musicians in this book, her teacher finally discovered that Orfield was learning all of her music by ear rather than reading it. In fifth grade, she heard a saxophone on the school bus's radio and decided that it was the instrument for her.

Orfield joined school band on tenor saxophone, which has remained her instrument of choice ever since. With her previous training and a good ear, she was soon experimenting in band.

> I played tenor. . . . The parts were whole notes for the most part, half notes once in a while—so I would listen to all the other parts in the band and then figure out what they were and then play them. Which I'm sure drove my band directors crazy. You're not supposed to do that, but at the time I was just all, like, "This is fun! I'm going to play the trumpet part here, and the trombone part here."

Under the relaxed but informed guidance of director Jim Borgaro at Menomonie High, Orfield played in a jazz band saxophone section with two other outstanding saxophonists who are still active professionals, Forrest "Woody" Mankowski (see chapter 18) and Marc Jimos. Current jazz star Ethan Iverson (see chapter 7), who was a few years behind these saxophonists in the Menomonie schools, told me that he looked up to them as local students whom he considered real musicians.[6]

After finishing high school, Orfield attended Lawrence University in Appleton, originally pursuing majors in music and chemistry. She adored Lawrence and says that Fred Sturm, the leader of the jazz program there, is still her hero. At Lawrence, she formed especially close relationships with Mary Louise Knutson and Rob Hudson, a Stevens Point native who is an active trombonist in New York City (and works full-time in the archives at Carnegie Hall).

Graduating from Lawrence in 1990, Orfield and her friend Heather decided to see the world and settled on Seattle as the place to start their adventure. Orfield has hilarious stories about the two small-town Midwestern girls learning the ways of the world, especially concerning employment opportunities. Eventually, Orfield landed a day job as a secretary/receptionist at a T-shirt company.

But she began pursuing her musical career right away, in the time-tested arenas of jam sessions and classified ads. Washington was the center of the grunge movement at that time, producing the eventual superstar area bands Pearl Jam and Nirvana, and Seattle was a musical hotbed. The first ad Orfield responded to was a request for a baritone saxophonist who was "into Ornette Coleman and Jimi Hendrix." She ended up working with the band Albert Figures, which Orfield describes as a garage band with "an incredible lyricist," for many years.

With Albert Figures, Orfield gained enough notoriety to get into other rock- and blues-based bands, including a group of transplanted musicians who had been in Chicago blues legend Koko Taylor's backup band. With this group, called Burnin' Chicago, Orfield went on her first tour, traveling through the United States for six months in a decrepit bus she describes as a "silver bullet-looking" thing that "smelled bad." It may have looked odd: a white female saxophonist in an otherwise all black male band. But, Orfield says, "There [was] a nice little cross-section of humanity in that group, and some of them were very much from the 'hood—rough and tough characters—and others were just very sweet." The pay was good (until the leader quit paying the others in order to, ostensibly, support his wife's drug habit), and Orfield always had her own hotel room. Six months with Burnin' Chicago, however, was long enough for her.

"I definitely stand out like a sore thumb," Orfield says of being a female instrumentalist in a man's world. "For the most part, I haven't really thought about that too much. You just do your thing and go for it," she says, echoing the attitude of Bev Dahlke-Smith (see chapter 8), another female musician who succeeded in a male-dominated environment. Orfield speculates that she has missed out on a few job opportunities because, as she says, men in "the good ol' boy network weren't comfortable having me around." On the other hand, she says,

> I think there have been gigs where I've been hired just because I'm a woman. . . . I took 'em! Of course I did. I didn't know; how could I possibly say no? . . . There are things that have been said to me that have been rude and sexist, and so what? You either get over it or you don't.

While working with bands that leaned toward rock, blues, and R&B, Orfield also started making inroads into the jazz scene in Seattle. Her first extended jazz gig was with the quintet of pianist Karin Kajita, a post-bop group that featured music that included, Orfield says, "really, really, really fast changes [*laughter*]. And . . . it was hard. I worked really hard at trying to keep up and do the thing."

Sometime in the 1990s, Orfield attended a performance by the Seattle-based Billy Tipton Memorial Saxophone Quartet. Billy Tipton was born Dorothy Lucille Tipton in the 1910s and, early in his successful musical career as a pianist and saxophonist, he began dressing and passing as a man onstage. Later, he also adopted a male persona in his personal life, eventually marrying a woman and adopting three sons. His biological sex was discovered by the general public only at his death.[7]

Orfield was immediately drawn to the group, which consisted of four female saxophonists and a drummer. Orfield gave her business card to the bandleader, Amy Denio, hoping against hope that the group might

Sue Orfield. PHOTO BY TEDDY SNIDER; COURTESY OF SUE ORFIELD

need a sub at some point. A few years later, after a member of the group heard Orfield playing with Albert Figures, she was asked to join. She says her first performance with this "amazingly cool group" was in the late 1990s in Milwaukee. The band's website states, "With concerts that cover musical territory from New Orleans 'second–line' to jazz, Afro-Cuban to Balkan, Klezmer and beyond, the Tiptons create some of the wildest sounds ever to come out of a sax quartet" (see online discography for recordings).[8] The Tiptons do not perform full-time, but Orfield travels to Europe with the group once or twice a year, as well as doing a couple of short US tours annually.

In the late 1990s, Orfield was having a very successful career in Seattle, and she was voted Best Horn by the Washington Blues Society in 1999 and every year from 2001 to 2004. However, around 2000, she developed a gambling addiction. Orfield's personal life began spiraling downward, and eventually she ended up homeless. Her parents traveled to Seattle and brought her back to Wisconsin, where she started a twelve-step program in which she remains active today. In the mid-2000s, she began her career anew in the Chippewa Valley of Wisconsin.

Since returning to Wisconsin, Orfield has become a real presence on the local scene around Eau Claire. Her popular quartet, the Sue Orfield Band, has been categorized as a rock band and a jazz band. (It contains elements of each, as well as blues.) It has cut three albums. Another of her groups, AcoustiHoo, shares some of the same band members and plays a few of the same originals but without the edge of electric guitar and drum set. Orfield keeps up her more straightforward jazz playing with the Chippewa Valley Jazz Orchestra, at occasional jam sessions, and on a variety of freelance dates in the Eau Claire area and in the Twin Cities. She also plays with the Twin Cities' soul and blues institution the Butanes. In 2014, Orfield began hosting *The Sue Orfield Show* for a community TV station in Eau Claire, showcasing area bands and musicians. She has also joined the staff of the Shell Lake summer jazz camps in northwestern Wisconsin.

She returns to Seattle on a semiregular basis to play not just with the Tiptons, but with other groups she used to play with when she lived there, including Junkyard Jane. With her personal and musical energies and abilities, Orfield should remain a force in the western Wisconsin musical scene for many years.

Michael Janisch

Bassist Michael Janisch was born in 1979 and grew up on a farm outside Ellsworth, in Pierce County, Wisconsin. Janisch began playing the family piano at age four and started on electric bass at ten. He came up in the school jazz program led by the respected Harvey Halpaus. This "inspirational teacher," as Janisch remembers him, took the band to the UW–Eau Claire and UW–La Crosse jazz festivals during Janisch's time at the school. "Every year we, his bands, would win," Janisch says, with only a bit of exaggeration. And one year at La Crosse, Janisch was chosen to go to Clark Terry's summer jazz camp.

Janisch took a little detour from music to play sports in college. He went to Mankato State University in Minnesota on scholarships for track and field, and football. While working on a history major and playing sports, he suffered an injury during his junior year. "To make a long story short," he says, "I was feeling sorry for myself one day, and then I went walking by the fine arts building, and I heard drums. And so I went and met the guy, and we started jamming, and I really got back into it, really got hooked." He called UW–La Crosse faculty member and jazz bassist Karyn Quinn (another Ellsworth native) and told her that he was ready to change his life. In 1999 he moved back to La Crosse and, as he recalls, "locked myself in an attic for an entire summer and just tried to catch up." After four semesters at La Crosse, he transferred to the Berklee College of Music in Boston, where he majored in music business, graduating in 2002.

Although feeling burned out by three years of intense practice, Janisch moved to New York after school. He remembers he "got inspired by all the people there and just practiced all the time." He toured quite a bit outside of the city, playing with some creative hip-hop bands and doing what he called "some groove playing," largely in order to pay bills and his school loans. But then Janisch met a girl from England.

"It's like a classic story," he says. "I went over [to England] to visit her, and . . . it's really all this fate stuff." While visiting London in 2004, he ended up playing at the Jazz Café, an important jazz venue. After the performance he was approached by an agent who was booking a tour for a rising-star singer and needed a bassist. Janisch accepted and toured for six months. Stardom was not in the cards for the singer, but through the connections Janisch had made, he began earning a living from his music for the first time in his life. While working his way into the London scene, he found that many of his friends from New York frequently toured Europe, so Janisch decided he might as well stay in England. He got

Michael Janisch at the 2013 Whirlwind Festival in London.
COURTESY OF MICHAEL JANISCH

married, had children, and is now deeply established in the London scene. By 2014 he was the head of bass at Trinity Laban Conservatoire and at the Royal Academy of Music, two of the city's respected music schools.

Janisch released his first album as leader in 2009 and started his own record label, Whirlwind Records, in 2010. Using the skills and knowledge he picked up at Berklee, Janisch and Whirlwind Records put out more than forty titles by early 2014. Additionally, Janisch has started a jazz festival and does a great deal of tour promotion, largely for American artists coming to the United Kingdom and Europe. He has facilitated the tours of such veterans as Lee Konitz, George Garzone, and Clarence Penn, as well as his contemporaries. But Janisch also had the urge to visit the States, which he did in early 2014. This led to a performance at the UW–La Crosse festival with a band that included Penn, saxophonist Patrick Cornelius, guitarist Matt Stevens, and Wisconsin trumpeter Philip Dizack. While Janisch's career is centered in the United Kingdom, it exemplifies the opportunities that are available to American jazz musicians, including those from Wisconsin.

Tom Gullion

Saxophonist Tom Gullion was born in 1965 and grew up in Kokomo, Indiana. He says he had "an amazing saxophone teacher" as well as friends who were into jazz; the group practiced regularly from play-along jazz recordings. When they were teenagers, they would drive an hour and half to Muncie to hear the Ball State University big band, and to Muncie's Shakey's Pizza joint once a month for more music.

Gullion was steered to Harry Miedema, a legendary saxophone teacher in Indianapolis. At the time, Miedema was touring extensively with the O'Jays, but in their sporadically scheduled lessons, Gullion says, "[I would] come over, wake him up, he'd come and teach me in his shorts, but I'd get a three- or four-hour lesson, and learn a boatload." This led Gullion to Indiana University, where he was schoolmates with future jazz stars: saxophonist Ralph Bowen, bassist Robert Hurst, trumpeters Scott Wendholt and Pharez Whitted, and pianist Jim Beard. (Wisconsin musicians David Bixler and Charles Ledvina were also at IU at that time.)

In 1988, IU's David Baker recommended Gullion for the musical opportunity of a lifetime. J. J. Johnson, arguably the most important trombonist in jazz history, had moved back to his hometown of Indianapolis after decades living in New York and southern California. Johnson put together a new, small touring band, and Gullion spent a month playing all over the country with some of the most distinguished players in jazz: Johnson, Cedar Walton, Rufus Reid, and Victor Lewis. Because Johnson's comeback tour was a big deal in the jazz world, jazz celebrities came out

Saxophonist Tom Gullion, with (left to right) Mark Urness (see earlier in this chapter), Ernie Adams, and Tim Whalen. COURTESY OF TOM GULLION

to hear the band, and the young Gullion played directly in front of tenor greats Stanley Turrentine and Stan Getz, and other jazz royalty like Dizzy Gillespie.

After the tour with Johnson, Gullion moved to New York for several years, staying alive largely by playing wedding gigs, often in a horn section with current trumpet star Chris Botti (another Indiana University product). But, Gullion says, "It wasn't really what I was interested in doing."

In 1992 he decided to move to a small town in Spain. "I had one of those magical years of . . . taking time, and practicing seven hours a day, for a year," he recalls. "And that helped me with a lot of things. It was really important to play for European audiences." Working with a Spanish rhythm section, Gullion toured constantly from 1992 to 1994. With corporate support, the band played clubs, festivals, and TV broadcasts, and cut a record as well.

After the touring in Spain, Gullion moved to Chicago, where he worked mostly with the South Side Hyde Park crowd, including Milwaukee native and drummer Ernie Adams. While raising his family, Gullion also began working in the computer software business. He completed a master's degree in music at Northwestern University while playing three or four gigs a week.

In 2000, he moved to Wisconsin.

> A couple friends had moved to this small town, Viroqua, Wisconsin, . . . to the country to breathe some fresh air, and [to have a] lower cost of living . . . [and to send their kids to] this arts-focused Waldorf School. It sounded all kind of pie-in-the-sky, and wonderful, and so I had this crazy notion that, well, I have this software career that pays the bills, and I can do that from anywhere; and we found this farm, and it has [an] attached building, and so that could be my music studio, and so I'd be able to practice whenever I want, . . . and write music, and write software.

The move allowed Gullion to, as he says, "open the [musical] vistas a little bit. And that's where it really felt like I could have a little bit of space to practice and envision something other than just doing the same old same old." He had studied and worked on bebop and its successor styles for many years, but he reached the point where he wanted to play and write. "I don't want to feel like I'm faking," he says, "and I don't want to feel like I'm playing somebody else's music."

While it hasn't panned out exactly as he expected, Gullion's work in software has remained a financial success, helping to support his musical pursuits. "It's been an incredible experience," he says, "transformative, in my life and in my music. . . . Whether you nurtured yourself in Brooklyn, or in Minneapolis, or Viroqua, it doesn't really matter."

Gullion works frequently in Wisconsin with a version of the quintet that recorded much of his 2009 recording *Carswell*. That band usually includes David Cooper, Matt Buchman, Mark Urness, and Dane Richeson.

Gullion made an important contribution to Wisconsin jazz besides his music. With his bassist friend Jeff Low, another Chicago transplant, Gullion is responsible for initiating what is now the Driftless Music Festival. The first Driftless Jazz Festival, in 2007, featured seven groups that Gullion brought to Viroqua to play on Memorial Day. Gullion pretty much ran the first few festivals, which have now been taken over by dedicated individuals and the local community radio station (WDRT), with the support of the city of Viroqua. The free festival now showcases interesting music of various styles other than jazz but continues to grow in attendance and remains a gift to the community.

Acknowledgments

Thanks:

For the funding of the Barbara Baldwin De Frees Chair in the Performing Arts at Ripon College, and a gift of Mary Jo and Christopher Wiedey, which allowed me to pursue these stories and the music.

To my colleagues at Ripon College, especially former Dean of Faculty Jerry Seaman.

To Andy Prellwitz and the rest of the staff (especially Kate Moody) at the Ripon College Library.

To Ted Messmer, for early encouragement, and a variety of materials.

To Julie Flemming, who runs the Bunny Berigan Jazz Jamboree and is "keeper" of the Berigan archive at the Fox Lake Public Library.

To Jan Uebelherr, formerly of the *Milwaukee Journal Sentinel*.

To Mark and Sharon Lewis for the materials about their father, Cappy Lewis.

To Milwaukee Symphony Orchestra bassists Laura Snyder and Catherine McGinn, for confirming information I received from other sources.

To Ben Barbera of the Milwaukee County Historical Society.

To Jillian Johnson at Lawrence University.

To Eddy Nix (of Driftless Books in Viroqua) for access to the research he's done on Freddie Slack.

To the Fond du Lac Public Library, and especially Mary Leb in Information Services, for information about Heinie Beau.

To Ann Guse at the Mayville Historical Society.

To Marc Myers for permission to extensively quote his interview at JazzWax.com with Jackie Cain.

To Eileen Millonzi and Stacey (Millonzi) Vojvodich for access to the materials about their husband and father, Sig Millonzi.

To Sue Shock and Theresa D'Orsi in the Alumni Office and Jay Satterfield, Special Collections Librarian, at Dartmouth College for information about Chris Swansen.

To John Schoenknect and Linda Hansen at the Waukesha County Museum.

To all the photographers who were so generous with their work.

To Editor in Chief Kate Thompson and everyone else at the Wisconsin Historical Society Press, but especially to my marvelous editor, Liz Wyckoff.

To my family—Maria, Erik, and Paul; my brother and sister, Rick and Krista; my late mother Frances; and my father Richard, "Dick," who with his critical eye read this manuscript multiple times.

To all the wonderful musicians and members of the musical community who shared their time with me (in alphabetical order): the late Joe Aaron, Adekola Adedapo, Carl Allen, Jackie Allen, the late Sam Armato, Lynne Arriale, Bob Baca, Greg Balfany, Dave Bayles, Sam Belton, Kaye Berigan, Michael Betz, David Bixler, Jamie Breiwick, Mike Britz, Matt Buchman, Claude Cailliet, Gerald Cannon, Jack Carr, Laura Caviani, Gary Christensen, David Cooper, Brad Curran, Beverly Dahlke-Smith, Larry Darling, Patty Darling, Mark Davis, Richard Davis, the late Doc De Haven, Kelly De Haven, Maggie Delaney-Potthoff, Sims Delaney-Potthoff, Frank DeMiles, Gerri DiMaggio, Luis

Diaz, Philip Dizack, Peter Dominguez, journalist Mike Drew, Pam Duronio, Manty Ellis, Jeff Erickson, Dan Fornero, Joel Frahm, Jim Frakes, Berkeley Fudge, Vince Fuh, Rick Germanson, John Gibson, Jack Grassel, Connie Grauer, Cliff Gribble, Tom Gullion, Mike Hale, Harvey Halpaus, Jeff Hamann, Curt Hanrahan, John Harmon, Zach Harmon, Milwaukee's "Second Mayor" Reuben Harpole, Paul Hastil, David Hazeltine, the late Chuck Hedges, Steve Houghton, Mike Irish, Ethan Iverson, Lovell Ives, Eric Jacobson, Michael Janisch, the late Al Jarreau, Allen Johnson, Karen Johnson, Russ Johnson, Greg Keel, Geoffrey Keezer, Ron Keezer, Dave Kiepert, John Kirchberger, Mary Louise Knutson, Laurie Lang, Steve Lewandoski, arts administrator Lynn Lucius, Tom Luer, Brian Lynch, Woody Mankowski, music publisher Keith Mardak, Lynette Margulies, Lyle Mays, Nick Moran, the late Michael Murphy, Tom Newburg, Dan Nimmer, Sue Orfield, Jim Paolo, Louka Patenaude, Tom Perry, the late Willie Pickens, the late Jeff Pietrangelo, Janet Planet, Karyn Quinn, Toty Ramos, Dane Richeson, Brian Ritter, Marty Robinson, Randy Sabien, Chris Salerno, John Salerno, historian George Sanders, Joe Sanders, Tom Sandquist, Eric Schoor, Bob Schulz, Andy Schumm, Ben Sidran, Dominic Spera, David Stoler, Tim Stemper, Daryl Stuermer, the late Fred Sturm, Hans Sturm, Ike Sturm, Dave Sullivan, John Sullivan, Tierney Sutton, Steve Sveum, Greg Tardy, Les Thimmig, John Thulin, Matt Turner, Mark Urness, Marshall Vente, Tom Washatka, Chris Washburne, Jeff Weiss, George Welland, Jan Wheaton, Warren Wiegratz, Ken Wiele, Joan Wildman, and Juli Wood.

Notes

Chapter 1

1. Beiderbecke's story is so seductive that it became the basis of a celebrated novel and movie, *Young Man with a Horn*.
2. Gunther Schuller, *The Swing Era: The Development of Jazz, 1930–1945* (New York: Oxford University Press, 1989), 463.
3. Much of the information on Berigan's early life and details from his career come from the exhaustive biography by Robert Dupuis, *Bunny Berigan: Elusive Legend of Jazz*, (Baton Rouge and London: Louisiana State University Press, 1993). After I wrote this chapter, Michael Zirpolo's *Mr. Trumpet: The Trials, Tribulations and Triumph of Bunny Berigan*, Studies in Jazz, no. 64 (Lanham, Toronto, Plymouth, UK: The Scarecrow Press, 2011) appeared. Zirpolo had access to more and newer information than did Dupuis. I have tried to reconcile the two accounts. Some similar information is in Richard Sudhalter's *Lost Chords: White Musicians and Their Contribution to Jazz, 1915–1945* (New York and Oxford: Oxford University Press, 1999).
4. Dupuis, *Bunny Berigan*, 12.
5. Ibid., 18–19, suggests that Bunny Berigan was coleading the band with Smith; Zirpolo implies that the band was led by Smith and Bob Berigan.
6. Ibid., 50.
7. Sudhalter, *Lost Chords*, 492–493.
8. Ibid., 492–493
9. Schuller, *The Swing Era*, 471–473, especially admires this performance and describes it at length.
10. Berigan also contributed notable solos to two other jazzed-up classics, Franz Liszt's "Liebestraum" and Felix Mendelssohn's "Spring Song," both recorded just weeks later on February 18.
11. John Chilton and Richard Sudhalter, liner notes to *Giants of Jazz: Bunny Berigan* (Alexandria, VA: Time-Life Records, 1982), 42.

12. Sudhalter, *Lost Chords*, 511, sees this as a pivotal event in Berigan's career, "crack[ing his] confidence." Zirpolo, *Mr. Trumpet*, 272–275, also reports on it at length.
13. Dupuis, *Bunny Berigan*, 192.
14. Ibid., 195
15. Ibid., 196–199.
16. Ibid., 233–234.
17. Ibid., 260.
18. Ibid., 262.
19. Ibid., 267.
20. Sudhalter, *Lost Chords*, 369. Schuller, *The Swing Era*, 464, also speaks to Berigan's fusion of elements of Armstrong and Beiderbecke.
21. Whitney Balliett, "Bunny Berigan," *The New Yorker* (November 8, 1982): 124, 127.

Chapter 2

1. Much of Herman's early history related here is derived from Gene Lees's definitive biography, *Leader of the Band: The Life of Woody Herman* (New York, Oxford: Oxford University Press, 1995). Lees reconstructed much of Herman's youth from conversations with Woody and his boyhood friend, Milwaukeean Ray Sherman. I also consulted William Clancy's *Woody Herman: Chronicles of the Herds* (New York: Schirmer Books, 1995), and Robert Kriebel's *Blue Flame: Woody Herman's Life in Music* (West Lafayette, IN: Purdue University Press, 1995).
2. Clancy, *Woody Herman*, 2.
3. Lees, *Leader of the Band*, 8.
4. Clancy, *Woody Herman*, 4.
5. Lees, *Leader of the Band*, 19. Quote from *Milwaukee Sentinel*, April 10, 1975.
6. Ibid., 57–58.
7. Kriebel, *Blue Flame*, 26.
8. Ibid., 34.
9. Ibid., 97.
10. Gunther Schuller, *The Swing Era: The Development of Jazz, 1930–1945* (New York: Oxford University Press, 1989), 730.
11. Kriebel, *Blue Flame*, 119.

12. Ibid., 152.
13. Doug Ramsey, liner notes for *The Complete Capitol Recordings of Woody Herman*, Mosaic Records MD6-196, 2000.
14. Ralph J. Gleason, liner notes for *My Kind of Broadway*, Columbia Records CS 9157, 1965.
15. Kriebel, *Blue Flame*, 219.
16. Ibid., *Blue Flame*, 218–219.
17. Lees, *Leader of the Band*, 333.
18. Clancy, *Woody Herman*, 372.
19. Schuller, *The Swing Era*, 729–730.

Chapter 3

1. Much of the biographical information presented here is from Mary Alice Shaughnessy's *Les Paul: An American Original* (New York: William Morrow and Company, Inc., 1993). One finds similar information in Robb Lawrence's two volumes of the *Les Paul Legacy—The Early Years of the Les Paul Legacy: 1915–1963* (Milwaukee: Hal Leonard, 2008) and *The Modern Era of the Les Paul Legacy: 1968–2009* (Milwaukee: Hal Leonard, 2009). Some time after I had written the chapter, I found Les Paul's *Les Paul In His Own Words*, centennial ed. (Milwaukee: Backbeat Books, 2016). I did my best to reconcile what I found there with the other sources. All quotes are from Shaughnessy unless otherwise noted.
2. Paul, *Les Paul In His Own Words*, 20–21.
3. Shaughnessy, *Les Paul*, 37.
4. Ibid., 48.
5. Ibid., 56.
6. Ibid., 59. Shaughnessy claims that Les later said it was a completely different club.
7. Ibid., 93–95.
8. Lawrence, *Les Paul Legacy*, vol. 1, 18–19.
9. The skits often had to do with Paul's inventions, real and imaginary, including his cleverly named Les Paulverizer, a device that enabled him to play backing tracks while performing onstage.
10. The history of the Les Paul guitar is the primary focus of Lawrence's books.
11. Shaughnessy, *Les Paul*, 204.

12. Ibid., 212.
13. Ibid., 214.
14. Ibid., 226.
15. Ibid., 266.
16. Ibid., 285. Shaughnessy's term.
17. "Les Paul Monument to Be Dedicated Saturday," *Milwaukee Journal Sentinel*, September 9, 2011.
18. Laurel Walker, "Plucking Some Les Paul Gems: Museum Brings Back 16 Items for Exhibit," *Milwaukee Journal Sentinel*, June 21, 2012; Mary Louise Schumacher, "Wizard of Waukesha gets Museum Home," *Milwaukee Journal Sentinel*, June 6, 2013.

Chapter 4

1. Information about Jabbo Smith is from Whitney Balliett, *Jelly Roll, Jabbo, and Fats: 19 Portraits in Jazz* (New York, Oxford: Oxford University Press, 1983); Sott Yanow, *Trumpet Kings: The Players Who Shaped the Sound of Jazz Trumpet* (Milwaukee: Backbeat Books, 2001); Gunther Schuller, *Early Jazz: Its Roots and Musical Development* (New York, Oxford: Oxford University Press, 1968); and especially Chip Deffaa, *Voices of the Jazz Age: Profiles of Eight Vintage Jazzmen* (Urbana and Chicago: University of Illinois Press, 1990). Some information is also from the website www.jazzhotbigstep.com/188.html.
2. This and the previous quote are from Yanow, *Trumpet Kings*, 339.
3. Benjamin Barbera, *An Improvised World: Jazz and Community in Milwaukee, 1950–1970* (master's dissertation, UW–Milwaukee, 2012), 19–20. Eldridge apparently lived in Milwaukee briefly around this date.
4. Yanow, *Trumpet Kings*, 339–340.
5. This is in the photo section in Deffaa, *Voices of the Jazz Age*.
6. "Cladys 'Jabbo' Smith Papers," University of South Carolina, South Caroliniana Library, University South Caroliniana Society, Manuscripts Collections. http://library.sc.edu/socar/uscs/1994/jabb094.html.
7. Yanow, *Trumpet Kings*, 340.
8. Information about Davison is from his entry by John Chilton in *The New Grove Dictionary of Jazz*, 2nd ed., ed. Barry Kernfeld, vol. 1 (London: Macmillan Publishers Limited, 2002), 582–583; Leonard Feather and Ira Gitler's *The Biographical Encyclopedia of Jazz* (New York: Oxford University

Press, 1999); and Hal Willard's book *The Wildest One: The Life of Wild Bill Davison* (Monkton, MD: Avondale Press, 1996).

9. In some sources, the Moon Glow is spelled Moonglow.
10. Willard, *The Wildest One*, 152–155.
11. Barbera, *An Improvised World*, 41. In a footnote, Barbera cites an article from *The Milwaukee Globe* in 1948 claiming that Dudley turned down offers to go on the road from both Duke Ellington and Count Basie.
12. Information on Sam Armato is from our July 2010 interview. We looked through his scrapbook and a biographical sketch his wife, Janet, had prepared.
13. Willard, *The Wildest One*, 120–150.
14. Ibid., 123.
15. Annysa Johnson, "Armato Known for Jazz, Kindness," *Milwaukee Journal Sentinel*, January 5, 2015.
16. Ibid.
17. Joe Aaron interview, July 2010. Additional material is from the obituary Jan Uebeherr wrote for the *Milwaukee Journal Sentinel*, "Musician Joe Aaron Loved Performing and Finding Students' Style," June 9, 2013.

Chapter 5

1. Eugene Chadbourne, "Abe Aaron Biography," AllMusic. www.allmusic.com/artist/abe-aaron-mn0000581536/biography. Information from this entry was, it seems, largely derived from the Abe Aaron entry in Leonard Feather's *The New Edition of the Encyclopedia of Jazz* (New York: Bonanza Books, 1960).
2. Information about Slack is compiled from entries in Feather's *The New Edition of the Encyclopedia of Jazz*; Leonard Feather and Ira Gitler's *The Biographical Encyclopedia of Jazz* (New York: Oxford University Press, 1999); the unsigned entry on Slack in *The New Grove Dictionary of Jazz*, 2nd ed., ed. Barry Kernfeld, vol. 3 (London: Macmillan Publishers Limited: 2002), 600; William F. Lee's *American Big Bands* (Milwaukee: Hal Leonard, 2005); George T. Simon's *The Big Bands*, 4th ed. (New York: Schirmer Books, 1981); and Mike Rowe's liner notes for *Freddie Slack: Down the Road A-Piece: The Definitive Boogie Woogie Collection, 1940–1955* (Fantastic Voyage Records FVDD111, 2011). Special thanks to Eddy Nix (of Driftless Books in Viroqua) for sharing his research about Freddie Slack and his family.

3. Rowe, *Freddie Slack*.
4. Simon, *The Big Bands*, 95.
5. Stephen Thomas Erlewine, "Ella Mae Morse Biography," AllMusic. www.allmusic.com/artist/ella-mae-morse-mn0000797881/biography. Eddy Nix has collected evidence that suggests that perhaps Slack should have been given a good-sized slice of the Capitol fortune, as it appears that he was in on the ground floor of its beginnings, along with songwriters Johnny Mercer and Buddy DeSylva, and businessman Glenn Wallichs.
6. Lee, *American Big Bands*, 271.
7. Walker is featured on the record "Riftette" with the Slack band (see online discography).
8. Simon, *The Big Bands*, 483.
9. Steve Jordan, with Tom Scanlan, *Rhythm Man: Fifty Years in Jazz* (Ann Arbor: University of Michigan Press, 1991), 24–31.
10. Ibid., 24–31.
11. Heinrich comes from John Chilton's *Who's Who of Jazz*, 4th ed. (New York: Da Capo, 1985). Articles from the *Fond du Lac Reporter* refer to Beau as Henry.
12. Most of the information in this chapter is from several articles from the *Fond du Lac Reporter*, generously supplied by the Fond du Lac Public Library. These include: Jean Sorg, "This Local Musician Made It to the 'Big Time,'" June 17, 1974; "Bands Honor Harvey Beau," May 3, 1977; Ellen Zyduck, "Heinie Beau, Famed Musician, Arranger, Composer Returns Home," August 5, 1979; and "Famed Clarinetist Heinie Beau Dies," April 20, 1987. Most helpful was the July 17, 1965, article by bandleader turned disc jockey Ron Harvey, "Hollywood Arranger Traces Success to Beau Family Orchestra Training."
13. An extant photo of Wally Beau and His Orchestra from 1936 includes all of the brothers but not Marie.
14. This and the previous quote are from "Hollywood Arranger Traces Success."
15. Ibid.
16. Ibid.
17. Marc Myers, "Heinie Beau: Moviesville Jazz," JazzWax. http://jazz.fm/index.php/music-a-video-mainmenu/jazzwax-mainmenu-153/9565-heinie-beau-moviesville-jazz, originally posted at JazzWax on February 19, 2014.
18. Ibid.

19. From the notes by Dave Dexter Jr. to *Heinie Beau and His Hollywood Sextet*, Henri Records, 1984.
20. Ibid.
21. Information on Schroeder is from Chilton's *Who's Who of Jazz*; Feather and Gitler's various editions of *The Encyclopedia of Jazz*; James M. Doran's entry on Schroeder in *The New Grove Dictionary of Jazz*, vol. 3, p. 525; and Owen Coyle, "Quiet Mastery," *The Mississippi Rag* 9, no. 3 (1982): 1–2.
22. Quotes and information in this and the previous two paragraphs are from Coyle, "Quiet Mastery."
23. Chilton, *Who's Who*, 293.
24. Kernfeld, ed., *The New Grove*, 525.
25. Coyle, "Quiet Mastery."
26. Max Harrison's notes to Mosaic CD set *The Complete CBS Recordings of Eddie Condon and His All Stars*.
27. Most of the information included here is the result of Ted Mesmer's labors. Ted sent me numerous internet articles that include information on Maxted. Specific references are cited as necessary.
28. This is from a report on Maxted's death that was posted at the website of Jazz at the Landing; date unknown. www.jazzhouse.org/gone/lastpost2.php3?edit=1008424902.
29. This information comes from an obituary that appeared in the paper of Local 802 (New York) of the American Federation of Musicians in January 2002.
30. The article by John Sheridan, "Remembering Billy," from 2001, appeared on various websites.
31. This appears in the standard press materials of the Allred band.
32. Adrian's real name was Wesley Adrianson. According to Mesmer, Wes's father never forgave him for shortening the family name.
33. Much of the information here comes from a variety of materials generously sent to me by Cappy Lewis's children, Mark and Sharon. This included newspaper clippings (some, unfortunately, without dates, or even the name of the newspaper evident) and a short interview with Lewis in some sort of history of the Woody Herman bands. Also consulted, Scott Yanow's *The Trumpet Kings: The Players Who Shaped the Sound of Jazz Trumpet* (Milwaukee: Backbeat Books, 2001), 232.
34. Herman materials.

Chapter 6

1. This and the next quote are from Michael Drew's article "Beautiful Music Together: For 25 Years, ex-Milwaukeean Jackie Cain Has Teamed with Roy Kral," *Milwaukee Journal*, August 11, 1974.
2. The interview was posted May 18, 2009 at www.jazzwax.com/2009/05/interview-jackie-cain-part-1.html and the subsequent parts (www.jazzwax.com/2009/05/interview-jackie-cain-part-2.html, etc.).
3. Cain told Myers about a number of incidents where Ventura clearly resented the attention that Kral and especially Cain were getting from audiences and the press.
4. This list was posted at jazzbackstory.blogspot.com/2014/09/jackie-cain-1928-2014.html, on September 20, 2014, after Cain's death, by Monk Rowe.
5. Being employed at Ripon College, I had access to many articles about Jarreau that are in the college archives. Citations are from Mary Kane's cover article "Complex Melody: The Joy and Pain of Al Jarreau," for the *Milwaukee Journal*'s Sunday publication *Wisconsin* (July 30, 1989); Jean Grant's two articles, "Heaven and Earth: Jarreau Tries to Stay True" and "Jarreau By Any Name," for the 1993 summer issue of *Ripon Magazine*, the college's alumni magazine; and articles for *Down Beat* by Lee Underwood, "Al Jarreau" (October 7, 1976); Steve Bloom, "Al Jarreau: Breaking Away," (February 1982); and Robin Tolleson, "A Troubador's New Tones: All Jarreau," (April 1989). Also cited is an unsigned 1994 in-house publication of WEA Records. Some information came from Jarreau's website, aljarreau.com. Unattributed quotes are from my conversation with Jarreau when he attended his class's fiftieth reunion at Ripon College, June 22, 2012.
6. Underwood, "Al Jarreau," 38, and Kane, "Complex Melody."
7. Bloom, "Al Jarreau," 26.
8. During our visit in June 2012, Jarreau sang "Too Fat Polka."
9. Jarreau has referred to this event in several interviews, and there is a picture of the flyer for the event, with Jarreau in a sailor's suit, in the WEA publication.
10. Kane, "Complex Melody."
11. Bloom, "Al Jarreau," 26.
12. WEA publication.

13. Being an NCAA Division III college, Ripon does not offer athletic scholarships. Either the practice was different in the late 1950s and early 1960s, or perhaps Jarreau had a job in the athletic department.
14. Grant, "Jarreau by Any Name," 8, and Jarreau interview.
15. Peter Bock, "The *Indigos* . . . Then and Now," *Ripon Magazine* (Summer 1993): 9–10.
16. Unsigned article, "Al Jarreau Featured Singer in Miss Wisconsin Pageant," *Oshkosh Northwestern*.
17. Donald H. Dooley, "Young Singer Seeks M.A. in Psychology," *Milwaukee Journal*, September 7, 1962.
18. The liner notes to Al Jarreau, *Still in Love with You*, state that although the band worked at the Tender Trap, the album was recorded due to the efforts of the owners of the Celebrity Club in Moline, Illinois. The recording location is not listed.
19. WEA publication.
20. Most of the preceding paragraph is from the WEA publication, with some information from Robert Palmer, "Al Jarreau: Scat Singer for the Seventies," *Rolling Stone* (January 25, 1979).
21. Underwood, "Al Jarreau," 38.
22. Michael Drew, "Singer Al Jarreau Displays New Skills," *Milwaukee Journal* (July 21, 1970).
23. Quoted in Grant, "Heaven," 3, and other places.
24. Underwood, "Al Jarreau," 38.
25. Bill Milkowski, "Jarreau Woos, Wins Hometowners,"*Milwaukee Journal* (September 18, 1980): 6.
26. This and the previous quote are from Bloom, "Al Jarreau," 25.
27. Ibid., 58.
28. That recording is *The Complete Miles Davis At Montreux 1973–1991*, a twenty-CD set released in 2002 on Warner Music Switzerland.
29. Other alumni receiving honorary degrees at the ceremony were Gail Dobish, a successful opera singer; Frances Lee McCain, who had recently starred in movie hits *Gremlins* and *Back to the Future*; and Ben Marcus, whose Wisconsin empire of movie theaters began with his first theater in Ripon, in 1935.
30. Wayne Lee, "Al Jarreau: The Fate of a Natural Winner," *Jazziz* (March 1989): 35.

31. One wonders what the reaction to this album would have created had it been released by an unknown singer.
32. *Down Beat* dedicated a page of its October 2014 issue to an interview with Jarreau about the album.
33. The biographical information here is from published interviews with Sutton, especially the 2011 interview conducted by Todd Gordon, "Tierney Sutton: In Union There is Strength," posted at All About Jazz (www.allaboutjazz.com/tierney-sutton-in-union-there-is-strength-tierney-sutton-by-todd-gordon.php), and the article by Mark Small, "A Novel Approach," posted at the Berklee College of Music website (www.berklee.edu/bt/204/coverstory.html). Unattributed quotes are from my interview with Sutton in the fall of 2011.
34. Sutton heard Jaye a few years later at Milwaukee's Jazz Estate, and Sutton found that "she was happening; she was totally happening. She had a great voice, great sound, she swung her little tail off."
35. The early recordings included just the trio; later ones added a second bassist to many of the selections.
36. Gordon, "Tierney Sutton."
37. Mitchell Seidel, "Tierney Sutton," *JazzTimes*, May 2007.

Chapter 7

1. Information and quotes in this chapter come largely from my interviews with Lyle Mays, March 18, 2014; Lynne Arriale, May 1, 2014; David Hazeltine, September 21, 2012; Geoffrey Keezer, September 4, 2010; Ron Keezer, June 29, 2011; Rick Germanson, May 2, 2014; Ethan Iverson, February 1, 2013; and Dan Nimmer, January 28, 2012.
2. Patrick T. Will in *The New Grove Dictionary of Jazz*, 2nd ed., ed. Barry Kernfeld, vol. 2 (London: Macmillan Publishers Limited, 2002), 737–738.
3. One can read about this work and see a performance of it in the article, "The Most Intriguing Performance in Jazz 2011" at Jazz Online. http://jazzonline.com/blogs/the-most-intriguing-performance-in-jazz-2011.html.
4. Ken Micallef, "Not Just for Jazz Lovers," *Down Beat*, September 2009, 32–35; Christian Wissmuller, "Lynne Arriale—Teaching Fearlessness," *JAZZed*, November 2009, 26–35; "Equal Time: On the Strength of Women in Jazz Today, Gender Lines Are Finally Being Erased," *Down Beat*, April 2011, 30–35.

5. Ira Gitler, "In the Trenches: David Hazeltine Provides the Invaluable Piano Grease That Keeps the Scene Swinging," *Down Beat*, May 2008, 44.
6. According to Ira Gitler, by 2008 Hazeltine had appeared on more than one hundred albums as a sideman.
7. Ed Berger, "Champagne Tastes: David Hazeltine's Modern Standards," *JazzTimes*, July/August 2005, 40.
8. Some of the information in this and the next paragraph is from Geoffrey Keezer's website, http://geoffreykeezer.com/.
9. See discography for Keezer's thoughts about his favorite albums.
10. Most of the biographical information here, and all unattributed quotes, came from my interview with Ethan Iverson. Also valuable were Iverson's blog, https://ethaniverson.com/, Howard Mandel's profile "Platonic Idealism" in the January 2000 issue of *Down Beat*, and Peter Kirn's "Bad, Not Bad," *Keyboard*, August 2005.
11. Known now for huge sweepstakes, during this period Publisher's Clearing House sent out a periodic catalog of books and records that publishers were trying to get rid of, sold for bargain prices.
12. Iverson said to be sure to put this in anything that I might write about him. It is to be a cautionary tale to young students.
13. This and the previous quote are from Mandel, "Platonic Idealism."
14. Ibid.
15. Ibid.
16. See the article about Rosoff by Iverson's wife, Sarah Deming, at Iverson's blog. https://ethaniverson.com/guest-posts/the-emotional-rhythm-of-sophia-rosoff-by-sarah-deming/.
17. Quoted in David Schimke, "King of the Throne," *Minnesota Monthly*, July 2004.
18. Andrew Bartlett, review of *These Are the Vistas*, *Jazziz*, August 2003; David R. Adler, review of *The Bad Plus*, AllMusic. www.allmusic.com/album/the-bad-plus-mw0000657163; David Fricke, review of *Give*, *Rolling Stone*, March 18, 2004.
19. Dan Ouellette, "The Bad Plus: Committed to a Concept," *Down Beat*, November 2010.
20. John Ephland review of *These Are the Vistas*, *Down Beat*, May 2003.
21. "Live at Smalls–Iverson, Ethan / Street, Ben," ArkivMusic. www.arkivmusic.com/classical/album.jsp?album_id=492510.

22. Jim Higgins, "Keys to His Big Success Began Here," *Milwaukee Journal Sentinel* (November 28, 2014), features a photograph of Nimmer in which he appears to still be a teenager.

Chapter 8

1. Information comes from Leonard Feather and Ira Gitler's *The Biographical Encyclopedia of Jazz* (New York: Oxford University Press, 1999); entry on Clark by Lawrence Koch in *The New Grove Dictionary of Jazz*, vol. 1, 2nd ed., ed. Barry Kernfeld, (London: Macmillan Publishers Limited, 2002), 447–448; and Harvey Siders, "Caught in the Act: Super Sax Plays Bird," *Down Beat*, February 15, 1973.
2. Kevin Brown, "Gumina, Jazz Accordionist, Tries Hand at the Classics," *Milwaukee Journal*, June 27, 1955.
3. Jan Uebelherr, who wrote Gumina's obituary for the *Milwaukee Journal Sentinel*, "'Mr. Fingers' Tommy Gumina Was an Accordion Innovator" (October 30, 2013), also supplied me with many of the archived articles (cited below) that she used for research for that obituary.
4. Dorothy Madle, "Accordionist Gumina Recounts Rise to Fame," *Milwaukee Sentinel*, September 7, 1954.
5. Larry Lawrence, "Squeeze Play by Sinatra Took Role from Milwaukee Accordion Player," *Milwaukee Journal*, May 18, 1955.
6. Madle, "Accordionist Gumina Recounts Rise to Fame."
7. Ibid.
8. Willie Pickens interview, April 11, 2013.
9. "Two New Groovings by Gumina Sure to Send Platter Shop Prexy," *Milwaukee Journal*, February 3, 1956.
10. "Accordionist Answers Call of 'The Horn,'" *Milwaukee Sentinel*, June 24, 1956.
11. Earl Wilson, "Accordion Acumen: Gumina: Jazz to Classics," *Milwaukee Journal*, April 7, 1957.
12. Larry Lawrence, "Squeeze Play."
13. "Accordionist Answers the Call of 'The Horn.'"
14. While some reports said that Gumina left the studios to work with DeFranco full time, the *Milwaukee Journal* reported in July 1961 that he was working on two TV series, *Route 66* and *Naked City*, writing and conducting for the former.

15. Information in this paragraph comes from Jordi Pujol's essay for the CD reissue of *Pacific Standard (Swingin'!) Time* and *Presenting the Buddy DeFranco–Tommy Gumina Quartet*, as well as the original notes to these albums, both by noted jazz critic Leonard Feather.
16. My copy of "Tommy Gumina Tries Some—Monkey Business," *Milwaukee Sentinel*, October 20, 1963, is incomplete and lists no author.
17. Madle, "Accordionist Gumina Recounts Rise to Fame."
18. "Tommy Gumina Tries Some—Monkey Business."
19. This and the previous quote are from Keith Spore's review of the Pepper recording, "Peppery Accordionist Finds Gold in Jazz" *Milwaukee Sentinel*, May 3, 1991.
20. Elliott Simon, "Tommy Gumina," All About Jazz, May 15, 2010. www.allaboutjazz.com/php/article.php?id=35987#.UpAmVGTErbw.
21. Information here is from Don Heckman's "Mike Melvoin Dies at 74; Studio Musician, Composer," *Los Angeles Times*, February 24, 2012; Robbie Gennet's "Mike Melvoin, 1937–2012," *Keyboard Magazine*, October 4, 2012; and Andrew Barker's "Former Recording Academy Prexy Was Jazz Pianist," *Variety*, February 27, 2012. There was a bit of other information in the February 2012 obituary in the *Milwaukee Journal Sentinel*.
22. Barker, "Former Recording Academy Prexy Was Jazz Pianist."
23. Gennet, "Mike Melvoin, 1937–2012."
24. Heckman, "Mike Melvoin Dies at 74."
25. Notes of Melvoin's album *The Capitol Sessions* (Naim Label, 2000).
26. Heckman, "Mike Melvoin Dies at 74."
27. Information and quotes from my June 26, 2014, interview with Steve Houghton, and follow-up meetings and correspondence.
28. Information and quotes from my August 11, 2014, interview with Beverly Dahlke and follow-up emails.
29. As of 2015, this video could easily be found on YouTube.
30. After Hall left, the band Jack Mack and the Heart Attack became the show's house band. Greg Smith was a member of that band.
31. The Wikipedia article on *The Late Show* states that Milwaukee affiliate WCVG, a prospective Fox affiliate, "would only sign with the network if they did not have to carry *The Late Show*." http://en.wikipedia.org/wiki/The_Late_Show_(Fox_TV_series).

32. Information and quotes from my June 28, 2013, interview with Tom Luer and follow-up conversations and correspondence.

Chapter 9

1. Information and quotes in this chapter come from interviews with Brian Lynch, November 6, 2009; Carl Allen, May 15, 2010; Gerald Cannon, May 27, 2014; Gregory Tardy, May 13, 2014; Joel Frahm, November 6, 2009; Ike Sturm, November 25, 2011; John Sullivan, March 16, 2014; Joe Sanders, April 6, 2013; and Philip Dizack, January 15, 2014.
2. Tom Erdmann, "A Commitment to Excellence: Brian Lynch," *International Trumpet Guild*, June 2007. Posted at Brian Lynch's website, http://brianlynchjazz.com/2007/06/international-trumpet-guild-journal-a-commitment-to-excellence-brian-lynch/.
3. Manty Ellis told me a very similar version of the same story.
4. Some information comes from Lynch's interview with Bob Rusch in the March 1993 issue of *Cadence*.
5. Much of the information in the next few paragraphs is derived from the standard reference books and Michael J. West's "Life of Brian: How Brian Lynch Became One of the Best and Busiest Trumpeters in Jazz and Latin Jazz," *JazzTimes*, October 2013.
6. West, "Life of Brian," 39.
7. Ted Panken "Brian Lynch: Expansive Presentation," *Down Beat* (February 2005): 28–29.
8. West, "Life of Brian," 39.
9. Michael Bourne, "Brian Lynch," *Down Beat* (August 1988): 14.
10. West, "Life of Brian," 40.
11. Some information on Carl Allen is from his entry by Gary Kennedy in *The New Grove Dictionary of Jazz*, vol. 1, 2nd ed., ed. Barry Kernfeld (London: Macmillan Publishers Limited, 2002), 33, and his website, http://carlallen.com/.
12. This is according to an interview by Skip Spratt, "Joel Frahm—MiniView," published at http://saxshed.com/joel-frahm-miniview-2/.
13. "Joel Frahm Biography," AllMusic. www.allmusic.com/artist/joel-frahm-mn0000215379/biography.
14. Spratt, "Joel Frahm."

15. Some background on John Sullivan was supplied in an earlier interview with his father, Dave, with commentary from his mother, Karen.
16. Some of the information here about the Milwaukee High School of the Arts combo was confirmed by the scrapbook of clippings that Cliff Gribble gave me.

Chapter 10

1. Much of the information on Dick Ruedebusch comes from Jack Baker's article "Dick Ruedebusch: Mr. Trumpet," in Michael Corenthal's *The Illustrated History of Wisconsin Music* (Milwaukee: Yesterdays Memories and MGC Publications, 1991). Other observations come from my interview with Chuck Hedges on June 8, 2010.
2. Baker, "Dick Ruedebusch," 371.
3. I was shown this program at the Mayville Historical Society.
4. Baker, "Dick Ruedebusch," 371.
5. Ibid., 372.
6. Ibid., 372.
7. Dominic Spera interview, July 13, 2015.
8. Baker, "Dick Ruedebusch," 373.
9. Hedges interview.
10. Baker, "Dick Ruedebusch," 373.
11. John Wilson, "New Jazz Leader Makes It Big," *New York Times*, January 13, 1962. Wilson wrote that Ruedebusch's "bull-like shoulders might qualify him for a line job on the Green Bay Packers."
12. Baker, "Dick Ruedebusch," 374.
13. Hedges interview.
14. Baker, "Dick Ruedebusch," 374.
15. "Jovial Jazzman," *Saturday Evening Post*, June 30, 1962.
16. Baker, "Dick Ruedebusch," 374.
17. Announcement, *Milwaukee Journal*, December 29, 1965.
18. Ruedebusch was with Herman in 1966, and in 1967 at least until late March, when the "Eastern" portion of the album *Woody Live—East and West* was recorded.
19. Baker, "Dick Ruedebusch," 375.
20. Hedges interview.

21. Baker, "Dick Ruedebusch," 375.
22. Information and quotes from my Hedges interview.
23. This legendary location thrived from the 1940s into the 1970s, and at its height "sprawled across more than 300 acres. It boasted attractions such as an air strip, golf course, restaurant, church, dinner theater and two ice skating rinks." "Remember When: Wagon Wheel Once Stretched over 300 Acres,"*Rockford Register Star* (online), posted April 24, 2009. www.rrstar.com/article/20090424/NEWS/304249852.
24. Bobby Tanzilo, "Jazz Clubs Upped Old Milwaukee's Hipster Quotient," *OnMilwaukee.com*, posted November 8, 2008 (https://onmilwaukee.com/music/articles/jazzpast.html), and various reports from Milwaukee newspapers. The club was a strip joint at the time of Pogrob's death. He was discovered blindfolded and shot numerous times. The slaying was never solved, but is generally considered to have been the work of organized crime.
25. Hal Willard, *The Wildest One: The Life of Wild Bill Davison* (Monkton, MD: Avondale Press, 1996), 310.
26. The information here is largely from newspaper clippings, programs, and other memorabilia generously made available to me by Sig Millonzi's widow, Eileen, and daughter Stacey Vojvodich. They also told me stories and facts that have informed this profile.
27. "Sig Millonzi—Milwaukee's Jazz Giant," *The Entertainer*, June 17–27, 1975.
28. *Billboard*, May 7, 1955.
29. "Jazz Fights for Place in Rock 'n' Roll Town," *Milwaukee Journal*, January 1970.
30. Dave Zurawik, "Never a Blue Monday at Club Garibaldi," *Milwaukee Sentinel*, August 8, 1975.
31. Information and quotes in the rest of this chapter are from April 4, 2014, interviews with Jack Carr, George Welland, and Steve Lewandowski.

Chapter 11

1. Information and quotes in this chapter come from interviews with Manty Ellis, March 8, 2012; Willie Pickens, April 11, 2013; Brian Lynch, November 6, 2009; Berkeley Fudge, January 28, 2012; Jim Paolo, June 7, 2012; Sam Belton, January 28, 2012; Mark Davis, June 12, 2012; Jeff Hamann and David Bayles, September 19, 2009; and Adekola Adedapo, January 28, 2012.

2. Derek J. Pinkham, *Milwaukee Jazz Profiles: Lives & Lessons of Musicians from the Cream City* (Milwaukee, WI: Marquette University Press, 2010), 200. Pinkham relates the story that Manty started sitting in with the Bert Bailey Big Band at this time. Billy Wallace was the regular pianist but brought the young Manty in to cover piano while Wallace worked on saxophone.
3. Aaron Cohen, "Manty Ellis," *Midwest Jazz Masters Journal* 4, no. 3 (1997): 29.
4. Ibid.
5. At the daylong events preceding the Eastside Jazz Fest of January 2012, a photograph was presented of a young Manty Ellis with a baby Berkeley Fudge. Mark Davis has related to me that at some point as a youth Fudge found his birth certificate and discovered that his first name was James; his middle name was Berkeley. He was never called James.
6. Evan Rytlewski, "Jazz Artists Hold Fundraiser for Berkeley Fudge: The Saxophonist Is Recovering from a Stroke," *Shepherd Express*, December 1, 2010. http://expressmilwaukee.com/blog-6121-jazz-artists-hold-fundraiser-for-berkeley-fudge.html.
7. Posted at jsonline on January 27, 2011.
8. Lapham Park is now known, at least in part, as Carver Park.
9. The information on Bunky Green is largely from his entry by Gary Kennedy in *The New Grove Dictionary of Jazz*, vol. 1, 2nd ed., ed. Barry Kernfeld, (London: Macmillan Publishers Limited, 2002), 86–87; the unsigned essay that accompanies the 2007 Lone Hill Jazz release of *Playin' for Keeps*; and Ted Panken "Bunky Green & Rudresh Mahanthappa: Breaking Free of the System," *Down Beat*, February 2011, 24–29.
10. Much of the information here is from standard sources (the entry on Morgan by Brian Priestley in Kernfeld, ed., *The New Grove*, vol. 2, p. 817, and others), but much of it is also from Manty Ellis's recollections. Ellis told me much more about Morgan than is included here.
11. Brandt Reiter, "Frank Morgan," All About Jazz, August 9, 2004. www.allaboutjazz.com/frank-morgan-frank-morgan-by-brandt-reiter.php.
12. Jeff Chambers's website, www.jeffchambersjazz.com/.
13. Biographical information on Buddy Montgomery is from standard sources and buddymontgomery.com.
14. Mike Drew, "Montgomery's Jazz Enlivened Pfister: Self-Taught Musician

Was Brother to Wes," *Milwaukee Journal Sentinel*, May 21, 2009. www.jsonline.com/entertainment/musicandnightlife/45798572.html.

15. Ellis related names and places to me. Rosie was possibly known as one of the higher-class "madams" in the area.
16. Drew, "Montgomery's Jazz."
17. Ben Barbera, *An Improvised World: Jazz and Community in Milwaukee, 1950–1970* (master's dissertation, UW–Milwaukee, 2012), 161–162.
18. Manty Ellis told me about missing the first day of recording because of travel and communication foul-ups as he returned to Milwaukee from California.
19. Some of this history is derived from Lora Rosner's notes to Rhyne's 1992 album *The Legend*.
20. This and the following block quote are from Jack Grassel, email to the author, June 5, 2012.
21. Liner notes to Jackie Allen's *Which?* (Naxos Jazz, 1999).

Chapter 12

1. Information and quotes are from interviews with Warren Wiegratz and Michael Murphy, August 25, 2011; Daryl Stuemer, April 22, 2014; John Kirchberger and Jim Paolo, June 7, 2012; Toty Ramos, November 27, 2011; Tom Sandquist, January 16 and 18, 2014; Larry Darling (email), February 2, 2014; and Curt Hanrahan, June 5, 2013.
2. Sometime around 2010, someone called Wiegratz's attention to a copy of the Mustard Men single selling on eBay—which it did, according to Wiegratz, for $68 to someone in Italy.
3. One of the auditionees was Michaela Carey, who, according to Daryl Stuermer, "sounded very good, but vocally she was a little bit too light for our kind of band." The audition was not in vain, however, as Carey and Stuermer eventually went on to a long and successful marriage.
4. Wiegratz believes he must have sold twenty-five or thirty thousand copies out of his basement.
5. Members of Toto, who were working in an adjoining studio, contributed some background vocals to the album.
6. On the Oceans album *Second Chance*, "Star Spangled Banner" was the opening cut.

7. Some of the following material is from Dave Zurawik, "Forecast for September: Carefree Days Ahead," *Milwaukee Sentinel*, March 19, 1976.
8. Ibid.
9. Some of the information about La Chazz comes from www.lachazz.com; some information and quotes are from Bill Milkowski, "Latin Group Offers Happy Mix of Salsa, Jazz," *Milwaukee Journal*, January 19, 1979.
10. Some material about Montage is from two newspaper articles: Dennis Getto, "A Kaleidoscope of Color in Music—That's Montage," *Milwaukee Sentinel*, February 25, 1977; Bill Milkowski, "Montage's 2 Year Wait Pays Off," *Milwaukee Journal*, March 5, 1977.
11. Much of the material here, including the quotes, is from Martin Hintz, "Symphonic to Rock—Matrix Crew Does It All, and Melodiously Well," *Milwaukee Sentinel*, December 16, 1972. Other information was supplied by Jack Grassel.
12. "2 Services Held Monday for David Phillips," *Milwaukee Sentinel*, November 28, 1981.
13. Eugene Chadbourne, "David Phillips Biography," AllMusic. www.allmusic.com/artist/david-phillips-mn0002042770/biography. Laura Snyder confirmed this in a conversation after an MSO concert in Ripon, Wisconsin, on October 5, 2014, lovingly showing me the instrument.
14. As a charter member of Matrix, I know most of the band's history. However, I was not in Wisconsin when the idea germinated. Some of the quotes here are from my interviews with John Harmon on June 28 and July 5, 2011.

Chapter 13

1. Information and quotes in this chapter come from interviews with Jan Wheaton, January 21, 2014; Gerri DiMaggio, August 20, 2012; Lynette Margulies, March 17, 2014; Jackie Allen and Hans Sturm, May 22, 2014; Kelly De Haven, June 6, 2012, and August 3, 2015; Sims and Maggie Delaney-Potthoff and Jeff Weiss, August 22, 2014; and Ben Sidran, July 17, 2014. Some information on Jan Wheaton comes from her website, www.jwvocalz.com.
2. Lue Allen, "With a Song in Her Heart: Jazz Vocalist Gerri DiMaggio Comes into Her Own," *Isthmus*, February 8, 2002.

3. Ibid.
4. The Jazz Showcase turned into the Dangle Lounge, a notorious adult club.
5. Some of the photos for Mitchell's album *Hejira*, including the one of Mitchell ice-skating, were shot on a frozen Lake Mendota.
6. Justine Kessler, "Gerri DiMaggio's Double Life," *Wisconsin Woman*, August 2006, contains much more information about Gerri's business career.
7. Allen, "With a Song."
8. Although I eventually visited with Sidran on July 17, 2014, quotes, unless noted, are from *Ben Sidran: A Life in the Music* (New York: Taylor Trade, 2003).
9. Ibid., 31. Sidran mentions two other regulars at the Pad who went on to some fame: musician Danny Kalb formed the band Blues Project, and Marshall Brickman became a writer for comedian/filmmaker Woody Allen.
10. Ibid., 68.
11. Daniel Kreps, "Clyde Stubblefield, James Brown's 'Funky Drummer,' Dead at 73," *Rolling Stone*, February 18, 2017.
12. On separate occasions, Mingus's drummer Dannie Richmond stayed at the Sidran home, and, later, Mingus himself spent a week there.
13. Ben Sidran, *Talking Jazz: An Illustrated Oral History*, (San Francisco: Pomegranate Artbooks, 1992). A paperback edition was published by Da Capo Press in 1995. In 2007, an expanded version with a booklet and twenty-four compact discs with interviews with sixty musicians was released by Unlimited Media.
14. Much of the information in the previous two paragraphs comes from Sidran's website, http://bensidran.com.
15. Ben Sidran, email to the author, July 18, 2014.

Chapter 14

1. Information and quotes in this chapter come from interviews (and follow-up emails and conversations) with Doc De Haven (and daughter Kelly and son-in-law David Cooper), June 6, 2012; Gerri DiMaggio, August 20, 2012, and Jan Wheaton, January 21, 2014; Les Thimmig, July 22, 2014; Joan Wildman, July 22, 2014; Richard Davis, January 14, 2013; Chris Washburne, November 16, 2013; and Hans Sturm (and Jackie Allen), May 22, 2014. Further information on Doc De Haven came from materials supplied to

me by his family, some of which were used as promotional materials during his career. Doc's family also supplied me with other materials, some of which were used as promotional materials during his career.

2. Much of this information is from Beebe's obituary that ran in the *Chicago Tribune* on September 2, 2004.
3. "Johnny Shacklett," *Wikibin*. http://wikibin.org/articles/johnny-shacklett.html.
4. Album notes for Sidran's album *Cien Noches*, CD Baby. www.cdbaby.com/cd/talkingjazz3.
5. Thanks to Greg Keel for sending me a copy of the program book, from which much of this information is derived. Keel, then in high school, attended the Camp Randall Stadium concert during the festival.
6. Information in the following paragraphs, including quotes, is from Stanley Dance's notes for the Pablo Records release *The Ellington Suites* (1976), which was released on compact disc in 1990 (Original Jazz Classics), and from Ellington's memoir, *Music Is My Mistress* (New York: Doubleday, 1973), 405–407.
7. Jeannie Cheatham, *Meet Me with Your Black Drawers On* (Austin: University of Texas Press, 2006), 226–227.
8. "Mayoral Proclamation of Cheatham Day," 2010. www.jeanniecheatham.com/cheathamproclamation.pdf.
9. Cheatham, *Meet Me*, 232–235.
10. Biographical information on Davis is from a variety of sources, including his entry by Bill Bennett in *The New Grove Dictionary of Jazz*, vol. 1, 2nd ed., ed. Barry Kernfeld, (London: Macmillan Publishers Limited, 2002), 578–579. When I interviewed Davis by phone in 2013, we talked about his life in Wisconsin, and especially his activities since 2000. Quotes are from that interview unless otherwise noted.
11. Sara Freeman, "Richard Davis: The Bassist's New Bag," *Isthmus*, July 14, 2000, posted online on April 7, 2011. www.thedailypage.com/daily/article.php?article=33013. *The New Grove* refers to Davis singing in an "informal trio with his brothers."
12. Kernfeld, ed., *New Grove*, 578.
13. Richard Davis's website, http://richarddavis.org/.
14. Ibid.
15. His awards include the Hilldale Award for distinguished teaching from

former chancellor Donna Shalala, and an honorary doctorate of humane letters from Edgewood College, in 1998; and in 2000, the Manfred E. Swarsensky Humanitarian Award from the Rotary Club of Madison. In 2001 he received the Governor of Wisconsin Arts Award. The city of Madison presented him with the Martin Luther King Jr. Humanitarian Award in 2003. In 2008, Richard Davis received a MAMA (Madison Area Music Award) Lifetime Achievement Award; in 2009 he received the Exceptional Service Award from the University of Wisconsin–Madison and the Spencer Tracy Award for Distinction in the Performing Arts from the Wisconsin Historical Society. This list was excerpted from http://richarddavis.org/.

16. Some information here is from "Seeking an Open Culture, New York Trombonist Chris Washburne Found It in Madison," UW–Madison website, November 8, 2013. https://uwmadisonschoolofmusic.wordpress.com/2013/11/08/washburne2013/. I also consulted information I collected about Washburne for my book *Jazz 'Bones: The World of Jazz Trombone* (Rottenburg, Germany: Advance Music, 2005). All quotes are from my interview with Washburne unless otherwise noted.
17. "Seeking an Open Culture."
18. Ibid.
19. Ibid.
20. Jason Gross, "Roscoe Mitchell Interview," *Perfect Sound Forever*, May 1998. http://furious.com/perfect/roscoemitchell.html.

Chapter 15

1. Information and quotes are from interviews (and some follow-up emails and conversations) with Kaye Berigan, May 19, 2011; Frank DeMiles, May 17, 2014; Jack Grassel, August 30, 2014; Jeff Pietrangelo and Tom Newburg, June 2, 2011; Luis Diaz, July 18, 2015; Juli Wood, August 23, 2013, and July 22, 2015; Connie Grauer, July 23, 2015; Eric Schoor, April 17, 2014; and Andy Schumm, January 13, 2014.
2. Howell showed up in the seventies in Chicago as a trombonist, among other things, recording with Eddie Harris.
3. Kaye Berigan, email to the author, May 20, 2011.
4. Eugene Kane, "Still in Session: But Only a Few Clubs Carry On the Struggle to Keep Jazz Alive in Milwaukee," *Milwaukee Journal*, May 3, 1988;

Mike Drew, "Not All Clubs Have Been Drummed Out of Town," *Milwaukee Journal*, May 3, 1988.

5. Drew, "Not All Clubs Have Been Drummed Out of Town."
6. At the 2014 Bunny Berigan Jazz Jubilee, Kaye presented me with this list.
7. Kaye Berigan, email to the author.
8. Amy Rabideau Silvers, "Billings Had Creative Hand in Cassette Lessons, Talking Books," *Milwaukee Journal Sentinel*, December 9, 2010.
9. Quotes in the section about Peter Dominguez are from Jon Liebman, "Peter Dominguez," *For Bass Players Only*, February 1, 2010 (http://forbassplayersonly.com/interview-peter-dominguez) unless noted otherwise. Also consulted was Kevin Johnson, "An Interview with Peter Dominguez," *No Treble: Nothing But Bass*, August 18, 2011. www.notreble.com/buzz/2011/08/18/an-interview-with-peter-dominguez. Dominguez and I also exchanged a number of emails.
10. Erich Burnett, "Here Comes the Judge," *Oberlin Conservatory Magazine*, 2014. http://issuu.com/oberlin/docs/oberlinconservatorymagazine2014/1.
11. Jack Grassel's Wikipedia entry. https://en.wikipedia.org/wiki/Jack_Grassel.
12. Jan Uebelherr, "Take Note: Pietrangelo's Specialty Was the Trumpet," *Milwaukee Journal Sentinel*, January 8, 2013. http://archive.jsonline.com/news/obituaries/take-note-pietrangelos-specialty-was-the-trumpet-e089gk3-186079811.html. Pietrangelo's friends had heard of him referring to himself as a member of this group on many occasions.
13. His sister Carol Wilson was probably the source for this information, which was in the obituary listed above.
14. Ken Orgel, email to the author, December 31, 2012. The quote appeared in Uebelherr, "Take Note."
15. Diaz owns a 45-rpm record that Narvaez's band put out sometime prior to this, perhaps in the early 1960s. He believes it must be one of the first Latin jazz (if it was jazz) recordings made in the city.
16. Mrs. Fun's website, http://mrsfun.com/about.

Chapter 16

1. Information and quotes in this chapter are from interviews with Vince Fuh, July 31, 2012; David Stoler, December 2, 2014; David Cooper, October 9, 2014; Paul Hastil, June 28, 2012; Nick Moran, July 31, 2012; Louka Patenoude, July 24, 2012; and Hanah Jon Taylor, June 11, 2015.

Chapter 17

1. Information and quotes in this chapter comes from interviews with Dominic Spera, July 13, 2015; Allen Johnson, January 3, 2012; Mike Hale, July 27, 2013; Claude Cailliet, September 1 and October 3, 2013; Dan Fornero, April 5, 2014; Russ Johnson, June 5, 2013; Eric Jacobson, July 13, 2015; Jamie Breiwick, July 17, 2013 (follow-up phone conversation June 2, 2015); and David Bixler, August 3, 2013.
2. Boutan later became a well-known piano bar player, singer, and radio personality in the Racine–Kenosha area.
3. This little bit of information about Hemkes was gleaned from several websites, as well as Elizabeth Blaustien's article "Music Teacher Also Gives Students Lessons on Life" in the *Journal Times* (March 7, 2000). http://journaltimes.com/music-teacher-also-gives-students-lessons-on-life/article_6eefa5ad-7f1a-5f22-b9ea-712208c92477.html.
4. Information on Lucien Cailliet comes from various internet resources and interviews with Claude Cailliet, including his entry on Bach Cantatas Website (www.bach-cantatas.com/Lib/Cailliet-Lucien.htm) and his biography on IMDb (www.imdb.com/name/nm0128838/bio?ref_=nm_ov_bio_sm).
5. Nelson went on to a successful career as a player in the area and as a middle school band director for years in Ripon, Wisconsin.
6. Most of the information here comes from several different obituaries for Robinson, mostly in British journals: "Jazz Saxophonist with Refined Tenor Style," *The Scotsman* (www.jazzhouse.org/gone/lastpost2.php3?edit=1004533565); Peter Vacher, "Spike Robinson," *The Guardian*, November 6, 2001, (www.theguardian.com/news/2001/nov/07/guardianobituaries); and "Spike Robinson," *The Telegraph*, November 2, 2001, (www.telegraph.co.uk/news/obituaries/1361199/Spike-Robinson.html).
7. Vacher, "Spike Robinson."
8. Ibid.
9. "Spike Robinson," *The Telegraph*.
10. Vacher, "Spike Robinson."
11. Ibid.
12. "Jazz Saxophonist with Refined Tenor Style."

Chapter 18

1. Information and quotes in this chapter come from interviews with John Harmon, June 28, and July 5, 2011; Zach Harmon, December 28, 2011; Janet Planet and Tom Washatka, June 9, 2011; John Gibson, July 27, 2013; Dane Richeson, August 9, 2011; Brad Curran, August 19, 2010; Lovell Ives, August 1, 2011; John and Christine Salerno, August 1, 2011; Woody Mankowski, May 8, 2012; Dave Sullivan, March 14, 2014; Marty Robinson and Matt Buchman, May 22, 2014; Fred Sturm, June 23, 2010; and Patty Darling, February 21, 2014.
2. When the album was reissued years later on compact disc, the error remained.
3. Jerry became Lorenzo Music and went on to fame as the television voice of Garfield the cat.
4. According to Gibson, Fred kept the bar open "because they built the Oshkosh Convention Center on his footprint. . . . He held out till the very end and got more money for the property, and then he built a new place north of there . . . that was called the Totem Lounge. He had a bar that was shaped like a piano, a grand piano."
5. Much of the information here was found in an article linked to a Dartmouth College site of obituaries of members of the class of 1961, "Christopher Crittenden Swansen." www.dartmouth.org/classes/61/In%20Memoriam/Sandreuter-Swanson/Swansen,%20Christopher%20Crittenden.pdf.
6. "Bob Moog Remembers," www.interstellar9.com/emerson/bobmoog.htm. Another description of the concert can be read in Lauren Rosati, "Sounds from Outer Space: The Moog at MoMA," *Inside / Out*, March 10, 2015. www.moma.org/explore/inside_out/2015/03/10/sounds-from-outer-space-the-moog-at-moma.
7. Moog's humorous recollections of the concert can be seen at "Bob Moog #2," www.youtube.com/watch?v=HO-NZzc1AJs&feature=related.
8. James P. Leary, ed., *Wisconsin Folklore* (Madison, WI: University of Wisconsin Press, 1999), 274–275. Duchow's signature tune, "Red Raven Polka," was named for the Red Raven Inn in Hilbert. At its peak, prior to World War II, the Duchow outfit traveled "from coast to coast and border to border . . . [and] played weekly at the Trianon Ballroom in Chicago and had a weekly coast-to-coast radio broadcast on WGN." www.ipapolkas

.com/blog/otw-portfolio/lawrence-duchow-deceased-category-inducted-1983.

9. "The Marching Band," University of Wisconsin–Green Bay website. https://50.uwgb.edu/the-marching-band/.
10. See discography for some of Burditt and Israel's recorded work with the Falconaires.
11. Woody Mankowski, email to the author, May 28, 2012.
12. When I visited Woody Mankowski, he had just finished a book of Coltrane transcriptions, including the epic "Chasin' the Trane," a solo that ended up being twenty-nine pages long.
13. Thanks to Steve Roberts of the Jackson Hole Historical Society and Museum for information about this production.
14. "Frenchy's Restaurant, Milwaukee," Restaurant Time Tunnel blog, posted July 14, 2008. http://restauranttimetunnel.blogspot.com/2008/07/frenchys-restaurant-milwaukee.html.
15. Karen Sullivan eventually moved to Sheboygan North High, teaching culinary arts. Her student ProStart team won a national championship in restaurant management and culinary arts in 2005.

Chapter 19

1. The information and quotes are from Bob Schulz's website, where there is an interview by Dr. Rosemary Hallum, and my two conversations with Schulz on May 17, 2014, and May 16, 2015.
2. Hallum interview.
3. Information and quotes in this chapter come from interviews with Steve Zenz, June 28, 2013; Randy Sabien, November 15, 2012; Matt Turner, September 17, 2010; Mark Urness, February 21, 2014; Greg Balfany, March 19, 2014; Karyn Quinn (and Harvey Halpaus), June 10, 2014; Jeff Erickson, January 30, 2014; Ron Keezer, June 29, 2011; Bob Baca, June 29, 2011, and June 23, 2015; Mary Louise Knutson, June 15, 2013; Sue Orfield, June 29, 2013; Michael Janisch, January 25, 2014; and Tom Gullion, February 20, 2014.
4. The La Crosse Jazz Orchestra website, www.lacrossejazzorchestra.com.
5. For more information, see Knutson's website, www.marylouiseknutson.com.
6. Ethan Iverson interview, February 1, 2013.

7. Upon Tipton's death, his story garnered national notice, even appearing in *People* magazine. One can read more about it in various places on the internet.
8. The band's name was shortened to the Tiptons Saxophone Quartet, and eventually to just the Tiptons.

Index

Page references in ***bold*** refer to photographs.